Alastair Sawday's

Special Places to Stay

FRENCH BED & BREAKFAST

5th EDITION

Typesetting, Conversion & Repro:	Avonset, Bath
Maps:	Bartholomew Mapping Services, a division of HarperCollins Publishers, Glasgow
Printing:	Jarrold Book Printing, Norfolk
Design:	Springboard Design, Bristol
UK Distribution:	Portfolio, London

First published in November 1999 by:
Alastair Sawday Publishing Co. Ltd
44 Ambra Vale East, Bristol BS8 4RE, UK

The Globe Pequot Press
P.O. Box 480
Guilford, Connecticut
06437
USA

Fifth edition 1999

Library of Congress Cataloging-in-Publication Data is available.

ISBN 1-9019700-7-6
ISBN 0-7627-0719-4 in the US

Printed in the UK

Alastair Sawday's
Special Places to Stay

FRENCH BED & BREAKFAST

5th EDITION

"He was the old buster who came down to breakfast one morning, lifted the first cover he saw, said "Eggs! Eggs! Eggs! Damn all eggs!" and instantly legged it for France.

P.G. Wodehouse - *Jeeves Takes Charge*

Guilford,
Connecticut, USA

ASP
Alastair Sawday Publishing
Bristol, UK

ACKNOWLEDGEMENTS

Ann Cooke-Yarborough, described in the last introduction as "impresario, dreamer, catalyst and galvaniser - the dynamo behind this edition", has stuck to that role for this one too. Indeed, this fifth edition is even more Ann's than ever, for it is her sympathy with the owners and her deepening understanding of what makes them tick that makes this book so very special. She hugely enjoys her contact with them, and their often beautiful houses, and takes delight in communicating that to you. Hence the charm - and value - of this book.

However, her work has involved an administrative load vast enough to sink two very ordinary mortals, so she hasn't been able to get out to meet enough of all the people who actually run the B&Bs. (There is a touch of poignancy to her briefings of inspectors; she would like to be doing it all herself.) So even Ann, more self-disciplined and devoted than most, has exhausted abundant stocks of energy and decided to inspect and write rather than shuffle paper. She is passing her editorial baton to Annie Shillito in this office, the Managing Editor of our 'foreign' books, and will - we all hope - start enjoying herself in a different role.

How to pay tribute to someone to whom one owes so much? How lucky I am to have enjoyed such a magnificent chunk of Ann's unflagging loyalty, huge ability and unfailing sense of fun. Her last creative contribution has been the commissioning, from a young artist friend in Paris, Aymeric Chastenet, of the intriguing prints that have replaced the regional title-page photos. They won't appeal to everyone, because they are bold and unusual, but that is Ann. I like them, and welcome the novelty. And I look forward to Ann's drive and imagination being applied to inspections and writing.

So if you are one of the many thousands who have enjoyed using previous editions of this book, do give a thought to the woman who has made it happen. She has been brilliant!

Alastair Sawday

Series Editor:	Alastair Sawday
Editor:	Ann Cooke-Yarborough
Production Manager:	Julia Richardson
Administration:	Kate Harris
Inspections:	Richard & Linda Armspach, Lillian Bell, Joanna Bell-Moore, Alyson & Colin Browne, Meredith Dickinson, Valerie Foix, Georgina Gabriel, Diana Harris, Susanna Isaac, Carol Lenthal, Joanna Morris, Caroline Portway, Lise Prentice, Eve Puddy, Pippa Ryder, Elizabeth Yates.
Additional writing:	Susanna Dammann, Brendan Flanagan, Grace Teshima, Sasha Lubetkin, Kristen Rainey
Accounts:	Sheila Clifton, Sandra Hasell, Maureen Humphries
Cover Design:	Caroline King
Illustrations:	Aymeric Chastenet
Additional photos:	Richard Armspach, Sara Hay, Hélicolor France, Joanna Morris

And our unseen but essential support teams. In Paris, they were Brendan Flanagan, Mathias Fournier and Lucie Nérot. In Bristol they were the staff of Alastair Sawday Publishing and Tours.

INTRODUCTION

You have probably heard of General de Gaulle's: "A country with 350 different sorts of cheese is ungovernable". Well, cheese, in all its noble guises is, once again, being hotly defended by the French. As I write, the French press throbs with stories of the *Confédération Paysanne's* resistance to the globalisation of the economy and of their proud French culture. Their leader has been imprisoned - and has become a national hero.

I hope that this book, too, in its own tiny way, will remain firmly on the side of those who encourage diversity, individuality... and the rural economy. Never has this been more important, as we reel under yet another onslaught from industrial agriculture and food processing, and from the insensitive apparatus of the global market.

We are proud of this book, and of the huge numbers of friendships that have been generated by the contacts it offers. It somehow gets better with every edition. We do hear tales, very occasionally, of the *"Tours Faltées"*... but essentially our readers write us wonderful thank-you letters.

Here are a few samples of the letters that make our work so satisfying:

"Our favourite had an almost tangible sense of peace and contentment, derived from Agathe's and Philippe's deep commitment to, and pleasure in, this little village. We loved the vast fireplaces, the old wicker chairs, the cool hall with its intriguing staircase and eclectic collection of old objects."

We hear much about those many hosts who have added an extra touch of kindness to your stay: "What a wonderful welcome! Lovely room (forget the dust and cobwebs!), relaxed and laid-back atmosphere, and the coffee/cognac as we arrived really did relax us. How can they be so cheerful, and cook for so many, all the time? And they showed great warmth and humanity to one guest whose daughter was ill at home."

And another: "Your book is the best of its kind yet. One night my wife was ill and Rhona insisted on accompanying us to the hospital and being our interpreter." (The same Rhona has been known, having had to refer guests to someone else's house, to take a bottle of wine to welcome them there.) Another hostess, realising that her guests would arrive - unaware - on a 'dead' night in the town, prepared a surprise welcome dinner for them.

The houses themselves, both aesthetically and with their 'service', often knock the grandest hotels into a cocked hat: "The bedroom was huge; we could have played cricket in it. The girls played with the goats, chickens, ducks and rabbits while we sat peacefully at the garden table under the whispering trees, sipping cool white wine. It was Heaven."

This book is about values, beauty, understanding, friendships, culture with both small and big 'c', and fun. We at the paper-shuffling end of the publishing business relish your pleasure in using it!

Alastair Sawday

INTRODUCTION

Places in the guide

We owe huge thanks to those readers who have taken the trouble to write about their French B&B experiences - good and bad - and to recommend new places. They have made a real contribution to this book.

• Poor reports are followed up with the owners in question: we need to see both sides but don't mention the writer's name, of course. Really bad reports lead to incognito visits after which we may exclude a house.

• All recommended places are inspected if appropriate.

Non-French owners

We receive bagfuls of requests from British and American B&B owners wanting to be in the guide and we have had to disappoint many. Our aim is essentially to guide you, our readers, to meetings with French families in their homes, so non-French owners have a smaller chance of being chosen.

However, many of you have written to say how restful it can be, after several evenings of valiant French conversation, to have a 'day off' and relax in your native tongue. Our Native Speaker homes are dotted around the country so we hope you find the linguistic break you need.

Payment

One last, important, point: owners pay a small fee to be included in the book, but the ability to pay is no 'Open Sesame' - it is a fee, not a bribe!

How to use this book

Finding the houses

The individual ENTRY NUMBER is at the bottom right of each entry. This is the number to use when looking for places in the book and when writing to us (with the Edition number please !). Each entry also has the 1/200,000 Michelin Regional Map reference as MMap followed by the relevant map and fold numbers, e.g. MMap 245-31 is Regional Map No 245, fold No 31 - we hope this helps with detailed pinpointing of houses.

Our maps

Designed for B&B flagging only, they will frustrate you if you try and use them as road maps! Take a detailed road map such as Michelin or Collins.

Directions

Apart from motorway exits, our directions take you to each house from one side only. If you approach another way, make adjustments. We give cardinal directions - N-S-E-W - where appropriate and name the French roads with the letters they carry on French maps and road signs :

A = Autoroute. Toll motorways with junctions that usually have the same name/number on both sides.

N = Route Nationale. The old trunk roads that are still pretty fast, don't charge tolls, but often go through towns.

D = Route Départementale. Smaller country roads with relatively little traffic.

If our directions are not perfect, PLEASE tell us how to improve them; you could save other people a major row over map-reading!

French words used in the entries are explained at the end of the book.

How to read this book

Whatever the caveats, all the places in this book are here because WE LIKE THEM. We hope you will quickly learn to read between our lines and pick up the subtleties of what one reader has called "Sawday-speak". If we love the people but find the décor odd, we often just describe it in factual terms. Quotation marks are for passages from readers' letters.

Telephoning
All telephone numbers in France have ten digits, e.g. (0)5 15 25 35 45. You should know that:

- the initial zero (bracketted here) is for use when telephoning inside France only, i.e. dial 05 15 25 35 45 from any private or public telephone;
- when dialling from outside France use the international access code then the country code for France - 33 - followed by the last 9 digits of the number you want, e.g. 00 33 5 15 25 35 45;
- numbers beginning (0)6 are mobile phone numbers and cost more;
- to telephone from France -
  - to Great Britain: 00 44 and your correspondent's number without the initial zero,
  - to the USA, dial 00 1 and your correspondent's number without the initial zero.

Rooms and bathrooms
French washing arrangements vary enormously and, if you have a sense of humour and are a good traveller, are part of the fun of France. A few are American-style luxurious, many are family-style. We try to tell you whether to expect shower or bath and whether the shower and/or wc are just curtained or screened off. Most baths will have a shower attachment but not necessarily a screen to go with it. It is impossible to tell you every detail.

Open season
When given in months, this means the WHOLE of both months named; thus April to November means 1 April to 30 November.

Prices
French Franc prices
They are indicative and not binding on the owners, but are presumed to be their 2000 prices. If you travel with this edition after 2000 you must expect an increase on both rooms and meals, though some owners are proud of not having put their prices up for years.

Where we give a price range, it generally means one of two things :

- different rooms have different prices
- prices vary according to season

As always, enquire when booking.

Euro prices
The single currency becomes legal in January 2002 but is already running alongside the Franc on many price tickets at the officially fixed rate of 6.59 French Francs for one Euro. We have given the basic price or price range for B&B for two in Euros. This should prepare you.

Reductions
Most French B&Bs offer reductions for long stays; some have attractive half-board terms, or special prices for children. Do enquire when booking.

Dinner prices
(VERY few places do lunch but the occasional picnic is available.) We have tried to show what the price quoted for dinner includes, but 'including wine' means many things. It may mean a standard quarter-litre carafe per person; it may mean a bottomless barrel of table wine; it may mean a very decent bottle of local produce or, in some rare cases, of excellent estate wine. Whatever it is, it is usually wonderful value.

Meals - 'Table d'Hôte'
You should seize the opportunity to eat honest - even gourmet - food in an authentic family atmosphere. However, dinner ABSOLUTELY MUST be booked beforehand, at least in the morning, sometimes the day before. Don't expect dinner every day! but do please come for dinner if you have booked it - nothing is more distressing than preparing a delicious meal that no-one comes to eat.

Where there is no *Table d'Hôte*, we have mentioned places to eat in the area but, here again, country restaurants stop taking orders at about 9pm and close one day a week.

Symbols
Identifies places where walkers can expect to find good hikes from the house or village, either in loops or on to another B&B, with luggage transported by your hosts. In a few cases, they will drive you to a starting point. Enquire when booking.

New this year, identifies houses with their own swimming pool available to guests, though not necessarily at all times.

Gîte space for ... people should tell you how many other people may be staying in holiday cottages on the property and give you an idea of what the total population is liable to be - the Happy-Families-Round-the-Pool Factor.

Tips for our American readers
We have a lot of lovely and utterly safe places for you to visit. But we also offer you the chance to venture forth and experience France off the beaten track.

One reader questioned our inclusion of widely differing places. Setting out to find "romantic, luxurious and exotic" places, she had experienced one quintessentially French house with chaotic plumbing and mismatching décor, and then a magnificently luxurious château. What she had missed was the significance of the price difference and the subtleties of the descriptions - which are designed to spell out the truth in a coded sort of way!

Experience tells us that many of you are coming over to Europe with a different 'vocabulary', so the following hints may be of help:

B&B
In the US, the standard of B&Bs is extremely high with superb plumbing and heating, lots of vast towels and good furniture. In France, it ranges from the basic farm, with a bath down the corridor or even in the bedroom, to the swishest private château. In between, there will be gorgeous châteaux with basic plumbing and lovely old houses with fine modern bathrooms. Do remember that we choose these places with mostly European readers in mind, so the more in tune you are with European thinking the more you will enjoy our selection. This book is for the open-minded traveller.

Plumbing
We deal with bathrooms elsewhere in this Introduction, but it is worth emphasising that US plumbing is magnificent compared to much of ours and that we Europeans have grown up with, even learned to love (?), rattling pipes, hip-baths behind curtains in bedrooms, exposed pipes and other oddities. If you are wary of such things then only go for the places which are obviously modernised... and probably more expensive.

This being said... if you come with a sense of adventure and are keen to meet interesting French people (often in beautiful homes), you will have a ball - many North Americans now swear by this book.

How to use Chambres d'Hôtes

Mutual Welcome
These are NOT hotels. *Chambre d'Hôte* owners will often bend over backwards for you (e.g. put the table on blocks to fit a wheelchair in), find rare or unusual objects (e.g. special courgette seeds), take you down the road to see an unknown treasure or up the mountain for a picnic. On the other hand, don't expect gin and tonic at 2am in your room or a chambermaid to pick up your strewn clothes every day.

And there is another side to the relationship. Owners tell us over and over again how much they appreciate guests who come bearing Alastair Sawday's guide - "they are educated and civilised, interesting and interested; really good people to have in one's house".

BUT - there has to be a but - I must mention here what some of our B&B owners would like to say to their less delicate guests - a tiny but annoying minority. Basically, they would like visitors to remember that "this house is a private home and we like to treat guests as friends we might have invited to stay". So they may happily lend their kitchen for a moment or accept your friends in their garden, but would like to be asked first. They appreciate guests who put things back where they came from and, above all, they like the civilised diner who does not abuse their *vin à volonté*.

Common courtesy is surely the least we can each expect and give. It opens the door, as so many readers tell us, to relationships that can lift a holiday into another dimension.

Your discontentments
If you are unhappy with the way you are treated at a *Chambre d'Hôte*, be it the welcome, the room, the bathroom or the food, I do urge you

to talk first to those who can do something about it immediately - the owners. They are eager to please you, willing to learn, and NEED your feedback. We welcome all your reports and letters and we do pass on your messages, positive and negative, but when you are on the spot, you are in a position of real influence - use it!

No-shows
Most owners hope you will treat them as friends too, with sensitivity, tidiness and punctuality. The most upsetting thing for them, apart from the perfunctory behaviour described above, is preparing rooms and waiting up late for 'guests' who never come, never ring, never give any further sign of life. They are asking if the English have lost their sense of "fair play"? So if you find you are not going to take up a booking, PLEASE telephone right away.

By the way, there is a tacit agreement among a number of B&B owners that no-show + no-call by 8pm can be taken as a refusal of the booking and they will re-let the room if another asker turns up. This can be a touch embarrassing...

Extras
There seems to be a growing tendency for owners to charge for 'extras' such as glasses of wine, soft drinks, even cups of tea. You may find a price list in your bedroom or displayed in the hall downstairs. I thoroughly understand that owners feel they cannot afford free drinks for all every day but I am not very happy about this way of dealing with it. One suggestion is that they add 10 or 20 Francs to the daily rate. I do believe that you should not feel obliged to pay for the "welcome glass" or the "unrefusable aperitif" that you didn't ask for but then turns up as an item on your bill. We will be glad to hear your views.

Booking
It is essential to book ahead in summer (July and August) and recommended in other months - these places often have very few rooms. You can, of course, travel spontaneously and try your luck. Otherwise, the fax is the ideal way of booking and avoiding misunderstandings over the telephone - more and more French B&Bs have fax machines, even e-mail.

You will occasionally receive a *Contrat de Location* ("Tenancy Contract") as confirmation (bureaucracy creeping into the most private corners, I fear). It must be filled in and sent back, probably with a deposit (see All about Money below) and commits both sides to the stated dates and terms.

Times for telephoning. Two points need making :

- The French never ring people they don't know intimately after 9.30pm, and some even put the deadline at 9pm;
- Do remember that Ireland and the UK are one hour behind the Continent so your latest time for ringing France from the UK is 8.30pm. Some country folk have been quite upset by enquiries coming through at midnight when they were fast asleep.

Arriving
Most owners expect you to arrive between 5pm and 7pm and definitely not during dinner. If you come earlier, you may find the rooms not finished or your hosts still out at work. Yet again, these are private houses and people have their private lives to get on with as well. We do

ask them to leave a note if they are going to be late or have an emergency errand to run, but some are chary of announcing 'House Empty' to the world at large. Similarly, if you are going to be late (or early, unavoidably), PLEASE telephone and say so.

Children
Don't expect charming Madame automatically to LOVE looking after your children while you sleep late or go out to dinner (I invent nothing - these are real cases quoted to us). She is not insured for unattended children falling in her pond or tumbling downstairs in search of comfort at ten o'clock at night. Anyway, she may have other things to do, such as go to bed herself.

Some owners will occasionally look after children but please don't take it for granted.

How to use Tables d'Hôtes

ALWAYS BOOK AHEAD - and if you book, please eat! If you are not going to be able to make it, do telephone to cancel immediately. Dinner will be at a fixed time but very seldom earlier than 7.30pm. In some houses, particularly in the south, it is normal to sit down at any time between 8.30 and 10 in the evening.

En famille or not *en famille*? Ideally, it should be, all at one welcoming communal table; very often, it is. Practically, there are reasons why it won't be. Two of these reasons will make sense to a lot of you :

- the owners' young family need their parents' presence at dinner and for homework time and/or are not considered 'civilised' enough to dine with guests;
- your hosts are minding their figures and simply cannot afford to eat as much as they serve their guests every day!

VEGETARIANS, please let your hosts know beforehand, otherwise they can't be expected to rustle up anything more original than the eternal '*omelette-salade*' or just offer you another helping of spinach. A handful of houses in this book actually specialise in vegetarian cooking but the  is given to all those who say they have a veggie dish or two up their sleeves if forewarned.

Practical Expectations

Voltage
American readers should be aware that the whole of Europe runs on 220-240 volts so leave your 110-volt appliances at home... or bring an adapter.

Towels, etc.
Towels may not always be up to scratch. There may not always be soap. Do ASK for things you lack. It is usually just an oversight when only two hand towels are provided for three people, though the French DO use smaller towels than we do. It's a good idea to take your favourite soap and towels with you.

Life in the country

If you choose one of our beautiful, ivy-covered farmhouses to spend three idyllic days breathing clean air, wallowing in Madame's fabulous country cooking and forgetting all your urban stresses, you've made the right decision. And part of the delight of a return to nature is renewing contact with local wildlife. One of the ivy's functions is to provide housing for creepy-crawlies - one may even get into your room through the open casement. Don't be afraid - you're bigger than he is! The horses you might have enjoyed riding in the morning will probably attract flies in the afternoon - it is a fact of summer life when there are cattle and stables nearby.

All about Money

Cash, cheque or credit card?

Most French B&B owners are not equipped to take plastic payment, though more and more of the plusher places are going over to plastic and the Internet. We feel it is reasonable for them to ask you to take your card to the nearest cash machine.

Travellers cheques and Eurocheques may also be a problem - French banks often charge a large lump-sum commission to honour them so the (smallish) amounts charged by B&Bs are half-annihilated by the charges. However, you CAN pay with either if the amount is stated in French francs (and your cheque guarantee card number is on the back of the cheque).

Deposits

Some owners ask for a deposit - many readers have found it virtually impossible or wickedly expensive to do this by direct transfer. One reader and one owner suggested the following solutions :

1. Have a number of French banknotes at home (you will need some for your travels anyway) and send the appropriate amount with your confirmation by 'International Recorded' mail.
2. Send a Eurocheque, or even an ordinary cheque, which the owner will destroy when you arrive (so no-one pays the charges); when you leave, they will ask you for cash for your whole stay.
3. Buy some French stamps while you're in France and send stamped addressed envelopes when planning your next trip to make sure you receive confirmation of your bookings.

Taxe de séjour

This is a small sum per person that local councils are allowed to levy on all visitors paying for accommodation. Some councils do, some don't. So you may find you bill increased by a petty 4, 5, or 9 Francs. Owners do not like this at all, are even embarrassed about it, and don't know how to present it. They would like to disguise it inside their quoted rate; some do, but it is against the rules. So do be understanding about their subjection, once again, to heedless bureaucracy.

DISCLAIMER

We make no claims to pure objectivity in judging B&Bs. We have included these ones because we have some powerful reason for considering them special. Our inspectors are as human as you are - and we cherish that. Please read the description carefully for hints that Madame may be a bit barmy or that the décor inside is somewhat kitsch, in spite of a splendid exterior. These are our choices. Our opinions and tastes are ours alone and this book is a statement of them; we hope you will share them. If you don't, it's not because we've been sloppy, but probably because things have changed or you are very different from the inspector! Do let us know.

SYMBOLS

Explanation of Symbols Treat each one as a guide rather than a concrete indicator.

 Working farm, vineyard or stud.

 Fairly good English is spoken here.

 One of your hosts speaks enough English for simple communication.

 Children are positively welcomed but cots, high chairs, etc., are not necessarily available. The text gives restrictions where relevant.

 You can either borrow or hire bikes here.

 Good hiking walks from house or village.

 Some, but not necessarily all, ingredients are organically grown.

 Vegetarians catered for with advance warning.

 Full disabled facilities provided.

 Accessible for people of limited mobility.

 Pets are welcome but may be housed in an outbuilding rather than in your room. Check when booking if restrictions/small supplements apply.

 This house has pets of its own: dog, cat, horse, duck, parrot,...

Applies to totally non-smoking houses.

 Swimming nearby – a pond, a lake, a river or the sea.

 Swimming pool on the property.

MMap Michelin Map reference: number of Michelin 1/200,000 regional map followed by number of fold in that map.

☐ Entry number of each inspected property.

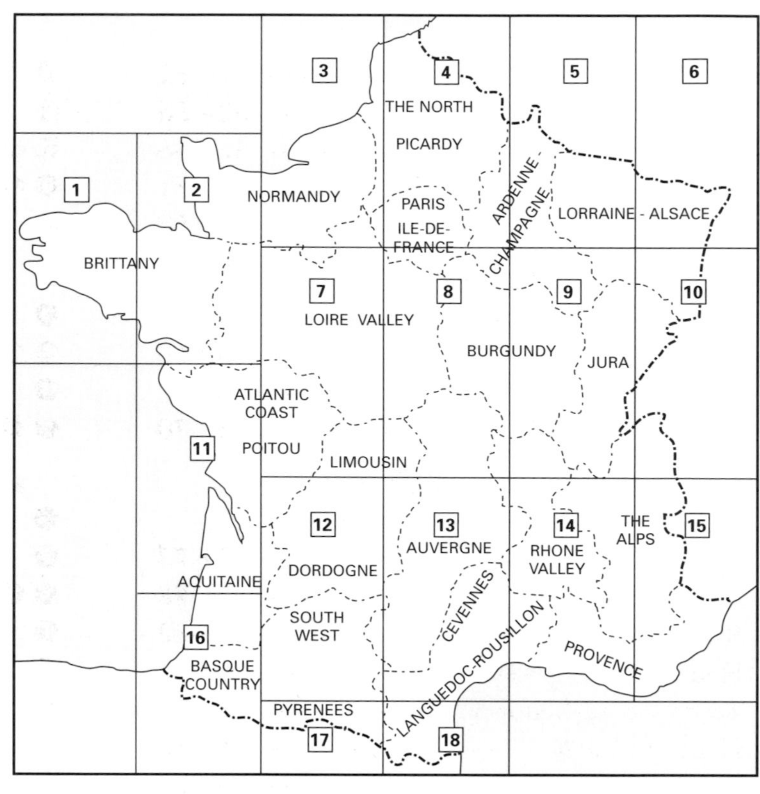

France : General Map

CONTENTS

CONTENTS

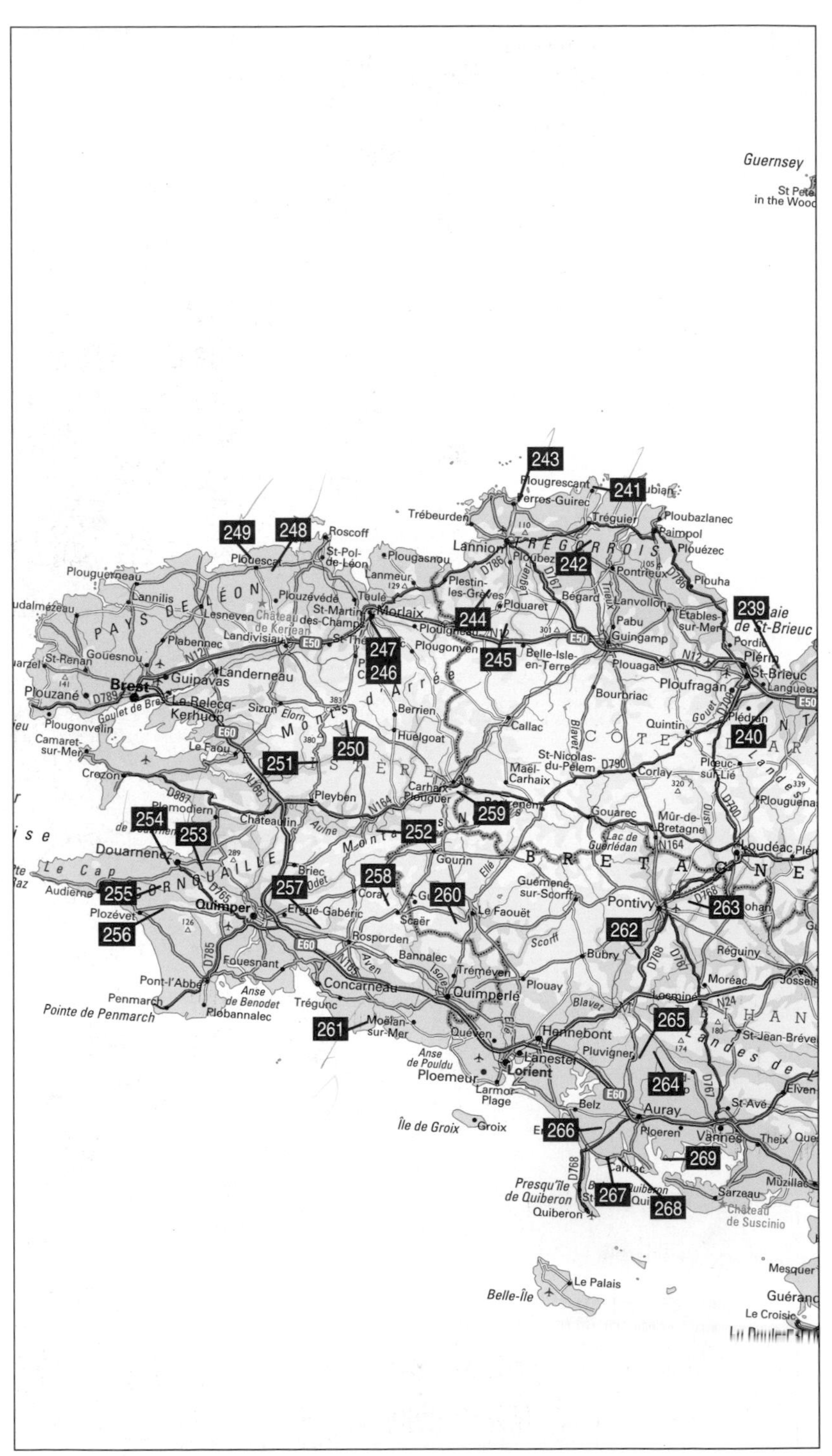

Scale for colour maps 1:1 600 000
(1cm:16km or 1 inch:25.25 miles)

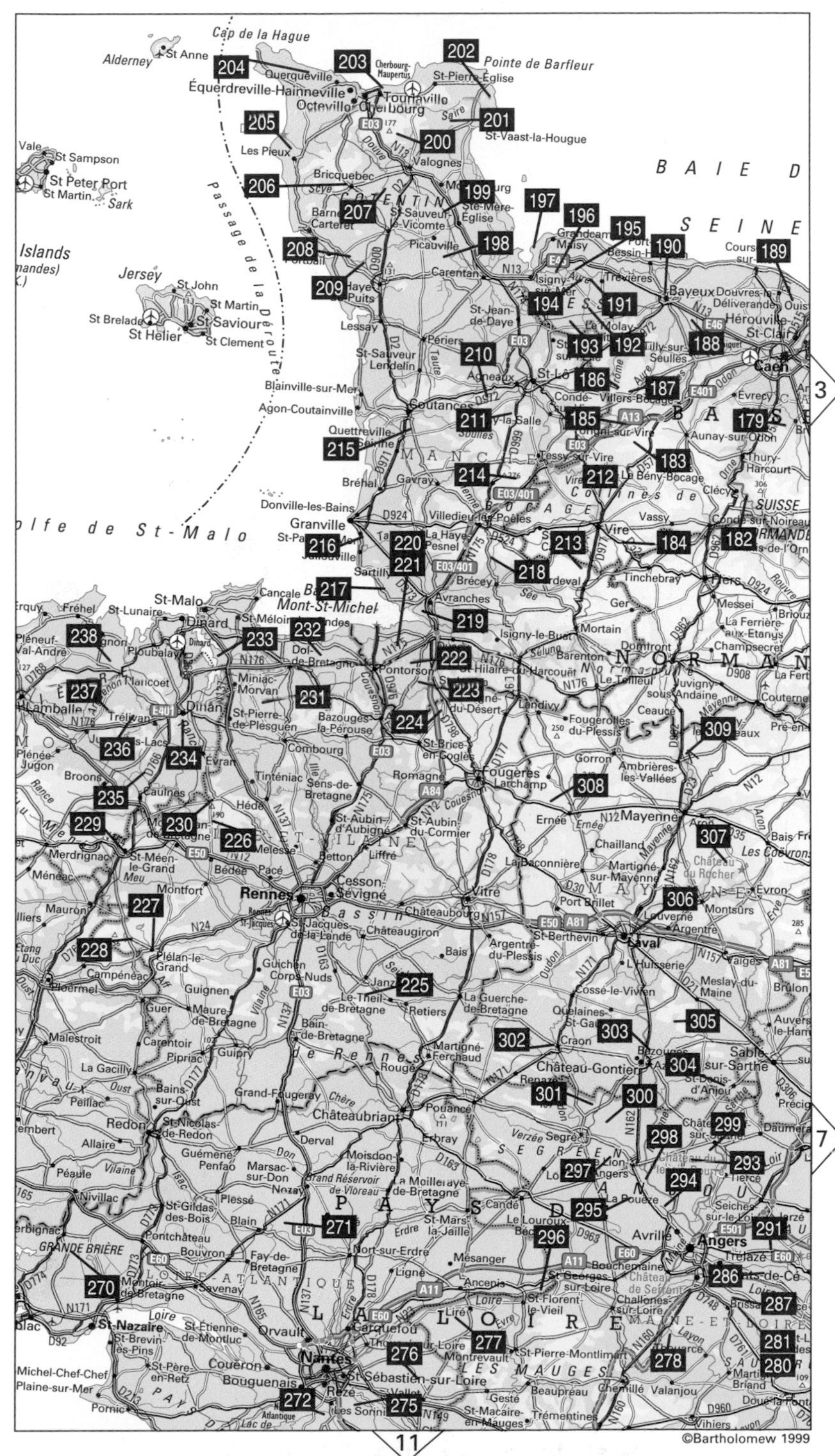

Cap de la Hague
Alderney
St Anne
204
203
202
Pointe de Barfleur
Querqueville
Équerdreville-Hainneville
Cherbourg-Maupertus
Tourlaville
St-Pierre-Église
Octeville
Cherbourg
205
201
St-Vaast-la-Hougue
Les Pieux
200
Valognes
Vale
St Sampson
St Peter Port
St Martin
Sark
206
Bricquebec
199
197
BAIE D
196
195
SEINE
Islands
Passage de la Déroute
Barneville-Carteret
207
St-Sauveur-le-Vicomte
Ste-Mère-Église
Grandcamp-Maisy
Bessin
208
198
Picauville
190
189
Jersey
St John
St Martin
St Saviour
St Brelade
St Helier
St Clement
209
La Haye-du-Puits
Carentan
Isigny-sur-Mer
Trévières
Bayeux
194
191
Douvres-la-Délivrande
Hérouville-St-Clair
Lessay
St-Jean-de-Daye
Le Molay
Périers
193
192
Tilly-sur-Seulles
188
St-Sauveur-Lendelin
210
Caen
Blainville-sur-Mer
Agneaux
St-Lô
186
187
3
Agon-Coutainville
Coutances
Condé-sur-Vire
Villers-Bocage
Évrecy
211
185
179
Quettreville-sur-Sienne
Canisy
Torigni-sur-Vire
Aunay-sur-Odon
215
MANCHE
Tessy-sur-Vire
183
Thury-Harcourt
Bréhal
214
Gavray
212
Le Bény-Bocage
Clécy
Collines de
BOCAGE
SUISSE
Donville-les-Bains
D924
Villedieu-les-Poêles
Vassy
Granville
Golfe de St-Malo
Condé-sur-Noireau
216
220
La Haye-Pesnel
213
Vire
184
182
221
Sartilly
218
Tinchebray
Flers
217
Brécey
Cancale
Baie du Mont-St-Michel
Avranches
Messei
St-Malo
St-Lunaire
Fréhel
Dinard
St-Méloir-des-Ondes
219
Isigny-le-Buat
Mortain
La Ferrière-aux-Étangs
238
233
232
Pléneuf-Val-André
Ploubalay
Dol-de-Bretagne
222
Barenton
NORMANDIE
Domfront
Champsecret
Pontorson
St-Hilaire-du-Harcouët
Juvigny-sous-Andaine
237
Miniac-Morvan
231
223
Le Teilleul
Lamballe
Dinan
Trélivan
St-Pierre-de-Plesguen
Bazouges-la-Pérouse
St-James
Landivy
Ceaucé
Couterne
Pré-en-Pail
236
224
Fougerolles-du-Plessis
309
Plénée-Jugon
234
Evran
Combourg
St-Brice-en-Coglès
Gorron
Broons
Tinténiac
Romagné
Fougères
Ambrières-les-Vallées
235
Caulnes
Sens-de-Bretagne
Larchamp
308
Hédé
St-Aubin-d'Aubigné
St-Aubin-du-Cormier
229
230
Ernée
Mayenne
ILLE-ET-VILAINE
226
307
Merdrignac
St-Méen-le-Grand
Melesse
Betton
Liffré
Chailland
Martigné-sur-Mayenne
Château du Rocher
Les Coëvrons
Ménéac
Bédée
Pacé
La Baconnière
Montfort
Rennes
Cesson-Sévigné
Vitré
306
Évron
Mauron
227
Châteaubourg
Port Brillet
Montsûrs
St-Jacques-de-la-Lande
Châteaugiron
Louverné
Argentré
Laval
228
Plélan-le-Grand
St-Berthevin
Argentré-du-Plessis
L'Huisserie
Vaiges
Campénéac
Bais
Ploërmel
Guichen
Corps-Nuds
Janzé
225
Meslay-du-Maine
Brûlon
Guignen
Le Theil-de-Bretagne
La Guerche-de-Bretagne
Cossé-le-Vivien
Guer
Maure-de-Bretagne
Retiers
Quelaines-St-Gault
305
Malestroit
Bain-de-Bretagne
302
Craon
303
Carentoir
Pipriac
Guipry
Martigné-Ferchaud
Bazouges
Sablé-sur-Sarthe
La Gacilly
Rougé
Château-Gontier
304
Renazé
St-Denis-d'Anjou
Bains-sur-Oust
301
300
Peillac
Grand-Fougeray
Pouancé
Redon
St-Nicolas-de-Redon
Châteaubriant
Allaire
Derval
Segré
299
298
Château-sur-Sarthe
7
Guémené-Penfao
Moisdon-la-Rivière
Erbray
SEGRÉEN
Péaule
Marsac-sur-Don
Grand Réservoir de Vioreau
Le Lion-d'Angers
293
Tiercé
La Moillerave-de-Bretagne
297
294
Nivillac
Nozay
PAYS DE
St-Gildas-des-Bois
Plessé
Candé
La Pouëze
Seiches-sur-le-Loir
271
295
Blain
St-Mars-la-Jaille
Le Louroux-Béconnais
Avrillé
Angers
291
Pontchâteau
296
GRANDE BRIÈRE
Bouvron
Mésanger
Fay-de-Bretagne
Trélazé
270
Montoir-de-Bretagne
LOIRE-ATLANTIQUE
Nort-sur-Erdre
Ligné
Bouchemaine
Savenay
Ancenis
St-Georges-sur-Loire
Château de Serrant
286
Ponts-de-Cé
St-Nazaire
Loire
Liré
St-Florent-le-Vieil
Chalonnes-sur-Loire
287
St-Étienne-de-Montluc
Orvault
Carquefou
LA LOIRE
MAINE-ET-LOIRE
Brissac
St-Brevin-les-Pins
277
281
Nantes
Thouarcé
St-Père-en-Retz
276
Montrevault
St-Pierre-Montlimart
278
280
Couëron
LES MAUGES
Michel-Chef-Chef
Bouguenais
St-Sébastien-sur-Loire
Martigné-Briand
Plaine-sur-Mer
PAYS DE RETZ
Rezé
Beaupréau
Chemillé
Valanjou
Doué-la-Fontaine
272
Vallet
Gesté
Pornic
275
Les Sorinières
St-Macaire-en-Mauges
Trémentines
Vihiers
11

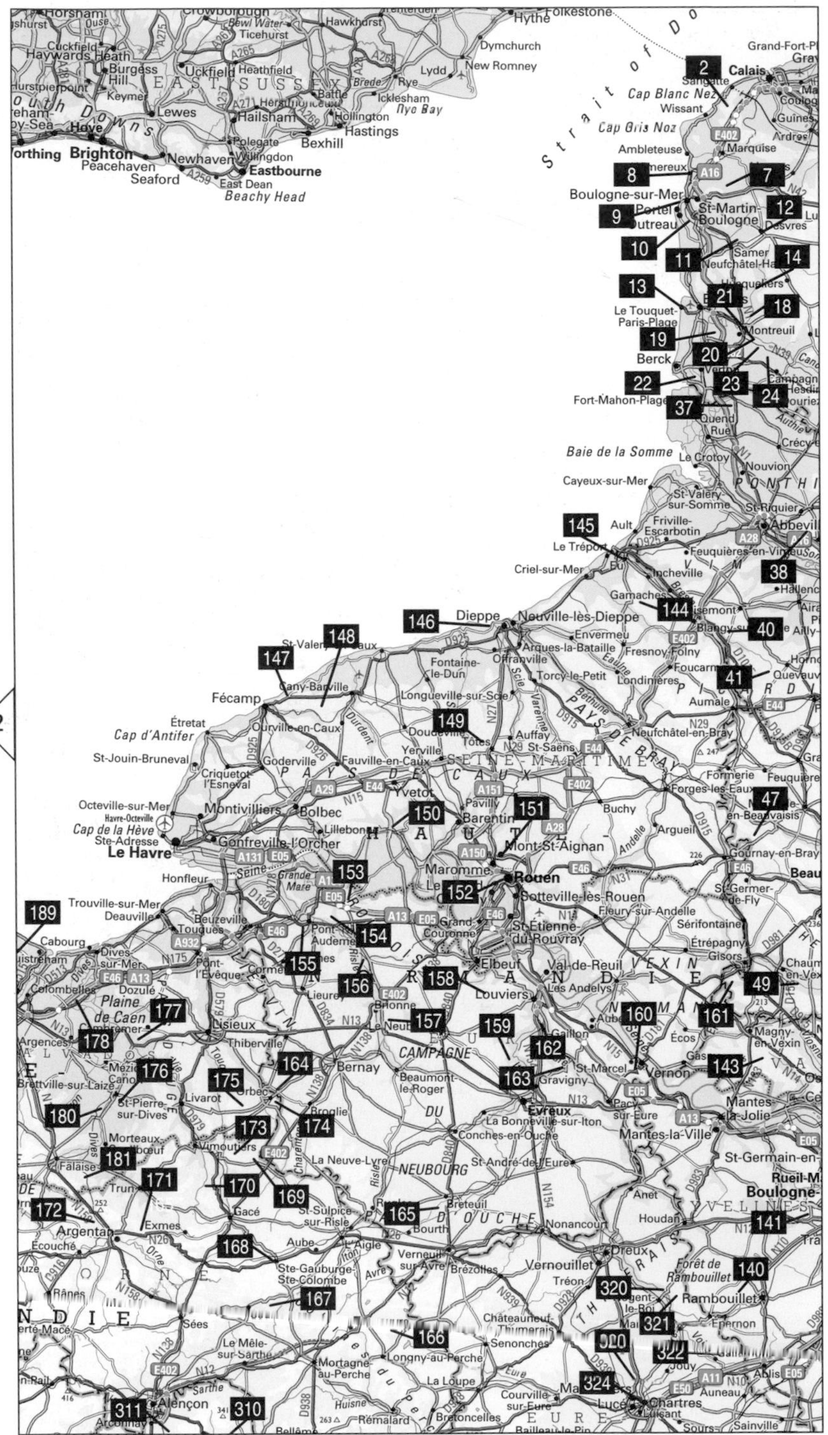

Folkestone
Hythe
Dymchurch
New Romney
Lydd
Hawkhurst
Ticehurst
Bewl Water
Crowborough
Horsham
Cuckfield
Haywards Heath
Burgess Hill
Hurstpierpoint
Keymer
Uckfield
Heathfield
EAST SUSSEX
Brede
Rye
Battle
Icklesham
Rye Bay
Hollington
Hastings
Hailsham
Lewes
South Downs
Hove
Brighton
Peacehaven
Seaford
Newhaven
Polegate
Willingdon
Eastbourne
East Dean
Beachy Head
Bexhill
Strait of Do
Calais
Sangatte
Grand-Fort-P
Cap Blanc Nez
Wissant
Cap Gris Noz
Ambleteuse
Marquise
Guînes
Ardres
Boulogne-sur-Mer
St-Martin-Boulogne
Desvres
Samer
Neufchâtel-Ha
Le Touquet-Paris-Plage
Montreuil
Berck
Fort-Mahon-Plage
Quend
Rue
Baie de la Somme
Le Crotoy
Nouvion
Crécy
Cayeux-sur-Mer
St-Valery-sur-Somme
St-Riquier
Abbevill
Ault
Friville-Escarbotin
Le Tréport
Eu
Feuquières-en-Vimeu
Criel-sur-Mer
Incheville
Gamaches
Blangy-sur
Dieppe
Neuville-lès-Dieppe
Envermeu
Arques-la-Bataille
Offranville
Fresnoy-Folny
St-Valery-en-Caux
Fontaine-le-Dun
Torcy-le-Petit
Londinières
Foucarm
Aumale
Fécamp
Cany-Barville
Longueville-sur-Scie
Étretat
Cap d'Antifer
Ourville-en-Caux
Doudeville
Tôtes
Auffay
St-Saëns
Neufchâtel-en-Bray
PAYS DE BRAY
St-Jouin-Bruneval
Criquetot-l'Esneval
Goderville
Fauville-en-Caux
Yerville
SEINE-MARITIME
PAYS DE CAUX
Forges-les-Eaux
Formerie
Feuquière
Octeville-sur-Mer
Havre-Octeville
Montivilliers
Bolbec
Yvetot
Pavilly
Barentin
Buchy
Argueil
Cap de la Hève
Ste-Adresse
Le Havre
Gonfreville-l'Orcher
Lillebonne
Mont-St-Aignan
Gournay-en-Bray
Honfleur
Seine
Grande Mare
Maromme
Rouen
Sotteville-lès-Rouen
St-Germer-de-Fly
Trouville-sur-Mer
Deauville
Beuzeville
Touques
Pont-Audemer
Grand-Couronne
St-Étienne-du-Rouvray
Fleury-sur-Andelle
Sérifontaine
Étrépagny
Gisors
Cabourg
Dives-sur-Mer
Pont-l'Évêque
Elbeuf
Val-de-Reuil
VEXIN
Colombelles
Dozulé
Plaine de Caen
Lieurey
Brionne
Louviers
Les Andelys
Argences
Lisieux
Thiberville
Le Neubourg
CAMPAGNE
Gaillon
Écos
Magny-en-Vexin
Bernay
Beaumont-le-Roger
St-Marcel
Vernon
Gravigny
Brettville-sur-Laize
Livarot
Orbec
Broglie
Évreux
Pacy-sur-Eure
Mantes-la-Jolie
Mantes-la-Ville
St-Pierre-sur-Dives
La Bonneville-sur-Iton
Conches-en-Ouche
Morteaux-Coulibœuf
Vimoutiers
La Neuve-Lyre
NEUBOURG
St-André-de-l'Eure
St-Germain-en-
Falaise
Trun
Gacé
St-Sulpice-sur-Risle
Breteuil
Anet
Houdan
YVELINES
Rueil-M
Boulogne-
Exmes
Argentan
Écouché
Aube
L'Aigle
Bourth
Nonancourt
Verneuil-sur-Avre
Brézolles
Dreux
Vernouillet
Ste-Gauburge-Ste-Colombe
Forêt de Rambouillet
Tréon
Rambouillet
ORNE
Rânes
NDIE
Sées
Châteauneuf-Thimerais
Épernon
Le Mêle-sur-Sarthe
Senonches
Mortagne-au-Perche
Longny-au-Perche
Jouy
La Loupe
Ablis
Auneau
Alençon
Rémalard
Courville-sur-Eure
Bretoncelles
Chartres
Lucé
EURE
Sainville
A16
E402
N1
A28
E44
A29
A151
A150
A28
A131
E05
A13
E46
A932
N13
N138
E402
A11
E50
2
3
8
7
9
12
10
11
14
13
21
18
19
20
22
23
24
37
145
38
144
146
40
148
147
41
149
47
150
151
153
152
189
154
155
49
156
158
177
157
160
161
178
159
162
143
176
175
164
163
180
173
174
181
171
170
169
172
165
141
168
140
320
167
321
166
322
324
311
310

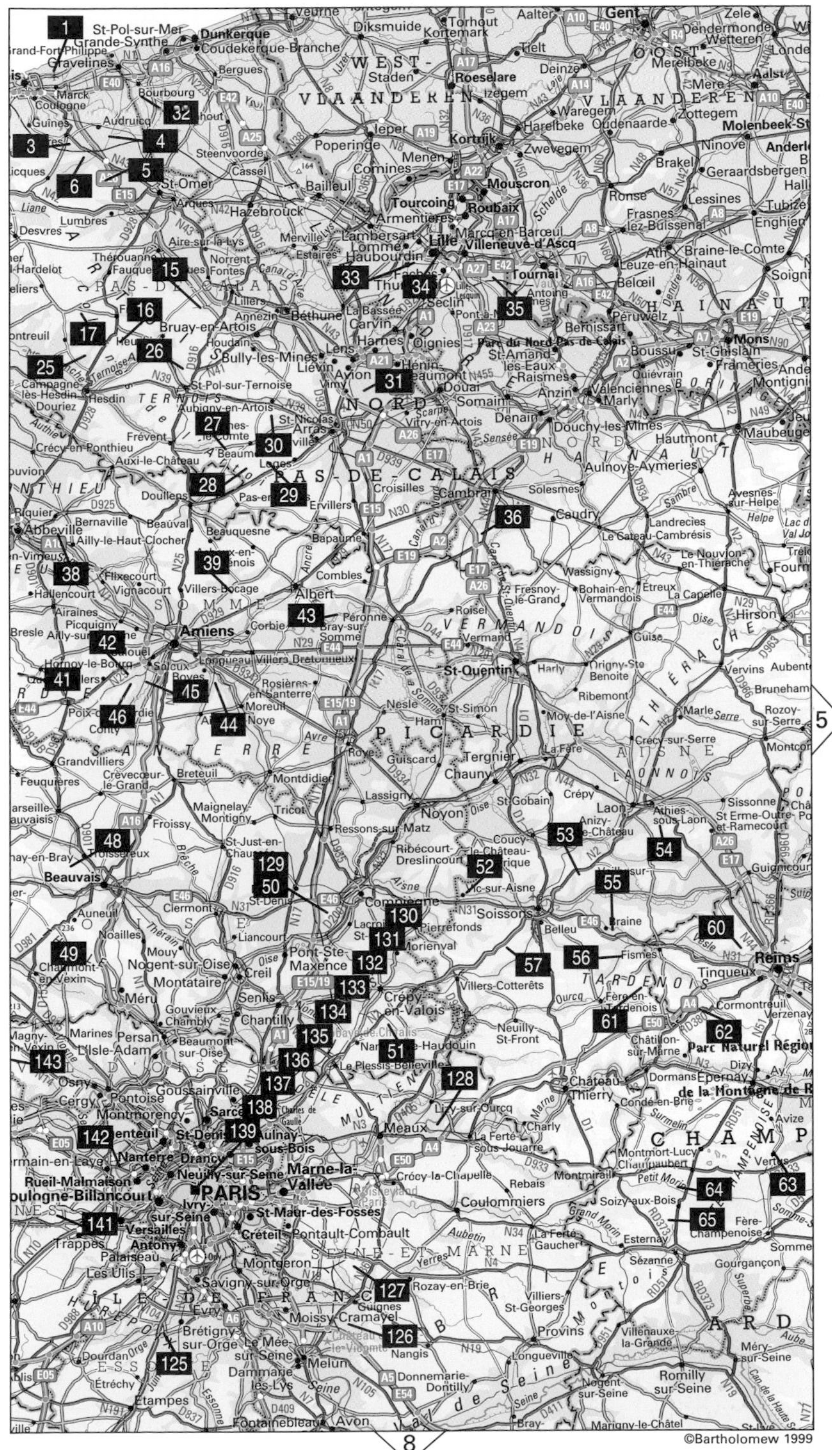

St-Pol-sur-Mer
Dunkerque
Grande-Synthe
Coudekerque-Branche
Gravelines
Bergues
Bourbourg
Marck
Coulogne
Guînes
Audruicq
Steenvoorde
Cassel
St-Omer
Arques
Hazebrouck
Lumbres
Desvres
Bailleul
Aire-sur-la-Lys
Thérouanne
Norrent-Fontes
Merville
Estaires
Lillers
Béthune
Bruay-en-Artois
Houdain
Bully-les-Mines
Liévin
Lens
Avion
Carvin
Harnes
Oignies
Hénin-Beaumont
Douai
Somain
Denain
Arras
St-Nicolas
Vitry-en-Artois
St-Pol-sur-Ternoise
Aubigny-en-Artois
Frévent
Hesdin
Campagne-lès-Hesdin
Douriez
Crécy-en-Ponthieu
Auxi-le-Château
Doullens
Beauval
Bernaville
Abbeville
Ailly-le-Haut-Clocher
Flixecourt
Vignacourt
Hallencourt
Airaines
Picquigny
Amiens
Corbie
Villers-Bocage
Beauquesne
Albert
Combles
Bapaume
Croisilles
Ervillers
Péronne
Bray-sur-Somme
Longueau
Villers-Bretonneux
Boves
Saleux
Rosières-en-Santerre
Moreuil
Hornoy-le-Bourg
Poix-de-Picardie
Conty
Grandvilliers
Feuquières
Crèvecœur-le-Grand
Breteuil
Montdidier
Roye
Nesle
Ham
St-Simon
Guiscard
Chauny
Tergnier
La Fère
Noyon
Lassigny
Maignelay-Montigny
Tricot
Ressons-sur-Matz
Froissy
St-Just-en-Chaussée
Ribécourt-Dreslincourt
Coucy-le-Château-Auffrique
Vic-sur-Aisne
Soissons
Belleu
Braine
Fismes
Beauvais
Troissereux
Auneuil
Noailles
Mouy
Clermont
Liancourt
Nogent-sur-Oise
Montataire
Creil
Pont-Ste-Maxence
Compiègne
Pierrefonds
Morienval
Senlis
Chantilly
Crépy-en-Valois
Villers-Cotterêts
Neuilly-St-Front
Nanteuil-le-Haudouin
Le Plessis-Belleville
Méru
Chambly
Persan
Beaumont-sur-Oise
L'Isle-Adam
Chaumont-en-Vexin
Magny-en-Vexin
Marines
Osny
Cergy
Pontoise
Goussainville
Montmorency
Sarcelles
St-Denis
Argenteuil
Nanterre
Drancy
Aulnay-sous-Bois
Neuilly-sur-Seine
Marne-la-Vallée
Rueil-Malmaison
Boulogne-Billancourt
PARIS
Ivry-sur-Seine
St-Maur-des-Fossés
Créteil
Pontault-Combault
Versailles
Trappes
Antony
Palaiseau
Les Ulis
Montgeron
Savigny-sur-Orge
Évry
Brétigny-sur-Orge
Moissy-Cramayel
Le Mée-sur-Seine
Melun
Dammarie-les-Lys
Dourdan
Étréchy
Étampes
Fontainebleau
Avon
Meaux
Lizy-sur-Ourcq
Crécy-la-Chapelle
La Ferté-sous-Jouarre
Charly
Coulommiers
Rebais
La Ferté-Gaucher
Rozay-en-Brie
Guignes
Nangis
Donnemarie-Dontilly
Provins
Villiers-St-Georges
Longueville
Nogent-sur-Seine
Bray
Marigny-le-Châtel
Romilly-sur-Seine
Villenauxe-la-Grande
Méry-sur-Seine
Château-Thierry
Condé-en-Brie
Montmirail
Montmort-Lucy
Champaubert
Soizy-aux-Bois
Esternay
Sézanne
Fère-Champenoise
Sommesous
Gourgançon
Vertus
Avize
Épernay
Dormans
Châtillon-sur-Marne
Dizy
Ay
Parc Naturel Régional de la Montagne de Reims
Reims
Tinqueux
Cormontreuil
Verzenay
Fère-en-Tardenois
Laon
Athies-sous-Laon
Anizy-le-Château
Crépy
St-Gobain
Sissonne
St Erme-Outre-et-Ramecourt
Guignicourt
Marle
Crécy-sur-Serre
Rozoy-sur-Serre
Montcornet
Vervins
Brunehamel
Aubenton
Hirson
La Capelle
Guise
Origny-Ste-Benoite
Ribemont
Moy-de-l'Aisne
Harly
St-Quentin
Vermand
Roisel
Fresnoy-le-Grand
Bohain-en-Vermandois
Étreux
Wassigny
Le Nouvion-en-Thiérache
Le Cateau-Cambrésis
Landrecies
Caudry
Cambrai
Solesmes
Aulnoye-Aymeries
Avesnes-sur-Helpe
Hautmont
Maubeuge
Douchy-les-Mines
Valenciennes
Marly
Anzin
Raismes
St-Amand-les-Eaux
Parc du Nord-Pas-de-Calais
Pont-à-Marcq
Seclin
Lille
Villeneuve-d'Ascq
Marcq-en-Barœul
Lambersart
Lomme
Haubourdin
Armentières
Tourcoing
Roubaix
Mouscron
Comines
Menen
Kortrijk
Zwevegem
Harelbeke
Waregem
Ieper
Poperinge
Staden
Roeselare
Izegem
Diksmuide
Torhout
Kortemark
Veurne
Tielt
Aalter
Deinze
Gent
Zele
Dendermonde
Wetteren
Merelbeke
Zottegem
Oudenaarde
Ninove
Aalst
Geraardsbergen
Brakel
Ronse
Lessines
Frasnes-lez-Buissenal
Ath
Leuze-en-Hainaut
Tournai
Antoing
Belœil
Péruwelz
Bernissart
Boussu
St-Ghislain
Quiévrain
Mons
Frameries
Enghien
Tubize
Braine-le-Comte
Soignies
WEST-VLAANDEREN
OOST-VLAANDEREN
HAINAUT
NORD
PAS-DE-CALAIS
SOMME
PICARDIE
AISNE
OISE
VAL-D'OISE
SEINE-ET-MARNE
ÎLE-DE-FRANCE
ESSONNE
CHAMPAGNE
THIÉRACHE
TARDENOIS
SANTERRE
TERNOIS
VERMANDOIS
LAONNOIS
MULTIEN
Val de Seine
1
3
4
5
6
15
16
17
25
26
27
28
29
30
31
32
33
34
35
36
38
39
41
42
43
44
45
46
48
49
50
51
52
53
54
55
56
57
60
61
62
63
64
65
125
126
127
128
129
130
131
132
133
134
135
136
137
138
139
141
142
143
5
8
©Bartholomew 1999

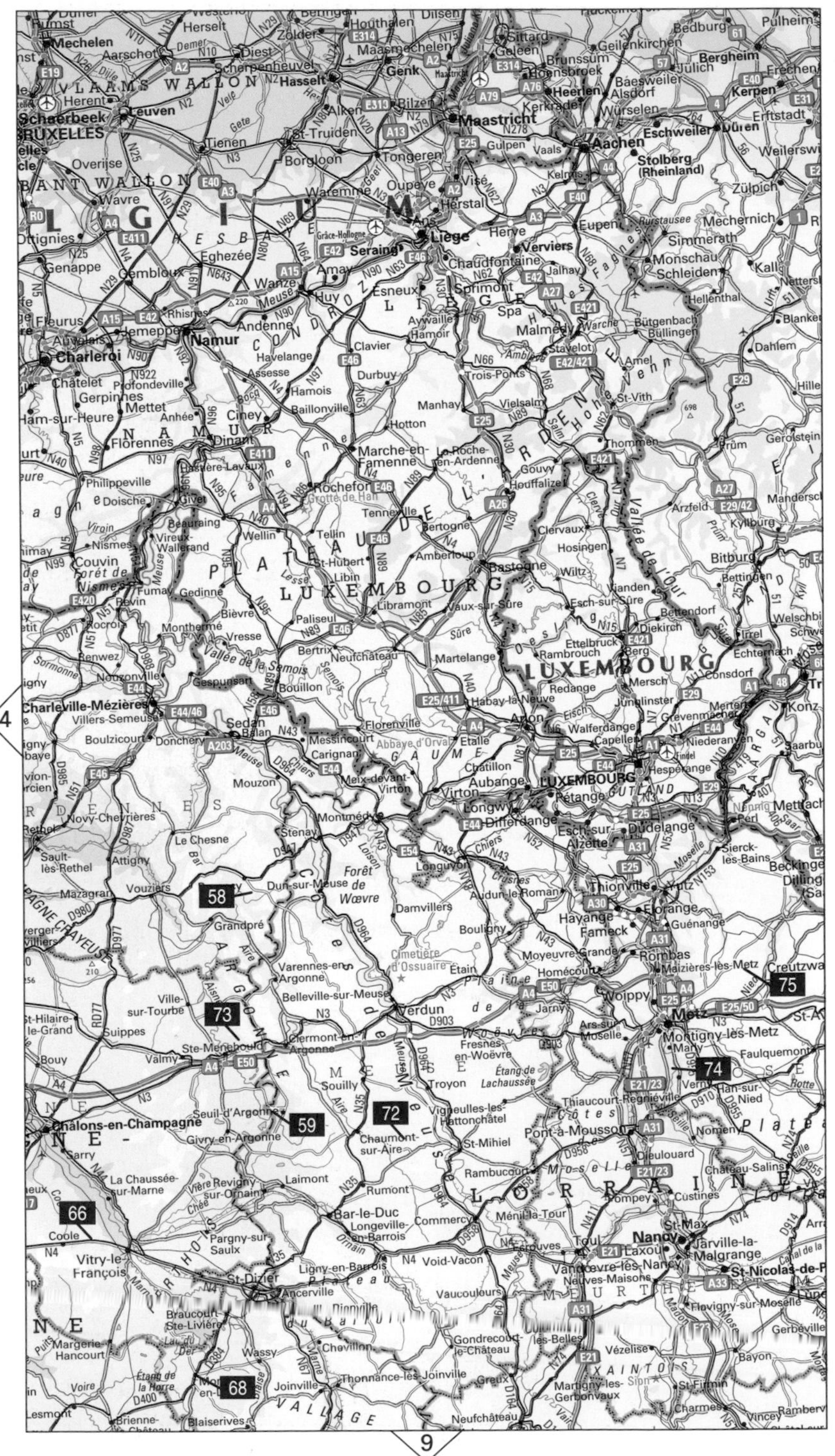

Mechelen
Aarschot
Diest
Zolder
Houthalen
Hasselt
Genk
Maasmechelen
Sittard
Geleen
Geilenkirchen
Bedburg
Pulheim
Bergheim
Jülich
Frechen
Brunssum
Hoensbroek
Heerlen
Baesweiler
Alsdorf
Kerpen
Kerkrade
Würselen
Erftstadt
Eschweiler
Düren
Maastricht
Aachen
Stolberg (Rheinland)
Weilerswist
Zülpich
Schaerbeek
BRUXELLES
Leuven
Herent
Tienen
St-Truiden
Alken
Bilzen
Borgloon
Tongeren
Gulpen
Vaals
Overijse
Wavre
Waremme
Oupeye
Visé
Herstal
Ans
Liège
Seraing
Herve
Verviers
Eupen
Mechernich
Simmerath
Monschau
Schleiden
Hellenthal
Ottignies
Genappe
Gembloux
Eghezée
Wanze
Huy
Amay
Chaudfontaine
Esneux
Sprimont
Spa
Jalhay
Malmedy
Bütgenbach
Büllingen
Dahlem
Fleurus
Charleroi
Jemeppe
Namur
Andenne
Aywaille
Hamoir
Stavelot
Amel
Châtelet
Gerpinnes
Profondeville
Havelange
Assesse
Clavier
Durbuy
Trois-Ponts
Vielsalm
St-Vith
Ham-sur-Heure
Mettet
Anhée
Ciney
Hamois
Baillonville
Manhay
Hotton
Florennes
Dinant
Marche-en-Famenne
La Roche-en-Ardenne
Thommen
Prüm
Gerolstein
Philippeville
Doische
Givet
Rochefort
Grotte de Han
Tenneville
Houffalize
Gouvy
Arzfeld
Beauraing
Wellin
Tellin
Bertogne
Clervaux
Hosingen
Kyllburg
Nismes
Vireux-Wallerand
Couvin
St-Hubert
Libin
Amberloup
Bastogne
Wiltz
Bitburg
Fumay
Revin
Gedinne
Libramont
Vaux-sur-Sûre
Vianden
Esch-sur-Sûre
Bettingen
Rocroi
Bièvre
Paliseul
Diekirch
Ettelbruck
Bettendorf
Monthermé
Vresse
Bertrix
Neufchâteau
Martelange
Rambrouch
Irrel
Echternach
LUXEMBOURG
Renwez
Nouzonville
Bouillon
Redange
Mersch
Consdorf
Charleville-Mézières
Villers-Semeuse
Sedan
Balan
Habay-la-Neuve
Arlon
Junglinster
Grevenmacher
Konz
Boulzicourt
Donchery
Florenville
Messincourt
Carignan
Abbaye d'Orval
Etalle
Walferdange
Capellen
Niederanven
Findel
Mouzon
Meix-devant-Virton
Virton
Châtillon
Aubange
Pétange
Hesperange
Novy-Chevrières
Montmédy
Longwy
Differdange
Esch-sur-Alzette
Dudelange
Perl
Mettlach
Le Chesne
Stenay
Longuyon
Sierck-les-Bains
Beckingen
Dillingen
Sault-lès-Rethel
Attigny
Forêt de Wœvre
Audun-le-Roman
Thionville
Yutz
Mazagran
Vouziers
Dun-sur-Meuse
Damvillers
Florange
Hayange
Fameck
Guénange
Grandpré
Bouligny
Moyeuvre-Grande
Rombas
Maizières-lès-Metz
Creutzwald
Varennes-en-Argonne
Cimetière d'Ossuaire
Étain
Homécourt
Woippy
Ville-sur-Tourbe
Belleville-sur-Meuse
Verdun
Jarny
Metz
St-Hilaire-le-Grand
Suippes
Clermont-en-Argonne
Ars-sur-Moselle
Montigny-lès-Metz
Marly
Faulquemont
Valmy
Ste-Menehould
Fresnes-en-Woëvre
Bouy
Souilly
Troyon
Étang de Lachaussée
Verny
Han-sur-Nied
Seuil-d'Argonne
Vigneulles-lès-Hattonchâtel
Thiaucourt-Regniéville
Châlons-en-Champagne
Givry-en-Argonne
Chaumont-sur-Aire
St-Mihiel
Pont-à-Mousson
Nomeny
Sarry
Dieulouard
Château-Salins
La Chaussée-sur-Marne
Revigny-sur-Ornain
Laimont
Rumont
Rambucourt
Pompey
Custines
Bar-le-Duc
Longeville-en-Barrois
Commercy
Ménil-la-Tour
Coole
Pargny-sur-Saulx
Nancy
St-Max
Jarville-la-Malgrange
Vitry-le-François
Ligny-en-Barrois
Void-Vacon
Toul
Laxou
Vandœuvre-lès-Nancy
Neuves-Maisons
St-Nicolas-de-Port
St-Dizier
Ancerville
Vaucouleurs
Flavigny-sur-Moselle
Braucourt
Ste-Livière
Gondrecourt-le-Château
Vézelise
Gerbéviller
Margerie-Hancourt
Wassy
Chevillon
Bayon
Thonnance-lès-Joinville
Joinville
Gréux
Mattaincourt-lès-Gerbonvaux
St-Firmin
Charmes
Vincey
Rambervillers
Lesmont
Brienne-le-Château
Blaiserives
Neufchâteau
Étang de la Horre
58
59
66
68
72
73
74
75

4

9

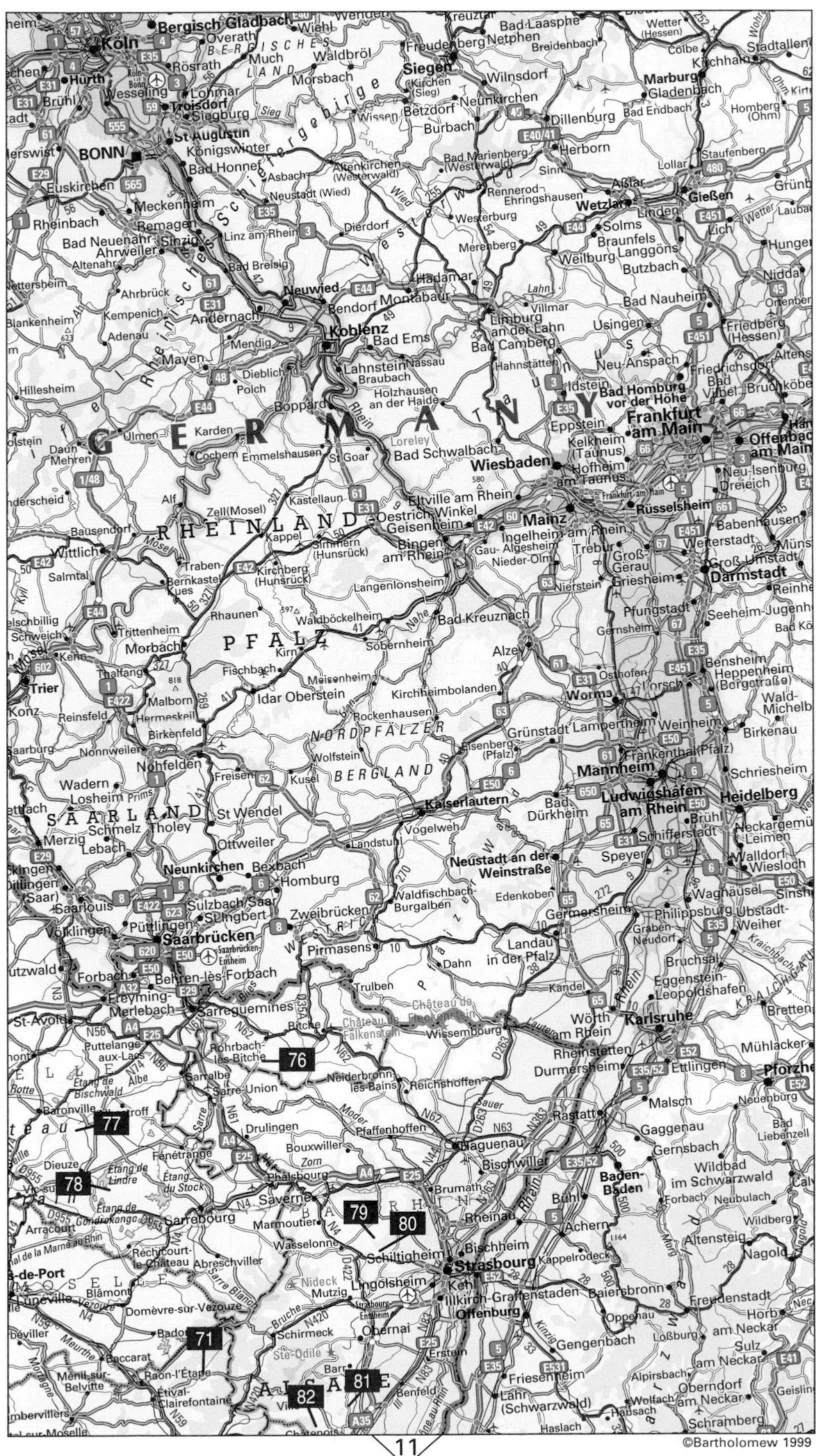

Köln
Bergisch Gladbach
Overath
Wiehl
Rösrath
Much
Waldbröl
Freudenberg
Netphen
Bad Laasphe
Wetter (Hessen)
Siegen
Marburg
Gladenbach
Hürth
Wesseling
Lohmar
Troisdorf
Siegburg
Morsbach
Wissen
Betzdorf
Neunkirchen
Wilnsdorf
Dillenburg
Bad Endbach
Homberg (Ohm)
Brühl
St Augustin
BONN
Königswinter
Bad Honnef
Asbach
Altenkirchen (Westerwald)
Burbach
Bad Marienberg (Westerwald)
Herborn
Staufenberg
Lollar
Euskirchen
Meckenheim
Neustadt (Wied)
Rennerod
Ehringshausen
Aßlar
Wetzlar
Gießen
Linden
Rheinbach
Remagen
Sinzig
Linz am Rhein
Dierdorf
Westerburg
Solms
Lich
Bad Neuenahr-Ahrweiler
Bad Breisig
Merenberg
Braunfels
Weilburg
Langgöns
Butzbach
Hungen
Nettersheim
Ahrbrück
Neuwied
Hadamar
Montabaur
Bendorf
Limburg an der Lahn
Villmar
Bad Nauheim
Nidda
Blankenheim
Kempenich
Andernach
Adenau
Koblenz
Bad Ems
Bad Camberg
Usingen
Friedberg (Hessen)
Mendig
Mayen
Dieblich
Lahnstein
Nassau
Braubach
Hahnstätten
Neu-Anspach
Friedrichsdorf
Bad Vilbel
Hillesheim
Polch
Holzhausen an der Haide
Idstein
Bad Homburg vor der Höhe
Boppard
GERMANY
Daun
Mehren
Ulmen
Karden
Cochem
Emmelshausen
St Goar
Loreley
Bad Schwalbach
Eppstein
Kelkheim (Taunus)
Hofheim am Taunus
Frankfurt am Main
Offenbach am Main
Wiesbaden
Neu-Isenburg
Dreieich
Eltville am Rhein
Oestrich-Winkel
Geisenheim
Kastellaun
Alf
Zell (Mosel)
RHEINLAND
Kappel
Simmern (Hunsrück)
Bingen am Rhein
Mainz
Ingelheim am Rhein
Rüsselsheim
Gau-Algesheim
Nieder-Olm
Trebur
Groß-Gerau
Babenhausen
Weiterstadt
Groß-Umstadt
Darmstadt
Bausendorf
Wittlich
Salmtal
Traben-Trarbach
Kirchberg (Hunsrück)
Bernkastel-Kues
Langenlonsheim
Nierstein
Griesheim
Pfungstadt
Seeheim-Jugenheim
Schweich
Trittenheim
Rhaunen
Waldböckelheim
Bad Kreuznach
Gernsheim
Morbach
PFALZ
Sobernheim
Kirn
Alzey
Trier
Thalfang
Fischbach
Meisenheim
Osthofen
Bensheim
Heppenheim (Bergstraße)
Idar Oberstein
Kirchheimbolanden
Worms
Konz
Reinsfeld
Malborn
Hermeskeil
Rockenhausen
Lampertheim
Weinheim
Birkenfeld
NORDPFÄLZER
BERGLAND
Grünstadt
Eisenberg (Pfalz)
Frankenthal (Pfalz)
Saarburg
Nonnweiler
Nohfelden
Freisen
Kusel
Wolfstein
Mannheim
Schriesheim
Wadern
Losheim
Ludwigshafen am Rhein
Heidelberg
SAARLAND
Schmelz
Tholey
St Wendel
Kaiserslautern
Bad Dürkheim
Brühl
Merzig
Lebach
Ottweiler
Landstuhl
Vogelweh
Schifferstadt
Neckargemünd
Leimen
Neunkirchen
Bexbach
Homburg
Neustadt an der Weinstraße
Speyer
Walldorf
Wiesloch
Dillingen (Saar)
Saarlouis
Sulzbach/Saar
St Ingbert
Waldfischbach-Burgalben
Edenkoben
Waghäusel
Püttlingen
Zweibrücken
Germersheim
Philippsburg
Ubstadt-Weiher
Völklingen
Saarbrücken
Pirmasens
Graben-Neudorf
Forbach
Behren-lès-Forbach
Dahn
Landau in der Pfalz
Bruchsal
Freyming-Merlebach
Sarreguemines
Trulben
Kandel
Eggenstein-Leopoldshafen
St-Avold
Bitche
Château de Fleckenstein
Wörth am Rhein
Karlsruhe
Puttelange-aux-Lacs
Rohrbach-lès-Bitche
Wissembourg
Rheinstetten
Ettlingen
Mühlacker
Pforzheim
Étang de Bischwald
Sarralbe
Sarre-Union
Niederbronn-les-Bains
Reichshoffen
Durmersheim
Neuenbürg
Baronville
Rastatt
Malsch
Bad Liebenzell
Drulingen
Pfaffenhoffen
Haguenau
Gaggenau
Bouxwiller
Fénétrange
Bischwiller
Gernsbach
Dieuze
Étang de Lindre
Étang du Stock
Phalsbourg
Baden-Baden
Wildbad im Schwarzwald
Saverne
Brumath
Forbach
Neubulach
Sarrebourg
Marmoutier
Rheinau
Bühl
Achern
Wildberg
Arracourt
Réchicourt-le-Château
Abreschviller
Wasselonne
Schiltigheim
Bischheim
Strasbourg
Kappelrodeck
Altensteig
Nagold
Nideck
Lingolsheim
Kehl
Lunéville
Blâmont
Mutzig
Illkirch-Graffenstaden
Baiersbronn
Freudenstadt
Domèvre-sur-Vezouze
Offenburg
Oppenau
Horb am Neckar
Badonviller
Schirmeck
Obernai
Loßburg
Gengenbach
Sulz am Neckar
Baccarat
Ste-Odile
Ménil-sur-Belvitte
Raon-l'Étape
Étival-Clairefontaine
Barr
Erstein
Benfeld
Friesenheim
Alpirsbach
Oberndorf am Neckar
ALSACE
Lahr (Schwarzwald)
Wolfach
Hausach
Haslach
Schramberg
76
77
78
79
80
71
81
82

11

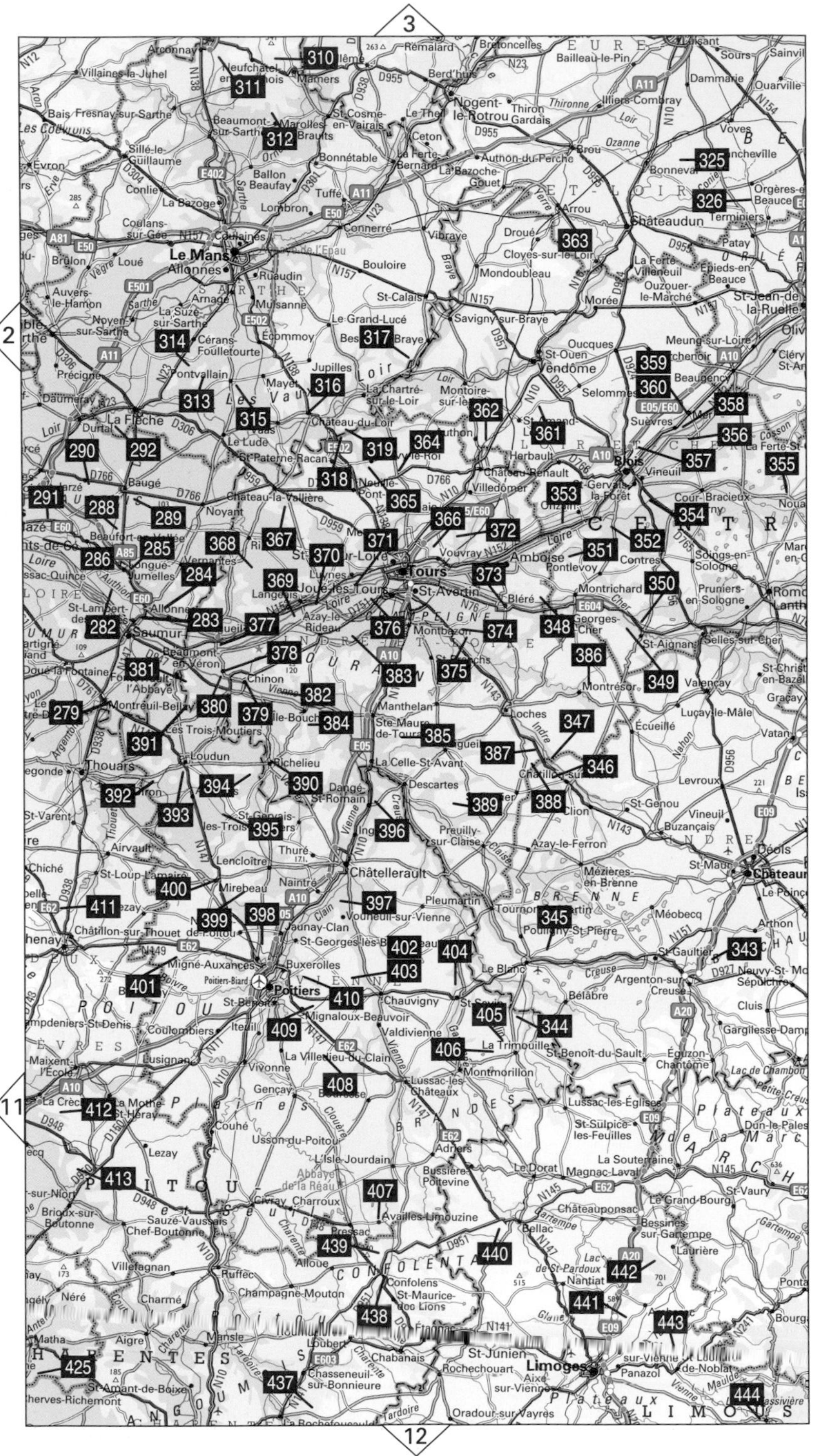
3
2
11
12
Le Mans
Tours
Poitiers
Limoges
Blois
Saumur
Châtellerault
Vendôme
Châteaudun
Amboise
Loches
Chinon
Thouars
Loudun
Nogent-le-Rotrou
La Flèche
Montmorillon
St-Junien

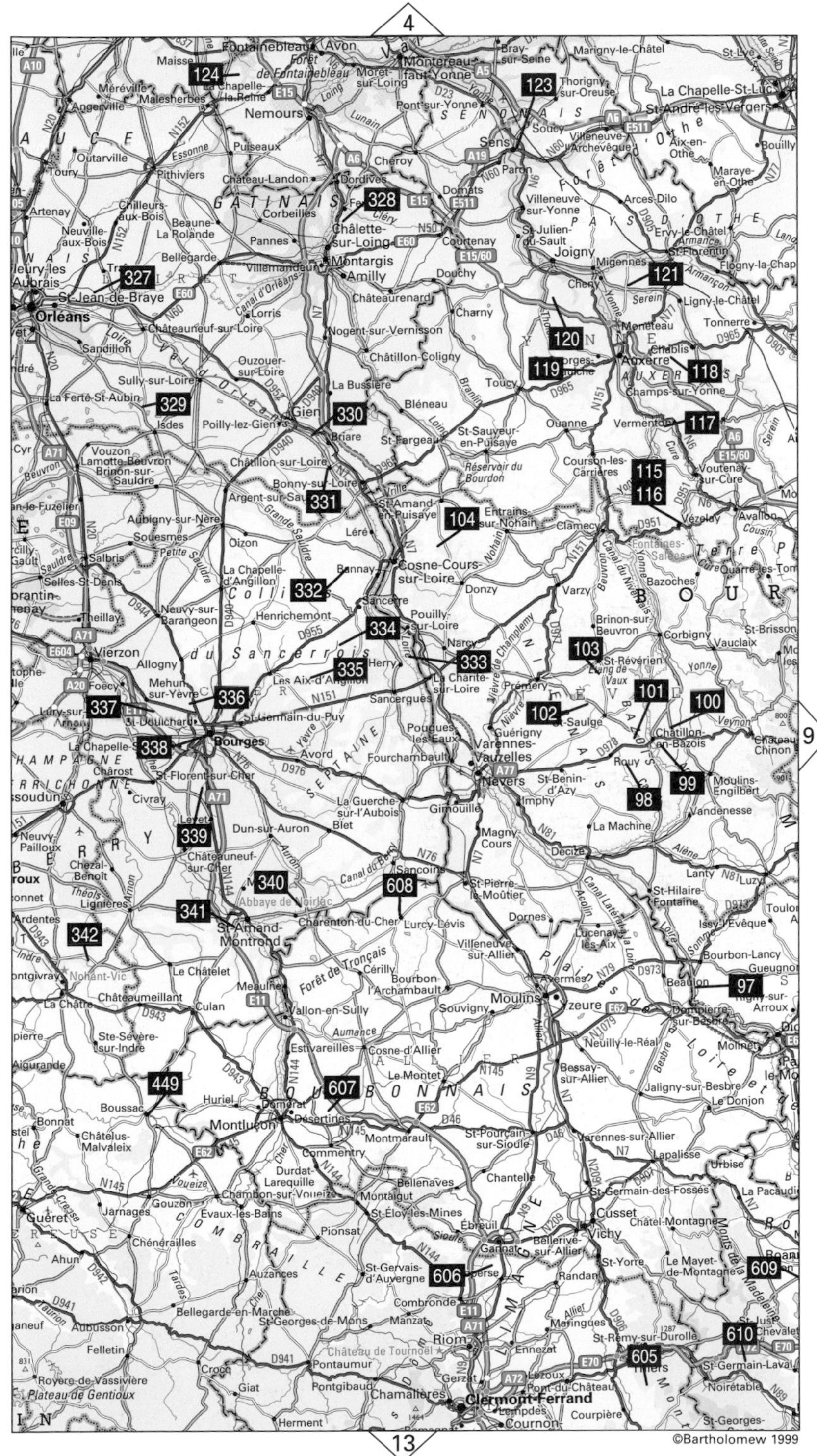

©Bartholomew 1999

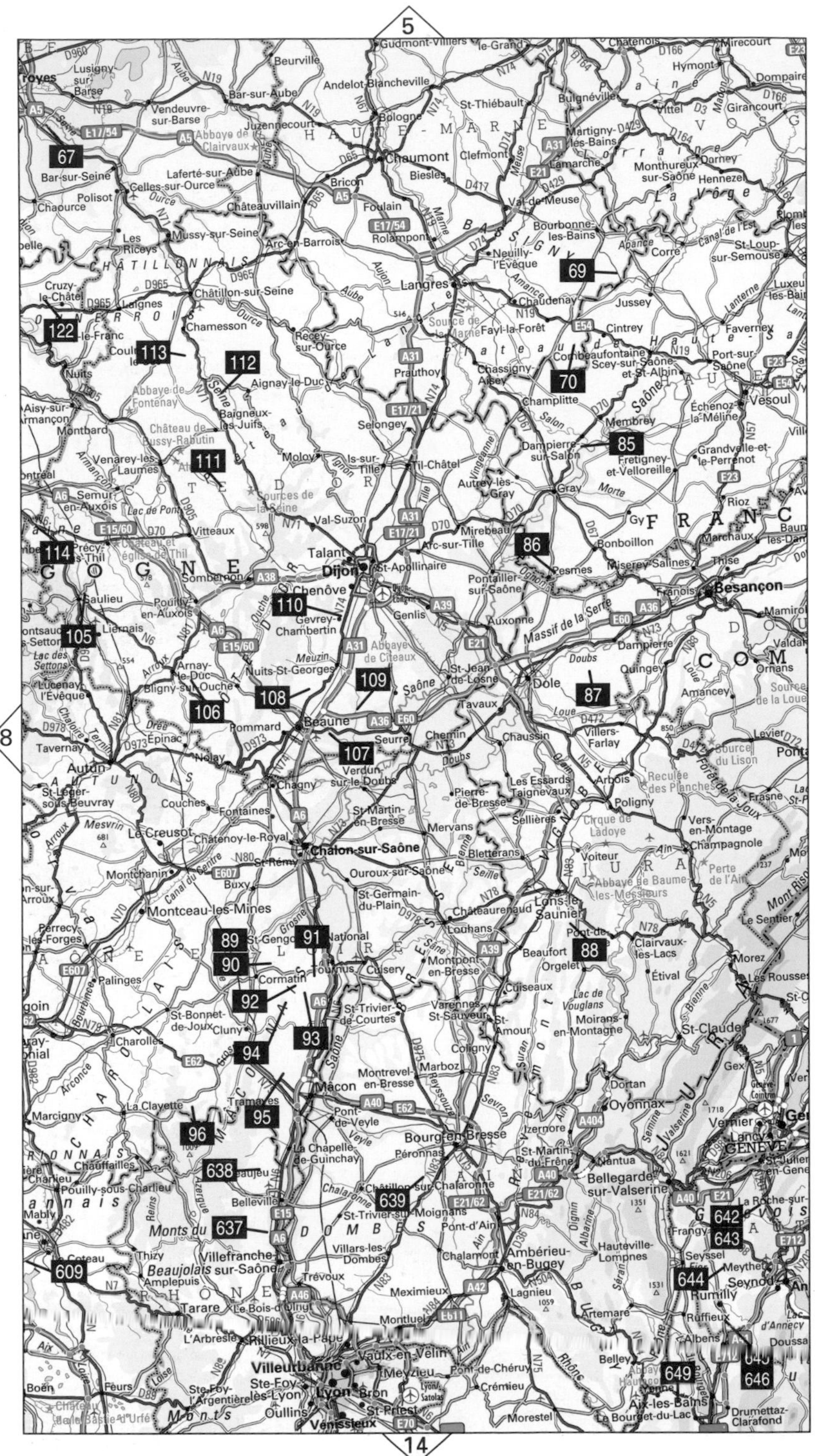
5
8
14
Troyes
Bar-sur-Aube
Bar-sur-Seine
Chaumont
Langres
Châtillon-sur-Seine
Dijon
Besançon
Vesoul
Gray
Dole
Beaune
Chalon-sur-Saône
Lons-le-Saunier
Autun
Le Creusot
Montceau-les-Mines
Cluny
Mâcon
Bourg-en-Bresse
Villefranche-sur-Saône
Lyon
Villeurbanne
Vénissieux
Oyonnax
Nantua
Bellegarde-sur-Valserine
St-Claude
Genève
Rumilly
Aix-les-Bains
Belley
Ambérieu-en-Bugey
Tarare
Pesmes
Auxonne
Genlis
Seurre
Louhans
Poligny
Arbois
Champagnole
Vittel
Langres
Saulieu
Semur-en-Auxois
Montbard
Nuits-St-Georges
Gevrey-Chambertin
Tournus
La Clayette
Charolles
Paray-le-Monial
Trévoux
Meximieux
67
69
70
85
86
87
88
89
90
91
92
93
94
95
96
105
106
107
108
109
110
111
112
113
114
122
609
637
638
639
642
643
644
645
646
649

6

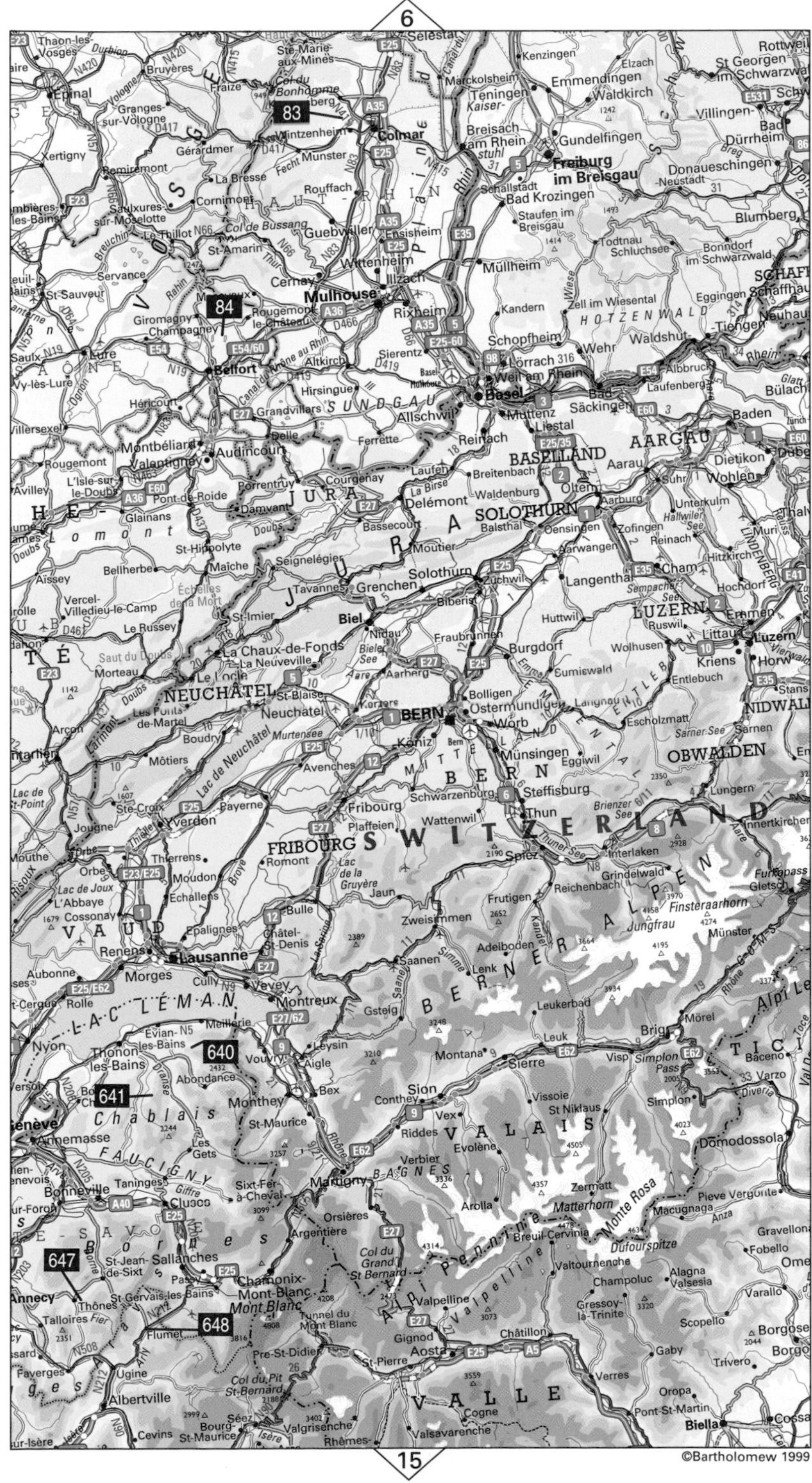

Epinal
Colmar
Freiburg im Breisgau
Mulhouse
Belfort
Basel
BASELLAND
AARGAU
SOLOTHURN
J U R A
Delémont
Solothurn
Biel
NEUCHÂTEL
Neuchâtel
BERN
B E R N
FRIBOURG
Fribourg
S W I T Z E R L A N D
LUZERN
Luzern
OBWALDEN
V A U D
Lausanne
L A C   L É M A N
Montreux
Genève
Annecy
Sion
V A L A I S
B E R N E R   A L P E N
Jungfrau
Finsteraarhorn
Matterhorn
Monte Rosa
Zermatt
Mont Blanc
Chamonix-Mont-Blanc
Aosta
V A L L E
Biella
Domodossola
Thun
Interlaken
Brig
Martigny
Albertville

15

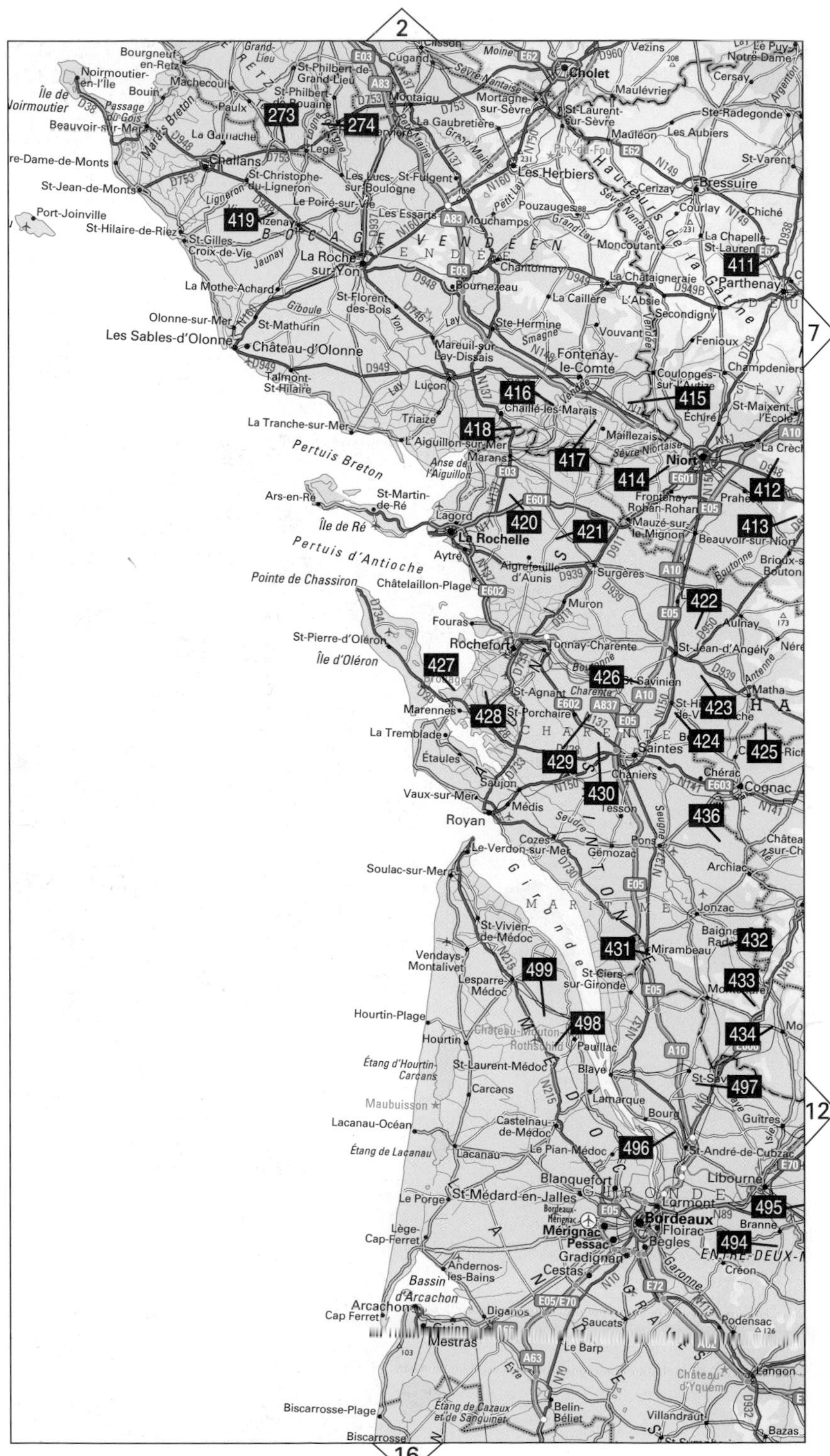
2
7
12
16
Bourgneuf-en-Retz
Noirmoutier-en-l'Île
Île de Noirmoutier
Machecoul
Bouin
Beauvoir-sur-Mer
Marais Breton
La Garnache
Paulx
St-Philbert-de-Grand-Lieu
St-Philbert-de-Bouaine
Cugand
Clisson
Montaigu
Cholet
Vezins
Le Puy-Notre-Dame
Cersay
Maulévrier
Mortagne-sur-Sèvre
St-Laurent-sur-Sèvre
Ste-Radegonde
La Gaubretière
Mauléon
Les Aubiers
Puy-du-Fou
St-Varent
Bressuire
Cerizay
Courlay
Chiché
Challans
Légé
St-Jean-de-Monts
St-Christophe-du-Ligneron
Les Lucs-sur-Boulogne
St-Fulgent
Les Herbiers
Port-Joinville
Le Poiré-sur-Vie
Les Essarts
Mouchamps
Pouzauges
St-Hilaire-de-Riez
St-Gilles-Croix-de-Vie
B O C A G E
V E N D É E N
La Roche-sur-Yon
Chantonnay
Moncoutant
La Chapelle-St-Laurent
Parthenay
La Châtaigneraie
Bournezeau
La Caillère
L'Absie
Secondigny
La Mothe-Achard
St-Florent-des-Bois
Olonne-sur-Mer
St-Mathurin
Les Sables-d'Olonne
Château-d'Olonne
Mareuil-sur-Lay-Dissais
Ste-Hermine
Vouvant
Fenioux
Fontenay-le-Comte
Champdeniers
Talmont-St-Hilaire
Luçon
Coulonges-sur-l'Autize
Chaillé-les-Marais
Échiré
St-Maixent-l'École
La Tranche-sur-Mer
Triaize
Maillezais
L'Aiguillon-sur-Mer
Pertuis Breton
Anse de l'Aiguillon
Marans
Niort
La Crèche
Ars-en-Ré
St-Martin-de-Ré
Île de Ré
Frontenay-Rohan-Rohan
Prahecq
Lagord
La Rochelle
Mauzé-sur-le-Mignon
Beauvoir-sur-Niort
Pertuis d'Antioche
Aytré
Aigrefeuille-d'Aunis
Surgères
Pointe de Chassiron
Châtelaillon-Plage
Muron
Aulnay
Fouras
St-Pierre-d'Oléron
Île d'Oléron
Rochefort
Tonnay-Charente
St-Jean-d'Angély
St-Savinien
Matha
St-Agnant
St-Porchaire
Marennes
La Tremblade
Saintes
Étaules
Chaniers
Chérac
Cognac
Saujon
Vaux-sur-Mer
Médis
Royan
Cozes
Le-Verdon-sur-Mer
Gémozac
Pons
Archiac
Soulac-sur-Mer
Jonzac
St-Vivien-de-Médoc
Mirambeau
Vendays-Montalivet
Lesparre-Médoc
St-Ciers-sur-Gironde
Hourtin-Plage
Hourtin
Château-Mouton-Rothschild
Pauillac
Étang d'Hourtin-Carcans
St-Laurent-Médoc
Blaye
Carcans
Maubuisson
Lamarque
Bourg
Lacanau-Océan
Castelnau-de-Médoc
Guîtres
Étang de Lacanau
Lacanau
Le Pian-Médoc
St-André-de-Cubzac
Blanquefort
Libourne
Le Porge
St-Médard-en-Jalles
Lormont
Bordeaux
Mérignac
Floirac
Branne
Pessac
Bègles
Lège-Cap-Ferret
Gradignan
Créon
Cestas
Andernos-les-Bains
Bassin d'Arcachon
Arcachon
Cap Ferret
Biganos
Saucats
Podensac
Mestras
Le Barp
Château d'Yquem
Langon
Biscarrosse-Plage
Étang de Cazaux et de Sanguinet
Belin-Béliet
Villandraut
Bazas
Biscarrosse
273
274
411
412
413
414
415
416
417
418
419
420
421
422
423
424
425
426
427
428
429
430
431
432
433
434
436
494
495
496
497
498
499

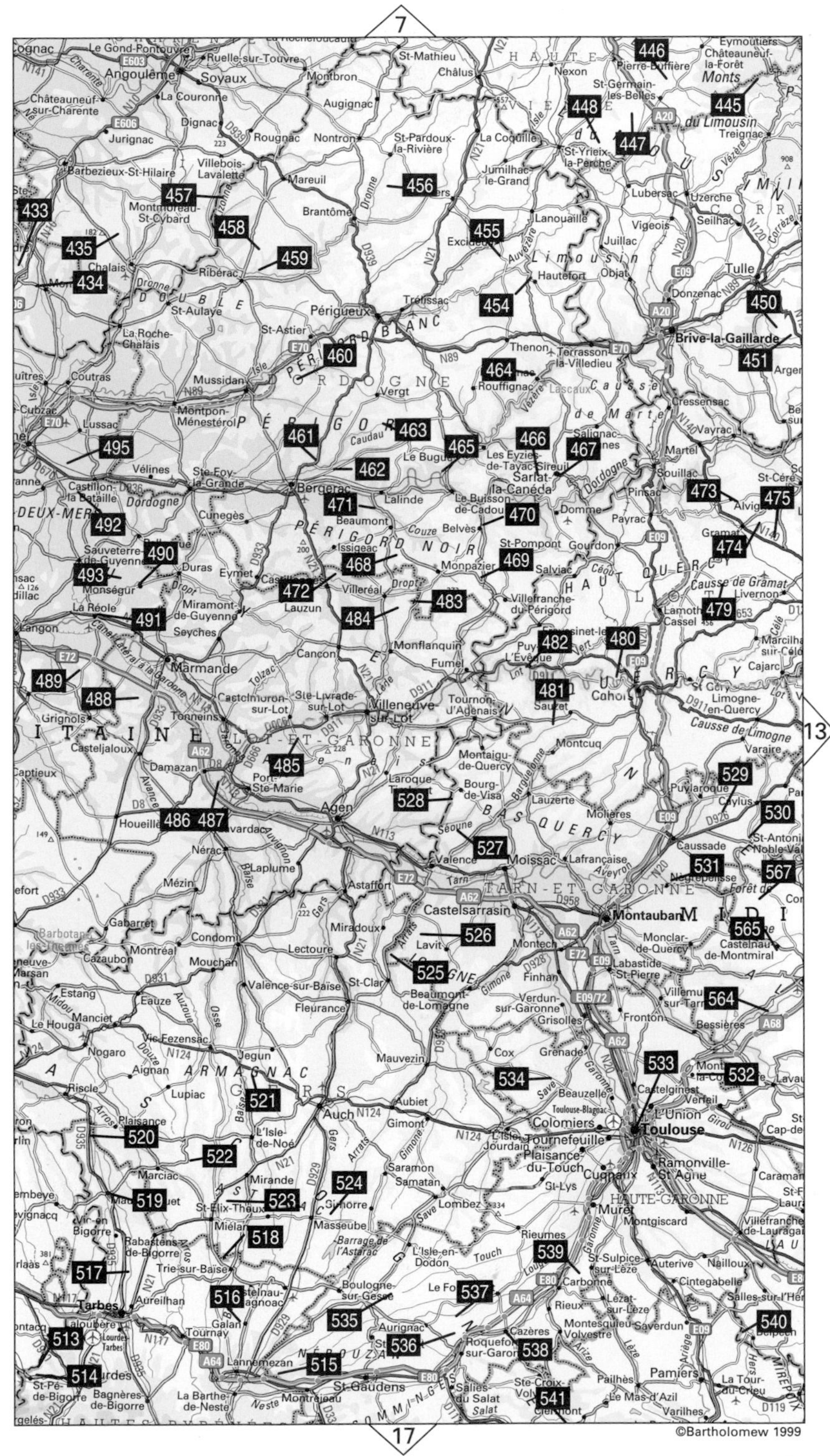

7
13
17
Angoulême
Soyaux
La Couronne
Châteauneuf-sur-Charente
Jurignac
Dignac
Barbezieux-St-Hilaire
Villebois-Lavalette
Montmoreau-St-Cybard
Chalais
Ribérac
St-Aulaye
La Roche-Chalais
Coutras
Mussidan
Montpon-Ménestérol
Lussac
Vélines
Ste-Foy-la-Grande
Castillon-la-Bataille
Sauveterre-de-Guyenne
Monségur
La Réole
Duras
Eymet
Bergerac
Lalinde
Beaumont
Issigeac
Villeréal
Lauzun
Miramont-de-Guyenne
Seyches
Marmande
Tonneins
Casteljaloux
Damazan
Castelmoron-sur-Lot
Ste-Livrade-sur-Lot
Villeneuve-sur-Lot
Cancon
Monflanquin
Fumel
Tournon-d'Agenais
Port-Ste-Marie
Agen
Nérac
Laplume
Mézin
Condom
Montréal
Gabarret
Cazaubon
Mouchan
Eauze
Estang
Manciet
Le Houga
Nogaro
Vic-Fezensac
Aignan
Riscle
Plaisance
Marciac
Lupiac
Jegun
Valence-sur-Baïse
Lectoure
Fleurance
Miradoux
Astaffort
St-Clar
Mauvezin
Auch
L'Isle-de-Noé
Mirande
St-Elix-Theux
Miélan
Masseube
Seissan
Gimont
Aubiet
Saramon
Samatan
Lombez
L'Isle-en-Dodon
Boulogne-sur-Gesse
Aurignac
Galan
Tournay
Lannemezan
Montréjeau
St-Gaudens
La Barthe-de-Neste
Bagnères-de-Bigorre
Tarbes
Aureilhan
Rabastens-de-Bigorre
Trie-sur-Baïse
Vic-en-Bigorre
Lourdes
St-Pé-de-Bigorre
Nontron
Montbron
Rougnac
Mareuil
Brantôme
St-Mathieu
Châlus
St-Pardoux-la-Rivière
La Coquille
Jumilhac-le-Grand
Excideuil
Lanouaille
Hautefort
Périgueux
Trélissac
St-Astier
Vergt
Thenon
Rouffignac
Le Bugue
Les Eyzies-de-Tayac-Sireuil
Sarlat-la-Canéda
Le Buisson-de-Cadouin
Belvès
Domme
St-Pompont
Monpazier
Gourdon
Salviac
Villefranche-du-Périgord
Puy-l'Évêque
Cahors
Sauzet
Montcuq
Lauzerte
Montaigu-de-Quercy
Bourg-de-Visa
Laroque-Timbaut
Valence
Moissac
Lafrançaise
Castelsarrasin
Lavit
Beaumont-de-Lomagne
Montech
Finhan
Verdun-sur-Garonne
Grisolles
Montauban
Caussade
Nègrepelisse
Monclar-de-Quercy
Castelnau-de-Montmiral
Fronton
Bessières
Villemur-sur-Tarn
Labastide-St-Pierre
Cox
Grenade
Beauzelle
Colomiers
Toulouse
L'Union
Castelginest
Verfeil
Tournefeuille
Plaisance-du-Touch
Cugnaux
Ramonville-St-Agne
St-Lys
Muret
Montgiscard
Rieumes
St-Sulpice-sur-Lèze
Carbonne
Rieux
Lézat-sur-Lèze
Montesquieu-Volvestre
Cazères
Saverdun
Pamiers
Le Mas-d'Azil
Pailhès
Varilhes
Autérive
Nailloux
Cintegabelle
Villefranche-de-Lauragais
Caraman
Nexon
Pierre-Buffière
St-Germain-les-Belles
St-Yrieix-la-Perche
Lubersac
Uzerche
Seilhac
Vigeois
Juillac
Objat
Tulle
Donzenac
Brive-la-Gaillarde
Terrasson-la-Villedieu
Lascaux
Cressensac
Vayrac
Martel
Souillac
Pinsac
Payrac
Gramat
Livernon
Lamothe-Cassel
Cajarc
Limogne-en-Quercy
Varaire
Puylaroque
Caylus
Eymoutiers
Châteauneuf-la-Forêt
Treignac
Monts du Limousin
Causse de Gramat
Causse de Limogne
DORDOGNE
LOT-ET-GARONNE
TARN-ET-GARONNE
HAUTE-GARONNE
PÉRIGORD BLANC
PÉRIGORD NOIR
HAUT QUERCY
BAS QUERCY
ARMAGNAC
LOMAGNE
GERS
Garonne
Dordogne
Lot
Tarn
A62
A64
A20
E70
E72
E80
E09
N21
N89
N124
N113
©Bartholomew 1999

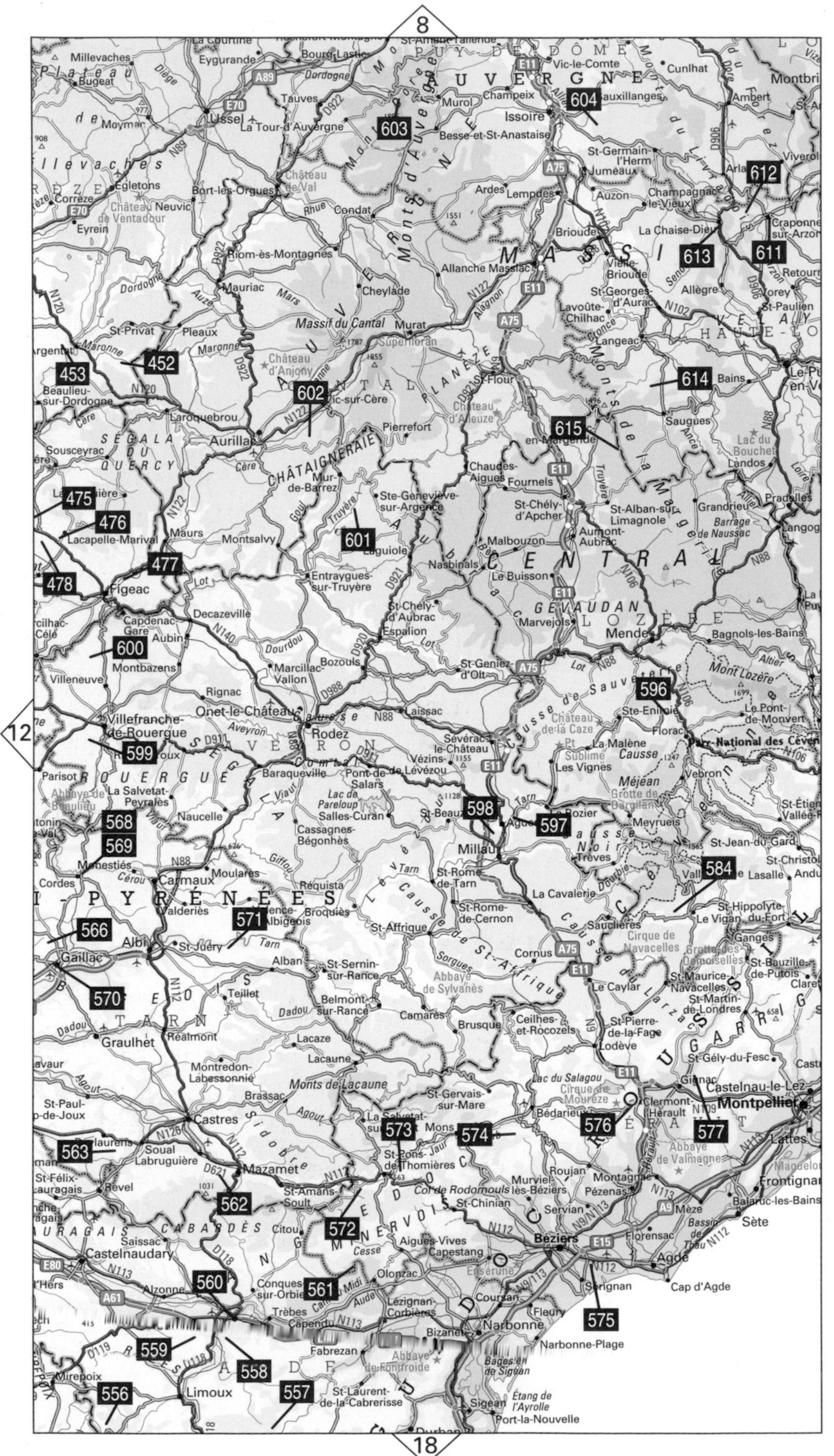

8
12
18
Millevaches
Eygurande
Bourg-Lastic
Bugeat
Ussel
La Tour-d'Auvergne
Tauves
Murol
Champeix
Vic-le-Comte
Cunlhat
Ambert
Montbrison
AUVERGNE
PUY-DE-DÔME
Issoire
Sauxillanges
Besse-et-St-Anastaise
Moymac
St-Germain-l'Herm
Jumeaux
Arlanc
Viverols
Egletons
Bort-les-Orgues
Château de Val
Corrèze
Neuvic
Château de Ventadour
Eyrein
Condat
Ardes
Lempdes
Auzon
Champagnac-le-Vieux
Brioude
La Chaise-Dieu
Craponne-sur-Arzon
Riom-ès-Montagnes
Allanche
Massiac
Vieille-Brioude
Retournac
Mauriac
Cheylade
St-Georges-d'Aurac
Allègre
Yssingeaux
Vorey
St-Paulien
Massif du Cantal
Murat
Lavoûte-Chilhac
Langeac
St-Privat
Pleaux
Superlioran
VELAY
HAUTE-LOIRE
Argentat
Château d'Anjony
Le Puy-en-Velay
Beaulieu-sur-Dordogne
Vic-sur-Cère
St-Flour
Bains
Château d'Alleuze
Laroquebrou
Aurillac
Pierrefort
Saugues
Lac du Bouchet
Landos
en-Margeride
Sousceyrac
SÉGALA DU QUERCY
CHÂTAIGNERAIE
Mur-de-Barrez
Chaudes-Aigues
Fournels
Ste-Geneviève-sur-Argence
St-Chély-d'Apcher
St-Alban-sur-Limagnole
Grandrieu
Pradelles
Barrage de Naussac
Langogne
Lacapelle-Marival
Maurs
Montsalvy
Laguiole
Malbouzon
Aumont-Aubrac
Nasbinals
Le Buisson
CENTRAL
Figeac
Entraygues-sur-Truyère
Decazeville
GÉVAUDAN
LOZÈRE
Marvejols
Mende
Capdenac-Gare
Aubin
St-Chély-d'Aubrac
Espalion
Bagnols-les-Bains
Montbazens
Bozouls
Marcillac-Vallon
St-Geniez-d'Olt
Mont Lozère
Villeneuve
Rignac
Causse de Sauveterre
Ste-Enimie
Le Pont-de-Montvert
Villefranche-de-Rouergue
Onet-le-Château
Rodez
Laissac
Château de la Caze
Florac
Parc National des Cévennes
Aveyron
Sévérac-le-Château
La Malène
Causse Méjean
Les Vignes
Parisot
ROUERGUE
Baraqueville
Vézins-de-Lévézou
Pont-de-Salars
Vebron
Abbaye de Beaulieu
La Salvetat-Peyralès
Lac de Pareloup
Salles-Curan
Grotte de Dargilan
St-Étienne-Vallée-Française
Naucelle
Cassagnes-Bégonhès
St-Beauzély
Aguessac
Le Rozier
Meyrueis
Causse Noir
St-Jean-du-Gard
Millau
Trèves
Ménestiés
Moularès
Carmaux
St-Rome-de-Tarn
Valleraugue
Lasalle
Cordes
MIDI-PYRÉNÉES
Réquista
La Cavalerie
Valdériès
Valence-d'Albigeois
Broquiès
St-Rome-de-Cernon
St-Hippolyte-du-Fort
Le Vigan
Albi
St-Juéry
St-Affrique
Causse de St-Affrique
Sauclières
Cirque de Navacelles
Grotte des Demoiselles
Ganges
Gaillac
Alban
St-Sernin-sur-Rance
Cornus
St-Bauzille-de-Putois
Teillet
Abbaye de Sylvanès
St-Maurice-Navacelles
Le Caylar
St-Martin-de-Londres
TARN
Belmont-sur-Rance
Camarès
Brusque
Ceilhes-et-Rocozels
St-Pierre-de-la-Fage
Graulhet
Réalmont
Lacaze
Lodève
Lacaune
St-Gély-du-Fesc
Montredon-Labessonnié
Lac du Salagou
Cirque de Mourèze
Monts de Lacaune
Brassac
St-Gervais-sur-Mare
Gignac
Castelnau-le-Lez
Montpellier
St-Paul-Cap-de-Joux
Castres
Bédarieux
Clermont-l'Hérault
HÉRAULT
La Salvetat-sur-Agout
Mons
Soual
Labruguière
St-Pons-de-Thomières
Abbaye de Valmagne
Lattes
Mazamet
Roujan
Montagnac
St-Félix-Lauragais
Revel
Murviel-lès-Béziers
Pézenas
Frontignan
St-Amans-Soult
Col de Rodomouls
St-Chinian
Servian
Mèze
Balaruc-les-Bains
LAURAGAIS
CABARDÈS
MINERVOIS
Sète
Saissac
Citou
Aigues-Vives
Capestang
Béziers
Florensac
Bassin de Thau
Castelnaudary
Cesse
Enserune
Agde
Conques-sur-Orbiel
Olonzac
Sérignan
Cap d'Agde
Alzonne
Lézignan-Corbières
Coursan
Trèbes
Capendu
Fleury
Bizanet
Narbonne
Narbonne-Plage
Fabrezan
Abbaye de Fontfroide
Bages en de Sigean
Mirepoix
Limoux
St-Laurent-de-la-Cabrerisse
Étang de l'Ayrolle
Sigean
Port-la-Nouvelle
Durban
603
604
612
613
611
452
453
602
614
615
475
476
601
477
478
600
596
599
568
569
598
597
584
566
571
570
563
573
574
576
577
562
572
560
561
575
559
558
556
557

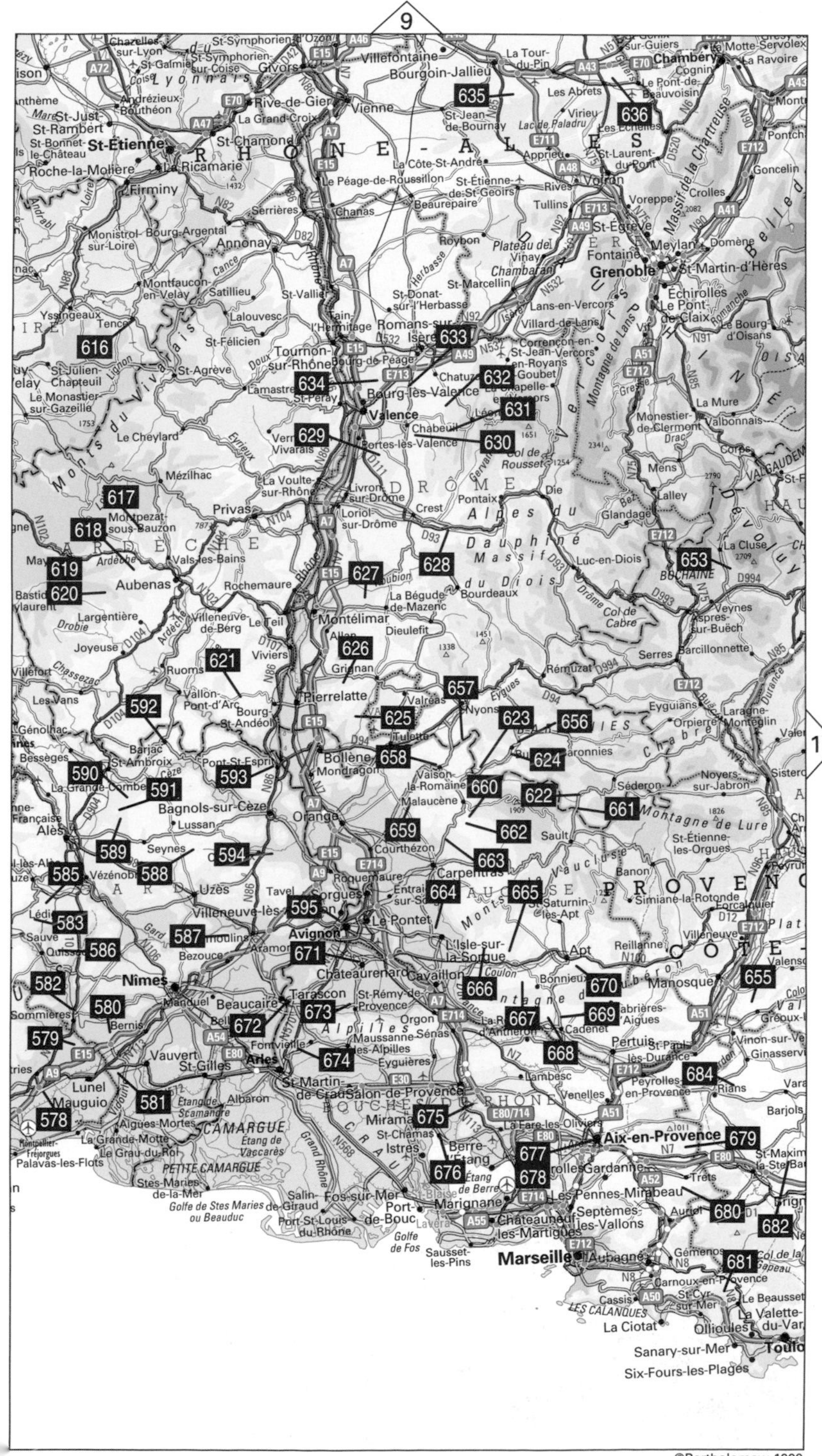

9
15
R H Ô N E - A L P E S
D R Ô M E
A R D È C H E
G A R D
V A U C L U S E
P R O V E N C E
B O U C H E S - D U - R H Ô N E
CAMARGUE
PETITE CAMARGUE
LES CALANQUES
Chambéry
La Motte-Servolex
La Ravoire
Villefontaine
Bourgoin-Jallieu
La Tour-du-Pin
Les Abrets
St-Symphorien-d'Ozon
Chazelles-sur-Lyon
St-Symphorien-sur-Coise
Givors
Rive-de-Gier
Vienne
La Grand-Croix
St-Just-St-Rambert
St-Étienne
St-Chamond
St-Bonnet-le-Château
Roche-la-Molière
La Ricamarie
Firminy
Andrézieux-Bouthéon
St-Jean-de-Bournay
Lac de Paladru
Virieu
Les Échelles
St-Laurent-du-Pont
Massif de la Chartreuse
Le Pont-de-Beauvoisin
Voiron
Apprieu
Rives
La Côte-St-André
Le Péage-de-Roussillon
St-Étienne-de-St-Geoirs
Beaurepaire
Chanas
Serrières
Tullins
Voreppe
Crolles
St-Égrève
Goncelin
Meylan
Domène
Grenoble
Fontaine
St-Martin-d'Hères
Échirolles
Le Pont-de-Claix
Monistrol-sur-Loire
Bourg-Argental
Annonay
Roybon
Plateau de Chambaran
Vinay
St-Marcellin
Montfaucon-en-Velay
Satillieu
St-Vallier
St-Donat-sur-l'Herbasse
Lans-en-Vercors
Villard-de-Lans
Yssingeaux
Tence
Lalouvesc
Tain-l'Hermitage
Romans-sur-Isère
Corrençon-en-Vercors
St-Jean-en-Royans
St-Félicien
Tournon-sur-Rhône
Bourg-de-Péage
Chatuzange-le-Goubet
La Chapelle-en-Vercors
Le Bourg-d'Oisans
St-Julien-Chapteuil
St-Agrève
Lamastre
St-Péray
Bourg-lès-Valence
Valence
Chabeuil
Le Monastier-sur-Gazeille
Le Cheylard
Vernoux-en-Vivarais
Portes-lès-Valence
Col de Rousset
Monestier-de-Clermont
La Mure
Valbonnais
Mézilhac
La Voulte-sur-Rhône
Livron-sur-Drôme
Loriol-sur-Drôme
Crest
Pontaix
Die
Mens
Lalley
Glandage
Privas
Montpezat-sous-Bauzon
Vals-les-Bains
Aubenas
Rochemaure
Alpes du Dauphiné
Massif du Diois
Luc-en-Diois
La Cluse
Col de Cabre
La Bégude-de-Mazenc
Bourdeaux
Montélimar
Dieulefit
Le Teil
Villeneuve-de-Berg
Largentière
Joyeuse
Viviers
Allan
Grignan
Veynes
Aspres-sur-Buëch
Serres
Barcillonnette
Rémuzat
Ruoms
Vallon-Pont-d'Arc
Bourg-St-Andéol
Pierrelatte
Valréas
Nyons
Les Vans
Génolhac
Barjac
St-Ambroix
Tulette
Pont-St-Esprit
Bollène
Mondragon
Vaison-la-Romaine
Baronnies
Eyguians
Orpierre
Laragne-Montéglin
Bessèges
La Grand-Combe
Bagnols-sur-Cèze
Lussan
Orange
Malaucène
Séderon
Noyers-sur-Jabron
Sisteron
Alès
Seynes
Courthézon
Sault
Montagne de Lure
St-Étienne-les-Orgues
Vézénobres
Uzès
Roquemaure
Carpentras
Banon
Tavel
Sorgues
Entraigues-sur-Sorgues
St-Saturnin-lès-Apt
Simiane-la-Rotonde
Forcalquier
Villeneuve-lès-Avignon
Avignon
Le Pontet
Sauve
Quissac
Bezouce
Aramon
L'Isle-sur-la-Sorgue
Apt
Reillanne
Villeneuve
Nîmes
Manduel
Châteaurenard
Cavaillon
Bonnieux
Manosque
Beaucaire
Tarascon
St-Rémy-de-Provence
Sommières
Bernis
Fontvieille
Alpilles
Maussanne-les-Alpilles
Orgon
Sénas
Cadenet
Grambois
Gréoux-les-Bains
Vauvert
St-Gilles
Arles
Eyguières
Lambesc
Pertuis
Vinon-sur-Verdon
Ginasservis
Lunel
Mauguio
St-Martin-de-Crau
Salon-de-Provence
Peyrolles-en-Provence
Rians
Aigues-Mortes
Étang de Vaccarès
Miramas
St-Chamas
Istres
Berre-l'Étang
Venelles
Aix-en-Provence
Barjols
Palavas-les-Flots
Le Grau-du-Roi
Grand Rhône
Gardanne
Trets
Stes-Maries-de-la-Mer
Golfe de Stes Maries ou Beauduc
Salin-de-Giraud
Fos-sur-Mer
Port-de-Bouc
Port-St-Louis-du-Rhône
Golfe de Fos
Marignane
Étang de Berre
Les Pennes-Mirabeau
Septèmes-les-Vallons
Châteauneuf-les-Martigues
Sausset-les-Pins
Marseille
Aubagne
Gémenos
Carnoux-en-Provence
Cassis
St-Cyr-sur-Mer
Le Beausset
La Ciotat
Ollioules
La Valette-du-Var
Sanary-sur-Mer
Six-Fours-les-Plages
Toulon
A7
A9
A43
A46
A47
A48
A49
A50
A51
A52
A54
A55
A72
E15
E70
E80
E711
E712
E713
E714
E80/714
N7
N85
N86
N100
N102
N113
N532
616
617
618
619
620
621
622
623
624
625
626
627
628
629
630
631
632
633
634
635
636
653
655
656
657
658
659
660
661
662
663
664
665
666
667
668
669
670
671
672
673
674
675
676
677
678
679
680
681
682
578
579
580
581
582
583
585
586
587
588
589
590
591
592
593
594
595

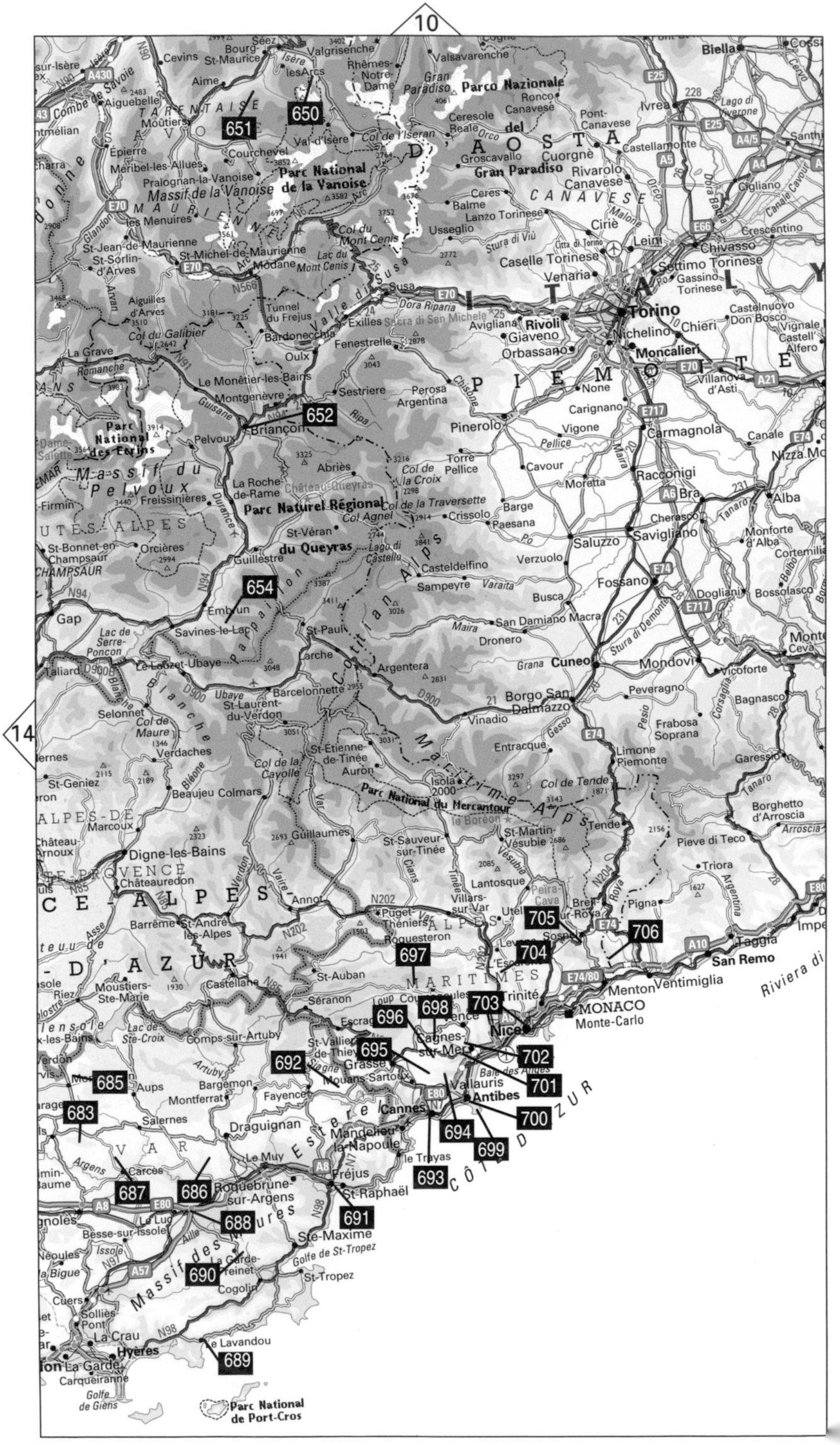
10
14
Biella
Ivrea
Lago di Viverone
Santhià
Parco Nazionale del Gran Paradiso
Valsavarenche
Rhêmes-Notre-Dame
Valgrisenche
Bourg-St-Maurice
Séez
les Arcs
Cevins
Aime
Aiguebelle
Combe de Savoie
Montmélian
Moûtiers
Épierre
Courchevel
Méribel-les-Allues
Pralognan-la-Vanoise
Massif de la Vanoise
Parc National de la Vanoise
Val-d'Isère
Col de l'Iseran
Ceresole Reale
Ronco Canavese
Pont-Canavese
Castellamonte
Cuorgnè
Rivarolo Canavese
Groscavallo
CANAVESE
Ceres
Balme
Lanzo Torinese
Usseglio
Ciriè
Leinì
Chivasso
Crescentino
Cigliano
Settimo Torinese
Gassino Torinese
Caselle Torinese
Venaria
Torino
Rivoli
Avigliana
Giaveno
Orbassano
Nichelino
Moncalieri
Chieri
Castelnuovo Don Bosco
Villanova d'Asti
Les Menuires
St-Jean-de-Maurienne
St-Sorlin-d'Arves
St-Michel-de-Maurienne
Modane
Col du Mont Cenis
Lac du Mont Cenis
Susa
Valle di Susa
Dora Riparia
Sacra di San Michele
Tunnel du Frejus
Exilles
Bardonecchia
Oulx
Fenestrelle
Aiguilles d'Arves
Col du Galibier
La Grave
Romanche
Le Monêtier-les-Bains
Montgenèvre
Sestriere
Perosa Argentina
Pinerolo
PIEMONTE
None
Carignano
Vigone
Carmagnola
Canale
Nizza Monferrato
Cavour
Torre Pellice
Moretta
Racconigi
Bra
Alba
Cherasco
Savigliano
Monforte d'Alba
Saluzzo
Barge
Paesana
Crissolo
Verzuolo
Fossano
Dogliani
Bossolasco
Busca
Briançon
Guisane
Parc National des Ecrins
Pelvoux
Massif du Pelvoux
Freissinières
La Roche-de-Rame
Château-Queyras
Abriès
Col de la Croix
Col de la Traversette
Col Agnel
Parc Naturel Régional du Queyras
St-Véran
Guillestre
Orcières
Champsaur
St-Bonnet-en-Champsaur
Casteldelfino
Sampeyre
Varaita
Lago di Castello
Cottian Alps
Embrun
Savines-le-Lac
Gap
Lac de Serre-Ponçon
St-Paul
Larche
Argentera
San Damiano Macra
Dronero
Maira
Cuneo
Mondovì
Vicoforte
Ceva
Borgo San Dalmazzo
Vinadio
Peveragno
Bagnasco
Le Lauzet-Ubaye
Ubaye
Barcelonnette
St-Laurent-du-Verdon
Selonnet
Col de Maure
Verdaches
St-Étienne-de-Tinée
Auron
Col de la Cayolle
Maritime Alps
Parc National du Mercantour
Isola 2000
Entracque
Limone Piemonte
Frabosa Soprana
Garessio
Col de Tende
Tende
Borghetto d'Arroscia
St-Geniez
Beaujeu
Colmars
Guillaumes
St-Sauveur-sur-Tinée
St-Martin-Vésubie
Le Boréon
Pieve di Teco
Triora
Digne-les-Bains
Marcoux
ALPES-DE-HAUTE-PROVENCE
Châteauredon
Annot
Lantosque
Villars-sur-Var
Puget-Théniers
Roquesteron
Sospel
Breil-sur-Roya
Pigna
Imperia
Taggia
San Remo
Riviera di Ponente
Barrême
St-André-les-Alpes
Castellane
St-Auban
Séranon
ALPES-MARITIMES
Moustiers-Ste-Marie
Riez
Comps-sur-Artuby
Artuby
Bargemon
Fayence
St-Vallier-de-Thiey
Grasse
Mouans-Sartoux
Cagnes-sur-Mer
Nice
Trinité
Levens
L'Escarène
Menton
Ventimiglia
MONACO
Monte-Carlo
Baie des Anges
Vallauris
Antibes
Cannes
Mandelieu-la-Napoule
Esterel
le Trayas
CÔTE D'AZUR
Aups
Montferrat
Salernes
Draguignan
Le Muy
Fréjus
St-Raphaël
Roquebrune-sur-Argens
Carcès
VAR
Argens
Le Luc
Besse-sur-Issole
Ste-Maxime
Golfe de St-Tropez
La Garde-Freinet
Cogolin
St-Tropez
Massif des Maures
Cuers
Solliès-Pont
La Crau
Hyères
La Garde
Carqueiranne
Golfe de Giens
Le Lavandou
Parc National de Port-Cros
650
651
652
654
683
685
686
687
688
689
690
691
692
693
694
695
696
697
698
699
700
701
702
703
704
705
706

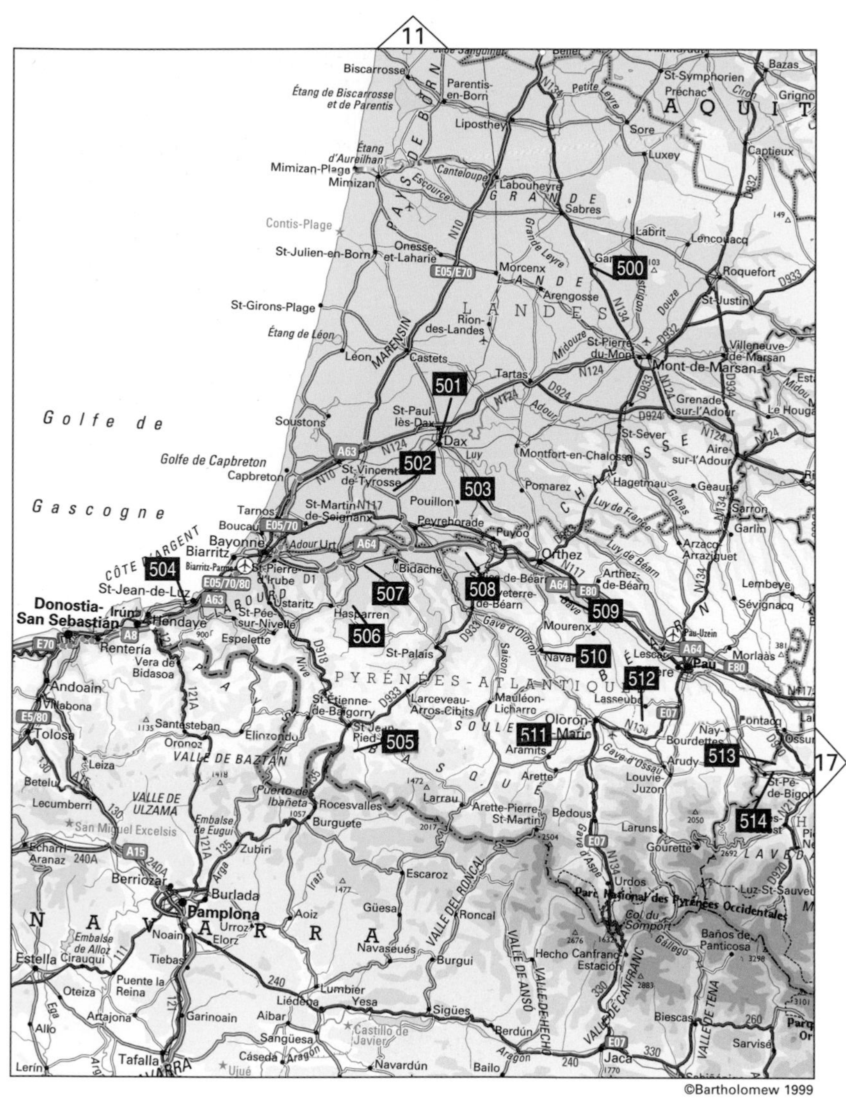
11
17
Biscarrosse
Étang de Biscarrosse et de Parentis
Parentis-en-Born
Liposthey
Bazas
St-Symphorien
Préchac
Sore
Luxey
Captieux
Mimizan-Plage
Mimizan
Étang d'Aureilhan
Labouheyre
Sabres
Contis-Plage
Labrit
Lencouacq
St-Julien-en-Born
Onesse-et-Laharie
Morcenx
Arengosse
500
Roquefort
St-Justin
St-Girons-Plage
Rion-des-Landes
Étang de Léon
Léon
Castets
St-Pierre-du-Mont
Mont-de-Marsan
Villeneuve-de-Marsan
Tartas
501
Grenade-sur-l'Adour
Golfe de
St-Paul-lès-Dax
Soustons
Dax
St-Sever
Aire-sur-l'Adour
Golfe de Capbreton
Capbreton
St-Vincent-de-Tyrosse
502
Montfort-en-Chalosse
Pomarez
503
Hagetmau
Geaune
Gascogne
Tarnos
St-Martin-de-Seignanx
Pouillon
Peyrehorade
Puyoo
Boucau
Bayonne
Biarritz
Orthez
Sarron
Garlin
Côte d'Argent
504
St-Jean-de-Luz
St-Pierre-d'Irube
Bidache
507
508
Salies-de-Béarn
Sauveterre-de-Béarn
Arthez-de-Béarn
Arzacq-Arraziguet
Lembeye
Sévignacq
Donostia-San Sebastián
Irún
Hendaye
Ustaritz
St-Pée-sur-Nivelle
Hasparren
506
509
Mourenx
Rentería
Espelette
St-Palais
Navarrenx
510
Lescar
Pau
Morlaàs
Vera de Bidasoa
Andoain
Villabona
Pyrénées-Atlantiques
St-Étienne-de-Baïgorry
Larceveau-Arros-Cibits
Mauléon-Licharre
512
Lasseube
Tolosa
Santesteban
Elizondo
Oronoz
Valle de Baztán
St-Jean-Pied-de-Port
505
Soule
511
Oloron-Ste-Marie
Aramits
Nay
Bourdettes
Arudy
513
Leiza
Betelu
Lecumberri
Valle de Ulzama
Puerto de Ibañeta
Roncesvalles
Burguete
Larrau
Arette
Arette-Pierre-St-Martin
Bedous
Louvie-Juzon
Laruns
Gourette
514
St-Pé-de-Bigorre
San Miguel Excelsis
Embalse de Eugui
Echarri-Aranaz
Zubiri
Escaroz
Berriozar
Burlada
Pamplona
Noain
Urroz
Elorz
Aoiz
Güesa
Roncal
Valle del Roncal
Urdos
Parc National des Pyrénées Occidentales
Col du Somport
Luz-St-Sauveur
Navarra
Embalse de Alloz
Estella
Cirauqui
Tiebas
Navascués
Burgui
Hecho
Canfranc Estación
Baños de Panticosa
Puente la Reina
Oteiza
Lumbier
Liédena
Yesa
Valle de Ansó
Valle de Hecho
Valle de Canfranc
Valle de Tena
Artajona
Garinoain
Aibar
Sigües
Castillo de Javier
Biescas
Sarvisé
Sangüesa
Cáseda
Berdún
Allo
Lerín
Tafalla
Ujué
Navardún
Bailo
Jaca

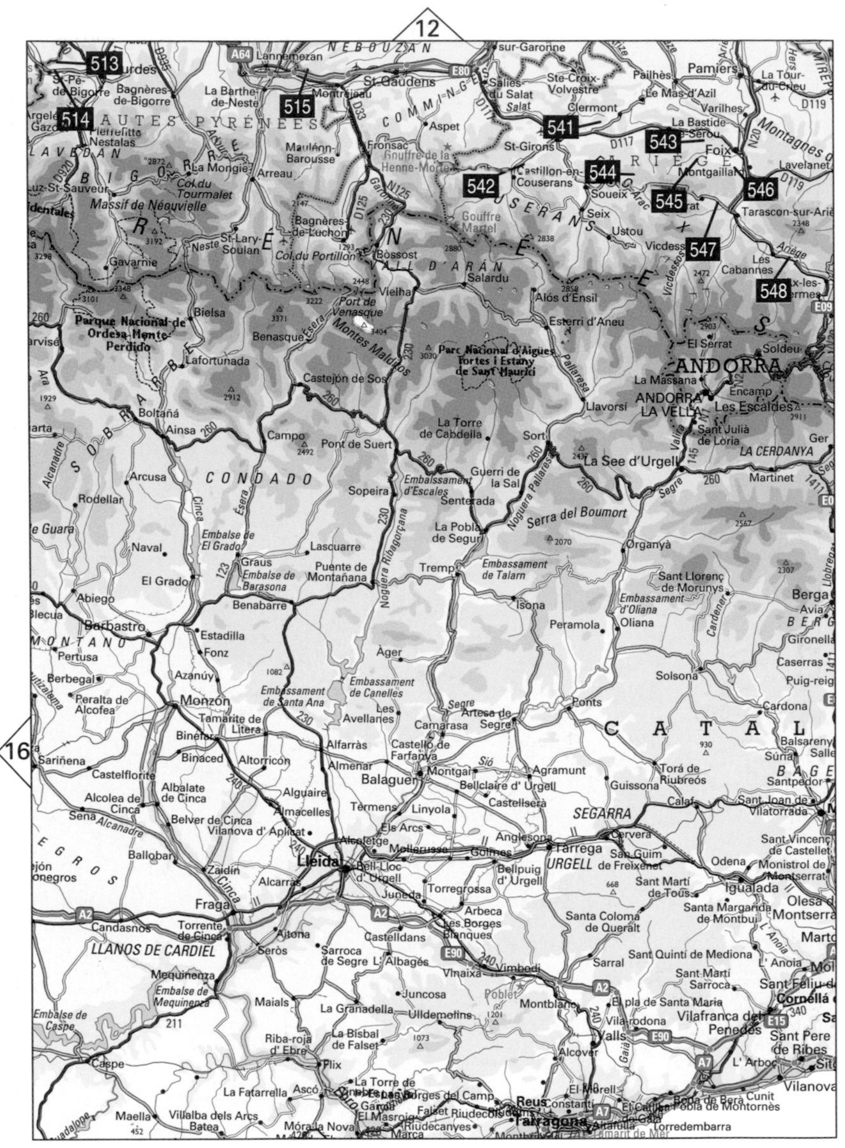
12
16
513
514
515
541
542
543
544
545
546
547
548
Lannemezan
St-Gaudens
Montréjeau
Aspet
Salies-du-Salat
Ste-Croix-Volvestre
Pailhès
Pamiers
La Tour-du-Crieu
Le Mas-d'Azil
Varilhes
Clermont
La Bastide-de-Sérou
Foix
Montgaillard
Lavelanet
St-Girons
Castillon-en-Couserans
Soueix
Seix
Ustou
Vicdessos
Tarascon-sur-Ariège
Les Cabannes
Bagnères-de-Bigorre
La Barthe-de-Neste
HAUTES-PYRÉNÉES
COMMINGES
COUSERANS
ARIÈGE
Nestalas
LAVEDAN
BIGORRE
La Mongie
Col du Tourmalet
Massif de Néouvielle
Arreau
Mauléon-Barousse
Fronsac
Gouffre de la Henne-Morte
Gouffre Martel
Bagnères-de-Luchon
Col du Portillon
Bòssost
VALL D'ARÁN
Salardu
St-Lary-Soulan
Gavarnie
Luz-St-Sauveur
Alós d'Ensil
Esterri d'Aneu
Vielha
Port de Venasque
Montes Malditos
Benasque
Bielsa
Parque Nacional de Ordesa-Monte-Perdido
Lafortunada
Parc Nacional d'Aigües Tortes i Estany de Sant Maurici
El Serrat
Soldeu
ANDORRA
La Massana
Encamp
ANDORRA LA VELLA
Les Escaldes
Sant Julià de Lòria
LA CERDANYA
Castejón de Sos
Llavorsí
Boltaña
Ainsa
SOBRARBE
Campo
Pont de Suert
La Torre de Cabdella
Sort
La See d'Urgell
Martinet
CONDADO
Arcusa
Rodellar
Sopeira
Embalsament d'Escales
Senterada
Guerri de la Sal
Noguera Pallaresa
Serra del Boumort
La Pobla de Segur
Naval
Embalse de El Grado
Lascuarre
Graus
Embalse de Barasona
Puente de Montañana
Tremp
Embassament de Talarn
Organyà
El Grado
Abiego
Benabarre
Isona
Sant Llorenç de Morunys
Embassament d'Oliana
Oliana
Berga
Barbastro
Estadilla
Fonz
Peramola
Àger
Pertusa
Berbegal
Azanúy
Peralta de Alcofea
Embassament de Canelles
Embassament de Santa Ana
Monzón
Tamarite de Litera
Les Avellanes
Solsona
Cardona
Ponts
Artesa de Segre
Camarasa
CATAL
Binéfar
Alfarràs
Castelló de Farfanya
Sariñena
Binaced
Altorricón
Almenar
Balaguer
Montgai
Agramunt
Guissona
Torá de Riubreós
Castelflorite
Albalate de Cinca
Alguaire
Bellcaire d'Urgell
Castellserà
Calaf
Alcolea de Cinca
Almacelles
Térmens
Linyola
SEGARRA
Sant Joan de Vilatorrada
Sena
Belver de Cinca
Vilanova d'Aplicat
Els Arcs
Anglesola
Cervera
Ballobar
Zaidín
Lleida
Alcoletge
Mollerussa
Golmes
Tàrrega
San Guim de Freixenet
Odena
Bell-Lloc d'Urgell
Bellpuig d'Urgell
URGELL
Sant Martí de Tous
Igualada
Alcarràs
Juneda
Torregrossa
Fraga
Candasnos
Torrente de Cinca
Arbeca
Les Borges Blanques
Santa Coloma de Queralt
Santa Margarida de Montbui
LLANOS DE CARDIEL
Aitona
Castelldans
Seròs
Sarroca de Segre
L'Albagés
Vimbodí
Vinaixa
Sarral
Sant Quintí de Mediona
Mequinenza
Embalse de Mequinenza
Juncosa
Poblet
Montblanc
El pla de Santa Maria
Sant Martí Sarroca
Maials
La Granadella
Ulldemolins
Vila-rodona
Vilafranca del Penedès
Embalse de Caspe
Riba-roja d'Ebre
La Bisbal de Falset
Valls
Sant Pere de Ribes
Caspe
Flix
Alcover
L'Arboç
La Fatarrella
Ascó
Reus
El Morell
Constantí
Vilanova
Maella
Villalba dels Arcs
Batea
Móra la Nova
Falset
Riudecols
Riudecanyes
Tarragona
Torredembarra
Cunit

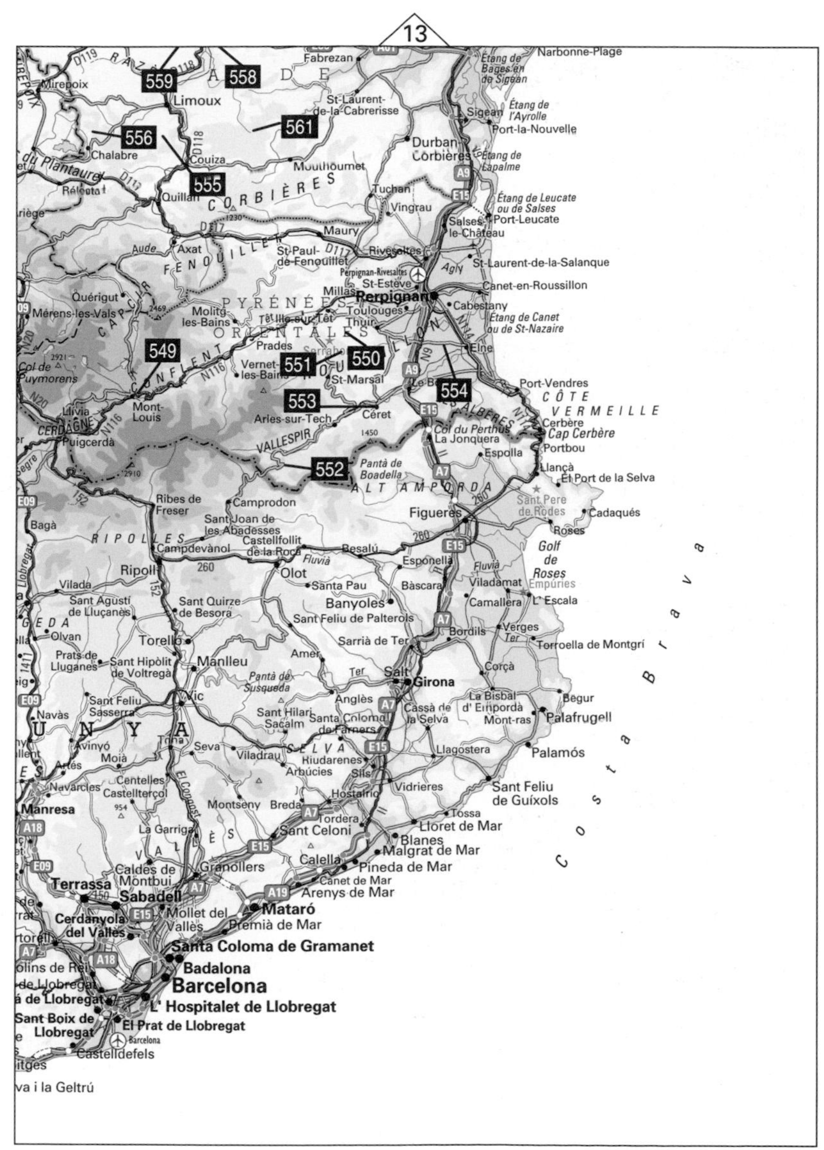
13
Fabrezan
Narbonne-Plage
Mirepoix
Limoux
St-Laurent-de-la-Cabrerisse
Sigean
Port-la-Nouvelle
Chalabre
Couiza
Durban-Corbières
Mouthoumet
CORBIÈRES
Quillan
Tuchan
Vingrau
Salses-le-Château
Port-Leucate
Maury
Axat
St-Paul-de-Fenouillet
Rivesaltes
FENOUILLÈDES
St-Laurent-de-la-Salanque
St-Estève
Canet-en-Roussillon
Quérigut
Perpignan
Millas
Cabestany
Mérens-les-Vals
Molitg-les-Bains
Toulouges
Thuir
PYRÉNÉES-ORIENTALES
Prades
Elne
Vernet-les-Bains
St-Marsal
Port-Vendres
CÔTE VERMEILLE
Mont-Louis
Llívia
Céret
Arles-sur-Tech
Cerbère
Cap Cerbère
Col du Perthus
La Jonquera
Portbou
Puigcerdà
Espolla
Llançà
El Port de la Selva
Pantà de Boadella
ALT AMPORDÀ
Ribes de Freser
Camprodon
Figueres
Cadaqués
Roses
Bagà
Sant Joan de les Abadesses
Castellfollit de la Roca
Golf de Roses
Campdevànol
Besalú
Ripoll
Olot
Esponellà
Santa Pau
Bàscara
Viladamat
Empúries
Vilada
Banyoles
Camallera
L'Escala
Sant Agustí de Lluçanès
Sant Quirze de Besora
Sant Feliu de Palterols
Verges
Bordils
Olvan
Torelló
Sarrià de Ter
Torroella de Montgrí
Prats de Lluçanès
Sant Hipòlit de Voltregà
Manlleu
Amer
Corçà
Salt
Girona
Pantà de Susqueda
Vic
Anglès
La Bisbal d' Empordà
Begur
Sant Feliu Sasserra
Navàs
Sant Hilari Sacalm
Santa Coloma de Farners
Cassà de la Selva
Mont-ras
Palafrugell
Avinyó
Moià
Tona
Seva
Viladrau
SELVA
Llagostera
Palamós
Artés
Riudarenes
Arbúcies
Sils
Navarcles
Centelles
Castellterçol
Hostalric
Vidrieres
Sant Feliu de Guíxols
Manresa
Montseny
Breda
Tossa
Tordera
Lloret de Mar
La Garriga
Sant Celoni
Blanes
Malgrat de Mar
Caldes de Montbui
Granollers
Calella
Pineda de Mar
Terrassa
Sabadell
Canet de Mar
Arenys de Mar
Mollet del Vallès
Mataró
Cerdanyola del Vallès
Premià de Mar
Santa Coloma de Gramanet
Badalona
Barcelona
L' Hospitalet de Llobregat
Sant Boi de Llobregat
El Prat de Llobregat
Castelldefels
Sitges
Costa Brava
Perpignan-Rivesaltes
Barcelona
559
558
561
556
555
549
551
550
553
554
552

On the flat, fertile plains of Flanders, among the swathes of wheat and maize, grow windmills, belfries and the arcaded streets of lovely old Arras.

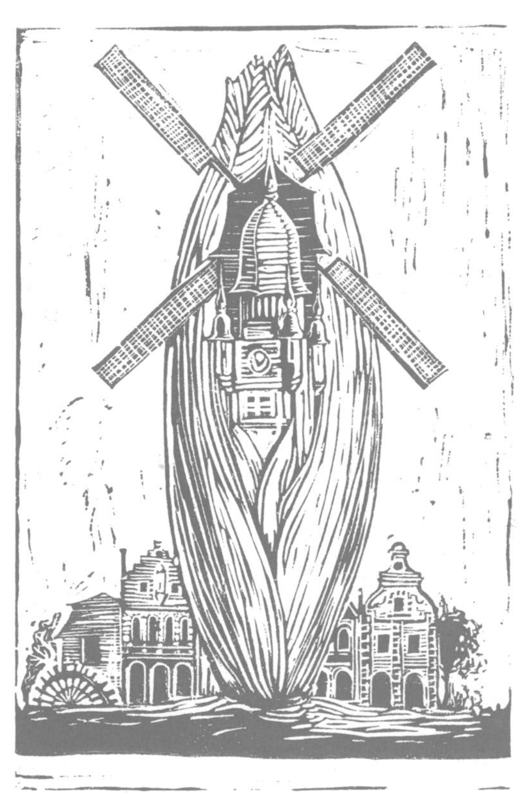

The North – Picardy

All is tranquil at Meldick. The long dining room windows look out onto the pond and the fields beyond — hard to imagine that two terrible wars were waged here, but one of Madame's fascinating treasures is a very real collection of medals and badges from those days. She has huge energy, a beautiful 1930s house that is a delight to be in and simply loves doing B&B because she enjoys the contact so much. Rooms are colour-themed, good-sized, carefully decorated and finely furnished; the family room is enormous! You are definitely welcomed as friends into the Houzets' home.

Rooms: 2 double, 2 twin, 1 room for 4, each with bath or shower & wc.

Price: 300 Frs (€ 45.73) for two, including breakfast. Extra bed 50 Frs.

Meals: Good restaurant 3km.

Open: All year.

From A16 exit 19 to Marck. There, right on D940 then immediately left to Le Fort Vert, through Marck. At Le Fort Vert, right on D119. House 3km along on right.

MMap 236-3 **ASP Map No: 4**

Jean & Danièle HOUZET
Manoir du Meldick
2528 av du Général de Gaulle
62730 Le Fort Vert
Pas-de-Calais
Tel: (0)3 21 85 74 34
Fax: (0)3 21 85 74 34

A good place to stay and visit this dramatic, cliff-lined coast. The enclosed farmyard envelops and protects; the old dovecote, its landing ledges intact, still welcomes pigeons; the roses bloom. Madame is always very busy and may be hard to get hold of. She serves breakfast, on time, in the newish conservatory where wooden birds fly. The rooms, in converted outbuildings with rafters and character, are a good size, nicely decorated, tempting. We would choose the studio over the stables... And there is a games room where children can play table tennis or paint on rainy afternoons. Three minutes from the sea, ten from the Tunnel.

Rooms: 3 triple, 2 double, 1 quadruple, all with bath or shower & wc.

Price: 240-300 Frs (€ 36.59-45.73) for two, including breakfast.

Meals: Choice 1km.

Open: All year.

Gîte space for 21 people

From A16 exit 11 into Peuplingues. 2km beyond, left at first houses in La Haute Escalle. Park in farmyard.

MMap 236-2 **ASP Map No: 3**

Jacqueline & Marc BOUTROY
La Grand'Maison
La Haute Escalle
62179 Escalles
Pas-de-Calais
Tel: (0)3 21 85 27 75
Fax: (0)3 21 85 27 75

The people are delightful — an open, smiling, intelligent family who 'do' wine-tastings and will sell you wine and honey. The big park is soft and appealing and lots of animals wander around; the closeness to ferry ports is seductive although the nearby main road and TGV line may disturb some people. Straightforward and simple are the key words here — no luxury (showers are behind curtains). Breakfast is in the separate guest quarters (or the family kitchen for very early starts), where basic pine furniture and slatting grace the smallish rooms, and windows look onto lawn and trees.

Rooms: 2 triple, each with shower, sharing wc; 1 quadruple with shower & wc.

Price: 230 Frs (€ 35.06) for two, including breakfast.

Meals: 1km or Ardres 5km. Self-catering.

Open: All year.

Gîte space for 11 people

From A26 (exit 2 on N43) dir. Calais. Wolphus is on left 1km after the junction, with woods beside road. Be careful turning in!

MMap 236-3 **ASP Map No: 4**

Jean-Jacques & Mimi BEHAGHEL
La Ferme de Wolphus
62890 Zouafques
Pas-de-Calais
Tel: (0)3 21 35 61 61
Fax: (0)3 21 35 61 61

She's a lovely old lady! She talks lots, in French, and otherwise relies on radio and telly for company. Hers is a piecemeal family house with comfortable old furniture and masses of photographs (17 grandchildren). Rooms are rustically attractive: well-decorated with good beds and windows onto the peace outside. Madame loves cooking her delicious country dishes for visitors and readers have praised her natural hospitality. Ask to see the exquisite vaulted stables — built for cows and carthorses, fit for thoroughbreds and prizewinners!

Rooms: 2 double, 1 with cot + child's bed, each with shower & wc.

Price: 210 Frs (€ 32.01) for two, including breakfast.

Meals: 90 Frs, including wine.

Open: April to October.

From A26 exit 2 for Tournehem; cross N43 & follow signs to Muncq Nieurlet; continue dir. Ruminghem; La Motte Obin on left ,approx. 1.5km after leaving Muncq Nieurlet, at signpost.

MMap 236-3 **ASP Map No: 4**

Mme Françoise BRETON
La Motte Obin
62890 Muncq Nieurlet
Pas-de-Calais
Tel: (0)3 21 82 79 63

In the plant-filled hall, bobble-edged curtains and squat, plush chairs fight for the retro stakes. Here you meet the nicest, simplest farming folk imaginable, worn and naturally gracious after a lifetime on the land, whose French country cooking, praised to the skies by readers, uses home-produced ingredients (even the kir is made with raspberry *maison*) and is eaten in true conviviality. Rooms are just as simply authentic with old wooden beds, floorboards, small showers, lots of light. Plus ducklings, chicks, kittens for children's delight. A real French experience — catch it before it disappears into the hi-tech millennium hole!

Rooms: 1 double, 1 twin, each with shower & wc.

Price: 210 Frs (€ 32.01) for two, including breakfast; extra bed 50 Frs.

Meals: 95 Frs, including aperitif & wine.

Open: All year.

Gîte space for 6 people

From A26 exit 2 on N43 dir. St Omer. 3km after Nordausques, right to Nortleulinghen. In village, right to church and right into Rue de la Mairie. Signed.

MMap 236-3 **ASP Map No: 4**

M & Mme NOEL MARTIN
8 rue de la Mairie
62890 Nortleulinghen
Pas-de-Calais
Tel: (0)3 21 35 64 60
www.sawdays.co.uk

A stunning house, not big but an architectural historian's delight. It is 'French traditional' with masses of original, highly perishable details intact such as stained glass, *trompe-l'œil* wall-paintings (admire the 1850s fake marble), superb green and white tiling in the kitchen and a fine, elegant dining/sitting room. The quiet rooms are trad-furnished too, with rich dark wardrobes and good beds. Madame is completely available for her guests and only too happy to talk and communicate her excellent local knowledge.

Rooms: 1 double with shower & wc; 1 twin with basin & shower, 1 double with basin, sharing bath & wc; 2 double with basin & shower, sharing wc (+ 3rd shower).

Price: 200-220 Frs (€ 30.49-33.54) for two, including breakfast.

Meals: Restaurant 3km. Ardres 10km.

Open: All year.

A26 exit 2 dir. Tournehem then immediately right to Zouafques then Tournehem. There D217 to Bonningues. House on right just after entering village.

MMap 236-3 **ASP Map No: 4**

Mme Christiane DUPONT
Le Manoir
Bonningues lès Ardres
62890 Tournehem sur Hem
Pas-de-Calais
Tel: (0)3 21 82 69 05
Fax: (0)3 21 82 69 05
www.sawdays.co.uk

Some say it's great fun, stupendously genuine hospitality with good food and antique-furnished rooms where sweeties and bathrobes are laid out — so it's immaterial that the loos are down a long corridor. Others have mentioned a chained dog and less-than-sparkling basins. Nicer than it looks in the picture though slightly scuffed and run in a comfortingly amateur way. Our inspector loved it for just being itself: "...so interesting and so real. My ideal place to stay; a big family home with special people". Your opinion would help. The main bedroom has walls panelled with painted cupboards and courtyard views.

Rooms: 2 twin, 2 double, each with shower, sharing 2 wcs.

Price: 175-200 Frs (€ 26.68-30.49) for two (+ 25 Frs for 2nd 'twin' bed), including breakfast. Extra person 60 Frs.

Meals: 75 Frs, including wine.

Open: All year.

From Calais A16 for Boulogne. At Marquise, D238 to Wierre Effroy; follow D234 S; left onto D233 and left to Le Breucq.

MMap 236-2 **ASP Map No: 3**

Jacques & Isabelle de MONTIGNY
Le Breucq
62142 Belle et Houllefort
Pas-de-Calais
Tel: (0)3 21 83 31 99
Fax: (0)3 21 83 31 99
www.sawdays.co.uk

7

A good base from which to explore the 'Opal Coast' made fashionable by the British in the thirties, or a perfect first or last night to your French holiday. Think *Monsieur Hulot's Holiday* and you will know the atmosphere of the town and this ravishingly exuberant house on the front. Mary has decorated it luxuriously in keeping with the period: white linen, wooden floors, carefully-chosen fabrics and furniture. She speaks excellent English and has acquired some good English habits, such as the cup of tea she may offer you in the beautiful room looking out to sea. Her huge and delicious breakfast takes place here too.

Rooms: 2 double, 2 twin, each with bath or shower & wc.

Price: 300-400 Frs (€ 45.73-60.98) for two, including breakfast (100 Frs more July/Aug).

Meals: Wide choice locally.

Open: All year.

From A16 exit 3 to Wimereux. In town, go to sea front. House about halfway along promenade, 100m left of Hôtel Atlantic (with your back to the sea).

MMap 236-1 **ASP Map No: 3**

Mary AVOT
La Goélette
13 Digue de Mer
62930 Wimereux
Pas-de-Calais
Tel: (0)3 21 32 62 44
Fax: (0)3 21 33 77 54
www.ifrance.com/lagoelette/

8

Distinctive it certainly is: well-groomed rooms and a very elegant hostess whose B&B philosophy is founded on trust and respect. She is an effervescent animal-lover whose guests have "opened the world anew to her". Huge, heavy family furniture, a great high-arched floral hall, dining space and French upholstered upright chairs for 12 are the common areas. The 'Big Bedroom' is fabulous, its bathroom almost more so; the top-floor suite is more Modern Rustic. All fascinating, capturing the flavour of one particular (and lovable) kind of France. Just 100 yards from the lovely old walled town of Boulogne.

Rooms: 1 double with bath & wc; 1 triple with shower & wc on different floor; 1 suite for 4 with shower, sharing wc.

Price: 250-350 Frs (€ 38.11-53.36) for two, including breakfast.

Meals: Wide choice within the ramparts (walking distance).

Open: All year except January.

Follow signs for 'Vieille Ville'. Rue Flahaut is off Boulevard Mariette which runs below the ramparts on the northern side of the city past the Porte des Dunes.

MMap 236-1 **ASP Map No: 3**

Simone & Édouard DELABIE
26 Rue Flahaut
62200 Boulogne sur Mer
Pas-de-Calais
Tel: (0)3 21 31 88 74
www.sawdays.co.uk

There are only a few horses in the stables now: the main stud farm is further away. This means that your hosts have a very busy life and may be a little preoccupied, though Madame is lively and fun when relaxed. The bedrooms, in a self-contained unit which looks out onto the courtyard and surrounding wooded hills, have simple, modern décor and the breakfast/living room is also very straightforward. The garden and orchard go down to the river and this is a good family stopover.

Rooms: 2 double, 2 twin, all with shower & wc.

Price: 250 Frs (€ 38.11) for two, including breakfast.

Meals: In village.

Open: All year except Christmas & New Year.

Gîte space for 9 people

From Boulogne sur Mer, D940 dir. St Léonard. There, at 2nd lights, left onto small road (to Echingen, not signed); in village centre, left into tiny street immediately after sharp bend then left into first gateway.

MMap 236-2 **ASP Map No: 3**

Jacqueline & Jean-Pierre BOUSSEMAERE
Rue de l'Eglise
62360 Echinghen
Pas-de-Calais
Tel: (0)3 21 91 14 34

This charming, genuine *Notaire*'s house (the shield on the front is his symbol of office) has a gloriously eccentric attic *salon* for guests with all the furniture gathered in the centre. The big bedrooms are decorated in traditional French style with antiques, shutters and modern bathrooms. Breakfast — including *clafoutis* if you're lucky — is served on the terrace in good weather. The pretty, authentic village makes no concessions to tourism, and the owners have a similar olde-worlde air to them, but modernity intrudes as traffic noise at the front so ask for a room over the garden.

Rooms: 2 double, 1 twin, each with bath or shower & wc. Extra beds available.

Price: 250 Frs (€ 38.11) for two, including breakfast.

Meals: In Samer or choice 5km.

Open: All year.

From Boulogne N1 S dir. St Léonard & Montreuil for approx. 15km. In Samer, take road that goes down to right of church — house on left.

MMap 236-12 **ASP Map No: 3**

Joëlle MAUCOTEL
127 rue du Breuil
62830 Samer
Pas-de-Calais
Tel: (0)3 21 33 50 87/(0)3 21 87 64 19
Fax: (0)3 21 83 00 43
www.sawdays.co.uk

The Desalases are friendly and helpful, eager to please and make friends. The house is simple and undemanding, a long low farm with plain rooms, beams, showers and loos curtained off among the rafters... all comfortable, scruffy in places and very pleasant. The bedrooms have forest views, their own entrance and a dayroom with refrigerator and a collection of books. Breakfast is a feast (try the smoked turkey) and you can work it off with a good walk. They welcome walkers and cyclists — you can even bring your horse.

Rooms: 2 double, each with shower & wc (curtained off).

Price: 250 Frs (€ 38.11) for two, including breakfast.

Meals: Barbecue available.

Open: All year.

From Boulogne sur Mer, D341 to Desvres, then D215 dir. Menneville; just outside Desvres, left at sign 'Le Mont Eventé'.

MMap 236-12 **ASP Map No: 3**

M & Mme DESALASE
Le Mont Eventé
Menneville
62240 Desvres
Pas-de-Calais
Tel: (0)3 21 91 77 65
e-mail: guydesalase@minitel.net
www.sawdays.co.uk

Georges is an Orson-Wellesian figure, larger than life and well able to talk at the same time as his wife... a sort of double act that is irresistible and lovable. The well-proportioned house is an architectural flourish, the contents are modern and in good taste, the rooms simple, with pretty bedding and one or two antiques. The only possible drawback is the Holiday Inn and all its vulgarity opposite, but the sea is only ten minutes away through the trees and there is stacks to do locally. It is all perfect for children, raucous and great fun.

Rooms: 1 double, 1 twin, each with bath & wc.

Price: 350 Frs (€ 53.36) for two, including breakfast.

Meals: Wide choice within walking distance.

Open: Easter to mid-November.

In Le Touquet follow signs to Holiday Inn — house is directly opposite.

MMap 236-11 **ASP Map No: 3**

Georges & Marie VERSMÉE
Birdy Land
Avenue du Maréchal Foch
62520 Le Touquet
Pas-de-Calais
Tel: (0)3 21 05 31 46 or
(0)3 27 46 39 41

Perfectly placed for touring, this old house sits on the quiet main street of a small village. The rooms are all somewhat stuck in a 1960s mode of dated wallpaper and flamenco dancing dollies — the cosiest is in the beamed attic. Madame is fairly elderly, anxious that you should enjoy your stay and she is so cheery and attentive a hostess we know her lack of English will not be a problem. There are bathrobes for 'detached' bathroom users, toothbrushes and toothpaste for the forgetful. Madame and her generous breakfast, with four sorts of home-made jam, yoghurt, cheese and *pain au chocolat,* make this address worth a mention.

Rooms: 2 double, 1 quintuple, each with shower & wc; 1 twin, 1 double, with basins, sharing shower & wc.

Price: 220-250 Frs (€ 33.54-38.11) for two, including breakfast. Extra bed 70 Frs. Children 2 to10 yrs 50 Frs.

Meals: 5km or wide choice10km; self-catering possible.

Open: All year.

From Hesdin D439 dir. Montreuil. At Brimeux right on D129 to Aix en Issart. House on right in village centre.

MMap 236-12 **ASP Map No: 3**

Mme Gilberte SANTUNE
42 rue Principale
62170 Aix en Issart
Pas-de-Calais
Tel: (0)3 21 81 39 46
Fax: (0)3 21 81 39 46

In calm countryside with neither cockerels nor dogs to alarm your early morning, Gina's welcome is as genuine and unpretentious as her house. There are informal wine-tastings at dinner and in the outbuilding — where guests are welcome to use the cooking equipment — and *pétanque* tournaments in summer. Madame calls her guestrooms *La Verte*, *La Rose*, *La Bleue*... and there are two other cosy ones under the roof of this 200-year-old farmhouse (mind your head up there!). Your hostess cares deeply that everyone should be happy and creates a really homely atmosphere.

Rooms: 3 double, 2 triple, each with bath or shower & wc.

Price: 240-280 Frs (€ 36.59-42.69) for two, including breakfast; extra bed 70 Frs.

Meals: 100 Frs, including aperitif, wine & coffee.

Open: All year.

Gîte space for 16 people

From Calais A26, exit 4 to Thérouanne then D341 to Auchy au Bois (12km). Right at Le Vert Dragon restaurant; 1st left: 2nd house on right after church.

MMap 236-14 **ASP Map No: 4**

Gina BULOT
Les Cohettes
28 rue de Pernes
62190 Auchy au Bois
Pas-de-Calais
Tel: (0)3 21 02 09 47
Fax: (0)3 21 02 81 68
www.sawdays.co.uk

The Battle of Agincourt (remember your *Henry V*?) was in 1415; this house, tower and all, was built in 1750. You imagine hearing the clanking of swords still? Open your eyes and you may indeed see medieval knights — that's just your hosts on their way to re-enact a battle: they love their local history and tales of ghosts and archers, soldiers and horses. The pretty guestrooms, called *Voyage*, *Romantique*, *Retro* and *Espace*, are in an adjoining wattle-and-daub house with its own dayroom and log fire. Breakfast is in a room crammed with bric-à-brac in the tower. Huge fun.

Rooms: 3 double, 1 triple, each with shower & wc (1 behind curtain).

Price: 300 Frs (€ 45.73) for two, including breakfast; extra bed 50 Frs.

Meals: Restaurant 1km; choice 6-15km.

Open: All year.

From St Omer D928 dir. Abbeville. At Ruisseauville left dir. Blangy-Tramecourt; at next crossroads, left dir. Tramecourt — house 100m along.

MMap 236-13 **ASP Map No: 4**

Patrick & Marie-Josée FENET
La Gacogne
62310 Azincourt
Pas-de-Calais
Tel: (0)3 21 04 45 61
Fax: (0)3 21 04 45 61

Both suites are generous in comforts and floral cosiness, both give onto the wide terrace and the green and flowery garden. One has a huge carved Henri III bed, a totally French heavy-framed mirror and loads of lace. The breakfast is as generous as the décor and your hosts, who are very young grandparents, will keep you informed and entertained. Madame makes superb jams, Monsieur's passion is Arab horses, but as he can no longer ride he keeps two animals from an equine refuge on his pasture.

Rooms: 1 suite for 4 with kitchen & dining room, 2 triple, all with own bath or shower & wc.

Price: 270 Frs (€ 41.16) for two, 450 Frs for 4, including breakfast.

Meals: Café-Musique-Restaurant 1.5km; bistro 4km.

Open: All year.

Gîte space for 4 people

From Montreuil N39 dir. Hesdin. Left on D928 dir. St Omer. After Hesdin Forest 2nd left on D155 to Sains lès Fressin. House is at PR5 milestone.

MMap 236-16 **ASP Map No: 4**

Jo & Jacques RIEBEN
Chantelouve
35 rue Principale
62310 Sains lès Fressin
Pas-de-Calais
Tel: (0)3 21 90 60 13
Fax: (0)3 21 90 60 13
www.sawdays.co.uk

The house feels almost monastic (it never was), even Gothic on a dark night, in its bare, white-stoned simplicity and eerie hush; it is a pure, pleasing renovation for lovers of the soberly authentic. The vaulted dining room is a triumph; bedrooms and bathrooms are remarkable with lit candles, old mirrors, large beds and views over the immaculate courtyard garden and its historic pigeon tower. Madame is flexible and helpful, her mornings are full of light, space and home-made jams, her passions include rescuing animals (there is a menagerie to delight any child) and collecting 1900s dress-dummies.

Rooms: 2 double, 1 suite for 4, each with bath & wc.

Price: 300 Frs (€ 45.73) for two, including breakfast.

Meals: Wide choice 5km.

Open: All year.

From Montreuil, D901 to Neuville. In Neuville, on sharp bend, D113 dir. Marles sur Canche. Shortly after La Chartreuse follow signposts for 3km.

MMap 236-12 **ASP Map No: 3**

Mme Dominique LEROY
Manoir Francis
62170 Marles sur Canche
Pas-de-Calais
Tel: (0)3 21 81 38 80
Fax: (0)3 21 81 38 56

Both Madame Horel and her *crêpes* are Breton: the former makes forty of the latter every morning to complete her already copious and delicious breakfast. You eat in the plant-filled conservatory, built onto one end of this modern house and overlooking the garden. This garden is Madame's ruling passion and she says she is incapable of letting someone sleep in a room without fresh flowers: choose the season of your visit according to your floral preferences. Her bedrooms are full of thoughtful touches — sweets by your bed, hairdryers — to add to the pretty, feminine, décor.

Rooms: 2 triple, 1 double, each with shower & wc.

Price: 270 Frs (€ 41.16) for two, including breakfast.

Meals: 3 restaurants in St Josse.

Open: All year.

From A16 exit 25 for Rang du Fliers, through roundabout on D143 dir. Le Touquet. At roundabout, right on D144E to St Josse & follow signs.

MMap 236-12 **ASP Map No: 3**

Marie-Thérèse & Maurice HOREL
Les Buissonnets
70 chemin des Corps Saints
62170 St Josse
Pas-de-Calais
Tel: (0)3 21 84 12 12
Fax: (0)3 21 84 12 12
www.sawdays.co.uk

This was indeed the home farm of the nearby Carthusian monastery and Anne, who manages to run the B&B, bring up three delightful children and teach part-time, is a charming, thoughtful hostess. Her talent and taste are in the guestrooms — hard to believe they were once pigsties! She has transformed them into pretty, not over-large, but comfortably-furnished bedrooms. Breakfast, which may include *crêpes*, is served in the enchantingly decorated kitchen/diner. Part of the monastery is open to visitors — a pleasant after-breakfast discovery, or play a game of tennis on the home court (lessons available too).

Rooms: 1 double, 1 triple, each with shower & wc.

Price: 240 Frs (€ 36.59) for two, including breakfast (+ 30 Frs for use of kitchenette).

Meals: Choice in Montreuil 4km.

Open: All year.

From A16 exit Montreuil sur Mer onto N1 dir. Le Touquet/Boulogne. At lights right to Neuville then right on D113. Pass 2 other Chambres d'Hôtes — house on left next to abbey.

MMap 236-12 **ASP Map No: 3**

Anne FOURDINIER
Ferme de la Chartreuse
62170 Neuville sous Montreuil
Pas-de-Calais
Tel: (0)3 21 81 07 31/
(0)6 86 71 26 15
Fax: (0)3 21 81 07 31

A modern bungalow with all the heart of traditional French country life. When your hosts handed the family farm on to the next generation, they wanted to go on doing B&B in their new house. Its big windows let in the green that wraps the land outside and it has a real family feel: photos and mementoes everywhere, in the comfortable guestrooms too, with their good, pretty bathrooms. Madame, clearly a natural at grandmothering, is happy to mind your baby if you want to go off to sample the bright lights of Montreuil. Friendly and impeccable, it is excellent value and an ideal stopover.

Rooms: 1 double with bath & wc, 1 triple with shower & wc.

Price: 240 Frs (€ 36.59) for two, including breakfast.

Meals: Choice in Montreuil 4km.

Open: All year.

From A16 exit Montreuil sur Mer onto N1 dir. Le Touquet/Boulogne. At lights right to Neuville then right on D113. After 200m, house on right.

MMap 236-12 **ASP Map No: 3**

Hubert & Christiane FOURDINIER
30 rue de la Chartreuse
62170 Neuville sous Montreuil
Pas-de-Calais
Tel: (0)3 21 81 95 05
Fax: (0)3 21 81 95 05

Built two decades ago to look like a little old thatched cottage, it is a real surprise in a bit of French suburbia — so is the splendidly 1930s breakfast room. All the Terriens' own work, their décor is a mix of the cosy-twee and the dramatic. Guest quarters are in the South Wing: 'Tower' has an all-white mezzanine in... the 'tower', 'Jaune' has a hand-painted wardrobe, 'Moderne' is amazingly all grey, black and white 1990s yuppie-style. Madame, as neat and bright as her ideas, makes sure the bathrooms are properly sparkling, all accessories just so and breakfast a feast of variety.

Rooms: 4 double, each with shower & wc.

Price: 290 Frs (€ 44.21) for two, including breakfast.

Meals: Choice within 3km.

Open: All year.

From A16 exit 25 towards Berck; at 3rd traffic light, left & follow signs for Chambres d'Hôtes or La Chaumière.

MMap 236-12 **ASP Map No: 3**

Geneviève TERRIEN
La Chaumière
19 rue du Bihen
62180 Verton
Pas-de-Calais
Tel: (0)3 21 84 27 10
http://perso.wanadoo.fr/lachaumiere

Perfect peace here, not even a cockerel to wake you, and a warm unaffected welcome, complete with *apéro* on arrival. Your hosts have nine grown-up children so it's not surprising their C18 house has a real family feel. Choose between the picturesque fabrics and wooden floor of the room in the main house or the convenience of a room opening off the old farmyard, now a rose garden. Breakfast can include cheese and yoghurt as well as home-made jam and baguettes and croissants collected at dawn. Excellent for a quiet stopover, but the Locquevilles love getting to know their guests properly, so do stay on if you can.

Rooms: 1 double, 1 twin, each with shower & wc.

Price: 230-270 Frs (€ 35.06-41.16) for two, including breakfast.

Meals: Montreuil sur Mer 2km.

Open: March to November.

From A16 exit 26 to Montreuil then D439 E dir. Hesdin. Go through Beaumerie St Martin & take first right at signpost.

MMap 236-12 **ASP Map No: 3**

Jeanne-Marie & Francis
LOCQUEVILLE
L'Overgne
62170 Beaumerie St Martin
Pas-de-Calais
Tel: (0)3 21 81 81 87

23

"The best cowshed I've ever stayed in" said one of the many recommenders of this house. Another claimed they'd had their "best breakfast in France" here. And we know that the Trunnets' smiles are genuine, their delight in your company unfeigned, their converted outbuilding handsome and perfectly finished (down to mosquito nets on windows), if a touch characterless, and beds excellent (one equally smart guestroom is in the main house). Monsieur is only too happy to show you the flax production process: it's fascinating. While Madame will be baking yet another superb cake for tomorrow's breakfast.

Rooms: 1 double, 3 triple, each with shower & wc.

Price: 275 Frs (€ 41.92) for two, including breakfast.

Meals: Choice in Montreuil 6km.

Open: All year.

From A16 exit 'Montreuil' dir. Hesdin. In Brimeux, left at junction, pass church, then house on right, signposted.

MMap 236-12 **ASP Map No: 3**

M & Mme Germain TRUNNET
Ferme du Saule
20 rue de l'Église
62170 Brimeux
Pas-de-Calais
Tel: (0)3 21 06 01 28
Fax: (0)3 21 81 40 14
www.sawdays.co.uk

24

This house has been allowed to keep its solid, genuine, elegant personality. Those bricks are original 18th-century, as are the bowed doorframes and drawing-room panelling inside. Mrs James's exquisite taste matches the house: unpretentious but stylish, harmonious and comfortable, chandeliers to light books, swags to hold fine textiles, excellent bedrooms, luxurious bathrooms. The small art gallery might inspire you to stay a while and paint the gentle views over the valley or the ghosts at Agincourt, 3km away.

Rooms: 2 twin, 1 family room, each with own bathroom.

Price: From 380 Frs (€ 57.93) for two, family room from 490 Frs, including breakfast.

Meals: In village or 5 minutes drive.

Open: All year.

From Hesdin, D928 dir. St Omer, then D155 left to Fressin. On entering village cross bridge, turn left & take 1st right; house is 200m on right.

MMap 236-13 **ASP Map No: 4**

Mrs Lesley JAMES
La Maison des Violettes
62140 Fressin
Pas-de-Calais
Tel: (0)3 21 81 80 94
Fax: (0)3 21 81 80 94

Looking for service? Madame has even guided guests up from St Pol rather than have them lose their way. She loves telling the story of the house and its contents: it is loaded with character and history. You will breakfast in both dining rooms if you stay two nights — one has a unique '1830s-Medieval' fireplace, the other is classically French with curly furniture. In an outbuilding, guestrooms are simpler, each with some old furniture and a neat shower room. The quiet garden (but weekend racetrack in the valley) has a couple of goats. Both your hosts work constantly on their beloved house and cope with teenage children. Good folk.

Rooms: 2 double, 2 twin (1 on ground floor), each with shower & wc. Kitchenette available.

Price: 240 Frs (€ 36.59) for two, including breakfast; extra bed 80Frs; under 5s free.

Meals: Choice within walking distance or self-catering.

Open: All year.

From St Pol sur Ternoise, D343 NW dir. Fruges. Just before entering Gauchin Verloingt, right Rue de Troisvaux then right Rue des Montifaux. House along on right.

MMap 236-14 **ASP Map No: 4**

Marie-Christine & Philippe VION
Le Loubarré
62130 Gauchin Verloingt
Pas-de-Calais
Tel: (0)3 21 03 05 05
e-mail: MCVion.Loubarre@wanadoo.fr
www.sawdays.co.uk

It feels miles from anywhere but the hospitality can be stupendous at weekends, when Madame is at home (if she isn't back from Paris on weekdays, an employee plays host but perhaps not housemaid enough). Great parties are sometimes held for village, family and guests — lawns dotted with pretty frocks and chandeliers ringing with laughter. Built in 1745, the château has striking grandeur, beautiful sitting and dining rooms, but still needs much restoration and redecoration (bedrooms are rather run down). Central heating is now in place and in any case the relaxed and friendly atmosphere should easily make up for a little damp.

Rooms: 5 double, each with bath or shower & wc.

Price: 500 Frs (€ 76.22) for two, including breakfast.

Meals: 100 Frs, including coffee.

Open: All year.

From Arras, N25 dir. Doullens. At L'Arbret, right on D8 to Avesnes le Comte. D75 to Grand Rullecourt (4km); château in village centre, on the square.

MMap 236-14 **ASP Map No: 4**

Patrice & Chantal de SAULIEU
Château de Grand Rullecourt
Avesnes le Comte
62810 Grand Rullecourt, Pas-de-Calais
Tel: (0)3 21 58 06 37
Fax: (0)1 41 27 97 30
e-mail: Routiers@Club-Internet.fr
www.saulieu.com/chateau

To all appearances a stately home, this is actually a warm, embracing country house. The hall/breakfast room has all the features of the stolid, studied early 19th century: black and white floor, moulded ceiling, arches framing (later) stained glass windows. Madame is as bustling and chatty as any busy young grandmother with guests to care for (and delicious 'real' apples to sell, the fruit of what is called Reasoned Agriculture). One room is in traditional French style, the other four have fresh modern pine furniture and pretty colours, all have space and quiet. *Only four available at any one time.*

Rooms: 5 triple, all with bath or shower & wc. Extra beds available.

Price: 290 Frs (€ 44.21) for two, including breakfast. Extra bed 80 Frs.

Meals: Choice 5-8km.

Open: All year except January.

Gîte space for 4 people

Between Doullens & Arras. N25 dir. Arras. In L'Arbret, first left to Saulty and follow signposts.

MMap 236-24 **ASP Map No: 4**

Pierre & Françoise DALLE
Rue de la Gare
62158 Saulty
Pas-de-Calais
Tel: (0)3 21 48 24 76
Fax: (0)3 21 48 18 32
www.sawdays.co.uk

We have heard much praise for this B&B. Well-placed for Arras, Calais and the military cemeteries of the Vimy Ridge, the 1847 timber-frame and stone house hides in a peaceful spot behind the church (whose clock chimes... peacefully). The rural simplicity of the outside contrasts with the handsome interior: stuffed owls in the new, floral hall and fine antiques. Madame provides those touches that make the difference, such as bathrobes and bottled water. She also serves a generous, imaginative breakfast ("the best of our trip") and is the sort of person who will spontaneously post back to you anything you leave behind.

Rooms: 2 double, 1 twin, all with bath or shower & wc.

Price: 200 Frs (€ 30.49) for two, including breakfast.

Meals: Basic bar/restaurant 7km.

Open: All year.

From Arras N25 dir. Doullens. At Bac du Sud right on D66 to Gouy en Artois and Fosseux. House is near village church.

MMap 236-15 **ASP Map No: 4**

Geneviève GUILLUY-DELACOURT
3 rue de l'Église
62810 Fosseux
Pas-de-Calais
Tel: (0)3 21 48 40 13

The sheltered garden is lovely (swings for the children too) and the lime trees are a fitting backdrop to this imposing manor built in soft grey stone between the 17th and 19th centuries. It originally belonged to the château next door and the drive is still flanked by a fine laurel hedge. Rooms are high-ceilinged, bright and comfortable, with some antique furniture (particularly the Grandparents' Room). Madame is warmly relaxed and attentive, very much the pivot of her family and has photographs of them everywhere.

Rooms: 1 family suite, 1 double, both with bath or shower & wc.

Price: 260 Frs (€ 39.64) for two, including breakfast.

Meals: Choice 4-7km.

Open: All year.

From Arras, N39 dir. Le Touquet. After 7km, left along D56 towards Duisans. House on left.

MMap 236-15 **ASP Map No: 4**

Annie & Patrick SENLIS
Le Clos Grincourt
18 rue du Château
62161 Duisans
Pas-de-Calais
Tel: (0)3 21 48 68 33
Fax: (0)3 21 48 68 33

This house is a fine example of northern French brick-building, as is the splendid C19 brewery across the road with its curious double swastika emblem. The Peugniez are lovely, gentle people whose children have grown and flown; they still farm (cereals only now, having given up beef) and enjoy good company. Their house is simple and most welcoming with a warm family feel and no pretentions. The attic-floor guestrooms have screened-off showers, old timbers and floorboards and make a good-value stopover. And don't forget that fascinating old Arras is thoroughly worth a day trip.

Rooms: 3 double, 1 twin, 1 quadruple, all with own shower, all sharing 2 wcs.

Price: 200 Frs (€ 30.49) for two, including breakfast.

Meals: In village or Arras 7km.

Open: All year except Christmas & New Year.

Gîte space for 12 people

From A1 exit 16 on N50 for 2km then left to Fampoux. In village follow Chambre d'Hôte signs. House on right in Rue Paul Verlaine.

MMap 236-16 **ASP Map No: 4**

Dominique & Marie-Thérèse PEUGNIEZ
17 rue Paul Verlaine
62118 Fampoux
Pas-de-Calais
Tel: (0)3 21 55 00 90
Fax: (0)3 21 55 00 90

The outside may be unprepossessing — don't be put off; you will get a marvellous welcome and be treated with immense care. Your hosts are eager to please, competent and pleasant. The hall of the house is striking with its real marble floor. There are lots of stuffed animals, a very sober breakfast room, another good room with painted panelling. All is impeccably clean and orderly and there is a lovely big garden at the back. A very good, and genteel, stop for those going to and from the ferry, just 2-3 minutes stroll from the town centre and excellent value.

Rooms: 2 double, each with shower & wc.

Price: 270 Frs (€ 41.16) for two, including breakfast.

Meals: Restaurant 100m.

Open: All year.

From Calais A16 E to exit 23b and into Bourbourg. From Place de l'Hôtel de Ville the street is left of the town hall as you face it.

MMap 236-3 **ASP Map No: 4**

Marilou & Jacques VAN DE WALLE
25 rue des Martyrs de la Résistance
59630 Bourbourg
Nord
Tel: (0)3 28 22 21 41

In this richly interesting city, Jeannine Hulin's beautiful townhouse reflects her personality: artistic, warm and friendly, and she takes obvious pleasure in both her house and her guests. You breakfast at a tiled table in the clean, bright kitchen or in the flower-filled, conservatory looking onto the garden. Original floor tiles, stripped pine doors and masses of plants add to the atmosphere. The big bedroom is lovely with matching *lit bateau*, wardrobe and desk, antique white linen and mirrors, and your delightful bathroom has a claw-footed bath.

Rooms: 1 double with private bath & shared wc on floor below.

Price: 255 Frs (€ 38.87) for two, incl. breakfast; extra bed 80 Frs.

Meals: Full choice in town.

Open: All year.

NON!

From A1 exit 19 onto D917 dir. Faches Ronchin Lille for 4km. At traffic light (Boulangerie Paul on corner) turn left; 1st right is Rue des Hannetons.

MMap 236-16 **ASP Map No: 4**

Jeannine HULIN
28 rue des Hannetons
59000 Lille
Nord
Tel: (0)3 20 53 46 12
Fax: (0)3 20 53 46 12
www.sawdays.co.uk

A charming hostess: her welcome more than compensates for an unremarkable modern house on a city street. And there's a lovely surprise: the picture window in the uncluttered living room gives onto a garden full of flowers where you can sit after exploring the treasures of Lille. The bedrooms are small, cosily-carpeted, pleasing and there's a little kitchen for guests. Chantal, bright, energetic and typically French, used to teach English (speaks it perfectly) then adapted her house specially to receive guests. Yves has good English too, and will dine with you — they both enjoy having an open house.

Rooms: 2 double with shower & wc; 1 twin with bath & wc.

Price: 220-260 Frs (€ 33.54-39.64) for two, including breakfast.

Meals: 100 Frs, including wine & coffee. Self-catering.

Open: All year.

From A1 exit 20/20b 'Centre Commercial'; at r'about dir. Wattignies; at T-junction right for 500m then left to Wattignies for 2km; at lights left for 'Le Village Centre' for 100m. At 'Pharmacie' right into Rue Faidherbe — house 500m on left (with front garden).

MMap 236-16 **ASP Map No: 4**

Yves & Chantal LE BOT
59 rue Faidherbe
59139 Wattignies
Nord
Tel: (0)3 20 60 24 51
www.sawdays.co.uk

You enter this classic French farmyard through a C17 archway facing the old stables (a fairly standard conversion job here) where you will find your bedroom. Rooms have been carefully colour-co-ordinated in simple cottagey style and the showers are welcomingly wide: a whole family could have fun in there. Your hosts particularly like having children (they have three of their own). Breakfast, which includes their own milk and yoghurt, wholemeal bread and waffles in winter, is a feast you can have at any time from 6am to noon. An ideal family base and really good value.

Rooms: 2 double, 1 twin, 1 triple, each with shower & wc.

Price: 200 Frs (€ 30.49) for two, including breakfast.

Meals: 70 Frs, including wine.

Open: All year.

From A27 (Lille-Doornik) exit 'Cité Scientifique' dir. Cysoing. In Sainghin, leave church on right, continue 600m, right on Rue du Cimetière, across junction into Rue Pasteur — farm 800m on right.

MMap 236-16 **ASP Map No: 4**

Dominique POLLET
Ferme de la Noyelle
832 rue Pasteur
59262 Sainghin en Mélantois
Nord
Tel: (0)3 20 41 29 82
Fax: (0)3 20 79 06 99

Originally a staging post on the windswept plain, this impressive house carries local history in its bones, including the ravages of C20 warfare: destroyed in 1916, it was rebuilt in 1920 then the staircase had to be replaced in 1945. The balcony room is splendid but all rooms have high ceilings, marble fireplaces and good old furniture. They are sober and peaceful. The breakfast room is more eclectically furnished with individual tables and toasters. Your wonderfully attentive hosts make it a perfect ferry stopover. The converted outbuilding contains a fully-equipped room for the disabled.

Rooms: 1 double, 2 twin, 1 triple, 1 suite for 6, each with shower & wc.

Price: 240-315 Frs (€ 36.59-48.02) for two, including breakfast.

Meals: Restaurant 100 metres.

Open: All year.

Gîte space for 8 people

20Frs

From A26 exit 9 dir. Masnières. Farm is at Bonavis junction where D917 and N44 meet, 2km north of Banteux.

MMap 236-27 **ASP Map No: 4**

Michel & Thérèse DELCAMBRE
Ferme de Bonavis
59266 Banteux
Nord
Tel: (0)3 27 78 55 08
Fax: (0)3 27 78 55 08

It glows with colour, comfort and good taste; everything is just so, almost like a dolls' house with a dolls' house clutter, Madame's perfect plaything. The impression is of character and antiques, with some modern bits. The living room is huge, with pink walls, beams, a black slate floor and a big fireplace and there is an almost overwhelmingly pretty breakfast room, full of *objets trouvés*, plants and a big crackling fire. The two first-floor rooms, which have a communicating door if you want a suite, are comfortable, with lovely bedding, good bathrooms, beams and views over church and garden.

Rooms: 2 double/triple, each with shower & wc.

Price: 360 Frs (€ 54.88) for two, including breakfast.

Meals: Choice 5km.

Open: All year.

From A16, exit 24. From Abbeville N1 N dir. Montreuil/Boulogne for 25km. In Vron left to Villers sur Authie. There, take Rue de l'Église (opposite café). At end of road, left up tree-lined lane; house on left.

MMap 236-12 **ASP Map No: 3**

Pierre & Sabine SINGER de WAZIÈRES
La Bergerie
80120 Villers sur Authie
Somme
Tel: (0)3 22 29 21 74
Fax: (0)3 22 29 39 58

The ancient garden, with its straight lines of dwarf box hedging and flower beds, is very attractive. (There is a roofed barbecue area which you are encouraged to use.) Joanna, a gentle and grandmotherly woman (who has seven children and yet more grandchildren), makes small ceramic figures — her kiln is in the barn. At breakfast, you eat jam made from her own organic fruit, sitting in the glass-fronted porch among her plants and *objets*, using very pretty crockery. One bedroom is off the kitchen, so not so private. In a pretty village and opposite the church.

Rooms: 3 double, each with shower or bath & wc.

Price: 280-300 Frs (€ 42.69-45.73) for two, including breakfast.

Meals: Barbecue available. Choice in Abbeville.

Open: All year.

From Boulogne A16, Abbeville/St Riquier exit. At first roundabout, to Vauchelles lès Quesnoy. House on main square opposite church.

MMap 236-22 **ASP Map No: 3**

Mme Joanna CRÉPELLE
121 place de l'Eglise
80132 Vauchelles lès Quesnoy
Somme
Tel: (0)3 22 24 18 17

A paradise for children, the rambling garden has stone love-seats and two ponds, the enclosed yard has swings and a play-house and the old manor house the feel of an adventure story. Behind the wrought-iron front door the emphasis is on country family hospitality and Madame, smiling, uncomplicated, often clad in a white linen apron, gives guests a big welcome. The redecorated living room has smart grey and white floor tiles and stylish blue stencilling on the ceiling beams. The fresh, rustic bedrooms have marble fireplaces, square French pillows on the beds, floral 1950s country-style décor and complicated bathroom arrangements.

Rooms: 1 double, gd floor, with bath & wc; 2 double, 1st floor, with showers sharing wc; 1 twin, 1 double, 2nd floor, sharing bath & wc. 2 small extra rooms for children.

Price: 250 Frs (€ 38.11) for two, including breakfast. Reservations only.

Meals: Restaurants 5-10km. Picnic possible.

Open: March to November.

From Amiens D929 dir. Albert. At Pont Noyelles, left onto D115 dir. Contay; signposted in Bavelincourt.

MMap 236-24 **ASP Map No: 4**

M & Mme Noël VALENGIN
Bavelincourt
80260 Villers Bocage
Somme
Tel: (0)3 22 40 51 51

This is above all a family house where Madame, mother of four beautifully-mannered children and lover of things outdoor — dogs, horses, gardening, shoring up the outbuildings — reigns with energy and a refreshingly natural attitude: what matter if a little mud is walked into the hall? In pleasing contrast is the formal dining room with its fabulous patterned parquet floor, vast table, family silver and chandeliers, plus very fine food. Rooms may seem slightly worn — renovation is laborious and there have been disastrous leaks — so come for lively hospitality not smart château bedrooms.

Rooms: 1 double, 1 suite for 4, each with bath or shower & wc; 2 double sharing bathroom.

Price: 400 Frs (€ 60.98) for two, including breakfast.

Meals: 110 Frs, including coffee.

Open: All year.

Gîte space for 20 people

From Abbeville, N28 dir. Rouen. At St Maxent, D29 to Oisemont, then D25 dir. Sénarpont. Signposted on outskirts of Foucaucourt.

MMap 236-22 **ASP Map No: 3**

Mme Elisabeth de ROCQUIGNY
Château de Foucaucourt
Hors Nesle
80140 Oisemont, Somme
Tel: (0)3 22 25 12 58
Fax: (0)3 22 25 15 58
e-mail: chateaudefoucaucourt@wanadoo.fr
www.sawdays.co.uk

Enfolded in rolling, wooded country, this very attractive house was the first to offer B&B hospitality in the Somme (though Rommel was not really invited, he just came) and the tradition holds. Madame is Mayor of their village and Monsieur, who is Dutch, makes cider, calvados and honey, keeps that supremely French animal a *trotteur* horse, and will happily tell you stories. They are calm, hospitable people, the rooms are comfortable, the views restful, the panelled dining room a proper setting for a fine breakfast. A good place to stay.

Rooms: 1 double with shower & wc; 3 triple, each with shower & handbasin, sharing wc.

Price: 230-250 Frs (€ 35.06-38.11) for two, including breakfast; extra bed 100 Frs.

Meals: Barbecue and guest kitchen available.

Open: All year.

Gîte space for 13 people

From Abbeville, N28 dir. Rouen. After 28km, left at Bouttencourt on D1015 to Sénarpont then D211 dir. Amiens. After 4.5km, left into Le Mazis; follow Chambres d'Hôtes signs.

MMap 236-22 **ASP Map No: 3**

Dorette & Aart ONDER DE LINDEN
80430 Le Mazis
Somme
Tel: (0)3 22 25 90 88
Fax: (0)3 22 25 76 04

The 'best' room is worth it: white all over with pools of colour in the bed hangings, soft kilim rugs, dark polished antiques, old oil paintings, gilt-framed prints. White doors lead to a gorgeous bathroom (antique basin and taps) and a private sitting alcove. The smaller rooms also have lovely furniture. Madame is a painter and the charm and peace of her garden, with bantams and rabbits all about, deepen the friendly atmosphere she creates without being intrusive. Breakfast, served in a delightful room next to Madame's studio, is a most happy affair.

Rooms: 3 double and 1 suite for 4, all with bath or shower & wc.

Price: 250-350 Frs (€ 38.11-53.36) for two, suite 500 Frs, including breakfast.

Meals: Restaurant 5km; choice 8km.

Open: April to October.

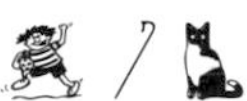

From Amiens, N29 dir. Poix, then left on D162 to Creuse; signposted.

MMap 236-23 **ASP Map No: 4**

Mme Monique LEMAÎTRE
26 rue Principale
80480 Creuse
Somme
Tel: (0)3 22 38 91 50

Come down into the valley as you approach the village and take in this spectacular view of the beautiful River Somme and a network of lakes. 15 hectares of it belong to the Randjias' working farm, an obvious attraction for those who enjoy fishing or boating. There are views of a bridge and the lock from the bedrooms. The friendly Madame Randjia offers adequate guestrooms and cooks excellent regional specialities, served in the flower-filled dining room. Families can have their noisy breakfasts in a separate room!

Rooms: 2 double, 1 twin, all with shower & wc.

Price: 280 Frs (€ 42.69) for two, including breakfast.

Meals: By arrangement 85 Frs, including coffee.

Open: All year.

Gîte space for 5 people

From A1, Péronne exit onto N29 westwards and immediately right on D146 dir. Feuillères. Before village, D146E to Frise. First farm after bridge.

MMap 236-25 **ASP Map No: 4**

Michel & Annick RANDJIA
La Ferme de l'Écluse
80340 Frise
Somme
Tel: (0)3 22 84 59 70
Fax: (0)3 22 83 17 56
www.sawdays.co.uk

This house has such a lovely face! The guest bedrooms and sitting room, however, are in a well-converted barn that gives onto the courtyard. They are furnished with a mix of old and new, adorned with fresh flowers in summer and double-glazed against winter chill and any road noise. If you arrive at a sensible time you will be offered a glass of home-made cider. Breakfast in the pretty room with its fireplace (in the main house) is a feast. Pony-and-trap rides in summer. The spire of Amiens Cathedral reaches up into the sky nearby.

Rooms: 3 double, 1 twin, each bath or shower & wc.

Price: 310 Frs (€ 47.26) for two, including breakfast.

Meals: Within walking distance.

Open: All year.

Gîte space for 11 people

From A16 Dury exit onto N1 S dir. Breteuil and Paris. Just before Dury, left dir. St Fuscien; signposted.

MMap 236-24 **ASP Map No: 4**

Alain & Maryse SAGUEZ
2 rue Grimaux
80480 Dury
Somme
Tel: (0)3 22 95 29 52

A typical, blessedly unmodernised, Picardy farm with low buildings, white walls and greenery. And a typically warm northern welcome from Madame, who used to be a social worker — she is at ease with all sorts and has the most infectious laugh. Guestrooms, each with separate entrance, are decorated and furnished with panache, personality and simple basics. Bathrooms have been recently redone. Ask for the big room in the *grenier* (loft). The lush green garden at the back has wrought-iron furniture, a lily pond and hens scratching in a large pen.

Rooms: 3 triple, all with shower, wc & kitchenette.

Price: 230-250 Frs (€ 35.06-38.11) for two, including breakfast.

Meals: 60 Frs, excluding wine.

Open: Easter to October.

From Amiens N1 south to Hébécourt. Opposite church follow Chambre d'Hôte signs to Plachy Buyon.

MMap 236-23 **ASP Map No: 4**

Mme Jacqueline PILLON
L'Herbe de Grâce
Buyon
80160 Plachy Buyon
Somme
Tel: (0)3 22 42 12 22
www.sawdays.co.uk

Most unusual! The ground floor of the converted chapel, also used by the *gîte d'étape* (B&B bookings are not taken when groups are expected), has a kitchen area, a free-standing fireplace shaped like an oil lamp (the local masonry students' masterpiece) and a massive dining table which converts for... snooker. Guests may light a fire, play snooker, use the kitchen, lounge in the garden. The smallish bedrooms, upstairs under the rafters, both have bath and loo in the room. The Richoux are eminently relaxed and likeable people. Nearby are water sports, fishing and Amiens' great Gothic Cathedral.

Rooms: 1 double, 1 triple, each with bath & wc in bedroom.

Price: 220 Frs (€ 33.54) for two, including breakfast.

Meals: Self-catering or restaurants 4km.

Open: All year.

Gîte space for 12 people

From Amiens, N1 dir. Beauvais. Between St Sauflieu and Essertaux, right on D153 to Lœuilly; signposted.

MMap 236-33 **ASP Map No: 4**

Claudine & Bernard RICHOUX
Route de Conty
80160 Lœuilly
Somme
Tel: (0)3 22 38 15 19

An idyllic village of handsome old houses surrounded by rolling farmland and green forests. There are cows in the field and apples in the small orchard beside the house. Guests sleep in a modern extension (though on beds that are a bit less modern?) to a fine old building of uncertain age. This is every bit the lived-in farmhouse and Madame is every inch the chatty, friendly, elderly farmer's wife. She is also a charming hostess who loves tending her orchard and kitchen garden... and her guests.

Rooms: 2 double, each with shower, bath & wc.

Price: 250 Frs (€ 38.11) for two, including breakfast.

Meals: 3 restaurants within 2km.

Open: All year.

From Beauvais dir. Le Tréport to Troissereux then D133 to Songeons, then D143 dir. Gournay en Bray. 1st village on leaving forest is Buicourt; house near church.

MMap 236-32 **ASP Map No: 3**

Eddy & Jacqueline VERHOEVEN
3 rue de la Mare
60380 Buicourt
Oise
Tel: (0)3 44 82 31 15

A very fine pigeon tower dominates the yard of this friendly working farm. Your rooms are in the former bakery where bread was made for humans and potatoes cooked for pigs — oven, beams and character have been preserved. The bedrooms are good-sized and simply furnished with an Indian cotton throw at each bedhead, original timbers and sober carpets. The active, quiet owners have turned several of their small farmhouse rooms into a lovely open-plan space with timber framing. Dine here with them in all simplicity, once the children are in bed, and soak up the warm, natural atmosphere.

Rooms: 1 quadruple, 1 triple, 2 double, all with shower & wc.

Price: 230 Frs (€ 35.06) for two, including breakfast. Extra bed 60 Frs.

Meals: 75 Frs, including wine & coffee.

Open: All year.

From Beauvais N31 dir. Rouen. Just on leaving Beauvais pick up signs to Savignies. Farm in village, 50m from church.

MMap 236-33 **ASP Map No: 4**

Annick & Jean-Claude LETURQUE
La Ferme du Colombier
60650 Savignies
Oise
Tel: (0)3 44 82 18 49
Fax: (0)3 44 82 53 70
www.sawdays.co.uk

The old C18 house is pretty, the 'new' (1927) wing by Auguste Perret, king of concrete, a piece of design history. His immense living room is squares in squares: panels, bookshelves, floor tiles, even the table, found languishing and unloved in an antique shop and brought 'home' by Madame. She loves her house and enjoys sharing its delights with you. Guestrooms are pleasing: ethnic fabrics, good colours and light, sophisticated bathrooms. Monsieur is mad about horses; their pasture is the foreground to the sweeping view from the quiet garden. And the train can carry you straight from the village to Paris... and back again.

Rooms: 2 double, 1 triple, each with bath or shower & wc.

Price: 300 Frs (€ 45.73) for two, including breakfast.

Meals: 120 Frs, including wine & coffee.

Open: All year.

From Calais A16 exit 13 (Méru) W dir. Chaumont en Vexin. In Loconville, left to Liancourt St Pierre; right to post office & follow left into rue du Donjon (impasse); high gate on left.

MMap 237-4 **ASP Map No: 3**

Monique & Luc GALLOT
La Pointe
60240 Liancourt St Pierre
Oise
Tel: (0)3 44 49 32 08
Fax: (0)3 44 49 32 08

Behind the austere brick walls and imposing archway you will discover a homely museum of exotica. Your hostess, a retired chemist, loves travelling; she also loves her dogs — and contact with visitors. Your beamed, fireplaced, mellow rooms, furnished with old pieces, are in the original house; she lives in the brilliantly-converted barn, and all is harmony and warm, natural living. Drink in her talk of France, the French and the rest of the world. Rest in peace, rouse to the dawn chorus, then enjoy breakfast in the sunshine. (Cats won't like it here.)

Rooms: 1 double with shower & basin, 1 double with bath & basin, sharing wc.

Price: 300 Frs (€ 45.73) for two, including breakfast.

Meals: Restaurants 4-6km.

Open: All year: booking essential.

Gîte space for 4 people

From A1 exit 10 dir. Compiègne/Arsy for 4km. By caravan yard right at small turning dir. Jaux. 1st right to Varanval, up hill then down. House on right opposite château gates (1.2km from N31 turning).

MMap 236-35 **ASP Map No: 4**

Françoise GAXOTTE
La Gaxottière
60880 Jaux Varanval
Oise
Tel: (0)3 44 83 22 41
Fax: (0)3 44 83 22 41
www.sawdays.co.uk

This cereal farm, surrounded by woods and fields, has an elegant, old, cobbled farmyard at its heart. Cleverly renovated farm cottages provide delightful, clean, modern rooms with pretty fabrics and good bedding. In a converted barn, under a brick-vault ceiling, are a games room with original mangers to catch the ping-pong balls and a stone-walled, log-fired sitting/dining room with an old dresser and painted jugs. The Hamelins, intelligent, smiling, light-hearted and keen to please, have thoughtfully installed swings and slides and a tennis court.

Rooms: 2 twin, 1 family suite (twin & bunks), all with bath or shower & wc.

Price: 300 Frs (€ 45.73) for two, including breakfast.

Meals: Choice in Crépy 9km.

Open: All year except January.

From A1 Senlis exit onto N324 to Crépy en Valois, then D332 dir. Lévignen and Betz. 3km after Lévignen right to Macquelines. Right at T-junction; farm immediately on right.

MMap 237-20 **ASP Map No: 4**

Philippe & Marthe HAMELIN
Ferme de Macquelines
60620 Betz
Oise
Tel: (0)3 44 87 20 21

The medieval keep looms over the attractive old village and this fine mansion, built in 1611, once belonged to Napoleon's Finance Minister. Bedrooms vary in quality, some are smarter than others, and breakfast is served at separate tables. The grounds run down to the river Aisne, creating an almost rural impression just three minutes' walk from the centre. Fish in the river, swim in the pool in summer (at the higher price), play tennis or, less energetically, draughts on the giant 10ft x 10ft board. A tranquil, clean-aired place where your hosts may be preoccupied with receptions or their *brocante* but babysitting is possible.

Rooms: 2 double, 3 triple, all with shower & wc.

Price: 330-390 Frs (€ 50.31-59.46) for two, including breakfast.

Meals: 100 Frs, excluding wine.

Open: All year.

Gîte space for 14 people

From Compiègne, N31 dir. Soissons; after 22km, left to Vic sur Aisne; opposite Mairie, right and first right again.

MMap 236-36 **ASP Map No: 4**

Jean & Anne MARTNER
Domaine des Jeanne
Rue Dubarle
02290 Vic sur Aisne
Aisne
Tel: (0)3 23 55 57 33
Fax: (0)3 23 55 57 33

If you want to sleep in a tower, try this: the vast bedroom and smaller room for children (across the hall from the main double room) have been imaginatively and attractively housed in the octagonal tower, which is one of the charms of this delicious *troubadour*-style château. Jacques' family have been here for five generations and are likely to remain, judging by the tribe of exquisitely-behaved children he and Marie-Catherine have produced. Breakfast and dinner (by arrangement) are served in summer in the enchanting orangery. It's a pleasure to see an old family home so well loved and used.

Rooms: 1 suite (double + single) for 3 with shower & wc.

Price: 300 Frs (€ 45.73) for two, including breakfast.

Meals: 120 Frs, including (good) wine.

Open: All year.

From A26 exit 13 dir. Laon; round Laon by-pass dir. Soissons onto N2 for about 15km then left on D423 to Nanteuil la Fosse. Through Nanteuil, following signs for La Quincy — château on right outside village.

MMap 236-37 **ASP Map No: 4**

Jacques & Marie-Catherine CORNU-LANGY
La Quincy
02880 Nanteuil la Fosse
Aisne
Tel: (0)3 23 54 67 76
Fax: (0)3 23 54 72 63
http://perso.wanadoo.fr/fc6/

Genuine French generosity and real contact are here in the big old house, welcoming and warmly tatty with mix 'n not-match wallpapers, posters on long corridors, funny old prints in bedrooms. The owners are great fun, energetic, and love their dinner parties in the dining room with its old family furniture, where guests of all nationalities communicate as the wine flows. They wouldn't dream of changing a thing for the sake of modern sanitising theories — may they prosper! The rooms are simple and good; one has a ship's shower room, another a Louis XVI bed, all look onto green pastures.

Rooms: 1 suite for 4, 2 double, 1 twin, each with bath or shower & wc; 1 double, 1 twin with basins, sharing bathroom.

Price: 200-280 Frs (€ 30.49-42.69) for two, including breakfast. Extra bed 100 Frs.

Meals: 95 Frs, including wine (not Sundays).

Open: 15 March to 15 October.

Gîte space for 12 people

From A26-E17, Laon/Chambry exit S on N2; 2nd left to Athies s/Laon; there D516 to Bruyères Monbérault; there left on D967 dir. Fismes — Chérêt signposted on leaving Bruyères.

MMap 238-38 **ASP Map No: 4**

Mme Monique SIMONNOT
Le Clos
02860 Chérêt
Aisne
Tel: (0)3 23 24 80 64

Come for Madame's personality: enthusiasm pours from her in an "outrageous French accent" (dixit her quietly charming English partner who speaks no French at all!) as she revels in being hostess, regional informer (all you need to know about local history, including two World Wars) and guide to magnificent forest walks. She loves her charmingly faded, almost ramshackle, formerly fine old house (newspapers found in the plaster were dated 1793) which has three huge rooms with superb old bath tubs (avoid the cramped attic room with shower and loo squeezed into a corner). If décor is haphazard and housework skimpy, breakfast is consistently generous.

Rooms: 2 twin with bath or shower & wc, 2 triple sharing a bathroom.

Price: 250 Frs (€ 38.11) for two, including breakfast.

Meals: 5 minutes walk to restaurants.

Open: All year.

From Soissons, N31 dir. Reims for 16km then right at signs for Braine centre. House is set back on right next to Peugeot garage — B&B sign.

MMap 237-9 **ASP Map No: 4**

Mme Jacqueline MARTIN
14 rue Saint Rémy
02220 Braine
Aisne
Tel: (0)3 23 74 12 74/(0)6 87 47 37 73
Fax: (0)3 23 74 12 74
e-mail: 106313.1301@compuserve.com

55

Out in the wilds, Ressons is a big, active farm (producing 'happy' veal), with an unspoilt house among rolling hills and champagne vineyards. Your hosts are hard-working, active and good company; they also hunt. Madame, an architect, works from home, brings up three small children AND nurtures her guests. The superb deeply-carved Henri III furniture is an admirable family heirloom; rooms are colour-co-ordinated, beds are beautiful, views are stunning, dinners cooked with home-grown produce are excellent; bring rod and permit and you can fish in the pond. Arms are open for you in this thoroughly civilised household.

Rooms: 1 double, 1 twin, each with own bath, sharing wc; 2 double & 1 twin, sharing bath & 2 wcs.

Price: 250-300 Frs (€ 38.11-45.73) for two, including breakfast.

Meals: 90 Frs, excluding wine (from 70 Frs).

Open: All year except Christmas.

Gîte space for 12 people

From Fismes D967 dir. Fère en Tardenois & Château Thierry for 4km. DON'T go to Mont St Martin. Continue 800m beyond turning; white house on left.

MMap 237-10 **ASP Map No: 4**

Valérie & Jean-Paul FERRY
Ferme de Ressons
02220 Mont St Martin
Aisne
Tel: (0)3 23 74 71 00
Fax: (0)3 23 74 28 88
www.sawdays.co.uk

56

This farm is utterly 'country French' and friendly to all (extra-special attention to children). Flagstones and stone benches, 12th-century cellars, coppers and big mirrors, plus a piano, old photographs and vases of flowers to add to the atmosphere. Madame deals with ease and energy with family and friends (that's you). Cottage-style bedrooms (one is particularly fine) with pretty linen and marble-topped washstands. Ample breakfasts; robust farmhouse dinners *en famille* if you wish and a pool for children.

Rooms: 1 double, 1 twin, with bath or shower & wc; 1 double, 1 twin, 1 single sharing shower & wc.

Price: 250 Frs (€ 38.11) for two, including breakfast.

Meals: 100 Frs, including coffee.

Open: All year.

From Soissons, N2 dir. Paris. At 4th main crossroads, D172 left dir. Chaudun. About 4km on, D177 left to Léchelle. (1 hour from Paris.)

MMap 237-9 **ASP Map No: 4**

Jacques & Nicole MAURICE
Ferme Léchelle
)2200 Berzy le Sec
isne
:l: (0)3 23 74 83 29
: (0)3 23 74 82 47

SOME FALSE FRIENDS

Biologique & Organic
English 'organic' is known as *de culture biologique* in French, *bio* for short. If you say *organique* people will imagine your organs are troubling you.

Biscuit & Gâteau
Biscuit: literally 'twice cooked' and properly applies to dehydrated army rations or the base for some sticky puddings. The usual words for sweet or savoury biscuits are *gâteaux secs, petits gâteaux*, also *gâteaux d'apéritif. Gâteau maison* at breakfast will probably be a simple sponge-cake with jam or a French-style fruit cake (called *le cake...*).

Tourte - Tarte - Tartine - Pie - Pis
Tourte: the closest the French have to 'pie', i.e. with pastry above and below.
Tarte: an open tart or flan.
Tartine: a half baguette (usually) sliced in half and buttered, i.e. breakfast food.
Une pie: magpie. *Un pis* (same pronunciation as *une pie*): a cow's udder.
Scotch: adhesive tape or whisky - the context should help.
Soda: a non-alcoholic, probably sweet, fizzy drink of some kind. Soda water you should is *eau gazeuse.*
Trouble: cloudy, murky – you can send a bottle of wine back for this.
Mousse: froth, foam, lather (beer, sea, soap) or foam rubber or... moss.
Pomme de pin: fircone; pineapple is *ananas; pamplemousse* is grapefruit.
Raisin: fresh grape or grapes as in Steinbeck's book *Les Raisins de la Colère.*
Grappe: a bunch of grapes -(*une grappe de raisins).*
Prune: fresh plum. A prune is *pruneau.*
Myrtille: bilberry – they grow wild and delicious on the hills of southern France.
Myrtle is *myrte.*
Verger: orchard – many greengrocer's shop are *Aux Fruits du Verger.*
Marmelade: stewed fruit. Marmalade is called *confiture d'oranges amères.*

The angel of Reims smiles eternally
upon the Kings of France anointed in his Cathedral
and upon the uncomprehending soldier
slain in the battlefields.
And the ephemeral bubbles burst on.

Ardennes – Champagne

The house is 800 years old — utterly splendid: no Holiday Inn or Novotel can conceivably put you up in a medieval tower. One of the three tower rooms has a Louis XV stone fireplace and a pale blue bathroom. Another huge old room has the usual fireplace, bedstead with family crest, wooden floor with rug. The *salon* has a 1567 painted ceiling, a huge Renaissance fireplace with family crest, formal chairs and sofas, desk and table. It is all very grand but your hosts are down-to-earth and charming people. Guests have admired the fantastic buildings and loved the warm welcome. Pets by arrangement.

Rooms: 4 double, each with own bath or shower & wc.

Price: 480-530 Frs (€ 73.18-80.80) for two, including breakfast; extra person 100-150 Frs.

Meals: Choice 10-20km.

Open: March to December.

From Reims, N46 then N47 dir. Luxembourg; go through Vouziers to Buzancy, turn right onto D12 and follow signs.

MMap 241-18 **ASP Map No: 5**

Jacques & Véronique de MEIXMORON
Château de Landreville
08240 Bayonville
Ardennes
Tel: (0)3 24 30 04 39
Fax: (0)3 24 30 04 39

Near the beautiful forest of Argonne, the farm is now run by M Patizel Junior while your hosts have converted the stables into a modern house. It has an attractive mixture of beautifully-restored antiques and good-quality new furniture, lovely linen and good mattresses, bright colours and clean-cut bathrooms. Madame is an excellent cook, Monsieur is a notable crafter of local wood and stone; both are proud of their country heritage, wonderful with children and deeply committed to 'real B&B'. Nothing is too much trouble for them.

Rooms: 2 double, 1 quadruple, all with shower & wc.

Price: 220 Frs (€ 33.54) for two, including breakfast.

Meals: 75 Frs, including wine & coffee.

Open: All year.

From A4 exit Ste Menehould on D982 (382 on some maps) to Givry en Argonne. There left on D54 to Les Charmontois (9km).

MMap 241-26 **ASP Map No: 5**

M & Mme Bernard PATIZEL
5 rue St Bernard
51330 Les Charmontois
Marne
Tel: (0)3 26 60 39 53
Fax: (0)3 26 60 39 53
www.sawdays.co.uk

You cannot forget this is a champagne-growing house: the Harlauts produce their own marque, the vines grow all around, there's champagne cake for breakfast, the dining table is a champagne barrel (part of) but it is for the first-class food and the atmosphere that guests return. This couple are perfect hosts: bright, welcoming and smiling, they love entertaining and are keen to provide good value. Dinner (except during grape harvest!) *en famille* is in the dining room or on the terrace overlooking the garden. Guestrooms are warm, uncluttered, Great Mastered and roof-windowed with simple shower rooms; steep narrow stairs up though.

Rooms: 1 double with shower & wc; 1 double & 1 twin, each with shower & washbasin, sharing wc.

Price: 230-260 Frs (€ 35.06-39.64) for two, including breakfast; extra bed 80 Frs.

Meals: 120 Frs, including wine & coffee.

Open: All year except Jan & Easter.

From A26 exit 15 'Reims La Neuvillette' onto N44 dir. Laon for 2km. Left to St Thierry. House in village.

MMap 237-11 **ASP Map No: 4**

Evelyne & Remi HARLAUT
5 rue du Paradis
51220 St Thierry
Marne
Tel: (0)3 26 03 13 75
Fax: (0)3 26 03 03 65

These independent champagne growers delight in showing guests round vineyards and cellars (tastings included). Up its own staircase, the bright, airy attic bedroom has beams, dormers, matching handmade curtains and covers, and wicker furniture. Breakfast is served in the lovely old family house with Madame's fine jams and the black dog Champagne (*naturellement*) lying under the table waiting for crumbs. Madame is a wonderful woman who started B&B for champagne buyers who did not want to leave after tasting! *Latest bookings taken at 7 pm.*

Rooms: 1 double with shower & wc.

Price: 235 Frs (€ 35.83) for two, including breakfast.

Meals: Choice in Fismes (11km).

Open: All year except 2 weeks in August.

Gîte space for 2 people

From Epernay N51 N dir. Reims for 4km then left on D386 dir. Fismes for 30km. At Crugny left on D23 to Brouillet. House with 'Ariston Fils' sign on right (Gîtes de France sign).

MMap 237-10 **ASP Map No:4**

Rémi & Marie ARISTON
Ariston Fils, 4 & 8 Grande Rue
51170 Brouillet
Marne
Tel: (0)3 26 97 43 46
Fax: (0)3 26 97 49 34
e-mail: champagne.ariston.fils@wanadoo

The guestrooms, and the terrace where you breakfast in summer, of this old family farmhouse (rebuilt in the '20s after war destruction), look out onto the quiet courtyard: you can't hear the road, only the sound of the two running springs. So sleep till 11 if you like — that's the latest Nathalie serves freshly-squeezed fruit juice and masses of croissants. The vast bedrooms are comfortably furnished and have everything you need. Éric works at the Crédit Agricole on the other side of the road — could be helpful... With their three children, they are a delightful young family, and there's a pony in the field next door.

Rooms: 4 suites for 3 or 4, each with shower & wc.

Price: 290 Frs (€ 44.21) for two, including breakfast.

Meals: Restaurant in village.

Open: All year.

From Reims RD980 SW to Ville en Tardenois (20km). House in town centre opposite Crédit Agricole.

MMap 237-10 **ASP Map No:4**

Nathalie & Éric LELARGE
Ferme du Grand Clos
51170 Ville en Tardenois
Marne
Tel: (0)3 26 61 83 78

It is so quiet here that the grandfather clock inside and the doves cooing in the trees outside can seem deafening. A timeless feel wafts through the newish house from that grandfather clock, the pretty, traditionally-decorated bedrooms (*lits bateau*, Louis Philippe furniture), the piano and the old Singer sewing machine in its corner. Huguette and her husband, who runs the beef and cattle farm, are generous hosts offering traditional unpretentious farmhouse hospitality. You can opt for champagne from their son-in-law's nearby vineyard, with a meal to match the quality of the wine and the welcome.

Rooms: 2 double, 1 triple, each with bath or shower & wc.

Price: 250 Frs (€ 38.11) for two, including breakfast.

Meals: 105 Frs (with wine) or 150 Frs (with champagne), including aperitif, wine/champagne, coffee.

Open: All year.

From Châlons en Champagne RD933 to Bergères (29km) then right on D9 to Vertus. Through Vertus and left, following signs to La Madeleine for 3km.

MMap 237-23 **ASP Map No:4**

Huguette CHARAGEAT
La Madeleine
51130 Vertus
Marne
Tel: (0)3 26 52 11 29
Fax: (0)3 26 59 22 09

Cows, chickens, ducks, guinea-fowl, turkeys, donkey, sheep, goats... children love it here, and love the higgledy-piggledy buildings too; school groups come for visits. The house is full of beams, the rooms are full of swags, flowers and antique bits, and one bathroom is behind a curtain. Our readers have loved the house, the family and the food. Little English is spoken but the welcome is so exceptional, the generosity so genuine, that communication is easy. Superb outings in the area for all.

Rooms: 1 suite with shower & wc; 3 double, each with bath & wc (1 curtained off). Extra beds available.

Price: 275-320 Frs (€ 41.92-48.78) for two, including breakfast.

Meals: 140 Frs, including wine & coffee.

Open: All year.

From Epernay, D51 dir. Sézanne. At Baye, just before church, right onto D343. At Bannay turn right. Farm is before small bridge.

MMap 237-22 **ASP Map No: 4**

Muguette & Jean-Pierre CURFS
Ferme de Bannay
51270 Bannay
Marne
Tel: (0)3 26 52 80 49
Fax: (0)3 26 59 47 78
www.sawdays.co.uk

There are fabulous walks to be had in the great Forêt du Gault that borders this C17 farmhouse (workmen recently discovered the date '1680' when reroofing the tower). The two rooms in the converted stable have a living room (original mangers still there), kitchenette, steep stairs up and modest, modern décor with carpeted floors. The third, in the main house, has old furniture and a view of the pond. You breakfast in another former stable on the courtyard but dine by the family fireplace on home-produced fruit, vegetables, eggs and poultry. "Madame is lovely", say our readers, "super welcome and food — people should stay a week!"

Rooms: 1 twin, 1 double, 1 triple, all with shower or bath & wc.

Price: 220 Frs (€ 33.54) for two, including breakfast; extra bed 80 Frs.

Meals: 95 Frs, including wine & coffee.

Open: All year.

From Calais A26 (Michelin map 61- 5) to St Quentin; D1 to Montmirail then D373 dir. Sézanne for 7 km. On leaving Le Gault left at silo; signposted.

MMap 237-22 **ASP Map No: 4**

Nicole & Guy BOUTOUR
Ferme de Désiré
51210 Le Gault Soigny
Marne
Tel: (0)3 26 81 60 09
Fax: (0)3 26 81 67 95

The Collots are hard-working, naturally welcoming farmers whose family has owned this house for several generations. The modernised C18 farmhouse has two newly-decorated sizeable guestrooms furnished with nice old beds and wardrobes and views over either the active farmyard, with its fine collection of agricultural machinery, or over the little village street. The family dining room where you have breakfast is pleasingly homely and cluttered and Madame takes the time to chat. Really excellent value.

Rooms: 2 double, each with shower & wc.

Price: 200 Frs (€ 30.49) for two, including breakfast; extra bed 60 Frs.

Meals: Choice in Vitry le François 6km. Barbecue available.

Open: All year.

From Vitry le François, N4 dir. Fère Champenoise. 3km after N4/D2 roundabout turn right. In village, left 100m after Mairie; signposted.

MMap 241-30 **ASP Map No: 4**

Brigitte & Michel COLLOT
19 rue de Coole
51300 Maisons en Champagne
Marne
Tel: (0)3 26 72 73 91

The key to the local church is with Madame; do look round it. Her own house is the medieval priory with two 11th-century towers... superb. She is an extremely friendly, busy, chatty young mother, originally from Quebec and definitely French-speaking, with teenage children, a farming husband and parents-in-law 'through the wall'. Splendid rooms; the ground floor one, for example, is enormous, with a huge stone fireplace, two queen beds, wattle walls between great timbers, a wooden roof with more beams, a basic bathroom — and breakfast is superb. "Better than any 5-star hotel on all counts", said one reader.

Rooms: 2 quadruple, 2 triple, 1 family room for 5, each with bath or shower & wc.

Price: 220-270 Frs (€ 33.54-41.16) for two, including breakfast.

Meals: Restaurant 5 mins walk.

Open: All year.

From Troyes N71 SE for 13 km. In Fouchères left onto D81 dir. Poligny — house just behind Fouchères church.

MMap 237-48 **ASP Map No: 9**

M & Mme Gilles BERTHELIN
Le Prieuré
Place de l'Église
10260 Fouchères
Aube
Tel: (0)3 25 40 98 09
Fax: (0)3 25 40 98 09

The pond area bathes in serene watery beauty. This is an irresistible spot for no-kill fishermen (including *carpistes*), water-sportsmen, walkers, bird-watchers and architecture buffs — the local half-timbered churches are considered one of the 100 most beautiful attractions in France. Afternoon tea is served in the elegantly panelled *salon*; later, a chandeliered dinner awaits you, possibly with home-raised boar or home-fished scaly things but not with your hosts, delightful as they are: they prefer to concentrate on the cooking. Bedrooms are comfortable and attractive. *Children over seven welcome.*

Rooms: 2 double, 2 twin, 1 suite, all with bath or shower & wc.

Price: 270-330 Frs (€ 41.16-50.31) for two, including breakfast.

Meals: 130 Frs, including wine & coffee.

Open: All year.

From Troyes, D960 to Brienne, D400 dir. St Dizier. At Louze, D182 to Longeville then D174 dir. Boulancourt; house on left at 1st crossroads.

MMap 241-34 **ASP Map No: 5**

Philippe & Christine VIEL-CAZAL
Domaine de Boulancourt
Boulancourt
52220 Montier en Der
Haute-Marne
Tel: (0)3 25 04 60 18
Fax: (0)3 25 04 60 18
www.sawdays.co.uk

If your family are straining at the leash, bring them here to let off steam: there is riding (and space for 15 guest horses), pony-trapping, walking, mountain-biking, archery, orienteering and a bit of gentle ping-pong. This is a most friendly place, simple and easy, with breakfasts (home-made jams, fresh *brioche*, lots of coffee) available until midday. The rooms are right for the price, warmly carpeted (after the corridor upstairs with its 'artexed' walls and 'lino' floor) with good storage space. You dine well in the nearby village (the Mayoress is the chef).

Rooms: 3 double, 1 twin sharing shower & wc.

Price: 190 Frs (€ 28.97) for two, including breakfast.

Meals: Good auberge 3km.

Open: All year.

Gîte space for 19 people

From Langres, N19 dir. Vesoul. Left on D460 dir. Bourbonne; right on D34; 3rd left to Velles. Through village to grass triangle; house on left.

MMap 241-48 **ASP Map No: 9**

Alain & Christine ROUSSELOT
Les [illegible] du Précheny
52500 Velles
Haute-Marne
Tel: (0)3 25 88 85 93

The bedrooms are named after members of the family who lived here before the Poopes: while Evelyne and Michel were restoring it they found the family photographs which inspired the decoration of each room. They clearly adore their life as B&B owners and go to immense trouble to make you feel comfortable and at home. Breakfast is as local as you can get — yoghurt from the farm, honey from the village and Evelyne's home-made jam all feature, while dinner may include such delicacies as blue cheese tart with artichokes or flamed turkey; Michel is chief pastry-cook.

Rooms: 1 double & 1 twin each with shower, sharing wc; 1 triple, 1 suite, each with shower & wc.

Price: 220-300 Frs (€ 33.54-45.73) for two, including breakfast.

Meals: 70 Frs, including wine.

Open: All year except Christmas & New Year.

From A31, exit 6 to Langres then N19 E dir. Vesoul for 30km. Right at Chambres d'Hôtes sign to Pressigny — house just after pond on left.

MMap 241-51 **ASP Map No: 9**

Evelyne & Michel POOPE
Maison Perrette
24 rue Augustin Massin
52500 Pressigny
Haute-Marne
Tel: (0)3 25 88 80 50
Fax: (0)3 25 88 80 49

The locals affectionately call it *"le petit coin"*, but that is to demean this fine little building, capable of so much more than its original designers intended. There is sitting room only, but it is deeply functional, a place where you can off-load the burdens of your day. A place to meditate in guaranteed peace, to rue your failures and celebrate your successes, to dream, to read. The architecture is thoroughly vernacular, the mood heavily influenced by the ebb and flow of generations of people bent on the same task.

Rooms: 1 small single, en suite.

Price: 1-2 Frs (€ 0.15-0.3) for one, including breakfast.

Meals: Al fresco recommended.

Open: All year except cleaning days.

Cross River Écoule into Aizance, straight on down Rue de la Lunette, 2nd left into Allée du Trône to pink house at end. Take path at side of house, through garden: Chalet at end of path.

Tinette GABINNETTI
Chalet de la Chasse
Allée du Trône 52525
Aizance sur Écoule
Haute-Marne
Tel: (0)3 04 05 06 07

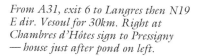

Storks still build their messy nests on the chimney stacks of breweries and biscuit factories where women once wore the giant bow as their traditional headdress.

Lorraine – Alsace – Franche-Comté

'Grandma's Fields' are surrounded by vast views across lakes, woods and hills. The house is like a chalet, all warm, glowing wood. Here, it's bed and breakfast PLUS afternoon tea and cake... and apparently Madame's chocolate-and-cherry is to die for. This is a quiet bookish, house (no telly), the perfect spot for a holiday of walking, swimming with the trout in the pond near the house, or reading. Go mushrooming in autumn and spring and cook your catch in Madame's kitchen where you also eat a breakfast which can be French, German or English, to taste. Supremely peaceful house, place and person.

Rooms: 2 double, sharing bathroom.

Price: 350 Frs (€ 53.36) for two, including breakfast & afternoon tea.

Meals: Use of kitchen and barbecue. Restaurants in Senones 2km.

Open: All year.

From Strasbourg A 352 W then N420 to St Blaise la Roche (45km); right on D424 14km dir. Senones to La Petite Raon; right after church dir. Moussey; 3rd left (after café) then left, left and left to house.

MMap 242-27 **ASP Map No: 6**

Judith LOTT
Les Champs Grandmère
Thiamont
88210 La Petite Raon, Vosges
Tel: (0)3 29 57 68 08
Fax: (0)3 29 57 68 83
e-mail: judelott@aol.com

There is now an 'artists' path' to explore in the nearby forest and a golf practice area laid out by Monsieur in the garden. They are very proud of their house and, although renovation may have hidden two centuries of history, it has produced very big, plush, slightly hotel-like guestrooms; the suite even boasts television and telephone... Dinner is authentic, however: a chance to sample some of the region's best dishes (*terrines, magret*, home-made pastries); Madame will join you for dessert and a chat. An excellent stopover between the ferries and Germany.

Rooms: 2 double, each with shower & wc, 1 suite with bath, shower & wc.

Price: 350-500 Frs (€ 53.36-76.22) for two, including breakfast.

Meals: 150 Frs, including wine & coffee.

Open: All year.

From Reims A4 exit 'Voie Sacrée' on N35 dir. Bar le Duc. At Chaumont sur Aire, D902 left to Longchamps sur Aire then D121 left to Thillombois. House is next to château.

MMap 241-27 **ASP Map No: 5**

Lise TANCHON
Le Clos du Pausa
Rue du Château
55260 Thillombois
Meuse
Tel: (0)3 29 75 07 85
Fax: (0)3 29 75 00 72
www.sawdays.co.uk

This is an ever-lasting project, so chat to Monsieur as he assiduously restores the house to its former glory — more rooms and bathrooms have been redecorated, some bits are still waiting — and enjoy Madame's charming affability, the goodnight chocolates and the kettle kit for the morning. There are elegant terraces, a super garden, stylish furniture to impress, lots of religion on view (bedside Bibles are French Catholic, not American Gideon), a genuine welcome to win you over. The house is beside a fairly busy road, so traffic noise may intrude, and some shower/loo rooms are pretty tight.

Rooms: 2 double, 1 twin, 1 triple, 1 suite with kitchenette & garden, each with shower & wc.

Price: 250-300 Frs (€ 38.11-45.73) for two, including breakfast; extra bed 100 Frs.

Meals: Self-catering in suite.

Open: All year.

Gîte space for 7 people

 10Frs

From A4, St Menehould exit onto N3 dir. Verdun-Chalons. House is signposted in La Vignette, the hamlet before Les Islettes.

MMap 241-22 **ASP Map No: 5**

M & Mme Léopold CHRISTIAENS
Villa des Roses
La Vignette, Les Islettes
55120 Clermont en Argonne
Meuse
Tel: (0)3 26 60 81 91
Fax: (0)3 26 60 23 09
www.sawdays.co.uk

Clearly not the place to stay if you want to be modern: some of it was part of the C13 defensive ring around Metz. It is now a typical farmhouse with 110 acres of cereal fields. Brigitte relishes her role as hostess, does it with great talent and makes friends easily. She also cooks superb, largely organic, meals and keeps goats, rabbits, donkey and dog. All the bedrooms are in another building, filled with her own paintings. There is a handsome dining room with great beams; try the local Moselle wine. A wonderful family and a friendly village.

Rooms: 1 triple, 1 double, each with bath & wc; 1 twin, 1 triple, each with shower, sharing wc.

Price: 270 Frs (€ 41.16) for two, including breakfast.

Meals: 100 Frs, including wine & coffee.

Open: March to November.

South of Metz on A31 Féy exit; right at junction; do not go into Féy but straight on for Cuvry. Farm on edge of village past 'Mairie'; signposted.

MMap 242-13 **ASP Map No: 5**

Brigitte & Jean-François MORHAIN
Ferme de Haute-Rive
57420 Cuvry
Moselle
Tel: (0)3 87 52 50 08
Fax: (0)3 87 52 60 20

A most interesting couple: he's a retired French architect (who's done wonders in the kitchen), she's a Polish painter (work in progress on the easel), patchworker (her bedcovers adorn your room) and dancer. They are both passionate about the environment and keen to chat over dinner. And good news for vegetarians who like a change: Alina is a 'veggie' and will happily rustle up a warm red *borsch* or a dish of *pierogi* (vegetable ravioli) though her talent stretches to delicious meaty things too. An excellent and friendly house.

Rooms: 1 twin room with shower & wc.

Price: 250 Frs (€ 38.11) for two, including breakfast.

Meals: 100 Frs (meat or fish) or 75 Frs (vegetarian), including wine & coffee.

Open: All year.

From Metz D3 NE dir. Bouzonville for about 21km then right on D53a to Burtoncourt. House on left in main street.

MMap 242-10 **ASP Map No: 5**

Alina & Gérard CAHEN
51 rue Lorraine
57220 Burtoncourt
Moselle
Tel: (0)3 87 35 72 65
Fax: (0)3 87 35 72 65

This house, built in 1750, has a chequered history: once a bistrot then a watermill, it was destroyed in the war. Louis's father restored the wheel. Inside, the house — deeply modernised, with lots of new wood and no particular trimmings — is a bit out of kilter with the charming exterior but it has very clean, comfortable rooms (showers curtained off from bedrooms) and a decent kitchen for guests' use. Breakfast, served in the living/dining room, is hosted by various members of the family who look down from two large studio-style family portraits. Madame has three children and is cheerful, hospitable and talkative.

Rooms: 1 double, 2 triple, all with shower & wc.

Price: 220 Frs (€ 33.54) for two, including breakfast.

Meals: Self-catering.

Open: All year.

From A4 exit 42 on N61 dir. Sarreguemines then onto N62 to Rohrbach. There right on D35 dir. Bining/Rahling. In village 1st right (after small bridge) then right again; signposted.

MMap 242-15 **ASP Map No: 6**

Louis & Annie BACH
2 rue du Vieux Moulin
57410 Rahling
Moselle
Tel: (0)3 87 09 86 85

Want to keep in touch with the office? All the gear is here, plus most of the modern extras that hotels provide, plus the wilder side. Set in the Lorraine Nature Park, the house is older than it looks, an ancient Lorraine farm, now a *Gîte Panda*, with two of the friendliest possible owners. They have done the restoration themselves; it is cluttered but comfortable... no shortage of chairs to sag into. Come for the walks — Bride Forest, lakes, a big bird sanctuary (they'll lend rucksacks and binoculars) — the vast breakfasts and the company.

Rooms: 2 double, 1 twin, each with shower or bath & wc.

Price: 310 Frs (€ 47.26) for two, including breakfast.

Meals: 120 Frs, including coffee.

Open: April to October.

From A31, exit 28 for St Avold (D910) for 30km. At Han sur Nied, D999 dir. Morhange and Dieuze. 10km after Morhange, left to Lidrezing.

MMap 242-14 **ASP Map No: 6**

René & Cécile MATHIS
La Musardière
2 rue le Faubourg, Lidrezing
57340 Morhange
Moselle
Tel: (0)3 87 86 14 05
Fax: (0)3 87 86 40 16

A night at this grand and very stylish château, the property of an engaging, lively and able couple, is really worth it and not at all daunting. Two utterly French *salons* with the right number of antiques and huge oils of the Napoleonic wars (French version) such as you normally only see in public galleries, a library with books and a billiards table, dinner with candles and flowers and the unadulterated pleasure of dining like a 17th-century French aristocrat (there may be wild boar in season). Guestrooms and bathrooms are suitably luxurious.

Rooms: 3 double and 3 twin, all with bath & wc.

Price: 590 Frs (€ 89.94) for two, including breakfast.

Meals: 250 Frs, including coffee.

Open: April to October.

Gîte space for 4 people

From Nancy, N74 dir. Sarreguemines & Château Salins. At Burthecourt crossroads D38 to Dieuzé, then D999 south; after 5km, left on D199F and D199G to the château.

MMap 242-18 **ASP Map No: 6**

Livier & Marie BARTHÉLÉMY
Château d'Alteville
Tarquimpol
57260 Dieuzé
Moselle
Tel: (0)3 87 86 92 40
Fax: (0)3 87 86 02 05
www.sawdays.co.uk

The gentle-mannered, softly-spoken owners live in another house but are present, attentive hosts. Their pride and joy is Monsieur's woodwork: he has built these rooms in the old stables, using different timbers (rooms are named elm, maple, beech...), fitting shower rooms ingeniously into the space available, making stairs, delicately painting the eaves. There is a quiet courtyard with garden; breakfast, with fresh juice, home-made jam and cakes, is in a room by the road. Rooms sparkle and English-speaking offspring are home after 8pm — ring then!

Rooms: 2 duplexes, 2 twin, 1 double, all with shower (1 behind curtain) & wc.

Price: 240-300 Frs (€ 36.59-45.73) for two, including breakfast.

Meals: Strasbourg 12km. Self-catering in duplexes.

Open: All year.

Gîte space for 11 people

From A4 exit 48 on N63 dir. Vendenheim/Strasbourg. Right on D64 dir. Lampertheim. At Pfulgriesheim right on D31 to Pfettisheim. In village follow main road; signposted.

MMap 242-20 **ASP Map No: 6**

Marie-Célestine GASS
La Maison du Charron
15 rue Principale
67370 Pfettisheim
Bas-Rhin
Tel: (0)3 88 69 60 35
Fax: (0)3 88 69 77 96

So close to expensive but gorgeous Strasbourg, yet such good value. You are also right at the start of the *Route des Vins*, in the heart of a pretty Alsatian village. The house used to be a working farm, producing rosé as well as milk, but your hosts have now retired and enjoy having more time for their guests. Although on a fairly busy main road its bedrooms are at the back where it's usually quiet; they are simple, small, yet comfortable. Marie teaches German; Paul, the ex-farmer, serves the breakfast in the garden or in the dining room with its brown tiles and blue walls. A great place to know in Alsace.

Rooms: 3 double, each with shower & wc.

Price: 200-220 Frs (€ 30.49-33.54) for two, including breakfast.

Meals: Restaurant in village.

Open: All year.

Gîte space for 6 people

From A4 exit 45 onto N404/N4 dir. Strasbourg for 16km. Farm is in middle of the village of Marlenheim on left, before post office.

MMap 242-19 **ASP Map No: 6**

Paul & Marie-Claire GOETZ
86 rue du Général de Gaulle
67520 Marlenheim
Bas-Rhin
Tel: (0)3 88 87 52 94

Readers have loved this place, and so do children — the house, the fun and *Le Petit Train* that tours the striking old village and the vineyards. The first Ruhlmann wine-grower built his lovely Alsatian house in 1688. Wine buffs will enjoy visiting the wine cellar and non-drinkers can taste the sweet water springing straight from the Vosges hills. The charming rooms under the sloping roof have new carpets and old family furniture; breakfast is served in a huge room full of relics: barrels, a wine press, a grape basket, a china stove. And you will meet the whole fun-loving family.

Rooms: 2 double, each with shower, sharing wc.

Price: 230 Frs (€ 35.06) for two, including breakfast and wine-tasting.

Meals: 6 choices within walking distance.

Open: April to November.

Dambach is about 8km north of Sélestat on D35. House in village centre, about equidistant between two gateways.

MMap 242-27 **ASP Map No: 6**

Jean Charles & Laurence
RUHLMANN
34 rue Maréchal Foch
67650 Dambach la Ville
Bas-Rhin
Tel: (0)3 88 92 41 86
Fax: (0)3 88 92 61 81
www.sawdays.co.uk

Young Madame Engel greets you with the warmest welcome and the finest Alsace cooking — she really loves receiving guests. The peaceful Swiss-style chalet, commanding breathtaking views of the mountains and forests, is just the place to enjoy both. All you need to do is take a deep breath, forget everything — and relax. The rooms are simply comfortable with signs of Monsieur's upholstering skills, geraniums cascading from every window, the views pouring in and a guest entrance. Breakfast tables are laden with goodies — try the home-made organic fruit jams and *kougelopf* (Alsace cake to the uninitiated).

Rooms: 2 double, 1 twin, each with shower & wc.

Price: 265-285 Frs (€ 40.40-43.45) for two, including breakfast.

Meals: Choice 4km.

Open: February to December.

From Colmar, A35 and N83 dir. Sélestat (exit 11) then N59 and D424 to Villé; D697 to Dieffenbach au Val. Careful: ask for exact address as 2 other Engels do B&B!

MMap 242-27 **ASP Map No: 6**

Doris ENGEL-GEIGER
Maison Fleurie
19 route de Neuve Eglise
Dieffenbach au Val
67220 Villé, Bas-Rhin
Tel: (0)3 88 85 60 48
Fax: (0)3 88 85 60 48
www.sawdays.co.uk

Two villages, two houses, one blue, one yellow, a mixture of B&B and self-catering, this is a special find. The enthusiastic owners, wine-growers and activity-providers (walks with donkeys, visits for the blind, wine-tastings, nature trails for children) offer one cosy, environmentally-conscious room at home and two others in exquisite Riquewihr where the C16 Blue House is run by friendly Nicole Sirot. Smallish rooms, organic breakfasts in baskets, roof terrace, holiday atmosphere and the only round cellar in Alsace.

Rooms: 1 suite for 4, 2 double, each with shower, wc & kitchenette.

Price: 360-480 Frs (€ 54.88-73.18) for two, 510 Frs for four, including breakfast (min. 3 nights).

Meals: Good choice in both villages.

Open: All year.

Gîte space for 12 people

From Colmar N83 dir. St Dié 'par le col' then N415 dir. Kaysersberg for 1km then left on D10 to Katzenthal. Enter village to fountain, fork left, house along on left. For Riquewihr, request directions by fax.

MMap 242-31 **ASP Map No: 10**

Francine & Clément KLUR-GRAFF
105 rue des Trois Épis
68230 Katzenthal
Haut-Rhin
Tel: (0)3 89 27 53 59
Fax: (0)3 89 27 30 17
e-mail: katz@newel.net
http://perso.wanadoo.fr/maisonbleue/

Madame has adorned her home with hand-painted stencils (she'll teach you if you like). She and her art student daughter often paint quietly together on the landing. The top-floor pine-clad sitting room is a delight, like being in a boat. Big cosy bedrooms, dinner with your hosts and possibly their daughters or son plus a few friends prove they know about conviviality... and Madame should charge extra for her conversation! "Lucky is the traveller who stops here," said the Canadian reader who led us to Le Montanjus. Nearby are golf and skiing (in equally breathtaking spots) and the *Ballons des Vosges* Regional Park.

Rooms: 1 double, 1 suite for 3, each with shower & wc.

Price: 295 Frs (€ 44.97) for two, including breakfast.

Meals: 105 Frs (weekdays) & 125 Frs (weekend), including wine & coffee.

Open: All year.

Gîte space for 5 people

From A36 exit 'Belfort Nord' on N83 dir. Mulhouse. In village of Les Errues, left dir. Anjoutey and on to Étueffont. At roundabout right dir. Rougemont and left at first bend — house at end.

MMap 243-10 **ASP Map No: 10**

Astride & Daniel ELBERT
Le Montanjus
8 rue de la Chapelle
90170 Étueffont
Territoire de Belfort
Tel: (0)3 84 54 68 63
e-mail: daniel.elbert@wanadoo.fr

As part of its 100m² suite, this château houses one of the most extraordinary bathrooms this side of the Saône: panels hung with old engravings, a sunken bath and an Italian chandelier contribute to an atmosphere of elegant luxury it would be hard to match, even with five stars; bedroom and sitting room are just as amazing. All this and a family feel! Antiques, attention to detail, a charmingly formal hostess with an easy laugh, make this a really special place. Dinner, carefully chosen to suit guests' tastes (if you want snails, you'll have to ask) is exquisitely presented on Gien porcelain and served on the terrace in summer.

Rooms: 1 suite with bathroom.

Price: 420 Frs (€ 64.03) for two, including breakfast.

Meals: By arrangement 100 Frs, including wine; 50 Frs light supper.

Open: Mid-May to September.

From A36, exit 3 onto D67 dir. Gray 35km. Entering Gray, right on D474 then fork left on D13 to Beaujeu and Motey sur Saône. There, left to Mercey : signposted in village.

MMap 242-41 **ASP Map No: 9**

Bernadette JANTET
Le Château
70130 Mercey sur Saône
Haute-Saône
Tel: (0)3 84 67 07 84

Once part of the C15 fortress of Pesmes, one of France's prettiest villages, it is vast. Guy bought only walls then built a house within them: it is his pride and joy. The staircase is grey-painted concrete with a wooden bannister; some of the rooms are magnificent, the sort you pay to visit on a wet Sunday afternoon. As the bedrooms are so huge the furniture can appear sparse, but they are colourful and stylish. There is a library plus a small *salon*, a 200m² reception room, a boat on the river and... too much to describe in this space. *Children over five welcome.*

Rooms: 4 double, 1 twin, 1 triple, 1 family room, each with bath or shower & wc.

Price: 400-450 Frs (€ 60.98-68.60) for two, including breakfast.

Meals: Choice within short walking distance.

Open: Mid-March to mid-October.

From A36, exit 2 onto D475 to Pesmes (20km). House is at top of village on left.

MMap 243-18 **ASP Map No: 9**

Guy HOYET
La Maison Royale
70140 Pesmes
Haute-Saône
Tel: (0)3 84 31 23 23
Fax: (0)3 84 31 23 23
www.sawdays.co.uk

La vie de château for all? This fabulously renovated neo-classical house and its stylish owners can be unhesitatingly recommended for an authentic taste of château living. All rooms, with proper period furniture, engravings and family portraits, look out over the fine *Directoire*-style park. Guests have their own breakfast and sitting rooms. Madame, as elegant as her house, unintrusively provides for all and Monsieur, whose pride and joy is the park, is pleased to be told that ten years of painstaking work have been worthwhile. They are most welcoming in English that is adequate but not fluent.

Rooms: 3 double rooms, 1 suite, all with bath & wc.

Price: 550 Frs (€ 83.85) for two, including breakfast.

Meals: Auberge 4km.

Open: All year.

From Besançon, N73 to St Vit. Then left through town and right onto D203 to Salans; château in village.

MMap 243-18 **ASP Map No: 9**

Béatrice & Claus OPPELT
Château de Salans
39700 Salans
Jura
Tel: (0)3 84 71 16 55
Fax: (0)3 84 79 41 54

A room under the roof, a lovely view of orchards and meadows, a brook to sing you to sleep. Your organic-wine-grower hosts are the gentlest, most generous couple imaginable; their son runs a wine-tasting sessions for them. Their fairly average home — a converted wine merchant's house — is distinguished by that wonderful welcome, a fine dresser carved with the lion of Franche-Comté, their delightful art gallery (Madame does embroidery but shows other artists' paintings) and a tempting garden at the back where a Wendy house awaits children. And anyone may play the piano here or golf just down the road.

Rooms: 1 twin, 1 suite for 4, both with shower & wc.

Price: 240 Frs (€ 36.59) for two, including breakfast; extra person 120 Frs.

Meals: 70 Frs, incl. coffee (wine 40 Frs).

Open: All year.

In Lons le Saunier dir. Chalon/Bourg en Bresse. After SNCF station left on D117 dir. Maconnay then D41 to Vernantois. Left before church & follow signs to 'Rose Arts'.

MMap 243-30 **ASP Map No: 9**

Monique & Michel RYON
'Rose Art'
8 rue Lacuzon
39570 Vernantois
Jura
Tel: (0)3 84 47 17 28
Fax: (0)3 84 47 17 28

St Claude makes the prince of pipes,
Canon Kir mixes his inimitable vine-fruit nectar,
the fat snail creeps to marry parsley and garlic,
the best wines fetch fabulous sums in the
courtyards of Beaune: *À table!*

Burgundy

A place to die for, and the owner, too, is passionate about it. He is a lovely man, bursting with ideas on further restoration; he also cultivates the vines. The bedrooms, in a renovated building near the main 15th-century château, are newly done (the bigger one is a gem, with superb beams and a vast mezzanine) and plain in the way so many are in France. You have a small veranda on which to sit and admire the view. Breakfast is in the château, which is a delightfully lived-in listed monument. Irresistible.

Rooms: 1 triple, 1 quadruple, each with bath or shower & wc.

Price: 400 Frs (€ 60.98) for two, including breakfast.

Meals: 5 restaurants within 5km.

Open: April to mid-November.

From Tournus D14 W dir. Cormatin. House is on this road 2km after Martailly lès Brancion (leave Brancion and La Chapelle on your right).

MMap 243-39 **ASP Map No: 9**

Bertrand & Françoise de CHERISEY
Château de Nobles
71700 La Chapelle sous Brancion
Saône-et-Loire
Tel: (0)3 85 51 00 55

A wonderful place for children, who can watch the goats being milked in the clean, enclosed farmyard, even help if they (and the nannies) like. There are horses too. Your hard-working hosts, with two children of their own and sensitive to the needs of families, have made a large family room at the top of the old stone farmhouse. Bathrobes are provided for grown-ups, so everyone feels cared for. All six rooms are sparkling and charmingly simple. People return, not only for the relaxing experience, but also to stock up on the home-made cheeses, mouth-watering *confitures* and local wines that are on sale and served at mealtimes.

Rooms: 2 double sharing shower & wc, 2 twin sharing shower & wc; 2 family suites with shower, wc and kitchen.

Price: 195-325 Frs (€ 29.73-49.55) for two, including breakfast.

Meals: Self-catering in two rooms. Nearby restaurant.

Open: All year.

Gîtes for 15 people

From Tournus, D14 dir. Cluny. At Chapaize, D314 dir. Bissy sous Uxelles. House next to church.

MMap 243-39 **ASP Map No: 9**

Pascale & Dominique de LA BUSSIÈRE
La Ferme
71460 Bissy sous Uxelles
Saône-et-Loire
Tel: (0)3 85 50 15 03
Fax: (0)3 85 50 15 03
e-mail: dominique.de-la-bussiere@wanadoo.fr

Do you long to know the secrets behind the scenes? You can discover how the theatre really works here, where farmhouse B&B is combined with a thriving theatre and art gallery. In June and July the local group of actor-winegrowers, *La Mère Folle*, founded in 1981 by Jean-Paul, perform in their converted barn. Régine, a musician, helps with productions. Busy, artistic people, they create an atmosphere of relaxed energy, take their B&B very seriously and offer good rooms with comfortable beds, modern décor of pale wood, original beams and, generously, *Grandpère's* excellent cubist paintings.

Rooms: 4 double, 1 twin, all with bath or shower & wc.

Price: 290 Frs (€ 44.21) for two, including breakfast.

Meals: Simple restaurant in village, otherwise 6km.

Open: All year.

From A6 exit Tournus onto D56 dir. Lugny through Chardonnay. 3km after Chardonnay right on D463 & follow signs to Chambres d'Hôtes/Théâtre Champvent.

MMap 243-39 **ASP Map No: 9**

Régine & Jean-Paul RULLIÈRE
Le Tinailler
Manoir de Champvent
71700 Chardonnay
Saône-et-Loire
Tel: (0)3 85 40 50 23
Fax: (0)3 85 40 50 18
www.sawdays.co.uk

Do wander through the woods and gardens of this C13 château — it's beautiful and tours of the *caves* and the *Route des Vins* can be arranged (Monsieur is a cellar master). One room, more 'period' with its small four-poster (and more expensive) is in the château, the rest (excellent too) are in the *maison vigneronne*, the old vine workers' cottages. Madame manages with charming efficiency, aperitifs in the cellar are part of the evening ritual and Monsieur may surprise you with an enormous bottle of cognac at dinner (regional food made with home-grown vegetables). A most welcoming place.

Rooms: 2 twin, 1 double/twin, 1 triple, all with bath & wc.

Price: 450-550 Frs (€ 68.60-83.85) for two, including breakfast.
Extra bed 120 Frs.

Meals: 100 Frs, including coffee.

Open: All year except January.

Gîte space for 16 people

From A6 exit at Tournus on D14 through Ozenay dir. Marthailly. 600m after Corcelles left at sign 'Caveau'.

MMap 243-39 **ASP Map No: 9**

Marie-Laurence FACHON
Maisons Vigneronnes
Château de Messey
71700 Ozenay, Saône-et-Loire
Tel: (0)3 85 51 33 83/16 11
Fax: (0)3 85 51 33 82
e-mail: bf@golfenfrance.com
www.demessey.com

The storm felled the great cedar, but not entirely: it now stands magnificently and fittingly guard in the form of St Vincent, patron saint of wine-growers. Father and son run the vineyard (1996 Mâcon Gold Medal for Chardonnay), Madame makes jam and cheese and loves spending time with guests, old and young (they have 6 grandchildren). All four bedrooms are big, have warm carpets, clean-cut modern furniture and distinctive colour schemes — two pastel, two strong dark — as well as excellent bathrooms. A supremely comfortable, friendly, relaxing place to stay.

Rooms: 2 double, 1 twin, 1 triple, all with own bath or shower & wc.

Price: 270 Frs (€ 41.16) for two, including breakfast.

Meals: Self-catering.

Open: All year.

From Tournus, N6 dir. Mâcon. After 10km, right on D163 to Uchizy; signposted.

MMap 243-39 **ASP Map No: 9**

Mme Annick SALLET
Domaine de l'Arfentière
Route de Chardonnay
71700 Uchizy
Saône-et-Loire
Tel: (0)3 85 40 50 46
Fax: (0)3 85 40 58 05

The view is of the C12 church, the house, only C17..., has been renovated with superb attention to detail, a welcoming log fire in winter — and wait till you see the excellent bathrooms. Monsieur is charming, chatty, with lots of tales to tell, and totally French, right down to his cigarettes. He'll take good care of you, will share his love of this famous wine-making region and provide a feast of local produce for breakfast (on the terrace when days are long and warm) — jams, honey, bread, cheeses and *pâtés* — which should set you up perfectly for a heady day's visit to the vineyards.

Rooms: 2 double, each with shower or bath & wc.

Price: 290 Frs (€ 44.21) for two, including breakfast.

Meals: Excellent restaurant nearby.

Open: All year.

From Tournus, D14 dir. Cormatin. After 12km left on D163 dir. Grévilly. After 200m, follow Grévilly on right. Straight on at T-junction. House 100m on left: outside village, just below church.

MMap 243-39 **ASP Map No: 9**

Claude DEPREAY
Le Pré Ménot
71700 Grévilly
Saône-et-Loire
Tel: (0)3 85 33 29 92
Fax: (0)3 85 33 02 79
www.sawdays.co.uk

There's an old-world charm to the lovely stones and tumbling geraniums outside, the silk flowers, frilly lampshades and polished furniture inside. The breakfast room is cosily stuffed with bric-à-brac, bedrooms are family-simple. Madame was a florist: she arranges her rooms as if they were bouquets and is always refreshing them; she may put a paper heart on your pillow wishing you *bonne nuit*. She doesn't refuse children but may well be happier if you arrive with a little dog under your arm. She or her husband can do winery visits for non-Francophones. Ask for one of the larger rooms; the smallest feels cramped.

Rooms: 1 suite for 4, 2 double, all with bath or shower & wc.

Price: 250-300 Frs (€ 38.11-45.73) for two, including breakfast.

Meals: Good choice 3-5km.

Open: All year except winter Sundays.

From N79 exit La Roche Vineuse. Go towards Chaunay lès Macon (NOT La Roche Vineuse) for 2km, then dir. Sommeré. Up hill following 'EH' signs-house at top of hill on left; bell on wall by gate with 4 big flowerpots.

MMap 243-39 **ASP Map No: 9**

Eliane HEINEN
Le Tinailler d'Aleane
Sommeré
71960 La Roche Vineuse
Saône-et-Loire
Tel: (0)3 85 37 80 68
Fax: (0)3 85 37 80 68

There's vast personality and an authentically worn feel to this old manor house. Madame, with her unorthodox sense of humour, is "quite a character" and wants visitors to see it was built by a C19 *parvenu* (some delightfully OTT bits) and is now inhabited by a couple of artists (watercolours and weavings). Choose activity: bicycling, walking, horse-riding; or gentility: contemplate mountain scenery, stroll round the mature gardens, play the Erard baby grand or browse through the rich collection of local guides and histories in the bibliothèque. Super old-decorated rooms, fine modern bathrooms.

Rooms: 1 double with bath, shower, wc; 1 suite for 5 with shower, wc & kitchen.

Price: 250 Frs (€ 38.11) for two, including breakfast.

Meals: Self-catering in suite; restaurant 5km.

Open: All year.

Gîte space for 10 people

From Mâcon, N79 dir. Cluny. At Berzé le Châtel, N79 on dir. Charolles, then D987 to Trambly. Left past church; house on left.

MMap 239-12 **ASP Map No: 9**

François & Florence GAUTHIER
Les Charrières
71520 Trambly
Saône-et-Loire
Tel: (0)3 85 50 43 17
Fax: (0)3 85 50 49 28
e-mail: gauthierflorence@minitel.net
www.sawdays.co.uk

A lovely spot, with the Loire at the bottom of the garden — Monsieur has retired to share his time between his house and his guests; Madame comes from her job in Paris at weekends. The C18 chateau has a fascinating amount of family furniture and treasures. He had an English nanny so is at home with the English language and culture and greatly enjoys discussing his many interests — the region, its history and architecture, his print and corkscrew collections — over a meal which might include *poulet au vinaigre* or *chou farci*. A chance to sample the pleasing lifestyle of the French provincial aristocracy.

Rooms: 2 double, 2 twin, 1 suite for 4, each with bath & wc.

Price: 300-450 Frs (€ 45.73-68.60) for two, including breakfast.

Meals: Light supper 70 Frs; dinner 140 Frs; including table wine.

Open: March to November.

From Digoin D979 dir. Bourbon Lancy for 25km. In St Aubin, 1st left at sign Les Lambeys — house on right through white gates.

MMap 238-47 **ASP Map No: 8**

Etienne de BUSSIERRE
Les Lambeys
71140 St Aubin sur Loire
Saône-et-Loire
Tel: (0)3 85 53 92 76

The garden goes down to the lake, the sun sets over it, you can borrow the owners' small boat and row on it... or fish, or canoe, or windsurf, and there's a private 'beach' that guests can use — a perfect place to unleash the children. Breakfast includes home-produced honey and *viennoiseries*. The big, bright rooms are French classic with gilt-framed mirrors, round tables in modern bathrooms and that particular type of wallpaper. The atmosphere is relaxedly family and Madame is taking English lessons, but her genuine welcome already transcends the language barrier. A super couple — she is level-headed and he loves to joke.

Rooms: 3 triple, 1 double, all with bath or shower & wc.

Price: 200-270 Frs (€ 30.49-41.16) for two, including breakfast.

Meals: Self-catering.

Open: All year.

Gîte space for 6 people

From Nevers, D978 to Rouy. There, D132 to Tintury; right on D112 to Fleury (signposted Fertrève) and first right after village: drive up to lake and turn right; signposted.

MMap 238-35 **ASP Map No: 8**

Michel & Marie-France GUÉNY
Fleury La Tour
58110 Tintury
Nièvre
Tel: (0)3 86 84 12 42
Fax: (0)3 86 84 12 42

What a welcoming place! Meeting guests with a glass of something special reflects the Perreaus' *joie de vivre*: they are wonderful, fun-loving folk, their house and farm are full of life, human and animal. It's a dairy farm with a sideline in organic vegetables — Madame, who is a delight, loves her big *potager*, you'll love its fruits. You stay in the old farmhouse's big loft where the bright, finely-furnished bedrooms share a large sitting room, but the little breakfast room is our favourite. The grounds and pool are most attractive, too. A tremendous place for enjoying the good things in life, including excellent company.

Rooms: 2 twin, 2 double, sharing 2 showers & separate wcs; 1 double with own shower & wc.

Price: 300 Frs (€ 45.73) for two, including breakfast.

Meals: By arrangement 100 Frs, including wine.

Open: All year.

From Nevers D978 dir. Château Chinon. 3km before Châtillon right on D10 dir. Alluy. In St Gratien left on C3 to La Marquise — 800m on right.

MMap 238-35 **ASP Map No: 8**

Huguette & Noël PERREAU
La Marquise
58340 St Gratien Savigny
Nièvre
Tel: (0)3 86 50 01 02/06 77
Fax: (0)3 86 50 07 14
e-mail: hcollot@aol.fr

If you are looking for a simple Deepest France experience, then leave the nerve-jangling N7 behind for this secluded C19 house where basic rooms have wallpapered ceilings, orange bedcovers and bathrooms in partitioned corners. Breakfast is at the long wooden table in the family's marvellous living room, where traditional oak furniture and a log fire create a farmhouse atmosphere. Your welcoming, sociable hosts have years of experience looking after guests. Take advantage of Monsieur's keen knowledge of regional history — he is very erudite and loves his subject — and enjoy Madame's fine dahlia collection.

Rooms: 1 double, 2 twin, all with bath or shower & wc.

Price: 230-270 Frs (€ 35.06-41.16) for two, including breakfast.

Meals: Barbecue possible.

Open: All year.

From Nevers, D978 dir. Château Chinon. At Châtillon en Bazois, D945 towards Corbigny; left on D259 dir. Mont et Marré; farm is 500m along.

MMap 238-35 **ASP Map No: 8**

Paul & Nicole DELTOUR
[illegible]
Mont et Marré
58110 Châtillon en Bazois
Nièvre
Tel: (0)3 86 84 13 94

Immaculately restored by the owners, the rooms sport good antique furniture and elegant décor with plenty of interesting wallpaper; the bathrooms are stupendous. Come at the right time of year and as far as your eye can see you'll be surrounded by fields of sunflowers. Your modest, friendly hosts clearly enjoy sharing their 1690s house in its 115 hectares of parkland. They are happy to suggest activities, from visiting local châteaux to lovely canalside walks and pony rides. Monsieur takes English lessons and is keen to flex his linguistic muscles with any willing volunteers — he has an impressive Burgundy accent!

Rooms: 4 double, each with bath or shower & wc.

Price: 280-350 Frs (€ 42.69-53.36) for two, including breakfast.

Meals: Self-catering. Restaurant 4km.

Open: All year.

From Château Chinon, D978 through Châtillon en Bazois dir. Nevers. 4km along (past Alluy), after service station, right on D112 towards Bernière; house on left after 1.5km.

MMap 238-35 **ASP Map No: 8**

Colette & André LEJAULT
Bouteuille
58110 Alluy
Nièvre
Tel: (0)3 86 84 06 65
Fax: (0)3 86 84 03 41

"The atmosphere is so comfortable, it feels like home", said a reader. Your hosts are cultured, intelligent, down-to-earth farmers with a good sense of humour — one could spend a lot of time with them. The room, in a converted outbuilding just 10m from the kitchen, is nothing lavish or luscious, just simple and clean. Come here with children, there are animals wild and domesticated to observe and horses to pat (but too old to ride). The energetic may choose to head for the national mountain bike centre (550km of marked track) and just 3km away you can immerse yourself in watersports. Then back to this all-embracing welcome.

Rooms: 1 double + bunk beds, with shower & wc.

Price: 250 Frs (€ 38.11) for two, including breakfast. Extra person 50 Frs.

Meals: 2 restaurants in St Saulge.

Open: All year.

Gîte space for 19 people

From Prémery, D38 dir. Châtillon en Bazois and St Saulge; signposted 'Gîte d'Étape' at junction of D38 and D181 to St Martin.

MMap 238-34 **ASP Map No: 8**

J-Patrick & Marie-Hélène JANDET
Basse Cour de St Martin
58330 Ste Marie
Nièvre
Tel: (0)3 86 58 35 15
Fax: (0)3 86 58 35 15
e-mail: Jpatrick.Jandet@wanadoo.fr

We wished breakfast could be more than once a day — Madame Bürgi's cakes and jams are incomparable and it's all organic and home-made. Indeed, the whole atmosphere of generous, efficient hospitality and rural peace generated by your hosts and their surroundings is exceptional. Bedroom shutters open out to country views and a curved double staircase leads down to a kempt lawn where, rather endearingly, chickens may be grazing. Inside are open fires, antique beds (with antique monogrammed bed clothes!), sympathetic period decorations and an atmosphere of secluded comfort.

Rooms: 6 double or twin with bath or shower & wc.

Price: 350-420 Frs (€ 53.36-64.03) for two, including breakfast. (No Eurocheques.)

Meals: By arrangement 100-150 Frs, including coffee. Or in village.

Open: All year.

From Nevers, D977 to Prémery. There, D977 bis dir. Corbigny; St Révérien is 15km along; signposted.

MMap 238-22 **ASP Map No: 8**

Bernadette BÜRGI & Florent de BEER
La Villa des Prés 58420
St Révérien
Nièvre
Tel: (0)3 86 29 04 57
Fax: (0)3 86 29 65 22
www.sawdays.co.uk

103

These people are genuine hosts who will easily get through any language barrier. Their engagingly cottagey C19 farmhouse has masses of character and space under its sweeping roof — exposed beams and old tiles are part of Monsieur's fine renovation job — and a charming, enthusiastic hostess, keen to provide her guests with authentic country hospitality. Rooms are traditionally decorated and comfortable. There is a pleasant living room with books and games. Breakfast (home-made jams) and dinner are eaten with the family; Madame is Portuguese and will make national specialities if asked — a real treat.

Rooms: 2 double, each with shower & wc.

Price: 300 Frs (€45.73) for two, including breakfast.

Meals: 120 Frs, including wine & coffee; children 60 Frs

Open: Easter to October.

From Cosne sur Loire D114 to Cours & St Loup des Bois; veer left on D114: Chauffour is between St Loup and St Vérain: follow signs for 'Musée de la Machine Agricole' then for 'Chambres d'Hôtes'.

MMap 231-27 **ASP Map No: 8**

Elvire & René DUCHET
Chez Elvire
Chauffour
58200 St Loup
Nièvre
Tel: (0)3 86 26 20 22

104

The Ayletts fell in love with a dilapidated C15 presbytery (one cold tap and an outside privy), bought it on the spot and set about their high-standard restoration, using old materials. Marjorie's artistry is evident in the elegantly comfortable bedrooms, where rich colours echo the hand-painted tiles in the luxurious bathrooms. Guests can enjoy excellent food, made with organically home-grown produce, in the attractive garden with superb Morvan views. Inside, there is an inglenook fireplace for cooler nights.

Rooms: 2 double, 1 twin, each with bath or shower & wc.

Price: 400 Frs (€ 60.98) for two, including breakfast.

Meals: By arrangement 130 Frs, including wine & coffee.

Open: All year.

From Avallon N6 to Saulieu. In centre, left at Hôtel Côte-d'Or onto D26 to La Motte Ternant. In village, follow signs for church.

MMap 243-13 **ASP Map No: 9**

Marjorie & Brian AYLETT
Le Presbytère
La Motte Ternant
21210 Saulieu
Côte-d'Or
Tel: (0)3 80 84 34 85
Fax: (0)3 80 84 35 32
www.sawdays.co.uk

Wooden beams and floors, huge old cupboards, shutters and stone fireplaces all contribute to the warm, relaxed feel of this lovely C18 presbytery. Claude Reny and her husband are Parisian bibliophiles and Claude is an enthusiastic gardener, supplying home-grown salads and always keen to swap horticultural hints. Breakfast, with home-made jam, is served round a large oval table in the *salle à manger*, and ageing bicycles are available for exploring. Monsieur is there in summer and speaks excellent English.

Rooms: 2 double, 1 twin, each with bath & wc.

Price: 400 Frs (€ 60.98) for two, including breakfast.

Meals: Choice within 6/7km.

Open: Easter to November.

From Arnay le Duc N6 dir. Châlons sur Saône for 1km then left onto D17 dir. Beaune. In village, house near church (signpost on D17).

MMap 243-14 **ASP Map No: 9**

Mme Claude RENY
La Cure
21230 Foissy
Côte-d'Or
Tel: (0)3 80 84 22 92
Fax: (0)3 80 84 22 92

A civilised house and family where you find space, warmth, good taste, intelligent company and a pretty terrace for breakfast — and so many musical events in summer. Madame is open and at ease — her house reflects her natural elegance. All is harmony in her renovated and not over-furnished manor with its pale colours, old tiles and rugs, modern art and big, soft-textured bedrooms (one more intimate and carpeted). The soft Burgundian light pours in through the big windows in the main rooms and the little village is quietly authentic.

Rooms: 2 triple, 1 double, each with bath or shower & wc.

Price: 380 Frs (€ 57.93) for two, including breakfast.

Meals: Simple place in village.

Open: May to mid-October.

From A6 Beaune/Chagny exit onto D973 dir. Dole & Seurre for 10km. In Corberon house signposted up on left.

MMap 243-28 **ASP Map No: 9**

Chantal & Alain BALMELLE
L'Ormeraie
21250 Corberon
Côte-d'Or
Tel: (0)3 80 26 53 19
Fax: (0)3 80 26 54 01

There's space and a welcome for all in this endearingly higgledy-piggledy yet simple C18 house in its attractive hill-top village. It has cheerful, plain rooms, all with independent entrances, that are lent an artistic flourish by Françoise's hand-decoration of some of the furniture: "neither marble nor satin, but wood and plaster, whiteness and colour" is how she defines her décor. Breakfast in the big, communal, all-in-together, kitchen/diner features honey from Henri's own hives. You may meet him in the evening and hear about life as a bee-keeper: he is genuinely fascinating, and Françoise clearly enjoys people.

Rooms: 1 quadruple, 1 triple, 3 double, 1 twin, all with shower & wc.

Price: 200-220 Frs (€ 30.49-33.54) for two, including breakfast.

Meals: By arrangement 90 Frs, including aperitif, wine & coffee.

Open: March to November.

From Nuits St Georges N74 dir. Beaune. At Corgoloin, D115 to Magny lès Villers. There, take road dir. Pernand Vergelesses; house almost imm'ly on right as you leave Magny, going uphill.

MMap 243-16 **ASP Map No: 9**

Françoise & Henri GIORGI
Maison des Abeilles
Route de Pernand Vergelesses
21700 Magny lès Villers
Côte-d'Or
Tel: (0)3 80 62 95 42

This is a C18 hunting lodge where the garden is full of flowers, the trees are centenarians and breakfast has the savour of yesteryear: yoghurt, fresh bread and home-made jam, a past one wouldn't mind revisiting regularly. Your hosts extend the warmest of genuine welcomes to the weary traveller — lots of towels, superb bed-linen, beautifully-judged colour schemes (Madame paints and knows about colour), fine furniture, a sprig of flowers, all combine to provide a soothing and reviving environment. The cottage is a deliciously independent blue hideaway with a working fireplace.

Rooms: 2 double, 1 twin, 1 cottage for 3, each with bath & wc.

Price: 450 Frs (€ 68.60) for two, cottage 600 Frs, including breakfast; extra bed 120 Frs.

Meals: Wide choice 10km.

Open: March to November.

From A31 exit 1 onto D35 E dir. Seurre. After about 3km right dir, Quincey, through Quincey and on to Antilly (4km). House on right.

MMap 243-16 **ASP Map No: 9**

Jean-François & Christiane BUGNET
Les Hêtres Rouges
Antilly
21700 Argilly
Côte-d'Or
Tel: (0)3 80 62 53 98
Fax: (0)3 80 62 54 85

Generously embracing, utterly French! Tall trees and terraces, for summer breakfasts, punctuate the lovely garden. Good old furniture, big rooms and snapshot collections create the family atmosphere of the elegant interior. Two grand, high-windowed, ground-floor rooms: *Style* has piano and plush, *Romantique* has superb original cupboards and is subtly pink; two cosier rooms up the narrow stairs have smaller windows and bathrooms. Your serene, welcoming hosts love having guests, and it shows.

Rooms: 2 double, each with bath & wc; 1 triple with shower & wc; 1 twin with hip-bath & wc.

Price: 400 Frs (€ 60.98) for two, including breakfast. Extra bed 200 Frs.

Meals: Choice in Gevrey, 7km.

Open: All year.

From Gevrey Chambertin, leave N74 westwards on D31 to Chambœuf. House well signposted in village.

MMap 243-16 **ASP Map No: 9**

Hubert & Michelle GIRARD
Le Relais de Chasse
Chambœuf
21220 Gevrey Chambertin
Côte-d'Or
Tel: (0)3 80 51 81 60
90)3 80 34 15 96
www.sawdays.co.uk

Expect a genuine welcome to this modern house with its lovely views over the valley of historic Alesia where the Roman colonisers fought the 'native' Gauls. Having lived long in Africa, the Gounands came home to build and decorate (slightly garishly) this house, become Mayor of the village (Monsieur will describe it all over a *kir*) and offer spotless rooms, new mattresses and high-quality bathrooms to lovers of walking, medieval villages and wine. Choose Madame's good cooking or your own in the well-equipped, open-sided summer house that Monsieur has designed in the garden.

Rooms: 1 double, 1 twin, each with curtained shower, sharing wc.

Price: 220 Frs (€ 33.54) for two, including breakfast. Extra bed 50 Frs.

Meals: By arrangement 80 Frs, including wine & coffee.

Open: Easter to October; by arrangement in winter.

From Dijon, N71 dir. Châtillon sur Seine. After Courceau, D6 left and follow signposts. (House is on D19A near junction with D6.)

MMap 243-2 **ASP Map No: 9**

Claude & Huguette GOUNAND
Villa Le Clos
Route de la Villeneuve D19A
21150 Darcey, Côte-d'Or
Tel: (0)3 80 96 23 20
Fax: (0)3 80 96 23 20
e-mail: cgounand@wanadoo.fr

The atmosphere is a deeply attractive mix of fine things — antiques, paintings, prints — and unstuffy informality. Soisick is good fun though you may find yourself waiting for her after the appointed hour and the cats may sneak in under the bedcovers, but relaxed animal-lovers enjoy the contrast between this casual attitude and the formal air of the ancient turrets of her pretty château (mostly restored by her). Rooms are comfortable with a lived-in, once-elegant look. Dinner, superbly cooked by Claudine, is served in the family dining room but do make sure your booking is firm. Lovely gardens, fly-fishing, painting courses.

Rooms: 3 double, 1 twin and 1 triple, each with bath or shower & wc.

Price: 360 Frs (€ 54.88) for two, including breakfast. Extra bed 120 Frs.

Meals: By arrangement 150 Frs, including wine & coffee.

Open: 21 March to 1 November.

From Dijon, N71 dir. Châtillon sur Seine. Before St Marc sur Seine, right on D32 and D901 dir. Aignay. Tarperon signposted on D901.

MMap 241-50 **ASP Map No: 9**

Soisick de CHAMPSAVIN &
Claudine BAILLARD
Manoir de Tarperon
21510 Aignay le Duc
Côte-d'Or
Tel: (0)3 80 93 83 74

The Dartois are porcelain collectors and fascinating hosts with wide knowledge of local history and archæology and, now that the farm is run by their children, lots of time to share with guests. Theirs is a big, interesting old house in a hamlet of only 80 people surrounded by tranquil countryside where the Seine is but a small stream and the Douix springs spectacularly in a grove near Châtillon. A lived-in, peaceful atmosphere, traditionally-furnished bedrooms, rather dated but adequate shared shower and loo and altogether exceptional value.

Rooms: 1 double & 1 twin, sharing bath, shower & wc

Price: 150 Frs (€ 22.87) for two, including breakfast.

Meals: Good restaurant 1km.

Open: All year.

From Châtillon sur Seine, N71 dir. Dijon. At Aisey sur Seine, right on D101 to Chemin d'Aisey; sharp right at church, house on left.

MMap 241-46 **ASP Map No: 9**

Simone & Jean DARTOIS
Chemin d'Aisey
21400 Châtillon sur Seine
Côte-d'Or
Tel: (0)3 80 93 22 51

Was that Rapunzel? Climb the winding stone stair to the top of the turret, push the big oak door, choose your four-poster, wallow in the ingenious gothicky bathroom then lie and admire the brilliant hangings and 'authentic' lights: no need to let down your hair. All is as 12th-century as Madame can make it. The medieval atmosphere, called strange, stagey, fascinating by some, is completed by objects from the château's history, some as old as the crusades. Madame is passionate about the place, most approachable and a talented cook — medieval dinners served in the candlelit baronial kitchen/dining room. A stylish and romantic retreat.

Rooms: 1 quadruple (2 four-posters) & own bathroom.

Price: 500 Frs (€ 76.22) for two, including breakfas; extra person 200 Frs.

Meals: 150-360 Frs, including coffee (state your budget).

Open: All year.

Gîte space for 4 people

From Avallon, N6 dir. Saulieu. As you enter Ste Magnance, first house on right.

MMap 238-24 **ASP Map No: 9**

Martine & Gérard COSTAILLE
Château Jacquot
RN6
89420 Ste Magnance
Yonne
Tel: (0)3 86 33 00 22
www.sawdays.co.uk

An ancient place steeped in history, Cabalus was an abbey hospice ("St Bernard and King Louis VII slept here") built in the shadow of the Basilica of this revered pilgrim city. An art gallery and coffee shop occupy the C12 vaulted room with its huge fireplace: guests have it to themselves for breakfast and share their hosts' sitting room where there's art everywhere and masses of books. Rooms are simple, authentic, with good beds. Eccentric, bearded and slightly shuffling, M Cabalus is the perfect gentleman with a fine sense of humour. Madame, also Swiss, is another warm, welcoming artist. An exceptional and inimitable house.

Rooms: 1 triple, 1 double, each with shower & wc; 2 triple, 1 double with showers but sharing wcs.

Price: 340-450 Frs (€ 51.83-68.60) for two, including breakfast.

Meals: 85 Frs, including coffee.

Open: All year.

In Vézelay centre, follow main street up to Basilique. House is last on left before reaching, Basilica, but next-to-last door (marked).

MMap 238-23 **ASP Map No: 8**

M CABALUS
Cabalus
Rue Saint Pierre
89450 Vézelay, Yonne
Tel: (0)3 86 33 20 66
Fax: (0)3 86 33 38 03
e-mail: cabalus@cabalus.com
www.cabalus.com

Soak up the physical and spiritual vibes from the great old stones and timbers of this house on the 'Eternal Hill', climbed b so many pilgrims over 500 years. A stone spiral staircase leads up to the bedrooms; the double has a terrace overlooking the sublime Basilica, both are full of simple character. Madame is easy, smiley, unintrusive and a passionate rider, so welcomes people riding or hiring horses. She serves breakfast in her dining room with its huge fireplace and readers have enjoyed the utter Frenchness of it all. Map and advice for hikers and cyclists and a pretty little self-catering flat for longer stay

Rooms: 1 double, 1 twin, sharing showe & wc.

Price: 280 Frs (€ 42.69) for two, including breakfast.

Meals: In Vézelay.

Open: All year.

Gîte space for 4 people

From Avallon, D957 to Vézelay. In town, go up towards Basilica (Rue St Étienne becomes Rue St Pierre). House, 100m from Basilica, identifiable by turret.

MMap 238-23 **ASP Map No: 8**

Monique & Bertrand GINISTY
Rue Saint Pierre
89450 Vézelay
Yonne
Tel: (0)3 86 33 25 74
www.sawdays.co.uk

Feel free to wander in the grounds or settle yourself totally without awkwardness in a corner of this handsome millhouse — it has a most inviting sitting room. Leigh and Gael's special brand of hospitality is so relaxed that you could fantasise that you own the place. Approached by a private bridge, the house is surrounded by a river, its own lake and rushing water. There's a canoe, (expensive) balloon flights from the garden, and a river beach. The big, light rooms have an English country feel, good bathrooms and the mill race generally drowns out the road...

Rooms: 2 double, 2 twin, 1 triple, 1 suite for 4, all with bath or shower & wc.

Price: 300-375 Frs (€ 45.73-57.17) for two, including breakfast.

Meals: Restaurant within walking distance.

Open: All year.

From Auxerre N6 dir. Avallon for 22km. Just before Vermenton village nameplate turn sharp right; signposted.

MMap 238-11 **ASP Map No: 8**

Leigh WOOTTON & Gael ROBERTSON
Le Moulinot
89270 Vermenton, Yonne
Tel: (0)3 86 81 60 42
Fax: (0)3 86 81 62 25
e-mail: lemoulinot@aol.com
www.sawdays.co.uk

They really are the nicest possible people. Simplicity and attention to detail are Madame's keynotes and her harmonious quirky house — 'Gothic' windows even in the attic, 'Victorian' panelling, superb old patterned floor tiles — is the warm and friendly central theme. Up two floors, the simply-furnished bedrooms have sloping ceilings, ancient rafters and not one common wall. Breakfast by the old bread oven or outside before learning to 'grow' truffles, consulting Monsieur on the estate wine you'll take home (the cellar is below the house), or setting off for Auxerre. A child-friendly house.

Rooms: 4 double, 1 suite for 4, all with bath or shower & wc.

Price: 280-340 Frs (€ 42.69-51.83) for two, including breakfast.

Meals: Restaurant 2km; Auxerre or Chablis 10km.

Open: Mid-January to mid-December.

From Auxerre, D965 dir. Chablis; after passing under the A6 motorway bridge, 3km on, house on right. DO NOT go to Venoy.

MMap 238-11 **ASP Map No: 8**

François & Françoise CHONÉ
Domaine de Montpierreux
89290 Venoy
Yonne
Tel: (0)3 86 40 20 91
Fax: (0)3 86 40 28 00

Ring at the huge gates, enter, and this superb château is your home for the night. You will indeed be welcomed as family by this young couple, their little boy, their pedigree Schnauzer dogs (Madame breeds them, passionately) and parakeets — all delightful. Downstairs, the thick-walled, vaulted dining and sitting rooms support the rest of the house, an impressive and original alternative to deep foundations. An oak staircase leads up to the charming, period-furnished bedrooms with views over roofs and woods (badgers to spot?). Meat-centred meals come with home-grown veg and good wine from the Septiers' cellar.

Rooms: 2 double with shower and basin each; 2 double without; all sharing 2 bathrooms and wcs in corridor.

Price: 350 Frs (€ 53.36) for two, including breakfast.

Meals: 200 Frs, including aperitif, wine and infusion.

Open: All year.

Gîte space for 5 people

From A6 exit Auxerre Nord on N6 dir. Auxerre for 0.5km; through Perrigny & St Georges dir. Villefargeau. At 'Relais de la Vallée' restaurant left and left again. Château at end of road.

MMap 238-10 **ASP Map No: 8**

Jacky & Marianne SEPTIER
1 allée du Château
89240 Villefargeau
Yonne
Tel: (0)3 86 41 33 32
Fax: (0)3 86 41 27 25
e-mail: marianne.septier@wanadoo.fr
http://perso.wanadoo.fr/marianne.septier

Very grand and so very French! The C19 manor is set back from the lime-tree-shaded square. Persian carpets on parquet floors, antiques and good, firm beds grace the large, luminous rooms and bathrooms are well fitted and finished. In winter a wood fire burns in the sitting room. Madame has taken great pains over her immaculate home; she puts you at your ease in these rather formal surroundings and enjoys talking to guests. Should she have to be out when you arrive, she'll leave a note on the door. "B&B perfection," wrote one reader, "for style, beds, hostess!" *Well-behaved children welcome.*

Rooms: 1 double/twin with shower & wc; 1 double,1 twin sharing bath, shower & wc.

Price: 300-420 Frs (€ 45.73-64.03) for two, including breakfast.

Meals: 120 Frs, including wine (by arrangement, low season only).

Open: All year.

From A6, Joigny exit onto D943 dir. Joigny then very shortly right onto D89 to Senan. Place de la Liberté is after church on right.

MMap 237-45 **ASP Map No: 8**

Mme Paule DEFRANCE
4 place de la Liberté
89710 Senan
Yonne
Tel: (0)3 86 91 59 00

You can see the river from your beautifully-furnished bedroom in this Burgundian manor house. It has been in the family for 400 years, standing in grand seclusion in its lovely gravel courtyard. The Brunots offer a near-professional degree of luxury (including prettily-tiled 'American-style' bathrooms) and genuine hospitality — they really appreciate getting to know people over two or three days. One bedroom is in a smart outbuilding and there is a comfortable guest sitting room; Madame is an accomplished cook; Monsieur has a superb wine cellar (you might even choose your own wine for dinner). Readers have sent glowing reports.

Rooms: 2 double, 1 suite for 3, each with bath or shower & wc. Extra bed available.

Price: 480 Frs (€ 73.18) for two, incl. breakfast; extra bed 100 Frs (2 nights min).

Meals: For more than 4 guests: 180 Frs, including wine & coffee.

Open: All year.

From A6, Auxerre-Nord exit on N6 dir. Joigny; right on D48, left on D84 dir. Brienon for 9km, past turning to Mt St Sulpice, right down road by river; house 0.5km on left with maroon gates.

MMap 237-46 **ASP Map No: 8**

Didier & Françoise BRUNOT
Domaine des Morillons
89250 Mont St Sulpice
Yonne
Tel: (0)3 86 56 18 87
Fax: (0)3 86 43 05 07

The farm is now run by the children so Henri just works "when he feels like it" and has plenty of time for his guests. These are long-standing local folk with a warm friendly attitude. The bedrooms are delightfully cosy, true to the spirit of an old-fashioned French farmhouse; shower rooms are clean and modern (one behind curtain). Isabelle serves what one reader called a "huge breakfast". A peaceful, rural spot where woods and all things bucolic abound. The village, with its little *auberge* for dinner, is 2km away.

Rooms: 1 double with shower & wc; 2 double sharing shower & separate wc.

Price: 240 Frs (€ 36.59) for two, including breakfast (less for long stays).

Meals: Auberge in village.

Open: Mid-March to October.

From Châtillon sur Seine, D965 dir. Tonnerre and Laignes. At Pimelles, D12 to Cruzy le Châtel; at T-junction right dir. Nicey, through Cruzy. House signed after village on right: small road up to farm.

MMap 237-48 **ASP Map No: 9**

Henri & Isabelle CHERVAUX
Les Musseaux
89740 Cruzy le Châtel
Yonne
Tel: (0)3 86 75 24 03

An oasis in a suburban 'railroady' desert: an unpretentious, family-lived-in farmhouse, in winter an open fire in the living room, in summer a terrace to breakfast on while squirrels play in the lovely tree-spread garden, and some flights of fancy. The décor ranges from pretty to kitsch to arty – son's black and white photographs, a hat collection, books everywhere. Madame, warm, generous and chatty, loves flowers and food (her fridge was stuffed with *pâtés*, cheeses, home-made jam) and is a mine of local information. Medieval Sens nearby, good regional cooking at home and a pot of jam when you go — sounds all right?

Rooms: 1 double, 1 twin, each with shower, sharing wc; 2 double sharing shower & wc; 1 double (+ child's bed) with shower & wc.

Price: 220-240 Frs (€ 33.54-36.59) for two, including breakfast.

Meals: 90 Frs, including wine.

Open: All year.

From Sens cross River Yonne W then right on D58 through St Martin to Courtois (5km). In village, 3rd right — house is last on left (no signs).

MMap 237-45 **ASP Map No: 8**

Hélène-Françoise & Daniel LAFOLIE
3 rue des Champs Rouges
Courtois
89100 Sens
Yonne
Tel: (0)3 86 97 00 33
Fax: (0)3 86 97 00 33

Please always telephone to CANCEL if you realise you are not going to take up your booking, even late in the day. It is the least of common courtesies.

"Ye who sit at a pavement café in Paris will see the whole world go by" under the all-seeing eye of the long-aproned, world-weary waiter who loves his City of Light but will never let you know it.

Paris – Ile de France

The natural air of real farm life. Tractors come and go in the farmyard, the old horse grazes in the field, the four young children play in the sandpit. The Desforges have done an excellent barn conversion. You climb the steep stairs to the lofty raftered dayroom (tea-making equipment, an old dresser, a comfortable sofa) and to the five good-sized bedrooms. They are furnished with grandmother's short-bedded but richly-carved Breton bridal suite, or grandfather's brass bed, old wardrobes and new mattresses. And Madame is delightful.

Rooms: 3 double, 2 twin, all with shower & wc.

Price: 250 Frs (€ 38.11) for two, including breakfast. Extra bed 60 Frs.

Meals: Choice in Milly 3km. Picnic possible.

Open: All year except mid-Dec to Jan.

From Fontainebleau D837 dir. Étampes into Milly centre. 300m after church left on D1 dir. Gironville for 3.5km. Farm on right.

MMap 237-30 **ASP Map No: 8**

Sophie & Jean-Charles DESFORGES
Ferme de la Grange Rouge
91490 Milly la Forêt
Essonne
Tel: (0)1 64 98 94 21
Fax: (0)1 64 98 99 91

The Art Deco style reigns supreme in this C19 hunting lodge that was exuberantly 'modernised' in the 1920s, from the high-windowed, fully-panelled dining room with its extraordinary dressers and unbelievably mustachioed grandfather to the fabulous bathroom fittings. The original features also include Versailles parquet floors and fine fireplaces: Tae uses her perfect sense of style and colour in decorating around and for these deeply-respected elements. Quiet spot, well-travelled hosts (especially South America), perfect for Chartres, Paris, Versailles...

Rooms: 2 suites for 5, each with bath & wc.

Price: 420 Frs (€ 64.03) for two, including breakfast.

Meals: Good restaurants in village.

Open: All year.

From A10 exit 10 to toll gate then right on D27 to St Cyr sous Dourdan then continue towards Arpajon — first house on left.

MMap 237-28 **ASP Map No: 4**

Claude & Tae-Lye DABASSE
Le Logis d'Arnières
1 rue du Pont-Rué
91410 St Cyr sous Dourdan
Essonne
Tel: (0)1 64 59 14 89
Fax: (0)1 64 59 07 46

A generous farmyard surrounded by beautiful warm stone buildings and set in wide open fields. Cereals, beets and show-jumpers — adding a definite touch of elegance to the landscape — flourish. Utter quiet and a genuine welcome, from hosts and Labradors alike, out here where Monsieur's family has come hunting for 200 years (his great-grandfather was a surgeon with Napoleon's army). Family furniture (the 1900s ensemble is most intriguing) in light-filled rooms, spotless mod cons and a vast sitting room for guests with piano and billiards table. And your hosts are excellent tour advisers who can direct you to little-known treasures.

Rooms: 1 triple with shower & wc; 1 apartment for 4 with mini-kitchen, shower & wc.

Price: 250 Frs (€ 38.11) for two, including breakfast; apartment 500 Frs for four.

Meals: In walking distance or 4-6km.

Open: All year except Christmas week.

From A5 exit 15 on N36 dir. Meaux for 200m; SECOND right to Crisenoy after TGV bridge, through village then 1.5km to farm (marked on Michelin No 106).

MMap 237-31 **ASP Map No: 4**

Philippe & Jeanne MAUBAN
Ferme Vert Saint-Père
77390 Crisenoy
Seine-et-Marne
Tel: (0)1 64 38 83 51
Fax: (0)1 64 38 83 52
e-mail: mauban.vert@wanadoo.fr
www.sawdays.co.uk

A pair of long, low stone buildings behind big blue porch doors, a narrow courtyard in between, the apse of the medieval church looking benignly over the wall and a charming garden with pond and terrace at the back. The Laurents are straightforward, gentle people; they are 'junk-shop' hunters (every bed is different) but they like to keep it uncluttered. The marble bathroom is NOT their doing! A friendly couple with two children who adopt stray cats, keep miniature ponies and will do all they can to make your stay restful and fruitful, including organising walks and making vegetarian meals if requested.

Rooms: 1 triple with bath & wc; 1 suite for 5/6 with shower & wc.

Price: 290 Frs (€ 44.21) for two, including breakfast. Extra bed 110 Frs.

Meals: 110 Frs, including wine & coffee.

Open: All year.

Gîte space for 7 people

From A4 exit on D231 to Villeneuve le Comte then right on D96 through Neufmoutiers to Châtres. House in village centre to left of church.

MMap 237-31 **ASP Map No: 4**

Dominique & Pierre LAURENT
Le Portail Bleu
2 route de Fontenay
77610 Châtres
Seine-et-Marne
Tel: (0)1 64 25 84 94
Fax: (0)1 64 25 84 94

For cat-lovers only — several felines here, plus one Labrador, some frogs, hedgehogs, rabbits. Home two centuries ago to a family of tax collectors and inn keepers — the bargemen would come to pay their tolls then stay on at the inn — the quiet grounds still go down to the river and lovely towpath walks. The balcony belongs to the *Champagne* suite, our favourite with its old paintings and wooden floor; the brilliantly Gothic dining room fireplace once belonged to Alexandre Dumas; your hosts once belonged to the travel industry and are excellent company.

Rooms: 1 suite for 3 with shower & wc, 1 suite for 5 with bath & wc.

Price: 280-340 Frs (€ 42.69-51.83) for two, including breakfast.

Meals: Two good restaurants nearby.

Open: March to October.

From A4 exit 18 onto N3 dir. Paris through St Jean then 1st right to Armentières; straight on at junction, past church — house is last but one on right in cul-de-sac.

MMap 237-20 **ASP Map No: 4**

Denise WOEHRLÉ
44 rue du Chef de Ville
77440 Armentières en Brie
Seine-et-Marne
Tel: (0)1 64 35 51 22
Fax: (0)1 64 35 42 95

What a mixture! A C13 farmhouse but super-luxy 1990s bathrooms; 20 minutes from high-tech CDG airport but a national hiking path (GR1) leading to forests just behind the house; a fluting Pan lording it over the manicured profusion of a prize-winning garden. Nothing is left to chance by your well-travelled, gracious and caring hostess. Royal breakfasts on rose-patterned porcelain in the peach-panelled *salon*; thirsty bathrobes in the marbled bathrooms for you to wear until changing for dinner which arrives under silver cloches. A form of perfection.

Rooms: 2 double/twin, 1 suite, each with bath & wc.

Price: 550-880 Frs (€ 83.85-134.16) for two, including breakfast.

Meals: 200-250 Frs, including aperitif & wine.

Open: All year except 2 weeks in February.

From A1 exit 'Soissons' on A104 dir. Marne la Vallée then N2 dir. Soissons 12km. Exit Othis. Through Othis on D13; at traffic light left to Beaumarchais. In village right after 1st speed bump.

MMap 237-19 **ASP Map No: 4**

Françoise MONTROZIER
12 rue des Suisses
Beaumarchais
77280 Othis
Seine-et-Marne
Tel: (0)1 60 03 33 98
Fax: (0)1 60 03 56 71

In one of the least artificial parts of Paris, where little old workshops still share the space with newer apartment blocks, your kind, smiling, artist hosts live between two tiny gardens and a tall house. The simple guestroom (good mattress!), which also has a sofa, shares one building with Sabine's studio and the next generation's ground-floor flat. Colours and fabrics are quiet and gentle, the bathroom is old-fashioned and perfectly adequate. The cosy family living room, in the main house, welcomes you for breakfast (French with a healthfood bias), or take it outside under the birdsung tree. Big, beautiful, black Janto, Jules's guide dog, loves people.

Rooms: 1 double with bath & wc.

Price: 350 Frs (€ 53.36) for two, including breakfast.

Meals: Choice within walking distance.

Open: All Year.

Metro: Jourdain or Place des Fêtes.
Car park: Place des Fêtes.

ASP Map No: 4

Sabine & Jules AÏM
Buttes Chaumont district
75019 Paris
Tel: (0)1 42 08 23 71
Fax: (0)1 42 40 56 04

On the sixth floor of one wing of a large and delightfully 1930s riverside block of flats with a superb view from its balconies across the Seine to the intriguingly modern André Citroën Park, this is a well-proportioned apartment with big rooms and a well-loved, lived-in patina. It is furnished with old family pieces, mementoes from distant travels (Iranian prayer mats and oriental rugs...). The guestroom is big too, with that same fine view, two narrow single beds, endearingly old-fashioned tiling in the shower and the loo just down the passage. If you open your window, you will naturally hear the traffic, somewhat muffled by leaves in summer, but the law has silenced the night-working barges. Madame, who still travels a lot, has lots of time for her guests and lends a very attentive yet gracious ear to their own travellers' tales.

Rooms: 1 twin with shower and basin, sharing wc.

Price: 300 Frs (€ 45.73) for two, including breakfast.

Meals: Choice within walking distance.

Open: Mid-September to June.

Metro: Mirabeau, Église d'Auteuil, Exelmans.
Buses: 72, 22, Petite Ceinture.
Car park: Rue Wilhem.

ASP Map No: 4

Auteuil district
75016 Paris
Tel: (0)1 42 88 87 66

The end of the road offers a breathtaking view of Notre Dame, buttresses flying in the setting sun. In this air, your skin absorbs the history of Paris, France, Europe through its pores. A few yards along, a great 17th-century doorway opens onto more ancient stones under the utterly Parisian porch. Old stone stairs bring you to a high-ceilinged, family-loved, unpretentious but ancient duplex flat where guests have a breakfast space beside the spiral staircase and a mezzanined, fireplaced room with high windows onto an unexpected green garden — a huge privilege in Paris. Madame is polyglot, active in the city and quietly welcoming.

Rooms: 1 room for 2-4 with bath & wc.

Price: 400 Frs (€ 60.98) for two, including breakfast.

Meals: Many restaurants nearby.

Open: All year.

Metro: Maubert-Mutualité; RER/Metro: St Michel-Notre Dame. Underground car park: 'Lagrange'.

ASP Map No: 4

Mme Brigitte CHATIGNOUX
Notre Dame/Saint Michel district
75005 Paris
Tel: (0)1 43 25 27 20
Fax: (0)1 43 25 27 20

From the table you can survey half the rooftops and domes of Paris. The compact living room is attractive with its deep sofas, upright piano and Madame's collection of decorative pill-boxes — altogether a clutter of curiosities that you will enjoy investigating. She likes treating her guests 'properly' and is happy to serve breakfast on fine linen in silver coffee pots. Bedrooms are less classy but perfectly comfortable. This is the trendy Mosque quarter (do drop into the Mosque tea-room one afternoon), with the colourful, animated Rue Mouffetard and the quieter Jardin des Plantes, once the Paris zoo, now the home of the fantastic Natural History Museum. Madame is quiet, a little shy, and most helpful. She also has a self-contained one-room apartment to let near Place de la République.

Rooms: 1 triple with shower; 1 double sharing bathroom; both sharing wc.

Price: 290-400 Frs (€ 44.21-60.98) (ie 290-330 sharing bathroom, 350-400 with shower) for two, incl. breakfast (min. 2 nights).

Meals: This is Paris!

Open: All year.

Metro Austerlitz. Car park Rue Censier. 8th floor, lift.

ASP Map No: 4

Madame Lélia COHEN-SCALI
Mouffetard district
75005 Paris
Tel: (0)1 43 36 51 62
www.sawdays.co.uk

A typical little Paris flat in a proudly moulded and bracketed 1900s building in a refreshingly popular yet residential area far from the massed bands of tourists — the famous Mount of Mars or Martyrs (Montmartre) is within walking distance but not so close that you feel harassed by charcoal-waving portraitists. The floorboards and ceiling plasterwork are original, as is the wooden fireplace; the décor is as young and lively as Françoise and Hervé themselves: theatrical bits and pieces, ivy growing all over your balcony, a castle scene on the duvet. They really look forward to their foreign guests and are happy to share their love of Paris, French food and good wine with you. You will like their youth, their spontaneity, their sense of fun.

Rooms: 1 double sharing shower & wc.

Price: 350 Frs (€ 53.36) for two, including breakfast.

Meals: Plenty of choice nearby.

Open: All year.

Metro: Guy Moquet or Lamarck-Caulaincourt.

ASP Map No: 4

Françoise & Hervé
Clair-Obscur, 8 bis rue Coysevox
Montmartre district
75018 Paris
Tel: (0)1 44 85 06 05
Fax: (0)1 44 85 06 14
e-mail: fforet@cybercable.fr
www.sawdays.co.uk

Quite a collection of contrasts here. Your very proper elderly hosts have moved from an isolated Mediterranean villa to this most populous, colourful quarter of Paris where you will hear a multitude of languages. But you leave the teeming pavement, pass the heavy gate and enter a leafy courtyard to zip up to the ninth floor. Their new apartment is all white walls, modern parquet floors, fine old family furniture and... great long views right across Paris from east to west, over to the Eiffel Tower and the Great Arch of La Défense, or up the hill to the little-known tree-filled Parc de Belleville. You breakfast on the balcony on fine days or by the amazing glass-fronted wardrobe with it haut relief carvings while Madame serves fresh pastries and tells you all you need to know about everything and Monsieur twinkles shyly.

Rooms: 1 double with shower & wc.

Price: 350 Frs (€ 53.36) for two, including breakfast.

Meals: Wide choice on the doorstep.

Open: Easter to September.

Metro: Belleville. Bus: 26.
Parking: Consult owners.

ASP Map No: 4

Danièle & Bernard de LA BROSSE
Belleville district
75019 Paris
Tel: (0)1 42 41 99 59
Fax: (0)1 42 41 99 59

Here are intelligence, sobriety and genuine style in one of the smartest of Left Bank streets. You enter a splendid vaulted porch designed in 1830 to take aristocrats' carriages, then mount a magnificent flight of stone steps to the lift. Madame welcomes you calmly into her vast, parquet-floored, high-windowed, sober-tinted apartment — nothing flashy, neither modern gadgets nor antique knick-knacks, just a few good pieces, space and light. Beyond the dining room, your smaller bedroom gives onto the big, silent, arcaded courtyard. Your multilingual hosts have lived all over the world, have deep knowledge of things of beauty and Monsieur, a retired engineer, still spends his days studying or teaching. Madame is as decided, stylish and genuine as her surroundings and enjoys, in equal parts, renovating her old mill near Chartres and the company of like-minded visitors — she is worth getting to know.

Rooms: 1 twin with bath & wc.

Price: 460 Frs (€ 70.13) for two, including breakfast (min. 3 nights).

Meals: Choice within 5 minutes walk; St Germain des Prés is 10 minutes away.

Open: All year.

Metro: Solférino. Car park: Invalides. 2nd floor: lift from street level.

ASP Map No: 4

Mme Elisabeth [illegible]
National Assembly/Invalides district
75007 Paris
Tel: (0)1 47 05 70 21/
(0)2 37 23 38 19

A narrow old building on a wide tree-lined boulevard where colourful street markets are held: here is a touch of pure unchanging Paris. The small flat's delightfully cluttered living room is 1800s with anachronistic timbers. There are books against every available wall, paintings and objects above and on top of them — from Africa, the Far East, America, they illustrate your hosts' eclectic tastes. Your room is quiet and snug over the inner courtyard. Cynthia is an intelligent, cosmopolitan American, Christian is quintessentially French and deeply informed by a professional life which includes exporting pedigree cattle and touring private châteaux in south-west France. He deals, expertly, in wine, is planning to write historical books and songs, and can guide you through the secret life of night-time Paris. Intimate, fun and fascinating.

Rooms: 1 double/twin with bath, shower & wc.

Price: 380 Frs (€ 57.93) for two, including breakfast.

Meals: Occasionally by arrangement. Varying prices.

Open: All year except August.

Metro: Edgar Quinet. Many bus and metro lines. Ask owners about parking.

ASP Map No: 4

Christian & Cynthia de MONBRISON
Montparnasse district.
75014 Paris
Tel: (0)1 45 38 68 72
Fax: (0)1 45 38 68 72

In a back street off a lively shopping district near the River Seine you find this C17 Parisian building and there, behind gently curved double doors, is a city home of charm and elegance whose owners managed to salvage some of the ancient timbers from the renovator's clean sweep and who live happily with one deliriously sloping wrought-iron balustrade (decorative but not structural...). It is warm, white-walled, antique-furnished and not at all imposing, with interesting artwork on the walls. Madame greatly enjoys her guests. Monsieur is a university professor of literature. Other inmates are plenty of plants and a gentle old cat called Campanule. The compact guest quarters are nicely private at the end of the corridor — good storage space, pretty quilts, lots of light.

Rooms: 1 twin with hip-bath/shower & wc.

Price: 420 Frs (€ 64.03) for two, including breakfast.

Meals: Both banks of the Seine beckon.

Open: All year except school holidays.

Metro: Châtelet or Pont-Neuf.
Car park: 'Conforama', via Rue du Pont Neuf then Rue Boucher.
3rd floor, lift.

ASP Map No: 4

Mme Mona PIERROT
Châtelet district
75001 Paris
Tel: (0)1 42 36 50 65

Nadine is lively, intense and intelligent: it is a privilege to sit in one of the deep soft chairs in her elegantly high-ceilinged C17 Paris flat — with lovely original windows onto the pedestrian street — and talk about Paris, art and exotic places with her. She is a busy Parisienne, juggling expertly with family, friends, profession and guests. Her activities as wildlife photographer, writer and purveyor (for friends) of native art by farflung tribes make for a fascinating and changing display on walls and shelves. You will sleep in complete quiet in the cosy, pale-peachy guestroom whose tall window gives onto the 'turreted' courtyard. The mattress is good beneath the Indian cotton cover, the shelves carry books and *objets*, the bathroom is... a bathroom. After breakfasting in the soft light of the half-timbered dining space, step out into the heart of Paris.

Rooms: 1 double with bath & wc.

Price: 480 Frs (€ 73.18) for two, including breakfast.

Meals: Paris at your feet.

Open: All year except August.

Metro: Hôtel de Ville or Châtelet.
Underground car park "Châtelet".
Gentle stairs to 2nd floor.

ASP Map No: 4

Nadine SAUNIER
Châtelet district
75004 Paris
Tel: (0)1 48 87 70 15
Fax: (0)1 48 87 70 15

Amazing! Goats, dogs, exotic fowl and stone boars outside, a collector's paradise and a housemaid's hell inside. This great traveller has amassed carvings and incrustations, inlays and filigrees in brass, lacquer and wood both rough and smooth, large and small, and filled his family mansion. All is exuberance and love of life and beautiful things and the rooms are a feast of almost baroque décor. Your host is also very good company. On weekdays his delightful polyglot assistant Taïeb will take excellent care of you. There is also a loo/library and a three-legged cat.

Rooms: 5 double with shower & wc, 1 suite for 5 with bath & wc.

Price: 320-395 Frs (€ 48.78-60.22) for two, including breakfast.

Meals: Three restaurants in village.

Open: All year.

From N10 north of Rambouillet take D937 then D936 towards Poigny la Forêt for 5km. Left on D107 to Poigny. Left up road by church; house is on right.

MMap 237-28 **ASP Map No: 3**

François LE BRET
2 rue de l'Église
78125 Poigny la Forêt
Yvelines
Tel: (0)1 34 84 73 42
Fax: (0)1 34 84 74 38

Such a soft, quiet woman! She's an art teacher — and definitely an artist — who loves her modern white-walled, white-curtained house under the wooded hillside and fills it elegantly with antiques large and small (she confesses to being a hoarder), as well as her own works in paint and wool. A peaceful feel, a caring hostess who gives you as much time as she has despite her early-morning exits. The big room (with en suite bathroom) is superb; the smaller one excellent value with its own bathroom across the landing. A short drive from Paris.

Rooms: 2 double (1 large, 1 small), each with bath & wc.

Price: 280-380 Frs (€ 42.69-57.93) for two, including breakfast.

Meals: 80 Frs, including wine & coffee.

Open: All year.

From Paris A13 onto A12 dir. St Quentin en Yvelines for 6km then exit on N12 towards Dreux. Exit to Plaisir CENTRE; 1st exit off roundabout dir. Plaisir Les Gâtines, 1st left for 400m; right into Domaine des Gâtines: consult roadside plan.

MMap 237-16 **ASP Map No: 3**

Mme Hélène CASTELNAU
7 rue Gustave Courbet
Domaine des Gâtines
78370 Plaisir
Yvelines
Tel: (0)1 30 54 05 15
Fax: (0)1 30 54 05 15

Only 25 train-minutes (Paris Region express network) from the heart of Paris, in a leafy residential suburb (with the occasional train at the far end of the road), this is a modern, light-filled house decorated with a mix of antique and contemporary furniture, plus some fascinating oriental treasures, mementoes of years in Indonesia. Your fully-equipped apartment is large and light; Madame is most welcoming. You can really make yourself at home here with your family for a few days. Leave the car and explore Paris at your ease.

Rooms: Apartment for 4 with bathroom & kitchen.

Price: 426 Frs (€ 64.94) for two per night (min 3 nights), including breakfast. Reduction one week and winter.

Meals: Choice locally.

Open: All year.

From Paris RER line 'A1' to Le Vésinet/Le Pecq station. Madame will fax street plan from station. At No 14, house is right-hand one.

MMap 237-17 **ASP Map No: 4**

Éveline ALBAUT
14 rue Anatole France
78110 Le Vésinet
Yvelines
Tel: (0)1 39 76 19 77
Fax: (0)1 39 76 19 77
e-mail: eveline@mail.com.fr

Hazeville is an exceptional experience: from your artist host to his highly aristocratic and refined home (built in 1560); from your rather exotic rooms in the (even older) pigeon-tower to the great farmyard where today the stables house hi-tech artisans rather than cart-horses. You will be flooded with history and art, given a generous breakfast on hand-painted china (painted by Monsieur to match the wall covering) and carefully directed to all the secret treasures of the Vexin. *Well-behaved children over seven welcome.*

Rooms: 1 double & 1 twin, both with bath, shower & wc.

Price: 650 Frs (€ 99.09) for two, including breakfast.

Meals: Wide choice within 5-10km.

Open: Weekends and school holidays.

From Rouen, N14 dir. Paris. 20km before Pontoise, at Magny en Vexin, right onto D983 to Arthies. Left onto D81, through Enfer; château on left.

MMap 237-16 **ASP Map No: 3**

Guy & Monique DENECK
Château d'Hazeville
95420 Wy dit Joli Village
Val-d'Oise
Tel: (0)1 34 67 06 17/
(0)1 42 88 67 00
Fax: (0)1 34 67 17 82

Fierce pagan Vikings sailed warlike
up the Seine in their long battle-boats...
and settled into the rolling pastures to milk cows for
Camembert and breed Christians for the Abbeys.

Normandy

An area of natural and historical delights: the Forest of Eu, lapping up to the edge of the farm, is 9,300 hectares of green space to explore and the Château of Eu is where Louis Philippe and Queen Victoria begat the Entente Cordiale. But come to La Marette for the uncanny silence at night, the birdsong at dawn, and your hosts' radiant smiles at all times. They want you to enjoy the house as it was when their daughters were here: a family atmosphere, the occasional shared shower, masses of human warmth, not an ounce of hotellishness.

Rooms: 1 suite with bath & wc; 1 suite & 1 double, each with wc, sharing shower.

Price: 200-280 Frs (€ 30.49 - 42.69) for two, including breakfast. Extra bed 100 Frs.

Meals: Choice 4/10/12km. Self-catering.

Open: All year.

From A28 exit Blangy sur Bresle dir. Le Tréport to Gamaches; left at lights on D14 to Guerville; follow signs to Melleville. Just before leaving village, right onto Route de la Marette.

MMap 231-12 **ASP Map No: 3**

Etienne & Nelly GARÇONNET
La Marette
Route de la Marette
76260 Melleville
Seine-Maritime
Tel: (0)2 35 50 81 65
Fax: (0)2 35 50 81 65

Did Queen Victoria 'stop' here once? We'll never know, but the hunting lodge (C17) is ideal for parties while the owners' house (C19 over C12 cellars) has one huge guestroom. Monsieur manages the Port and the Chamber of Commerce, Madame the house and garden, masterfully — she has lived here since she was six. Both are proud of their region, keen to share their knowledge and advise on explorations: nature, hiking, historical visits, excellent suggestions for wet days, dry days... A delightful, welcoming couple with natural generosity, elegance, taste and manners and an open-minded approach to all mankind.

Rooms: 1 triple, 1 double, 1 apartment for 5, each with shower & wc.

Price: 280 Frs (€ 42.69) for two, including breakfast; extra bed 70 Frs.

Meals: In Eu 2km, Le Tréport 4km. Self-catering in apartment.

Open: All year.

At Eu, head for Ponts et Marais (D49). As you leave Eu, right on Route de Beaumont (2km).

MMap 231-12 **ASP Map No: 3**

Catherine & Jean-Marie DEMARQUET
Manoir de Beaumont
76260 Eu
Seine-Maritime
Tel: (0)2 35 50 91 91
e-mail: qentin.demarque@netclic.fr

The parrot arrived five years ago... and stayed. If you're a golfer you may do the same: you are bang next to the third green. Green is the dominant colour inside, too, thanks not least to the exotic palms. The light, modern house is creature-comfortable and copes well with the transition between '80s daring and '90s pleasing. There is a television set in each room and the sitting area is really the owners' territory, but they are extremely nice people and Madame can give you a yoga lesson. Bedroom comfort is plush, bordering on the professional.

Rooms: 2 twin, 1 double, each with bath or shower & wc.

Price: 320-350 Frs (€ 48.78-53.36) for two, including breakfast.

Meals: Full choice in Dieppe.

Open: All year.

From Dieppe, D75 ('Route du Littoral') W along coast dir. Pourville. Once you reach golf course, 1st left, 3rd house on right (signposted).

MMap 231-11 **ASP Map No: 3**

Alain & Danièle NOËL
24 chemin du Golf
76200 Dieppe
Seine-Maritime
Tel: (0)2 35 84 40 37
Fax: (0)2 35 84 32 51

You'd never know this venerable Norman farmhouse was built by Monsieur himself: he used old materials, original designs, and was as careful as they both are about getting things right — indeed, they may seem a bit perfectionist. But it has a genuinely good feel to it. Inside there are old beams, lovely furniture (admire the fine *comtoise* clock), spotless guestrooms with good bathrooms and a low, beamed, big-tabled room for breakfast (not available for the rest of the day, though). Then you can take the path hewn out of the cliff face down to the wild rugged beaches, in superb contrast to the cosiness you have just left.

Rooms: 2 double, 1 twin, each with bath or shower & wc.

Price: 320 Frs (€ 48.78) for two, including breakfast.

Meals: Choice in Fécamp.

Open: All year except 3 weeks in August.

Gîte space for 8 people

Leave Fécamp by D925; left at signpost to Senneville. In village take bumpy road towards the sea; house is first on left.

MMap 231-8 **ASP Map No: 3**

M & Mme LETHUILLIER
Val de la Mer
76400 Senneville sur Fécamp
Seine-Maritime
Tel: (0)2 35 28 41 93

Nature lovers rejoice! Start with a view from your bed of the immaculate garden where pigeons, ducks and cats scurry. Take a long shower and enjoy fluffy towels and bathrobes, then breakfast on four kinds of bread. Fishing and hiking are at your back door, tennis a few miles away; the family suite has welcome wet-weather entertainments. Return from an afternoon jaunt to read Madame's books, relax among the lovely antiques or make yourself something in the kitchen. The owner is most amicable and gracefully succeeds in caring for her teenage children while giving time to guests — and space for everyone's privacy.

Rooms: 1 triple with bath & wc, 1 suite with bath, shower & wc.

Price: 480-530 Frs (€ 73.18-80.80) for two, including breakfast. Children under 3 free. Reservations only.

Meals: In Valmont, 1km.

Open: All year.

From Dieppe D925 W dir. Fécamp for approx. 60km then left on D17 to Valmont. In centre, left on D150 dir. Ourville for 1.2km; right on Chemin du Vivier — house is 2nd entrance on right.

MMap 231-9 **ASP Map No: 3**

Dominique CACHERA
Le Clos du Vivier
4 chemin du Vivier
76540 Valmont, Seine-Maritime
Tel: (0)2 35 29 90 95
Fax: (0)2 35 27 44 49
e-mail: Le.clos.du.vivier.@wanadoo.fr
www.sawdays.co.uk

Madame loves to talk (in French) and has a winning smile. Her house (she was born here), which stands in a classic square, poplar-sheltered Seine-Maritime farmyard, is 300 years old; the worn old stones, bricks and flints (less worn!) bear witness to its age — so does the fine timberwork inside. Otherwise it has been fairly deeply modernised, but the long lace-clothed breakfast table before the log fire (in winter) is most welcoming. The pleasant rooms are good if unremarkable and the only sounds are the occasional lowing of the herd and the breeze blowing in the poplars.

Rooms: 1 triple with bath & wc; 1 double with shower & wc; 2 double sharing shower & wc.

Price: 220 Frs (€ 33.54) for two, including breakfast.

Meals: Auberge 1km.

Open: All year.

Gîte space for 10 people

From Dieppe N27 dir. Rouen for 29km; right on N29 through Yerville & dir. Yvetot for 4.5km; left on D20 to Motteville; right to Flamanville. In village, Rue Verte is road behind church. Farm 300m on left; signposted.

MMap 231-22 **ASP Map No: 3**

Yves & Béatrice QUEVILLY BARET
La Ferme de la Rue Verte
76970 Flamanville
Seine-Maritime
Tel: (0)2 35 96 81 27

Madame is a blithe soul who proclaims that she's "on holiday all year" and her welcome is terrific — nothing is too much trouble. The colourful, flowerful garden, her great love, is a wonder in almost any season, a hillside oasis of tumbling vegetation in the town (the road can be noisy but it's all right at night). Her guestrooms are cosy and tempting, reflecting the history of the old house and her collecting flair. There is a dayroom for guests but breakfast is in the pretty family dining room. A very French address, full of character, excellent value and a good base for exploring the churches and villages that fill this area.

Rooms: 1 double, 2 triple, 1 quadruple, each with shower & wc.

Price: 275 Frs (€ 41.92) for two, including breakfast.

Meals: In village or self-catering.

Open: All year.

Gîte space for 4 people

From Rouen D982 dir. Le Havre; under Pont de Brotonne, into Caudebec, right onto rue de la République (D131) dir. Yvetot; No 68 is 500m on the right.

MMap 231-21 **ASP Map No: 3**

Christiane VILLAMAUX
68 rue de la République
76490 Caudebec en Caux
Seine-Maritime
Tel: (0)2 35 96 10 15
Fax: (0)2 35 96 75 25
www.sawdays.co.uk

The stern black front door of this solid townhouse hides a light, stylish interior with views across the old town to the spires of Rouen Cathedral. Dominique, a keen and cultured Egyptologist, has a flair for refined decoration — see her paintings, coverings and country furniture. There are rugs on the wooden floor in the sitting room and French windows lead to a balcony and the garden. Nothing standard, nothing too studied, a real personal home and a lovely setting for an unhurried feast at her flower-decked breakfast table and a chance to quiz her (her English is excellent) about her latest digs in Egypt.

Rooms: 1 double with bath & wc; 2 double, each with bath, sharing wc.

Price: 270-300 Frs (€ 41.16-45.73) for two, including breakfast. Extra bed 80 Frs.

Meals: 110 Frs, including wine & coffee.

Open: All year except Oct & Nov.

In Rouen, follow signs to Gare SNCF (railway station); take Rue Rochefoucault imm'ly to right of station; left into Rue des Champs des Oiseaux, across 2 sets of lights, straight over into Rue Vigné, left at fork into Rue Hénault. Black door on left.

MMap 231-23 **ASP Map No: 3**

Mme Dominique GOGNY
22 rue Hénault
76130 Mont St Aignan
Seine-Maritime
Tel: (0)2 35 70 26 95
Fax: (0)2 35 52 03 52
www.sawdays.co.uk

In an ancient street in the historic centre of lovely old Rouen, 100m from the Cathedral, stands the C17 family home of Philippe Aunay. He enjoys sharing, in English, German or Norman and with much wry, dry humour, the history of Rouen and the informal comfort of his lovely (quiet) townhouse. It is a treasure-trove of curios, with huge beams, big windows and genuine Norman antiques. Bathrooms are crisply modern, breakfast generous and your reception cheerful. *Car park a short walk from house.*

Rooms: 2 double, 1 twin, with bathrooms (can be a suite with kitchen); 1 single, sharing bathroom.

Price: 290-300 Frs (€ 44.21-45.73) for two, incl. breakfast.

Meals: Vast choice on the spot.

Open: All year.

On cathedral-side embankment: at Théâtre des Arts, take Rue Jeanne d'Arc; Rue aux Ours is 2nd on right but NO parking. Leave car in 'Bourse' or 'Pucelle' car park, near house, and walk.

MMap 231-23 **ASP Map No: 3**

Philippe & Annick AUNAY-STANGUENNEC
45 rue aux Ours
76000 Rouen
Seine-Maritime
Tel: (0)2 35 70 99 68
www.sawdays.co.uk

Expect to see a brightly-coloured tanker appear from behind the trees heading for the Channel, or the great annual armada sailing past — such is the magic of this site on the banks of the Seine just below Rouen. The Laurents' garden goes down to the water's edge and they offer binoculars for bird-watching, maps and books for trail-exploring — it is a Panda (WWF) house. The big house is for guests, the owners occupy a thatched cottage next door. There are beams and panelling, antiques and windows onto that stunning view, a kitchen/diner, a very comfortable sitting room and Madame has all the time in the world for you.

Rooms: 2 suites for 3, 2 quadruple, each with bath or shower & wc,

Price: 260 Frs (€ 39.64) for two, including breakfast; extra bed 60 Frs.

Meals: 85 Frs, excluding wine (wine 50 Frs, cider 25 Frs); self-catering.

Open: All year.

Gîte space for 14 people

From Pont Audemer D139 NE for 10km to Bourneville & continue D139 to Aizier. In village, left at 'Mairie' dir. Vieux Port — house on right.

MMap 231-21 **ASP Map No: 3**

Yves & Marie-Thérèse LAURENT
Les Sources Bleues
Le Bourg
27500 Aizier
Eure
Tel: (0)2 32 57 26 58
www.sawdays.co.uk

It's prettier every year: nothing's nicer than waking up in one of the attractive, antique- or ethnic-furnished rooms of this superbly-renovated farmhouse (super bathrooms too). The kitchen/dining room with its open fire is the hub: colourful, full of pictures, plants, a collection of cheese boxes and one hundredweight of human warmth and dynamism, this is where English Nicky concocts her culinary wonders using lamb, cheese, veg and cider produced by French Régis. They are young, charming, work like beavers and are always available for guests. Paradise in an ideal base for exploring Normandy. *Please come after 4.30pm.*

Rooms: 2 double, 1 twin, 1 triple, 1 quadruple, all with bath or shower & wc.

Price: 280 Frs (€ 42.69) for two, including breakfast.

Meals: 120 Frs, including wine & coffee.

Open: All year.

From A13, Le Havre exit, on D139 dir. Pont Audemer. In Fourmetot, left dir. Corneville. Farm 1km from turning on left.

MMap 231-21 **ASP Map No: 3**

Régis & Nicky DUSSARTRE
L'Aufragère
La Croisée
27500 Fourmetot
Eure
Tel: (0)2 32 56 91 92
Fax: (0)2 32 57 75 34
www.sawdays.co.uk

A long drive leads past carefully-tended flowerbeds up to the old *pressoir*, built during the French Revolution and now restored by this exceptional couple — he a gentle ex-sailor who can tell a tale or two, she quiet and engaging. Bedrooms were a labour of love for her — fabrics and papers carefully chosen, flowers cut and dried to match, old trunks and carved *armoires* chosen from family treasure stores. Breakfast on home-made cake to classical music, dine on local specialities with flowers on the table.

Rooms: 2 double, each with shower & wc.

Price: 280 Frs (€ 42.69) for two, including breakfast.

Meals: 120 Frs, including wine & coffee.

Open: All year.

From Le Havre dir. Paris & Rouen; over Pont de Tancarville on A131 then right on D810 to Pont Audemer; D87 through St Germain Village; continue D87 then right into Tricqueville on CV19; signposted.

MMap 231-20 **ASP Map No: 3**

Gaston & Michelle LE PLEUX
La Clé des Champs
27500 Tricqueville
Eure
Tel: (0)2 32 41 37 99

Its atmosphere is as pleasing as its looks: this is a genuinely old, Normandy house (even apple trees abound), its lovely external timber frame enclosing a heart-warming antique clutter spread with excellent taste over bricks and beams, original tiles and carved furniture. The delicious bedrooms are subtly lit by dormer windows, softly furnished country-style, pastel-hued and comfortably bathroomed. Monsieur is a charming gentleman, full of smiles. Madame is more serious and most attentive. Both are proud of their warmly cosy house and its ravishing garden with long views of the peaceful valley.

Rooms: 2 double/twin, 1 suite for 4, each with bath or shower & wc.

Price: 250-270 Frs (€ 38.11-41.16) for two, including breakfast.

Meals: 110 Frs, including aperitif, wine & coffee.

Open: Mid-March to September.

From Paris A13 exit 26; left on D89 to 'Médine' r'about. Straight across dir. Evreux/Appeville-Annebault; left imm'ly after 'Les Marettes' sign then follow 'Chambres d'Hôtes' signs.

MMap 231-15 **ASP Map No: 3**

Françoise & Yves CLOSSON MAZÉ
Les Aubépines
Aux Chauffourniers
27290 Appeville dit Annebault
Eure
Tel: (0)2 32 56 14 25
Fax: (0)2 32 56 14 25

In a softly wooded environment, with pastoral meadow and lake spread before it, Hermos is a house full of quiet history and family atmosphere. Outside, a typical C16 marriage of brick and stone and a baronial double staircase, inside, panels, mouldings, parquet floors, flowers all over. Madame is a most welcoming hostess, full of spontaneous smiles, whose family has owned the house for 100 years. She also gardens, organises seminars (not when B&B guests are here) and cares for two children. The large panelled bedrooms have refreshing colours, good beds, old wardrobes and windows onto the gentle world outside. Elegant and restful.

Rooms: 1 quadruple with bath & wc; 1 triple with shower & wc.

Price: 250-350 Frs (€ 38.11-53.36) for two, including breakfast.

Meals: Choice 2km.

Open: All year.

Gîte space for 20 people

From A13 exit Maison Brulée on N138 dir. Bourgthéroulde & Brionne. 8km after Bourgthéroulde left on D83 to Le Gros Theil; on entering village sharp right on D92 & follow signs for 2km.

MMap 231-22 **ASP Map No: 3**

Béatrice & Patrice NOËL-WINDSOR
Manoir d'Hermos
27800 St Eloi de Fourques
Eure
Tel: (0)2 32 35 51 32
Fax: (0)2 32 35 51 32

French in every way: old and new furnishings, tailored and natural garden, cultural references (Saint-Exupéry, author of the immortal *Petit Prince* and a friend of Madame's father's, stayed here). The sensuous garden is full of old favourites: lilac, peonies, honeysuckle, fruit trees. In the middle of the village, the house is very old (1500s), very quiet and has an atmosphere that inspires ease and rest. Madame used to be an antique dealer so breakfast is served on old silver. She sculpts and paints and also restores statues in the C15 church opposite the house.

Rooms: 2 double, 1 triple, 1 quadruple (in cottage), each with shower & wc.

Price: 260 Frs (€ 39.64) for two, including breakfast.

Meals: 90 Frs, excluding wine.

Open: All year.

Gîte space for 12 people

From A13 exit 19 to Louviers; D313 dir. Elbeuf for 11km; left on D60 to St Didier des Bois. House with white iron gate opposite church.

MMap 231-22 **ASP Map No: 3**

Mme Annick AUZOUX
1 place de l'Église
27370 St Didier des Bois
Eure
Tel: (0)2 32 50 60 93
www.sawdays.co.uk

Close to perfection... not surprising given Janine's bubbling enthusiasm and sprightly energy. She is, nevertheless, 'classic' in her dress and appearance and creates a very special breakfast with pewter service and folded napkins. She is deeply intolerant of dust and dirt, so the immensely comfortable bedrooms might even be cleaner than your own. The downstairs sitting room is vast, about 80m², the staircase is beautifully sculpted, the garden goes down to the river and you are halfway between Giverny and Rouen.

Rooms: 1 double/twin, 1 suite for 5, each with bath & wc.

Price: 250-280 Frs (€ 38.11-42.69) for two, including breakfast.

Meals: In village or 6km away.

Open: All year.

Gîte space for 4 people

From Evreux, D155 north. 300m after Les Faulx hamlet, right for Heudreville. House in cul-de-sac opposite church.

MMap 231-35 **ASP Map No: 3**

Mme Janine BOURGEOIS
La Ferme
4 rue de l'Ancienne Poste
27400 Heudreville sur Eure
Eure
Tel: (0)2 32 50 20 69
Fax: (0)2 32 50 20 69

Exquisite!... and without a whiff of pretension. The Brunets, as delightful as their house, have the lightness of touch to combine the fresh best of modern French taste with an eye for authenticity — in a brand new house. There are recycled château windows, light flooding in from both sides of this classical narrow *maison de campagne*, eye-catching stretches of pine-floored corridor, handsome rugs, a brave mix of old and modern furniture, massive comfort. Gorgeous.

Rooms: 3 twin, 2 double, each with bath or shower & wc.

Price: 480-680 Frs (€ 73.18-103.67) for two, including breakfast; child 200 Frs.

Meals: In village or 5km.

Open: April to Nov (by arrangement in winter).

Gîte space for 10 people

From A13 exit 14 dir. Vernon/Giverny. Entering Giverny left on Rue Claude Monet. After church, left on Rue Blanche Hoshedé Monet for 1.2km; left on white arrow, imm'ly right on track for 800m then left to 'La Réserve'.

MMap 231-36 **ASP Map No: 3**

Didier & Marie Lorraine BRUNET
La Réserve
27620 Giverny
Eure
Tel: (0)2 32 21 99 09
Fax: (0)2 32 21 99 09
www.giverny.org/hotels/brunet/index.htm

The clean, cool River Epte, which Monet diverted at nearby Giverny to create the ponds for his famous *Nymphéas*, runs at the bottom of the pretty garden and bestows the same quality of serenity here. The house is beautifully furnished with family antiques and Madame, a strong, intelligent and inherently elegant person, willingly shares her extensive knowledge of all things Norman (including food). Rooms are stylish and quiet; one has an Art Deco brass bed designed by *Grandpère*. The attic twin is up steep stairs and under sloping ceilings.

Rooms: 2 double, each with shower or bath & wc; 1 twin sharing bathroom.

Price: 300-330 Frs (€ 45.73-50.31) for two, including breakfast.

Meals: 130 Frs, including wine & coffee.

Open: 15 March to 15 December.

From Dieppe, D915 to Gisors. Cross Gisors then D181 dir. Vernon. In Dangu, rue du Gué is beside the river Epte. Look for house with green shutters.

MMap 237-3 **ASP Map No: 3**

Nicole de SAINT PÈRE
Les Ombelles
4 rue du Gué
27720 Dangu
Eure
Tel: (0)2 32 55 04 95
Fax: (0)2 32 55 59 87
e-mail: vextour@aol.com

A lovely, elegant address of listed château and gardens (landscaped and formal), vast woodlands for walking (and shooting, in autumn), a tennis court, an ancient fallen mulberry tree that has rebuilt itself, two suites full of canopied beds in the C18 château, other fine rooms in the converted dovecote (illustrated). The lady of the manor's exquisite taste has weaved its magic from floor to ceiling, from Jouy print to antique wardrobe and you will feel like prince and princess here, just 40km from Giverny.

Rooms: 2 double, 1 double/twin, 2 suites for 4/5, each with bath or shower & wc.

Price: 450-850 Frs (€ 68.60-129.58) for two, including breakfast.

Meals: Restaurant 8km.

Open: All year.

From A13 exit 'Louviers' on A154 dir. Évreux, exit Caër/Gravigny on D155 dir. Acquigny; through Boulay Morin; 500m after village, left to Émalleville — chateau opposite church.

MMap 231-35 **ASP Map No: 3**

M & Mme Christian THIEBLOT
Château d'Émalleville
17 rue de l'Église
27930 Émalleville, Eure
Tel: (0)2 32 34 01 87
Fax: (0)2 32 34 30 27
e-mail: chateau-emalleville@yahoo.fr
www.multimania.com/chateauemallevil

This Franco-Spanish couple lived in Latin America for over 20 years before retiring to their small manor house in Normandy — spot the mementoes. Monsieur prides himself on having immaculately clean bathrooms — one English guest said she would happily sleep in the bath! The small bedrooms are decorated with good furniture, dried flowers and prints, giving an atmosphere of solid comfort (though not always an armchair!). There's now a fully telecommunicating study too. Enjoy fresh fruit juice and home-made jams over breakfast sitting at the huge olive-wood breakfast table and find time to visit the C11 chapel in the village.

Rooms: 1 suite for 2, 1 family room for 4, 1 double, each with bath or shower & wc.

Price: 250-320 Frs (€ 38.11-48.78) for two, including breakfast. Extra bed 50 Frs.

Meals: Auberges 5km.

Open: All year.

From A13 exit 17 for Gaillon then W dir. Evreux on D316 through Autheuil, St Vigor & up hill then right for Reuilly. House on road, 200m past 'Mairie' on right.

MMap 231-35 **ASP Map No: 3**

Jean-Pierre & Amaia TREVISANI
Clair Matin
19 rue de l'Église
27930 Reuilly
Eure
Tel: (0)2 32 34 71 47
Fax: (0)2 32 34 97 64
e-mail: clair_matin@compuserve.com

Madame, tall, sophisticated and immaculate, did all the wallpapering herself and is naturally relaxed and welcoming. She finds it normal that everyone sit at the same big table in the ochre and scarlet breakfast room. There is a family-friendly common room with billiards, table tennis, picnic table, refrigerator. Bedrooms are big and beautifully decorated (*merci Madame!*); *La Jaune* has superb views. No finery, a touch of faded grandeur and all-pervasive warmth characterise this splendid house of friendship.

Rooms: 2 family rooms, 1 double, 1 twin, each with bath or shower & wc.

Price: 280 Frs (€ 42.69) for two, including breakfast.

Meals: Choice in Orbec.

Open: All year.

From Lisieux, D519 dir. Orbec. At Orbiquet, left on D2 (Calvados)/D145 (Eure). Go through St Germain la Campagne; château on left as you leave village.

MMap 231-32 **ASP Map No: 3**

Bruno & Laurence de PRÉAUMONT
Château du Grand Bus
St Germain la Campagne
27230 Thiberville
Eure
Tel: (0)2 32 44 71 14
Fax: (0)2 32 46 45 81

Just one loo between three bedrooms but we think one loo is a small price to pay for being in such a remarkable old house (rebuilt from nought in the '50s!). It was an important site in the Hundred Years War. The rickety wooden bridge across the moat is a good introduction, followed by the affable old nanny goat by the door. Madame has a touch of charming eccentricity and is an excellent hostess. The service is elegant: silver teapot, fruit juice in crystal glasses at breakfast, tea in the afternoon — and the rooms are perfect.

Rooms: 2 double, 1 twin, each with bath or shower; sharing wc.

Price: 400 Frs (€ 60.98) for two, including breakfast.

Meals: 130 Frs, including wine & coffee.

Open: March to December.

From Breteuil, D141 dir. Rugles; through forest. At Bémécourt, take left turn; 300m after the traffic lights, right into Allée du Vieux Château.

MMap 231-34 **ASP Map No: 3**

Mme Maryvonne LALLEMAND-LEGRAS
Le Vieux Château
27160 Bémécourt
Eure
Tel: (0)2 32 29 90 47

Delightful people and a fascinating house. An ancestor fled to Scotland in 1789 and returned an Adam fan, hence the *trompe l'œil* marble and Wedgwood-moulded staircase. A civilised, friendly couple welcome you: she organises chamber music in their big, log-fired drawing room; he makes top-class Camembert and mows his acres on Sundays. The elegant bedrooms have antiques, books, ancestral portraits, much soft comfort and a loo in a tower. The dining room has wrap-around oak panelling inlaid with precious woods — eat here with the family and belong briefly to this wonderful world. Good walks start 2km away.

Rooms: 1 twin, 2 double, each with bath & wc.

Price: 500-600 Frs (€ 76.22-91.47) for two, including breakfast.

Meals: 250 Frs, including wine & coffee.

Open: All year (by arrangement Dec to March).

From Verneuil sur Avre, N12 SW 24km to Carrefour Ste Anne. Left on D918 dir. Longny au Perche for 4.5km; left on D289 dir. Moulicent. House 800m on right.

MMap 231-45 **ASP Map No: 3**

Jacques & Pascale de LONGCAMP
La Grande Noë
61290 Moulicent
Orne
Tel: (0)2 33 73 63 30
Fax: (0)2 33 83 62 92
e-mail: grandenoe@wanadoo.fr
www.sawdays.co.uk

Utter peace among the cattle-dotted Norman pastures — one woman, her horses, dogs and cats in a low-lying farmhouse, beautifully rebuilt "from a pile of stones", where old and new mix easily and flowers rampage all around. Barbara calls it her "corner of paradise" and her delight is contagious. The lovely sloping garden is all her own work too — she appears to have endless energy. The pastel guestrooms, two upstairs, one with garden access on the ground floor, are attractive and have brand new bathrooms. Come by horse, or walk. Beautiful country and a sociable, interesting, horse-loving woman to welcome you.

Rooms: 2 twin, 1 double, each with bath or shower & wc.

Price: 250 Frs (€ 38.11) for two, including breakfast.

Meals: 100 Frs, including wine & coffee.

Open: All year.

From Courtomer, past Mairie then right after last building towards Tellières. 2km from turning, left at crossroads towards Le Marnis.

MMap 231-44 **ASP Map No: 3**

Barbara GOFF
Le Marnis
Tellières le Plessis
61390 Courtomer, Orne
Tel: (0)2 33 27 47 55
Fax: (0)2 33 27 29 55
e-mail: barbaragoff@minitel.net
www.sawdays.co.uk

Inside is as angular as outside: the staircase is a monumental piece of carpentry elbowing its way up to the 2nd floor where a panoramic window lets in the whole sky. Grandmother's toy camel stands here in its 1905 skin: the house was built by her parents in 1910 to an open, American-style plan and sliding glass partitions give generous ground-floor spaces. Guestrooms are good too, much-windowed, with soft colours, marble fireplaces and old mirrors. All spotless, it is the pride and joy of your alert, eager hostess who talks and laughs readily and manages four children and guests expertly.

Rooms: 1 twin with bath & wc, 1 suite for 4 with shower & wc.

Price: 310 Frs (€ 47.26) for two, including breakfast.

Meals: 145 Frs, including aperitif, wine & coffee.

Open: March to November.

From Argentan N26 E for 37km. Entrance 4km after Planches on right by small crucifix — long lime-bordered drive.

MMap 231-44 **ASP Map No: 3**

Antoine & Nathalie LE BRETHON
La Bussière
61370 Ste Gauburge-Ste Colombe
Orne
Tel: (0)2 33 34 05 23
Fax: (0)2 33 34 71 47

They somehow keep going with the farm, although they long for a younger farmer to take over. Any takers? We are delighted to have the Bourgaults in the book for there is something quintessentially *chambre d'hôte* about them and their house. It is unaffected, authentic, low-ceilinged and comfortable. The rooms have a very personal mix of old and new furniture... another traditional B&B touch. Madame bubbles with energy, loves children and gives you the sort of welcome that makes you glow.

Rooms: 1 double, 1 triple, all with bath or shower & wc (overflow room available).

Price: 250 Frs (€ 38.11) for two, including breakfast.

Meals: Choice within 3km.

Open: All year.

From Rouen, N138 dir. Alençon, through Bernay to Monnai. There, right onto D12; after 2km, follow signs to Chambres d'Hôtes.

MMap 231-32 **ASP Map No: 3**

Gérard & Emilienne BOURGAULT
Les Roches
61470 Le Sap
Orne
Tel: (0)2 33 39 47 39
www.sawdays.co.uk

These are caring, generous, sensitive farmers who like contact and share their quiet sense of humour with each other, their guests and their children. Rooms, called *Spring*, *Summer*, *Autumn* and... *Cashmere*, have cane or brass bedsteads, plain country décor and fresh flowers. Madame spoils you at breakfast and dinner with local honey and Camembert, her own poultry and rabbit from the field across the stream. Her home-made jam repertoire includes dandelion-flower and apple. Meals are normally taken with the family — most convivial despite limited English. The sitting room, playroom and kitchen facilities are a bonus.

Rooms: 2 double, 1 triple, 1 quadruple, each with shower & wc.

Price: 230 Frs (€ 35.06) for two, including breakfast.

Meals: 90 Frs, including wine & coffee.

Open: All year.

From Argentan, N26 dir. L'Aigle and Paris. Left at Silli en Gouffern. At Ste Eugénie, last farm on left.

MMap 231-31 **ASP Map No: 3**

Pierre & Ghislaine MAURICE
La Grande Ferme
Ste Eugénie
61160 Aubry en Exmes
Orne
Tel: (0)2 33 36 82 36
Fax: (0)2 33 36 99 52

You buy into fun, a real unfussy family atmosphere and a most successful mix of things English and French in this converted manor-farm with its pigeon-tower and duck stream. Your hosts have sheep, dairy cows, 300 apple trees (*Normandie oblige!*) and are thoroughly integrated, as are their two young daughters. Their guestrooms in the old camembert-making dairy are light, soberly furnished with touches of *fantaisie* and Diana's very decorative stencils. Breakfast is superb, dinner should be an occasion to linger over and remember.

Rooms: 1 triple, 1 double, 1 twin, each with bath or shower & wc. Extra beds available.

Price: 300 Frs (€ 45.73) for two, including breakfast (one-night stay +30 Frs).

Meals: 130 Frs, including wine, coffee and home-baked bread.

Open: March to November.

From Vimoutiers, D916 dir. Argentan. Just outside Vimoutiers take left fork D16 signed Exmes then D26 signed Survie & Exmes.

MMap 231-43 **ASP Map No: 3**

Diana & Christopher WORDSWORTH
Les Gains, Survie
61310 Exmes
Orne
Tel: (0)2 33 36 05 56
Fax: (0)2 33 35 03 65
www.sawdays.co.uk

In a deeply rural spot where peace is the norm not the exception, you are unhesitatingly received into a warm and lively family and it feels GOOD. Two rooms are in a converted outbuilding and have an appropriately rustic air — the upstairs room is bigger and lighter, the ground-floor room has a little private garden; both have beams, old wardrobes and mini-kitchens. The suite, ideal for families, is in the main house. Meals are taken at the family table, there are fresh flowers everywhere and your hosts have a genuine sense of country hospitality. Children are welcome to visit their son's farm next door.

Rooms: 2 double, each with shower, wc & mini-kitchen; 1 suite for 4 with bath & wc.

Price: 220 Frs (€ 33.54) for two, including breakfast. Extra bed 50 Frs.

Meals: By arrangement 80 Frs, including cider & coffee. Self-catering in 2 rooms.

Open: All year.

Gîte space for 6 people

From Argentan N158 dir. Caen. After sign for Moulin sur Orne, take next left. House 800m on left; signposted. (3.5km from Argentan.)

MMap 231-31 **ASP Map No: 3**

Janine & Rémy LAIGNEL
Le Mesnil
61200 Occagnes
Orne
Tel: (0)2 33 67 11 12

Real gourmet, organic, vegetarian food is served and vegans are catered for here — rare in the depths of rural France. "We aren't vegetarians but might well convert with this sort of fare," said one reader. The Butlers, now thoroughly integrated, are most knowledgeable about local lore and full of enthusiasm for their project. In the 'guest house', you find sitting and reading rooms (books galore), crawling space for toddlers, bedrooms of character; there's a big garden and medieval Ticheville is within walking distance. Bayeux and Camembert are driveable.

Rooms: 4 double, all with shower & wc.

Price: 300 Frs (€ 45.73) for two, including breakfast.

Meals: 105 Frs excellent vegetarian meal; wine & coffee extra.

Open: Easter to October.

D579 from Lisieux to Vimoutiers then D979 dir. Alençon. 5km on, left on D12 towards l'Aigle. In Ticheville: house signposted on left.

MMap 231-32 **ASP Map No: 3**

Jill & Colin KIRK
La Maison du Vert
Le Bourg
61120 Ticheville, Orne
Tel: (0)2 33 36 95 84
Fax: (0)2 33 39 37 78
e-mail: colin.kirk@wanadoo.fr
http://perso.wanadoo.fr/lamaisonduvert

You would never guess the size of 62 Rue Grande from the outside: from a small façade it stretches deep into the garden where Dorothea and Claude, a charming and elegant couple, have worked wonders with rose, wisteria and myriad colourful plants. The two quiet suites are in the old stables; the former coachman's room, now a lovely guestroom, is up an extraordinary wooden spiral staircase which climbs to huge windows overlooking the light and lusciously rich garden. This polyglot home reflects its owners' polytravels as well as their passion for gardening — and they choose to illustrate their house with... their garden.

Rooms: Apartment for 2/4, 1 double, both with shower and wc .

Price: 280-300 Frs (€ 42.69-45.73) for two, including breakfast. Extra person 70 Frs.

Meals: Choice in Orbec.

Open: All year.

Orbec is 19km S of Lisieux on D519. Turn into village — house is on main street next to 'L'Orbecquoise' restaurant.

MMap 231-32 **ASP Map No: 3**

Dorothea VAILLÈRE
62 rue Grande
14290 Orbec
Calvados
Tel: (0)2 31 32 77 99
Fax: (0)2 31 32 77 99

A measured arrival up the drive to the main house, across the mosaic-floored hallway and up heavy wooden stairs to richly decorated, south-facing rooms. The Masliahs left Paris to renovate this imposing C18 chateau and have accomplished the task with panache. Every rug, curtain, curio and even tap was carefully chosen. Though the rooms are formal, your hosts are not. They happily rise to prepare the odd early breakfast but do try their special brunch after a lie-in. There is a little guest sitting room or you can soak up the sun in your bedroom.

Rooms: 2 triple, 1 twin, each with bath & wc.

Price: 370 Frs (€ 56.41) for two, including breakfast.

Meals: Restaurant 6km.

Open: All year.

Gîte space for 8 people

From Caen, N13 to Lisieux; D519 to Orbec; D4 dir. Livarot for 6km. Right dir. St Martin de Bienfaite; first house on right after 1km.

MMap 231-32 **ASP Map No: 3**

Chantal & Didier MASLIAH
Château de la Lande
Cerqueux
14290 Orbec
Calvados
Tel: (0)2 31 32 00 50
Fax: (0)2 31 32 00 50

The date is precisely 1462; Annick thinks the building (not all of an age) belonged to the Abbey of Saint Pierre. The old beams are particularly impressive. It is a lovely, green place, in three acres of orchards overlooking the valley of the Auge. The garden is yours and there is fishing for coloured carp in the pond. Good rooms, a charming hostess and lots to do nearby. She often has to be out after lunch, by the way, so prefers you to arrive in the late afternoon if possible.

Rooms: 1 double with shower & wc; 2 triple, 1 family room, all with bath or shower, sharing 3 separate wcs.

Price: 270 Frs (€ 41.16) for two, including breakfast.

Meals: Choice nearby.

Open: All year.

Gîte space for 10 people

From Lisieux D511 dir. St Pierre sur Dives. Just before St Pierre D40 left dir. Livarot. After 1.5km, right to Berville; signposted.

MMap 231-31 **ASP Map No: 3**

Annick DUHAMEL
Le Pressoir
Berville
14170 St Pierre sur Dives
Calvados
Tel: (0)2 31 20 51 26
Fax: (0)2 31 20 03 03
www.sawdays.co.uk

It may look like a film set but it is genuine early 17th century. Inside, there is an equally astounding dining room, added on by one Monsieur Swann and resplendently carved, panelled and painted. Two big rooms — *Jaune* and *Verte* — catch the morning sun but *Saumon* is even better with its heavenly sunset prospect; all are incredible value. Madame, a beautiful lady, made all the curtains and covers. She and her diplomat husband are well-travelled, polyglot, cultured — they help make a stay here as special as any in France.

Rooms: 2 double, 1 twin, each with bath or shower & wc (1 downstairs).

Price: 300 Frs (€ 45.73) for two, including breakfast. Extra bed 70 Frs.

Meals: Restaurant 1km away.

Open: All year.

Gîte space for 6 people

From Caen N13 E dir. Lisieux for 25km. At Carrefour St Jean, D50 (virtually straight on) dir. Cambremer. 5km from junction, house signposted on right.

MMap 231-31 **ASP Map No: 3**

Christine & Arnauld GHERRAK
Manoir de Cantepie
Le Cadran
14340 Cambremer
Calvados
Tel: (0)2 31 62 87 27

This Franco-American couple are brilliant hosts and we love their place — the bucolic setting by the little river, the fine old square house beneath the church, the refined and subtle decoration of the rooms, the books, pictures and antiques and, above all, the alive, lived-in, loving atmosphere. Breakfast is a candlelit feast that can last some time. The biggest room is superb with its own fireplace for intimate evenings; another has mahogany furniture; the deliciously cosy, red attic room has beams and dormers, all have superb river views, and all guests may wallow in the great antique copper bath.

Rooms: 1 double, 2 triple, all with bath or shower & wc. Extra bathroom for all with antique copper bath!

Price: 300 Frs (€ 45.73) for two, including breakfast.

Meals: Restaurants 2-7 km. Picnic possible.

Open: Mid-March to mid-November.

Gîte space for 6 people

From A13 exit 29b on N175 to Troarn. There, right after church on D95 to Bures 2km. Go into village: house is just after church wall (sign).

MMap 231-30 **ASP Map No: 3**

Marie-Catherine LANDON &
Michael CASSADY
Manoir des Tourpes,Chemin de l'Église
14670 Bures sur Dives, Calvados
Tel: (0)2 31 23 63 47
Fax: (0)2 31 23 86 10
e-mail: mcassady@mail.cpod.fr
www.cpod.com/monoweb/mantourpes

A handsome square-set château where you can taste the "world's best cider" (dixit Monsieur), admire yourself in innumerable gilt-framed mirrors, luxuriate in a jacuzzi or bare your chest to a hydromassage shower, play the piano, watch pop-up telly, appreciate Monsieur's very dry sense of humour and Madame's superb cooking, and at last lie down in an antique, new-mattressed bed in one of the enormous bedrooms. The period ceilings, tapestries and furniture make this a real château experience; the people make it very human.

Rooms: 2 double, 2 suites, all with bath or shower & wc.

Price: 550 Frs (€ 83.85) for two, including breakfast.

Meals: 240 Frs, including aperitif, cider or wine, coffee, calvados.

Open: All year.

From Caen, N158 dir. Falaise. At La Jalousie, right on D23; right on D235 just before Bretteville sur Laize; signposted.

MMap 231-30 **ASP Map No: 2**

Anne-Marie & Alain CANTEL
Château des Riffets
14680 Bretteville sur Laize
Calvados
Tel: (0)2 31 23 53 21
Fax: (0)2 31 23 75 14

In their restored C18 farmhouse surrounded by two open fields, the Vanhouttes positively welcome an exchange of ideas and cultures. Don't miss the chance to enjoy their company at dinner as well: the food is delicious, with most produce straight from the farm. You are just as cosily cossetted in your room, where the indefatigable Annick, a linen-maker, has made the curtains, padded bedheads, table cloths and even the cross-stitch pictures. Talk to her about how linen is made — she has samples for sale — and to him about cattle or crops: theirs is real country knowledge.

Rooms: 1 double, 1 triple, each with shower & wc; 1 overflow room.

Price: 230 Frs (€ 35.06) for two, including breakfast. Extra bed 50 Frs.

Meals: 85 Frs, including wine & coffee.

Open: All year.

From St Pierre sur Dives D511 dir. Falaise and follow signs to Château de Vendeuvre. In front of château, cross bridge and follow signs to farm.

MMap 231-31 **ASP Map No: 3**

Jean & Annick VANHOUTTE
Ferme du Bois de Tilly
14170 Vendeuvre
Calvados
Tel: (0)2 31 40 91 87
Fax: (0)2 31 90 58 13

Monsieur's family have owned this pretty house for 100 years, he was born here and married a local girl. They are a sweet couple, quietly and unobtrusively attentive, and you will feel well cared for. The large garden is clearly much loved and has a flowery bower with a stone table. Inside you will find some superb pieces of family furniture — country French at its best — as well as crinkly pink lights and little bits of *brocante.* Falaise was Duke William's home until he left his native Normandy to conquer other shores but this typical Falaise house is quite young, only dating from the 1600s, in a dear, quiet little Norman village.

Rooms: 1 suite for 4, 1 double/triple, both with shower & wc.

Price: 220 Frs (€ 33.54) for two, including breakfast.

Meals: Falaise 3km. Barbecue & picnic possible.

Open: All year.

From Falaise D63 dir. Trun for 3km. 2nd left onto D69 for 1km. At junction, cross over, go round bend — farm signposted on left.

MMap 231-30 **ASP Map No: 3**

Alice & Gilbert THOMAS
Ferme la Croix
14700 Villy lez Falaise
Calvados
Tel: (0)2 31 90 19 98

Here is pure, down-to-earth Norman hospitality so what matter that the house lacks years? They are close to all things natural, plough their big veg patch with the cob in harness, will drive you through the secret byways of the area in a pony-drawn trap while telling local legends, take you on night-time discovery walks, share dinners made with organic produce to old forgotten regional recipes, offer good rooms where you wake to stunning views over the hushed hills of *La Suisse Normande*. Nothing gushy or corny, these are independent, strong, comforting people who genuinely care for your well-being and that of the land.

Rooms: 2 double, 1 twin, 1 suite, each with own shower & wc.

Price: 220 Frs (€ 33.54) for two, including breakfast.

Meals: 80 Frs, including aperitif, cider & coffee (not Sundays).

Open: All year.

From Caen, D562 dir. Flers. About 35km on at Le Fresne, D1 dir. Falaise. After 4km, house on right; signposted.

MMap 231-30 **ASP Map No: 2**

Roland & Claudine LEBATARD
Arclais
14690 Pont d'Ouilly
Calvados
Tel: (0)2 31 69 81 65
Fax: (0)2 31 69 81 65

The setting is gorgeously flowered, the walks peaceful (itineraries provided) and the farm feathered, including geese for *foie gras* (Madame knows how and does it all herself) and spit-roasting in winter. You are warmly greeted by your youngish hosts, the atmosphere is relaxed and if the big bedrooms are unremarkable, they are clean, with their own entrance, kitchen and sitting room. But you will come above all for Madame's talented cooking and genuine hospitality. Children welcome: there are cots, games and bikes for them.

Rooms: 2 triple (1 on ground floor), each with shower & wc.

Price: 205 Frs (€ 31.25) for two, including breakfast.

Meals: By arrangement 80 Frs, including aperitif, cider & coffee.

Open: March to November.

Gîte space for 7 people

From Caen dir. Cherbourg then A84 dir. Avranches; exit St Martin des Besaces on D53 then left onto D165 dir. Brémoy; house is on right, 4km from St Martin.

MMap 231-28 **ASP Map No: 2**

Jacqueline & Gilbert LALLEMAN
Carrefour des Fosses
14260 Brémoy
Calvados
Tel: (0)2 31 77 83 22
e-mail: Jg-lalleman@yahoo.fr

With a few sheep in the background, this is a typical old farmhouse, even down to the corrugated iron roof. The guest wing is in the converted stables where the kitchen/diner has its original stone flags and the manger. The rooms are country-comfortable, nicely decorated, functional and spotless; one has a balcony onto the farm and the apple orchard (and road at the bottom) where all sorts of games await your pleasure — as does Mireille the donkey. Your elderly hostess is friendly and glad of your company.

Rooms: 1 double, 1 triple, each with shower & wc.

Price: 240 Frs (€ 36.59) for two, including breakfast.

Meals: In Vire 2km. Self-catering.

Open: All year.

From Vire centre, D524 dir. Tinchebray & Flers; house on right after 2km — signposted.

MMap 231-28 **ASP Map No: 2**

Mme Marcelle MARIE
La Gage
14500 Roullours
Calvados
Tel: (0)2 31 68 17 40

There is a fun-loving, relaxed atmosphere about this place: you could scarcely find easier, friendlier hosts than Joseph and Marie-Thé. There are animals and milking for children, table football and volley-ball for teenagers, *pétanque* for all. Your hosts, who have quantities of local lore and advice to communicate, will join you for a farm supper at the long table in the log-fired (winter), fresh-flowered, guests' dayroom. They are simple and genuine; so are their rooms (one has an ancient dresser set into the stone wall) and their welcome. This is superb value and far enough from the road not to suffer from much traffic noise.

Rooms: 5 rooms/suites for 3 or 4, each with own bath or shower & wc, 1 with kitchen.

Price: 200 Frs (€ 30.49) for two, including breakfast. Extra person 30 Frs.

Meals: 80 Frs, including wine & coffee.

Open: All year.

From A84/E401 Caen-Rennes motorway exit 42 onto N175 dir. Cahagnes for 2km then right following Chambres d'Hôtes signs to farm.

MMap 231-28 **ASP Map No: 2**

Joseph & Marie-Thé GUILBERT
Le Mesnil de Benneville
14240 Cahagnes
Calvados
Tel: (0)2 31 77 58 05
Fax: (0)2 31 77 37 84

Well off the busy road, down its own drive, this old stone house, built in 1714, is now a dairy farm. The *salon* is very French and just the place for a quiet read. There are other fine period rooms. The big bedrooms, looking out over the large pond, are light and sunny with country furniture (one has a four-poster) and not crammed in next to each other. The family is charming, hospitable and helpful but not intrusive. Special extras are comfortable garden chairs, that pond for fishing, a horse for riding, paths for walking, home-made yoghurt and cider. Some stay a week.

Rooms: 2 double & 1 suite, all with shower & wc.

Price: 255 Frs (€ 38.87) for two, including breakfast.

Meals: 120 Frs, including wine & coffee.

Open: All year.

From Caen, A13 dir. Cherbourg then exit for Carpiquet and Caumont. 500m before Caumont, left at Chambres d'Hôtes sign into private drive.

MMap 231-28 **ASP Map No: 2**

Alain & Françoise PETITON
La Suhardière
14240 Livry
Calvados
Tel: (0)2 31 77 51 02

The new English owners here have built a tennis court, turned the old pool into a pretty lily pond and made a new one in a more discreet spot, installed a sauna, redone bathrooms with soft beige tiles and wooden accessories, put up fresh calico curtains... and it is still a fascinating old inn (parts are C12) with medieval beams, old flagstones and a couple of fine fireplaces. The attic/mezzanine suite for four or five, our favourite room, is an exciting space under the rafters. The Bamfords are relaxed, easy hosts, providing masses of activities in this quiet village where the only sounds are the odd car and regular church chimes.

Rooms: 1 quadruple, 2 double, 1 suite for 4/5, 1 triple in annexe, each with bath or shower & wc.

Price: 350 Frs (€ 53.36) for two, including breakfast; extra bed 60 Frs.

Meals: 120 Frs, including wine & coffee.

Open: All year.

Gîte space for 7 people

From Bayeux, D6 to Juvigny then D9 to Caumont l'Eventé. Opposite Caumont church, D28 dir. Balleroy. After 200m, Gîtes de France sign on right.

MMap 231-28 **ASP Map No: 2**

Elizabeth & Andrew BAMFORD
Le Relais
19 rue Thiers
14240 Caumont l'Eventé, Calvados
Tel: (0)2 31 77 47 85
Fax: (0)2 31 77 59 27
e-mail: lerelais19@aol.com
www.sawdays.co.uk

Through the wood and across the stream to the simplest, friendliest house you could imagine. It is about a century old while the Ameys have that timeless quality of solid country dwellers and will wrap you in blue-eyed smiles. Their welcome is all unstylish comfort and warmth. Most furnishings are 'rustic', bar two superb Norman *armoires*, the walls are pastel, the curtains lace, the bathroom pink, the towels small. Breakfast comes with incomparably good farm milk and butter; dinners are reliably Norman; the wisteria blooms. Excellent value.

Rooms: 3 double, each with handbasin, sharing bathroom & separate wc.

Price: 190 Frs (€ 28.97) for two, including breakfast.

Meals: 85 Frs, including cider & coffee.

Open: All year.

Gîte space for 10 people

From Caen A84 dir. Mt St Michel, exit 46 'Noyers Bocage'. Right on D83 dir. Cheux for 1.5km then left to Tessel; signposted.

MMap 231-29 **ASP Map No: 2**

Paul & Éliane AMEY
La Londe
14250 Tessel
Calvados
Tel: (0)2 31 80 81 12
Fax: (0)2 31 80 81 12
www.sawdays.co.uk

A converted mill (no-one knows how old it is) with a delightful bridge and terrace. The guest quarters are in the separate 'Hunting Lodge' where Madame's talented decoration marries things past and designer-colourful present and you have your own dining room and kitchen. There are nuts to be gathered in the woods, beaches nearby, the stream for entertainment on the spot. Your hosts are sweet and love having families. "My kids spent hours by the shallow stream — not dangerous if they're supervised", said a reader.

Rooms: 1 double with shower & wc, 1 double & 1 twin sharing shower & wc.

Price: 290 Frs (€ 44.21) for two, including breakfast.

Meals: Restaurants 2-3km. Self-catering.

Open: All year.

Gîte space for 6 people

From Ouistreham D35 through Douvres & Tailleville. Cross D404. At roundabout entering Reviers, turn right. House on left (NOT first Chambres d'Hôtes).

MMap 231-17 **ASP Map No: 2**

Patricia & Jean-Michel BLANLOT
La Malposte
15 rue des Moulins
14470 Reviers
Calvados
Tel: (0)2 31 37 51 29
Fax: (0)2 31 37 51 29

Through the great arched gate is a lovely old house, its C17 golden stones now proudly on view, its courtyard housing several tribes of animal and a games room; a cider-apple orchard; a fascinating military historian who takes battlefield tours — arrange yours with him — and loves sharing his passion for the dramas that took place here; a gentle lady who serves her own jams plus fresh breads and croissants for breakfast; stone stairs to big, comfortably casual guestrooms; and above all a genuine family-friendly welcome just 15 minutes walk from the Cathedral.

Rooms: 2 double, 2 triple, each with shower & wc; 2 'dormitories' for 4 and 5 sharing 2 showers & wcs.

Price: 250 Frs (€ 38.11) for two, dormitory bed 100 Frs each, including breakfast.

Meals: Full choice Bayeux 1km.

Open: All year.

Gîte space for 4 people/6

On Bayeux by-pass, at Campanile Hotel take D572 dir. St Lô. Take 2nd right and follow signs to arched gateway.

MMap 231-17 **ASP Map No: 2**

Lt-Col & Mrs CHILCOTT
Manoir du Doyen (ex Pont Rouge)
Saint Loup Hors
14400 Bayeux, Calvados
Tel: (0)2 31 22 39 09
Fax: (0)2 31 21 97 84
e-mail: chilcott@mail.cpod.fr
www.VRBO.com/VRBO/352.htm

How old can a house be? This one is C11, renovated in 1801... The brass-railed staircase and the drawing room are gracious but not grand. The dining room, with its huge fireplace and modern bar, is relaxed in its yellow and green garb; breakfast crockery is yellow and green, too. Colour is important to Madame and she uses it well, mixing bright with soft, just as she mixes antiques with artificial flowers. These genuinely warm folk take you naturally into their family circle. The comfortable bedrooms look onto wide fields, the new smaller attic room is perfect and the 'Norman' dinners have been praised to the skies by our readers.

Rooms: 1 double, 2 quadruple, all with shower or bath & wc.

Price: 250 Frs (€ 38.11) for two, including breakfast. Extra bed 60 Frs.

Meals: 100 Frs, including wine & coffee.

Open: All year.

From Bayeux N13 dir. Cherbourg; through Tour en Bessin then left on D100 dir. Crouay for about 1km. House on right with cartwheel.

MMap 231-16 **ASP Map No: 2**

Catherine & Bertrand GIRARD
Le Relais de la Vignette
Route de Crouay, Tour en Bessin
14400 Bayeux
Calvados
Tel: (0)2 31 21 52 83/
(0)6 80 45 69 95
Fax: (0)2 31 21 52 83

You may sleep like angels; this was a monks' dormitory in the 15th century. The Abbey is right there, floodlit at night, and the whole setting is exquisitely peaceful. The house is beguiling with its stone staircase, exposed beams, old columns and big fireplace. Monsieur, a recently retired breeder of cattle and horses, is quietly contemplative while Madame, a lively grandmother, is bright and attentive — a most pleasant pair of hosts though they don't dine with guests. It is a no-frills, and thoroughly good, place.

Rooms: 1 twin, 2 suites for 3, each with shower or bath & wc.

Price: 240 Frs (€ 36.59) for two, including breakfast.

Meals: 90 Frs, including wine & coffee.

Open: All year.

Gîte space for 11 people

From Bayeux, N13 W for 14km; D30 dir. Trévières; 2nd right, 1st right, right again on D29 dir. St Lô for 1km; right on D124 to Écrammeville, and follow signs (farm near church).

MMap 231-16 **ASP Map No: 2**

Louis & Annick FAUVEL
Ferme de l'Abbaye
14710 Écrammeville
Calvados
Tel: (0)2 31 22 52 32
Fax: (0)2 31 22 47 25
www.sawdays.co.uk

History throbs in every corner of this old farmhouse, which has been in Madame's family for three generations — parts of the building date back to the 11th century when it belonged to *Richard Cœur de Lion*. Rooms are hardly regal now but are perfectly adequate and have small showers. It is at table that the farm comes into its own. The cooking and conviviality are pure *Normandie*. Monsieur sometimes plays the harmonica after dinner, there is song and free-flowing *pommeau*. In the morning you may still hear singing as the cows are milked.

Rooms: 3 double, 1 triple, 1 family for 4, each with shower & wc.

Price: 200 Frs (€ 30.49) for two, including breakfast.

Meals: 80 Frs, including own cider.

Open: All year.

From Bayeux D5 to Molay Littry then continue on to Tournières. At entrance to village, left (next to 'Boucherie') at their sign.

MMap 231-16 **ASP Map No: 2**

Solange & Pierre ISIDOR
Ferme de Marcelet
14330 Tournières
Calvados
Tel: (0)2 31 22 90 86

Madame's son bakes the most delicious bread in the C18 oven he has restored. He also produces cakes and *patisseries* of all sorts for afternoon tea. Madame is a quiet, kindly woman and has created an easy family atmosphere. Ask for *La Chambre Ancienne*, definitely the best, with its low ceiling, antique beds and planked floor; the others lack character, though they are big and have that country feel. If you have a spare moment, do take a boat ride in the bird-full *Marais* — they'll organise it for you. There is a small camping site on the farm.

Rooms: 2 twin,1 triple, all with shower & wc. Extra beds available.

Price: 230 Frs (€ 35.06) for two, including breakfast; extra bed 50 Frs.

Meals: Ferme-auberge 3km.

Open: All year.

From Bayeux D5 W through Le Molay Littry dir. Bernesq and Briqueville. Right about 0.75km before Bernesq; Le Ruppaley on this road, signposted.

MMap 231-16 **ASP Map No: 2**

Marcelle MARIE
Le Ruppaley
14710 Bernesq
Calvados
Tel: (0)2 31 22 54 44
www.sawdays.co.uk

Go to great lengths to stay here; the solid beauty of the old fortified farmhouse, its simplicity, and the serenity of the *Marais* lapping at the edge of the lawn all make it near-perfect. Your hosts, too, are amiable and generous, happy to wait up for you if you arrive late; the rooms are comfortably simple. This is a WWF *Gîte Panda*, a place to learn all about local flora and fauna — nature guides distributed, binoculars on loan. Stretch your eyes across a luminous landscape of marshes and fields, eat well, enjoy the cider, and sleep in bliss.

Rooms: 1 double, 1 twin, 1 suite for 4, all with bath or shower & wc.

Price: 260 Frs (€ 39.64) for two, including breakfast.

Meals: 90 Frs, including cider & coffee.

Open: Easter to October.

From Bayeux, N13 to La Cambe, then D113 south. After 1km, D124 dir. St Germain du Pert (1.5km).

MMap 231-16 **ASP Map No: 2**

Paulette & Hervé MARIE
Ferme de la Rivière
14230 St Germain du Pert
Calvados
Tel: (0)2 31 22 72 92
Fax: (0)2 31 22 01 63
www.sawdays.co.uk

The dining room is the centrepiece: panelling, old tiles, windows facing both ways, sun pouring in. You eat at separate tables where the views are across the moat, over the formal garden with its swings and profusion of plants, and down to the orangery. Some of the parquet floors are magnificent, as is the whole house, which is littered with wood-carvings and furniture made by Monsieur's father. The bedrooms are, of course, splendid. The US Press Corps camped here in 1944 — sensibly. *Pets by arrangement.*

Rooms: 5 double, all with bath or shower & wc.

Price: 320-380 Frs (€ 48.78-57.93) for two, including breakfast.

Meals: Choice 6-10km.

Open: March to December.

From Cherbourg, N13 to Isigny. There, right on D5 dir. Le Molay. Left near Vouilly church. Château on right after 500m.

MMap 231-15 **ASP Map No: 2**

Marie-José & James HAMEL
Château de Vouilly
Vouilly
14230 Isigny sur Mer
Calvados
Tel: (0)2 31 22 08 59
Fax: (0)2 31 22 90 58

This ancient fortress of a farm has a stupendous tithe barn and a little watch tower transformed into a delightful gîte for two. Madame's energy is boundless, she is ever redecorating, cooking (excellent Norman cuisine), improving, much supported by her farmer husband. She is proud of her family home, its flagstones worn smooth with age and its fine country antiques so suited to the sober, high-ceilinged rooms (one has a shower in a tower, another looks over the calving field). Breakfast by the massive fireplace may be candle or oil-lamp lit on dark mornings and is *à volonté.*

Rooms: 2 triple, 1 double, each with shower & wc.

Price: 280 Frs (€ 42.69) for two, including breakfast.

Meals: 100 Frs, excluding wine.

Open: All year.

Gîte space for 6 people

From Bayeux N13 for 30km; exit on D514 to Osmanville and on dir. Grandchamp for 5km. Left dir. Géfosse Fontenay; house 800m along on left before church.

MMap 231-15 **ASP Map No: 2**

Gérard & Isabelle LEHARIVEL
Ferme de la Rivière
14230 Géfosse Fontenay
Calvados
Tel: (0)2 31 22 64 45

Inside the stately 16th-century manor, up a twisty stone staircase, along a creaky corridor, is one of the finest B&B suites we know: a half tester, carved fireplaces, a boudoir, rugs, prints and antiques, a claw-footed bath, windows onto lush gardens with ancient trees. The panelled dining room fills with light, the tiled, be-rugged guest sitting room is grand yet welcoming, your hosts are lively, cultured and fun: Belgian Yves still partly runs his family business and English Lynne can offer wonderful aromatherapy sessions.

Rooms: 1 apartment (D + TW + child's bed) with bath & wc.

Price: 520 Frs (€ 79.27) for two, including breakfast; extra bed 250 Frs.

Meals: Good restaurant 3km.

Open: Mid-March to Oct (by arrangement in winter).

From Carentan D903 dir. La Haye du Puits. At Baupte (5km) right on D69 to Appeville. At Appeville continue D69 dir. Houtteville, take second lane on right — house on left.

MMap 231-15 **ASP Map No: 2**

Yves LEJOUR & Lynne WOOSTER
Le Manoir d'Ozeville
Appeville
50500 Carentan
Manche
Tel: (0)2 33 71 55 98
Fax: (0)2 33 42 17 79
e-mail: ozeville@aol.com

"A real corker" enthused the inspector. "They are a delight. He has a fine dry wit and loves to chat, about everything — but especially politics. She, too, holds her own and anyone with a smattering of French would enjoy them enormously." They are farmers, and proud of it. The old manor has huge character and a small private chapel; we found the shabbiness and the haphazard décor most endearing. There is even some Art Deco furniture. Wonderful value in a natural and unsophisticated manner.

Rooms: 1 triple with bath & wc; 1 triple, 1 double sharing shower & wc.

Price: 190-210 Frs (€ 28.97-32.01) for two, including breakfast.

Meals: Small good-value restaurants locally.

Open: All year.

From Cherbourg, N13 south; leave at Ste Mère l'Eglise exit. Go into Ste Mère l'Eglise & follow signs for Pont l'Abbé; house signposted on right after 3km.

MMap 231-15 **ASP Map No: 2**

Albert & Michèle BLANCHET
La Fière
Route de Pont l'Abbé
50480 Ste Mère l'Eglise
Manche
Tel: (0)2 33 41 32 66

A delightful couple live in this thoroughly ramshackle, unspoiled, even dilapidated château with their two small boys and all the guests who come to share the hugely relaxed, some might say over-casual, atmosphere, the big garden, the variegated rooms and basic bathing spaces. The cavernous Mussolini Room has the balcony with views across the heart-shaped lawn. The Colonial Room has pith-helmets and mementoes, while the Hat Room... A very special place — not for the stuffy, though the winter chill is now warded off by brand new central heating — and they do energetic themed weekends.

Rooms: 2 double & 1 twin, each with bath & wc (1 screened off); 1 quadruple, 1 triple sharing a bathroom.

Price: 240-280 Frs (€ 36.59-42.69) for two, including breakfast (children half price).

Meals: Choice locally.

Open: All year except Jan, Feb & Aug.

Gîte space for 15 people

From Cherbourg, N13 dir. Valognes. After 8 miles, right on D119 dir. Ruffosses. Cross motorway bridge; follow blue & white signs.

MMap 231-14 **ASP Map No: 2**

Mark & Fiona BERRIDGE
Château Mont Épinguet
50700 Brix
Manche
Tel: (0)2 33 41 96 31
Fax: (0)2 33 41 98 77

Words are inadequate... Incredibly, your beautiful, energetic hostess is a grandmother! A farmer's wife! He now breeds race horses, she indulges her passion for interior decoration — her spotless rooms are a festival of colours, textures, antiques, embroidered linen. You cannot fail to enjoy staying in this wonderful old building — they love having guests. The great granite fireplace is always lit for the delicious breakfast which includes local specialities. There is a richly-carved 'throne' at the head of the long table. A stupendous place, very special people.

Rooms: 2 double with shower & wc; 1 twin with bath & wc; (+ 1 overflow room for children).

Price: 300-350 Frs (€ 45.73-53.36) for two, including breakfast.

Meals: Choice in Barfleur 3km.

Open: All year.

Gîte space for 5 people

From Barfleur dir. Quettehous then branch right on D25 dir. Valcanville. Take 2nd right and follow signs.

MMap 231-3 **ASP Map No: 2**

Marie-France & Maurice CAILLET
La Fèvrerie
50760 Ste Geneviève
Manche
Tel: (0)2 33 54 33 53
www.sawdays.co.uk

Great swaying pines, a wild coast and the sea have guarded this site for over 800 years (the English burnt the first castle in 1346). Lush lawns, myriad flowers and white geese soften Nature's wildness. The manor's stern stone façade hides a warm, gentle, elegant welcome in rooms with superb fireplaces, good beds, big windows to let in the light and truly personal decoration: pictures, books (breakfast is taken in the library) and antiques. Madame will enthral you with tales from Norman history and provide detailed maps for hikers.

Rooms: 1 suite for 3, 1 double, each with shower & wc.

Price: 300 Frs (€ 45.73) for two, including breakfast.

Meals: Auberge within walking distance.

Open: All year.

Gîte space for 6 people

From Cherbourg, D901 to Barfleur. There, D1 dir. St Vaast. After signpost marking the end of Barfleur, 2nd right and 1st left.

MMap 231-3 **ASP Map No: 2**

Mme Claudette GABROY
Le Manoir
50760 Montfarville
Manche
Tel: (0)2 33 23 14 21

In quiet country, just 6km from the ferries (the separate room with its own outside entrance is ideal for early ferry-catchers), this old stone manor stands proudly on the Normandy Coast hiking path looking across the town and out to sea. It is spotless, not over-modernised, and furnished in very French style with lots of velvet, floral linen and marble-topped chests. Retired from farming, the sociable Guérards enjoy welcoming both their own family and guests whom they happily point towards the cliff walks and other sights worth the detour.

Rooms: Main house: 1 double, 1 twin, each with bath & wc; outside stairs to triple room with shower & wc.

Price: 220-250 Frs (€ 33.54-38.11) for two, including breakfast.

Meals: Cherbourg 3km.

Open: All year.

Gîte space for 7 people

From Cherbourg, D901 to Tourlaville & dir. St Pierre Église. Right at lights dir. Château des Ravalet/Hameau St Jean; up hill to 'Centre Aéré', then follow Chambres d'Hôtes signs (3km from lights).

MMap 231-2 **ASP Map No: 2**

Mme GUÉRARD
Manoir Saint Jean
50110 Tourlaville
Manche
Tel: (0)2 33 22 00 86
www.sawdays.co.uk

Old-fashioned hospitality is the keyword here. You are just a mile from the (often) glittering sea and Michel, who makes submarines, is happy to share his passion for sailing and take you coast-hopping or out in the open sea. The shipbuilder's skill is evident in this modern house with its modern floors: the attic space has been cleverly used to make two snug rooms with showers and kitchenettes. The décor is simple, the rooms spotless and Éliane is an easy, relaxed hostess who will rise early for dawn ferry catchers. It is brilliantly quiet and ideal for beach and ferry alike.

Rooms: 2 double, each with shower & wc.

Price: 220-230 Frs (€ 33.54-35.06) for two, including breakfast.

Meals: 2 restaurants 2km.

Open: All year.

From Cherbourg take D901 then D45 W along coast 13km to Urville Nacqueville; 1st left by Hôtel Le Beau Rivage; up hill on D22 for 2km then 2nd left; signposted.

MMap 231-1 **ASP Map No: 2**

Michel & Éliane THOMAS
Eudal de Bas
50460 Urville Nacqueville
Manche
Tel: (0)2 33 03 58 16
Fax: (0)2 33 03 58 16

This splendid group of buildings is a spectacular historical ensemble where hefty medieval walls shelter an elegant C18 manor from the wild sea (you can hear it one mile away). Hosts and furnishings are irreproachably French and civilisation is the keynote — books, fine china, panelling, gilt mirrors, plush chairs, engravings. Your suite has ancient floor tiles, brand new bedding, a loo in a tower. Stay a while, do your own breakfast in exchange for using the very grand dining room and get to know your literary *châtelaine.*

Rooms: 2 double, each with shower & wc.

Price: 480 Frs (€ 73.18) for two, including breakfast. Terms for children.

Meals: Good choice 2-15km.

Open: All year.

Gîte space for 8 people

From Cherbourg, D904 dir. Coutances. 3km after Les Pieux, right on D62 dir. Le Rozel, then right on D117 into village; house is just after you leave village — signposted.

MMap 231-13 **ASP Map No: 2**

Josiane & Jean-Claude GRANDCHAMP
Le Château
50340 Le Rozel
Manche
Tel: (0)2 33 52 95 08
www.sawdays.co.uk

Full of laughter and talk, covered in sincere smiles, your hosts hope to give you "the best of France, the best of England": an old Norman house with Laura Ashley fabrics, antiques from both countries, a collection of English china inside, wild French hares, kestrels and owls outside (there's a spyhole for observation). Two rooms are smallish, the attic room larger, all have good bathrooms and oodles of fluffy towels. Linda varies the daily menu, down to napkin colours and china; Ted, an expert on the Second World War, will take you round the landing beaches. Both are passionate about their house and region, and their delight is catching.

Rooms: 2 double, each with bath & wc, 1 twin with shower & wc.

Price: 300-350 Frs (€ 45.73-53.36) for two, including breakfast.

Meals: 100 Frs, including wine.

Open: All year.

From Cherbourg S dir. Caen/Rennes then D900 to Bricquebec (via Le Pont); cont. dir. Valognes, past Intermarché, left at T junction, 1st left after 'Sapeurs Pompiers' dir. Les Grosmonts — 300m on right.

MMap 231-14 **ASP Map No: 2**

Ted & Linda MALINDINE
La Lande
Les Grosmonts
50260 Bricquebec
Manche
Tel: (0)2 33 52 24 78
Fax: (0)2 33 52 24 78

In attractive farmland and well placed for the attractions of Valognes, this secluded village house is run by a sweetly and peacefully hospitable elderly couple. They are very informative on local history and sights and their house, with its open fireplace, is typically French country style. The rooms, not big but comfortable, have new bedding and wallpaper and nice old family furnishings; we definitely preferred the attic room, even if the loo is down a flight of stairs. There is a kitchen specially for guests.

Rooms: 1 double with shower & wc; 1 double with shower, wc on floor below.

Price: 180 Frs (€ 27.44) for two, including breakfast.

Meals: Self-catering.

Open: All year.

From Cherbourg, N13 to Valognes (slow down: signs hard to see entering Valognes); D902 dir. Bricquebec. After 2km left on D87 to Yvetot Bocage. At the church, go towards Morville and take first left.

MMap 231-14 **ASP Map No: 2**

Léon & Lucienne DUBOST
Le Haut Billy
Route de Morville
50700 Yvetot Bocage, Valognes
Manche
Tel: (0)2 33 40 06 74
www.sawdays.co.uk

Madame is as Norman as this house, where she was born: solidly earthed and used to welcoming strangers with kindness and a strong country accent. She shares her time between family, guests and dairy cows and is extremely proud of her breakfasts. They are indeed very generous, include fresh farm eggs and are served in the wonderful family dining room amid photographs, copper pans and old beams. Less characterful, the bedrooms have country furniture, old-style wallpapers and... more photographs. A super person and remarkable value B&B.

Rooms: 2 triple, each with bath or shower & wc (1 curtained off).

Price: 200 Frs (€ 30.49) for two, including breakfast.

Meals: Restaurants 3km.

Open: All year.

From Cherbourg, N13 past Valognes then right on D2 to St Sauveur le Vicomte. There, D15 dir. Port Bail. Farm is on right after about 1km before Château d'Ollonde.

MMap 231-13 **ASP Map No: 2**

Bernadette VASSELIN
La Roque de Bas
Canville la Roque
50580 Port Bail
Manche
Tel: (0)2 33 04 80 27

In their long, converted Norman farmhouse, Richard and Jay practise perfect hospitality and serve a superb breakfast. Our readers bear witness: "Blissful, a paradise for the children who played in all safety with goats, ducks and rabbits while their parents sipped their white wine (kept in the Clays' fridge) in peace". They say they feel like personal guests and often become firm friends. The rooms are big and beautifully furnished, the peace complete (even 7am church bells are in keeping), the value hard to beat.

Rooms: 2 double, 1 with bath/shower & wc, 1 with shower & wc.

Price: 200 Frs (€ 30.49) for two, including breakfast.

Meals: Restaurants 5km.

Open: All year.

Gîte space for 12 people

From La Haye du Puits, D903 dir. Barneville Carteret. At Bolleville, right on D127 to St Nicolas de Pierrepont; left before church; house on right after cemetery.

MMap 231-14 **ASP Map No: 2**

Richard & Jay CLAY
La Ferme de l'Eglise
50250 St Nicolas de Pierrepont
Manche
Tel: (0)2 33 45 53 40
Fax: (0)2 33 45 53 40
e-mail: theclays@wanadoo.fr
www.sawdays.co.uk

When asked why she chose to open her farmhouse (rebuilt in 1856) to guests, the bright-eyed Madame Lepoittevin's simple reply is disarming: *"C'est la convivialité"*. You cannot fail to be won over by the warmth and friendliness of both the house and your hostess as you chat with her over a leisurely breakfast and sleep soundly in a spotless bedroom where magazines, knick-knacks, carpets and heavy old wardrobes are utterly *famille*. Though dinner is not offered, you can picnic in the garden or cook your own on the barbecue.

Rooms: 2 double, each with shower & wc.

Price: 205 Frs (€ 31.25) for two, including breakfast. Extra bed 50 Frs.

Meals: Choice 4-10km.

Open: All year.

From St Lô D972 dir. Coutances, through St Gilles; house signposted on left, 4km after St Gilles, on D972.

MMap 231-27 **ASP Map No: 2**

Jean & Micheline LEPOITTEVIN
Saint Léger
50750 Quibou
Manche
Tel: (0)2 33 57 18 41
Fax: (0)2 33 55 00 01

The Osmonds are such spontaneously welcoming, down-to-earth country folk, greeting guests with big smiles, stories and much useful local information, that people come back year after year. Madame, a delightful, humorous woman, plays the organ in the village church. Bedrooms have old family furniture (admire *grand-mère's* elaborately crocheted bedcover), really good mattresses, simple washing arrangements. It is all spotless and there is a roomy dayroom with lots of plants, and a kitchen in the old cider press.

Rooms: 1 double with shower & wc; 1 twin, 1 triple, each with shower, sharing 2 wcs.

Price: 205 Frs (€ 31.25) for two, including breakfast.

Meals: Restaurant 1km; choice St Lô 4km; self-catering.

Open: All year.

From St Lô D999 dir. Villedieu for 3km; right on D38 dir. Canisy. House 1km along on right.

MMap 231-27 **ASP Map No: 2**

Marie-Thérèse & Roger OSMOND
La Rhétorerie
Route de Canisy
50750 St Ebremond de Bonfossé
Manche
Tel: (0)2 33 56 62 98

Miles from anywhere, apparently, but pilgrims once rested in this C12 farmhouse on their journey to and from the shrine at Santiago de Compostela. Today's new pilgrims can rest their weary bones at L'Orgerie during their travels in France. Four dogs greet you as you sip your *pommeau* aperitif with delightful hosts and dinner is then taken in the towering dining room with its gallery and huge fireplace. The house has a truly ancient feel but the guestrooms are snug and few will mind the loo being down the corridor. Amazing value.

Rooms: 1 double, 1 twin (family suite), sharing shower & separate wc.

Price: 180 Frs (€ 27.44) for two, including breakfast.

Meals: 70 Frs, including wine & coffee.

Open: All year.

From Caen N175 SW dir. Villedieu/Rennes. At Pont Farcy left on D52 dir. Vire for 3km — house signposted on right (DON'T turn to St Vigor).

MMap 231-27 **ASP Map No: 2**

Jacques & Jacqueline GOUDE
L'Orgerie
50420 St Vigor des Monts
Manche
Tel: (0)2 31 68 85 58

These are solid, earthy, farming folk and Madame, who is a bit shy, has a lovely sunny smile. They are planning to breed rare animals such as Norman rabbit and Rouen duck and always encourage guests to visit Sourdeval on Tuesdays to see the cattle market in full swing. The rooms are unpretentiously simple with candlewick bedcovers, old floor tiles, wooden wardrobes and views across the valley. The family room has two beds on a mezzanine. Guests breakfast at one long table and are welcome to watch the milking. Really good value.

Rooms: Main house: 1 triple, 1 double sharing shower & separate wc. Cottage: family room for 5, shower & wc.

Price: 185 Frs (€ 28.20) for two, including breakfast. Extra person 70 Frs.

Meals: Choice 5km.

Open: All year.

Gîte space for 2 people

From Sourdeval D977 dir. Vire for 6km. Just before 'end of Manche' sign right dir. Le Val. House 2km along on right.

MMap 231-40 **ASP Map No: 2**

Jeanne & Raymond DESDOITS
Le Val
Vengeons
50150 Sourdeval
Manche
Tel: (0)2 33 59 64 16

From the new conservatory, enjoy wraparound views across the abundantly flowered garden — it's Madame's pride and joy and she'll tell you all about gardening and medicinal plants -, spy on the squirrels in the lime tree and indulge in a sinfully laden breakfast table (dare try the *Kousmine*: a muesli-type concoction to keep you energised all day). Three rooms are in a converted outbuilding, two in the enchanting main house. Beds are brass or carved wood; there are lace and pink and granny-style touches, in keeping with an old farmhouse, plus some fine antiques.

Rooms: 1 twin, 3 double, 1 triple, all with shower & wc, 1 with kitchenette.

Price: 230-260 Frs (€ 35.06-39.64) for two, including breakfast.

Meals: In village, 1.5km.

Open: All year except a week each in Jan & Sept.

Gîte space for 2 people

30Frs

From Percy D58 dir. Hambye then immediately left on D98 dir. Sourdeval for 1.5km. House signposted on right.

MMap 231-27 **ASP Map No: 2**

Daniel & Maryclaude DUCHEMIN
Le Cottage de la Voisinière
Route de Sourdeval D98
50410 Percy, Manche
Tel: (0)2 33 61 18 47/
(0)6 85 81 81 75
Fax: (0)2 33 61 43 47
www.sawdays.co.uk

Monsieur breeds horses and there is riding available, but only for very experienced riders. The less horsey can enjoy an interesting visit to stables which have produced some great racers (including *La Belle Tière*). The place is a gem, though the guestrooms are up a steep wooden staircase, and Madame cooks all the food, including her own bread and *croissants*. Meals are served in the beamed dining/breakfast room. The setting is charming, among hills, woods and fields; this would be a delightful place for a winter visit, too.

Rooms: 1 double, 1 twin, each with shower & wc; 1 twin for children.

Price: 200 Frs (€ 30.49) for two, including breakfast.

Meals: 100 Frs, including wine & coffee. Cold meal 60 Frs (summer).

Open: All year.

Gîte space for 3 people

Leave Coutances on D971 S dir. Granville and fork quickly left on D7 dir. Gavray for 1.5km; then left on D27 to Nicorps. Through village and first right — house on left, signposted.

MMap 231-26 **ASP Map No: 2**

M & Mme POSLOUX
Les Hauts Champs
La Moinerie de Haut
50200 Nicorps
Manche
Tel: (0)2 33 45 30 56
Fax: (0)2 33 07 60 21

Remarkable value, even for Normandy, and such likeable hosts. This is a small dairy farm with a large, plain guestroom looking out over the old cider press and the fields: cider has been made here for two centuries — make sure you try it. Breakfast will be straightforward French, with the added bonus of milk fresh from the cows and Madame's home-made jam. The sea is within walking distance (2km), pretty Granville with its fish restaurants is just 5km away or you can easily nip across to the Channel Islands.

Rooms: 1 room for up to 4 people, with shower & wc.

Price: 190 Frs (€ 28.97) for two, including breakfast.

Meals: Choice in Granville.

Open: All year.

Gîte space for 9 people

From Granville, D973 dir. Avranches. After about 3km, left at Gîtes de France & 'Déchetterie' sign, left after 200m; house on left.

MMap 231-26 **ASP Map No: 2**

Jean-Claude & Liliane LAISNÉ
Mallouet
50400 Granville
Manche
Tel: (0)2 33 50 26 41

From this hillside perch above the village, all guests can stand, some can even lie, and look across the bay to the mystical outline of Mont St Michel, then *walk* there along the coastal path. The bedrooms are airy and light — try the *Eisenhower* (yes, he did), or the balconied *Tulipes* with its super Art Deco furniture. The original tap-making owner left some magnificent basins and fittings. The Leroys farm (organically, some miles away), keep a lovely garden, allow guests to buy their produce and use their kitchen, organise concerts in the garden, visits to Mt St Michel... Breakfast is a help-yourself buffet feast.

Rooms: 3 double, 2 twin, each with bath or shower & wc. 2 overflow rooms.

Price: 320-530 Frs (€ 48.78-80.80) for two, including breakfast.

Meals: 75-250 Frs, including aperitif, cider or wine & coffee (bookings only low season). Self-catering high season.

Open: All year.

Gîte space for 15 people

From Cherbourg, N13 to Valognes; D2 to Coutances; D971 to Granville; D911 (along coast) to Jullouville and on to Carolles and St Jean le Thomas (6.5km from Jullouville).

MMap 231-26 **ASP Map No: 2**

André & Suzanne LEROY
Les Hauts
7 avenue de la Libération
50530 St Jean le Thomas, Manche
Tel: (0)2 33 60 10 02
Fax: (0)2 33 60 15 40
e-mail: leshauts@club-internet.fr
www.chateau-les-hauts.com

Madame is easy-going, independent and has a fine sense of humour. Thoroughly French, she has lived in Paris, the rural south-west and now Normandy with her four wonderfully-mannered children, her Dutch partner and their peaceful Labrador. A delightful family, lush grounds, rolling views that carry your eye for miles and a welcoming old original-tiled and floor-boarded château decorated with strong colours, friends' paintings, antiques and a certain pleasing austerity. Home-made cake with breakfast, refined regional dinners (vegetarian if asked for early) which may include home-grown strawberries and herbs.

Rooms: 2 double, each with bath & wc, 1 single with shower & wc.

Price: 350-430 Frs (€ 53.36-65.55) for two, including breakfast.

Meals: 80 Frs, excluding wine (50-100 Frs bottle).

Open: All year except Christmas & New Year.

From Villedieu les Poêles N175 /D524 dir. Vire for 1.5km; right on D999 dir. Brecey. After Chérencé le Héron left to St Martin Bouillant, through village to sawmill & follow signs to Loges sur Brecey. House 2km along, 1st right after wood.

MMap 231-27 **ASP Map No: 2**

Nathalie de DROUAS
Château des Boulais
Loges sur Brecey
50800 St Martin le Bouillant
Manche
Tel: (0)2 33 60 32 20
Fax: (0)2 33 60 45 20

Madame is the sweetest old lady, not too reserved, not gushing, just smiling and eager to please. Hers is a typical, C19 village house. Pleasant, country-style bedrooms have floral wallpapers and mats on polished wood floors. There's an inviting, armchaired reading corner on the landing plus a big dayroom with a fireplace. Breakfast is served here at the long 10-seater table. There are (free) tennis courts, a swimming pool and restaurants close at hand, and the proximity to Mont Saint Michel is a natural advantage. (When calling to book, better to have a French speaker to hand.)

Rooms: 1 double, 1 triple, sharing bath & wc; 1 twin with shower & wc.

Price: 190 Frs (€ 28.97) for two, including breakfast.

Meals: Gourmet auberge next door.

Open: All year.

From Avranches, N175 dir. Pontorson. 3km after Precey, right to Servon.

MMap 231-38 **ASP Map No: 2**

Mme LESÉNÉCHAL
Le Bourg
50170 Servon
Manche
Tel: (0)2 33 48 92 13

Ask for the room facing Mont St Michel — it's the nicest... and that view! You can walk there in two hours; or they have bikes for you. In the enclosed courtyard there are passion-fruit and fig trees. The Gédouins have cows and pigs; Annick makes delicious jams; Jean is Mayor — the council meets in his kitchen. Rooms are clean and compact, if short on storage space. There is a warm and kindly welcome, though, and the once-thin walls have now been properly soundproofed. Honey for breakfast, the sea only 500 yards away.

Rooms: 2 double, each with shower & wc.

Price: 220 Frs (€ 33.54) for two, including breakfast; extra bed 50 Frs.

Meals: 80 Frs, including cider & coffee. Excellent auberge in village.

Open: All year.

From Mt St Michel, D275 dir. Pontaubault. At Montitier, D107 to Servon. There, take D113 left. House on left; signposted.

MMap 231-38 **ASP Map No: 2**

Annick, Jean & Valérie GÉDOUIN
Le Petit Manoir
21 rue de la Pierre du Tertre
50170 Servon
Manche
Tel: (0)2 33 60 03 44
Fax: (0)2 33 60 17 79

Although the C18 château has been renovated and modernised virtually beyond recognition, the farm buildings are genuine. Set back from the (still audible) main road, the house 'lives' on the other side: there, you discover the original pediment, facing splendid views of hills and woods. Bedrooms, freshly decorated in pink/dark green or blue/white, are simply furnished with brass or wooden beds and mirrored *armoires*. Breakfast is taken at the long family dining table and Madame is eager to help you plan your day. The Botanical Gardens in Avranches are superb.

Rooms: 1 double, with shower & wc; 3 double, each with shower, sharing wc.

Price: 200-220 Frs (€ 30.49-33.54) for two, including breakfast.

Meals: Locally 1.5km or Avranches 3km.

Open: All year.

From Avranches, D973 dir. Granville, across Pont Gilbert; 300m after shopping precinct, take 1st drive on left.

MMap 231-38 **ASP Map No: 2**

Eugène & Huguette TURGOT
Le Château
Marcey les Grèves
50300 Avranches
Manche
Tel: (0)2 33 58 08 65

This place is as real, unpretentious and comfortable as ever. Definitely a working farm with 800 pigs and a high-tech milking shed that attracts interest from far and wide; you can watch too. Masses of flowers sweeten the air. The young owners enjoy contact with visitors and Madame pays special attention to breakfast — her apple tart is delicious. Then you can walk directly out into the lovely countryside to see the little chapel or the local château. The guestrooms, one in the house, the other with its own entrance, are simple and good.

Rooms: 2 double with own shower and wc.

Price: 180 Frs (€ 27.44) for two, including breakfast; extra person 50 Frs.

Meals: Good choice 5km.

Open: All year.

Gîte space for 14 people

From Pontorson N175 to Aucey la Plaine, then follow signs to Chambres d'Hôtes La Provostière for 3km. Farm is between Pontorson & Vessey.

MMap 231-38 **ASP Map No: 2**

Maryvonne & René FEUVRIER
La Provostière
50170 Aucey la Plaine
Manche
Tel: (0)2 33 60 33 67
Fax: (0)2 33 60 37 00

Only one dog remains but this is still one of the most natural of 'family' houses, very *sympa* and the family still descends at weekends. They are an interesting couple, travel a lot and talk well. Jean-Paul is an arbitrator and Brigitte is on the council. Meals (they are delicious) are taken in the lovely dining room with its huge fireplace. A splendid staircase leads you up to the good guestrooms. The setting of the house is glorious with a lake and a château next door. There are games galore, and it is still a working farm.

Rooms: 2 double, 2 family rooms, all with bath or shower & wc. Extra beds and cot available.

Price: 220 Frs (€ 33.54) for two, including breakfast.

Meals: 85 Frs, including wine & coffee.

Open: All year.

From Cherbourg A84, exit 34 dir. Mt St Michel for 600m then exit dir. Mt St Michel and onto D43 dir. Rennes. At roundabout, D40 dir. Rennes for 5.5km, then D308 left; signposted.

MMap 231-38 **ASP Map No: 2**

Jean-Paul & Brigitte GAVARD
La Ferme de l'Etang
Boucéel, Vergoncey
50240 St James
Manche
Tel: (0)2 33 48 34 68
Fax: (0)2 33 48 48 53
www.sawdays.co.uk

It is all clean and comfortable, in solid farmhouse style. The old stable block, entirely modernised for B&B in the 1970s, has stripped wooden floors and easy furnishings, cots in the attic rooms and a kitchenette, all making it ideal for family stopovers. The Balcony Room is in a league of its own with exposed timbers, country antiques and... even a (glassed-in) balcony. Madame is very quiet, "makes a superb soufflé" and mouthwatering Norman cuisine. The poetically-named but perfectly ordinary Two Estuaries motorway now provides quick access 1km away.

Rooms: 1 triple, 1 double, 1 twin, 1 room for 4, all with bath or shower & wc.

Price: 220-240 Frs (€ 33.54-36.59) for two, including breakfast.

Meals: 83 Frs, including wine & coffee.

Open: All year.

Gîte space for 6 people

From A84 exit 32 at St James then onto D12, following signs for 'Super U' store for 900m dir. Antrain. House is on right.

MMap 231-38 **ASP Map No: 2**

François & Catherine TIFFAINE
La Gautrais
50240 St James
Manche
Tel: (0)2 33 48 31 86
Fax: (0)2 33 48 58 17
www.sawdays.co.uk

Previous occupants have left their mark. Decorative style, one might admit, is not 'of the essence' here. But authenticity is. We seek it out, and it is rare to find it in such honest profusion. Rooms are frill-free. Facilities are close enough to be described as thoroughly en suite, the pipes are engagingly open. The eating arrangements are primitive; you all dine together at a long, low 'table'. Our own research suggests that warmth was originally only available from other occupants. But some indefinable quality will draw you here... curiosity, perhaps?

Rooms: Two family rooms with low dividing wall.

Price: 300 Frs (€ 54.73) per family (12 max.), including breakfast; single occupancy by arrangement.

Meals: 40 Frs full organic trough; 15 Frs vegetarian snacks, truffles by arrangement.

Open: Every day except market days.

From A84 exit St Aubin; turn south, keep nose to slurry signs 3km to St Jean. There, left after 'Charcuterie': inn 200m along on right; pork in yard.

M & Mme Travers de Porque
L'Auberge du Sanglier
Chemin du Groin
50005 St Jean Pied de Porc
Manche
Tel: (0)2 22 33 44 55

The sea! The rocks! Fear not fisherfolk –
if the lighthouse cannot save you from
wrecking on the reefs, the carved calvaries will
send up prayers for your souls ashore.

Brittany

Madame wanted us to mention her passion for embroidery; there is much of it about, together with Laura Ashley fabrics, flounces, friezes and fantasy... and she is enthusing about her new *salon-showroom* where you can sit and read on an antique chair then buy it as you leave, or the table, or... They are a delightful couple but you will perhaps see less of them now they have installed a guest dining room in the converted barn. So, not always very *familiale* but thoroughly caring. Count on Beethoven, *crêpes* and an indoor garden for breakfast. It is in a tiny hamlet.

Rooms: 1 large suite for 5, 1 triple, both with shower & wc. 'Studio' also available.

Price: 300-350 Frs (€ 45.73-53.36) for two, including breakfast. Lovers' night 780 Frs.

Meals: 100 Frs, excluding wine.

Open: All year.

Gîte space for 8 people

From Rennes, S on new road to Janzé (D163/D41). Here, right on D92 for La Couyère for approx. 6km. House is on right in La Tremblais: yellow gate; signposted. Park behind.

MMap 230-41 **ASP Map No: 2**

Claudine & Raymond GOMIS
La Raimonderie
La Tremblais
35320 La Couyère
Ille-et-Vilaine
Tel: (0)2 99 43 14 39
Fax: (0)2 99 43 14 39
www.pageszoom.com/gomis

People come back to Quengo for its atmosphere, its history and the utter silence, not because it's cosy or squeaky clean. Madame, a straightforward, friendly *Bretonne*, used to run the 9,000 egg-laying hens here. The fascinating château has a private chapel, a monumental oak staircase, marble fireplaces, 1900s wallpaper and about 30 rooms in all — too many corners for housework to reach every day; underfoot is a mosaic floor by Italian craftsmen, overhead are hand-painted beams by a C19 artist from Rennes who 'did' for all the local gentry. The bathroom has a claw-footed bath, bedrooms are old-fashioned too. Amazing.

Rooms: 2 double, 1 triple, all with basin & bidet, sharing bathroom & 2 separate wcs.

Price: 200-220 Frs (€ 30.49-33.54) for two, including breakfast; extra bed 60 Frs.

Meals: Choice 4-6km.

Open: April to mid-October.

From N24 (Rennes-Lorient) exit at Bédée on D72 to Irodouer. Arriving in Irodouer, 1st right before church — château entrance 600m along on left.

MMap 230-25 **ASP Map No: 2**

Mme de LORGERIE
Château du Quengo
35850 Irodouer
Ille-et-Vilaine
Tel: (0)2 99 39 81 47

The lovely C18 townhouse on the church square has a delicious little 'French' garden — low walls, box hedges, a giant camellia, masses of flowers and a herb patch. Inside, there are hand-decorated beams, antiques from 25 years of dealing and from Madame's family (her grandmother lived here), plus an ocean-themed loo. A sumptuous breakfast is supplied by your lovely, leisurely hostess, she's all covered in smiles with a soft young voice. She has Breton, Creuzois, Basque and Flemish origins and spent her childhood 'commuting' between Morocco and Brittany. This makes for a powerfully interesting old lady!

Rooms: 1 double, 1 suite, each with bath & wc.

Price: 300 Frs (€ 45.73) for two, 450 Frs suite for 4, including breakfast.

Meals: In town.

Open: All year.

From Rennes N24 W for 27km to Plélan le Grand. House on church square: granite façade & ivy hedge.

MMap 230-39 **ASP Map No: 2**

Mme Hubert de FLORIS
La Tréberdière
Place de l'Église
35380 Plélan le Grand
Ille-et-Vilaine
Tel: (0)2 99 06 83 05

Just the place to visit Merlin's forest — everyone knows he was a Breton, not a Cornish, wizard and did his sorcery right here in Brocéliande... From one bedroom you can see the forest only 500m away, from another, which has a little C18 marble fireplace (it still works), you look out over fields. Big, bright, interesting decoration throughout thanks to Madame's good taste and new ideas in handling her lovely old house: mainly 1760s, the big manor house actually has some C15 bits. She serves breakfast as late as you want with real squeezed orange juice and is a most unusual, interesting companion.

Rooms: 2 double, 1 suite for 4, each with bath or shower & wc.

Price: 300 Frs (€ 45.73) for two, including breakfast.

Meals: Choice 1-5km.

Open: All year.

From Rennes N24 for 27km. Right into Plélan le Grand; right at church on D59 dir St Malon sur Mel; 1st left: Chemin des Châteaux for 1km. House on top of small hill, entrance behind on left.

MMap 230-38 **ASP Map No: 2**

Mme HERMENIER
La Ruisselère
35380 Paimpont
Ille-et-Vilaine
Tel: (0)2 99 06 85 94

All that a French townhouse should be: elegant, refined, light yet solidly comfortable, inside and out. The owners, he a photographer, she a watercolourist, have applied all their talent and taste to renovating it. The guest suite, above Madame's studio in a separate little house, is fresh and romantic with home-sewn furnishings in restful colours (admire the curtains cleverly made from antique linen sheets). You may dine with your gentle, artistic hosts in their delicious white dining/sitting room and even take a painting course.

Rooms: Duplex for 4 with shower & wc.

Price: 260 Frs (€ 39.64) for two, 400 Frs for 4, including breakfast.

Meals: 80 Frs, including wine.

Open: all year.

From Rennes N12 W for 36km exit St Méen le Grand. In town centre, back to 'Mairie', take Ave Foch between Crédit Agricole & Pharmacie. No 39 on left.

MMap 230-24 **ASP Map No: 2**

Catherine & Luc RUAN
Le Clos Constantin
39 avenue Foch
35290 St Méen le Grand
Ille-et-Vilaine
Tel: (0)2 99 09 53 09
www.sawdays.co.uk

This, the oldest house (1490s) in beautiful old Bécherel, right on the splendid Place du Vieux Marché, is as elegant inside as out with long country views at the back. Monique has talent and refined taste (see her renovation and décor), speaks perfect English, loves people, books, calligraphy and gardens and does garden and architecture tours. The guestrooms are across the patio. *Juliette* has space, a huge stone fireplace, beams, cool blue and warm ochre tones; *Joséphine* is prettily pink, checked and striped with pine furniture and garden view; both have super bathrooms. Monique is a good cook and is exceptionally attentive.

Rooms: 1 double, 1 double/triple, each with bath or shower & wc.

Price: 300-380 Frs (€ 45.73-57.93) for two, including breakfast; extra bed 100 Frs.

Meals: 120 Frs, including wine & coffee. Picnic basket 85 Frs.

Open: All year.

From St Malo N137 S dir. Rennes for 43km. At Tinténiac exit, right on D20 to Bécherel. House in town centre, on main square near church.

MMap 230-25 **ASP Map No: 2**

Monique LECOURTOIS-CANET
Le Logis de la Filanderie
3 rue de la Filanderie
35190 Bécherel
Ille-et-Vilaine
Tel: (0)2 99 66 73 17
Fax: (0)2 99 66 79 07
e-mail: filanderie@aol.com

It is as idyllic, as bucolic as it looks; the beauty of the setting takes you by surprise and the little guesthouse is a dream. In what used to be the bakery, it is just a yard or two from the lake, where you can fish or observe all sorts of water-dwelling folk, far enough from the main house to feel secluded, snugly romantic and utterly seductive. If your need for intimacy is deep then Catherine will deliver breakfast and dinner (course by course) to your hideaway. But nicer still to join them at table; they are young and delightful and we have received nothing but praise for them.

Rooms: 1 twin/quadruple in cottage with *salon*, shower & wc.

Price: 250 Frs (€ 38.11) for two, including breakfast.

Meals: 80 Frs, including wine & coffee.

Open: All year.

Gîte space for 4 people

From St Malo, N137 into St Pierre de Plesguen. On church square take D10 dir. Lanhelin for 1.5km, then follow signs on right to 'Le Pont Ricoul Chambre d'Hôte'

MMap 230-25 **ASP Map No: 2**

Catherine & François GROSSET
Le Pont Ricoul
35720 St Pierre de Plesguen
Ille-et-Vilaine
Tel: (0)2 99 73 92 65
Fax: (0)2 99 73 94 17
e-mail: pontricoul@aol.com

Between St Malo and Mont St Michel, with the sea just 3km away, this is a dairy farm with a neatly-converted stone house. The comfortable rooms include two with mezzanines; the others are smaller. Marie-Madeleine is all care and attention: in winter she is up before breakfast to lay the fire in the huge hearth where you can toast bread; in summer, the garden and orchard beckon. Jean, gentle and bright-eyed, says that, although he's tied to the farm, he "travels through his guests". They both know and love their region and walks in detail.

Rooms: 5 rooms for 2-4 people, all with shower or bath & wc.

Price: 250 Frs (€ 38.11) for two, including breakfast. Extra bed 80 Frs.

Meals: Choice in Dol de Bretagne.

Open: All year.

From St Malo N137 S dir. Rennes for 15km; exit on N176 dir. Mt St Michel for 12km. At Dol de Bretagne, D80 dir. St Broladre for 3km; left on D85 dir. Cherrueix; house (signed) on right before 3rd little bridge.

MMap 230-12 **ASP Map No: 2**

Jean & Marie-Madeleine GLÉMOT
La Hamelinais
35120 Cherrueix
Ille-et-Vilaine
Tel: (0)2 99 48 95 26
Fax: (0)2 99 48 89 23
www.sawdays.co.uk

The atmosphere of quiet simplicity of both house and owner are like the calm of a balmy summer's morning, but you are not cut off: modernity bustles on the village street outside the front door. Isabelle's talent seems to touch the very air that fills her old family house. There is nothing superfluous: simple carved pine furniture, an antique wrought-iron cot, dhurries on scrubbed plank floors, palest yellow or mauve walls to reflect the ocean-borne light, harmonious striped or gingham curtains. Starfish and many-splendoured pebbles keep the house sea-connected. The unspoilt seaside village is worth the trip too.

Rooms: 2 double & 1 twin with bath & wc, 2 double with shower & wc (1 fully equipped for the disabled).

Price: 250-290 Frs (€ 38.11-44.21) for two, including breakfast.

Meals: Choice in village.

Open: All year.

From St Malo, N137 dir. Rennes. 6km after St Malo, right on D117 to St Suliac (3km from N137 exit to village entrance). Road leads to main street (Grande Rue) down to port — house at top on right.

MMap 230-11 **ASP Map No: 2**

Isabelle ROUVRAIS
Les Mouettes
Grande Rue
35430 St Suliac
Ille-et-Vilaine
Tel: (0)2 99 58 30 41
Fax: (0)2 99 58 39 41

Sheer delight for lovers of the utterly personal, even eccentric. In this miniature museum of a house, the infectiously vibrant Rhona will introduce you to her wiggly Chinese sofa, her husband's regimental drum, the C18 looking-glass in your room and other cherished household gods. A home like no other, a remarkable garden (climb up to the second terrace with a drink and a book), a supremely comfortable bed (with view of a fine bathroom through the glass door), a generous and elegant breakfast, a short run to the beach. Unforgettable. The second room and sitting room, to be finished mid-2000, will be just as temptingly personal.

Rooms: 1 double with bath, shower & wc. 2nd double with bath & wc, summer 2000.

Price: 300 Frs (€ 45.73) for two, including breakfast.

Meals: Wide choice within walking distance.

Open: March to October.

From Dinan central square, take Rue de Lehon, through Porte St Louis, follow road down, bear left below ramparts, straight across into Rue de Coëtquen.

MMap 230-25 **ASP Map No: 2**

Rhona LOCKWOOD
55 rue de Coëtquen
22100 Dinan
Côtes-d'Armor
Tel: (0)2 96 85 23 49
Fax: (0)2 96 87 51 44
www.sawdays.co.uk

Janine's love is her vegetarian cooking, Steve's is his sculpture that decorates the rambling, rose-filled garden. Our inspector loved it for its isolation, lack of pretension, and daring to be different. It is the sort of 'alternative' that we like: simple, attractive, comfortable-yet-humble... and interesting. Guests eat at separate tables, tasting, perhaps, the artichoke *aioli* or roasted cherry tomatoes. Use the living room and garden, browse through the books, make yourself coffee... your hosts are young and easy. Advance bookings only.

Rooms: 1 family room for 4 with shower & wc; 1 twin, 1 double, sharing bath & wc.

Price: 300-340 Frs (€ 45.73-51.83) for two, incl. breakfast (min. 2 nights).

Meals: 100 Frs for 3-course vegetarian meal incl. wine & coffee. Packed lunch 30-40 Frs.

Open: March to November.

Gîte space for 6 people

From Dinan D766 S for Caulnes approx. 13km; right on D64 to Plumaudan; left for Caulnes for approx 150m; 2nd right for Le Plessis; house on right after 2km.

MMap 230-25 **ASP Map No: 2**

Janine & Steve JUDGES
Le Plessis Vegetarian Guesthouse
Le Plessis
22350 Plumaudan
Côtes-d'Armor
Tel: (0)2 96 86 00 44
Fax: (0)2 96 86 00 44
e-mail: janine.leplessis@wanadoo.fr

These people turn the everyday into the remarkable: modern houses have a hard time getting into this book but this one sailed in. Clad in red cedar, open-plan to provide space for six children, its wood, metal and glass are in perfect harmony; only the best materials are used and every tiny detail has been taken care of: plain white covers on beds, Eastern-style cushions and wall hangings on plain walls, superb beds and towels, shower-pressure just right. Breakfast is *un peu brunch*, as carefully thought out as the house. Lovely people and an exquisite, serene house that seems to hug its garden to its heart.

Rooms: 1 suite for 2 with *salon*, 1 suite of 2 bedrooms, each with shower & wc.

Price: 310 Frs (€ 47.26) for two, including breakfast.

Meals: Within walking distance.

Open: All year.

From Dinan N176 W dir. St Brieuc for about 12km. Exit right to Plélan le Petit. Follow signs to 'Centre/Mairie'; at 'Mairie' right dir. St Maudez then 2nd right.

MMap 230-24 **ASP Map No: 2**

Martine & Hubert VIANNAY
Malik
Chemin de l'Étoupe
22980 Plélan le Petit
Côtes-d'Armor
Tel: (0)2 96 27 62 71/
(0)6 09 92 35 21

This is a place for golfers — 9-hole golf course plus all the trappings (clubhouse, lessons, socialising) — with the added charm of a farm atmosphere, a cosy house and carp ponds for those with a rod. The grand C15 Breton *longère*, has been in the Beaupère family for four generations. Madame has a flair for decorating with velvet and florals and her rooms are very comfortable. Guests are welcome to eat *en famille*: few will resist *Petits Pigeons, Lardons et Raisins* and local cheeses with a choice of good wines. The old Breton bread oven is working again for the baking of bread or even, occasionally, the roasting of sucking pig.

Rooms: 2 twin, 2 double (1 with extra bed), all with bath or shower & wc.

Price: 270 Frs (€ 41.16) for two, including breakfast.

Meals: 80 Frs, excluding wine (30-50 Frs).

Open: All year.

From Dinan, N176 dir. St Brieuc. At Plélan le Petit, take D19 (right) to St Michel de Plélan. House signposted left, 1km after village.

MMap 230-24 **ASP Map No: 2**

Odile & Henri BEAUPÈRE
La Corbinais
22980 St Michel de Plélan
Côtes-d'Armor
Tel: (0)2 96 27 64 81
Fax: (0)2 96 27 48 65
e-mail: corbinais@wanadoo.fr
www.pro.wanadoo.fr/corbinais/golf

A long low Breton house built on hard Breton granite, guarded by a soft Breton spaniel and kept by a relaxed and friendly Breton woman whose family has owned it for generations (she lives in the little house). There is old wood everywhere — ceilings, wardrobes, beams, beds; there are gingham cloths, floral curtains and lace cushions. Breakfasts and evening meals (these must be requested) are cooked on a wood-fired range and served on attractive rough pottery at separate tables in the guests' dining room.

Rooms: 3 double, 1 twin, 1 triple, 1 double + bunks, all with bath or shower & wc.

Price: 240-255 Frs (€ 36.59-38.87) for two, including breakfast (booking essential).

Meals: 90 Frs, including wine & coffee (not Sundays).

Open: All year.

Gîte space for 14 people

From Dinard, D168 to Ploubalay and D768 to Plancoët; D19 to St Lormel; left opposite school at far end of village then follow signs for 1.5km.

MMap 230-10 **ASP Map No: 2**

Évelyne LEDÉ
La Pastourelle
St Lormel
22130 Plancoët
Côtes-d'Armor
Tel: (0)2 96 84 03 77
Fax: (0)2 96 84 03 77

There's no other like it: the sea at the bottom of the drive, an extraordinary, rather crumbly old château (Monsieur's ancestor built it in 1373!), vast and wonderful guestrooms, a lively, lovable couple of aristocratic hosts, bent on riding, hunting and entertaining you. You breakfast in the upstairs *salon*, or downstairs, through the low stone arch in the room with the boar's head and other bits of personality — such fun. Madame is applying energy and good taste to renovating some of the 30 rooms. One suite is pink, another blue and yellow. Beds are canopied, windows high, portraits ancestral, rugs cotton — atmosphere unreal.

Rooms: 2 suites, 1 double, each with bath or shower & wc.

Price: 450-700 Frs (€ 68.60-106.71) for two, including breakfast. Extra bed 150 Frs.

Meals: Good choice 5km.

Open: May to September.

From St Brieuc N12 dir. Lamballe exit Yffigniac-Hillion. After Yffigniac left on D80 to Hillion; D34 dir. Morieux. 200m after Hillion, roadside crucifix on left by château gates.

MMap 230-9 **ASP Map No: 1**

Vicomte & Vicomtesse Louis du FOU de KERDANIEL
Château de Bonabry
22120 Hillion
Côtes-d'Armor
Tel: (0)2 96 32 21 06

You will have gentle piped music and Breton pancakes for breakfast in the big traditional dining room. Madame collects dolls and other items of folklore which peek out at you from nooks and corners. Great carved mirror-fronted wardrobes are standard here, beds are firm and comfortable, floors are polished wood, bathrooms are modern and the dominant colour is blue (even the radiators). You will feel well looked after in this quiet country place with genuine farming folk, nice, simple and direct. There is a kitchen annexe for self-catering and climbing frames for children in the front field.

Rooms: 2 double, 1 triple, each with bath or shower and wc.

Price: 230 Frs (€ 35.06) for two, including breakfast; extra bed 80 Frs.

Meals: Choice in Yffiniac 4km. Self-catering.

Open: All year.

Gîte space for 25 people

From N12 exit Yffiniac (NOT 'Yffiniac Gare') into village. Go 1km then left dir. Plédran, through La Croix Orin: Le Grenier is down hill on left, 3.5km from Yffiniac centre.

MMap 230-23 **ASP Map No: 1**

Marie-Reine & Fernand LOQUIN
Le Grenier
22120 [illegible]
Côtes-d'Armor
Tel: (0)2 96 72 64 55
Fax: (0)2 96 72 68 74

Looking for perfect *château* B&B? It is here, with a couple of perfect *châtelains* to receive you. Exposed to the wild Breton elements, this fortified Bishop's seat, now a vegetable farm, has superb grounds and a luxurious interior of marble fireplaces, gilt mirrors, antiques and a classically French *salon*. Guestrooms are big and richly decorated, the tower room deliciously different, more 'rustic', with its timbers and mezzanine and the new loo fitted to the original, still functioning, C14 drain! The twin-basined bathrooms are all quite lovely. Breakfast is a Breton feast to linger over in good company.

Rooms: 2 double, 1 twin, 1 triple, and 2 suites for 3-4; all with private bathrooms.

Price: 600 Frs (€ 91.47) for two, including breakfast.

Meals: Walking distance in summer; choice 10km.

Open: All year.

From Guingamp, D8 to Plougrescant. In Plougrescant, right after the church (leaning spire) and right again 200m along.

MMap 230-7 **ASP Map No: 1**

Vicomte & Vicomtesse de ROQUEFEUIL
Manoir de Kergrec'h
22820 Plougrescant
Côtes-d'Armor
Tel: (0)2 96 92 59 13
Fax: (0)2 96 92 51 27

The estate has been in the family for 600 years and their 'latest' house (C17-C19) is a masterpiece of understated elegance. Ceilings are high, windows generous, guests rejoice in a granite-hearthed, tapestry-walled sitting room where old books and family portraits remind them this is 'just an ordinary family house'. Madame, dynamic and adorable, loves her visitors. The bedrooms vary in size and character, all are fascinating, though we preferred *La Jaune* for its panelling and lovely view. Worth every centime.

Rooms: 3 double, 2 twin rooms, all with bath, shower & wc.

Price: 460-550 Frs (€ 70.13-83.85) for two, including breakfast. Extra bed 130 Frs.

Meals: Crêperie in village; excellent restaurant nearby.

Open: All year.

Gîte space for 10 people

From St Brieuc, N12 to Guingamp, then D8 dir. Tréguier. At Pommerit Jaudy turn left at the lights.

MMap 230-7 **ASP Map No: 1**

Comte & Comtesse de KERMEL
Château de Kermezen
22450 Pommerit Jaudy
Côtes-d'Armor
Tel: (0)2 96 91 35 75
Fax: (0)2 96 91 35 75
www.sawdays.co.uk

Once inside this enlarged 1930s house you will understand why it is in this book: the ever-changing light of the great bay shimmers in through the vast expanse of glass whence you can watch the boats come and go, or walk to the beach (10 minutes). Guy chose the house so he could see his small boat at anchor out there (lucky guests may be taken for a sail) and Marie-Clo has enlivened the interior with her talented patchwork and embroidery. It is calm, light, bright; they are attentive hosts and breakfast is seriously good.

Rooms: 2 double, each with sitting area, sea view, shower & wc.

Price: 300 Frs (€ 45.73) for two, including breakfast.

Meals: Lots of choice in Perros Guirec.

Open: All year.

Gîte space for 4 people

From Lannion D788 N to Perros Guirec; follow signs to 'Port' then to 'Centre ville par la corniche'; follow round bay for approx. 1km then left at sign 'Nid Vacances'. (Will fax plan or collect you from railway station.)

MMap 230-6 **ASP Map No: 1**

Marie-Clo & Guy BIARNÈS
41 rue de la Petite Corniche
BP 24
22700 Perros Guirec, Côtes-d'Armor
Tel: (0)2 96 23 28 08
Fax: (0)2 96 23 28 23
e-mail: guy.biarnes@wanadoo.fr
www.sawdays.co.uk

A fine C15 manor that exudes character and history, inside and out. There are monumental fireplaces, a worn spiral staircase, ancestral portraits (including a Marquise among oriental faces on an embroidered screen), fine furniture. The bedrooms have space, taste, arched doors and good bathrooms. Breakfast, a fine Breton spread, can be brought to your room if you wish. Madame planted the lovely garden 40 years ago and still tends it; Monsieur is gracious and well-travelled. Their welcome is elegant, their conversation intelligent, their house a delight and their son breeds racehorses on the other half of the estate.

Rooms: 2 twin, each with bath & wc.

Price: 500 Frs (€ 76.22) for two, including breakfast.

Meals: Choice 7-10 km.

Open: All year.

From N12 exit at Beg ar Chra/ Plouaret (bet. Guingamp & Morlaix) to Plouaret; D11 dir. Lannion to Kerauzern; D30 left dir. St Michel en Grève & Ploumilliau; cross railway; cont. 3km; left at signpost 100m, left again, go to end.

MMap 230-6 **ASP Map No: 1**

M & Mme Gérard de BELLEFON
Manoir de Kerguéréon
Ploubezre
22300 Lannion
Côtes-d'Armor
Tel: (0)2 96 38 91 46

Enter the enclosed courtyard and you will discover the charms of this C17 grey stone presbytery with its blue shutters and climbing roses. Walled gardens and an orchard for picnics complete the peaceful, private mood. Rooms are finely furnished, particularly the biggest which is high and stylish, the style reflected in its amazing bathroom. The cosy attic rooms have great character, low beams and small shower rooms (not for taller people). Madame knows the area 'like her pocket' and has itineraries for your deeper discovery of secret delights — plan two or three days if possible.

Rooms: 1 double and 2 twin, all with bath or shower & wc.

Price: 300 Frs (€ 45.73) for two, including breakfast; terms for longer stays (exc. July & Aug).

Meals: 150 Frs, including wine & coffee.

Open: All year.

Gîte space for 6 people

From Guingamp N12 dir. Morlaix, then Louargat exit. From Louargat church, D33 to Tregrom (7km). House in village centre, opposite church (blue door in wall).

MMap 230-6 **ASP Map No: 1**

Nicole de MORCHOVEN
Le Presbytère Tregrom
22420 Plouaret
Côtes-d'Armor
Tel: (0)2 96 47 94 15
www.sawdays.co.uk

Built in the 1840s by well-travelled writer/merchant Corbière, whose better-known poet son Tristan was a protégé of Verlaine's, *Crow's Rock Manor* has always had these big, airy, wood-floored, lofty-ceilinged, chandeliered rooms with superb views of the generous grounds. Now admirably restored by your young and sociable hosts, it is definitely a special place with its air of old-style, refined but not overstated luxury. For a modern touch, step up to your marble bath to gaze out to hills and woods on two sides. Breakfast may include *far breton* and *crêpes*, strawberries and home-made jam.

Rooms: 2 twin, each with bath & wc; 1 additional twin.

Price: 420 Frs (€ 64.03) for two, including breakfast (2 nights min. July & Aug).

Meals: Bistro 1km; choice in Morlaix 3km.

Open: All year.

From Morlaix follow right bank of river N, take SECOND right signed Ploujean (hairpin bend) for 500m; right dir. Ploujean — house 3rd on right.

MMap 230-5 **ASP Map No: 1**

Etienne & Armelle DELAISI
Manoir de Roch ar Brini
29600 Ploujean Morlaix
Finistère
Tel: (0)2 98 72 01 44
Fax: (0)2 98 88 04 49
e-mail: rochbrini@aol.com
www.acdev.com/rocharbrini

Ring back 2.00

Charlick is the most sociable workaholic you could find, Yolande a smiling, helpful mother of four. Having beautifully converted this old Breton weavers' house, they now convert other ruins as well as running their small *auberge* that serves *crêpes* galore and meats grilled on the open fire. They are active, artistic (he has momentarily set his darkly expressive painting aside) and fun. The rooms have clever layouts, colour schemes and fabrics informed by an artist's creative imagination, two beds on mezzanines for the quadruples — superb. All is gentle and soft; there are animals and swings for children's delight — and more *crêpes.*

Rooms: 2 quadruple, 1 double, all with bath or shower & wc.

Price: 250-350 Frs (€ 38.11-53.36) for two, including breakfast.

Meals: About 130 Frs, including wine & coffee.

Open: April to mid-November.

From St Brieuc N12 dir. Morlaix, exit 'Plouigneau' dir. Plougonven. There dir. Plourin lès Morlaix for 5km. House on right; signposted.

MMap 230-5 **ASP Map No: 1**

Charlick & Yolande de TERNAY
La Grange de Coatelan
29640 Plougonven
Finistère
Tel: (0)2 98 72 60 16

Squarely planted in its Breton soil, this is without doubt a family house open to guests not a purpose-converted undertaking. The children now run the farm and the Gralls have time for visitors. After a blissful night (warm traditional décor, excellent mattresses, neat modern bathrooms) and a bucolic awakening to birdsong in the fields, come down to Madame's home-made *crêpes* or *far breton* at their square Breton table beside the deeply-carved sideboard. Family antiques, family warmth, peace and unity that reassure and relax.

Rooms: 2 double, 1 twin, each with shower & wc.

Price: 250 Frs (€ 38.11) for two, including breakfast.

Meals: Restaurant 2.5km.

Open: All year.

From St Pol de Léon D10 W to Cléder (8km). Arriving in Cléder, take road to sea for 2km then left following signs to 'Ferme de Kernévez'.

MMap 230-4 **ASP Map No: 1**

François & Marceline GRALL
Kernévez
29233 Cléder
Finistère
Tel: (0)2 98 69 41 14

Ring back

The veranda is a modern appendage on this much-altered C19 house but the welcome inside is genuine enough. Your hosts are relaxed and friendly without being effusive. Monsieur gave up farming because he preferred dealing with guests! They have mixed ancient and modern in their furniture and décor, bolting on the odd manorial fireplace and fake beam, and the whole house is comfortable without being exciting, unless you count the electrically-operated double mattress (wall-mounted televisions too). Breakfast is more like brunch with cheeses and meats and cake… and you are so near the sea.

Rooms: 1 double/twin, 1 suite for 4, both with own bath & wc.

Price: 380 Frs (€ 57.93) for two, including breakfast.

Meals: Choice within walking distance.

Open: All year.

Gîte space for 10 people

From St Pol de Léon D10 to Plouescat. Just after town name sign right towards 'Plages' & Pen-Kear. Signposted.

MMap 230-4 **ASP Map No: 1**

Marie-Thérèse & Raymond LE DUFF
Pen-Kear
29430 Plouescat
Finistère
Tel: (0)2 98 69 62 87
Fax: (0)2 98 69 67 33

In a tiny, incredibly quiet hamlet on the fascinating, desolate heath of the Monts d'Arée, in the *Armorique* National Park, Kreisker is a sensitive, utterly Breton conversion, all local stone, slate roofs and giant slabs of schist from the old floors. Inside there is scrubbed wood, more stone, ethnic rugs, fresh cotton and pretty china. The independent guestroom has a lovely blue/grey-clothed brass bed and a fine bathroom. After the feast that is breakfast, your ears ringing with Madame's knowledgeable talk of Breton culture, go and explore this ancient land. *Children welcome if you bring a child's bed; good-value dinner 3km away but book ahead.*

Rooms: 1 double with bathroom.

Price: 250 Frs (€ 38.11) for two, including breakfast.

Meals: Crêperies and restaurants 3-15km (book ahead).

Open: All year.

Gîte space for 8 people

From Morlaix, D785 dir. Quimper. At La Croix Cassée, D42 to Botmeur; house is on right on leaving village dir. La Feuillée.

MMap 230-19 **ASP Map No: 1**

Marie-Thérèse & Jean-Bernard SOLLIEC
Kreisker
29690 Botmeur
Finistère
Tel: (0)2 98 99 63 02
e-mail: jbsol@club-internet.fr

Sleep in the old cider-press; father still brews his magic (for private use) but not in your bathroom. The two most memorable things here are Marie-Christine's radiant and passionate smile as she talks about her native Brittany, its myths, its pathways and its soul; and the sympathetic use of wood on floor, ceilings and walls. Breakfasts are enormous, perhaps with Breton music in the background. It is quiet and cosy, the setting is lovely, Marie-Christine is delightful. Her daughter now runs an 'annexe' in her converted stables 1.5km away, and this is also where dinners are served. All feedback welcome!

Rooms: 2 triple, each with shower & wc. 3 double, 1 twin, all with shower & wc, at 2nd house 1.5km away.

Price: 260 Frs (€ 39.64) for two, including breakfast.

Meals: 90 Frs, including wine & coffee. Good crêperie in Brasparts.

Open: All year.

Gîte space for 14 people

From Morlaix D785 S dir. Quimper for about 35km. 800m before Brasparts, turn right (on bend) & follow signs.

MMap 230-19 **ASP Map No: 1**

Marie-Christine CHAUSSY
Garz ar Bik
29190 Brasparts
Finistère
Tel: (0)2 98 81 47 14
Fax: (0)2 98 81 47 99

English people in a very French house. Gill, a senior member of the Quilters' Guild and much-appreciated teacher of patchwork, and Clive, a retired banker and accomplished cook of four-course dinners, are quietly friendly hosts, enjoying their year-round flowering garden, where they are constantly creating new features (pond, rockery) in the balmy Breton air. Their house (a resurrected ruin) has soft furnishings, soft cats, a nice mix of old and new. Their welcome includes good simple rooms with non-matching beds (one or two a bit short), tea trays and informed help on what to see in the adopted country they so love.

Rooms: 1 twin, 1 family room for 4, both with shower or hip bath & wc; 1 twin sharing bathroom.

Price: 240 Frs (€ 36.59) for two, including breakfast.

Meals: 120 Frs, including aperitif, wine & coffee.

Open: All year.

From Morlaix, D785 dir. Pleyben for 23km. Left on D764 dir. Huelgoat for 7km. Right on D36 dir. Châteauneuf du Faou. Laz is on the D36 after Châteauneuf; house at end of village on left. (Secure parking.)

MMap 230-19 **ASP Map No: 1**

Gill & Clive THOMPSON
Les Deux Aiguilles
3 Grand'Rue
29520 Laz
Finistère
Tel: (0)2 98 26 87 23

This neat old farmhouse has kept watch over the bay for generations. Typically Breton, the entrance is guarded by a religious statue and, as you would expect, the *Bretonne* room has proper Breton furniture while the *Romantique* room has a canopied bed with bunches of roses. There are flowers everywhere, indoors and out, on the walls, on the balconies, in the garden, in the rustic, flagstoned dining room where you have breakfast. A peaceful house, charming hosts and just five minutes walk from the sea.

Rooms: 2 double (1 on ground floor), each with shower & wc.

Price: 250 Frs (€ 38.11) for two, including breakfast.

Meals: Choice in Douarnenez.

Open: All year.

Gîte space for 12 people

small   

From Douarnenez, D7 dir. Locronan. House is before village, on first road on left after sign for 'La plage du Ris'; signposted.

MMap 230-17 **ASP Map No: 1**

Henri & Henriette GONIDEC
Lanévry
Kerlaz
29100 Douarnenez
Finistère
Tel: (0)2 98 92 19 12
www.sawdays.co.uk

A beautiful house, 3km from the sea, smelling of real countryside — mown grass and birds and the surrounding woods — it contains some brilliant examples of Old Breton furniture — a *lit clos* (big carved wooden box with doors concealing a small double bed), dresser, chests, wardrobes — and a fine chestnut staircase. The living room is light and generous, like its owner; bedrooms have more old pieces, pretty fabrics, parquet throughout; one has a shower behind a curtain. Madame is one of the most attractive, humorous people we know and her unusually-qualified son makes barrels for Breton *eau-de-vie* on the premises.

Rooms: 1 family room for 4, 1 double, 1triple, 1 twin, all with shower & wc.

Price: 250-280 Frs (€ 38.11-42.69) for two, including breakfast.

Meals: Town very near.

Open: All year.

Gîte space for 10 people

From Douarnenez D765 W dir. Audierne for 2km (Pouldavid is a suburb of Douarnenez). 400m after lights, right following signs for Chambres d'Hôtes.

MMap 230-17 **ASP Map No: 1**

Mme Marie-Paule LEFLOCH
Manoir de Kervent
Pouldavid
29100 Douarnenez
Finistère
Tel: (0)2 98 92 04 90
Fax: (0)2 98 92 04 90

The farm is now let out so the Oliers can concentrate on their B&B. This uncomplicated couple, who have led a simple farming life, are real weatherbeaten Bretons who have converted an old pighouse into three good modern rooms with restfully plain white walls, extra-wide beds, thermostatic showers (*très moderne*) and a comfortable wicker-chaired dayroom. Madame serves a Breton breakfast in her dining room; Monsieur may offer you a bunch of flowers. Their smile is a great gift. There are walks across two valleys from the house; beaches and ports are 10km away and the guest kitchen appeals to families.

Rooms: 1 double, 1 triple, 1 twin/quadruple all with shower & wc.

Price: 260 Frs (€ 39.64) for two, including breakfast; extra person 70 Frs.

Meals: Good choice 5km. Guest kitchen.

Open: All year.

From Douarnenez D765 dir. Audierne. On entering Confort Meilars, 1st left and follow signs for 2.5km.

MMap 230-17 **ASP Map No: 1**

Anne & Jean OLIER
Kerantum
29790 Mahalon
Finistère
Tel: (0)2 98 74 51 93

The bewitching name (of the warring knight who became first baron in 1010), the splendidness of the place, its vast, opulent rooms and magnificent grounds, seduced us utterly: a powerful experience, grand rather than intimate, but unforgettable. Built with stones from the C11 fortress, it is a jewel of C18 aristocratic architecture, inside and out. M Davy, the latest descendant, is passionate about buildings, his ancient family seat in particular, and applies all his energy and intelligence to restoring château and park, planting thousands of bulbs and bushes, and converting visitors to the same devotion. Deeply interesting and unusual.

Rooms: 4 double, 2 suites, each with bath or shower & wc.

Price: 650-800 Frs (€ 99.09-121.96) (double) for two, suite 900-1300 Frs, including breakfast.

Meals: Choice nearby.

Open: March to November.

Gîte space for 5 people

From Quimper D765 W for 5km then left on D784 dir. Landudec for 13km; left following signs to Guilguiffin.

MMap 230-17 **ASP Map No: 1**

Philippe DAVY
Domaine du Guilguiffin
29710 Landudec
Finistère
Tel: (0)2 98 91 52 11
Fax: (0)2 98 91 52 52
e-mail: chateau@guilguiffin.com
www.guilguiffin.com

The view across fields and wooded hills is perfectly wonderful. Your quarters are in a converted outbuilding, separate from the owners' house, and the window in each smallish room is a double-glazed door onto the long terrace where chairs await. There is a big modern veranda room for breakfast (with *crêpes* or croissants), where a richly-carved Breton wardrobe takes pride of place. Modern-furnished rooms and bathrooms are identical and impeccable. Madame is efficient, full of information about Breton culture, and very purposeful. Only suitable for older children who can sleep alone.

Rooms: 4 double, 2 twin, all with shower & wc.

Price: 250 Frs (€ 38.11) for two, including breakfast.

Meals: 90 Frs (September-mid-June only). Self-catering. Restaurant 10km.

Open: All year.

  older  small 

From Quimper, D765 dir. Rosporden. At St Yvi left dir. Kervren; at very end of lane (2.5km).

MMap 230-33 **ASP Map No: 1**

Odile LE GALL
Kervren
29140 St Yvi
Finistère
Tel: (0)2 98 94 70 34
Fax: (0)2 98 94 81 19

This rural haven lies between *Armor*, the land by the sea and *Argoat*, the land of woods. It is a Breton house with naturally hospitable Breton owners, Breton furniture and a huge Breton brass pot once used for mixing *crêpes.* They love children, who may explore the dairy farm. Madame is welcoming and chatty (in French), Monsieur has a reassuring earthy calmness. One of the large, light, country-style rooms has been redone in sunny yellow. Copious breakfasts include those *crêpes* (though not mixed in the brass pot) and home-grown kiwi fruit in season.

Rooms: 4 double and 1 twin, all with shower & wc.

Price: 260 Frs (€ 39.64) for two, including breakfast.

Meals: Restaurant 4km.

Open: All year.

From Scaër, D50 dir. Coray Briec; after 3km, left at 'Ty Ru' and follow signpost for Kerloaï.

MMap 230-19 **ASP Map No: 1**

Louis & Thérèse PENN
Kerloaï
29390 Scaër
Finistère
Tel: (0)2 98 59 42 60
Fax: (0)2 98 59 05 67

A haven is what guests call this exquisitely-renovated manor house, where ancient stones are set off by plain white walls and its own chapel still stands. Big, beamed guestrooms with antique furniture, modern beds and four-star bathrooms, relaxed and knowledgeable hosts who want to communicate their feel for 'real' Brittany (Peter hunts treasure), serve refined dinners made with home-grown organic vegetables and organise fungus-hunting holidays. Work up your appetite on miles of canal towpath or by visiting the beautiful unsung Breton hinterland.

Rooms: 2 double, 2 twin, 1 family room for 4, all with own bath or shower & wc.

Price: 260-330 Frs (€ 39.64-50.31) for two, including breakfast.

Meals: By arrangement 120 Frs, including wine & coffee.

Open: Easter to October.

At Carhaix Plouguer (midway between Roscoff & Lorient), take N164 southern bypass; turn off at 'Districenter' (big warehouse/shop) & follow signs to Prevasy; right at triangular green, straight on to house.

MMap 230-20 **ASP Map No: 1**

Peter & Clarissa NOVAK
Manoir de Prevasy
29270 Carhaix
Finistère
Tel: (0)2 98 93 24 36
Fax: (0)2 98 93 24 36
www.sawdays.co.uk

The setting is out of this world, the welcome just right, so what matter the youth of the house? You can boat on the lake with the wild duck, walk by the babbling stream through the woods and wild rhododendron, sit on the bank under the palm tree and gaze across the valley to the distant hills. And you can barbecue in the orchard. Hospitality comes naturally to this serene retired couple who are happy to share their truly privileged environment in a quiet hamlet. The rooms are perfectly adequate in their ubiquitous pink and blue, the atmosphere incomparable.

Rooms: 1 triple, 1 double, both with shower & wc.

Price: 230 Frs (€ 35.06) for two, including breakfast.

Meals: Choice 1.5km. Barbecue possible.

Open: All year.

From Quimperlé D790 dir. le Faouët 9km. Left to Querrien; follow signs dir. Mellac. 1km after village, 1st left to Kerfaro. There left after stone house. Last house in lane.

MMap 230-34 **ASP Map No: 1**

Renée & Yves LE GALLIC
Kerfaro
29310 Querrien
Finistère
Tel: (0)2 98 71 30 02/
(0)6 85 17 96 43
Fax: (0)2 98 71 30 02

Madame is a darling — quiet, serene and immensely kind — and really treats her guests as friends. The long, low, granite house has been in the family for all of its 300 years, enjoying the peace of this wind-blown, bird-sung spot just five minutes walk from the sea and that gorgeous coastal path. Most of the building consists of gîtes; the *chambres d'hôtes* are squeezed into the far end — definitely small, impeccably simple, like the dining room. With charming Port Manech and some handsome beaches nearby, it is a wonderful holiday spot.

Rooms: 2 double, 2 twin, all with shower & wc.

Price: 250 Frs (€ 38.11) for two, including breakfast.

Meals: In village: walking distance.

Open: All year.

Gîte space for 14 people

From Pont Aven, D77 dir. Port Manech: right just before the signpost Port Manech, and 1st left. Signposted 'Chambres d'Hôtes'.

MMap 230-33 **ASP Map No: 1**

Yveline GOURLAOUEN
Kerambris
Port Manech
29920 Nevez
Finistère
Tel: (0)2 98 06 83 82

The situation is heavenly, cradled in a quiet hamlet 200 yards from the river in a particularly lovely corner of Brittany. The people are delightful: Martine looks after old folk and young Melissa, Philippe pots and teaches aikido, both have lots of time for their guests. The two big, superbly-converted, uncluttered attic rooms have been decorated with flair in subtle pastels and fitted with good shower rooms. Guests have their own sitting/breakfast room and kitchen. Birds sing. The cat is one of the best ever. The welcome is genuine and you may get a different kind of cake for breakfast every day. Readers' letters are full of praise.

Rooms: 2 twin, each with shower & wc.

Price: 230 Frs (€ 35.06) for two, including breakfast.

Meals: Wide choice in St Nicolas 3km. Kitchen for guests' use.

Open: Easter to October; otherwise by arrangement.

From Pontivy, D768 dir. Lorient; exit for Port Arthur/St Nicolas des Eaux to St Nicolas; right immediately after bridge; follow signs 'Chambres d'Hôtes & Poterie' for 3km.

MMap 230-35 **ASP Map No: 1**

Martine MAIGNAN & Philippe BOIVIN
Lezerhy
56310 Bieuzy les Eaux
Morbihan
Tel: (0)2 97 27 74 59
Fax: (0)2 97 27 74 59
www.sawdays.co.uk

Here in the heart of rural Brittany, where you feel the clock stopped 50 years ago, a forgotten peace descends, your pace slows, *la tranquillité* sets in. Peter and Pat, a warm, good-humoured couple, have converted an old farmhouse and its barns into a wonderful holiday spot, a place full of laughter and the happiness of being there. The house now sports finely-crafted (by Peter) 'Jacobean' panelling — it may be imitation but it feels deeply cosy and utterly English. The giant weekly international barbecue with guests and locals is highly appreciated, the three acres of garden give space for all (there are seven gîtes and a pool too); it is ideal for families.

Rooms: 1 twin with shower & wc, 1 2-room suite for 4 with shower & wc.

Price: 250 Frs (€ 38.11) for two, including breakfast.

Meals: In village or good choice 5km.

Open: All year.

Gîte space for 35 people

From Pontivy D764 dir. Josselin for 5km; straight on through C4 (Noyal Pontivy/St Thuriau) crossroads; 100m after crossroads, right to Pennerest.

MMap 230-22 **ASP Map No: 1**

Peter & Pat ROBERTS
Pennerest
56920 Noyal Pontivy
Morbihan
Tel: (0)2 97 38 35 76
Fax: (0)2 97 38 23 80
e-mail: p.roberts@wanadoo.fr
www.sawdays.co.uk

Madame, an elegant and wonderfully French country lady, serves generous breakfasts ("a little different every day") in her pretty beamed dining room by the great fireplace and the grandfather clock. It used to be a farmhouse, still has a pond where you can do some desultory fishing and is just 20 minutes from those little harbour towns, the beaches and the ferry to Belle Ile. Within the old walls, the B&B conversion is fairly standard but each room has its own private outside area and such restful views all round.

Rooms: 5 double/triple, each with shower & wc.

Price: 250 Frs (€ 38.11) for two, including breakfast.

Meals: Good restaurants nearby. Self-catering.

Open: All year.

From N24 Baud exit on D768 dir. Auray for 16km. At first Pluvigner roundabout left onto D16 dir. Locminé for 4km then turn right and follow signs.

MMap 230-36 **ASP Map No: 1**

Marie-Claire COLLET
Kerdavid Duchentil
56330 Pluvigner
Morbihan
Tel: (0)2 97 56 00 59

Before concentrating on the privileged few, including you, at Kerreo, Gérard used his skills as a chef for the wealthy of this world (châteaux-hotels) and the deprived (catering schools for troubled youths). The B&B is all his: Nelly works in town. He has revived the old bread oven in the lush little garden, renovated and decorated the 'cottage' with great flair and faithfulness — the rooms, named after Breton fairies, are enchanting. He is quietly welcoming and the whole family is deeply Breton, doing *Fest-Noz* with costumes, dances, bagpipes and songs, though the odd moonlight game of *boules* or darts gives a foreign flavour.

Rooms: 4 double, 1 twin, each with bath or shower & wc.

Price: 290-320 Frs (€ 44.21-48.78) for two, including breakfast.

Meals: 100 Frs, including wine/cider.

Open: All year.

From Lorient N165 E for 20km; exit 'Landevant' onto D24 N for approx. 8km then left at sign to Chaumière de Kerreo — thatched house with fuschia-pink paintwork at hamlet crossroads.

MMap 230-36 **ASP Map No: 1**

Gérard GREVÈS & Nelly Le GLEHUIR
Chaumière de Kerreo
56330 Pluvigner
Morbihan
Tel: (0)2 97 50 90 48
Fax: (0)2 97 50 90 69

In a beautiful setting among the fields, the standing stones of Carnac minutes away, beaches and coastal pathways close by, Kerimel is a handsome group of granite farm buildings. The bedrooms are beauties: plain walls, some panelling, pale blue covers and curtains, old stone and beams plus modern comfort. The dining room is cottage perfection: dried flowers hanging from beams over wooden table, tiled floor, vast blackened chimney, stone walls. Gentle, generous people... "We talked of flowers", wrote one guest.

Rooms: 5 double/twin, each with shower & wc.

Price: 290-350 Frs (€ 44.21-53.36) for two, including breakfast. Extra bed 90 Frs.

Meals: Good place 3km away.

Open: All year.

From N165 exit for Quiberon/Carnac on D768 for 4km then right to Ploemel. There D105 W dir. Erdeven; house signposted on right after 1.5km.

MMap 230-35 **ASP Map No: 1**

Babeth & Pierre MALHERBE
Kerimel
56400 Ploemel (Carnac)
Morbihan
Tel: (0)2 97 56 84 72
Fax: (0)2 97 56 84 72
e-mail: elisabeth.malherbe@wanadoo.fr
www.sawdays.co.uk

The spreading creeper has softened the tautly-lifted face of the Balsans' thoroughly-renovated farmhouse, but lovers of all things clean and efficient will still delight in the order restored. The dayroom is large and light, with a lovely fire and large French windows leading onto the patio and garden. Rooms lead off a long, white passage upstairs and are extremely comfortable with proof of Monsieur's upholstering expertise. No stunning views but the sea is 500 yards away, historic towns are close and so are the mystical standing stones of Carnac. Home-made Breton cakes and jams for breakfast with genuinely friendly people.

Rooms: 3 double, 2 twin, all with shower & wc.

Price: 300-350 Frs (€ 45.73-53.36) for two, incl. breakfast; extra bed 100 Frs.

Meals: Good choice 1km.

Open: All year.

From Carnac town take Avenue des Druides dir. Beaumer. At crossroads left on Chemin de Beaumer. Impasse de Beaumer is 2nd on left.

MMap 230-35 **ASP Map No: 1**

Marie-France & Daniel BALSAN
L'Alcyone
Impasse de Beaumer
56340 Carnac Plage
Morbihan
Tel: (0)2 97 52 78 11
Fax: (0)2 97 52 13 02

An oyster farm, bang there on the quayside! All bedrooms have the view so close that you could dream of staying here alone with paint and brushes to soak up and capture that lovely (almost Cornish) atmosphere while drinking coffee on the balcony, smelling the sea and listening with utter contentment to the chugging of fishing boats. Madame, from northern France, was a legal advisor to businesses in England, Germany and USA — alert, efficient and chatty, she came to Brittany to help François farm oysters , and never looked back. He'll take you out there too, if you ask. Unusual and very welcoming.

Rooms: 1 twin, 1 triple, 1 apartment for 3, each with shower & wc.

Price: 300-400 Frs (€ 45.73-60.98) for two, including breakfast.

Meals: Restaurant 500m.

Open: All year.

Gîte space for 10 people

From Auray D28/D781 to Crach & La Trinité sur Mer; right at lights before bridge across to La Trinité — house 400m along on left, signed 'François Gouzer'.

MMap 230-35 **ASP Map No: 1**

Christine & François GOUZER
Kernivilit
St Philibert
56470 La Trinité sur Mer
Morbihan
Tel: (0)2 97 55 17 78
Fax: (0)2 97 30 04 11
e-mail: fgouzer@club-internet.fr

Gaze across garden and terrace at the ever-changing blue-green sea from the three attractive simply-furnished ground-floor bedrooms of this modern house of character. There are oyster beds nearby and a little beach at the end of the garden (for shallow high-tide bathing). A vast carved four-poster reigns imposingly in a first-floor bedroom that leads to an even more startling dayroom with billiard table, books all round, an oak altar, a 1950's juke box, a telescope, a child-size Louis XV armchair, — all neatly arranged as if in a stately home. Madame, brisk and practical, has a style that features marked contrasts — you will warm to her.

Rooms: 1 double with bath; 3 double with basin & bidet sharing 2 showers; all sharing 6 wcs.

Price: 310-370 Frs (€ 47.26-56.41) for two, including breakfast.

Meals: In Larmor Baden 1.5km.

Open: All year except mid-July & Aug.

shallow

From Auray D101 S to Baden; D316 S to Larmor Baden; through village N/NE to Locqueltas: small white sign on right — house 10m along on right.

MMap 230-36 **ASP Map No: 1**

Mme MC HECKER
Locqueltas
56870 Larmor Baden
Morbihan
Tel: (0)2 97 57 05 85
Fax: (0)2 97 57 25 02
www.sawdays.co.uk

Your graceful, cultured hosts always dine with you, creating an authentic taste of life with the French country aristocracy; dress for it, and enjoy a game of billiards afterwards. It may seem (rather endearingly) formal, with breakfast at 9am sharp and a touch of old-fashioned primness about table manners but they are good company and enjoy introducing guests to each other. Inevitably, the bedrooms are magnificent. The château has its own lake and 100 hectares of superb parkland... all within the Brière Regional Park where water and land are inextricably mingled and wildlife abounds.

Rooms: 2 double, 1 twin, all with own bath or shower and wc.

Price: 500-550 Frs (€ 76.22-83.85) for two, including breakfast.

Meals: Candlelit dinner 220 Frs, including aperitif, wine & coffee.

Open: All year.

Gîte space for 10 people

From N165 exit 15 for La Roche Bernard dir. La Baule to Herbignac. Here, fork left on D47 dir. St Lyphard for 4km; house on right.

MMap 232-13 **ASP Map No: 2**

François & Cécile de la MONNERAYE
Château de Coët Caret
44410 Herbignac, Loire-Atlantique
Tel: (0)2 40 91 41 20
Fax: (0)2 40 91 37 46
e-mail: coetcaret@multimania.com
www.multimania.com/coetcaret/

These are the sweetest people, even if their somewhat kitschy taste is not everyone's cup of tea! They really do "treat their guests as friends". Madame is bright and sparkling with a smiling open face, very proud to show you her decorated books, musical scores and hats with the dried flower and gold spray touch; Monsieur is a retired farmer, less chatty but equally friendly. The house is warm (log fire in winter), cosily country-furnished and the rooms are soft and welcoming (but mind your head on the way up) with great attention to detail. Breakfast is served in pretty little baskets at the long table.

Rooms: 2 triple (D + S), each with shower & wc; 1 triple (D + S) sharing bath & separate wc.

Price: 265 Frs (€ 40.40) for two, including breakfast.

Meals: Good restaurant 3km. Self-catering in summer.

Open: All year.

Gîte space for 4 people

From Rennes N137 dir. Nantes for 63km. Exit at Nozay on N171 dir. Blain for 8km. At bottom of hill, left at roadside cross; signposted.

MMap 232-15 **ASP Map No: 2**

[illegible] & Marcel PINEAU
La Mercerais
44130 Blain
Loire-Atlantique
Tel: (0)2 40 79 04 30

Deep connections here: Le Plessis once belonged to the Roche family who crossed with William in 1066, settled in Fermoy, Ireland, then returned to France. Now very Breton, there are velvet curtains and high-back chairs in the *salon*; silver coffee pots and freshly-squeezed orange juice at breakfast; 3,000 rosebushes in the garden and bedrooms with huge character. The Belordes bought back the family seat after decades of 'alien owners'. Her father was in London with de Gaulle; she loves the English, enjoys cosmopolitan conversation (lots) and offers candlelit champagne dinners (supplement...). Expensive but special.

Rooms: 1 suite for 5, 1 double, 1 twin/quadruple, all with bath & wc.

Price: 550-900 Frs (€ 83.85-137.20) for two, including breakfást.

Meals: 275-350 Frs, including wine & coffee.

Open: All year.

Gîte space for 4 people

From Nantes leave A83 ring-road on D85 past airport. At T-junction at 'Champ de Foire' left through Pont St Martin & follow signs to Le Plessis.

MMap 232-28 **ASP Map No: 2**

M & Mme BELORDE
Château du Plessis-Atlantique
44860 Pont St Martin
Loire-Atlantique
Tel: (0)2 40 26 81 72
Fax: (0)2 40 32 76 67
www.chateaux-france.com/-plessisatlantique

The typical long low 18th-century house in its vineyard setting is perfect for a quiet escape. The friendly, unobtrusive Desbrosses particularly enjoy the company of foreign visitors who may use their library and the drawing room with its deeply comfortable chairs around an imposing fireplace. Madame is an artist and potter — the strong colours are her (successful) choice, guestrooms are individually styled and dinner is served on matching blue and yellow plates. You will be taken very good care of at La Mozardière.

Rooms: 1 suite, 1 double, both with bath & wc.

Price: 295 Frs (€ 44.97) for two, including breakfast.

Meals: 120 Frs, including wine.

Open: All year.

From Nantes D937 dir. La Roche. At Rocheservière D753 to Legé. In village centre dir. Challans. Left just after 'Le Paradis' restaurant. Signed 'Richebonne'.

MMap 232-40 **ASP Map No: 11**

Christine & Gérard DESBROSSES
La Mozardière
Richebonne
44650 Legé
Loire-Atlantique
Tel: (0)2 40 04 98 51
Fax: (0)2 40 26 31 61

A fine welcome awaits you at this young couple's farmhouse out in the sunflower fields. Francette has put her considerable flair into turning the top of the house, previously empty space, into an attractive communal sitting area and two delightful guestrooms, all white walls, local furniture, old tiled floors, exposed stone and pretty yet unfussy décor. There are delicious dinners, a shop selling René's duck preserves (served at breakfast too), a little flower garden and a peaceful night guaranteed.

Rooms: 1 room for 4/5, 1 double, both with shower and wc.

Price: 280 Frs (€ 42.69) for two, including breakfast. Extra person 40 Frs.

Meals: 5-10km.

Open: All year.

From Nantes ringroad dir. Bordeaux then D937 through Rocheservière and on for 4.5km. At first crossroads after town right on D84/D94 to Ferme des Forges. Signposted on left.

MMap 232-40 **ASP Map No: 11**

Francette & René PEAUDEAU
La Ferme des Forges
44650 Legé
Loire-Atlantique
Tel: (0)2 40 04 92 99
Fax: (0)2 40 26 31 90

The lofty dining room has massive beams, a massive table, massive old flags; the panelling took 500 hours to restore, fine period furniture gleams — Monsieur is passionate about buildings and an avid auction-goer. A feeling of Renaissance nobility (the old staircase tower was hidden under plaster five years ago...) extends everywhere except to the bathrooms, which are reassuringly modern. Madame seems charmingly eccentric and, under daughter Gaëlle's management, the estate produce a Muscadet from the surrounding vineyards that is served as an aperitif at about seven before you sally forth for dinner.

Rooms: 5 double with bath or shower & wc.

Price: 470-670 Frs (€ 71.65-102.14) for two, including breakfast.

Meals: Wide choice within 5 minutes.

Open: April to Oct; by arrangement in winter.

Gîte space for 10 people

    50Frs

From Nantes N249 dir. Poitiers then N149 dir. Le Pallet/La Haie Fouassière. 1km before Le Pallet D7 right to Monnières. In village follow signs to Gorges — château 1km along on left.

MMap 232-29 **ASP Map No: 2**

Annick & Didier CALONNE
Château Plessis-Brezot
44690 Monnières
Loire-Atlantique
Tel: (0)2 40 54 63 24
Fax: (0)2 40 54 66 07
www.sawdays.co.uk

Such a pretty old coaching inn in the middle of the flat Muscadet country, with its Midi-style courtyard for turning the carriages... it was actually built just before the motor came in and the horse went out. Your ever-charming hosts have brought their fine carved *armoires* from their previous B&B in Normandy to add some character to the rather heavily renovated interior. Madame's dynamism and sense of fun are, of course, intact. The guestrooms, two in an annexe with kitchenette and a steep, uneven staircase, have nice parquet floors and good new bathrooms; fresh flowers and peace are the keynotes.

Rooms: 4 double, 1 twin, each with shower & wc.

Price: 260 Frs (€ 39.64) for two, including breakfast; extra bed 60 Frs.

Meals: Choice 6km. Self-catering in annexe.

Open: All year.

Gîte space for 6 people

From Nantes N249 E dir. Poitiers, exit 'Vallet' dir. Loroux Bottereau then Le Landreau for 5km. 600m before Le Landreau right and follow signs to La Rinière (3km).

MMap 232-29 **ASP Map No: 2**

Françoise & Louis LEBARILLIER
Le Relais de La Rinière
44430 Le Landreau
Loire-Atlantique
Tel: (0)2 40 06 41 44
Fax: (0)2 51 13 10 52
e-mail: lariniere@chez.com
www.chez.com/lariniere

Oh gentle living that was here – and deep,
dark intrigue – when the Renaissance blossomed
by the banks of France's mightiest river and
kings and courtiers rode out to hunt the noble stag.

The Loire Valley

The house is just eight metres thick but behind it you will find a big barn-enclosed courtyard, two large towers, a 300-year-old oak and a covered terrace for lounging. The Migons couldn't be nicer, their house is a labour of love — and they are still labouring. Bedrooms — big, north-facing windows with shutters — are pretty, elegant, comfortable; the dining room fireplace has spits, the furniture is antique and you see the beams; the games room has two billiards tables, a piano, a set of drums: Monsieur plays bass guitar and will share his passion for old cars (admire his veteran collection). Fear not: *Drain* is old French for 'oak'.

Rooms: 4 doubles, each with bath or shower & wc.

Price: 450-500 Frs (€ 68.60-76.22) for two, including breakfast.

Meals: 120 Frs, including wine & coffee. Wide choice 4-10 km.

Open: All year.

From A11 exit 20 on D923. Cross Loire to Liré on D763; right on D751 to Drain; left on D154 dir. St Laurent des Autels. Gateway to drive about 5km along on left.

MMap 232-29 **ASP Map No: 2**

Brigitte & Gérard MIGON
Le Mésangeau
49530 Drain
Maine-et-Loire
Tel: (0)2 40 98 21 57
e-mail: Le.Mesangeau@wanadoo.fr

A fine house restored with thoughtful sensitivity by its energetic young owners, its view rolls across the little river and the water meadows and its soft green shutters blend with stones and slates. The two large, old-furnished, modern-bathroomed, arched-windowed bedrooms in the main house are lovely with ingenious use of sloping ceilings and rafter space. One has a *pantalonnière*, a chest of drawers specially designed for trousers. The little cottage with its spiral stair to the sleeping platform is delicious. You will be well cared for by hospitable people in country peace.

Rooms: 2 triple with bath or shower & wc; 1 cottage for 2/3 with shower and kitchen.

Price: 280-320 Frs (€ 42.69-48.78) for two, including breakfast.

Meals: Choice 3-7km. Barbecue and picnic in garden.

Open: All year (by arrangement in winter).

From Angers N160 dir. Cholet. Exit at Mûrs Érigné & take D751 dir. Chalonnes. House is 3km after Mûrs Érigné on right.

MMap 232-31 **ASP Map No: 2**

Philippe & Anita CATROUILLET
Les Roches
49610 Mozé sur Louet
Maine-et-Loire
Tel: (0)2 41 78 84 29

The house was a convent in the 1500s, a courtier's residence in the 1600s, a police station in the 1900s and is now a *Chambre d'Hôte* with superb stone staircases. The *Suite Blanche* (an orange room leads to the white room) has beams, tiles, mirrors, fireplaces, carved *armoires*. Other rooms are big too, a little less stunning, and maintenance may be needed. But the glorious living room with its mystifying high-level door, high beamed ceiling and old built-in cupboards is worth the visit by itself. Monsieur restores antiques — his house speaks well of his trade; Madame is pleasant and efficient; restoration continues.

Rooms: 2 suites, 1 triple (with kitchenette), all with bath or shower & wc (very occasionally sharing).

Price: 320 Frs (€ 48.78) for two, including breakfast.

Meals: Choice in town or self-catering.

Open: March to October.

From Saumur, D147 dir. Poitiers. In Montreuil Bellay, follow signs to Les Petits Augustins — entrance to house opposite chapel.

MMap 232-33 **ASP Map No: 7**

Monique & Jacques GUÉZÉNEC
Demeure des Petits Augustins
Place des Augustins
49260 Montreuil Bellay
Maine-et-Loire
Tel: (0)2 41 52 33 88
Fax: (0)2 41 52 33 88

There is heady scent in the air and the design of this farm makes you want to sing — the gentle green woodwork and the stone arches soften the square symmetry of the courtyard, which has virtually no farm mess to spoil it. Yet these intelligent, good-natured farmers work hard, growing fields of lupins, hollyhocks and thyme for seed. Your hosts' wing (and yours while you stay — other family members live in other wings) has been done with simple good taste; each room has a personal touch; there are landing chairs for guests to watch farmyard life go by. Martine is most likeable, young, dynamic and conscious of what B&B enthusiasts really want.

Rooms: 1 double with shower & wc; 1 double, 1 twin, each with own shower, sharing 2 wcs (showers behind curtains).

Price: 230 Frs (€ 35.06) for two, including breakfast.

Meals: Restaurants 3 or 7km.

Open: All year.

Gîte space for 18 people

From Angers, N260 dir. Cholet, then D748 dir. Poitiers. After Brissac, D761 dir. Poitiers. Continue for 2km; house signposted on left, at end of avenue of chestnut trees.

MMap 232-32 **ASP Map No: 2**

Jean-Claude & Martine COLIBET
La Pichonnière
49320 Charcé
Maine-et-Loire
Tel: (0)2 41 91 29 37 (mealtimes)
Fax: (0)2 41 91 29 37

The key words here are serenity, harmony, restfulness. The countryside may not be the most spectacular but the house is utterly peaceful in its little hamlet and Monsieur will guide beginners in the art of billiards if they wish. Madame is shy but kind, spontaneously welcoming and properly proud of her pretty, unfussy rooms where pastel colours, tiled floors and oriental rugs sit well under old rafters and stones and all is spotlessly clean. Breakfast, with home-made jams, can be in the garden on fine mornings and you can picnic there too or bicycle down to the banks of the Loire.

Rooms: 2 double, 1 triple, all with shower & wc.

Price: 260 Frs (€ 39.64) for two, including breakfast.

Meals: 110 Frs, including wine & coffee.

Open: All year.

From Angers N761 dir. Brissac & Doué. At les Alleuds left on D90 dir. Chemellier. After 3km hamlet on left.

MMap 232-32 **ASP Map No: 2**

Eliette EDON
49320 Maunit Chemellier
Maine-et-Loire
Tel: (0)2 41 45 59 50
Fax: (0)2 41 45 01 44

Once the servants' quarters of the château (wealthy people who housed their servants grandly...), it is in a quiet, deep and secluded valley, right on the GR3 long-distance path and the Loire Valley walk. The bedrooms are under the high exposed roof beams, elegantly and discreetly done and with good antiques, matching wallpaper and fabrics (flowery English?), and impeccable bathrooms and loos. Breakfast is beautifully served, with linen table napkins and silver teapot; it is refined but relaxed, and you can picnic in the garden if you wish.

Rooms: 1 suite for 4, 1 twin/triple, both with shower & wc.

Price: 350 Frs (€ 53.36) for two, including breakfast; extra bed 70 Frs.

Meals: Wide choice in the area.

Open: Easter to Nov. By arrangement in winter.

Gîte space for 4 people

From Saumur D751 W along Loire for 15km. In Gennes D69 S dir. Doué la Fontaine up hill, past church & police station. At r'bout take road past Super U: drive to house is 500m along on left.

MMap 232-32 **ASP Map No: 7**

Annick & Jean-Baptiste BOISSET
Le Haut Joreau
49350 Gennes
Maine-et-Loire
Tel: (0)2 41 38 02 58
Fax: (0)2 41 67 37 46

This solid old manor, between town and country, is a thoroughly French family house: the energetic Bastids have a health-food shop in town, four lovely children and an open and genuinely welcoming attitude. The generous reception rooms, furnished with antiques and heirlooms, are naturally elegant but not imposing. The pleasant guestrooms are altogether simpler (two shower rooms are just curtained off) with quaint touches such as an old stone sink and a wallpapered safe as bedside tables while the big bosky garden is a good barrier against the road. On request, all diets can be catered for at breakfast.

Rooms: 1 suite, 1 triple, 1 double, 1 twin each with bath or shower & wc.

Price: 250-370 Frs (€ 38.11-56.41) for two, including breakfast.

Meals: Wide choice in Saumur.

Open: All year (by arrangement in winter).

Gîte space for 5 people

From Saumur centre N147 dir. Angers. Cross Loire & railway, straight on for 200m to Renault garage; left on Ave des Maraîchers dir. St Lambert. After 400m, right into Rue Grange Couronne — house first on right, signposted.

MMap 232-33 **ASP Map No: 7**

Catherine & Emmanuel BASTID
La Bouère Salée
Rue Grange Couronne
49400 St Lambert des Levées, Saumur
Maine-et-Loire
Tel: (0)2 41 67 38 85/ 51 12 52
Fax: (0)2 41 51 12 52
www.sawdays.co.uk

The rambling C19 château stands in a 10-acre oasis of semi-wild vegetation where endangered flora and fauna take refuge. A wonderful woman greets you, a gentle artist and nature-lover with a sure and personal approach to interiors, both house and human. The suite is superb in dramatic red, white and blue (yes, it works!), the children's room deeply child-friendly. It is warm and authentic, offering timeless comfort and silence in the lush green surroundings: "magical". The woodwork has been stripped back, walls are richly clothed (all Madame's work), the furniture is old but not wealthy, the light pours in and you bask in harmony.

Rooms: 1 double, 1 triple & 1 suite for 5, all with bath or shower & wc.

Price: 350-460 Frs (€ 53.36-70.13), suite 760 Frs.

Meals: Saumur 9km.

Open: All year (by arrangement in winter).

From Saumur, N147 dir. Longué. At la Ronde, D767 dir. Vernantes; left on D129 dir. Neuillé. 1km before Neuillé take Fontaine Suzon road; signposted.

MMap 232-33 **ASP Map No: 7**

Mme Monique CALOT
Château du Goupillon
49680 Neuillé
Maine-et-Loire
Tel: (0)2 41 52 51 89

Your hosts are charming, unselfconscious aristocrats living in a Neo-Gothic folly with lots of cheerfully active children. There's a properly dark and spooky baronial hall, light, elegant reception rooms with ancestors on the walls, lots of plush and gilt. If you splurge on the 'suite' (in fact one vast room), you will have a sitting area and a library corner in an alcove. The smaller double has its shower up in a turret, its loo in another on the corridor. Both are elegantly, unfussily decorated with period French pieces and some modern fabrics. The park is huge, wild boar roam, boarlets scamper in spring. Altogether an amazing experience.

Rooms: 1 double with shower & private wc; 1 suite with bath & wc.

Price: 300-900 Frs (€ 45.73-137.20) for two, including breakfast.

Meals: 220 Frs, excluding wine (Saumur 65 Frs). Lunch 180 Frs.

Open: All year.

From A85 exit 'Saumur' on D767 dir. Le Lude. After 1km, left on D129 to Neuillé. Signposted.

MMap 232-33 **ASP Map No: 7**

Monica LE PELLETIER de GLATIGNY
Château de Salvert
Salvert
49680 Neuillé
Maine-et-Loire
Tel: (0)2 41 52 55 89
Fax: (0)2 41 52 56 14

Not only a fine house, also a door onto cultural initiations of all sorts. Set proudly on the Loire embankment, the house has an unbeatable view of the mighty river but the road is busy (little traffic at night). Guests have a cobblestoned kitchen/diner whence the original slate stairs lead up to the house and four well-furnished double-glazed rooms (two with that view). Other, pretty rooms in the old stables in the courtyard, alongside the architecturally-correct dog kennel. Young and lively, Claudine offers a monthly cultural event: take one of her mystery tours, join a traditional Songs-of-the-Loire dinner or a story-telling cocktail party.

Rooms: 1 suite for 4, 2 triple, 2 double, 1 twin, each with shower & wc; 2 have kitchenette.

Price: 300-350 Frs (€ 45.73-53.36) for two, including breakfast; extra bed 50 Frs.

Meals: 125 Frs, incl. wine & coffee.

Open: All year.

From Angers, D952 dir. Saumur. House is on left hand side of road (signposted) as you enter St Mathurin sur Loire.

MMap 232-32 **ASP Map No: 2**

Mme Claudine PINIER
Verger de la Bouquetterie
118 rue du Roi René
49250 St Mathurin sur Loire
Maine-et-Loire
Tel: (0)2 41 57 02 00
Fax: (0)2 41 57 31 90

The Arnaults, retired farmers, are a quiet, welcoming couple who may offer you a glass of home-made rosé in their wine cellar under the old windmill. They are real country people, their traditional ivy-covered farmhouse, set among vineyards and wheat fields, has an authentic country interior — not falsely pretty but muted, practical and clean — and they enjoy the contact with guests. There are many craft and cultural events in the area, including the Artichoke Fair in Coutures in September.

Rooms: 2 triple with washbasins, sharing a bathroom & separate wc.

Price: 200 Frs (€ 30.49) for two, including breakfast.

Meals: Wide choice within 10km.

Open: February to October.

From Saumur, D751 to Coutures, through Gennes. 2km after Coutures, left on rue des Alleuds, following signs to Chambres d'Hôtes.

MMap 232-32 **ASP Map No: 2**

Marcel & Thérèse ARNAULT
Fredelin
49320 Coutures
Maine-et-Loire
Tel: (0)2 41 91 21 26

A refreshingly young and enthusiastic family welcomes you to this C18 barn which has modern eyes in the back of its head — huge windows onto the garden — and is full of light inside. The old wine press (*pressoir*) has become the ping-pong and pool house. Lovingly-restored original beams, tiles and stones (Monsieur restores houses — very well) are the perfect setting for simple old *armoires* and bedheads. Each room has its own entrance, the suites have steep stairs up to the children's rooms, everything is in unpretentious good taste. You all eat together at the long dining table — Madame is sociable, easy-going and a good cook!

Rooms: 1 double, 1 twin, 1 triple, 2 suites, each with bath or shower & wc.

Price: 280-350 Frs (€ 42.69-53.36) for two, including breakfast.

Meals: 120 Frs, including wine. Children 50 Frs.

Open: All year.

From Saumur N147 N/NW 15km to Longué. After Longué right on D938 dir. Baugé for 2.5km then left to Brion. House signposted in village opposite church.

MMap 232-33 **ASP Map No: 7**

Anne & Jean-Marc LE FOULGOCQ
Le Logis du Pressoir, Villeneuve
49250 Brion
Maine-et-Loire
Tel: (0)2 41 57 27 33
Fax: (0)2 41 57 27 33
e-mail: pressoir@wanadoo.fr
www.sawdays.co.uk

Michael and Jill have just moved into this very French house with their two young and lively children who specialise in talking to the horse, fluffing the sheep and hunting the morning's eggs. They are new to B&B and are loving it — there is a generally cheerful, friendly, family atmosphere. The house has a fresh, rejuvenated feel to it, the big room under the roof with its beams, stripped (and new-rugged) pine floor and good views through low roof windows is charming and the ground-floor 'suite' has its own garden entrance straight onto the clean chlorophyll-loaded air.

Rooms: 1 triple, 1 suite, each with shower or bath & wc.

Price: 280 Frs (€ 42.69) for two, including breakfast.

Meals: 95 Frs, including wine.

Open: All year.

Gîte space for 4 people

From La Flèche, D308/D938 dir. Baugé. There, follow sign for Tours & Saumur; right at traffic lights on D61 to Vieil-Baugé. Signposted after 2km.

MMap 232-21 **ASP Map No: 7**

Michael & Jill COYLE
La Chalopinière
49150 Le Vieil Baugé
Maine-et-Loire
Tel: (0)2 41 89 04 38
Fax: (0)2 41 89 04 38
e-mail: rigbycoyle@aol.com

The atmosphere is artistic, relaxed, convivial. Madame delights in decorating her wonderful house; Monsieur is an artist: his Venus emerges from a bathroom wall. In a quiet wooded spot, the house is all dormers, balconies and Victorian extravaganza; the little tower, once dovecote and chapel, is older. Furnishings are a study in disorganised elegance, masses of antiques, *brocante*, modernities — sophisticated and fun. There are relaxation sessions, billiards, piano, and coffee-roasting on the spot; a sense of magic in the park with its groves of mature trees, the odd statue peering from the bushes, a pond fed by a miraculous spring. Good food, too.

Rooms: 1 suite for 5, 4 double, all with bath & wc.

Price: 340 Frs (€ 51.83) for two, including breakfast. Extra bed 85 Frs.

Meals: 120 Frs, including wine & coffee.

Open: All year.

From Angers A11 E for 20km then A85 dir. Tours; exit 2 on D938 dir. Baugé for 5km; right on D62 dir. Mouliherne. House 5km along on right.

MMap 232-33 **ASP Map No:** [illegible]

Françoise & Michel TOUTAIN
Le Prieuré de Vendanger
49150 Le Guédeniau, Maine-et-Loire
Tel: (0)2 41 67 82 37/
(0)6 12 63 03 74
Fax: (0)2 41 67 82 43
e-mail: toutainf@wanadoo.fr
www.sawdays.co.uk

What a splendid woman she is! Down to earth, fun-loving and decent, offering authentic farmhouse hospitality. They are both delighted to show you their exclusively grass-fed brown oxen, even sell you beef direct. You breakfast in the simple dining room which is alive with the desire to please. The attic has been converted into three good rooms and a children's room. Great old roof timbers share the space with new rustic-style beds and old *armoires*. It is simple and clean-cut with discreet plastic flooring, pastel walls, sparkling new shower rooms. They have two lively kids, there are toys and games and swings for yours.

Rooms: 2 triple, 1 twin, each with shower & wc. Extra room with handbasin.

Price: 220 Frs (€ 33.54) for two, including breakfast. Extra bed 70 Frs.

Meals: Choice 5km.

Open: All year.

From Angers N23 to Seiches sur le Loir; right on D766 dir. Tours for 9km; right into Jarzé on D59 dir. Beaufort en Vallé. House on left 700m after Jarzé.

MMap 232-20 **ASP Map No: 2**

Véronique & Vincent PAPIAU
Le Point du Jour
49140 Jarzé
Maine-et-Loire
Tel: (0)2 41 95 46 04
Fax: (0)2 41 95 46 04

The word could be *alternative*: it is different and great for the informal. Joyce, a thoroughly relaxed, welcoming aromatherapist, has an organic kitchen garden, cooks good veggie food, receives art, yoga and meditation workshops (lovely meditation room) and may invite guests to "come and join in". The old farm has been here for 300 years in its soft, leafy stand of poplars; beams are everywhere — take care going to bed. One room has steps down to the courtyard, the other looks over the pond, both have warm-hued furnishings in harmony with the old wood and stone. Old it feels, mature alternative it sings. Small camping site, lots of animals.

Rooms: 1 triple, 1 double, sharing bath & wc.

Price: 250 Frs (€ 38.11) for two, including breakfast.

Meals: Vegetarian 75 Frs, including wine & coffee.

Open: All year.

Gîte space for 6 people

From Le Mans N23 to La Flèche. There D37 to Fougeré then N217 dir. Baugé for 1.5km. House behind poplars on left.

MMap 232-21 **ASP Map No: 7**

Joyce RIMELL
La Besnardière
Route de Baugé
49150 Fougeré
Maine-et-Loire
Tel: (0)2 41 90 15 20

An old farmhouse on the family estate transformed from tumbledown dereliction to rural idyll to house this charming, cultured, artistic, unpretentious couple and their four beautifully-behaved children — the place exudes age-old peace and youthful freshness. Rooms are decorated with flair and simplicity — white walls, sea-grass flooring, good fabrics. A perfect retreat for music and nature lovers — join Tuesday choir practice at the château, take singing lessons with a sister; fish, boat, walk in the unspoilt countryside. A very special place.

Rooms: 1 twin, 1 double, 1 triple, each with bath or shower & wc.

Price: 350 Frs (€ 53.36) for two, including breakfast.

Meals: 130 Frs, including wine & coffee.

Open: All year.

From Angers dir. Lion d'Angers. At Montreuil Juigné right on D768 dir. Champigné. 500m after crossroads at La Croix de Beauvais right up drive to La Roche & Malvoisine.

MMap 232-29 **ASP Map No: 2**

Patrice & Regina de LA BASTILLE
Malvoisine
49460 Ecuillé, Maine-et-Loire
Tel: (0)2 41 93 34 44/
(0)6 80 57 54 84
Fax: (0)2 41 93 34 44
e-mail: bastille-pr@wanadoo.fr
www.sawdays.co.uk

A big old house protected from the encroaching town by the floodlands it overlooks, so the views across open fields may not be destroyed by developers. The heavy furniture is old-fashionedly elegant and if a degree of clutter disguises the antiqueness, the lived-in feel is comforting and guests have space and independence with their own sitting area. In the attractive breakfast/dining room, the huge television and the stone fireplace vie for supremacy. Your retired hosts are unintrusive, Monsieur has a nice dry sense of humour and they welcome children.

Rooms: 2 double, 1 twin, 1 family room for 3/4; all with shower & wc (1 behind curtain).

Price: 250 Frs (€ 38.11) for two, including breakfast.

Meals: In village: son's restaurant.

Open: All year.

From Angers, N162 dir. Le Lion d'Angers for about 7km; right on D768 dir. Montreuil centre & immediately right on Ave d'Europe for about 2km to end of built-up area; left into Rue Espéranto; signposted.

MMap 232-19 **ASP Map No: 2**

Jean-Louis & Suzanne HUEZ
Le Plateau
Rue Espéranto
49460 Montreuil Juigné
Maine-et-Loire
Tel: (0)2 41 42 32 35

The cheerful, cosy sitting room with its open fire immediately sets the tone — this is a charming, friendly house run by an equally welcoming young couple who have small twin sons and guest-loving dogs. Many readers have praised the hospitality shown to both young and old and the "remarkable" food — vegetarians catered for — served in the lovely light dining room. The rooms, up steep stairs, are delightful (the largest room rather more ordinary) with showers behind curtains, two separate shared wcs and French towels (i.e. smaller than ours — bring your own?).

Rooms: 2 double, 2 twin, all with shower & sharing 2 separate wcs.

Price: 220-250 Frs (€ 33.54-38.11) for two, including breakfast (min. 2 nights July & August).

Meals: 120 Frs, including wine & coffee.

Open: Mid-April to October.

From Angers, N162 dir. Laval. At Le Lion d'Angers, D770 W dir. Candé. Pass garden centre & after 1.5km left at big wooden roadside cross; signposted.

MMap 232-19 **ASP Map No: 2**

M & Mme Patrick CARCAILLET
Le Petit Carqueron
49220 Le Lion d'Angers
Maine-et-Loire
Tel: (0)2 41 95 62 65

Racine, the supreme C17 French playwright, was made Prior here by his uncle but was removed by the Bishop; the incident inspired *Les Plaideurs.* Rooms are in a converted priory outbuilding, each one a two-floor suite, well-but-simply furnished. The main house has a friendly family kitchen and a dining room with stacks of books and a pianola in the fireplace. The old chapel is now a garden room for breakfasts and there's a big garden with a swimming pool. Your hosts are lovely people, interesting and educated. We love the area too... and its wines.

Rooms: 2 suites for 4, each with bath & 2 wcs; 1 twin with bath & wc.

Price: 400 Frs (€ 60.98) for two, including breakfast. Extra person 100 Frs.

Meals: 140 Frs, including wine & coffee.

Open: March to October.

From Angers N23 W dir. Nantes for 13km. Go through St Georges, cont. for about 1.5km; left after a garage. Pass château: house is on left. Park outside and walk through gate.

MMap 232-31 **ASP Map No: 2**

Bernard & Geneviève GAULTIER
Prieuré de l'Epinay
49170 St Georges sur Loire
Maine-et-Loire
Tel: (0)2 41 39 14 44
Fax: (0)2 41 39 14 44
e-mail: bgaultier@compuserve.com
www.sawdays.co.uk

You cannot fail to warm to Madame's easy vivacity and infectious laugh. She virtually lives in her kitchen (in the house just opposite), making jams, pastries and bread in the old bread oven. This couple have lovingly preserved their typical old Segré farmhouse with its long deep roof and curious *outeau* openings (some might have put in modern dormers). The living room has great beams, a big brick fireplace, exposed stone walls and new country furniture. Rooms are deliciously rustic: crochet, terracotta, pine, sloping ceilings. The woods are full of birdlife and the cows graze peacefully under the children's window.

Rooms: 2 quadruple, 1 double, all with bath or shower & wc.

Price: 210-230 Frs (€ 32.01-35.06) for two, including breakfast. Extra bed 80 Frs.

Meals: Choice 2-5km. Picnic in garden.

Open: All year.

Gîte space for 10 people

From Angers N162 dir. Le Lion d'Angers; follow dir. Rennes then D863 dir. Segré for 3km. Left at Chambre d'Hôte sign. House 1km along on left.

MMap 232-19 **ASP Map No: 2**

Jocelyne & François VIVIER
Les Travaillères
49220 Le Lion d'Angers
Maine-et-Loire
Tel: (0)2 41 61 33 56/
(0)6 80 82 02 49

Cheeky red squirrels run along the stone balustrade, the wide river flows past the large, lush riverside garden: it feels like deep country but this handsome manor has urban elegance in its very stones. Panels, cornices, mouldings, subtly-muted floor tiles bring grace while traditional French furnishings add softness. In these formal surroundings Madame, energetic, relaxed and communicative, adores having guests and pampering them with luxury. Monsieur is jovial and loves fishing! Fine, plush bedrooms, three with river views, all with superb bathrooms. Walking and cycling paths now marked.

Rooms: 2 double, 1 twin room, each with bath/shower & wc.

Price: 380-480 Frs (€ 57.93-73.18) for two, including breakfast; extra bed 100 Frs.

Meals: 150 Frs, excluding wine.

Open: Easter to 31 October.

From Angers, N162 dir. Lion d'Angers. At Grieul (20km) right on D291 to Grez Neuville. At church (1.5km), Rue de l'Écluse towards river on left.

MMap 232-19 **ASP Map No: 2**

Jacqueline & Auguste BAHUAUD
La Croix d'Étain
2 rue de l'Écluse
49220 Grez Neuville
Maine-et-Loire
Tel: (0)2 41 95 68 49
Fax: (0)2 41 18 02 72
www.sawdays.co.uk

A neo-Gothic surprise with a bucolic stork-nested, deer-roamed park that runs down to the river and an interior worthy of Hollywood: the sitting room is wildly mock-medieval, the panelled drawing room was taken whole from an C18 château. This was once a fully self-sufficient country estate and there are the remains of a chapel, dovecote and mill (you can swim or row a boat in the river). Any proper château has a Bishop's Room, of course: you can sleep in this one; the corner room has a splendid four-poster. An elegantly warm welcome from lovely people who fill the house with friends and family and might even play bridge with you.

Rooms: 2 triple, 1 double, each with bath or shower & wc.

Price: 380 Frs (€ 57.93) for two, including breakfast.

Meals: 135 Frs, including wine & coffee.

Open: Easter to 31 October.

From Angers, N23 north. At Seiches sur Loir, D74 dir. Châteauneuf sur Sarthe for 5.5km. Château on right as you leave Montreuil village.

MMap 232-20 **ASP Map No: 2**

Jacques & Marie BAILLIOU
Château de Montreuil
49140 Montreuil sur Loir
Maine-et-Loire
Tel: (0)2 41 76 21 03

Golfers are particularly welcome here but design buffs will be thrilled by the originality of this 200-year-old village house with its curious fenestration (half a curvy-glazed triangle in your bathroom) and extraordinarily complicated dining table. Everyone will love the big peaceful garden, the deep-seated, welcoming sitting room and the well-decorated, simply furnished bedrooms. English Claire is a knowledgeable hostess, anxious to please, who organizes golfing tours; French Éric, who has deliciously Maurice Chevalier English, loves sharing the cooking and includes vegetarian specialities.

Rooms: 1 triple, 2 double, 1 twin, all with hip-bath/shower & wc.

Price: 260 Frs (€ 39.64) for two, including breakfast. Extra bed 100 Frs.

Meals: 95 Frs, including coffee.

Open: April to October.

From Laval N162 through Château Gontier & 16km dir. Angers. Right on D78 to St Martin du Bois. Past 'Tabac' then 1st left. House along on right.

MMap 232-19 **ASP Map No: 2**

Claire DIGARD & Éric PAJAK
La Pigeonnerie
18 rue du Prieuré
49500 St Martin du Bois
Maine-et-Loire
Tel: (0)2 41 61 33 52
e-mail: golf_anjou@hotmail.com
www.sawdays.co.uk

Madame, a history teacher, is a great source of local knowledge (old slate mines, model villages, river trips...). The converted farm building, in the grounds of the Château du Teilleul, has a big, convivial, cedar-panelled sitting room. The bedroom, charmingly decorated and beamed with a sloping roof, has the bath behind a bookcase/bar and its own loo in the corridor. This splendid home, littered with heirlooms, has been called "homely if chaotic, with super conversation and ambience". Madame has been called "the perfect, elegant hostess". Four lovely children too. We like it a lot.

Rooms: 1 twin with own bath & basin in room, wc down corridor.

Price: 280 Frs (€ 42.69) for two, including breakfast.

Meals: 110 Frs, including wine.

Open: All year.

Take D923 from St. Sauveur dir. Segré. Driveway is on right, 200m after village.

MMap 232-19 **ASP Map No: 2**

Marie-Alice & Michel de VITTON
Le Domaine du Teilleul
49500 St Sauveur de Flée
Maine-et-Loire
Tel: (0)2 41 61 38 84
Fax: (0)2 41 61 38 84

Sprightly Monsieur le Comte is the patriarch of this very close family which extends to include guests to whom Loïk and Hélène, the younger generation, give a wonderfully relaxed welcome. This very special place has so many ways of expressing its personality: oval windows, canopied beds, sunken marble bath, children's room, lift to bathroom, ancient oaks, bread oven, ice house, pigeon house, endless reception rooms, magnificent stone staircase, pool like a 'mini-Versailles'. Teresa Berganza stayed and practised at the grand piano — she too enjoyed that gracious and natural sense of hospitality.

Rooms: 2 double, 1 twin, 3 single, each with bath or shower & wc. Extra space for children.

Price: 600-900 Frs (€ 91.47-137.20) for two, 350-550 Frs for one, incl. breakfast.

Meals: In village or picnic in park.

Open: All year except mid-Dec to mid-Jan.

From Château Gontier, N171 to Craon. Château clearly signposted as you enter town.

MMap 232-18 **ASP Map No: 2**

Comte Louis de GUÉBRIANT, Loïk & Hélène de GUÉBRIANT
Château de Craon
53400 Craon
Mayenne
Tel: (0)2 43 06 11 02
Fax: (0)2 43 06 05 18
www.sawdays.co.uk

A fine château next to the River Mayenne and, thanks to surrounding park and farmland, surprisingly quiet although just off the road. There is a large, formal sitting room and, across the central hallway with its grand piano and staircase, an elegant dining room with separate tables for breakfast. The house has been much added to since it came into the family 400 years ago but every object, antique and picture tells a story. Bedrooms include a suite with a double four-poster and river views and a tiny double with two single four-posters — pretty grand, we feel, and grandly welcoming people to receive you.

Rooms: 1 double, 1 twin, 1 suite, each with bath & wc.

Price: 400 Frs (€ 60.98) for two, including breakfast. Extra bed 100 Frs.

Meals: Choice in town.

Open: All year.

In Château Gontier N162 N dir. Laval. Château entrance is 50 metres after last roundabout as you leave the town.

MMap 232-19 **ASP Map No: 2**

Brigitte & François d' AMBRIÈRES
Château de Mirvault
Mirvault Azé
53200 Château Gontier
Mayenne
Tel: (0)2 43 07 10 82
Fax: (0)2 43 07 10 82
www.sawdays.co.uk

Hard to beat! The atmosphere is elegant yet relaxed and supremely friendly, the rooms are exquisite, the hospitality utterly natural, the noble horse and love of beautiful things inform house and hosts. In this lovely medieval village, your hosts run one of only six carriage-driving schools in France. As well as fine dinners there are superb pony-and-trap picnics — a treat not to be missed. It is peacefully off the beaten track and genuinely civilised. Our readers have been highly enthusiastic.

Rooms: 2 double, 1 triple, all with own shower and wc.

Price: 350-395 Frs (€ 53.36-60.22) for two, including breakfast; extra bed 150 Frs.

Meals: Saturdays, for at least 6: 160 Frs, including wine & coffee.

Open: All year.

From Sablé sur Sarthe, D309 (D27) dir. Angers. On entering St Denis, 1st left at 'Renov Cuir' sign. House is 100m along, signposted.

MMap 232-20 **ASP Map No: 2**

Martine & Jacques LEFEBVRE
Le Logis Du Ray
53290 St Denis d'Anjou
Mayenne
Tel: (0)2 43 70 64 10
Fax: (0)2 43 70 65 53

Three peacocks wander the garden, ducks and geese paddle in the enchanting pond, cows graze in the fields and apples are transformed into cider. When you walk into the house you walk into another world. It is a beam-lover's delight and the amazing oak staircase takes off in several directions. There are nooks and crannies, odd angles and crooked lines; terracotta-tiled floors, big windows, half-timbered walls, a canopied bed, antiques here for over 150 years. Madame is brightly friendly and blessed with a laugh that sings.

Rooms: 2 double, 1 triple, 1 family room, each with shower or hip bath & wc.

Price: 250 Frs (€ 38.11) for two, including breakfast. Extra bed 50 Frs.

Meals: 80 Frs, including coffee.

Open: All year.

Gîte space for 6 people

From Laval N162 S dir. Château Gontier for 14km then left through Villiers Charlemagne to Ruille Froid Fonds. In village left on C4 for Bignon. Signposted.

MMap 232-19 **ASP Map No: 2**

Claudette DAVENEL
Villeprouvé
53170 Ruille Froid Fonds
Mayenne
Tel: (0)2 43 07 71 62

Mansion house and *chambre d'hôte* on the grandest of scales gracefully combined in a splendid château in the heart of the town. The surrounding park with its formal, box-lined French garden and wild, romantic 'English' garden creates a sylvan setting. The hosts are exquisitely courteous and the rooms large and light, each one decorated in individual style. You will find an easy mix of luxury and comfort in the cavernous bathrooms, marble fireplaces and beautiful original panelling, some of it delicate blue against striking yellow curtains and bedcovers. Exceptional position, exceptional style.

Rooms: 3 double, 1 suite, each with bath & shower & wc.

Price: 650-750 Frs (€ 99.09-114.34) for two, including breakfast.

Meals: Full choice in Laval.

Open: All year except December & January.

In Laval centre follow signs to 'Mairie' then to 'Le Bas du Gast' — opposite 'Salle Polyvalente' and 'Bibliothèque'.

MMap 232-7 **ASP Map No: 2**

M & Mme François WILLIOT
Le Bas du Gast
6 rue de la Halle aux Toiles
53000 Laval
Mayenne
Tel: (0)2 43 49 22 79
Fax: (0)2 43 56 44 71
www.sawdays.co.uk

Old stones, indeed, as they say in French and readers have loved the "real character of the place". It is an enchanting C15th manor with staircase tower to the upstairs bedroom, bread oven and a fine dining room where breakfast is served to the chiming of the church clock. This is the Nays' old family home, well restored and really lived in (they have two small sons). They weave baskets, make music, will teach you French and radiate enthusiasm. A wonderful atmosphere in delectable countryside.

Rooms: 1 double, 1 triple, both with bath or shower & wc.

Price: 220-250 Frs (€ 33.54-38.11) for two, including breakfast.

Meals: In village or 3km.

Open: All year.

Gîte space for 6 people

From Laval, N157 dir. Le Mans. At Soulgé sur Ouette, D20 left to Evron then D7 dir. Mayenne. Signposted in Mézangers.

MMap 232-8 **ASP Map No: 2**

Léopold & Marie-Thérèse NAY
Le Cruchet
53600 Mézangers
Mayenne
Tel: (0)2 43 90 65 55

An exceptional and engaging couple; Thérèse is vivacious and the conversation at their table is the very heart and soul of this marvellous place. At dinner, everything is home-made, from *pâté* to *potage* to *patisserie*... all *Normand* and attractively presented. Breakfast is a feast at which you help yourself to freshly-squeezed juice, eggs, cheese and buckets of coffee. The bedrooms are average-sized, decorated with Japanese grass paper and a few antiquey bits and bobs. Good people, and one or two sons may also be there.

Rooms: 1 triple, 2 double, 1 twin, each with shower or bath & wc.

Price: 250 Frs (€ 38.11) for two, including breakfast; extra bed 80 Frs.

Meals: 95 Frs, including wine & coffee.

Open: April to November.

From Fougères N12 east towards Laval for 15km when farm signposted on right.

MMap 232-6 **ASP Map No: 2**

Maurice & Thérèse TRIHAN
La Rouaudière
Mégaudais
53500 Ernée
Mayenne
Tel: (0)2 43 05 13 57
Fax: (0)2 43 05 71 15

The house is indisputably French, the owners Franco-British, the breakfast sometimes 'Scandinavian' and the squirrels on the green sward red. In this haven of quiet, Denis and Patricia will fascinate you with tales of their days as foreign correspondents. Guests enjoy good beds, their own cosy sitting room with the old bread oven, a complete kitchen and a lovely path down to the stream. After visiting villages, walking the trails, dreaming in the rolling country, return to good conversation and real hospitality.

Rooms: 2 double/twin, each with bath & wc.

Price: 320 Frs (€ 48.78) for two, including generous breakfast.

Meals: Auberge in village; good restaurant nearby; guest kitchen.

Open: March to October.

On N12 from Mayenne dir. Alençon; after 5km, left on D34 dir. Lassay. In Montreuil Poulay, left on D160; house is 700m along.

MMap 231-41 **ASP Map No: 1**

Denis & Patricia LEGRAS-WOOD
Le Vieux Presbytère
53640 Montreuil Poulay
Mayenne
Tel: (0)2 43 00 86 32
Fax: (0)2 43 00 81 42
e-mail: 101512.245@compuserve.com

A house of great character and charm, it has memories of the English occupation during the 100 Years War and a turret turned into a bedroom for children — a little stone nest with exposed stone walls, old tiled floor, narrow windows and fireplace. Madame is an utterly delightful hostess, an excellent cook of regional specialities and the atmosphere of the house is one of simple, unaffected hospitality. 20-mile views across the beautiful Sarthe countryside from all rooms, space, parquet floors and period furnishings.

Rooms: 1 quadruple with bath & wc; 1 triple with shower, 1 double with shower, sharing wc.

Price: 250-300 Frs (€ 38.11-45.73) for two, including breakfast. Extra bed 80 Frs.

Meals: 90 Frs, including cider & coffee.

Open: All year.

From Mamers, D3 dir La Mêle for 6km. Do not go into Aillières. Farm on left.

MMap 231-44 **ASP Map No: 3**

Marie-Rose & Moïse LORIEUX
La Locherie
Aillières
72600 Mamers
Sarthe
Tel: (0)2 43 97 76 03
www.sawdays.co.uk

The whole atmosphere is deliciously casual and shambolic and dinner, with masses of home-produced ingredients, is a large, gregarious affair that may last some time — wonderful for lovers of French family cooking. The guestrooms and their shower rooms, in converted outbuildings, may show signs of the passing of time... and the family cats, but you will enjoy the Langlais. They are a lively, active couple with children and a farm to run who still find time to handpaint lampshades, take you to watch the milking or search for freshly-laid eggs. "Beautiful rooms and big smiles all round."

Rooms: 2 double, 1 twin, 1 triple, plus 1 suite in 'La Petite Maison', all with shower & wc.

Price: 260 Frs (€ 39.64) for two, including breakfast.

Meals: 110 Frs, including wine & coffee.

Open: All year.

Gîte space for 6 people

From Alençon south on N138. After 4km, left onto D55, through Champfleur towards Bourg le Roi; farm signposted 1km after Champfleur.

MMap 231-43 **ASP Map No: 3**

Denis & Christine LANGLAIS
Garencière
72610 Champfleur
Sarthe
Tel: (0)2 33 31 75 84
www.sawdays.co.uk

A jewel, in rolling parkland with sheep grazing under mature trees, horses in the paddock, swans on a bit of the moat, deer, boar... Your hosts are the nicest, easiest of aristocrats, determined to keep the ancestral home alive in a dignified manner. Bedrooms: antique furniture on parquet floors, good rugs, modern beds, bathrooms and loos in turrets, cupboards, alcoves. Downstairs: an elegant dining room with family silver, sitting room with log fire, family portraits, and a small book-lined library. Hunting trophies on walls; timeless tranquillity, lovely people.

Rooms: 1 suite for 3, 4 double, 1 twin, each with bath or shower & wc.

Price: 450-650 Frs (€ 68.60-99.09) for two, including breakfast.

Meals: 195 Frs including wine; 'Dîner Prestige' 320 Frs.

Open: All year.

From Alençon N138 S dir. Le Mans for approx. 14km. At La Hutte left on D310 for 10km, right on D19 through Courgains, left on D132 to Monhoudou; signposted.

MMap 232-10 **ASP Map No: 7**

Michel & Marie-Christine de MONHOUDOU
Château de Monhoudou
72260 Monhoudou
Sarthe
Tel: (0)2 43 97 40 05
Fax: (0)2 43 33 11 58
www.chateaux-france.com/-monhoudou

This creeper-clothed house is extremely and prettily flowery. Rooms have flower names that inspire the décor of floral colours, cushions, bedcovers, friezes; all sorts of chairs and side tables found in *brocante* shops then lovingly restored and painted with... flowers. Madame, determined, energetic and most hospitable, is a perfectionist. Her garden blooms as wonderfully as her house, the rich and copious breakfast is served in the old-tiled, wood-fired extension and she runs the whole show with the help of her friendly, well-behaved Alsatian.

Rooms: 1 suite (triple+single), 1 double, 1 twin, 1 quadruple, each with bath or shower & wc.

Price: 280-380 Frs (€ 42.69-57.93) for two, including breakfast; extra bed 60 Frs.

Meals: Choice 3-7 km.

Open: April to September, other months by arrangement.

From Le Mans, D147 S to Arnage (8km); left fork on D307 for 15km then right on D77 dir. Mansigné for 5km; Route de Tulièvre is tiny road on left, 3km after Requeil.

MMap 232-22 **ASP Map No: 7**

Marie-Dominique BLANCHARD
La Maridaumière
Route de Tulièvre
72510 Mansigné
Sarthe
Tel: (0)2 43 46 58 52
Fax: (0)2 43 46 58 52

This delightful couple breathe a real sense of harmonious complicity. And theirs is so French a château: not overwhelming, just peaceful loveliness with a big garden set among farmland and woods. Guests who swear they never sleep beyond 6 arrive sheepishly for breakfast at 10. The sitting room, narrow and panelled, feels like the inside of an old ship and the homey atmosphere is sustained by some gratifyingly untidy corners, pretty small shower rooms and much unselfconscious good taste. Dine at one big table where the wine flows unstinted and all nations commune under the smiles of such warm-hearted hosts. Ideal for families.

Rooms: 2 double/triple, 3 suites for 4/5, all with bath or shower & wc; 2 separate wcs.

Price: 280-320 Frs (€ 42.69-48.78) for two, including breakfast. Extra bed 85 Frs.

Meals: 110 Frs, including wine & coffee.

Open: All year.

Gîte space for 5 people

From Le Mans, N23 dir. La Flèche. At Cérans Foulletourte, D31 to Oizé; left onto D32; signposted on right.

MMap 232-22 **ASP Map No: 7**

Alain DAVID & Nicole DUBOIS
Château de Montaupin
72330 Oizé
Sarthe
Tel: (0)2 43 87 81 70
Fax: (0)2 43 87 26 25

This is a lovely old townhouse (parts are C14) with a plain façade hiding a beautifully-decorated interior, bedrooms with masses of personality, a large garden and a properly-concealed pool, all stretching back from the street. Once in the garden, you would scarcely know you're in town. The rooms, in renovated outbuildings, are pleasantly independent, while convivial meals are shared in the dining room — and delicious they sound. There is a big table with benches on the terrace, Madame is a peaceful feminine presence and Monsieur prides himself on his choice of Loire wines from small, unpublicised wine-growers.

Rooms: 1 double, 1 triple, 1 suite for 4/5 with small kitchen, all with own shower & wc.

Price: 260-300 Frs (€ 39.64-45.73) for two, including breakfast; extra bed 120 Frs.

Meals: 90 Frs, including table wine (Loire wines 50 Frs).

Open: All year.

Gîte space for 4 people

From Le Mans, D147 to Arnage, then D307 to Pontvallain. House in town centre; signposted.

MMap 232-22 **ASP Map No: 7**

Guy VIEILLET
Place Jean Graffin
72510 Pontvallain
Sarthe
Tel: (0)2 43 46 36 70
Fax: (0)2 43 46 36 70

A warm, open-armed welcome is guaranteed in this square house on the town square where you can sit at a pavement café and soak up the atmosphere of a typical French market town. The big rooms are square too, with original mouldings and lovely tiles in the hall, blue-clothed tables in the neat dining room. The skylit landing (actually a 'bridge' between two parts of the building) is fun. The décor and furnishings are mostly recent, functional, plush and pastel with the odd daring turquoise room. You will find it noisy in the front, quieter at the back. Claude is warmly bear-like, while Dianne is gentle, quiet and efficient.

Rooms: 1 double, 1 triple, 1 quadruple, each with bath or shower & wc.

Price: 270 Frs (€ 41.16) for two, including breakfast.

Meals: Good eating places very near.

Open: March to September.

From Le Mans, N138 dir. Tours. House in town centre, set back from town square, behind the bandstand.

MMap 232-23 **ASP Map No: 7**

Dianne & Claude LE GOFF
22 rue de l'Hôtel de Ville
72500 Château du Loir
Sarthe
Tel: (0)2 43 44 03 38
www.sawdays.co.uk

A group of low buildings in a picture of a place by a three-acre, tree-reflecting pond full of fish, frogs and ducks with a view up to a hilltop village — peace and space for all. There are games (croquet, table tennis, *pétanque*), a boat, even a sauna. Rooms are smallish, well-fitted, with separate entrances and mixed modern and old furnishings — you have a degree of independence, somewhat at the price of homeliness perhaps. Madame loves to have guests and to feed them. Monsieur twinkles and gets on with the garden. They are a charming, caring couple. Breakfast includes cheese and cold meats. Dinner is an important event, so indulge!

Rooms: 2 triple, 2 double, 1 twin, all with shower & wc.

Price: 270 Frs (€ 41.16) for two, including breakfast.

Meals: 90 Frs, including wine & coffee.

Open: March to mid-November.

From Le Mans D304 to Grand Lucé and La Chartre. Left on D305 through Pont de Braye. Left on D303 to Lavenay & follow signs (2km).

MMap 232-24 **ASP Map No: 7**

Monique & Jacques DÉAGE
Le Patis du Vergas
72310 Lavenay
Sarthe
Tel: (0)2 43 35 38 18
Fax: (0)2 43 35 38 18

Marie-Claire is so relaxed, such good adult company, so unflappably efficient that it's hard to believe she has four children under six! She and Martin, an ardent Anglophile, have converted this C18 watermill brilliantly — a labour of love, even down to the cogwheels that turn in the great kitchen where breakfast is served at the huge oak table. The double-height sitting room is full of books and videos for all to peruse. Rooms are attractive, simple, with good beds, old tiled floors, bare stone walls. The atmosphere embraces you, the country sounds of stream, cockerel and Angelus prayer bells soothe, the unsung area brims with interest.

Rooms: 2 double, 1 family room, each with bath or shower & wc.

Price: 250 Frs (€ 38.11) for two, including breakfast. Under 12s free.

Meals: Restaurant opposite.

Open: All year.

From Tours N138 dir. Le Mans to Dissay sous Courcillon (35km). In village, left at lights — mill is just past church.

MMap 232-23 **ASP Map No: 7**

Marie-Claire BRETONNEAU
Le Moulin du Prieuré
3 rue de la Gare
72500 Dissay sous Courcillon
Sarthe
Tel: (0)2 43 44 59 79

A fairytale cottage: mellow old stone, white shutters, green ivy, a large leafy garden, a clematis-covered well, a little wood and glimpses of the C12 castle round the corner (this house used to be the castle's servants' quarters). Green-eyed Michèle is modern, intelligent and interested in people; she and Michel share the hosting. The suite is three gentle Laura Ashley-inspired interconnecting bedrooms that look onto garden or endless fields. Stay a while and connect with the gentle hills, woods, streams and châteaux. Guests can be as independent as they like (separate entrance) and can take one, two or three rooms.

Rooms: 1 3-room suite for 5 with bathroom and separate wc.

Price: 260 Frs (€ 39.64) for two, including breakfast. Extra person 120 Frs.

Meals: Occasionally 80-90 Frs, including coffee.

Open: April to October.

From Le Mans, N138 dir. Tours. After Dissay/Courcillon, left onto small road on the bend & follow signs to 'Chambres d'Hôtes' & Château Courcillon.

MMap 232-23 **ASP Map No: 7**

Michèle LETANNEUX & Michel GUYON
La Châtaigneraie
72500 Dissay sous Courcillon
Sarthe
Tel: (0)2 43 79 45 30
www.sawdays.co.uk

The house has that easy lived-in air, the welcome is genuine, so what matter if the French is sometimes hard to follow? The Maréchals are amiable, elderly, hard-working farmers who are renovating their house, lead a sociable life and love having their grandchildren around. The low-beamed bedrooms are modest but comfortable. Expect meals, eaten *en famille*, to be just that: good, honest, family fare, often using home-grown, chemical-free vegetables, that readers have found excellent. One reader wrote: "unique ambience and thoroughly relaxed timetable". The farm buildings include a gîte.

Rooms: 4 double, each with bath or shower & wc.

Price: 240-250 Frs (€ 36.59-38.11) for two, including breakfast.

Meals: 80 Frs, including wine.

Open: All year.

Gîte space for 18 people

From Dreux, N12 to Brouais; D115 to Boutigny; D101 dir. Prouais; farm is between the two villages, signposted 'Chambres d'Hôtes'.

MMap 231-48 **ASP Map No: 3**

Serge & Jeanne-Marie MARÉCHAL
La Ferme des Tourelles
11 rue des Tourelles, La Musse
28410 Boutigny Prouais
Eure-et-Loir
Tel: (0)2 37 65 18 74/
(0)6 08 06 29 98 (mob)
Fax: (0)2 37 65 18 74

The furniture and decoration of this fine old farmhouse are in truly impeccable taste. Bedrooms with exposed timbers and excellent beds overlook the garden. There's an attractive *salon* and prettily-presented breakfasts. The Lothons are proud of their home with its refined, rather exclusive air — Monsieur is an antiques dealer, Madame a gentle hostess — and they thoroughly enjoy guests. Groups taking both rooms can have their own cooking and laundry facilities (supplement).

Rooms: 1 triple, 1 double, each with bath & wc.

Price: 380 Frs (€ 57.93) for two, including breakfast.

Meals: Choice 5km.

Open: All year.

Gîte space for 4 people

From Houdan, D61 dir. Bourdonné; right on D115 to Dannemarie. There, follow D101 to Faverolles. In village, signposted 'La Cour Beaudeval Antiquités'.

MMap 231-48 **ASP Map No: 3**

Mireille & Jean-Claude LOTHON
La Cour Beaudeval
28210 Faverolles
Eure-et-Loir
Tel: (0)2 37 51 47 67

They are delightful! Virginie beautifully French, Richard a gentle American/European, their two sons small but perfectly behaved. The old family house with its tall windows and fine proportions feels properly lived in — deep comfortable armchairs by the marble fireplace under crystal chandeliers. The top floor has been converted into five good rooms with sound-proofing, big American-size beds, masses of hot water, mix 'n' match colour schemes... and little decorative family clutter! They are easy, fun and intelligent; and Virginie loves cooking (simply).

Rooms: 1 triple, 3 double, 1 twin, all with shower & wc.

Price: 300-350 Frs (€ 45.73-53.36) for two, including breakfast.

Meals: Simple dinner: 100 Frs, including wine & coffee.

Open: March to October.

From A11 exit Ablis on N10 dir. Chartres. At Essars, right to St Symphorien, Bleury & Ecrosnes. There right & immediately left to Jonvilliers for 2.5km. White château gates straight ahead.

MMap 240-16 **ASP Map No: 3**

Virginie & Richard THOMPSON
Château de Jonvilliers
17 rue d'Épernon
28320 Jonvilliers, Eure-et-Loir
Tel: (0)2 37 31 41 26
Fax: (0)2 37 31 56 74
e-mail: information@chateaudejonvilliers.com
www.chateaudejonvilliers.com

"One of the best nights I have ever spent in a *chambre d'hôte.*" Our inspector loved it, largely because of the Vasseurs. Only 15 minutes from Chartres, it is totally quiet in a blanket of fields. Bruno works out there single-handedly but is no typical farmer; he went to the Lycée Français in London, so conversation can be in either language. Dinner is unforgettable — try the goat cheese — and breakfast is orgiastic with farm-laid eggs. Deeply comfortable bedrooms, simple sitting/dining room, nice children, relaxed, refined people.

Rooms: 2 double, 1 twin, each with bath or shower & wc.

Price: 290-320 Frs (€ 44.21-48.78) for two, including breakfast. Extra person 90 Frs.

Meals: 100 Frs, including wine & coffee. Under 12s 50 Frs.

Open: All year.

From Chartres N154 N for Dreux. Shortly after leaving Chartres, left on D133 for Fresnay and follow signs for 'Chambres d'Hôtes' to Levéville (or Levesville).

MMap 231-48 **ASP Map No: 3**

Nathalie & Bruno VASSEUR
Ferme du Château
Levéville
28300 Bailleau l'Évêque
Eure-et-Loir
Tel: (0)2 37 22 97 02
Fax: (0)2 37 22 97 02

Up two flights of a spiral staircase, in the attic (fear not, Monsieur will carry your bags), the bedroom feels not unlike sleeping in a church with unexpectedly comfortable beds, lots of books, and good shower on the floor below. There are reminders of pilgrimage and religion everywhere — indeed, the little prayer room is your sitting room — but they don't intrude. So close to the great Cathedral... we are delighted to have discovered this slightly eccentric and welcoming place. Your host is a charmer and enjoys a chuckle.

Rooms: 1 twin room with shower & wc.

Price: 270 Frs (€ 41.16) for two, including breakfast.

Meals: Choice at your doorstep.

Open: All year.

On arriving in Chartres, follow signs for IBIS Centre and park as you reach Hotel IBIS (Place Drouaise) then walk 20m along Rue de la Porte Drouaise and on Rue Muret to No 80 (approx. 100m car to house).

MMap 231-48 **ASP Map No: 3**

Jean-Loup & Nathalie CUISINIEZ
Maison JLN
80 rue Muret
28000 Chartres
Eure-et-Loir
Tel: (0)2 37 21 98 36
Fax: (0)2 37 21 98 36

Eulogies for these people have reached us. A beautiful painted sign leads to the well-restored old house which still retains a certain quaintness. It has three cosy, white guestrooms and one very large ground-floor room, all with excellent bedding. Madame is matronly and trusting and the house has a warm family atmosphere, with old pieces of furniture. Birdsong soothes your ear and wheat fields sway before your eye as you rest in the pretty garden. Your hosts can teach you lots about the various bird species. In summer there is a children's pool. *Bookings not confirmed by 5pm on day of arrival may be re-allocated.*

Rooms: 1 double, 1 triple, 2 quadruple, all with shower & wc en suite or on landing.

Price: 250 Frs (€ 38.11) for two, including breakfast.

Meals: Choice 7km.

Open: All year.

From Châteaudun, N10 dir. Chartres. At Bonneval, D17 to Moriers; there, D153 to Pré St Martin; signposted. (Or A11 exit 'Thivars'.)

MMap 237-39 **ASP Map No: 7**

Bernadette & Jean-Baptiste VIOLETTE
Le Carcotage Beauceron
8 rue Saint Martin
28800 Pré St Martin
Eure-et-Loir
Tel: (0)2 37 47 27 21
Fax: (0)2 37 47 38 09

An unusual kind of farmer, Michel has a rare expertise of which he is very proud: growing poppies for use in pharmaceuticals. Géraldine's lively manner and easy welcome into her delightful family relieve the dreariness of the ever-flat Beauce. The farm is set round a quiet, tidy courtyard where rabbits and hens lead their short lives, the good guestrooms are light and pleasantly if simply furnished, the bathrooms brand new. "Remarkable value. Real people. They've got it just right," said one reader, but don't expect designer décor or gourmet food at these amazing prices.

Rooms: 2 triple, 1 double, 1 twin, all with shower & wc.

Price: 190 Frs (€ 28.97) for two, including breakfast.

Meals: By arrangement 60 Frs, including wine.

Open: All year.

Gîte space for 5 people

From A10, Allaine exit on D927 dir. Châteaudun. At La Maladrerie, D39 to Loigny. Signposted opposite church.

MMap 237-39 **ASP Map No: 7**

Géraldine & Michel NIVET
8 rue Chanzy
28140 Loigny la Bataille
Eure-et-Loir
Tel: (0)2 37 99 70 71

This elegant C18th townhouse has retained the expansive atmosphere one associates with its wine merchant builders. They were loading their wine onto barges on the canal which flows under the windows until the 1930s. So much for the past; for the present: dine with your refined hostess in the antique-furnished, chandeliered dining room, sleep in one of her good, very individual rooms, breakfast off ravishing Gien china with fruit from the garden, meet Lutiz the black Labrador who helps her owner welcome guests over a glass of local white wine. Madame is happy to arrange visits to wine growers.

Rooms: 1 apartment for 4, 1 triple, each with bath & wc; 1 apartment for 5 with bath & wc downstairs.

Price: 300 Frs (€ 45.73) for two, including breakfast.

Meals: 100 Frs, including wine.

Open: All year.

From Orléans N60 E dir. Montargis/Nevers, exit to Fay aux Loges, through Fay, cross canal, left on D709 — house is 1st on left arriving in Donnery.

MMap 237-41 **ASP Map No: 8**

Nicole & Jacques SICOT
Les Charmettes
45450 Donnery
Loiret
Tel: (0)2 38 59 22 50
Fax: (0)2 38 59 26 96
e-mail: nsicot@mail.club-internet.fr

There is much horsiness here: the suite is over the stables, other rooms are full of equine reminders, including Toulouse-Lautrec lithographs — a taste of real French provincial aristocratic style. You sleep in great comfort under period rafters, dine *en famille* by candlelight (outside in summer), and breakfast whenever you like — "people are on holiday", says Madame expansively. Both your hosts were members of the French National Driving team: they offer rides in their prize-winning equipage. Lots of other outdoor activities are to be found in the huge forest which surrounds the quietly elegant building.

Rooms: 2 double, 1 twin, 1 suite, each with bath & wc.

Price: 560-700 Frs (€ 85.37-106.71) for two, suite 900 Frs, including breakfast.

Meals: 180 Frs, including aperitif & wine. Lunch 100 Frs.

Open: All year.

From Montargis N7 dir. Paris for 6km then right through forest to Paucourt. On entering village take 1st right Route de la Grotte aux Loups for 200m. House on left with ivy-covered wall.

MMap 237-43 **ASP Map No: 8**

Emmanuelle & Antoine de JESSÉ CHARLEVAL
Domaine de Bel Ebat
45200 Paucourt, Loiret
Tel: (0)2 38 98 38 47/
(0)6 81 34 68 99
Fax: (0)2 38 85 66 43

Your bubbling, smiling hostess, who left Paris for country calm, is keen on hunting and horses: hence horses and dogs outside, horns and antlers inside. Hers is a typical old Sologne house in brick and stone with great beams and lovely flagstones, the talking telly in contemporary contrast. The double room is brilliantly done, small but cosy, with steeply sloping roofs — no good for the over-stretched; the suites are larger (one $60m^2$); all are differently furnished and clothed — this is very much a family house. Madame, genuinely eager to please, cooks only exceptionally but will happily drive you to and from the restaurant!

Rooms: 1 double, 2 suites for 4 & 5, each with bath or shower & wc.

Price: 300-500 Frs (€ 45.73-76.22) for two, including breakfast; extra bed 100 Frs.

Meals: Exceptionally: 150-200 Frs, incl. wine & coffee; 2 restaurants 1km; self-catering possible.

Open: All year.

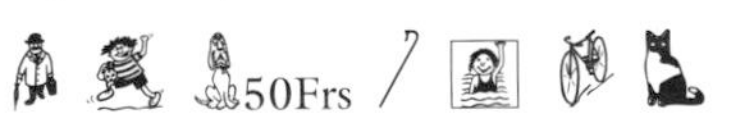

From Orléans N60 E to Châteauneuf sur Loire then right onto D11/D83 to Vannes. Go through village — house approx. 1km after village on right.

MMap 238-6 **ASP Map No: 8**

Agnès CELERIER NOULHIANE
Domaine de Sainte-Hélène
Route d'Isdes
45510 Vannes sur Cosson
Loiret
Tel: (0)2 38 58 04 55
Fax: (0)2 38 58 28 38

This vast estate by the Loire even has a private hunting reserve (long-stay guests may visit it). Trees and garden surround the manor. The interior is carefully decorated and the rooms have lovely old furnishings. Breakfast is in the *salon* (games and hi-fi) or on the flowered terrace. The young hosts — he is a vet, she looks after the house, their small children and you — make it feel friendly despite the grand appearance. They themselves live in another house just nearby. Children welcome. Don't miss the canal bridge at Briare.

Rooms: 3 double, all with shower or bath & wc; 1 suite for 3 with bathroom & kitchen.

Price: 250-320 Frs (€ 38.11-48.78) for two, including breakfast.

Meals: Briare or Gien 4km. Self-catering in suite.

Open: All year.

Gîte space for 3 people

From A6, Dordives exit onto N7 to Briare then D952 dir. Gien. Signposted by the nurseries, midway between Briare and Gien.

MMap 238-8 **ASP Map No: 8**

Mme Bénédicte FRANÇOIS
Domaine de la Thiau
45250 Briare
Loiret
Tel: (0)2 38 38 20 92
Fax: (0)2 38 67 40 50
e-mail: JMFRANC@club-internet.fr
http://perso.club-internet.fr/JMFRANC/

The canal flows gently past this handsome old village house but you may hear the less gentle road in the morning. The guestrooms are rustic-furnished and very appealing — the suite in the loft in the main house with its exposed beams is particularly good-looking — and there are two cosy self-contained cottages with kitchens. Your hosts are kind, well-educated and welcoming: their breakfast room is decorated with lots of pretty, personal knick-knacks. There's a barge restaurant in summer just a stroll from the house and do walk to the great C19 canal bridge over the Loire in Briare — a stupendous and handsome alliance of engineering and nature.

Rooms: 1 double, 1 suite for 3, each with shower & wc.

Price: 270 Frs (€ 41.16) for two, including breakfast.

Meals: In village.

Open: All year.

Gîte space for 4 people

From Châteauneuf sur Loire D952 to Gien then towards Poilly lez Gien and on D951 to Châtillon sur Loire; signposted.

MMap 238-8 **ASP Map No: 8**

M & Mme Gilbert LEFRANC
La Giloutière
13 rue du Port
45360 Châtillon sur Loire
Loiret
Tel: (0)2 38 31 10 61

No problem with English here: Madame is married to an Englishman and her artistic daughter, who clearly inherited her talent from her mother, is studying in Manchester. The guestrooms are furnished with elegance, taste and those touches of luxury which make you feel pampered. You will be greeted with a glass of Sancerre in the wonderful *salon*, whose old tiles continue into the bedrooms of this C15 *logis*. The whole house is full of worldwide travel memories and there's a romantic and shady walled garden where you can breakfast in traditional French fashion on *brioches*, *croissants* and garden fruits in season.

Rooms: 1 double, 1 twin, sharing shower & wc.

Price: 320 Frs (€ 48.78) for two, including breakfast.

Meals: Choice 10km.

Open: April to September.

Gîte space for 4 people

From Cosne sur Loire D55 W to Ste Gemme & on to Subligny (13km). House just beneath church in walled garden.

MMap 238-20 **ASP Map No: 8**

Agnès SINGER
La Chenevière
18260 Subligny
Cher
Tel: (0)2 48 73 89 93
e-mail: agnes.singer@universal.fr
www.sawdays.co.uk

This was the village notary's house; the tastes of the present owner show in the names she gives her rooms: *Monet, Picasso, Van Gogh*, each decorated to suit. Marie-Christine is into painting herself: the panelling of the dining room/entrance hall is punctuated by stencilled flowerpots atop columns and the whole room is a tour de painting force. Her warm welcome and her colour schemes, are worthy of the hospitable Monet: you can breakfast in the garden on fine days and she will even babysit — an extra Monet probably wouldn't have offered: Picasso possibly? The less agile should ask for *Monet* which has no mezzanine.

Rooms: 1 double, 2 quadruple, each with shower & wc.

Price: 260-290 Frs (€ 39.64-44.21) for two, including breakfast.

Meals: La Charité 7km. Delivery possible in summer.

Open: All year.

From N7 exit dir. Sancerre. Cross river, turn left & follow canal S to Herry. House signposted on village green.

MMap 238-20 **ASP Map No: 8**

Marie-Christine GENOUD
10 place du Champ de Foire
18140 Herry
Cher
Tel: (0)2 48 79 59 02
Fax: (0)2 48 79 59 02
www.sawdays.co.uk

Design married to old stones: the stables of this big farmhouse have been turned into brilliant guest quarters. Pale wood clothes the space with architectural features such as a double-height staircase, 14-foot wooden columns and sliding shutters. The breakfast room is a union of new wood and antique treasures; in the bedrooms, contemporary fabrics couple perfectly with lacey linen and crocheted covers. The house is full of light, the garden, where guests have a terrace, has an abundance of green and flowery things. Meals sound delicious and Madame quietly and graciously looks after you. La Reculée breathes a good air.

Rooms: 3 double, 2 twin, all with bath or shower & wc (2 on ground floor).

Price: 290 Frs (€ 44.21) for two, including breakfast.

Meals: 110 Frs, including wine & coffee.

Open: Mid-March to mid-November.

From Sancerre, D958 dir. Bourges. At Les Salmons, left on D93 to Montigny. Take D44 for 5km; signposted.

MMap 238-19 **ASP Map No: 8**

Elizabeth GRESSIN
La Reculée
18250 Montigny
Cher
Tel: (0)2 48 69 59 18
Fax: (0)2 48 69 52 51
e-mail: scarroir@terre-net.fr

Reached through a big stand of poplars with mowed verges and daffodils in spring, this early C20 house is surrounded by 125 hectares of wheat and maize — and its quiet, leafy front garden and donkey paddock. The Proffits are typical farmers, busy with work and children but friendly hosts. Guests lodge in a separate 'modern rustic-style' wing where bedrooms are plainly furnished, with the occasional knick-knack, and they have their own large long-tabled living room. Madame will join you here for (slightly basic?) meals if you wish. She is open and most helpful, especially about what to do and see.

Rooms: 1 double, 2 twin, all with shower & wc.

Price: 240 Frs (€ 36.59) for two, including breakfast.

Meals: 80 Frs, excluding wine & coffee (not Sundays).

Open: All year.

From Bourges, N151 dir. la Charité. At St Germain du Puy, D955 dir. Sancerre. At Les Aix d'Angillon, 2nd right dir. Ste Solange & follow Chambre d'Hôte signs for 4km.

MMap 238-19 **ASP Map No: 8**

Odile & Yves PROFFIT
La Chaume
18220 Rians
Cher
Tel: (0)2 48 64 41 58
Fax: (0)2 48 64 29 71
e-mail: proffityve@aol.com
www.sawdays.co.uk

He's a kindly, straightforward, young grandfather, she's teaches infants, they have come to this rustic haven to bring up their new family where the natural garden flows into woods and fields, deer roam and birdlife astounds. The house reflects their past: interesting bits from journeys to distant places: Indian rugs and Moroccan brasses in the pleasant ground-floor guestrooms, a collection of fossils in a vast glass cabinet in the duplex. African memorabilia and lots of old farmhouse stuff, nothing too sophisticated, and Jean will give you a light history lesson if you like. Return after contemplating Bourges to meditate in God's harmonious garden.

Rooms: 2 triple, 1 quadruple, all with shower & wc; duplex for 4/5 with bath & wc.

Price: 240 Frs (€ 36.59) for two, including breakfast. Extra bed 65 Frs.

Meals: 70 Frs, including wine & coffee.

Open: All year.

From Bourges D944 dir. Orléans. In Bourgneuf left and immediately right and follow signs 1.5km.

MMap 238-18 **ASP Map No: 8**

Jean MALOT & Chantal CHARLON
La Grande Mouline
Bourgneuf
18110 St Eloy de Gy
Cher
Tel: (0)2 48 25 40 44
www.sawdays.co.uk

Here, in the heartland of unspoilt rural France, an articulate husband-and-wife team run their beef and cereals farm, taxi their children to school and dancing classes, make their own jam and still have time for their guests. Laurence is vivacious and casually elegant and runs an intelligent, welcoming house. The big, simple yet stylishly attractive bedrooms of her superior C18 farmhouse are of pleasing proportions — one of them in an unusual round brick-and-timber tower. Guests may use the swimming pool, which nestles discreetly out of sight, at agreed times.

Rooms: 2 double, 1 twin, 1 triple, 1 quadruple, each with bath or shower & wc.

Price: 250-270 Frs (€ 38.11-41.16) for two, including breakfast.

Meals: In village or choice 6km.

Open: All year.

From Vierzon N76 dir. Bourges to Mehun sur Yèvre. After town, right on D60 to Berry Bouy. Continue on D60: farm on right approx. 3km after village.

MMap 238-30 **ASP Map No: 8**

Laurence & Géraud de LA FARGE
Domaine de l'Ermitage
18500 Berry Bouy
Cher
Tel: (0)2 48 26 87 46
Fax: (0)2 48 26 03 28

To the privilege of sleeping beneath that unsurpassed Cathedral add the company of an articulate, intelligent couple — she exudes warm serenity, he an eager interest in each visitor — and the walls of a C15 guesthouse to enclose you and it's a gift! In the dining room those old stones are crumbly in places where ancient timbers, niches, cupboards have been exposed in all their mixed-up glory. Bedrooms are wonderful too, if some plumbing seems only just younger than the walls, and the 'knight of the house' who beckons you upstairs is a fine touch of humour. The family live on the other side of the quiet courtyard that is in fact a leafy secret garden.

Rooms: 2 suites for 3/4 each with bath & wc; 2 double with bath or shower & wc.

Price: 380-450 Frs (€ 57.93-68.60) for two, including breakfast.

Meals: Full choice within walking distance.

Open: All year.

In the centre of Bourges, at the foot of the cathedral. Park in yard if space permits.

MMap 238-30 **ASP Map No: 8**

Marie-Ange & Joël BROUSTE
Les Bonnets Rouges
3 rue de la Thaumassière
18000 Bourges
Cher
Tel: (0)2 48 65 79 92
Fax: (0)2 48 69 82 05
www.sawdays.co.uk

The Chambrins are quiet country folk with tanned faces, clear eyes and much gentle reality — the most honest, no-fuss, genuinely hospitable couple you could hope to meet. Special touches, such as great swathes of creeper outside and dried flowers and an old iron cot inside, give character to this simple old farmhouse set among the sunflower fields. The kitchen-cum-breakfast room, with its carved dresser, is small and intimate. The rooms are comfortable, though not huge, but there is a nice guests' sitting area on the landing with well-worn, quilt-thrown sofas, books and games.

Rooms: 1 double, 1 twin, 1 triple, each with shower & wc. Extra bed 80 Frs.

Price: 200 Frs (€ 30.49) for two, including breakfast.

Meals: Choice 4-10km.

Open: All year.

Gîte space for 5 people

From Bourges, N144 to Levet; then D28 dir. Dun sur Auron. After 2km turn right. House 300m from junction.

MMap 238-31 **ASP Map No: 8**

larie-Jo & Jean CHAMBRIN
nnay
340 St Germain des Bois

(0)2 48 25 31 03
)2 48 25 31 03

They are a great couple! Conversation flows effortlessly over glass and ashtray. Their 1940s manor is entirely Art Deco and houses an eclectic collection of modern art. Monsieur paints and runs an antique shop. You find original art and good beds in the rooms (including an ingenious system for making twin-to-double beds), can learn how to make a properly formal French garden and breakfast whenever you want. Dine — until the small hours — in the long room with its huge collage at one end in the congenial Bohemian, fun-loving, intelligent atmosphere created by your down-to-earth hosts (both called Claude). Out of the ordinary.

Rooms: 2 double and 1 twin, all with own bath, shower, wc.

Price: 380-450 Frs (€ 57.93-68.60) for two, including breakfast.

Meals: 150-200 Frs, including wine & coffee.

Open: All year.

From St Amand Montrond, D951 dir. Sancoins and Nevers. At Charenton Laugère, D953 dir. Dun sur Auron; house is 300m along on left.

MMap 238-31 **ASP Map No: 8**

M & Mme Claude MOREAU
La Serre
18210 Charenton Laugère
Cher
Tel: (0)2 48 60 75 82

"Quite the most beautiful house we've ever stayed in", said a reader, "a unique experience of French hospitality and taste". In the family for 200 years now, it is indeed beautifully proportioned, standing in its large, shady garden. The sitting room is a cool blue/grey symphony, the dining room smart yellow/grey with a most unusual maroon and grey marble table — breakfast is in here while dinner *en famille* is in the big beamed kitchen. Each room has individual character, both elegant and comfortable, and Madame has a fine eye for detail. She is charming, dynamic, casually elegant and genuinely welcoming.

Rooms: 1 double, 2 twin, each with bath or shower & wc.

Price: 270-320 Frs (€ 41.16-48.78) for two, including breakfast.

Meals: 80-120 Frs, including wine.

Open: All year.

Gîte space for 6 people

From A71 exit 8. At roundabout take D925 W dir. Lignières & Châteauroux. House signposted 500m on right.

MMap 238-31 **ASP Map No: 8**

Marie-Claude & Régis DUSSERT
Domaine de la Trolière
18200 Orval
Cher
Tel: (0)2 48 96 47 45

Teacher and hurdy-gurdy player involved in the summer folk festival, Solange Frenkel has converted an 18th-century *grange* (barn) into one of the friendliest *chambres d'hôtes* we know. In the remote rural area where George Sand held her salons and consorted with Chopin, it has high ceilings, huge beams, a vast fireplace in the sunken cosy living-room 'pit' and pretty bedrooms with garden entrances. You can have unlimited breakfast while Lasco the Labrador waits patiently to take you walking. One reader simply wrote, "The best".

Rooms: 1 double, 1 twin, each with bath or shower & wc.

Price: 280 Frs (€ 42.69) for two, including breakfast.

Meals: By arrangement 95 Frs, including wine.

Open: All year.

From Bourges, N144 dir. Montluçon. At Levet D940 dir. La Châtre. At Thevet St Julien, D69 dir. St Chartier. After 2km, left; after 1km, left again. Signposted.

MMap 238-41 **ASP Map No: 8**

Solange FRENKEL
La Garenne
36400 Thevet St Julien
Indre
Tel: (0)2 54 30 04 51
www.sawdays.co.uk

A brave and endearing young English couple who came to farm in France, with their rabbit-eared sheep (they now have two small children, and cattle, too), invite you to drive 2km through the woods for a taste of rural French tranquillity with an English flavour. Their house still has some old beams and a stone fireplace. Rooms are big, pale-floored, simply-furnished, supremely peaceful: pilgrims to Compostela often stay here. Alison will take good care of you and Robin may tell you tales of shearing French sheep and settling into this other land. He can also show you where to gaze on rare orchids. Argenton, 'Venice of the Indre', is a must.

Rooms: 1 double with bath & wc; 2 double, 1 triple, sharing bathroom & separate wc.

Price: 260-290 Frs (€ 39.64-44.21) for two, including breakfast.

Meals: 90 Frs, including wine & coffee.

Open: April to December.

From Châteauroux A20 exit 16 to Tendu taking 1st left into village. Pass 'Mairie' then fork left at church dir. Chavin & Pommiers. House 2km up track.

MMap 238-40 **ASP Map No: 7**

Robin & Alison MITCHELL
La Chasse
36200 Tendu
Indre
Tel: (0)2 54 24 07 76

Don't you love those brick portholes? Set in a large park where protected species of flora and fauna thrive, it is a most striking house. Your hostess fell in love with it too and left her beloved Paris to be here, but she needs lots of people to make it hum. Relaxed and sociable, she will treat you very much as part of the family. The generous rooms have beams and old furniture, the ochre-walled hall is a homely clutter of riding gear, the dining room feels definitely lived in and the open view across parkland to the woods beyond is supremely restful.

Rooms: 1 double, 1 double/twin, 1 suite for 4, each with bath or shower & wc.

Price: 320 Frs (€ 48.78) for two, including breakfast.

Meals: 90 Frs, including wine.

Open: April to October.

Gîte space for 4 people

From Poitiers N151 E to Le Blanc (60km). Right BEFORE river on D10 to Bélâbre then left on D927 NE dir. St Gaultier. House on right after about 5km.

MMap 238-38 **ASP Map No: 7**

Aude de LA JONQUIÈRE-AYMÉ
Le Grand Ajoux
36370 Chalais
Indre
Tel: (0)2 54 37 72 92
Fax: (0)2 54 37 56 60
e-mail: grandajoux@aol.com
http://members.aol.com/grandajoux

These environment-passionate people — courageously agin' huntin' in France's royal hunting grounds, nature photographer (wonderful pics of local fauna) and bird-knower (binoculars for ornithologists) — are quiet and serious. Their elegant house has an amazing mound, created by a fallen and resuscitated judas tree, for spring splendour, great-grandmother's solid Second Empire furniture and amusing sculptural plastic works created by father and son for artefact interest. The Brenne nature reserve is all here: take Alain's deeply informed accompanied walks in spring and autumn.

Rooms: 2 double, each with bath or shower & wc.

Price: 270-300 Frs (€ 41.16-45.73) for two, including breakfast; extra bed 70 Frs.

Meals: Choice in Le Blanc.

Open: All year (book ahead).

From Argenton sur Creuse, N151 dir. Poitiers. At Le Blanc, D975 dir. Martizay; then D27 dir. Rosnay. After 2km right to Les Chézeaux; signposted.

MMap 238-38 **ASP Map No: 7**

Annie & Alain JUBARD
Les Chézeaux
36300 Le Blanc
Indre
Tel: (0)2 54 37 32 17
www.gites-de-france.fr

Your charming, talented, partly-Parisian hosts — one a window-dresser, the other a theatre hair-and-make-up artist — have created a stylish home of simple sophistication with a relaxed atmosphere. The elegant, well-proportioned rooms have canopied beds, subtle colour schemes (*Les Mûriers* just avoids being blackberry-lurid) and good tiled bathrooms. The sitting room has white walls, matting on old tiles, good country antiques and an old fireplace. Enjoy the lime-tree-shaded garden and your hosts' genuine hospitality. Interesting terms for long stays.

Rooms: 1 double, 1 twin, each with shower & wc; 1 suite for 4 with bath & wc.

Price: 330 Frs (€ 50.31) for two, suite 550 Frs, including breakfast. Extra bed 100 Frs.

Meals: Restaurant in village.

Open: Mid-June to mid-Sept (winter weekends by arrangement).

From Loches, N143 S dir. Châteauroux for 16km. Go through Fléré; 1km after village, right on D10a for Cléré du Bois; signposted.

MMap 238-26 **ASP Map No: 7**

Claude RENOULT
Le Clos Vincents
36700 Fléré la Rivière
Indre
Tel: (0)2 54 39 30 98
Fax: (0)2 54 39 30 98

Like so many watermills, this place is just a delight to look at and the ground-floor double has its own door to the stream-side terrace — the soothing sound of water should drown out any overhead floorboard creaks or road noise. Pretty rooms all, with antiques and lace, a good sitting room with wonderful beam structure in the former milling area (look out for graffiti on the stone walls) and breakfast feasts. The owners have done a sensitive restoration, are genuinely interested and caring and have a flexible approach to your needs.

Rooms: 1 double, 1 triple, 1 suite for 4, each with shower & wc.

Price: 250 Frs (€ 38.11) for two, including breakfast.

Meals: 105 Frs, including wine & coffee.

Open: All year.

From Loches N143 S dir. Châteauroux for 16km. On entering Fléré, village square is on right — Moulin clearly signed at bottom of square.

MMap 238-26 **ASP Map No:** 7

Danielle AUMERCIER
Le Moulin
36700 Fléré la Rivière
Indre
Tel: (0)2 54 39 34 41
Fax: (0)2 54 39 34 93
www.sawdays.co.uk

The C13 chapel is still used on the village feast day and the manor house, somewhat newer (C16), drips with history... which the modern décor manages to respect. The sitting and dining rooms are huge, the bedrooms are smallish and cosy. One has a large stone fireplace, stone floor, painted beams and very successful Laura Ashley fabrics. The setting is superb: high up and overlooking the Cher Valley. Fine mature trees shade the garden, and you can put your horse in the paddock. A stunning place — and you'll like your hosts, too.

Rooms: 1 suite, 2 double, each with bath or shower & wc.

Price: 400 Frs (€ 60.98) for two, including breakfast.

Meals: Wide range locally.

Open: All year.

St Georges is on N76 between Chenonceau & Montrichard. In town centre, turn up hill following signs to 'La Chaise'. There, continue up Rue du Prieuré. No 8 has heavy wooden gates.

MMap 238-14 **ASP Map No:** 7

Danièle DURET-THERIZOLS
Prieuré de la Chaise
8 rue du Prieuré
41400 St Georges sur Cher
Loir-et-Cher
Tel: (0)2 54 32 59 77
Fax: (0)2 54 32 59 77
e-mail: ctgduret@club-internet.fr

Here you are instantly one of the family, which is Hector the gentle giant hound, Persian Puss, two fine horses, a bright and friendly little girl, her congenial artist father and her relaxed linguist mother. Rooms — two in the main house, two in the garden house, where you can also study painting or French — are subtly colourful with good family furniture, vibrant bathrooms and... Jean-Lou's works on the walls. Some Aubusson tapestry cartoons too, and understated elegance in the sitting and dining rooms. A house of tradition and great originality, a joy of a garden, interesting, fun-loving hosts and a big welcoming table in the evening,

Rooms: 4 doubles, each with bath & wc.

Price: 350 Frs (€ 53.36) for two, including breakfast.

Meals: 120 Frs, including wine.

Open: All year.

From Blois D956 to Contres then D675 to St Aignan. After bridge right on D17 to Mareuil sur Cher. House on left in hamlet of 'La Maison des Marchands' (just before cat breeder sign) before main village.

MMap 238-15 **ASP Map No: 7**

Martine & Jean-Lou COURSAGET
Le Moutier
13 rue de la République
41110 Mareuil sur Cher, Loir-et-Cher
Tel: (0)2 54 75 20 48
Fax: (0)2 54 75 20 48
e-mail: lemoutier.coursaget@wanadoo.fr
www.sawdays.co.uk

A fine family house on the edge of this village in the lovely Cher valley, set against a steep hillside with fields and woods above. Madame is a most amiable lady with a nice sense of humour, living with her cats and Gigi, the Heinz 57 dog. Her son looks after the horses. The bedrooms are comfortable, light and medium-sized with traditional French family décor. The sitting room manages to be both big and cosy, with an open fireplace — a real family room where friends and family relax for a drink and a smoke.

Rooms: 4 double, all with bath or shower & wc, 1 double sharing bathroom.

Price: 260 Frs (€ 39.64) for two, including breakfast.

Meals: Good restaurant nearby.

Open: All year except 2 weeks in March.

From Blois, D956 to Contres, then D675 for St Aignan. At Noyers sur Cher, right before intersection of D675 and N76: Rue de la Mardelle is the last street before the level crossing.

MMap 238-15 **ASP Map No: 7**

Mme CHOQUET
La Mardelle
68 rue de la Mardelle
41140 Noyers
Loir-et-Cher
Tel: (0)2 54 71 70 55

People are always amazed at how quiet it is here. The drive is a half-mile pine-lined tunnel; the garden disappears into fields which disappear into woods... yet there are châteaux and wine cellars galore to be visited just down the road (even the 'big house' next door has a moat). Your dynamic, youthfully-retired hosts are new to B&B and eager to make your stay 'just right' in their converted C19 'stables' (horses lived like kings in those days). The big living room with its fine stone fireplace is a splendid double-aspect space, guestrooms are big, simple and attractively furnished and the welcome is warmly genuine.

Rooms: 2 double, 1 twin, 2 quadruple, each with bath or shower & wc.

Price: 280 Frs (€ 42.69) for two, including breakfast.

Meals: By arrangement 100 Frs, including aperitif, wine & coffee.

Open: April to December.

From Amboise D23 for 3km to Sauvigny then D30 to Vallières les Grandes. In village right dir. Montrichard on D27/D28. Lane 2nd left after water tower; house just after manor house.

MMap 238-14 **ASP Map No:** 7

Annie & Daniel DOYER
Ferme de la Quantinière
41400 Vallières les Grandes
Loir-et-Cher
Tel: (0)2 54 20 99 53
Fax: (0)2 54 20 99 53
e-mail: fermequantiniere@minitel.net

A house of endless happy discoveries. Your hostess, easy-going, chatty Marie-France, has created an oasis of sophisticated rusticity and enjoys playing shepherdess – she has some sheep and hens and loves to take children to look for fresh eggs – and working in the garden in combat gear. The house itself – open, airy and connected to the bedrooms by a glass walkway, has a soft, attractive feel (despite the marble tiles!) and a gorgeous woodsy view of the valley. There is an astonishing cylindrical shower in the centre of one of the double bedrooms – and another room sports a billiards table. A treat.

Rooms: 2 double, 1 suite, each with shower & wc.

Price: 380-550 Frs (€ 57.93-83.85) for two, including breakfast.

Meals: 2 restaurants 3km.

Open: May to October.

From Blois D751 13km to Candé; left after bridge dir. Valaire; pass War Memorial & grain silo; keep right at next fork then left at sign 'Le Chêne Vert' — house on left after small bridge

MMap 238-15 **ASP Map No:** 7

Marie-France TOHIER
Le Chêne Vert
41120 Monthou sur Bièvre
Loir-et-Cher
Tel: (0)2 54 44 07 28
Fax: (0)2 54 44 07 28

What a delightful couple: welcoming, sensitive and fun! So eager to make real contact that they have taken English lessons and will 'brief' guests at length on where to go. Madame rightly calls her C18 farmhouse *le petit trésor caché* — it has that serendipity touch. Its shutters open onto a garden (with over 100 sorts of flower) which rambles down to the small River Cisse and water meadows; its rooms are pretty, cosy, quiet; the sitting/dining room is beamed and book-lined. Fires in winter, breakfast outside in summer — a dream of a place.

Rooms: 2 double, 2 twin, all with bath or shower & wc.

Price: 350 Frs (€ 53.36) for two, including breakfast.

Meals: Choice locally.

Open: Easter to November.

Leave N152 Blois/Tours road dir. Onzain opposite bridge to Chaumont. Left immediately after underpass (chemin du Roy). After 2.5km, right. Left at stop sign. House 100m on left.

MMap 238-14 **ASP Map No: 7**

Martine LANGLAIS
46 rue de Meuves
41150 Onzain
Loir-et-Cher
Tel: (0)2 54 20 78 82/
(0)6 07 69 74 78
Fax: (0)2 54 20 78 82

Anita is charmingly Dutch; Didier, a French chef with cross-Channel experiences, speaks lovely English with accents as needed (Scots, London,...) to colour his charming sense of humour. He will take you mushrooming, as well as cooking excellent dinners with things like home-smoked salmon, rabbit stew with... wild mushrooms, chocolate mousse. The farm has three spotlessly clean, attractively-furnished bedrooms with high dormer windows overlooking fields towards the forest, and firm comfortable beds. Add a shallow swimming pool well away from the house and, if you like, cookery lessons!

Rooms: 2 suites, 2 double, 1 twin, each with bath or shower & wc.

Price: 285-320 Frs (€ 43.45-48.78) for two, including breakfast.

Meals: 125 Frs, including wine (not Tuesdays).

Open: All year except mid-December to mid-January.

From A10 exit Blois dir. Vierzon. Join D765 to Cour Cheverny then D102 dir Contres. Lane to farm about 1.5km after Cheverny château on right. Signposted.

MMap 238-15 **ASP Map No: 7**

Anita & Didier MERLIN
Ferme des Saules
41700 Cheverny
Loir-et-Cher
Tel: (0)2 54 79 97 54
Fax: (0)2 54 79 97 54
e-mail: merlin.cheverny@infonie.fr
www.chez.com/fermedessaules

They are Irish, and delighted to be very much part of their French village. Mary, brimming with energy and optimism, teaches English to French businessmen. Patrick, soft-spoken with a lovely sense of humour, has renovated the house and now finds much enjoyment in running the B&B — you are very well looked after. Rooms, up steep stairs under the (new) rafters, with lots of floral patterns and pictures, are a good size, with rather small bathrooms. The garden apartment is nicely independent. You all breakfast together in the warm-hearted Crehans' cheerful dining room. Super spot for walking and bird-watching.

Rooms: 2 double, 1 twin, 1 apartment for 4/5, each with bath or shower & wc.

Price: 280 Frs (€ 42.69) for two, including breakfast.

Meals: Choice in village.

Open: April to October.

From A71 exit 3 onto D923 through La Ferté Beauharnais to Neung sur Beuvron. Go through village — house on right just after turning to La Marolle.

MMap 238-16 **ASP Map No: 7**

Mary Ellen & Patrick CREHAN
Breffni Cottage
16 rue du 11 novembre
41210 Neung sur Beuvron
Loir-et-Cher
Tel: (0)2 54 83 66 56
Fax: (0)2 54 83 66 56

Fascinating and delightful people in a house full of style, originality and happy surprises. Madame, an art historian, talks exuberantly about everything and creates beauty with her hands. (The shimmering patchwork quilts are her work.) Monsieur has a great sense of fun too, yet their house hums with serenity. Rooms are period-themed with family pieces: the *1930s* has an old typewriter, a valve radio and an authentic, garish green bathroom; the *1900s* has a splendid carved bed. The romantic garden is a fitting mixture of French geometric and English informal and the house set back enough for the road not to be a problem.

Rooms: 1 double, 1 twin, 1 triple, 1 single, each with bath or shower & wc.

Price: 300-350 Frs (€ 45.73-53.36) for two, including breakfast.

Meals: 2 restaurants in village.

Open: April to Oct or by arrangement.

From A10 exit 16 & follow signs to Chambord, crossing Loire river at Mer. After bridge right on D951 — house on right at end of village.

MMap 238-3 **ASP Map No: 7**

Francis & Béatrice BONNEFOY
L'Échappée Belle
120 rue Nationale
41500 St Dyé sur Loire
Loir-et-Cher
Tel: (0)2 54 81 60 01
e-mail: fbbonnefoy@aol.com
www.sawdays.co.uk

Muriel is a flower-loving perfectionist of immaculate taste and has let loose her considerable decorative flair on this miniature Italian villa where Queen Marie de Médicis used to take the waters: the fine garden still has a hot spring and the River Loire flows past behind the trees. The interior is unmistakably French in its careful colours, lush fabrics and fine details — fresh flowers too. Carved wardrobes and brass beds grace some rooms. The suite is a wonderful 1930s surprise and has a super-smart bathroom. You will be thoroughly coddled in this very elegant and stylish house.

Rooms: 1 suite, 1 quadruple, 2 double, 2 twin, all with bath or shower & wc.

Price: 420 Frs (€ 64.03) for two, including breakfast.

Meals: By arrangement 200 Frs, including wine & coffee.

Open: All year (by arrangement in winter).

Macé is 3km north of Blois along N152 dir. Orléans. Go into village & follow signs. House is 500m on right before church.

MMap 238-3 **ASP Map No: 7**

Muriel CABIN-SAINT-MARCEL
La Villa Médicis
Macé
41000 St Denis sur Loire
Loir-et-Cher
Tel: (0)2 54 74 46 38
Fax: (0)2 54 78 20 27

The white duck is a symbol of friendship and Roudoudou is, quite rightly, the house mascot. Inside, a warmly sensitive atmosphere radiates from the beautiful old floor tiles, fabulous timbered ceilings, lovely family furniture. From the ground-floor bathroom you look straight onto the mill wheel (restored by Monsieur); Madame uses her innate feeling for history to advise on places to see. Both are quietly, gently caring about their guests' well-being. Bedrooms, each in a different style, are big, harmonious in fabric and colour, and look over the rambling, peaceful garden. Huge selection of teas for breakfast.

Rooms: 2 double, 2 triple, 1 suite, each with bath or shower & wc.

Price: 320-450 Frs (€ 48.78-68.60) for two, including breakfast.

Meals: Excellent choice within 7km.

Open: All year.

From A10, exit 16 onto N152 dir Blois. 3.5km after Mer, right towards Diziers and follow signs 'chambres d'hôtes'.

MMap 238-3 **ASP Map No: 7**

Marie-Françoise & André SEGUIN
Le Moulin de Choiseaux
8 rue des Choiseaux
41500 Suèvres, Loir-et-Cher
Tel: (0)2 54 87 85 01
Fax: (0)2 54 87 86 44
e-mail: choiseaux@wanadoo.fr
www.antipode.le-village.com/choiseaux

Perfect for Chambord and for walks in the Sologne, this C18 house stands in seven acres of woodland that cut out all sight of the nuclear power station. A quiet, leafy place to rest after château-visiting exertions: one owner went through Revolution, Restoration, Napoleon, three prisons, three death sentences... and then died in his bed. Traditionally-furnished bedrooms are light, sunny, attractive: there are nice old things everywhere, including grandfather's paintings. Madame, who speaks little English, shares her time between guests and the two of her five children who are still here — her welcome is appropriately formal.

Rooms: 1 double, 1 twin, 1 quadruple, all with shower & wc.

Price: 280 Frs (€ 42.69) for two, including breakfast.

Meals: 2 restaurants in village; choice 8km.

Open: All year.

From Orléans, D951 dir. Blois. On entering St Laurent, follow signs to 'Chambres d'Hôtes'.

MMap 238-4 **ASP Map No: 7**

Catherine & Maurice LIBEAUT
L'Ormoie, 26 rue de l'Ormoie
St Laurent des Eaux
41220 St Laurent Nouan, Loir-et-Cher
Tel: (0)2 54 87 24 72
Fax: (0)2 54 87 24 93
e-mail: maurice.catherine.libeaut@wanadoo.fr
www.sawdays.co.uk

The picture-framing workshop is where Madame is found; her jovial husband farms outside town and will serve your breakfast. The rooms are light and simple, decorated in understated good taste and subdued shades of off-white, grey and blue. There are beams, floors of polished parquet or tiles, billiards in the sitting room and a kitchenette for you. The garden at the back is charming, the miniature trees at the bottom screen the outbuildings. A C16th townhouse, but you feel you are in the countryside.

Rooms: 3 triple, 1 double/twin, 1 suite, each with bath or shower & wc.

Price: 290-350 Frs (€ 44.21-53.36) for two, including breakfast.

Meals: Choice in Mer.

Open: All year except January.

Gîte space for 6 people

Leave N152 Orléans-Blois road in Mer and park by church. House is short walk up main shopping street: entrance in picture-framing shop on left. (Instructions for car access given on arrival.)

MMap 238-3 **ASP Map No: 7**

Joëlle & Claude MORMICHE
9 rue Dutems
41500 Mer
Loir-et-Cher
Tel: (0)2 54 81 17 36
Fax: (0)2 54 81 70 19

As one reader said: "A little gem of a B&B" with its sweeping farmyard, its pond and such a welcome. You can see for miles across fields filled with larksong and cereals. It is peaceful, pretty and a place for picnics. The owners are a smiling couple who give you their time without invading your space but are delighted to show you their immaculate farm, orchard and vegetable garden if you're interested. Their rooms have gentle colours, soft materials and firm mattresses. The furniture is simple and rustic, the bedrooms and bathrooms are deeply raftered, the old farmhouse breathes through its timbers.

Rooms: 1 double with shower & wc; 2 double sharing bath & wc.

Price: 215-260 Frs (€ 32.78-39.64) for two, including breakfast. Extra bed 90 Frs.

Meals: 80 Frs, including wine (for 2-night stay min). Restaurant 6km.

Open: All year.

From Vendôme D957 dir. Blois for 6km. Right at sign to Crucheray & 'Chambre d'Hôte'. House 4km from turning; signposted.

MMap 238-2 **ASP Map No: 7**

Élisabeth & Guy TONDEREAU
Les Bordes
41100 Crucheray
Loir-et-Cher
Tel: (0)2 54 77 05 43
Fax: (0)2 54 77 05 43

Back to school? The History of the World on the old school room/sitting room ceiling covers the Creation, Noah's Ark, the Karma Sutra... Artists, literary folk, musicians love this place. Claude and Ariane, both wordsmiths, are articulate, cultivated, delightfully 'bohemian': children come and go to his parents' house via a ladder over the wall. The unspoilt schoolhouse has white rooms and bright paintwork; the cottage feels older; woods and fields lie just beyond the semi-wild garden where you can sit in a live willow *gloriette*. Home production is king here: hams, sheepskins, wild-boar rugs, dandelion jam ...

Rooms: 1 double, 1 twin, 1 triple, each with bath or shower, sharing wc; 1 cottage for 6/7 with kitchen, sitting room, shower & wc.

Price: 210 Frs (€ 32.01) for two, including breakfast.

Meals: 80 Frs, including aperitif, wine & digestif. Self-catering in cottage.

Open: All year.

From Vendôme N10 S dir. Tours for 19km; right on D71 to Villechauve. Go into village — house on right just after church.

MMap 238-2 **ASP Map No: 7**

Claude & Ariane LABALLE
La Lune et les Feux
Le Bourg
41310 Villechauve
Loir-et-Cher
Tel: (0)2 54 80 37 80

Extraordinary! a paradox of epicurean asceticism. Alain is a musical, artistic craftsman, cultivator of the senses, seeker of harmony; Isabelle is lovely, warm, welcoming, serene — and a superb cook. In the bedrooms, almost monastic in their simplicity, nothing distracts from the natural warmth of old tiles and Alain's beautiful furniture: all is light, space, harmony. The magnificent room under the rafters is used for recitals and furniture display. Isabelle's vegetable garden centres on a lily pond and there's a little path through the 'wild' wood beyond: this house is a meeting of market place and wilderness. Humans grow here.

Rooms: 1 double, 2 triple, 1 suite for 6/7, each with bath or shower & wc.

Price: 250-290 Frs (€ 38.11-44.21) for two, including breakfast; extra bed 75 Frs.

Meals: 100 Frs, including wine.

Open: April to October.

Mondoubleau is just north of the N157 between Orléans & Le Mans. Carrefour de l'Ormeau is main crossroads in centre of village — house on corner opposite Ford garage.

MMap 232-12 **ASP Map No: 7**

Alain GAUBERT & Isabelle PEYRON
Carrefour de l'Ormeau
41170 Mondoubleau
Loir-et-Cher
Tel: (0)2 54 80 93 76
Fax: (0)2 54 80 88 85

There are touches of fun in this simple characterful old farmhouse: a couple of parrots perch in the children's room, for example. Madame is charming, clearly delighting in her role as hostess; Monsieur quietly gets on with his gardening. Now retired, they are both active in their community, caring and unpretentious (he is Deputy Mayor). Traditionally furnished, the rooms have subtle, well-chosen colour schemes, the bathroom is new and clean. Breakfast is served in the dining room with home-made jams and crusty bread. The house backs onto the gardens of the château, is surrounded by chestnut trees and wonderfully quiet.

Rooms: 1 triple, 1 twin, 1 suite for 5, each with bath or shower & wc.

Price: 250 Frs (€ 38.11) for two, including breakfast. Extra bed 70 Frs.

Meals: Auberge 300m.

Open: All year.

From Tours D29 to Beaumont la Ronce. House signposted in village.

MMap 232-24 **ASP Map No: 7**

Michel & Andrée CAMPION
La Louisière
37360 Beaumont la Ronce
Indre-et-Loire
Tel: (0)2 47 24 42 24

In the lesser-known and lovely Loir valley you have a little old house in the garden all to yourselves. It has a kitchen and a bathroom downstairs, two little bedrooms up a steep staircase, all recently renovated, and its own piece of flower-filled garden for intimate breakfasts. Or you can join Madame in her light and cheerful kitchen at the long check-clothed table with baskets hanging from the beams. She is friendly, cultivated and dynamic, very involved in the local music festival and tourist activities so an excellent adviser for guests, and also a great maker of jams. It's not luxurious, but elegantly homely, quiet and welcoming.

Rooms: 2 double in cottage with 1 bathroom.

Price: 300 Frs (€ 45.73) for two, 520 Frs for four, including breakfast.

Meals: 120 Frs, incl. wine & coffee.

Open: All year.

From Tours/La Membrolle N138 dir. Le Mans. At Neuillé Pont Pierre D68 to Neuvy le Roy. House on road through village: blue front door, opposite turning to Louestault.

MMap 232-23 **ASP Map No: 7**

Ghislaine & Gérard de COUESNONGLE
20 rue Pilate
37370 Neuvy le Roi
Indre-et-Loire
Tel: (0)2 47 24 41 48
www.sawdays.co.uk

365

High on a cliff above the Loire, it looks over the village and across the vineyards and valley to a château. Only four years old but done in *Tourangeau* style with reproduction furniture, the house is immaculate and meticulously kept: one room is in Louis XIV style, plus orangey carpet and flowery paper. There is a big dining/sitting area with tiled floor and rugs, an insert fireplace and views over the large sloping garden... under which there is a troglodyte dwelling. Mountain bikes to borrow, giant breakfasts... great value for the Loire.

Rooms: 1 suite, 3 double, each with bath & wc.

Price: 260-295 Frs (€ 39.64-44.97) for two, including breakfast.

Meals: Wide choice locally & in Tours.

Open: All year.

From Tours A10 N dir. Paris; cross River Loire then leave exit 20. Follow signs to Rochecorbon. In village left at lights then right up steep narrow lane; signposted.

MMap 232-36 **ASP Map No: 7**

Mme Jacqueline GAY
7 chemin de Bois Soleil
37210 Rochecorbon
Indre-et-Loire
Tel: (0)2 47 52 88 08
Fax: (0)2 47 52 85 90
e-mail: jacquelinegay@minitel.net
www.sawdays.co.uk

366

A working goat-farm producing its own delicious cheese. Sleep in the pigsty (or is it the stable block?), swim in their beautiful pool then carouse over dinner in the lovely old room in the main house with its beams and large open fireplace; the meal, very much *en famille*, starts after the evening's milking. The atmosphere around the table, the unusual and lovely setting and the easy good nature of your hosts make the fairly basic rooms utterly acceptable. Bits of the house are 13th century: it was built by a glass-maker, a very superior trade in those days, and overlooks the extraordinary ruins of a large castle.

Rooms: 2 double, 1 twin, 1 quadruple, each with shower & wc.

Price: 240 Frs (€ 36.59) for two, including breakfast. Extra bed 60 Frs.

Meals: 85 Frs, including wine & coffee.

Open: March to December.

Château la Vallière is 33km NW of Tours. From Château la Vallière take D34 S dir. Langeais — first right then right again, past ruined castle: house at top of track.

MMap 232-22 **ASP Map No: 7**

Gérard & Martine RIBERT
Vaujours
37330 Château la Vallière
Indre-et-Loire
Tel: (0)2 47 24 08 55
e-mail: rib007@aol.com

An imposing lodge set in a big 'English' garden and surrounded by forest, it has a harmonious, almost mellow feeling despite being built recently — but in C17 Angevin style with old materials from the château next door. An unusual and refreshingly natural place, it reflects the family's plan to return to country simplicity. They are relaxed and relaxing, chatty and creative, as proved by the delightful, carefully-designed and decorated bedrooms and living-dining area with their terracotta tiles and scrubbed rafters. *Children over 10 welcome.*

Rooms: 1 double, 2 twin, each with shower (1 behind curtain) & wc.

Price: 300-330 Frs (€ 45.73-50.31) for two, including breakfast.

Meals: In village.

Open: All year except 20 December to 5 January.

From Tours, N152 dir. Saumur. At St Patrice, D35 to Bourgueil. There, D749 to Gizeux then D15 to Continvoir. In village, left on D64; signposted.

MMap 232-34 **ASP Map No: 7**

Michel & Claudette BODET
La Butte de l'Épine
37340 Continvoir
Indre-et-Loire
Tel: (0)2 47 96 62 25
Fax: (0)2 47 96 07 36
www.sawdays.co.uk

Such a French family house: *Oncle Vincent*'s room has two BIG single beds, one made for Vincent with matching wardrobe and chest of drawers, the other, brass-knobbed and not matching the cane chair... *Tante Angèle* did the samplers in HER room, and Madame is properly proud of her fine linen. The cottage snuggles demurely in its *Jardin Secret*, rose scent wafts, Monsieur takes you to his favourite wine-growers and craftsmen (for a small fee). They love having guests and opening doors onto unknown treasures of the Loire area.

Rooms: 1 double with bath, 1 twin with shower, sharing wc. 1 cottage for 3 with shower & wc.

Price: 240-260 Frs (€ 36.59-39.64) for rooms; cottage 300 Frs, for two, incl. breakfast; extra bed 80 Frs.

Meals: Auberge 50m away.

Open: All year.

From Chinon, D16 to Huismes. In village go under arch between church and large house, then 1st street on left & 2nd house on right.

MMap 232-34 **ASP Map No: 7**

Anne & Jean-Marc BUREAU
Le Clos de l'Ormeau
37420 Huismes
Indre-et-Loire
Tel: (0)2 47 95 41 54
Fax: (0)2 47 95 41 54

A dream place! Rarely does one see so masterly a renovation and that open gallery is exceptionally rare. So is the serene and genuinely medieval atmosphere of the great square drawing room — worn flagstones, monumental fireplace, low low doors, no curtains (not authentic), soft pink furnishings against whitewashed stone walls... and, in contrast, furniture from France, Africa, Vietnam. Magical. One bedroom has a brick-and-timber wall, a great plain wooden bed, lace covers; the other a marble washstand and a monkish mirror; the deep-tubbed, small-paned bathroom is a delight. Your hosts are excellent, cultured company. Really special — book early.

Rooms: 1 suite for 3/4 with bath & wc.

Price: 650 Frs (€ 99.09) for two, 950 Frs for 3/4, including breakfast.

Meals: Choice in Villandry.

Open: April to September.

From Tours D7 to Savonnières. There, right across bridge then immediately left. House 3km along on right.

MMap 232-35 **ASP Map No: 7**

Michel & Marie-Françoise SALLES
Manoir de Foncher
37510 Villandry
Indre-et-Loire
Tel: (0)2 47 50 02 40
Fax: (0)2 47 50 09 94

Éric was the first Frenchman to join the Campaign for Real Ale! He is a charming, artistic Anglophile, with a sense of fun and a real interest in people. The four downstairs rooms have their own terraces, stone beams and fireplaces. All rooms have magnificent bath or shower rooms and a stylish use of colour while the white panelled dining room has attractive blue and white fabrics and a crystal chandelier over the big oval table. There's a smallish, cosy sitting room with a wooden fireplace. The whole place is a haven of history, culture, peace — magical.

Rooms: 2 triple, 1 twin, 3 double, 1 suite of 2 twins, each with bath or shower & wc.

Price: 420-580 Frs (€ 64.03-88.42), suite 750 Frs, for two, including breakfast. Min. 2 nights.

Meals: In village or wide choice 3km.

Open: March to November.

From Savonnières left at Hôtel Faisan dir. Ballan Miré and up hill about 1km. House on left (signposted).

MMap 232-35 **ASP Map No: 7**

Éric & Christine SALMON
Prieuré des Granges
15 rue des Fontaines
37510 Savonnières, Indre-et-Loire
Tel: (0)2 47 50 09 67
Fax: (0)2 47 50 06 43
e-mail: salmon.eric@wanadoo.fr
www.sawdays.co.uk

The owners, a likeable, cosmopolitan couple with gentle voices and masses of energy, are proud of their smart château with its listed garden (stupendous trees) and lavish much civilised care on house and guests. Three rooms are in the château (lots of stairs to the top room but what a view), three in the *Closerie*, one with a dramatic oval window onto the setting sun. Superb décor with lovely materials, subtle colours, fine furniture, attention to origins. One 'monastic' room (plain walls, exposed brick and timber) contrasts pleasingly with the plushness. Good company, PLUS a heated outdoor swimming pool! Worth every penny.

Rooms: 2 suites for 3, 2 double, 2 twin, all with bath & wc.

Price: 590-790 Frs (€ 89.94-120.43) doubles, 790-1050 Frs suites, for two, including breakfast.

Meals: 235 Frs, including wine & coffee. Choice within walking distance.

Open: All year.

From Tours N152 dir. Blois for 4km. At St Georges left and follow signs 1km to château.

MMap 232-36 **ASP Map No: 7**

Christine & Jacques DESVIGNES
Château de Montgouverne
37210 Rochecorbon
Indre-et-Loire
Tel: (0)2 47 52 84 59
Fax: (0)2 47 52 84 61
www.sawdays.co.uk

Go from common street to stately courtyard magnolias to circular marble domed staircase and you have a *Monument Historique*, a miniature Bagatelle Palace, a bachelor's folly with a semicircular *salon*. The light, airy, elegant rooms, small and perfectly proportioned, are softly pink-and-grey; lean out and pick a grape from the vine-clad pergola. Monsieur was a pilot and still flys vintage aircraft. Madame was an air hostess and English teacher and is casually sophisticated and articulate about her love of fine things, places and buildings. Wonderful, and a stone's throw from Chenonceaux.

Rooms: 1 double, 1 suite for 4, each with shower & wc.

Price: 250-400 Frs (€ 38.11-60.98) for two, including breakfast.

Meals: Good choice within walking distance.

Open: April to November (by arrangement in winter).

From Amboise D32 S to Bléré through La Croix en Touraine. Cross bridge: Rue des Déportés imm'ly opposite but one-way so turn left, imm'ly right, 1st right, right again. Guests can be collected from private airport 5km.

MMap 238-14 **ASP Map No: 7**

Dominique GUILLEMOT
Le Belvédère
24 rue des Déportés
37150 Bléré
Indre-et-Loire
Tel: (0)2 47 30 30 25
Fax: (0)2 47 30 30 25
www.sawdays.co.uk

Susanna is a special person: calm, cultured, full of knowledge and taste. You will enjoy her warm generosity, log fires, books and food (she's an excellent cook). Her background is Anglo-Irish-American-Scottish — so are her rooms, beautifully low-key and elegant with muted décor, nice bits of furniture and modern bathrooms. The finely-restored high-ceilinged main room has a relaid C17 tiled floor of great beauty. The style is perfect yet without pretension. A Romanesque arch, floodlit at night for aperitifs and coffee, enhances the garden and the church tower stands protectively above.

Rooms: 2 triple, 1 twin, 1 double, all with bath or shower & wc.

Price: 310-350 Frs (€ 47.26-53.36) for two, including breakfast.

Meals: 150 Frs, including aperitif, wine & coffee (not summer Saturdays).

Open: All year except Christmas.

From Tours N143 dir. Loches for 15km. In Cormery, cross bridge & take, very quickly, 3rd left. House 100m up on left (signposted).

MMap 232-36 **ASP Map No: 7**

Susanna McGRATH
Le Logis du Sacriste
3 rue Alcuin
37320 Cormery, Indre-et-Loire
Tel: (0)2 47 43 08 23
Fax: (0)2 47 43 05 48
e-mail: sacriste@creaweb.fr
www.sawdays.co.uk

Madame loves flowers — she won 2nd prize in a *gîtes fleuris* competition for her glorious summer garden — and hates winter. She is relaxed and pleased to make you feel at home in her pretty farmhouse (sunflowers grow in all the surrounding fields). Rooms, predictably flower-themed and fresh-flower decorated, are smallish but bright and cheerful, the guests' dayroom opens onto the terrace and the family dining room is most welcoming. In 2000 you should be able to have a little billiards practice before dinner. Try not to miss the spectacular maze created every summer with cereal crops at Reignac.

Rooms: 1 double, 1 twin, 2 triple, each with bath or shower & wc.

Price: 250-270 Frs (€ 38.11-41.16) for two, including breakfast.

Meals: 85 Frs, including wine & coffee.

Open: All year.

From Tours N143 dir. Loches, through Cormery and on for 10km. Here, see Massy-Ferguson garage on left and turn left for Azay sur Indre/Chambre d'Hôte; house 700m along, signposted.

MMap 238-14 **ASP Map No: 7**

Marie-Agnès BOUIN
La Bihourderie
37310 Azay sur Indre
Indre-et-Loire
Tel: (0)2 47 92 58 58
Fax: (0)2 47 92 22 19
www.sawdays.co.uk

Bruno, a philosopher and former teacher, is as casually refined and interesting as his family château. The roomy and engagingly shabby bedrooms have large windows over the park, big, old-fashioned baths, fireplaces and rugs. Use the charming sitting/dining room with its stone-tiled floor, pretty blue-and-white curtains, fireplace and cosy armchairs, or play in the 100-hectare park with its fine old cedars and the surrounding fields of grazing sheep — "rather like a Gainsborough" and the over-stressed find it all supremely restful. The estate makes *foie gras*, so not for convinced vegetarians.

Rooms: 2 double, 1 twin, each with bath/shower & wc.

Price: 510 Frs (€ 77.75) for two, including breakfast.

Meals: In village or Tours (5km).

Open: All year by arrangement.

From Tours D751 SW dir. Chinon for 5km. In Ballan Miré, right at lights just before level crossing. Signposted — entrance opposite golf course.

MMap 232-35 **ASP Map No: 7**

Monsieur Bruno CLÉMENT
Château du Vau
37510 Ballan Miré
Indre-et-Loire
Tel: (0)2 47 67 84 04
Fax: (0)2 47 67 55 77

An elegant dressed-stone house, a well-converted stable block, the inimitable limpid light of the Loire Valley on the edge of a quiet little village — this is a protected wetland area between Loire and Vienne rivers. The guest quarters have ancient beams, stone walls and new floors, space to sit or cook, even a little terrace. The uncluttered, sizeable rooms have the same happy mix of old and new with some fine pieces of furniture. You will be welcomed by a couple who are proud of their house and area and will direct you to less obvious places of interest. "Very clean, very friendly, very good food", say readers' letters.

Rooms: 2 triple, each with bath & wc; 1 double with shower & wc.

Price: 230-280 Frs (€ 35.06-42.69) for two, including breakfast.

Meals: 85 Frs, including wine & coffee (not Sunday). Self-catering.

Open: All year.

From Chinon D749 dir. Bourgueil for 6km. Left dir. Savigny en Véron & follow signs to 'Camping'. House 1km after campsite on right.

MMap 232-34 **ASP Map No: 7**

Marie-Françoise & Michel CHAUVELIN
Chevíré
11 rue Basse
37420 Savigny en Veron
Indre-et-Loire
Tel: (0)2 47 58 42 49

What a splendid person! What a sensitive restoration of her old farmhouse (some of it C15). Intelligent, well-travelled, cultured, she took a course on food and taste awareness, started doing B&B and simply loves bringing people together over an excellent meal where all her interests are nourished. A big fire crackles in the sitting room, the old tiles and timbers glow rich and mellow, summer dinners are in the little walled courtyard, the shady garden has private corners, rooms play variations on the theme of good fabrics and furniture (the small, lower-priced room is real value). Swathes of conviviality and light envelop the place.

Rooms: 1 double, 1 suite for 4, 1 apartment for 4, each with bath or shower & wc.

Price: 220-300 Frs (€ 33.54-45.73) for two, including breakfast.

Meals: 120 Frs, including wine & coffee.

Open: All year.

Gîte space for 4 people

From Chinon D749 dir. Bourgueil. At roundabout in Beaumont, 3rd exit dir. La Roche Honneur. Left at sign to Grézille; left again at painted sign La Balastière.

MMap 232-34 **ASP Map No: 7**

Antoinette DEGRÉMONT
La Balastière, Hameau de Grezille
37420 Beaumont en Véron
Indre-et-Loire
Tel: (0)2 47 58 87 93/
(0)6 81 69 35 06
Fax: (0)2 47 58 82 41
e-mail: balastiere@infonie.fr

Jany and Jean, back in Chinon after many years in Paris, create a thoroughly civilised atmosphere where guests bask in refined but unpretentious comfort. Their well-renovated C19 townhouse stands on the bank of the stately River Vienne with the little streets of medieval Chinon rising behind it up to the old castle. Both bedrooms (*Iris* and *Loriette*) overlook the water and have Jany's unmistakable personal touch. Jean sings in the local choir and his amazing CD and record collection covers two walls of his study. They are an articulate, music- and art-loving couple, and excellent hosts.

Rooms: 2 double, each with shower or bath & wc.

Price: 320-350 Frs (€ 48.78-53.36) for two, including breakfast.

meals: Good choice within walking distance.

Open: May to September.

Entering Chinon on D751 from Tours, drive along river past bridge and Rabelais statue. House is just after Post Office.

MMap 232-34 **ASP Map No: 7**

Jany & Jean GROSSET
84 quai Jeanne d'Arc
37500 Chinon
Indre-et-Loire
Tel: (0)2 47 98 42 78
www.sawdays.co.uk

The cool, softly blue-grey drawing room with its air of faded C18 elegance and its two large, dramatic, contemporary paintings sets the tone of a uniquely atmospheric, austerely sober old *manoir*. Bought by an energetic, artistic young mother who loves its simple authenticity, it has been treated to respectful improvement. No slick bathrooms — one bath behind thick curtains, a loo in a cupboard, but new (old-style) fittings, a sympathetically restored staircase and brand-new linen for the old-tiled bedrooms. You are drawn to intimate corners in the garden and orchard, there are water meadows beyond, and ancient peace.

Rooms: 1 double, 1 triple, 1 quadruple, each with bath & wc.

Price: 360 Frs (€ 54.88) for two, including breakfast.

Meals: Good choice 1-5km.

Open: Easter to 31 October.

 30Frs  

From Chinon, D749 dir. Bourgueil. Little road to Montour is first on left; house easily found behind imposing gates. (2km off D749, 8km from Chinon.)

MMap 232-34 **ASP Map No: 7**

Mme Valérie ARBON
Manoir de Montour
37420 Beaumont en Véron
Indre-et-Loire
Tel: (0)2 47 58 43 76
Fax: (0)2 47 58 43 76
e-mail: valerie.arbon@wanadoo.fr

In a magical garden on a steep secluded slope where troglodytes once lived (the cave with its original fireplace now houses preserves and pans), the pretty little creeper-covered old house (illustrated) and its renovated outbuilding with two excellent guestrooms, make a gentle C20 retreat from the crowds visiting the châteaux. One room has a superbly carved Norman bridal bed (doves and sheaves meaning peace and prosperity), the other has a fine great family *armoire*, both are softly furnished with good bathrooms. Madame, relaxed, cultivated and welcoming, is most knowledgeable about her beloved Loire Valley.

Rooms: 2 dble, each with shower & wc.

Price: 270 Frs (€ 41.16) for two, including breakfast; extra bed 70 Frs.

Meals: Wide choice within 5km.

Open: March to October.

From Saumur D947 dir. Chinon to Montsoreau (10km); D751 through Candes & St Germain sur Vienne. 500m on, at the 'Goujon Frétillant' restaurant, right and follow signs for 1.5km.

MMap 232-34 **ASP Map No: 7**

Anne DUBARRY
7 La Vallée des Grottes
37500 St Germain sur Vienne
Indre-et-Loire
Tel: (0)2 47 95 96 45

A modern house (1980s) in old style (C18 Loire), with modern comforts (heating and bathrooms) and old materials (beams, stones), carved chests and contemporary sculptures: these ex-Parisians clearly have a gift for marrying old and new, city sophistication and country earthiness. A place of warmth and luxury, superb rooms, beautiful furniture, a long and spectacular vineyard-to-Vienne River view. Madame is humorous, cultured and happy to guide you round the estate. Guests have their own sitting and utility rooms.

Rooms: 1 suite for 3/4 in main house; 2 double in pool-side cabin; all with bath or shower & wc.

Price: 450-480 Frs (€ 68.60-73.18) for two, including breakfast; extra bed 100 Frs.

Meals: Possibilities 2-9km.

Open: All year.

Gîte space for 4 people

From Chinon, D21 to Cravant les Coteaux. Continue towards Panzoult; house is on left after 2km.

MMap 232-35 **ASP Map No: 7**

Marie-Claude CHAUVEAU
Domaine de Beauséjour
37220 Panzoult
Indre-et-Loire
Tel: (0)2 47 58 64 64

The house had lost most of its original features but Michelle has created a cosy atmosphere with an open fireplace and lots of antiques and ornaments. Chatty, energetic and direct, she is a keen gardener and her garden, full of hidden corners, is a riot of foliage and flowers, with plenty of shade in summer. Rooms are immaculate and stylish, here some blue stripey wallpaper and old prints, there a brass bed and white table lamps. The Indre valley is charming and Saché has strong artistic vibes: Balzac lived and wrote here; Alexander Calder lived and sculpted here. *Children over 12 welcome.*

Rooms: 2 triple, 1 double, 1 suite for 4, each with shower & wc.

Price: 400 Frs (€ 60.98) for two, including breakfast.

Meals: Wide choice 10 minutes drive.

Open: Mid-March to mid-November.

From Azay le Rideau D84 E dir. Artannes. Hamlet of Sablonnière is 6km along; house clearly marked on left in centre of hamlet.

MMap 232-35 **ASP Map No: 7**

Mme Michelle PILLER
Les Tilleuls
16 rue de la Sablonnière
37190 Saché
Indre-et-Loire
Tel: (0)2 47 26 81 45
Fax: (0)2 47 26 84 00

The lovely cross-shaped symmetry envelopes you, glazed fanlights on each arm of the cross look through onto trees, the welcome is open-armed. Christian, a sweet, lively, amusing, naturally hospitable host, teaches yoga, used to deal in Asian objects — the eclectic furnishings tell fascinating tales — and opens his house to walkers, yoga students (big light dojo on the top floor), gentle therapy groups as well as B&B guests (there are other bedrooms). Expect lots of laughter and good imaginative cooking. A house of surprises and delights where you feel utterly at home, it is warm, human, harmonious and unforgettable. Doug the dog's great too.

Rooms: 2 twin, 2 double, each with shower & wc; 7 others sharing showers & wcs.

Price: 250-330 Frs (€ 38.11-50.31) for two, including breakfast.

Meals: 130 Frs, including wine & coffee.

Open: All year.

From Chinon cross River Vienne & take D749 then D760 to Ile Bouchard. After entering town, 2nd right and follow signs.

MMap 232-35 **ASP Map No: 7**

Christian VAURIE
La Commanderie
16 rue de la Commanderie
37220 Brizay, Indre-et-Loire
Tel: (0)2 47 58 63 13
Fax: (0)2 47 58 55 81
e-mail: info@lacommanderie.com
www.lacommanderie.com

Writing a novel? Then that L-shaped room with stone fireplace and old desk is ideal for you. But all the rooms are large, light, old-tiled, well-bathroomed and the newly-restored outbuilding has a fine family room in the old hayloft. A calm, homely atmosphere is cultivated by these educated farmers who have the gift of working hard yet apparently having all the time in the world for you. Breakfast includes goat's cheese and *saucisson* from the village and Madame cooks delicious, wholesome country dinners.

Rooms: 1 twin, 4 double, 1 suite, 1 family room, all with bath or shower & wc.

Price: 250-290 Frs (€ 38.11-44.21) for two, including breakfast.

Meals: 110 Frs, including wine & coffee.

Open: All year except Christmas.

From A10, Ste Maure de Touraine exit on D760, then D50 dir. Ligueil. Go through Sepmes. Farm is on left as you leave village; signposted.

MMap 232-35 **ASP Map No: 7**

Anne-Marie & Joseph VERGNAUD
La Ferme les Berthiers
37800 Sepmes
Indre-et-Loire
Tel: (0)2 47 65 50 61

Watermills make wonderful houses and your charming hosts have recently converted theirs, near the magnificent château of Montrésor, in stylish and simple good taste: plain beige carpets, attractive lined curtains, co-ordinated colour schemes. A plain wooden staircase leads up to the coconut-matted landing, good linen, good towels. The atmosphere is welcoming, very warm, with lots of original features... and quiet flows the water beneath the glass panel in the dining room. Madame is as educated as she is travelled and her family has been in the château for 200 years — there is a sense of timeless peace here, off the beaten track.

Rooms: 1 double, 1 twin, 2 triple, each with bath or shower & wc.

Price: 290-340 Frs (€ 44.21-51.83) for two, including breakfast. Extra bed 80 Frs. Under 4s free.

Meals: Choice within 5km.

Open: All year.

Gîte space for 10 people

From Loches D760 to Montrésor. In village, left dir. Chemillé and mill is on left; signposted.

MMap 238-14 **ASP Map No: 7**

Sophie & Alain WILLEMS de LADERSOUS
Le Moulin de Montrésor
37460 Montrésor
Indre-et-Loire
Tel: (0)2 47 92 68 20
Fax: (0)2 47 92 74 61

We are swamped with praise — for Andrew's superb cooking, Sue's fabulous welcome, the setting, the décor, the fun. They really are delightful, in their different ways. Their deliciously watery home, a carefully restored mill on an island, is all ups and downs, nooks and crannies, big rooms and small, character and variety with skilful use of Sue's speciality stencils and sponging. Plus a restful shady garden, private waterside spot and the added temptation of about 1,000 paperbacks. They may have brilliant blue and yellow macaw too but... not really suitable for young children because of the water.

Rooms: 2 double, 2 triple, 1 twin, all with bath or shower & wc.

Price: 300-340 Frs (€ 45.73-51.83) for two, including breakfast.

Meals: 150 Frs, including aperitif, wine & coffee.

Open: All year except Dec & Jan.

From Loches, N143 dir. Châteauroux; pass Perusson then left at sign to St Jean-St Germain; house is last over the bridge on the left.

MMap 238-14 **ASP Map No: 7**

Andrew PAGE & Sue HUTTON
Le Moulin
St Jean-St Germain
37600 Loches, Indre-et-Loire
Tel: (0)2 47 94 70 12
Fax: (0)2 47 94 77 98
e-mail: millstjean@aol.com
www.sawdays.co.uk

387

Yet another easy-going, happy family — dogs, cats, children — that will sweep you inside with real warmth: several readers have confirmed our impression. Malvina has all the time in the world for guests... a great art. Bedrooms are upstairs in a barn, under the roof, with low beams, sloping ceilings, lots of light. The floors are parquet, the walls creamy-limed, the beams scrubbed, the furniture attractively simple, and there is a small kitchen for you. In the sitting/dining room, more beams, a fireplace, a heavy oak table invite relaxation, and there is a fenced-in pool behind the barn.

Rooms: 2 twin, 2 triple (can be connecting), each with shower & wc.

Price: 290-310 Frs (€ 44.21-47.26) for two, including breakfast.

Meals: By arrangement 110 Frs, including wine & coffee.

Open: All year.

Gîte space for 14 people

From Loches N143 S dir. Châteauroux. After Perrusson right onto D41 to Verneuil (approx. 2km). Left in village; signposted.

MMap 238-26 **ASP Map No: 7**

Malvina & Olivier MASSELOT
La Capitainerie
37600 Verneuil sur Indre
Indre-et-Loire
Tel: (0)2 47 94 88 15
Fax: (0)2 47 94 70 75
e-mail: captain@creaweb.fr
www.sawdays.co.uk

388

The Dallais Restaurant opposite has a Michelin star! People come to this tiny village and stay in this unassuming B&B, just for that special dinner (there's a more modest eating house in the village too). But there is more: Natacha, a busy, bubbly, intelligent young mother, is sweetly attentive, her quiet, affable husband is grounded here in his family goat-cheese business (almost 200 goats 3km away — guests can visit) and Le Grand Pressigny, 10km away, has a superb museum of prehistory. The fairly basic guestrooms (French cheap 'n' cheerful) are in a separate wing with a good dayroom and real disabled facilities in one room.

Rooms: 4 double, each with shower & wc.

Price: 250 Frs (€ 38.11) for two, including breakfast. Extra bed 80 Frs.

Meals: Two restaurants in village, one starred, one simple 'family'.

Open: All year.

From Châtellerault D725 through La Roche Posay & Preuilly sur Claise. 1km after Preuilly left on D50/D41 to Le Petit Pressigny. House in centre opp. Restaurant Dallais.

MMap 232-48 **ASP Map No: 7**

Bernard & Natacha LIMOUZIN
La Pressignoise
37350 Le Petit Pressigny
Indre-et-Loire
Tel: (0)2 47 91 06 06

Unusual, historic Richelieu, France's first grid-based new town built from scratch in the 1600s, was almighty Cardinal Richelieu's creation. The Lawrences have set up their English-language and music schools in a long C17 townhouse with studios on the street side and a beamed entrance through to a sunny courtyard garden (hibiscus and banana trees) and the main house. The big rooms are softly decorated, beds are canopied with attractive fabrics chosen with flair and imagination, and have good lighting. Tim and Marion are welcoming, considerate hosts and provide bountiful breakfasts.

Rooms: 1 double, 2 quadruple, all with own bath or shower & wc.

Price: 310 Frs (€ 47.26) for two, including breakfast. Extra bed 90 Frs.

Meals: Wide choice within 200m. Picnic and barbecue possible.

Open: All year.

A10 motorway, Richelieu exit. After entering Richelieu, take 2nd left. House 300m down on right.

MMap 232-46 **ASP Map No: 7**

Marion & Tim LAWRENCE
L'Escale
30 rue de la Galère
37120 Richelieu
Indre-et-Loire
Tel: (0)2 47 58 25 55/
(0)6 85 59 16 39

The details are brilliant: on every pillow a cotton nightcap, in every room a religious book; the house looks like a museum but feels like a (very refined) home. It is fascinating, compelling, utterly seductive and the rooms are close to perfection. The very special gardens with some vastly ancient trees (the giant plane is a wonder in itself) are open to the public, at certain hours, and to guests night and day. The kitchen garden grows botanical throwbacks and plants for witches' brews. Your host is endlessly inventive: breakfast is "as our country forebears ate" with cheese, cold meats and wine. Extra special.

Rooms: 2 double, each with own bath & wc.

Price: 640 Frs (€ 97.57) for two, including (superb) fork breakfast.

Meals: Auberge 4km; choice 10km.

Open: March to November.

From Tours bypass Chinon then towards La Devinière, past La Devinière/La Roche Clermault & on to Bournand. Go to War Memorial, turn left then 1st left for 100m. House on left, grey gate.

MMap 232-33 **ASP Map No: 7**

Christian LAURENS
Château de Bournand
86120 Bournand
Vienne
Tel: (0)5 49 98 77 82
Fax: (0)5 49 98 97 30

Please remember that dinner is NEVER automatic at a **Chambre d'Hôte**, *must always be booked ahead and may not be available every day.*

That golden liquid is distilled near
ancient wetlands where flat-bottoms already
carried marksmen and waterfowl rose when the
Catholic Royalists put their hearts into
bitter battles against the Revolution.

Poitou – Atlantic Coast

This pretty château in its large park is an old family seat with period pieces, family portraits and trees — your hosts have provided more twigs for those trees in the form of 11 grandchildren. Madame has a twinkly brightness and will greet you like a long-lost friend in intelligent if slightly impeded French; Monsieur is a genial, English-speaking field sportsman. Rooms and washing arrangements are also rather eccentric and other-worldly, all made of antiques, alcoves and showers in cupboards. Your hosts will gladly discuss visits to Loire châteaux, Futuroscope and other fascinations.

Rooms: 1 triple, 1 double, each with shower; 1 single with basin; 1 bathroom, 2 wcs for all (1 on another floor).

Price: 240 Frs (€ 36.59) for two, including breakfast.

Meals: 100 Frs, including wine & coffee.

Open: All year.

From Loudun, D759 dir. Thouars. After 7km, left on D19 to Arçay, 1km along; château on right behind big gates as you enter village (no signs).

MMap 232-45 **ASP Map No: 7**

Hilaire & Sabine LEROUX de LENS
Château du Puy d'Arçay
86200 Arçay
Vienne
Tel: (0)5 49 98 29 11

Come and experience the daily life of farmers in a small hilltop village with a fine 12th-century church. After 20-odd years of B&B, your hosts still enjoy their guests enormously. He, a jovial retired farmer (their son now runs the farm), knows his local lore; she smiles quietly and gets on with her cooking in the big homely kitchen — they are the salt of the earth. Up the superb old solid oak staircase, bedrooms are clean and bright with good beds, curtained-off showers and separate loos. A warm and generous welcome is assured plus masses of things to do and see.

Rooms: 3 double, 1 with extra bed for child, each with shower & wc.

Price: 215 Frs (€ 32.78) for two, including breakfast.

Meals: 75 Frs, including wine & coffee.

Open: All year.

From Loudon, follow signs for Thouars then take D60 towards Moncontour. At Mouterre Silly, find the church; house is 50m along towards Silly, signposted 'Chambres d'Hôtes'.

MMap 232-45 **ASP Map No: 7**

Agnès & Henri BRÉMAUD
Le Bourg
86200 Mouterre Silly
Vienne
Tel: (0)5 49 98 09 72
Fax: (0)5 49 22 33 40
www.sawdays.co.uk

It really is a lovely old farmhouse, built in the late C15, proudly set at the end of its drive. The Picards, five generations of whom have lived here, are quiet, welcoming, if busy, cereal farmers who will treat you as part of the family. Overlooking the chestnut-treed garden are the generous bedrooms where good furnishings include handsome wardrobes and firm new mattresses. Sunlight streams into the huge sitting room with its well-matched beams, white walls and terracotta-tiled floor. Breakfast is in the yellow dining room or on the leafy terrace and there are now simple cooking facilities for guests.

Rooms: 2 double, 1 twin, each with shower & wc.

Price: 260 Frs (€ 39.64) for two, including breakfast. Children 60 Frs.

Meals: In village or Richelieu; self-catering.

Open: All year.

Gîte space for 6 people

From Richelieu, D7 dir. Loudun. After 4km, right onto a drive with lime trees on both sides.

MMap [illegible] **ASP Map No: 7**

Jean & Marie-Christine PICARD
Le Bois Goulu
86200 Pouant
Vienne
Tel: (0)5 49 22 52 05

The fortified farmhouse is set in highly roamable parkland. The guestrooms, slightly squeezed into the converted stables, are furnished with high old beds and family pieces. The conversion was almost all Pierre-Claude's own work, as was the replacement of the courtyard laurel by a coyly naked lady in a bower! After a game of *pétanque*, he regales guests with family history over candlelit dinners in the vast family kitchen while Chantal cooks to her own excellent recipes. Come for the food and entertainment — no matter if you roll from the shower straight into bed. Superb value and well-placed for ancient Fontevraud and modern Futuroscope.

Rooms: 3 double, 1 room for 3-6, 1 room for 2-4, each with shower & wc.

Price: 205 Frs (€ 31.25) for two, including breakfast; extra bed 75 Frs.

Meals: 115 Frs, including wine & coffee.

Open: All year.

Gîte space for 10 people

From Saumur, D947 to Candes, then D147 to Loudun. There, D14 to Monts sur Guesnes; left at post office — signposted.

MMap 232-46 **ASP Map No: 7**

Pierre-Claude & Chantal FOUQUENET
Domaine de Bourg-Ville
86420 Monts sur Guesnes, Vienne
Tel: (0)5 49 22 81 58
Fax: (0)5 49 22 89 89
e-mail: pierre-claude@wanadoo.fr
www.bourgville.com

You will be mollycoddled by these delightful people. One bedroom (full wheel-chair access) is in a converted woodshed, with beams, pretty curtains, blue and yellow tiled floor and view over the large, rambling garden with its frog pond (hence *Grenouillère*). Two rooms are upstairs in a separate house across the courtyard where Madame's mother, a charming lady, lives. Pleasant, comfortable rooms, and the buildings are most attractive. Meals can be served on the shaded terrace and you can mess about in the small rowing boat.

Rooms: 2 triple, 3 double, each with bath or shower & wc.

Price: 220-280 Frs (€ 33.54-42.69) for two, including breakfast. Extra bed 70 Frs.

Meals: By arrangement 90 Frs, including wine & coffee.

Open: All year.

From Tours N10 S dir. Châtellerault for 55km. In Dangé St Romain, right at 3rd traffic lights; cross river; keep left on little square; house 200m along on left; signposted.

MMap 232-47 **ASP Map No: 7**

Annie & Noël BRAGUIER
La Grenouillère
17 rue de la Grenouillère
86220 Dangé St Romain
Vienne
Tel: (0)5 49 86 48 68
Fax: (0)5 49 86 46 56

This is a charming young couple. They have two small boys, are frank, sociable and very good company, spending time with guests after dinner when the new baby allows. They have converted a fine big barn into guest quarters — older than the main house, it has been very well done, muted colour schemes in the largish rooms harmonising with ethnic rugs. The superb cobbled terrace that runs the full length of the building invites you to sit on balmy evenings gazing across the wide landscape, listening to the music of the wind in the poplars. With a nature reserve on the doorstep this is a little-known corner waiting to be discovered.

Rooms: 4 triple, 1 double, all with bath & wc.

Price: 270-290 Frs (€ 41.16-44.21) for two, including breakfast. Extra bed 80 Frs.

Meals: 95 Frs, including wine.

Open: All year.

Gîte space for 15 people

From Châtellerault D749 to Vouneuil sur Vienne. Left in church square & follow Chambre d'Hôte signs. Last house on right in small hamlet of Chabonne.

MMap 232-47 **ASP Map No: 7**

Florence & Antoine PENOT
Chabonne
86210 Vouneuil sur Vienne
Vienne
Tel: (0)5 49 85 28 25
Fax: (0)5 49 85 22 75
www.sawdays.co.uk

So close to the lovely, lively old city of Poitiers and even closer to the high-tech *Futuroscope*, yet only the ping-pong of the little white ball or the splish-splosh of swimmers disturbs the hush of the tiny village. Madame, vivacious and dynamic, is delighted to welcome you to sleep in her simple, pretty, rooms in the converted outbuilding, and to breakfast so copiously in courtyard or dining room that children are given doggy bags. The two rooms sharing cooking facilities have good, trad French furnishings. The duplex, with its two smallish rooms, is more 'rustic' with an intriguing window layout. All are excellent value.

Rooms: 1 double, 1 triple, 1 duplex for 4/5, each with bath or shower & wc.

Price: 260-280 Frs (€ 39.64-42.69) for two, including breakfast.

Meals: Choice 3km. Self-catering (excluding duplex).

Open: All year.

From A10 exit 28 onto D18 W dir. Avanton for about 2km. Signposted in hamlet of Martigny.

MMap 232-16 **ASP Map No: 7**

Annie & Didier ARRONDEAU
La Ferme du Château de Martigny
86170 Avanton
Vienne
Tel: (0)5 49 51 04 57
Fax: (0)5 49 51 04 57
www.sawdays.co.uk

The château, begun in the 1400s, 'finished' in the 1700s, has a properly aged face. From the dramatic dark-panelled, orange-walled hall up the superbly banistered staircase, through a great carved screen, you reach the *salon* gallery that runs majestically the length of the house. Here you may sit, read, write, dream of benevolent ghosts. Off the gallery, the bedrooms, loaded with personality, are perfectly fitting; Madame's hand-painted tiles adorn a shower, her laughter accompanies your breakfast. Monsieur tends his trees, joins in making jam and knows all there is to do in the area. A great couple in a genuine family château.

Rooms: 1 suite, 2 twin, all with bath or shower & wc. Extra children's room.

Price: 370-390 Frs (€ 56.41-59.46) for two, including breakfast. Extra bed 100 Frs.

Meals: Nearby inn; choice 10km.

Open: All year.

Gîte space for 4 people

From A10 Futuroscope exit onto D62 dir. Neuville; at Quatre Vents r'about D757 to Vendeuvre; left on D15 to Chéneché & cont. dir. Thurageau. Labarom 800m on right after leaving Chéneché.

MMap 232-46 **ASP Map No: 7**

Eric & Henriette LE GALLAIS
Château de Labarom
86380 Chéneché
Vienne
Tel: (0)5 49 51 24 22/
(0)6 80 46 17 66
Fax: (0)5 49 51 47 38
e-mail: chateau.de.labarom@wanadoo.com

An utterly delightful couple who just cannot do enough for you. Monsieur, who once resuscitated cars for a living, now takes much more pleasure in reviving tired travellers. Their house is on the old ramparts and the pretty garden looks directly out over the boulevard below where you would expect there to be a moat (quiet enough at night). The two rooms are neat, with good beds and old *armoires.* One has surprising big-flower wallpaper, the smaller is plain blue; both have space and the shower room has been prettily retiled. Breakfast in high-backed chairs at the long table in the converted stables beneath the old hay rack.

Rooms: 2 twin rooms, each with shower or bath & wc.

Price: 230 Frs (€ 35.06) for two, including breakfast. Extra bed 70 Frs.

Meals: Restaurants in village.

Open: All year.

From Châtellerault D725 dir. Parthenay for 30km. In Mirebeau, left immediately after traffic lights next to 'Gendarmerie' — No 19 about 50m on right.

MMap 232-46 **ASP Map No: 7**

Jacques & Annette JEANNIN
19 rue Jacquard
86110 Mirebeau
Vienne
Tel: (0)5 49 50 54 06

Vivaldi would have delighted in this fine C18 coaching inn, attractively converted by Monsieur Flambeau and his vivacious English wife. The rooms are named after the seasons, *Summer* has a brass four-poster, *Winter* a white canopied bed, *Four Seasons* looks almost English with its old-style pine furniture and pretty children's bed/playroom leading to the peach-pink, Laura Ashley-draped double. All bathrooms are beautifully tiled to match the bedrooms. On the main square of a quiet village, it has a charming courtyard and a large garden planted with mature trees: an oasis of peace and greenery. *Baby-sitting available.*

Rooms: 1 suite for 4, 1 quadruple, 3 double, each with bath or shower & wc.

Price: 250 Frs (€ 38.11) for two, including breakfast.

Meals: 115 Frs, including wine & coffee.

Open: February to mid-November.

From Poitiers N149 W dir. Nantes for 14km. At Vouillé left on D62 to Latillé. House is the largest in main village square. (Poitiers-Latillé 24km.)

MMap 233-7 **ASP Map No: 7**

Yvonne FLAMBEAU
La Demeure de Latillé
1 place Robert Gerbier
86190 Latillé, Vienne
Tel: (0)5 49 51 54 74
Fax: (0)5 49 51 56 32
e-mail: latille@chez.com
www.chez.com/latille

This kind, hospitable, interesting couple live in the converted château stables and the whole estate is still shared by Madame's family (her brother does B&B in the orangery). She is discreetly warm; Monsieur is a true bibliophile and vastly erudite, with a living room full of books, pictures, treasures and a sense of history. The rooms are soft and comfortable with old furniture and pale walls. The one in the house has an old raised stone fireplace occupied, surprisingly, by a spinning wheel. The cottage has its own little garden and an amusing three-hole alcove for hens' nests. Natural elegance and traditional comfort combined.

Rooms: Main house: 1 twin with shower & wc. Cottage: 1 quadruple with hip-bath/shower & wc.

Price: 330-350 Frs (€ 50.31-53.36) for two, including breakfast.

Meals: 140 Frs, including wine & coffee.

Open: All year.

From A10 Poitiers Nord exit on N10 dir. Limoges for 7km. Left to Bignoux & follow signs to Bois Dousset/Les Godiers.

MMap 233-9 **ASP Map No: 7**

M & Mme Philippe RABANY
Les Godiers
86800 Lavoux
Vienne
Tel: (0)5 49 61 05 18
Fax: (0)5 49 61 05 18

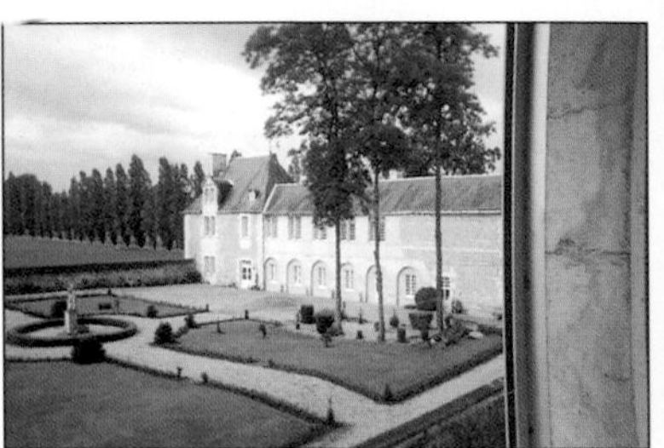

It is SO French, this former orangery in the fine château park — not stilted, just natural. The stone-flagged *salon* has a fine jumble of ten French chairs, bits of ancient furniture, pictures, ornaments and lamps. The dining room has traditional elegance. Every object tells a story, there are statues here and there, indoors and out; bedrooms are large, bursting with character; bathrooms too. The family is lively and fun with many interests: Monsieur's are history and his family, Madame's are art and life — they combine unselfconscious class with flashes of southern non-conformism and their daughter is an art student.

Rooms: 2 double, 1 twin, 1 suite, all with own bathrooms (1 on separate floor).

Price: 350 Frs (€ 53.36) for two, including breakfast. Terms for children.

Meals: 60 Frs, including wine & coffee.

Open: All year.

From A10, Poitiers Nord exit, N10 dir. Limoges. After 7km, left to Bignoux; follow signs to Bois Dousset.

MMap 233-9 **ASP Map No: 7**

Vicomte & Vicomtesse Hilaire de VILLOUTREYS de BRIGNAC
Logis du Château du Bois Dousset
86800 Lavoux
Vienne
Tel: (0)5 49 44 20 26
Fax: (0)5 49 44 20 26

A bee farm! Yes, the humble bee reigns royal here where several honeys and other bee products are made — the small shop in the courtyard is a hive of activity. Charline welcomes you with an uplifting smile and, while Jacky actually does the bee-tending, is excellent at explaining (in French) the arcana of bee-keeping and the ancient complicity between man and insect, over breakfast in the separate guest building. If the décor is a little garish and synthetic in the velux-windowed bedrooms, the warmly human and relaxed atmosphere draws a veil over critical eyes. Great for children too.

Rooms: 2 double, 1 twin, each with bath or shower & wc. Extra beds available.

Price: 240 Frs (€ 36.59) for two, including breakfast.

Meals: Restaurant in St Savin. Barbecue available.

Open: Mid-February to mid-October.

From Chauvigny, N151 dir. St Savin. 2km before St Savin, left to Siouvre; signposted.

MMap 233-10 **ASP Map No: 7**

Charline & Jacky BARBARIN
Siouvre
86310 St Savin
Vienne
Tel: (0)5 49 48 10 19
Fax: (0)5 49 48 46 89
www.sawdays.co.uk

The G.R.48 path goes past the house — this is a great place for walkers. Your delightful hosts, much involved in local life, are a friendly family with three children. Deby's brother (the sheep farmer) and parents (antique-dealers) also live on the estate. Guests are in the main family house which is comfortable and attractive, with interesting and original antiques, prints and good fabrics in the bedrooms. The sitting room is cosy, the dining room elegant. A wonderful place for nature lovers. One reader simply said "Outstanding".

Rooms: 2 double, 2 twin, all with bath or shower & wc.

Price: 420 Frs (€ 64.03) for two, including breakfast.

Meals: 95 Frs, including wine & coffee.

Open: All year.

Gîte space for 8 people

From Chauvigny, D54 to Montmorillon then D727 dir. La Trimouille. House is on right 10km along this road: signposted.

MMap 233-11 **ASP Map No: 7**

Richard & Deby EARLS
La Boulinière
Journet
86290 La Trimouille, Vienne
Tel: (0)5 49 91 55 88
Fax: (0)5 49 91 72 82
e-mail: jr-earls@interpc.fr
www.interpc.fr/jr-earls

These are true farming folk (their son now 'does' the goats) with their roots in village life: they sing in the choir, act with the drama group, Madame shows her embroidery, Monsieur is the Mayor. And they love sharing their simple, stylish house with intelligent, cultured, like-minded guests. The suite is in the converted coach house, its kitchen in the old bread oven. All rooms, with their good fabrics and Madame's exquisite samplers, blend harmoniously with the garden and woodlands (golden orioles, hoopoes, wild orchids...). You may visit the goats, watch cheese being made, fish in their big lake.

Rooms: 2 double, 1 suite for 4/5 with kitchen/diner, each with bath or shower & wc. Extra room for children.

Price: 280 Frs (€ 42.69) for two, including breakfast.

Meals: 100 Frs, including wine. Self-catering in annexe.

Open: All year.

From Poitiers N147 SE to Lussac les Châteaux then D727 E for 21km; left on D121 to Journet. In village, N towards Haims — house 1km on left.

MMap 233-10 **ASP Map No. ?**

Jacques & Chantal COCHIN
Le Haut Peu
86290 Journet
Vienne
Tel: (0)5 49 91 62 02
Fax: (0)5 49 91 59 71

Working the land has real meaning to the Salvaudons. They are educated, intelligent farmers — he energetic and down-to-earth, she gentle and smiling — committed to the natural way ("there's more to the Vienne than the Futuroscope"), who like swapping travellers' tales and sharing simple, lasting values. Their sheep farm lies in unspoilt, rolling, stream-run country where fishing competitions are held. All the farm produce is organic: don't miss the chance to try Madame's Limousin specialities — lamb, chicken cooked in honey, vegetable pies — round the family table.

Rooms: 1 triple, 1 double, with showers and basins; shared wc.

Price: 190 Frs (€ 28.97) for two, breakfast included.

Meals: 80 Frs, including wine & coffee.

Open: All year.

Gîte space for 6 people

From Poitiers, D741 to Civray. There, D148 east and D34 to Availles. There D100 dir. Mauprévoir. After 3km, signposted.

MMap 233-20 **ASP Map No: 7**

Pierre & Line SALVAUDON
Les Ecots
86460 Availles Limousine
Vienne
Tel: (0)5 49 48 59 17
Fax: (0)5 49 48 59 17

Elegant and sophisticated is the feel. This fine château is soberly but immaculately decorated with a mix of antique and modern furniture. The dining room has a remarkable carved wooden fireplace with doors and drawers for plate-warming, practicalities that date from well before the days of electricity. The finely-proportioned bedrooms are full of character, the suite has windows on three sides onto the peaceful, unspoilt park. Madame is small, dark and loquacious; Monsieur is tall, blond and reserved; together they are delicious hosts who will do anything for you.

Rooms: 1 suite for 3, 3 double, 1 triple, each with bath or shower & wc.

Price: 350-550 Frs (€ 53.36-83.85) for two, including breakfast.

Meals: Supper tray *Assiette Gourmande*: 70 Frs; wine 60 Frs.

Open: All year.

Gîte space for 4 people

From Poitiers N147 S dir. Limoges. At Fleuré, right on D2 dir. Gençay for 4km. Château entrance signed on left.

MMap 233-9 **ASP Map No: 7**

M & Mme Georges REBILLARD
Château de la Guillonnière
86410 Dienné
Vienne
Tel: (0)5 49 42 05 46
Fax: (0)5 49 42 48 34
e-mail: contact@rent-a-castle.com
www.rent-a-castle.com

Sophisticated, simple luxury is the keynote of this ravishing C17 château where each bedroom is named after the marble used in its bathroom. Michel, a retired lawyer, has not lost his professional gift of the gab and Monique is an inspired interior designer. You may eat locally-grown and often home-reared food (*foie gras*) by candlelight, sleep in a four-poster under a magnificent beamed ceiling and breakfast hugely next morning in the garden; this is the perfect spot for a honeymoon, first or second or — who says you can't have a honeymoon every year?

Rooms: 2 double, 1 twin, each with bath & wc.

Price: 500-700 Frs (€ 76.22-106.71) for two, including breakfast.

Meals: 150 Frs, including wine.

Open: All year.

From Poitiers N147 dir. Limoges; first left dir. Savigny l'Évescault then first right on D89 for 5km. First right on entering village.

MMap 233-9 **ASP Map No: 7**

Monique & Michel TABAU
Château de la Touche
86800 Savigny l'Évescault
Vienne
Tel: (0)5 49 01 10 38
Fax: (0)5 49 56 47 82
www.oudormir.com/chateaudelatouche

The guest quarters, in the generous château outbuildings, are decorated with a wonderful flair for fabrics and colours — mats and tablecloth match crockery, bathrooms match bedrooms. It's smart yet utterly welcoming, as befits a converted bakery — the largest room, finely renovated with exposed beams, stones and thick white curtains, houses the old bread oven. Your hosts are well-travelled, sociable people who will happily chat (Monsieur in perfect English) in the pleasant sitting area about all the things in the cultural treasure-chest that is the Poitou.

Rooms: 2 rooms for 3/4, 2 double, 2 twin, all with bath, shower & wc.

Price: 350-430 Frs (€ 53.36-65.55) for two, including breakfast.

Meals: Self-catering. Restaurants 2-8km.

Open: All year.

From A10 exit 29, take Rocade Est (ringroad) dir. Limoges/Châteauroux for 5km, exit left on D3 dir. Montamisé for 3km, then right on D18 for 2.5km. Château on right.

MMap 233-8 **ASP Map No: 7**

Daniel & Agnès VAUCAMP
Château de Vaumoret
Rue du Breuil Mingot
86000 Poitiers
Vienne
Tel: (0)5 49 61 32 11
Fax: (0)5 49 01 04 54

The picture tells it all — moat, keep, drawbridge, dreams. Up two spiral stone flights is "the biggest bedroom in France" — solid granite windowsills, a giant fireplace, a canopied bed and the shower snug in the former *garde-robe* (water closet). Breakfast under the 5-metre guardroom vault, your feet on the original C14 flagstones. The old stones are exposed, the furniture sober and the fires always laid, just like olden times. Indeed, the whole place is brilliantly authentic, the magnificent gardens glow from loving care and Pippa is eager and attentive — flowers, bubbly, fishing in the moat, all on the house!

Rooms: 2 double, each with shower & wc.

Price: 625 Frs (€ 95) for one room, 950 Frs (€145) for both, including breakfast.

Meals: Restaurant 4km; choice 9km.

Open: All year.

From A10 exit 29 on N147 then N149 W to Parthenay. Round Parthenay northbound, cont. N149 dir. Bressuire; 7km N of Parthenay, right at sign for château

MMap 232-44 **ASP Map No: 7**

Nicholas & Philippa FREELAND
Château de Tennessus
79350 Amailloux
Deux-Sèvres
Tel: (0)5 49 95 50 60
Fax: (0)5 49 95 50 62
e-mail: tennessus@csi.com
www.tennessus.com

History and Nature meet here: this used to be a Protestant area, in the days of religious strife, and the nearby *Marais Poitevin*, a common hiding place for both sides, is worth a visit. Your hosts make a delightful partnership — she teaches, he cooks. One reader especially enjoyed the way he did his pigeons. He pops in and out of the kitchen to chat while cooking dinner, so the atmosphere is very relaxed. Much of the food is home-produced. Guests are free to use the big dining room and sitting room and the pleasant bedrooms are up two flights of stairs in the attic. Excellent value in an easy and attractive village house.

Rooms: 1 triple with curtained-off shower & wc; 2 double sharing shower & wc.

Price: 240 Frs (€ 36.59) for two, including breakfast.

Meals: 90 Frs, including wine & coffee.

Open: All year.

From A10 exit 32 on D7 dir. Mougon for 1km; left on D5 dir. La Mothe St Héray for 7km; right for Prailles; sign on left on entering village — continue up & turn right to house.

MMap 233-6 **ASP Map No: 7**

Michel & Marie-Claude DUVALLON
Le Colombier des Rivières
79370 Prailles
Deux-Sèvres
Tel: (0)5 49 32 84 43

The family snapped the house up after the Revolution, the only time it has changed hands since the 15th century. Come not for the rooms but for the idyllic setting. It is all slightly shambolic and aristocratically faded in a way that quite won us over: utterly 'family', they serve splendid dinners, enjoy the conversation around the table and may suggest a game of bridge as well. Children love the enormous park and the boat. Monsieur uses a limpid and charming French; Madame smokes *Gauloises* and speaks with a husky voice — a most likeable pair.

Rooms: 1 triple, 2 double, 1 twin, each with bath or shower & wc; 2 double sharing shower & wc.

Price: 350 Frs (€ 53.36) for two, including breakfast.

Meals: 100 Frs, including wine & coffee.

Open: All year.

From A10 exit 'Poitiers Sud' on N10 dir. Angoulême for 3km; right on N11 dir. Niort for 14km. From Lusignan D950 to Melle then dir. Brioux for 3km; right on D301 to St Romans. House in village, near church.

MMap 233-17 **ASP Map No: 11**

François RABANY & Odile de NOUËL
Le Logis
79500 St Romans lès Melle
Deux-Sèvres
Tel: (0)5 49 27 04 15
Fax: (0)5 49 29 18 37

This riverside setting is idyllic, with its views out to the Sèvre Niortaise, and very quiet in the evenings when the trippers have gone. There's a small boat and Monsieur, who is most knowledgeable about the utterly fascinating *Marais* ('marsh') area, will escort guests on boat trips (at reasonable rates). Madame is justifiably proud of this pretty single-storey house where she was born and which has a charming old-world atmosphere, rooms crammed with a lifetime's collection of objects, solid repro furniture and is good value in a touristy area. Families welcome, preferably without toddlers (unfenced water).

Rooms: 1 double, 1 triple, each with own shower & wc.

Price: 250-280 Frs (€ 38.11-42.69) for two, including breakfast. Extra person 80 Frs.

Meals: Restaurants within walking distance.

Open: All year.

From Coulon centre D23 dir. Irleau. At end of village, immediately left along bank of River Sèvre which is Rue Élise Lucas.

MMap 233-5 **ASP Map No: 11**

Ginette & Michel CHOLLET
68 rue Élise Lucas
79510 Coulon
Deux-Sèvres
Tel: (0)5 49 35 91 55/42 59

A solidly reliable address, this 18th-century village house is just yards from the beautiful cloisters of the Royal Abbey where Eleanor of Aquitaine was born and her mother buried. The rooms are recently converted, simply and with subdued rustic good taste (one is very big), and look over the walled garden. The dining room is in the old stable block and there is a small sitting room in the former wash-house where Christine will make up a fire if it's cold. She and her parents, who live in the main house, are most welcoming,

Rooms: 2 triple, 1 double, 1 twin, each with shower & wc.

Price: 270-290 Frs (€ 41.16-44.21) for two, including breakfast.

Meals: 85 Frs, incl. aperitif, wine & coffee. Under 8s 45 Frs. Book previous day.

Open: April to October.

From Niort N148 NW dir. Fontenay le Comte for 20km. After Oulmes right to Nieul sur l'Autize; follow signs to Abbey — house just before it on left.

MMap 233-5 **ASP Map No: 11**

Christine CHASTAIN-POUPIN
Le Rosier Sauvage
1 rue de l'Abbaye
85240 Nieul sur l'Autize
Vendée
Tel: (0)2 51 52 49 39
Fax: (0)2 51 52 49 46

At the very end of the lane, just yards from the river, Massigny is a secret corner of marshy Vendée. The rooms are as handsome as you'll find: Jean-Claude used to teach cabinet-making and his delight in wood is evident. Add beds made for deep sleep, unfussy fabrics, papers and painted beams for æsthetic satisfaction, a guest sitting room with two carved *armoires* and a lovely copper tub for plants, and all you need is to sit a while with these friendly, open people and share their wide-ranging conversation. Remarkable value in a memorable and unsung spot.

Rooms: 2 double, each with shower & wc.

Price: 250 Frs (€ 38.11) for two, including breakfast; extra bed 60 Frs.

Meals: Choice 3-10 km.

Open: All year.

From A83 exit at Fontenay le Comte on D938ter and go SW dir. La Rochelle for 6km, then right at small sign for Massigny.

MMap 233-4 **ASP Map No: 11**

Marie-Françoise & Jean-Claude NEAU
Massigny
85770 Velluire
Vendée
Tel: (0)2 51 52 30 32
Fax: (0)2 51 52 30 32
www.sawdays.co.uk

A dream... a fine house with its own boat to drift you deep into the *Marais*, or *Venise Verte* (as they call it here — oddly). The old *maison de maître*, in the village, has a glorious walled garden with over 70 varieties of iris. Monsieur is a doctor; Liliane, bright and enthusiastic, is a local guide. The bedrooms: parquet floors, photos of the *Marais*, regional furniture, in one a four-poster with views of the water. Downstairs: books, a chess table, more parquet. Rabelais lived in the Abbey, a stone's throw away. All rather poetic and very special.

Rooms: 3 double, 1 triple, 1 twin, each with bath or shower & wc.

Price: 340-370 Frs (€ 51.83-56.41) for two, including breakfast. Extra bed 50 Frs.

Meals: In village.

Open: All year.

From Fontenay le Comte N148 dir. Niort for 9km then right on D15 to Maillezais. There, follow signs for L'Abbaye. House on left, signposted.

MMap 233-4 **ASP Map No: 11**

Liliane BONNET
69 rue de l'Abbaye
85420 Maillezais
Vendée
Tel: (0)2 51 87 23 00
Fax: (0)2 51 00 72 44

A fisherman's paradise, this charming traditional house beside the River Vendée on the edge of the village is owned by the delightful and welcoming Riberts. They completely renovated it five years ago and the big, light, airy rooms with their stripped doors and traditional furniture are full of fresh flowers from the secluded walled garden. You have the freedom of *salon* and library and eat excellent breakfast (cooked if requested) and dinner in the family room or in a larger dining room, depending how many you are. Lots to do in the area; they have plans for canoes on the river. Remarkable people, remarkable value.

Rooms: 5 triple rooms, all with own bath or shower & wc.

Price: 280 Frs (€ 42.69) for two, including breakfast. Extra person 70 Frs.

Meals: 100 Frs, including wine & coffee.

Open: Mid-January to mid-November.

From Fontenay le Comte, D938ter for 13km then right on D25. Le Gué de Velluire is 4.5km on. At end of village, turn left — beside river.

MMap 233-4 **ASP Map No: 11**

Christiane & Michel RIBERT
Le Logis
5 rue de la Rivière
85770 Le Gué de Velluire
Vendée
Tel: (0)2 51 52 59 10
Fax: (0)2 51 52 57 21

Most aptly named: the Pikes have two sets of identical twin sons! It is a simple, old-fashioned, pleasantly-renovated 1900s farmhouse with a large garden where children play and adults barbecue then climb the outside stair to the two quiet, comfortable rooms that are much appreciated after days at the seaside. Your lively, welcoming hosts came from farming in England and are thoroughly integrated here. They enjoy having guests on the farm — Ian manages while Janty helps with lambing and eggs (quail, pheasant) —, will tell you what there is to be discovered in this area that they love and take you to see the sheep if you're interested.

Rooms: 1 double with bath, shower & wc, 1 twin with shower & wc.

Price: 240 Frs (€ 36.59) for two, including breakfast.

Meals: Good restaurant 5km.

Open: All year (by arrangement only mid-September to mid-June).

From La Roche sur Yon D948 NW 25km through Aizenay; at Bel Air left on D94 dir. Commequiers for about 1km (signs to La Fraternité); turn left, house on right

MMap 232-40 **ASP Map No: 11**

Janty & Ian PIKE
La Fraternité
Maché
85190 Aizenay
Vendée
Tel: (0)2 51 55 42 58/
(0)6 62 02 42 58
Fax: (0)2 51 60 16 01

An interesting young couple, fairly new to B&B and great Anglophiles. Madame knows about nutrition and serves good, fresh, balanced meals with home-grown poultry, rabbit and eggs from the farm next door. Monsieur teaches engineering in nearby La Rochelle, where they'll point you towards the lesser-known things to see. The old farmhouse, lovingly restored and decorated by themselves, is simple, pristine, with big, comfortable rooms and they love children of any age. Their quiet lane invites cyclists; they have table-tennis but no telly – country peace and excellent value. *No pets in rooms.*

Rooms: 1 family room for 4 and/or 1 double, with bath, shower & wc; 1 triple with shower & wc.

Price: 240-290 Frs (€ 36.59-44.21) for two, including breakfast.

Meals: 90 Frs, including wine.

Open: All year.

From La Rochelle N11 E for 11km; north on D112 to Longèves; in village, right at 'Alimentation', first left, past 'Mairie' — house 700m on left.

MMap 233-4 **ASP Map No: 11**

Marie-Christine PROU
43 rue du Marais
17230 Longèves
Charente-Maritime
Tel: (0)5 46 37 11 15
e-mail: prou@eigsi.fr
www.sawdays.co.uk

They are a lively young family who all enjoy having guests, parents cook together (lots of organic ingredients) while three children entertain young visitors — an excellent team. Theirs is a lovingly-restored old house where old and modern each have their place. Antique *armoires* and big new beds, a collection of old scales and full disabled facilities (in the slightly more modern-décor cottage), lots of treasures and a tennis court. The air is full of warm smiles, harmony breathes from the old walls and woodwork. They have thought of everything to make you comfortable and families are positively welcome.

Rooms: 1 triple, 1 suite for 6, 1 cottage for 5, each with bath or shower & wc.

Price: 350 Frs (€ 53.36) for two, including breakfast.

Meals: 120 Frs, including wine & coffee.

Open: All year.

From Surgères 'Gendarmerie' & fire station, take D115 NW dir. Marans & Puyravault & follow signs for 5km.

MMap 233-3 **ASP Map No: 11**

Brigitte & Patrick FRANÇOIS
Le Clos de la Garenne
9 rue de la Garenne
17700 Puyravault, Charente-Maritime
Tel: (0)5 46 35 47 71
Fax: (0)5 46 35 47 91
e-mail: BPAML.Francois@wanadoo.fr
http://perso.wanadoo.fr/la-garenne/

This old farmhouse — built in 1600, renovated in 1720 — stands in a garden of mature trees that goes right down to the River Boutonne for peaceful walks and shallow swimming. Guests have a big dayroom with comfortable chairs, games and a full-size French billiards table. The clean, fresh bedrooms have good beds and large *armoires.* Indeed, the whole place has a totally French country feel to it: you might be staying with your favourite granny. There are good bike trails and you can visit the one and only place in France that produces angelica.

Rooms: 1 double/twin with shower & wc; 1 suite for 4 with bath & wc.

Price: 270 Frs (€ 41.16) for two, including breakfast.

Meals: 95 Frs, including wine & coffee.

Open: All year.

From Gendarmerie in St Jean d'Angély, D127 dir. Dampierre Antezant. In Antezant, first right.

MMap 233-16 **ASP Map No: 11**

Pierre & Marie-Claude FALLELOUR
Les Moulins
17400 Antezant
Charente-Maritime
Tel: (0)5 46 59 94 52
Fax: (0)5 46 59 94 52
www.sawdays.co.uk

We know why people come back again and again: the Deschamps just love doing B&B and it shows. Madame delights in cooking delicious meals for her guests and Monsieur enjoys talking English. They have enlarged their dining room to take a bigger table and their generosity is legendary (they once delayed a friend's party to dine with late-arriving guests), so what matter a slightly unkempt façade? Huge wardrobes dominate the bright-papered bedrooms, beds and bedding are traditional French, and the best room has three lovely windows.

Rooms: 1 double, 2 suites, each with bath or shower & wc.

Price: 230-250 Frs (€ 35.06-38.11) for two, including breakfast; extra bed 50 Frs.

Meals: 90 Frs, including wine & coffee.

Open: Easter to 30 October.

From St Jean d'Angély, D939 dir. Matha. 3km after crossroads to Varaize, D229 towards Aumagne. House [illegible] on left

MMap 233-17 **ASP Map No: 11**

Eliane & Maurice DESCHAMPS
La Clé des Champs
17770 Aumagne
Charente-Maritime
Tel: (0)5 46 58 23 80
Fax: (0)5 46 58 23 91

Madame's *galettes* are famous in the area — enjoy them, and other specialities, in the warm and homely dining room where the television is blessedly hidden in a cupboard. The Forgets are a sweet, welcoming couple who have made great efforts with their French country furniture, pretty curtains and scattered treasures. The rooms are named after flowers in a genuine country family atmosphere. There are bikes for rent, swings to play on, wonderful cookery weekends. One guest found "Food, drink and company all excellent".

Rooms: 2 double, 1 triple, 1 family room, each with bath or shower & wc.

Price: 215-255 Frs (€ 32.78-38.87) for two, including breakfast.

Meals: 90 Frs, including wine & coffee.

Open: All year.

From Saintes, N150 dir. Niort. After 6km, D129 dir. Ecoyeux; signposted (red & white).

MMap 233-16 **ASP Map No: 11**

Henri & Marie-Andrée FORGET
Chez Quimand
17770 Ecoyeux
Charente-Maritime
Tel: (0)5 46 95 92 55
Fax: (0)5 46 95 92 55

This professional couple left Paris for the country – and what country it is! With nearby Romanesque delights, Cognac at 19 km, the beaches of Ile de Ré and Ile d'Oléron not too far, and even the well-known 'free-range' zoo of La Palmyre (France's first), you find culture and beauty as well as a warm, relaxing place to stay. The creamy, indigenous stone of the old farmhouse — part C17, part C19 — is a perfect foil for flowers everywhere. Madame, an enthusiastic gardener, grows her own organic veg; there are hand-painted touches plus a kitchen designed so she can cook and entertain guests at the same time — she knows what comes first.

Rooms: 3 double, each with bath or shower & wc, 1 twin to make family 'suite' with double.

Price: 240-260 Frs (€ 36.59-39.64) for two, including breakfast; extra bed 80 Frs.

Meals: 85 Frs, including aperitif & wine.

Open: All year.

From A10 exit 34 dir. St Jean d'Angély then E on D939 to Matha (20km). In Matha, right dir. Thors (D121). Entering Thors, turn left — Le Goulet on right.

MMap 233-17 **ASP Map No: 11**

Frédérique THILL-TOUSSAINT
Le Clos du Plantis
1 rue du Pont, Le Goulet
17160 Sonnac
Charente-Maritime
Tel: (0)5 46 25 07 91/
(0)6 81 99 07 98
Fax: (0)5 46 25 07 91

Jenny loves cooking and writing, John is building a boat to sail across the Atlantic in, together they have lovingly restored their *Charentais* farmhouse and they delight in having guests. The atmosphere is convivial and you are welcome to socialise and dine *en famille*. Or feel free to go your own way (separate guest entrance). The beautifully-landscaped garden, with its pretty windmill (let separately), has an English feel — and a croquet lawn — but the 'sense of place' remains unmistakably French. And pretty St Savinien is a painters' delight.

Rooms: 1 room for 2-4 with bath & wc.

Price: 240-280 Frs (€ 36.59-42.69) for two (depending on length of stay), including breakfast.

Meals: 85 Frs, including wine & coffee.

Open: All year except Christmas.

Gîte space for 2 people

From bridge in St Savinien D14 along river, under railway bridge, left on D124 dir. Bords. After 2km, 2nd left after 'Le Pontreau' sign; house 200m on right.

MMap 233-16 **ASP Map No: 11**

John & Jenny ELMES
Le Moulin de la Quine
17350 St Savinien
Charente-Maritime
Tel: (0)5 46 90 19 31
Fax: (0)5 46 90 28 37

Your hosts speak no English but are gently welcoming to all nations. They moved south on retirement to enjoy the balmy climate here — guests respond to it as willingly as do all those flowers and... pumpkins. Country-style rooms have big pieces of furniture in smallish spaces, good mattresses and smallish towels. The area is flat — where else could those millions of oysters bed down for their short lives? — but lovely beaches are just 10 minutes away, there are forests for walking or bicycling, birdlife for hours of watching and fortified Brouage on the Ile d'Oléron to visit.

Rooms: 1 double with bath & wc; 1 double with shower & wc.

Price: 250-300 Frs (€ 38.11-45.73) for two, including breakfast.

Meals: Full choice in Marennes 3km.

Open: All year except October.

Gîte space for 5 people

Take D123 dir. Ile d'Oléron. At Marennes, right dir. Château de la Gataudière then follow signs.

MMap 233-14 **ASP Map No: 11**

Jean & Jacqueline FERCHAUD
11 rue des Lilas
La Ménardière
17320 Marennes
Charente-Maritime
Tel: (0)5 46 85 41 77

Your hosts simply love their superb farmhouse and you can tell they have lavished care, money and time on it since they settled here after their years in Morocco. A delightful, interesting couple — Anne-Marie is a talented artist whose stylish painted furniture, patchwork, painstakingly-constructed rag rugs and co-ordinated colour schemes adorn the house, her husband is Mayor of the village. Good breakfasts and dinners are eaten with your hosts in the dining room or by the swimming pool. The gardens are landscaped, the terrace paved, flowers bloom and the bedrooms are big. *Quiet children over six welcome.*

Rooms: 4 double, each with bath & wc.

Price: 380 Frs (€ 57.93) for two, including breakfast. Extra person 80 Frs.

Meals: 150 Frs, including wine & coffee.

Open: All year.

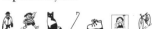

From Saintes N150 west for 5km then fork right on N728 for 29km. Right on D118 to St Sornin. In village centre take Rue du Petit Moulin opposite church door.

MMap 233-15 **ASP Map No: 11**

M & Mme PINEL-PESCHARDIÈRE
La Caussolière
10 rue du Petit Moulin
17600 St Sornin, Charente-Maritime
Tel: (0)5 46 85 44 62
Fax: (0)5 46 85 44 62
e-mail: caussoliere@wanadoo.fr
www.caussoliere.com

You are clearly in a family home not a guesthouse here — the big antique wardrobes were Madame's mother's, the lacy covers on the lovely old boat beds (*lits bateau*) are even older, the well-furnished, old-fashioned atmosphere is so comfortable. Madame keeps a good home-produced table; Monsieur organises outings to distilleries and quarries; both enjoy their guests, especially those who help catch escaping rabbits. They are kindly farmers, really worth getting to know — stay a few days, even if the plumbing is a touch noisy.

Rooms: 1 triple on ground floor, 1 suite for 2-4, both with shower & wc.

Price: 260-280 Frs (€ 39.64-42.69) for two, including breakfast.

Meals: 90 Frs, including wine.

Open: All year.

From A10, Saintes exit on N137 dir. Rochefort/La Rochelle. After about 11km, D119 to Plassay. House on left on entering village.

MMap 233-15 **ASP Map No: 11**

Michelle & Jacques LOURADOUR
La Jaquetterie
17250 Plassay
Charente-Maritime
Tel: (0)5 46 93 91 88

Madame, a likeable, lively person, interested in people (that includes you), and Monsieur, a wizard on local tourist info, really care for your comfort. Your quarters are a huge, many-beamed barn: there's sitting space with a big log fire, billiards and rocking chairs downstairs, gallery access to bedrooms above. These, called *Agatha Christie*, *Picardie*..., have books, lace bedcovers and garden views. Your hosts love to chat with guests about the best places to explore in this beautiful area. And we have heard of "breakfasts on the sunlit terrace with home-made jams" and you may use Madame's kitchen (leave it tidy!).

Rooms: 3 double, 1 twin each with own shower & wc.

Price: 270 Frs (€ 41.16) for two, including breakfast. Extra bed 80 Frs.

Meals: In village.

Open: April to mid-November.

From Saintes N137 dir. Rochefort for 6km then left onto D127 to St Georges. Rue de l'Eglise is in village centre. House on left.

MMap 233-15 **ASP Map No: 11**

Anne & Dominique TROUVÉ
5 rue de l'Église
17810 St Georges des Coteaux
Charente-Maritime
Tel: (0)5 46 92 96 66
Fax: (0)5 46 92 96 66
www.sawdays.co.uk

This is genuine château stuff: gilt, marble, mouldings and period furniture to match the 1850s building. Both house and garden are being brilliantly restored. Monsieur, who was a designer and teaches history of art, has a natural feel for colour and fabric; he loves arches too, and has put one over each bath; rooms are large and finely-proportioned, overlooking the park (where guests can picnic and admire the botanical wonders) — it is all superb and he talks most interestingly about bringing his château back to life. He also plays the piano and serves candlelit dinners of traditional regional cooking in a most congenial atmosphere.

Rooms: 3 double, each with bath, shower & wc.

Price: 380-450 Frs (€ 57.93-68.60) for two, including breakfast; extra bed 90 Frs.

Meals: 180 Frs, including aperitif, wine & coffee.

Open: All year (by arrangement in winter).

From A10 exit 37 to Mirambeau Centre. Ave de la République is after & opposite Tourist Office & swimming pool, behind trees on your right.

MMap 233-27 **ASP Map No: 11**

René VENTOLA
Le Parc Casamène
95 avenue de la République
17150 Mirambeau
Charente-Maritime
Tel: (0)5 46 49 74 38
Fax: (0)5 46 49 74 38
www.sawdays.co.uk

Our readers wax poetical in their praises: "one of the best", "close to perfection"... Agathe and Philippe both knew La Loge as children but never imagined they might one day own the big C19 house (they actually live next door). They've transformed it with sensitivity, flair and country furniture and clearly have a fine instinct for natural hospitality — people come, are greeted with a cool drink, use the kitchen, sit chatting while Agathe does her sewing... and want to stay. Big, simple bedrooms and lots of home-grown fruit and vegetables at dinner. The peace is almost monastic beneath the 300-year-old oak trees. Ideal for families.

Rooms: 2 double, 1 twin each with bath, shower and wc.

Price: 270 Frs (€ 41.16) for two, including breakfast. Extra person 60 Frs.

Meals: 90 Frs, including wine & coffee.

Open: Mid-April to September.

From A10 exit 26 to Pons then D142 to Jonzac. There D134 through Ozillac and Fontaines d'Ozillac. On leaving village, Chaunac is signposted (5km).

MMap 233-28 **ASP Map No: 11**

Agathe & Philippe PICQ
La Loge
17130 Chaunac
Charente-Maritime
Tel: (0)5 46 70 68 50
Fax: (0)5 46 86 13 02

A fine family house with beautiful mature gardens — formerly a cognac-making 'château', really a farm — set in excellent walking country and forest. It has been immaculately restored by the owners, émigrés from Paris, and is well decorated, beautifully (almost over-) furnished, sparklingly clean; Madame's food is excellent and everything is done properly, without fuss, despite Monsieur's health-imposed rest from helping her. Just relax and enjoy the nearby River Dordogne and the sea. Readers have praised the place and the convivial dinner party atmosphere in the evenings and the road has not caused any problems.

Rooms: 2 twin, 1 triple, 1 quadruple, each with shower & wc (1 behind curtain).

Price: 290 Frs (€ 44.21) for two, including breakfast.

Meals: 105 Frs, including wine & coffee.

Open: All year except October.

From Paris, A10 Mirambeau exit on D730 dir. Montlieu la Garde; then N10 dir. Angoulême. After Pouillac, first left after 2nd closed petrol station; signposted after 800m.

MMap 233-39 **ASP Map No: 11**

Denise & Pierre BILLAT
La Thébaïde
Pouillac
17210 Montlieu la Garde
Charente-Maritime
Tel: (0)5 46 04 65 17
Fax: (0)5 46 04 65 26
www.sawdays.co.uk

Once a modest inn for train travellers, it still overlooks the former station, now an attractive and lived-in house. Their brochure says: 'La Font Bétou is one of those very rare places in the world that does not pretend but just is.' Both are ex-market researchers, Gordon from London, Laure from Paris, and they thoroughly enjoy people. Laure cooks (rather well) because she loves it. There are two big rooms in the annexe, two others in the house; all four are pretty and welcoming, everyone can use the hosts' sitting room or lounge by the pool and the kitchen door is always open.

Rooms: In house: 1 double, 1 twin, sharing bath & wc. In cottage: 1 split-level double, 1 twin, each with shower & wc + sitting space downstairs.

Price: 300-320 Frs (€ 45.73-48.78) for two, including breakfast.

Meals: 120 Frs, including wine & coffee.

Open: All year except January.

From Angoulême N10 S for 45km then left onto D730 through Montlieu la Garde dir. Montguyon. 1km after Orignolles, right to house.

MMap 233-39 **ASP Map No: 11**

Laure TARROU & Gordon FLUDE
La Font Bétou
17210 Orignolles
Charente-Maritime
Tel: (0)5 46 04 02 52
Fax: (0)5 46 04 02 52
e-mail: tarrou@la-font-betou.com
www.la-font-betou.com

An exquisitely French neo-Gothic château which Béatrice inherited and lovingly protects from the worst ravages of modernisation (good bathrooms, separate loos). She, a primary school teacher, and Christopher, a philosophy teacher, like eating with their guests. Sleep between old linen sheets, sit in handsome old chairs and wallow in a superb bathroom. The sitting room has a most unusual window over the fireplace, in the chimney breast — whither the smoke? This is a gem, perfect for those who definitely do not want a hotel.

Rooms: 1 family suite, 2 double, 1 twin, each with bath or shower, sharing 2 wcs on guestroom floor + 1 downstairs.

Price: 280 Frs (€ 42.69) for two, including breakfast.

Meals: 70 Frs, including wine (book ahead).

Open: All year.

From A10 exit 36 E to Pons, Archiac & Barbezieux (D732/D700/D731); continue D731 dir. Chalais for 12km. After Passirac, 1st right at roadside cross and up leafy drive.

MMap 233-29 **ASP Map No: 12**

Mme Béatrice de CASTELBAJAC
Le Chatelard
Passirac
16480 Brossac
Charente
Tel: (0)5 45 98 71 03
Fax: (0)5 45 98 71 03
e-mail: cmacann@aol.com

This interesting house has an old-fashioned, well-lived-in, much-loved air to it. The bedrooms have parquet floors, old-style wallpapers, pretty old beds (new mattresses) and built-in cupboards. Madame's regional cooking is highly appreciated and dinner is worth coming back for. A conservatory is being built to seat more people round a bigger table where your hosts hope to stay and chat a while if not too busy serving you. Their huge and lovely Pyrenean sheepdog, and occasional grandchildren, extend the same warm welcome.

Rooms: 2 triple, each with basin & shower; 2 double, 1 twin, with basins, sharing shower. ALL sharing 2 wcs.

Price: 220 Frs (€ 33.54) for two, including breakfast.

Meals: 75 Frs, including wine & coffee.

Open: All year.

From A10, Pons exit on D700 dir. Barbezieux Archiac. After Echebrune, D148 (1st left) dir. Lonzac-Celles. Right onto D151, then follow signposts.

MMap 233-28 **ASP Map No: 11**

Micheline & Jacky CHAINIER
Le Chiron
16130 Salles d'Angles
Charente
Tel: (0)5 45 83 72 79
Fax: (0)5 45 83 64 80

The old house stands proudly on its wooded hill. The guestrooms, in a well-converted stable-block overlooking the garden and the pool-and-waterfall feature, are done with thoughtful taste, antiques and good, tiled shower rooms. Madame, busy with her successful horse breeding (gorgeous foals in summer), always has time to tell guests what to see in the area, arrange cognac-distillery visits or invite you to relax in a hammock after a game of badminton. Monsieur is most sociable and offers a local aperitif to guests of an evening.

Rooms: 1 double & 1 twin, each with shower & wc.

Price: 300 Frs (€ 45.73) for two, including breakfast.

Meals: Restaurant nearby. Self-catering possible.

Open: All year.

Gîte space for 8 people

From Angoulême, N141 to La Rochefoucauld; right at 3rd traffic light on D162 to St Adjutory; in village 2nd right & follow signs.

MMap 233-31 **ASP Map No: 7**

Sylviane & Vincent CASPER
La Grenouille
16310 St Adjutory
Charente
Tel: (0)5 45 62 00 34
Fax: (0)5 45 63 06 41

A young English farming couple now live in this prosperous-looking country house with their family antiques and their bilingual children (excellent company for small visitors, who are positively welcomed). They grow corn, sunflowers, ostrich and turkey but are happy to sit and talk round the big table (try them on Anglo-French farming contrasts!). From the panelled dining hall with its polished wood, soft colours and floor-to-ceiling doors, a splendid staircase leads up to the simple rooms. The big one has a romantic air and a claw-footed bath; others are smaller but all have good lighting and towels and are excellent value.

Rooms: 2 double, each with bath or shower & wc; 1 double, 1 twin, each with shower, sharing wc.

Price: 200 Frs (€ 30.49) for two, including breakfast.

Meals: 90 Frs, including wine.

Open: All year.

From Confolens, D948 dir. Limoges for 4km — signposted on road.

MMap **ASP Map No: [illegible]**

Stephen & Polly HOARE
Lesterie
Ste Marie des Lions
16500 Confolens
Charente
Tel: (0)5 45 84 18 33
Fax: (0)5 45 84 01 45

With Alex fresh from music-publishing, they took on Hélène's family farm and have worked hard to make a go of it. It now produces venison and ostrich meat: if you want to try some, ask for dinner; you will be offered a glass of local *Pineau des Charentes* too. There are wallabies and llamas, of course, and sheep, chickens, dogs and cats; it is a perfect place for family holidays, which the Everitts encourage. Breakfast is in the oak-and-stone kitchen. Bedrooms are newly-converted in a farm outbuilding, clean and fresh, one small, one big.

Rooms: 1 quadruple, 1 triple, each with bath or shower & wc.

Price: 240 Frs (€ 36.59) for two, including breakfast.

Meals: 90 Frs, including coffee.

Open: All year.

Gîte space for 4 people

From Poitiers D741 S dir. Confolens for 50km. 10km after Pressac, left on D168 for St Germain de Confolens; signed after [illegible].

MMap 233-20 **ASP Map No: 7**

Alex & Hélène EVERITT
Le Pit
Lessac
16500 Confolens, Charente
Tel: (0)5 45 84 27 65
Fax: (0)5 45 85 41 34
e-mail: Everitt16@aol.com
www.sawdays.co.uk

Food and religion already occupied the minds of the prehistoric cave painters all those millenia ago, though there are more geese than bison nowadays to stew with the truffles.

Limousin – Dordog

French country cooking enthusiasts, including vegetarians, sing the praises of Mother's meals made with home-grown vegetables, lamb, duck, pigeon and rabbit (delicious *pâtés*): she just loves to cook (try her tomato jam too). Myriam has lots of time for guests while Pierre looks after the 20 sheep and works hard on house improvement. The C18 farmhouse, with its magnificent wooden staircase and original beams and timber framing, has country antiques, functioning fireplaces, restfully simple bedrooms, a garden full of toys, and... excitement on a microlight(!). Wonderful French value with interesting hosts.

Rooms: 1 double, 1 triple, each with bath or shower & wc; 2 quadruple, each with shower, sharing wc in passage.

Price: 200 Frs (€ 30.49) for two, including breakfast.

Meals: 80 Frs, including wine & coffee.

Open: March to October.

Gîte space for 6 people

In Bellac follow signs to Limoges; just before leaving Bellac right on D3 dir. Blond. 4km to Thoveyrat. House [illegible]nposted on left.

Map 233-22 **ASP Map No: 7**

& Myriam MORICE
[illegible]yrat
Bellac
[illegible]ienne
55 68 86 86
55 68 86 86

A really super, nature-loving, chemical-free house where natural materials come into their own: wood everywhere including under the tiles, cork insulation, organic food that includes meat and home-made bread, and they've done it for the last 30 years! The central heating is provided by steam ducts leading from the cooking-pot over the open fire. He is a painter of Italian extraction; she made all the upholstery, bedheads and patchworks. Rooms have soothing, simple, successful colour schemes and lots of wood. And there are more fabulous colours, and walks, to be found outside.

Rooms: 2 double, 1 triple, each with shower & wc.

Price: 260 Frs (€ 39.64) for two, including breakfast.

Meals: 85 Frs, including wine.

Open: All year.

From Paris A20 exit 25 on D44 dir. St Sylvestre; left on D78 dir. Grandmont & St Léger la Montagne; through Grandmont then right dir. Les Sauvages after 200m.

MMap 239-1 **ASP Map No: 7**

Lorenzo & Édith RAPPELLI
Les Chênes
Les Sauvages
87240 St Sylvestre, Haute-Vienne
Tel: (0)5 55 71 33 12
Fax: (0)5 55 71 33 12
e-mail: les.chenes@wanadoo.fr
www.haute-vienne.com/chenes.htm

Eight centuries ago Knights Templar farmed here; four centuries ago dashing King Henri IV hunted wolves here; the same family has always owned these 750 acres and pilgrims have always passed through on the way to Compostela — such is the tapestry of history that your intelligent, sociable hosts weave for you beneath the Aubusson or across the grand dinner table. They are absolutely the right mix of friendliness and formality. All rooms are properly period-furnished, but pay the extra for the superb suite and enjoy its mighty bathroom (shower rooms smaller).

Rooms: 1 suite for 4, 1 double, 1 twin, each with bath or shower & wc.

Price: 320-400 Frs (€ 48.78-60.98) for two, including breakfast.

Meals: 100 Frs, excluding wine (50 Frs).

Open: April to October.

From A20 exit 24 onto D27 to Bersac; continue dir. Laurière then left after railway bridge and follow signs for 3km to château.

MMap 239-1 **ASP Map No: 7**

Éric & Annie PERRIN des MARAIS
Le Château du Chambon
Le Chambon
87370 Bersac sur Rivalier
Haute-Vienne
Tel: (0)5 55 71 47 04
Fax: (0)5 55 71 51 41
e-mail: perrin-desmarais.eric@wanadoo.fr

Go through your own entrance, covered in wisteria and rose, to your own kitchen area with stairs up to the rather appealing bedroom with its white walls, off-white carpet and sea-grass wallpaper. The other bedroom is useful for overflow. You have your own living room too, with an open fire. (It can all be let as a gîte.) Néline is a wonderful hostess, both gentle and energetic. The house is lovely, splashed with colour and imaginative gestures, and the 2½-acre garden makes further demands upon a willing pair of owners.

Rooms: 1 double/twin, 1 twin, sharing shower, wc & small kitchen with dishwasher & washing machine (same group only).

Price: 300 Frs (€ 45.73) for two, including breakfast. Extra bed 100 Frs. Reduction 2 nights.

Meals: Self-Catering.

Open: All year.

Gîte space for 4 people

From Limoges, N141 to St Léonard then D39 towards St Priest; after 5km right dir. Lajoumard; first left and follow signs.

MMap 239-14 **ASP Map No: 7**

Mme Néline JANSEN de VOMÉCOURT
La Réserve
Bassoleil
87400 St Léonard de Noblat
Haute-Vienne
Tel: (0)5 55 56 18 39

A glorious touch of eccentricity here. The house, once C12th, is now entirely 16th/17th and has been in the family for generations. You may share a bath or creep down a floor for the loo, but one room is authentic Charles X and all are deeply evocative. The main house has a spectacular stone staircase with Egyptian vases pillaged from a Pharaoh's tomb, huge bedrooms and modern bathrooms. The great dining hall has wood panelling but breakfast is in a small guest *salon* or in the cottage kitchen. Monsieur, who plays jazz on those two pianos, runs his own model train museum. Definitely different.

Rooms: In gatehouse: 1 double with shower, 2 double sharing bathroom, all 3 sharing wc; in main house: 1 triple, 1 suite, each with bath & wc.

Price: 300 Frs (€ 45.73) for two, including breakfast; extra bed 60 Frs.

Meals: 80 Frs, including wine & coffee.

Open: All year.

Gîte space for 6 people

From Limoges, D979 dir. Eymoutiers; Fougeolles on left just before entering Eymoutiers, signposted Chambres d'Hôtes.

MMap 239-15 **ASP Map No: 7**

Jacques & Frédérique du MONTANT
Fougeolles
87120 Eymoutiers
Haute-Vienne
Tel: (0)5 55 69 11 44

The atmosphere is more traditional than the photo suggests, lively yet restful. Michel's modern sculptures add magic to the garden and his work is everywhere: handmade door handles, towel rails, shelf supports,... mainly in brass and steel. Bedrooms and bathrooms are biggish and the house glories in an extravagant use of materials: opulent floor-length curtains, off-white material instead of wallpaper and a tented ceiling of it in the dayroom (all Madame's work). The living and dining rooms have a studio feel with 'works in progress'. He loves showing his forge and studio, she loves making cakes — a very likeable couple.

Rooms: 2 double, each with shower & wc.

Price: 290 Frs (€ 44.21) for two, including breakfast.

Meals: 90 Frs, including wine & coffee.

Open: April to December.

From Eymoutiers, D30 dir. Chamberet. House in village of La Roche, 7km beyond Eymoutiers.

MMap 239-15 **ASP Map No: 12**

Michel & Josette JAUBERT
La Roche
87120 Eymoutiers
Haute-Vienne
Tel: (0)5 55 69 61 88

Deep in the country, this demure little guesthouse was built in the 1700s for the farm manager's family and would be idyllic for the more independent modern traveller. There is a flagstoned, beamed and chimneyed sitting room with books, ancient dresser and old photos... and a bread oven that is still occasionally used. A roped wooden staircase leads to the two bedrooms, planked and pine-clad, not unlike a boat. The kindly Desmaisons live next door, are passionate about the area and will point you towards fabulous walks. You can use the barbecue, make picnics, and you breakfast in your own quarters.

Rooms: Suite of 1 double, 1 twin, sharing shower & wc on floor below.

Price: 300 Frs (€ 45.73) for two, including breakfast. Extra person 50 Frs.

Meals: Barbecue + hotplate; auberge 10km.

Open: May to September.

From A20 exit 41 onto D82 dir. Glanges. Cross railway line then 1st right onto D120 & follow signs for 5km.

MMap 239-14 **ASP Map No: 12**

Anne-Marie & Jean-Luc DESMAISON
Lancournet
87380 Glanges
Haute-Vienne
Tel: (0)5 55 00 81 27
Fax: (0)5 55 00 81 27

These are real farmers who like to be as bio-dynamic (i.e. respectful of natural life systems) and self-sufficient as possible, so meals are home-grown and nourishing. The four rooms share a living room with kitchen, but dine with your hosts if you can: they are completely unpretentious, very good company and know their region intimately. Two rooms are on the ground floor, two in the roof, with pine-clad sloping ceilings, white walls and roof windows. The farm is surrounded by woods (superb walking), and children love helping to milk the goats and collect the eggs. So do some adults.

Rooms: 3 double, 1 triple, each with own shower & wc.

Price: 240 Frs (€ 36.59) for two, including breakfast.

Meals: By arrangement 85 Frs, including wine.

Open: All year.

From A20, exit 41 to Magnac Bourg then D215 (between 'Total' service station & 'Brasserie des Sports') SW then follow signs 4km to La Chapelle.

MMap 239-13 **ASP Map No: 12**

Patrick & Mayder LESPAGNOL
La Chapelle
87380 Château Chervix
Haute-Vienne
Tel: (0)5 55 00 86 67
Fax: (0)5 55 00 70 78
e-mail: lespagno@club-internet.fr

There once stood a forge here, producing cannon balls. They now produce *pâtés, confits* and *rillettes...* and keep ducks, horses, a pig, dogs, a cat and two children (six and nine); the latter are very much part of life here and the atmosphere is easy and *familiale.* Nothing fancy about the bedrooms — they are cosy and comfortable. A huge sitting room with enormous hearth, stone walls, tatty sofa, and the nicest possible people. Stay for dinner; most ingredients are home-grown or home-raised. Boating on the lake. Guests love it all. *Ask about pets when booking.*

Rooms: 3 double, each with shower & wc.

Price: 240 Frs (€ 36.59) for two, including breakfast. Extra bed 70 Frs.

Meals: 90 Frs, including wine & coffee.

Open: All year.

From A20 exit 40 to Pierre Buffière; W across river onto D15 then D19 dir. St Yrieix la Perche for 18km. At La Croix d'Hervy, left on D57 for Coussac Bonneval. Mill on left after approx. 4km.

MMap 239-13 **ASP Map No: 12**

Valérie & Renaud GIZARDIN
Moulin de Marsaguet
87500 Coussac Bonneval
Haute-Vienne
Tel: (0)5 55 75 28 29

If the quaint, quirky and creative appeal, come to this C18 house on the edge of town. The bouncy dog, the exquisite handmade patchwork quilts that contrast with fading wallpaper and cluttered terrace (stunning views of medieval Château de Boussac), the jolly, genuine hostess and her delightful husband who live in amiable confusion, all add up to a totally French experience. They both used to be in *haute couture*: he talks fascinatingly about that strange world. Good-sized, clean rooms — ask for one with a view; the new triple has a kitchenette. A good place for exploring town and country.

Rooms: 2 double, 1 triple, 1 suite, all with bath or shower & wc.

Price: 280 Frs (€ 42.69) for two, including breakfast. Extra bed 80 Frs.

Meals: 80 Frs, including wine & coffee.

Open: All year except October.

Gîte space for 4 people

From A71 exit 10 onto D94 W by-passing Montluçon (15km) then right onto D916 through Domérat, Huriel, Trégnat to Boussac. On Boussac main square, take road to left of Mairie, left again at butcher's — house on right.

MMap 238-42 **ASP Map No: 8**

Françoise GROS & Daniel COLSENET
La Courtepointe
3 rue des Loges
23600 Boussac, Creuse
Tel: (0)5 55 65 80 09
Fax: (0)5 55 65 80 09
www.sawdays.co.uk

They have been given "10/10 for welcome, comfort, food — everything". The kitchen is a wonderful place with its display of farm things and Anne's sunny presence — she delights in texture, smell and colour, her cooking reflects her pleasure and you catch the vibes easily. Their house restoration job is (extremely well) finished and Jim can spend time coaching the village football team; many local farmers are the Lardners' friends so visits can be arranged; regional dinners are served with good wine — all proof of thorough integration among the rolling hills of rural France. Excellent value, plus deep peace.

Rooms: 1 twin with bath & wc. Extra room for children.

Price: 200 Frs (€ 30.49) for two, including breakfast.

Meals: 95 Frs, including wine & coffee.

Open: All year.

Gîte space for 2 people

From Argentat, N120 dir. Tulle then left onto D921 dir. Brive. Pass sign to Albussac; 300m on, left to Le Prézat, through hamlet; house on right with lawn.

MMap 239-27 **ASP Map No: 12**

Anne and Jim LARDNER
Le Prézat
19380 Albussac
Corrèze
Tel: (0)5 55 28 62 36
Fax: (0)5 55 28 62 36

Jacquie, half French, and Ian, half Hungarian, are fervent Francophiles: it's all very cosmopolitan. Their renovation of this old village house is an achievement to be proud of, with remarkable bathrooms and Laura Ashley-style décor. They are very organised and will tell you absolutely everything about the locality and its people, history, flora and building regs. A professional chef, Ian produces food of superb quality and amazing variety which he serves with a flourish and wines from his own cellar. Aperitifs and dinner *en famille* are occasions for stimulating conversation — not a time for shrinking violets.

Rooms: 2 double/twin, 1 twin, each with bath or shower & wc.

Price: 180-200 Frs (€ 27.44-30.49) for two, including breakfast.

Meals: By arrangement 80 Frs, including wine & coffee.

Open: All year.

From Tulle N120 to Forgès. Left into Place de la Mairie and park in church square behind.

MMap 239-27 **ASP Map No: 12**

Ian & Jacquie HOARE
La Souvigne
1 impasse La Fontaine
19380 Forgès, Corrèze
Tel: (0)5 55 28 63 99
Fax: (0)5 55 28 65 62
e-mail: ianhoare@wanadoo.fr
http://perso.wanadoo.fr/souvigne

The stones are as big and the house as tiny inside as out. It was just a hut for drying chestnuts, at the time when French peasants found their only protein in that rich chuffy fruit. The vast (non-working) fireplace still occupies one wall of the room. The restoration is perfect in its simplicity of stone and plaster, tile and beam; the big bed is excellent, the lighting subtle, the space too pure for large furniture and the neighbourhood too remote for any night life. A little gem for seekers of utter peace. Madame, an interesting, sociable teacher, loves having guests (except Mondays). Visit the remarkable nearby Tours de Merle, the C11 skyscrapers.

Rooms: 1 double with shower & wc.

Price: 230 Frs (€ 35.06) for two, including breakfast.

Meals: Restaurant 400m; choice 8km.

Open: May to November.

Gîte space for 2 people

From Argentat D980 dir. St Privat and follow signs to 'Tours de Merle' for 9km. In St Geniez ô Merle straight over crossroads; after cemetery, through stone pillars on right then through pastures to houses.

MMap 239-28 **ASP Map No: 13**

Marie-José JUBERT
Le Cros
19220 St Geniez ô Merle
Corrèze
Tel: (0)5 55 28 44 47

You will be part of life on the farm while you stay and you'll understand why Madame, born in the area, has no desire ever to move away. Ideal for families, with its expanse of grass within eyesight, canoes for hire and fishing down on the River Dordogne (ask about their own piece of river bank) in what is now a conservation area, and a proper kitchen for guests, Saulières has a superbly 'family, friends and farming' atmosphere. They are a highly likeable couple — he raises beef cattle and grows walnuts while she makes pretty curtains, soft bedcovers and paints pictures for the guestrooms in the modern extension.

Rooms: 1 quadruple, 1 triple, 1 double & 1 twin, each with own shower & wc.

Price: 250 Frs (€ 38.11) for two, including breakfast. Extra bed 50 Frs.

Meals: Self-catering or good choice 2km.

Open: All year.

Gîte space for 8 people

From Tulle, N120 to Argentat then D12 along River Dordogne dir. Beaulieu; past Monceaux to Saulières (6km from Argentat).

MMap 239-27 **ASP Map No: 13**

Marie-Jo & Jean-Marie LAFOND
Saulières
Monceaux sur Dordogne
19400 Argentat
Corrèze
Tel: (0)5 55 28 09 22

Your interesting hosts are in the peasant heritage movement... and go to Glynebourne whenever they can. The sensitive restoration of this lovely, listed group of ancient buildings, with a shingle-roofed bread oven, illustrates their commitment. Bedrooms, at opposite ends of the long building, have odd bathroom layouts: one has the shower in a (big) cupboard next to the fireplace, an antique washbasin that tips straight into the drain (genuine period feature) and a 120cm brass bed. They founded the local music/dance festival, are still very involved in the cultural life of the community and have a huge classical CD collection.

Rooms: 1 suite for 4 with bath & wc, 1 double with shower & wc.

Price: 320-350 Frs (€ 48.78-53.36) for two, incl. breakfast; extra bed 50 Frs. (Min. 2 nights.)

Meals: 2 restaurants 1.5km.

Open: All year except January & 2nd fortnight in October.

From Périgueux N21 N 11km to Sarliac sur l'Isle; right on D705 to Coulaures (12km); right on D73 to Tourtoirac. Right after bridge, pass cemetery then left on D67 dir. St Orse — house 1km on left

MMap 233-44 **ASP Map No: 12**

Danièle & Jean-Pierre MOUGIN
Bas Portail
Tourtoirac
24390 Hautefort
Dordogne
Tel: (0)5 53 51 14 35
e-mail: bestofperigord@perigord.com

There is an island for loners, a dream of a garden (all John's work), a swimming pool in the walled garden and superb, light, airy rooms with pretty soft furnishings and bathrooms across the corridor. Diana, a passionate and excellent cook (readers have confirmed), is happy for people to come into her marvellous great kitchen to enjoy her company and the views from all four sides of this very finely converted C17 millhouse on the banks of the Auvezère river. They have been here for eight years and will happily direct you towards the many nearby treasures and pleasures. *Children over 12 welcome.*

Rooms: 1 double, 1 twin, each with bath or shower & wc.

Price: 700 Frs (€ 106.71) for two, including breakfast; extra bed 100 Frs.

Meals: 200 Frs, including coffee.

Open: All year.

From Périgueux, N21 dir. Limoges. About 2 km on, right over bridge dir. airport. Left at next r'about on D5 dir. Hautefort. 1.5km after Tourtoirac, left dir. La Crouzille. Cross the Auvezère. 1st drive on right.

MMap 233-44 **ASP Map No: 12**

John & Diana ARMITAGE
Le Moulin de la Crouzille
Tourtoirac
24390 Hautefort
Dordogne
Tel: (0)5 53 51 11 94
Fax: (0)5 53 51 11 94

In a really pretty hamlet, this is a civilised place for the independently-minded to stay. You sleep and breakfast in the well-converted barn where original beams and stones are married with white walls, plain furniture and good old cupboard doors. Beds and bathrooms are all good, breakfast is served until late and the Rubbens enjoy chatting to their guests. The fine big pool, out of sight or hearing of the guest quarters, is inviting with its diving board and barbecue, service is excellent and well-behaved children are tolerated!

Rooms: 1 triple, 2 double, each with bath or shower & wc.

Price: 390 Frs (€ 59.46) for two, including breakfast.

Meals: Restaurant in village.

Open: Easter to October.

From Périgueux, D939 to Brantôme. There, D78 & D83 dir. Champagnac de Belair; D82 & D3 to Villars and 'Grottes de Villars'. Left to Lavergne; signposted.

MMap 233-32 **ASP Map No: 12**

Mme Eliane RUBBENS
'Enclos
avergne
4530 Villars
ordogne
el: (0)5 53 54 82 17
ax: (0)5 53 54 82 17
ww.sawdays.co.uk

Come to this deliciously rustic hamlet to experience true French *paysan* hospitality in the Durieux's converted barn. Furniture is properly dark, bathrooms authentically simple, Madame's regional cuisine (you can watch her cook) a daily marvel. She uses fine ingredients, many home-produced: vegetables, nuts, honey, fruits and free-range chickens. The history-charged area has ancient caves and stately châteaux; add spice to sightseeing with a sprinkling of local folklore, available courtesy of Monsieur who acts, if requested, as a willing and knowledgeable guide and plies guests with his own fruit liqueurs when they return.

Rooms: 2 triple rooms with showers and wash-basins behind screens, sharing a wc.

Price: 390 Frs (€ 59.46) for two, half-board only, including breakfast & dinner.

Meals: Dinner with aperitif, wine & coffee included in price.

Open: All year.

From Angoulême D939 south. After Dignac D23 to Villebois Luvalette, D17 to Gurat then D102 dir. Vendoire for 2km then left for Le Bouchaud.

MMap 233-30 **ASP Map No: 12**

André & Pierrette DURIEUX
Le Bouchaud D17
24320 Vendoire
Dordogne
Tel: (0)5 53 91 00 82

Once a lovers' retreat, this peaceful, long-viewed stone cottage stands in two acres of woods and fields. Your genial Flemish hostess paints, plays the flute, teaches French, shares her library and her talent for good conversation, drawing on a long and interesting life. Her house, filled with Belgian antiques and exceptional paintings, has a split-level sitting room opening onto a sun terrace, modest but adequate bedrooms, a bread oven and a large heated pool. Madame welcomes single visitors for week-long rest cures, or French immersion, and excellent guided tours of the area — enquire about full-board terms.

Rooms: 1 double, 1 twin, sharing shower & wc (2nd wc on ground floor).

Price: 220 Frs (€ 33.54) for two, incl. breakfast (min. 2 nights).

Meals: 80 Frs, including wine.

Open: All year.

Gîte space for 4 people

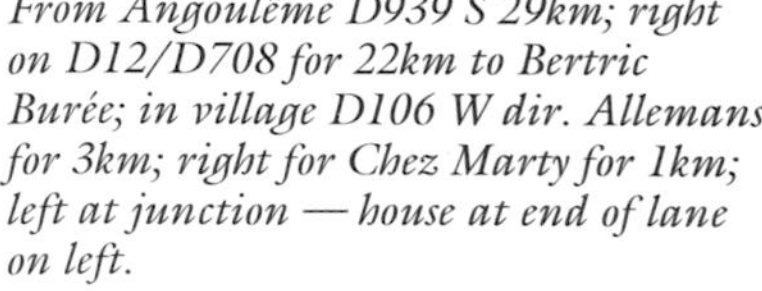

From Angoulême D939 S 29km; right on D12/D708 for 22km to Bertric Burée; in village D106 W dir. Allemans for 3km; right for Chez Marty for 1km; left at junction — house at end of lane on left.

MMap 233-41 **ASP Map No: 12**

Anne HART
La Fournière
Chez Marty
24320 Bertric Burée
Dordogne
Tel: (0)5 53 91 93 58
Fax: (0)5 53 91 93 58
www.sawdays.co.uk

We love this place — the bright, rustic dining room with its limed walls, white tablecloths and ticking chair covers, the level changes upstairs, the bedrooms with their berugged wooden floors and simple furnishings (good taste and African throws), the inviting bathrooms. The cool, overflowing stone plunge pool in the green and pleasant garden is unforgettable (there's a shallow one for children). Delightful, energetic Jane creates a relaxed atmosphere, offers superb and imaginative food and early supper for children in this lovely tranquil spot. And John "is a joy to be with".

Rooms: 2 dble, 1 twin each with shower & wc; 1 dble, 1 twin sharing bath & wc.

Price: 290-325 Frs (€ 44.21-49.55) for two, including breakfast.

Meals: 100 Frs, including coffee.

Open: All year.

Gîte space for 5 people

From Ribérac dir. Verteillac for 2km. At La Borie right on D99 for 4km, continue through Celles; 4km to right turn dir.Pauliac. Signposted in hamlet.

MMap 233-41 **ASP Map No: 12**

Jane & John EDWARDS
Pauliac
Celles
24600 Ribérac, Dordogne
Tel: (0)5 53 91 97 45
Fax: (0)5 53 90 43 46
e-mail: pauliac@infonie.fr
www.sawdays.co.uk

A little bit of Alsace in the Dordogne is what the Kieffers have created. Their *moulin* in a valley gives the impression of being a Swiss mountain inn. Levels change, steep original stairs rise, brilliantly chosen colours give huge character, Alsace rugs and antiques warm the atmosphere — as does the sitting room fireplace — and if bedrooms are on the small side the welcome from your easy-going hostess is huge. The whole effect is rich and brave. Add fully organic home-grown ingredients (*foie gras*, lamb, poultry, veg) for delicious dinners and you have excellent value.

Rooms: 1 twin (+ child's room), 1 double, each with shower & wc.

Price: 250 Frs (€ 38.11) for two, including breakfast.

Meals: 80 Frs, excluding wine (price according to quality chosen).

Open: All year.

From Périgueux N89 SW dir. Mussidan/Bordeaux. After end of dual carriageway, follow blue signs: left/right on D39e dir. St Séverin for 3km — house on right after small lake.

MMap 233-41 **ASP Map No: 12**

Jacques & Ginette KIEFFER
Le Moulin de Leymonie du Maupas
24400 Issac
Dordogne
Tel: (0)5 53 81 24 02

All power to this deeply united family and their desire to keep local tradition alive raising poultry and hand-crafting *pâtés* and *foie gras*. Marie-Jeanne and her son and daughter-in-law (a brilliant cook and teacher, though not for vegetarians) now 'share' the B&B tasks. Marie-Jeanne will welcome you with her natural good humour, settle you into your genuinely French Rustic room, give you time to admire the view then drive you the 7km across the Dordogne River to her son's lovely old house for a memorable dinner. One of France's most exquisite areas and an exceptional experience of genuine French country warmth.

Rooms: 1 double, 1 triple, 1 quadruple, all with shower & wc (1 curtained).

Price: 260 Frs (€ 39.64) for two, including breakfast (min. 2 nights).

Meals: 110 Frs, including wine & coffee.

Open: March to November.

Gîte space for 5 people

From Bergerac, D32 dir. St Alvère. After 10km, look for signpost 'Périgord — Bienvenue à la Ferme'.

MMap [illegible] **ASP Map No: 12**

Marie-Jeanne & Marie-Thérèse ARCHER
La Barabie — D32
Lamonzie Montastruc
24520 Mouleydier
Dordogne
Tel: (0)5 53 23 22 47
Fax: (0)5 53 22 81 20

This Belgian couple know their adopted region 'like their pocket' and are keen that you discover the hidden treasures of the Dordogne not just the oversubscribed star sights. Their fine set of Périgord buildings sits high on a wooded, hawk-hunted hill, the big, solar-heated pool is at a decent distance and the house has been beautifully restored (the garden is still being conquered). In the biggest room, you sleep under a soaring timber canopy supporting a crystal chandelier... Easy décor, good furniture, a friendly welcome and the run of the kitchen. You may even be able to paint your own souvenir tile.

Rooms: 1 double, 1 triple, 1 quadruple, each with bath and wc.

Price: 250-315 Frs (€ 38.11-48.02) for two, incl. breakfast; extra bed 85 Frs.

Meals: Auberge 4km; choice in Bergerac 9km. Use of kitchen.

Open: All year.

Gîte space for 6 people

From Bergerac N21 N dir. Périgueux. 4km after Lembras, Les Rocailles sign on right.

MMap 234-4 **ASP Map No: 12**

Marcel VANHEMELRYCK & Nicole DENYS
Les Rocailles de la Fourtaunie
24520 Lamonzie Montastruc
Dordogne
Tel: (0)5 53 58 20 16
Fax: (0)5 53 58 20 16
e-mail: marcel.vanhemelryck@wanadoo.fr

Staying as guests of Robert and Stuart in this charming watermill, where they serve their own spring water, is a delight. Views over a perfect landscape of deep, willow-dotted meadow, green lawns, stream coursing under the house and a reedy lake, can be enjoyed from all the smallish, ever-immaculate rooms in the separate guest house and there's a good dayroom with a white piano. Breakfast tables are set out here or on the idyllic, vine-shaded little terrace beside the old bread oven. It is all lovingly tended, nearby is unspoilt Paunat with its huge church and peace, perfect peace. *Small pets on request; careful children only (unfenced water).*

Rooms: 3 double, 2 twin, 1 triple, all with bath or shower & wc.

Price: 394 Frs (€ 60.06) for two, including breakfast.

Meals: Good choice in nearby towns.

Open: All year.

 small  

From Le Bugue D703 dir. Limeuil; le on D31 through Limeuil. At crossroc D2 dir. Ste Alvère; after 100m fork house is on left 2km along — driv down from small crossroads.

MMap 233-43 **ASP Ma**

Robert CHAPPELL & St
SHIPPEY
Le Moulin Neuf, Pauna
24510 Ste Alvère, Do
Tel: (0)5 53 63 30 1
Fax: (0)5 53 73 33
e-mail: moulin-neuf

Even for the Dordogne, this is a particularly lovely area and the small isolated hamlet is calm and simple. La Licorne is three unspoiled old buildings; a stream bounds the pretty courtyard — it feels rather medieval. Rooms, one in the C13 barn overlooking the nut trees and garden, are small, white, patchwork-quilted with modern furniture and the occasional old carved cupboard door. The dining room is superb with its big fireplace and gallery at each end where you can sit and read; food is light and vegetable-orientated. Relaxed, well-travelled, cultured owners, eager to put you at your ease. *Children over 12 welcome.*

Rooms: 2 double, 1 suite for 4, each with bath or shower & wc.

Price: 346-376 Frs (€ 52.75-57.32) for two, including breakfast.

Meals: By arrangement 130 Frs, excluding wine (carafe 36 Frs).

Open: April to mid-November.

...n Montignac D65 south for 6km ...eft on minor road dir. Valojoulx. ...in centre of hamlet to left of ...

...3-44 **ASP Map No: 12**

...LIEZ & Astrid VAN ...

...

Lascaux

...7

Madame, an old hand at B&B (providing badminton, swings, a solar-heated pool), speaks excellent English (more Anglo than Americanophile), has enthusiastically adopted meat-loving Périgord cuisine and recently opened a little *brocante*. In the golden triangle between Périgueux, Sarlat and Bergerac, the converted C18 barn, farm buildings and log cabin (cosily our favourite) are enveloped in lovely woodland where tempting paths beckon. The conservatory has a summer kitchen so guests can be as independent as they like. Well-behaved children welcome. *Please arrive after 5pm.*

Rooms: 1 double, 1 suite for 5 in house, 1 suite for 3 in log cabin, each with bath or shower & wc.

Price: 350 Frs (€ 53.36) for two, including breakfast. Extra person 100 Frs.

Meals: By arrangement 125 Frs, light meal 50 Frs, incl. wine & coffee.

Open: All year.

Gîte space for 6 people

From Le Bugue D703 towards Pezuls for 10km then left towards Vaudunes for about 1.5km across first junction; house is on right.

MMap 235-5 **ASP Map No: 12**

Xavière SIMAND
La Maison des Bois
Maison Neuve
24510 Paunat, Dordogne
Tel: (0)5 53 22 75 74/
(0)6 82 75 79 32
Fax: (0)5 53 22 75 74
www.sawdays.co.uk

"Wow!", wrote the inspector "What a beautiful house," ... and immensely friendly hosts too. Set in pretty grounds with a lake overlooking a wooded valley, it has been lovingly restored to a sophisticated standard, with lots of Laura Ashley and superb bathrooms, four of them behind magnificent curtains. Pictures, antiques, tapestries, harmonised colours, comfortable sofas, three superb 'public' rooms for guests, a playroom: elegance yet homeliness... almost a château-hotel, but much friendlier and far better value. Readers have confirmed that luxury and welcome do indeed go hand in hand here.

Rooms: 2 twin, 3 double, 1 extra child's room, each with bath or shower & wc.

Price: 400-500 Frs (€ 60.98-76.22) for two, including breakfast.

Meals: Choice in Sarlat 5km.

Open: All year.

From Sarlat S on D57 dir. Beynac then very quickly right onto D25 dir. Le Bugue for 4km; right at Ventojols & La Métairie signs for 800m, then right for 400m of drive.

MMap 235-6 **ASP Map No: 12**

Michel & Martine PINARD-LEGRY
La Metairie Haute
Lasserre
24200 Sarlat
Dordogne
Tel: (0)5 53 30 31 17
Fax: (0)5 53 59 62 66
www.abscisse.com/perigord/plegry/plegry1.html

Hard by medieval Sarlat, this much-visited château (free tour for B&B guests!) is like a dream. Painted beams draw the eye, the carved stone staircase and the ancient floors are utterly lovely, history oozes from every corner (there may even be a ghost). All furniture is authentic C17 Perigordian — no concessions to C20 chic. The twin? two four-posters; the suite? one room perfect Louis XVI with claw-footed bath behind curtains and loo in an archer's turret, the other classic red Jouy fabric-clad (slightly showing its age). Madame is elegant, friendly, very French; her son, who helps in the château, speaks good English; both are delightful.

Rooms: 1 twin (+ single), 1 suite, both with bath, shower & wc.

Price: 750 Frs (€ 114.34) for two, including breakfast.

Meals: Good restaurant 5km away; choice in Sarlat.

Open: April to October.

Gîte space for 10 people

From Sarlat D47 dir. Les Eyzies for 8km. Château signposted regularly.

MMap 235-6 **ASP Map No: 12**

Comte & Comtesse de MONTBRON
Château de Puymartin
24200 Sarlat la Canéda
Dordogne
Tel: (0)5 53 59 29 97
Fax: (0)5 53 29 87 52
e-mail: ch.puymartin@lemel.fr

It's not all truffles and romance, y'know — here are French country people still working the land with their priorities and values still intact. They are busy, capable farmers living in an utterly typical French farmhouse, down to that very special colour of orangey-brown wallpaper and those highly-polished *lits bateau*. There are walnuts galore, dairy cows, a vegetable garden and you can visit the prune ovens. Succulent regional dishes are eaten with the family and the house is altogether an excellent and welcoming stopping place. One reader says it's "huge fun but don't talk while the weather report is on".

Rooms: 2 double, 1 triple each with bath or shower & wc (1 ground-floor room).

Price: 220 Frs (€ 33.54) for two, including breakfast.

Meals: 80 Frs, including wine.

Open: All year.

Gîte space for 5 people

From Beaumont du Périgord, D660 5km dir. Montpazier; second farm on right after sign for Petit Brassac.

MMap 235-5 **ASP Map No: 12**

Gilbert & Reine MARESCASSIER
Petit Brassac
Labouquerie
24440 Beaumont du Périgord
Dordogne
Tel: (0)5 53 22 32 51
Fax: (0)5 53 22 32 51
www.sawdays.co.uk

A homely farming couple with much enthusiasm for their natural, healthy home-produced food, they give you an insight into rural France, love having you at their own table where the gastronomic traditions of Périgord are vaunted (though modernity in the form of a noisy telly can force its way in) and Monsieur serves his own liqueurs. The setting is blissfully peaceful, the new local-style house was built with old stones and beams, the bedrooms are old in style — so much so that three have shower and loo virtually in the room, just screened off. Tours in a horse-drawn buggy can be arranged.

Rooms: 3 twin, 1 double, all with shower & wc (3 in room).

Price: 220 Frs (€ 33.54) for two, including breakfast.

Meals: 80 Frs, including aperitif, wine & coffee.

Open: 1 March to 30 November.

From Périgueux, N89 dir. Brive then D710 dir. Cahors/Fumel. At 'Le Périgord en Calèche' sign, turn right. It is the first house.

MMap 235-9 **ASP Map No: 12**

Jacqueline & Robert MARESCASSIER
Le Bourg
24550 Mazeyrolles
Dordogne
Tel: (0)5 53 29 93 38
Fax: (0)5 53 29 93 38

Come for the opulent 'marbled halls' feel of the main rooms, for the poolside set-up, for Richard, half Spanish, half Bordelais, who encourages deer, has hens (and will have ducks and horses) running loose, grows fruits and nuts to bursting point (they make their own oil). He's a young, enthusiastic, attractive ex-hotelier; he paints too. Breakfast consists of own eggs and anything you want. Isabelle is a part-time air-hostess and they will share their imaginatively-cooked dinner with you if you are a small group. Simple bedrooms with plain beds and white walls are in ideally restful contrast to the spectacular style below.

Rooms: 3 double, 2 twin, each with shower & wc (2 connect for family use).

Price: 340-410 Frs (€ 51.83-62.50) for two, including breakfast.

Meals: 115 Frs, including aperitif & wine.

Open: All year.

Gîte space for 5 people

From Périgueux D710 S through Siorac and 6km further dir. Belvès. Do NOT take right fork up into Belvès, stay on D710 for 500m then left dir. Sagelat Église. House 600m along on left.

MMap 235-5 **ASP Map No: 12**

Richard & Isabelle GINIOUX
Le Branchat
24170 Belvès
Dordogne
Tel: (0)5 53 28 98 80
Fax: (0)5 53 28 90 82
e-mail: le.branchat@wanadoo.fr
…v.perigord.com/belves

The pale gold stones, the curvy roof, the entrance arch, the tough old beams and the wafer bricks round the fireplaces are well-preserved old friends that we are always happy to see again; the first-floor alcove enclosing the original long-drop privy is rarer. Splendid main rooms combine simplicity and taste, antique and modern furniture; smaller, tempting bedrooms have hand-stencilled doors. The two easy, articulate former Parisiennes who live here may offer you their irresistible chocolate courgette cake, a browse in their library and a chance to share their genuine pleasure in people.

Rooms: 3 double, 1 twin, 1 triple, each with bath or shower & wc.

Price: 320 Frs (€ 48.78) for two, including breakfast.

Meals: 110 Frs, including wine & coffee.

Open: All year.

Gîte space for 6 people

From Bergerac D660 W dir. Lalir… Sarlat for 19km. Right across Ri… Dordogne at Pont de Couze (st… D660). At Bayac right onto I… Issigeac — house on left afte…

MMap 235-5 **AS…**

Francine PILLEBOU…
CALMETTES
Le Relais de Lave…
Lavergne
24150 Bayac, …
Tel: (0)5 53…
Fax: (0)5 5…
www.sawd…

Madame is a refined, well-travelled, forthright lady who enjoys having visitors, especially English — she worked in England some time ago. Now she shares this handsome country manor, of 17th and 18th-century origin, and its fine garden with her guests, whom she likes to "welcome as friends". Her freshly-papered, painted, floral-curtained drawing room is full of antiques from her past and flowers from the garden. Bedrooms are normal *Vieux France*. You can picnic and barbecue, play table tennis and *pétanque* outside. This is a house with no set rules and lots of charm.

Rooms: 2 double, 1 triple, each with bath or shower & wc.

Price: 320 Frs (€ 48.78) for two, including breakfast.

Meals: Barbecue available. Restaurants 2km.

Open: Easter to end October.

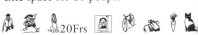

…rgerac, N21 south for 11km, …n D14 to Issigeac, then D21 …nnes. At Monmarves; …urn into green gate.

ASP Map No: 12

…OON

With its steep roofs and dark stone, and now that the Bells have accomplished that vast labour of love called restoration, the old farmhouse is quaint and inviting. Inside, the original character of beams, old floors and twisty corners has been carefully preserved and it is furnished in all simplicity with genuine cast-iron beds, carpets on tiles, pictures and, in the huge open-plan living-kitchen, an open hearth and a closed stove. It is not smart, just family-comfortable and a thoroughly relaxed atmosphere reigns — Gavin an artist and potter, Lillian a happy (and excellent) cook, young Michael a boisterous boy, will take you to their hearts.

Rooms: 1 triple, 1 double + bunks, 1 suite for 3, all with bath or shower & wc.

Price: 240 Frs (€ 36.59) for two, including breakfast.

Meals: 90 Frs, including wine & coffee.

Open: All year.

Gîte space for 10 people

20Frs

From Brive, N… S for 10km then N140 dir. Gram…/Rocamadour for 21km; D36 l… to Rignac; at church, left then l… right; cont. D36 dir. Lavergne for 50m; left for Pouch by green bottle bank. 2km: first house, signed.

MMap 235-6 **ASP Map No: 12**

Gavin & Lillian BELL
Pouch
46500 Rignac
Lot
Tel: (0)5 65 33 66 84
Fax: (0)5 65 33 71 31
www.sawdays.co.uk

The owners have restored this lovely old mill, some of it 600 years old, to make space for you and space for them. It stands in colourful gardens, the stream runs round it, nearly all the guestrooms, with their sand/lime-rendered or old stone walls and fine wall hangings, lead off a ground-floor corridor and have French windows onto the garden. A new barn conversion will include kitchen, TV room, *salon* and dining conservatory for guests. Here, you will eat Madame's fine food while Monsieur's paintings of typical local houses are on view. Their near-professional welcome is superb, the area full of fascinating treasures.

Rooms: 4 double & 1 twin, all with shower & wc.

Price: 310-420 Frs (€ 47.26-64.03) for two, including breakfast.

Meals: 120 Frs, including wine.

Open: March to October.

From Gramat, N140 dir. Figeac; after 500m, left onto a small road leading to the mill.

MMap 235-6 **ASP Map No: 12**

Gérard & Claude RAMELOT
Moulin de Fresquet
46500 Gramat
Lot
Tel: (0)5 65 38 70 60/
(0)6 08 85 09 21
Fax: (0)5 65 38 70 60

You instantly feel at home in this converted C18 barn with its great Lot views. Madame, who spent many years in America, is an avid patchworker and her creative touches are everywhere, including the garden and terrace area, full of shrubs and ferns and secluded spots. The open-plan living room, where old rooflights deliver splashes of sky, is full of artistic character with its oak floors, woodburning stove and pretty antiques beneath paintings of all periods. The airy ground-floor guestroom has its own antique writing table, watercolours and a glazed stable door onto the garden. A privilege for two.

Rooms: 1 twin with bath & wc.

Price: 270 Frs (€ 41.16) for two, including breakfast.

Meals: Within walking distance.

Open: All year.

From Figeac N140 NW 24km dir. Gramat; before Thémines exit, right for 'Le Bout du Lieu' — house 200m on left, large wooden gates in stone wall.

MMap 235-6 **ASP Map No: 12**

Élisabeth de LAPÉROUSE-COLEMAN
La Buissonnière
Le Bout du Lieu
46120 Thémines
Lot
Tel: (0)5 65 40 88 58
www.sawdays.co.uk

A multi-talented, cosmopolitan couple keep house here in the summer and live in Japan in the winter. Charles cooks — the huge kitchen/entrance hall is his domain and meals, French or Franco-Japanese, are memorable. Kako paints — even the wooden coat hangers bear her flowers. The house is French and spotless. All bedrooms, in the older, lower part of the house, have an exceptionally tranquil view of rolling meadows, superb mattresses and lush bathrooms; the oldest has an ancient stone fireplace and traditional stone sink. They are delightful people and Figeac is said to be "one of the best-renovated towns in Europe".

Rooms: 2 twin, 1 suite for 3, each with bath or shower & wc,

Price: 270 Frs (€ 41.16) for two, including breakfast.

Meals: 100 Frs, including aperitif & wine.

Open: May to November.

From Gramat SE on N140 dir. Figeac for 17km, through Le Bourg, sharp left immediately after small bridge on edge of village. House signed on left, 1km.

MMap 235-11 **ASP Map No: 13**

Kako & Charles LARROQUE
Mas de la Feuille
46120 Le Bourg
Lot
Tel: (0)5 65 11 00 17
Fax: (0)5 65 11 00 17
www.sawdays.co.uk

Anthony, a powerfully articulate and enthusiastic English wine-dealer, will chat while cooking; his aristocratic French wife is genteel and charming; both like to dine with their guests and enjoy good wine and company when their wine-trade and guesthouse duties allow. The old stone barn has been attractively converted into cosy B&B rooms with antiques, deep armchairs and restful colours (and ubiquitous tellies). There's a warm sitting room, which the owners (who live in the unconverted farmhouse) share with thei visitors, and a cool pool outside.

Rooms: 4 double, 1 triple, 1 quadruple all with bath or shower & wc.

Price: 360 Frs (€ 54.88) for two, including breakfast.

Meals: 160 Frs, including wine & coffee.

Open: All year (book ahead, esp. in winter).

From Figeac centre N140 dir. Decazeville. Outside town left on D2 dir. Montredon for 3km then right on D210 dir. Lunan then follow signs.

MMap 235-11 **ASP Map No: 13**

Anthony & Dominique NIELSON de LAMOTHE
Liffernet Grange
Lunan
46100 Figeac
Lot
Tel: (0)5 65 34 69 76
Fax: (0)5 65 50 06 24

In the hills between Figeac and Rocamadour, Isabelle and her young son live in a converted barn — it is beautiful, with one of those plunging rooflines. The superb conversion, with very green bathrooms, has created a wonderful beamed living/eating area which opens out through big barn doors — now glazed — onto a pretty garden. Isabelle is a lovely, open-hearted person with all the energy and enthusiasm of youth and a new project. Meals at the big convivial table are good Périgord style and she grows her own vegetables. A relaxed atmosphere combining intelligent conversation and practical guidance on things to see in the Lot.

Rooms: 1 double, 3 triple, each with shower & wc.

Price: 250 Frs (€ 38.11) for two, including breakfast; extra bed 70 Frs.

Meals: 90 Frs, including wine.

Open: All year.

From Figeac, N140 NW dir. Gramat for 21.5km then left on D38 to Théminettes. House well signposted, 1st on left about 400m after N140.

MMap 235-11 **ASP Map No: 13**

Isabelle NGUYEN
La Gaoulière
Friaulens Haut
46120 Théminettes
Lot
Tel: (0)5 65 40 97 52
Fax: (0)5 65 40 97 52

A charming 1730's presbytery in a stupendous setting and a warm relaxed couple, he a genial English gentleman, she talkative and very French. French cooking too: home-made cakes, home-grown vegetables are all part of her refined regional fare. Their house is a successful mix of cottage-style and antique furniture and a brave modern approach to colour, all in excellent taste. The big garden is ideal for children (toys and games on hand) and *al fresco* dinners; Robert is happy to take you to see the seven fountains that give the village its name or direct you to long hikes, caves, local woods and wildlife.

Rooms: 1 double with shower & wc; adj. single + 2nd double across landing for same party sharing shower + wc.

Price: 240 Frs (€ 36.59) for two, including breakfast.

Meals: 95 Frs, including wine.

Open: All year.

From Souillac N20 S for 24km. At Peyrebrune left on D1 to Séniergues; D2 dir. Figeac to Fontanes du Causse (16km from Peyrebrune). In village, house on right with maroon shutters.

MMap 235-18 **ASP Map No: 12**

Martine & Robert MORCOM-HARNEIS
L'Ancien Presbytère
46240 Fontanes du Causse
Lot
Tel: (0)5 65 31 17 15
Fax: (0)5 65 31 17 15

A heart-warming and very French experience, staying with this lovely cheerful couple who are always ready for a drink and a chat (in French) — their wonderful love of life is infectious. Use the peaceful terrace where your hosts are happy for you to sit all day over your breakfast, revelling in the setting, the vast views and the flowering garden. Inside, the décor is in keeping with the farmhouse, with floral papers and family furniture. No dinner but lots of home-grown wine and aperitif, fruit from their trees and *gâteau de noix* with their own honey — flowing as if you were in paradise.

Rooms: 2 double, 1 triple each with curtained-off shower & wc.

Price: 240 Frs (€ 36.59) for two, including breakfast.

Meals: Good restaurant 2 km.

Open: All year.

Gîte space for 6 people

From Cahors D8 west for 10km. Just before Flaynac right at Chambres d'Hôtes sign then right and right again.

MMap 235-14 **ASP Map No: 12**

& Mme Jean FAYDI
ynac
90 Pradines

(0)5 65 35 33 36

Built of genuine Lot stone, the C17 farmhouse (a gîte in summer, extra B&B in winter) and barn (where the family and first B&B rooms are), are being restored by the Scotts to look like the old characters they are, with modern comforts too and those stunning views over two valleys. The bedrooms are small and storage space is limited but the pool (solar-heated, salt-purified) and sunbeds beckon you out. Friendly, gregarious hosts who want you to have a good time; breakfast served any time, anywhere; dinner, sometimes a poolside barbecue, is fun, friendly, relaxed and informal. Pool-house kitchen and fridge for picnic lunches.

Rooms: 1 double with bathroom; 2 double sharing bathroom.

Price: 250-300 Frs (€ 38.11-45.73) for two, including breakfast.

Meals: By arrangement 100 Frs, including wine & coffee.

Open: All year (please telephone).

Gîte space for 22 people

By-pass Cahors dir. Toulouse; at roundabout take D653 dir. Agen; at fork turn right on D656. Pass Villeseque, Sauzet, Bovila then take 3rd left on straight stretch; signposted.

MMap 235-13 **ASP Map No: 12**

Peter & Zoé SCOTT
Mondounet
46800 Fargues
Lot
Tel: (0)5 65 36 96 32
Fax: (0)5 65 31 84 89
e-mail: scotsprops@aol.com
www.frenchconnections.co.uk/accom/oll/html

Once the laundry house to the C16 château that rises above it, in a perfect medieval village, it is old, tiny, three-levelled, and space is brilliantly used: convertible sofa beds, pullout barbecue, miniature kitchen. The bedroom under the eaves is richly decorated with a mix of French antiques and treasures from faraway places (Egypt, China...). Your Franco-English hosts are delightfully relaxed and cosmopolitan — fish with him in the river at the bottom of the garden, chat to her in their sitting room, a shrine to their many travels. Breakfast is set out in your kitchen, get up when you like.

Rooms: Cottage with 2 double & 2 twin beds, shower & wc, kitchen.

Price: 250 Frs (€ 38.11) for two, including breakfast.

Meals: Self-catering or in village.

Open: All year.

Gîte space for 4 people

From Cahors W on D911 30km to Puy l'Évêque. At r'about take road towards bridge; before bridge, right in Rue des Teinturiers. Park by river between 2 plane trees & take steps up to house.

MMap 235-13 **ASP Map No: 12**

Mme Françoise PILLON
4 rue des Mariniers
46700 Puy l'Évêque
Lot
Tel: (0)5 65 36 56 03
Fax: (0)5 65 36 56 47
e-mail: fanfan@wanadoo.fr
www.sawdays.co.uk

Horses are a passion with this family and you will often find them riding down in the valley. Within striking distance of three famous *bastides* (strongholds), this old farm grows, typically, tobacco, maize and sunflowers and there's a château thrown in for the view. The house is a converted pigeon tower (hawks and owls now nest in the holes outside); there are good bedrooms, a log-fired, country-style sitting room, highchair, bottle-warmer and games for children, a fine swimming pool for all. Madame has an infectious energy and speaks fluent English; her affable husband is quieter. Our readers are enthusiastic — it's good value.

Rooms: 2 double, each with shower & wc, 1 with mini-kitchen.

Price: 300 Frs (€ 45.73) for two, including breakfast.

Meals: 100 Frs, including wine & coffee. Self-catering 60 Frs per day.

Open: All year.

Gîte space for 8 people

From Villeneuve sur Lot D676 to Monflanquin and D272 dir. Monpazier. 1.5km after crossroads to Dévillac, left up small road just before small bridge — house is 2nd on right.

MMap 235-9 **ASP Map No: 12**

Michel & Maryse PANNETIER
Colombié
47210 Dévillac
Lot-et-Garonne
Tel: (0)5 53 36 62 34
Fax: (0)5 53 36 04 79

Deep in the Périgord countryside, Salarial is a typical local farmhouse unexpectedly furnished with the fruits of an informed traveller's choice: antiques, wall-hangings and paintings from distant lands bring sophisticated originality to rustic beams, old country doors and low ceilings. Madame has lived in China, can tell many a tale of the Orient (the Chinese Room is witness) whilst being extremely knowledgeable about what to see and do just here. Breakfast when you're ready, on the terrace in summer; embroidered sheets and spotless bathrooms; good conversation or bucolic peace — you choose. An ideal getaway.

Rooms: 1 duplex for 4 with bath & wc, 1 double with shower & wc.

Price: 300-350 Frs (€ 45.73-53.36) for two, including breakfast

Meals: In Villeréal 3.5km, Monflanquin 9km.

Open: All year.

From Bergerac N21 S for 9.5km; fork left on D14 to Villeréal (24km); D676 S dir. Monflanquin for 2.5km; left dir. St Etienne de Villeréal. Salarial signed on right after 800m.

MMap 235-9 **ASP Map No: 12**

Jacqueline DELLETERY
Salarial
47210 St Etienne de Villeréal
Lot-et-Garonne
Tel: (0)5 53 36 08 71/
(0)6 07 14 09 05
www.sawdays.co.uk

Madame, small, neat, well-dressed, very French and attractive, is starting again, having lived most of her life in Provence. Her house is a fine *maison de maître*, the ground floor of which is her domain and classically French in style. Upstairs is for guests, and reached by a separate entrance. There is a big dayroom with books, board games and light cane furniture. The bedrooms have plain, painted walls and a light, uncluttered feel, plus long views down the valley. Historic villages and lovely countryside are all around.

Rooms: 2 double, 1 twin, each with bath or shower & wc.

Price: 245-275 Frs (€ 37.35-41.92) for two, including breakfast.

Meals: 82 Frs, including wine & coffee.

Open: All year.

From Agen N21 N for 6km; fork left on D13 to Montpezat. In village turn right to church (Église St Jean). After passing church on right take 1st left and follow signs.

MMap 234-16 **ASP Map No: 12**

Madeleine GASQUY
Pince-Guerre
47360 Montpezat d'Agenais
Lot-et-Garonne
Tel: (0)5 53 95 07 71

Ann knows her design — she and Alain have clearly enjoyed doing the conversion using interesting paint techniques. There are lovely gardens and three acres of ancient trees around the château. It has salmon-coloured shutters, open fires, lots of high windows, brightly-coloured walls, palm trees, polished wooden floors, some Empire furniture. The superb bedrooms are very plush and new-mattressed, one with a Rice Bed from Ann's native South Carolina. Dinner is delicious and your hosts are gregarious yet efficient.

Rooms: 1 duplex for 5 with 2 bathrooms; 4 double, each with bath or shower & wc.

Price: 650 Frs (€ 99.09) for two, including breakfast. Third person in duplex 200 Frs; other extra beds 100 Frs.

Meals: 150 Frs, including wine & coffee.

Open: All year.

From A62 exit 6 dir. Aiguillon. Take 2nd right, D642, dir. Buzet. Château on right, signposted, shortly before Buzet.

MMap 234-16 **ASP Map No: 12**

Ann & Alain Doherty GELIX
Château de Coustet
47160 Buzet sur Baïse
Lot-et-Garonne
Tel: (0)5 53 79 26 60
Fax: (0)5 53 79 14 16
e-mail: ccoustet@csi.com

A great place if you enjoy large, scatty tribes: artistic and energetic, Madame reigns over a happy household where adults and children roam through house and garden, free as air. Balous is a typical Gascon manor: masses of old wood, a certain worn style, big wrought-iron or polished *bateau* beds, lots of space. There are paintings everywhere, from inherited ancestral portraits to relatively modern (some of Madame's six children are painters). The big tree-filled park keeps both neighbouring houses and the motorway out of sight, out of earshot; happiness enfolds you.

Rooms: 1 triple, 2 double, each with bath or shower & wc.

Price: 250 Frs (€ 38.11) for two, including breakfast.

Meals: 75 Frs, including wine & coffee.

Open: All year.

From A62 exit 6, then right on D108 dir. Buzet sur Baïse/Nérac; right immediately after Renault garage for 'Lac-Baignade': house 300m on left.

MMap 234-16 **ASP Map No: 12**

Mme Françoise SAVY-TAQUET
Château Balous
47160 Damazan
Lot-et-Garonne
Tel: (0)5 53 79 42 96

A wonderfully welcoming hostess (Monsieur runs the farm), brilliant big bedrooms in the best French provincial (unflouncy) style looking across the garden to meadows and woods, opulent but unostentatious white bathrooms, acres of parkland for walks from your door, space for 8,000 free-range chickens and myriad other animals: sheep, horses, ducks, dogs (but no cats). Despite its size, the C17 château is a comfortable, informal home, ideal for children. You can play billiards, table tennis, croquet, *boules.* Breakfast — with the inevitable eggs — and dinner are very much *en famille.* French B&B *par excellence.*

Rooms: 1 double, 1 twin, 1 suite, all with bath or shower & wc.

Price: 320-380 Frs (€ 48.78-57.93) for two, including breakfast.

Meals: 120 Frs, including wine & coffee.

Open: All year.

From Marmande, D933 S dir. Casteljaloux for 10km. Château signposted on right opposite D289.

MMap 234-16 **ASP Map No. 12**

M & Mme de LA RAITRIE
Château de Cantet
Samazan
47250 Bouglon
Lot-et-Garonne
Tel: (0)5 53 20 60 60
Fax: (0)5 53 89 63 53

Do remember these are private houses: even if you think it's all right to use the kitchen or invite friends round, you must get the owners' permission first.

Stilted shepherds once herded their flocks in swamps
but pine plantations drained the land so
stilts just dance at country fairs where northern
neighbours sell the fermented juice of the world's best
grapes.

Aquitaine

Visitors eat round a 10ft-diameter table made from an outsize wine barrel, in a C19 barn with beams, cantilevered gallery and a magnificent two-storey fireplace. Antoine teaches cookery and still loves to whip up regional feasts in his own sensational stainless steel kitchen then serve rather special wines from his contacts in the trade. Children have a sandpit, climbing frame and pool (and the company of Claire and Antoine's three young children). Canoeing, canal trips, fishing, riding and cycling are available locally. Readers write reams of praise.

Rooms: 4 double, 1 twin, each with bath and/or shower & wc.

Price: 300 Frs (€ 45.73) for two, including breakfast; extra bed 100 Frs.

Meals: 120 Frs, including wine & coffee.

Open: All year.

From A62 exit 4 for La Réole. At junction with D9 left dir. Bazas Grignols then 1st left 250m after bridge — La Tuilerie signed for remaining 3km.

MMap 234-11 **ASP Map No: 12**

Claire & Antoine LABORDE
La Tuilerie
33190 Noaillac
Gironde
Tel: (0)5 56 71 05 51
Fax: (0)5 56 71 05 51
www.sawdays.co.uk

Madame was an interior designer and her house is straight out of *Maisons et Jardins.* Walls taken back to the original stones and a plethora of stripped woodwork marry supremely well with a catholic mix of features and flourishes. This is THE area for wine buffs and Monsieur, who used to be a wine merchant, will happily share his knowledge at wine tastings. The pool was specially built for guests. The food is simple but delicious and in warm weather is served on the terrace overlooking the large garden.

Rooms: 2 double, 1 twin, each with bath or shower & wc.

Price: 360 Frs (€ 54.88) for two, including breakfast; extra bed 100 Frs.

Meals: From 120 Frs, including wine & coffee.

Open: All year.

From A62 exit 4 on D9 to La Réole. There, D670 then D668 dir. Monségur. At roundabout, D21 for St Sève. Through village, down hill, right after bridge into lane to house; signed on left.

MMap 234-11 **ASP Map No: 12**

Paul & France CHAVEROU
Domaine de la Charmaie
33190 St Sève
Gironde
Tel: (0)5 56 61 10 72
Fax: (0)5 56 61 27 21

Don't be fooled by the modest exterior — go through the main buildings, and splendour strikes! Discover delightful gardens and a great pool enclosed by charming guest quarters: your dynamic, fun-loving hosts have done a brilliant conversion of the old stables. They have kept much of the original wood and added elegant antique furniture to each of the large, individually-styled bedrooms. Fine attention to detail includes *armoires* lined with sophisticated contemporary fabrics that match curtains and wallpaper, good bathrooms, superb breakfasts. Overall, excellent value.

Rooms: 2 double, 1 twin, each with bath or shower & wc.

Price: 450 Frs (€ 68.60) for two, including breakfast.

Meals: Restaurant 300m; choice in town.

Open: All year.

Gîte space for 6 people

From Libourne D670 S 45km to La Réole; left on N113 dir. Agen. House on left on edge of town opp. Automobile Museum.

MMap 234-11 **ASP Map No: 12**

Christian & Danielle HENRY
Les Charmettes
Henry's Lodge
33190 La Réole
Gironde
Tel: (0)5 56 71 09 23
www.sawdays.co.uk

This spotlessly clean and comfortable 1750s farmhouse was Monsieur's family holiday home for years. Born in Senegal, he has been in Madagascar, Tahiti and many other places: quantities of fascinating souvenirs tell the tale. Madame, pleasant and attractive, was a nursery school teacher and is very keen to please her guests: we were naturally offered coffee and cakes on the terrace. Beautiful bedrooms, simple yet not stark, have white or clean stone walls, built-in cupboards often with genuine wall-to-wall doors. Excellent for fishing, canoeing or riverside walking (50m to the River Dordogne) and St Emilion just 7km away.

Rooms: 1 double/twin, 1 double, each with own shower & wc; 1 double, 1 triple, sharing bathroom & wc.

Price: 280-320 Frs (€ 42.69-48.78) for two, including breakfast.

Meals: In village or choice 2km.

Open: All year.

Gîte space for 4 people

From Bordeaux D936 E for 36km; 4km after Branne right on D670 dir. Agen. At Lavagnac (1km) left after 'Boucherie/Charcuterie' — house on left.

MMap 234-7 **ASP Map No: 12**

France PRAT
3 chemin de Courbestey
Lavagnac
33350 Ste Terre, Gironde
Tel: (0)5 57 47 13 74
Fax: (0)5 57 47 13 74
e-mail: france.prat@wanadoo.fr
www.sawdays.co.uk

Food and wine buffs will love it here. Madame, a keen cook who includes vegetarian and diabetic food on her menu, was making *pâté/terrine* when we arrived; Monsieur is a wine expert. Their early 19th-century farmhouse, set in an area of fields and vineyards, is simply but attractively furnished and the beamed, wallpapered guestrooms are big and comfortable. The dining room is decorated in Art Deco style with modern pictures. The Lévys do Sunday lunches for non-guests and are booked weeks, even months in advance.

Rooms: 1 double, 2 triple, each with bath, shower & wc.

Price: 330 Frs (€ 50.31) for two, including breakfast.

Meals: 120-200 Frs, excluding wine & coffee.

Open: January to September.

From Libourne, D670 through Sauveterre, then left on D230 to Rimons. Just outside Rimons, at sawmill on right, take first left; signposted.

MMap 234-12 **ASP Map No: 12**

Dominique & Patrick LÉVY
Grand Boucaud
Rimons
33580 Monségur
Gironde
Tel: (0)5 56 71 88 57
Fax: (0)5 56 71 88 57

Parts of this priory are C12, when it provided rest for pilgrims. Susie now sees that C20 guests are also refreshed. Her warm personality (she does personal development workshops) and the serenity of the setting are worth coming for. Lie in a hammock under the walnut tree, let the fan-tail pigeons coo you into a blissful siesta, the nightingales serenade your dawn. The house is decorated with a sophisticated combination of good antiques and modern pieces, opulent curtains and cheerful bedcovers. No routine — breakfast served whenever it suits, candlelit dinners on request. The lower price is for travellers not using garden or pool.

Rooms: 1 triple, 3 double: 2 with shower, bath & wc; 2 sharing shower & wc.

Price: 400-500 Frs (€ 60.98-76.22) for two, including breakfast; extra bed 150 Frs.

Meals: Restaurant 3km.

Open: All year.

Gîte space for 6 people

From Bordeaux D936 dir. Bergerac through St Quentin de Baron. Exactly 1km after village, house signposted on right.

MMap 234-7 **ASP Map No: 11**

Susie de CASTILHO
Le Prieuré
33750 St Quentin de Baron
Gironde
Tel: (0)5 57 24 16 75
Fax: (0)5 57 24 13 80
e-mail: susiedecastilho@wanadoo.fr
www.sawdays.co.uk

Tradition has deep, proud roots here; you sense it in the ancient walls. The *Girondin* farmhouse has stood for three centuries, the vines are mature, the wine superb; the lovely linen and lace bedcovers are family heirlooms, the family itself is busy, lively, full of character, all three generations have a strong presence. Madame's eagle eye for detail, her spotless care of the stone-walled, old-furnished guestrooms, her attention to your every need and her beautiful breakfast table in the cosy family dining room make it special indeed (though she's sometimes away, then Madame Mère reigns supreme and powerful).

Rooms: 2 double, 2 twin, 1 triple, all with bath or shower & wc.

Price: 300-320 Frs (€ 45.73-48.78) for two, including breakfast.

Meals: Choice locally.

Open: February to December.

From Libourne, D243 dir. St Emilion. 3km before St Emilion, D245 dir. Pomerol; signposted.

MMap 234-3 **ASP Map No: 11**

Claude & Jacqueline BRIEUX
Château Millaud-Montlabert
33330 St Emilion
Gironde
Tel: (0)5 57 24 71 85
Fax: (0)5 57 24 62 78

A hard-working young couple in a C18 château, without quite enough money to make it over-stylish; but they have three good and very big bedrooms, a stone entrance hall, a wrought-iron balcony terrace for a glass of (their own dry white Semillon) château wine, and decorative bantams all over the garden. It is relaxed and easy — even busy — with three young children, and deer in the woods. Breakfast is on the terrace, wine-tasting in the magnificent *salle de dégustation*. The small pool is for evening dippers rather than sun-worshippers.

Rooms: 3 triple, each with shower & wc.

Price: 300 Frs (€ 45.73) for two, including breakfast.

Meals: Choice in Bourg.

Open: All year except Feb & 1 week in Aug.

From A10 exit 40a or 40b through St André de Cubzac, W on D669 through Bourg dir. Blaye and very soon right on D251 dir. Berson for 1km; signed on right up lane/drive.

MMap 233-38 **ASP Map No: 11**

M & Mme BASSEREAU
Château de la Grave
33710 Bourg sur Gironde
Gironde
Tel: (0)5 57 68 41 49
Fax: (0)5 57 68 49 26
e-mail: chateau.de.la.grave@wanado
www.sawdays.co.uk

There are five comfortable, old-furnished guestrooms in this generous C18 mansion, built on the foundations of a medieval château in a place loaded with history. It surveys vineyards (the fulsome Côtes de Blaye are here), fields and forest. The Chartiers keep about a dozen horses and ponies and their daughters might give your children rides. The large, quiet, sunny rooms have their own entrance, kitchen and living room. This is well-organised, 'no-nonsense' hospitality and Monsieur will arrange vineyard tours for you.

Rooms: 3 triple with en suite shower & wc; 1 triple with separate shower & wc.

Price: 200-240 Frs (€ 30.49-36.59) for two, including breakfast.

Meals: Self-catering possible. Restaurants nearby.

Open: All year.

From A10, exit 38 on D132 and D115 to St Savin. There, D18 to St Mariens. Left just before village; signposted.

MMap 233-38 **ASP Map No: 11**

aniel & Yvonne CHARTIER
âteau de Gourdet
20 Saint Mariens
nde
(0)5 57 58 05 37

The New Hebrides, Brazil, New Zealand, the Sahara... Michèle has lived in them all; it is enough to make one feel parochial. But her family has been here for five generations and they built this hacienda-style house where the old farm crumbled away. The imitation zebra and tiger-skin upholstery in the living room pales into insignificance beside all the memorabilia and African sculptures. Bedrooms are traditional, with fine views across oceans of vines. Their own wine comes with dinner and the nearby ferry comes from Blaye.

Rooms: 1 double with bath & wc; 1 twin with shower & wc.

Price: 300-320 Frs (€ 45.73-48.78) for two, including breakfast.

Meals: 150 Frs, including aperitif, wine & coffee.

Open: All year.

From Bordeaux Rocade (by-pass) exit 7 on D1 to Castelnau; N215 through St Laurent and on for 4km; right for St Sauveur & Vertheuil. Through village, leave abbey on right, over level crossing, white house approx. 1km on left.

MMap 233-37 **ASP Map No: 11**

Michèle TARDAT
Cantemerle
9 rue des Châtaigniers
33180 Vertheuil Médoc
Gironde
Tel: (0)5 56 41 96 24/
(0)6 08 98 71 02
Fax: (0)5 56 41 96 24

Ideal for wine buffs! Old meets new here — the house is a successful mixture of both. The rooms have modern fabrics alongside nice old pieces of furniture, Philippe is Cellar Master for a *Grand Cru Classé* steeped in tradition, and is also an Internet convert; Monika, who is German and nursed in Vietnam for a while, may give you home-baked bread and muesli for breakfast. They are urbane, helpful, well-travelled polyglots and can obtain entry to most big wine châteaux for their guests. The large fish-and-lily pond adds a note of serenity. You may breakfast on the terrace and the beach is just 20 minutes away.

Rooms: 2 double/twin, 1 double, 1 suite, each with bath or shower & wc.

Price: 260-320 Frs (€ 39.64-48.78) for two, including breakfast; 320 Frs for cottage without breakfast.

Meals: Possibility 7km.

Open: All year.

Gîte space for 4 people

From Bordeaux ring road exit 7 on D1 dir. Le Verdon, past Castelnau & St Laurent. 4km after St Laurent right on D104 to Cissac. In village, right at War Memorial into Rue du Luc. House 1km on left, after water tower.

MMap 233-37 **ASP Map No: 11**

Philippe & Monika ACHENER
Le Luc
6 route de Larrivaux
33250 Cissac Médoc, Gironde
Tel: (0)5 56 59 52 90
Fax: (0)5 56 59 52 90
e-mail: ph.achener@GMX.net
www.sawdays.co.uk

Lost in the middle of a pine forest, its windows onto endless young oaks and pines, with duck pond and river beyond, the Jehl house will satisfy your soul. Madame, a lovable person, teaches yoga (for guests too, and she's trilingual); her artist son's hand-painted decoration (marbling, stencilling, *trompe l'œil*) brings blessed originality without offence to old stone and brickwork (he also teaches); grandchildren live next door, all in harmony with nature, and summer walks yield wildflower treasures. The simple rooms are not large but there is real family space at the piano or around the huge kitchen fireplace during delicious dinners.

Rooms: 1 double, 1 twin, 1 triple, each with shower & wc (+ 2 small 'dormitories')

Price: 220-250 Frs (€ 33.54-38.11) for two, including breakfast.

Meals: 80 Frs, including wine. Children 60 Frs.

Open: All year.

From Mont de Marsan N134 NW to Garein (20km); left on D57 dir. Ygos & Tartas then follow their signs — 1km of lane before arriving at house.

MMap 234-18 **ASP Map No: 16**

Mme Liliane JEHL
Moulin Vieux
40420 Garein
Landes
Tel: (0)5 58 51 61 43
Fax: (0)5 58 51 61 43

All the floors of this grand and appealing old French country house are original oak and it has an atmosphere of dream-like tranquillity. Just outside the park gates is the beautiful River Adour, rich in bird and wildlife — every 10 years or so it comes up and kisses the terrace steps. The two south-facing bedrooms overlook the river and a great spread of communal meadows where animals graze freely. There is a vast choice for 'flexitime' breakfast on the terrace or in the dining room. Madame, an attractively energetic and interesting hostess, was a publisher in Paris for 35 years and also speaks Spanish.

Rooms: 3 double, 1 triple, each with bath or shower & wc.

Price: 300-350 Frs (€ 45.73-53.36) for two, including breakfast.

Meals: Wide choice 2-5km.

Open: All year.

From A63 exit 8 to St Geours de Marene then south on D17 for 5km to Saubusse; right just before bridge — château 800m on right.

MMap 234-26 **ASP Map No: 16**

Claude DOURLET
Château de Bezincam,
Route de l'Adour
Saubusse les Bains
40180 Dax
Landes
Tel: (0)5 58 57 70 27

Madame is a gem, gracious and charming, her husband is more reserved, Braco the dog loves company. In its secluded setting, their miniature château rejoices in a fine chestnut staircase with iron banister, a veranda paved with rare Bidache stone, high ceilings, old prints, a glimpse of the Pyrenees and the call of a peacock. Madame teaches yoga, paints, is a long-distance walker and a committed vegetarian. Children can freely roam the 20 hectares of parkland — they love it. The rooms, large and properly decorated, have gorgeous parquet floors and relatively little 'château' furniture. We think the smaller ones give better value.

Rooms: 1 double, 1 twin, each with shower & wc; 2 large doubles with bathrooms en-suite.

Price: 300-500 Frs (€ 45.73-76.22) for two, including breakfast.

Meals: Vegetarian dinner 100 Frs, including wine & coffee (min. 3 nights).

Open: April to Oct (other times by arrangement).

From A10 or A63 motorways: exit St Geours de Maremne to Orist. Or, from A64 exit Peyrehorade to Dax. In both cases, 10km to Monbet.

MMap 234-30 **ASP Map No: 16**

M & Mme Hubert de LATAILLADE
Château du Monbet
40300 St Lon les Mines
Landes
Tel: (0)5 58 57 80 68
Fax: (0)5 58 57 89 29

"The whole place is special! The furniture is astounding, the house captivating. I love it." Our inspector was obviously moved. The house (1610) and contents have been accumulated by Colette's family for 14 generations: there are portraits from C12 onwards. The bedrooms are spectacular: antique beds with canopies and drapes, strong colours, wonderful old furniture; two have open fireplaces. Dining room and *salon* are handsome, too: antiques, terracotta tiles and huge stone fireplace. Colette is elegant, attentive, helpful and hugely resourceful.

Rooms: 3 double, each with bath or shower & wc.

Price: 260-300 Frs (€ 39.64-45.73) for two, including breakfast.

Meals: 100 Frs, including wine & coffee.

Open: All year.

From Dax D947 for Pau/Orthez for 10km. Stay on D947, ignoring sign for Mimbaste and take NEXT right onto D16 then follow discreet little blue and white signs to house.

MMap 234-26 **ASP Map No: 16**

Colette DUFOURCET-ALBERCA
Maison Capcazal de Pachioü
40350 Mimbaste
Landes
Tel: (0)5 58 55 30 54
Fax: (0)5 58 55 30 54
www.sawdays.co.uk

FORMS OF ADDRESS

We 'Anglo-Saxons' drop far more easily into first-name terms than the French. This reluctance on their part is not a sign of coldness, it's simply an Old National Custom, to be respected, we feel, like any of our own tribal rituals. So it's advisable to wait for the signal from them as to when you have achieved more intimate status. many of them have, of course, grown used to foreign ways, whereas some will stick to the ideas they were brought up with for ever.

The French do not say "Bonjour Monsieur Wilson" or "Bonsoir Madame Cook" – this is considered rather familiar. They just say "Bonjour Monsieur" or "Bonsoir Madame" – which makes it easy to be lazy about remembering people's names.

The Basques still play Pelote against a finely-shaped wall,
the eagle still reigns high over the Pyrenees,
the shaggy sheep graze the pastures and
beret-wearers grow old interestingly.

Basque Country – SW – Pyrenees

The brand new old-style Basque house was designed by Monsieur; his subtle use of pastels, fabrics and simple furniture makes for delightful bedrooms which all have a fine view of the stunning Rhune mountain. Hall, living and dining areas have a touch of Morocco, where your hosts used to live, and big windows facing those fabulous mountains. They are wonderful people, open and easy to talk to; he can educate you in the finer aspects of the *corrida*, she can be counted on to dissuade you! He cooks too.

Rooms: 4 double, each with bath or shower, 2 with own wc, two sharing wc.

Price: 280-330 Frs (€ 42.69-50.31) for two, including breakfast.

Meals: From 110 Frs, including wine & coffee.

Open: All year except mid-December to mid-January.

From A63 exit 2 dir. Urrugne/Col d'Ibardine. At roundabout, 3rd exit dir. Col d'Ibardine. At next roundabout, 2nd exit then next left for 500m; follow signs for Maison Haizean.

MMap 234-33 **ASP Map No: 16**

Murielle NARDOU
Maison Haizean
Chemin Rural d'Acharry Ttipy
64122 Urrugne
Pyrénées-Atlantiques
Tel: (0)5 59 47 45 37
Fax: (0)5 59 47 45 37

All the cosily-decorated rooms have steep stairs up to a mezzanine (ideal for children), lovely views over the valley of the Cize, and doors onto the large, communal balcony. There is an open-plan sitting/breakfast area where you can also make your lunch. Madame is a genteel country lady who has spent time in California and now lives here with her brother, the retired shepherd, and her other brother, the priest. Dine in the main house with these interesting people and taste the shepherd brother's *soupe du berger*. Then perhaps continue on to Compostela — you are on the path here.

Rooms: 3 quadruple, 1 triple, 1 twin, each with bath or shower & wc.

Price: 240 Frs (€ 36.59) for two, including breakfast. Extra person 60 Frs.

Meals: 85 Frs, including aperitif & wine.

Open: All year.

Gîte space for 18 people

From St Jean Pied de Port D428 dir. St Michel and follow signs.

MMap 234-37 **ASP Map No: 16**

Jeanne OURTIAGUE
Ferme Ithurburia
64220 St Michel
Pyrénées-Atlantiques
Tel: (0)5 59 37 11 17

A huge hall leads to the *salon* where leather chairs wait round the open fireplace. You are up above the village in a C14 Basque farmhouse: the vast lintel stones, the original heart-of-oak staircase, the split levels, nooks and crannies on the first floor speak of great age, the distant hills echo the message. The former attic, restored with imagination and colour by Isabelle, successfully combines ancient and modern. Indulge in daughter Charlotte's delicious desserts, hear tales of yore from Isabelle, who has adopted her new land by training as a native storyteller, and visit the prehistoric caves of Isturitz for a taste of things more ancient still.

Rooms: 2 double, 3 triple, each with shower & wc.

Price: 270-350 Frs (€ 41.16-53.36) for two, including breakfast.

Meals: 100 Frs, including wine.

Open: All year.

From A64, Briscous exit on D21 S to Hasparren. There, left on D10 dir. Labastide Clairence for 3km then right on D251 through Ayherre to Isturitz. Signposted.

MMap 234-33 **ASP Map No: 16**

Isabelle & Charlotte AIROLDI
Urruti Zaharria
Route D251
64240 Isturitz, Pyrénées-Atlantiques
Tel: (0)5 59 29 14 53
Fax: (0)5 59 29 14 53
e-mail: urruti.zaharria@wanadoo.fr
http://perso.wanadoo.fr/urruti.zaharria

This 16th-century Basque farmhouse in a superb listed village has had new life breathed into it by its French/Irish owners who revel in sharing their home with guests. Dinners around the enormous oak dining table are lively; local dishes, like *daube* (a thick stew) and *garbure* (soup with *confit de canard*), often grace the menu. The rooms are big, light and airy, with exposed wafer bricks, beams and hand-stencilling. An excellent breakfast is served on the terrace in warm weather and Gilbert will teach you to play *pelote basque* — wildly.

Rooms: 1 triple, 4 double, all with bath or shower & wc.

Price: 280-360 Frs (€ 42.69-54.88) for two, including breakfast.

Meals: By arrangement 80 Frs excl. wine or coffee;120-150 Frs (gastronomic), with wine & coffee.

Open: All year (check ahead).

From A64 junction 4 dir. Urt/Bidache; right on D123 to La Bastide Clairence. House is on left in main street.

MMap 234-29 **ASP Map No: 16**

Valerie & Gilbert FOIX
Maison Marchand
64240 La Bastide Clairence
Pyrénées-Atlantiques
Tel: (0)5 59 29 18 27
Fax: (0)5 59 29 14 97
e-mail: valerie.et.gilbert.foix@wanadoo.fr
http://perso.wanadoo.fr/maison.marchand

She is passionate about her garden with its huge old trees, lovingly developed by generations of nurserymen into a collector's paradise of old evergreens, magnolia, azalea, rhododendron, with benches discreetly placed for quiet reading... and the Pyrenees as a backdrop. The word for these Béarn houses is 'sturdy', with solid old furniture and traditional decoration. There are modern touches too: colourful wallpapers in the bedrooms and small but modern bathrooms. Madame is elegant and very on the ball... doing nearly all the work herself and longing to show you round the garden. Local delights include golf, gambling, fitness and fishing.

Rooms: 2 twin, 1 double, 1 for 3 or 4, each with bath or shower & wc.

Price: 295-360 Frs (€ 44.97-54.88) for two, including breakfast. Extra person 70 Frs.

Meals: 95 Frs, including coffee (carafe from 18 Frs).

Open: All year.

Gîte space for 10 people

From A64 exit 7; right for Salies '<5 tonnes' then next right signed to Le Guilhat for 1.8km. La Closerie on left beside Despaux nurseries at crossroads with Chemin des Bois.

MMap 234-30 **ASP Map No: 16**

Marie-Christine POTIRON
La Closerie du Guilhat
64270 Salies de Béarn
Pyrénées-Atlantiques
Tel: (0)5 59 38 08 80
Fax: (0)5 59 38 08 80
www.sawdays.co.uk

Come for the calm, the views from the terrace over lush greenness, the forest and the river at the bottom of the field (with an occasional heron). Nicole, a cheerful, lively hostess, was a hairdresser, Jean-Marie has an agricultural background and they create an easy, informal mood. The bedrooms (dull, rear views) have plain walls, country antiques, built-in formica cupboards, beams, pretty country fabrics. Superb Basque dishes with fresh farm produce are served in the attractive dining room. *Children over seven welcome.*

Rooms: 2 double, 1 twin, each with bath or shower & wc.

Price: 240 Frs (€ 36.59) for two, including breakfast.

Meals: 85 Frs, including wine & coffee.

Open: All year except January.

From Bayonne A64 dir. Pau. Leave at exit 5 and follow Chambres d'Hôtes signs. House about 3km from exit 5.

MMap 234-29 **ASP Map No: 16**

Nicole & Jean-Marie LAPLACE
Maison Huntagneres
64520 Guiche
Pyrénées-Atlantiques
Tel: (0)5 59 56 87 48/
(0)6 80 70 64 90

This grand C18 village house and its owners are quiet, elegant, sophisticated. Dinner is a chance to talk with your hosts about the region; you can delve into their extensive library (she binds books). They have completely renovated the house since finding it and this sleepy village in the foothills of the Pyrenees. The bedrooms are light and airy with interesting old furniture and lovely wooden floors. *La Rose* is very chic and *La Verte* is a dream — enormous, beautifully furnished, with views out to the mountains and a 'waltz-in' bathroom. Readers are ecstatic.

Rooms: 2 double with own shower or bath & wc.

Price: 270 Frs (€ 41.16) for two, including breakfast.

Meals: 90 Frs, including wine & coffee.

Open: All year.

From Navarrenx D2 dir. Monein to Jasses. There D27 dir. Oloron Sainte Marie. In Lay Lamidou turn left then first right; 2nd house on right.

MMap 234-34 **ASP Map No: 16**

Marie-France DESBONNET
64190 Lay Lamidou
Pyrénées-Atlantiques
Tel: (0)5 59 66 00 44/
(0)6 86 22 02 76
www.sawdays.co.uk

An exceptional couple: Heather, warmly communicative, Desmond, a retired architect with a great sense of fun, have brilliantly restored Agnos and still do all the cooking. Julian Wedgwood (yes, that family) came for one night, stayed and laboured for nine and told us we should put them in this book! Admire the high ceilings framing remarkable mirrors, paintings set into panelling, fine period furniture, the black marble dining room fountain... François I is said to have escaped by a secret tunnel (can you find it?), there's a medieval kitchen and an old prison. It's huge and you will feel completely at home.

Rooms: 3 suites, 1 double, 1 twin, each with bath and/or shower & wc.

Price: 380-650 Frs (€ 57.93-99.09) for two, including breakfast; extra bed 100 Frs.

Meals: 100-120 Frs, excluding wine (60 Frs).

Open: All year except February.

Gîte space for 14 people

From Pau N134 for 35km to Oloron Ste Marie; through town and S on N134 dir. Zaragoza for 1km. In Bidos, turn right for Agnos.

MMap 234-38 **ASP Map No: 16**

Heather & Desmond NEARS-CROUCH
Château d'Agnos
64400 Agnos
Pyrénées-Atlantiques
Tel: (0)5 59 36 12 52
Fax: (0)5 59 36 12 52

From the terrace you can see for ever into the great Pyrenees — sunlit snowy in winter, awesomely coloured in summer: the Brownes own the land around so no danger of encroaching uglies and it's ideal for landscape painters. They have converted the old *gîte* into three delightful cosy rooms — exposed stonework, beams, living room — with a fourth in the main house, all with good bathrooms. Your hosts are multinational (Polish, French, South African), they and their young children are a happy, relaxed and thoroughly integrated family. It is not smart, just deliciously easily friendly — and super food.

Rooms: 2 double, 2 twin, each with bath or shower & wc.

Price: 280 Frs (€ 42.69) for two, including breakfast.

Meals: 110 Frs, including wine & coffee.

Open: All year.

From Pau N134 S dir. Saragosse for 10km. At Gan right on D24 dir. Lasseube for c. 9km then left on D324. Follow Chambres d'Hôtes signs, cross 2 small bridges. House on left up hill.

MMap 234-39 **ASP Map No: 16**

Simon & Isabelle BROWNE
Maison Rancès
Quartier Rey
64290 Lasseube
Pyrénées-Atlantiques
Tel: (0)5 59 04 26 37
Fax: (0)5 59 04 26 37
www.sawdays.co.uk

Marie-Luce and Jean-Vincent, a delightful salt-of-the-earth couple, have created four guestrooms in one of their barns that are small, deliberately functional and clean with linoleum floors, neat little shower rooms and no particularly memorable style, but the windows and terrace onto a stunning, even majestic, view give them that special something. So, too, do your hosts. Marie-Luce will happily give children a guided tour of her farm — the ducks and geese, chickens and rabbits (they don't seem to grow vegetables) — some of whose relatives will doubtless be served at the very meaty dinner. Lourdes is 13km away.

Rooms: 1 double, 2 triple, 1 twin, all with own shower & wc.

Price: 220 Frs (€ 33.54) for two, including breakfast.

Meals: 75 Frs, including wine & coffee.

Open: All year.

From Lourdes D937 dir. Pau ('par Bétharram'). In St Pé de Bigorre right between church and Mairie then climb steep, winding, mountainous road 4km to top of hill; signposted.

MMap 234-39 **ASP Map No: 12**

Marie-Luce & Jean-Vincent ARRAMONDE
Ferme Campseissillou
65270 St Pé de Bigorre
Hautes-Pyrénées
Tel: (0)5 62 41 80 92
e-mail: camparra@club-internet.fr

Cedar and sequoia shade this imposing 400-year-old house. The large bedrooms, with old, uneven, stained wooden floors and curtained four-posters, have regal titles and modern bathrooms. Buffet breakfast and formal dinner are at separate tables set with silver, linen and candelabras. Besides restoring house and garden (including a French-style kitchen garden), Monsieur's passions are computers (games for children), music (he has an excellent CD collection) and receiving guests. Rafting and canoeing close by.

Rooms: 3 double, 1 triple, all with bath or shower & wc (1 behind curtain).

Price: 350 Frs (€ 53.36) for two, including breakfast.

Meals: 130 Frs, including wine & coffee.

Open: All year.

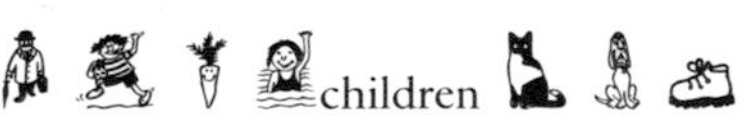
children

From Pau D938/937 for 31km dir. Lourdes. In St Pé, facing 'Mairie', take road to its right — house 50m up on right.

MMap 234-39 **ASP Map No: 11**

Christian PETERS
Le Grand Cèdre, 6 rue du Barry
65270 St Pé de Bigorre
Hautes-Pyrénées
Tel: (0)5 62 41 82 04
Fax: (0)5 62 41 85 89
e-mail: cp@grandcedre.com
www.grandcedre.com

Madame is heavenly, a person of enormous grace; her *domaine* is an oasis of calm where peace reigns and you may make a lifelong friend, sharing her delight in playing the piano or golf (good course 3km). Built during the Napoleonic Wars, the house has a coolly elegant hall, big, airy bedrooms and superb bathrooms while fine furniture and linen sheets reflect her pride in her ancestral home. A beautifully-presented breakfast is further enhanced by civilised conversation. Come to unwind — you may never want to leave.

Rooms: 1 double, 1 triple, 1 quadruple, all with bath & wc.

Price: 280 Frs (€ 42.69) for two, including breakfast.

Meals: Restaurant 2km.

Open: All year.

From A64 exit 16 to Lannemezan; there, D117 dir. Toulouse for 5km. In Pinas, at church take road towards Villeneuve. House on right after 1km.

MMap 234-40 **ASP Map No: 12**

Mme Marie-Sabine COLOMBIER
Domaine de Jean-Pierre
20 route de Villeneuve
65300 Pinas (Lannemezan)
Hautes-Pyrénées
Tel: (0)5 62 98 15 08
Fax: (0)5 62 98 15 08
e-mail: marie.colombier@wanadoo.fr
www.sawdays.co.uk

The Hindu greeting *namaste* to name it, star-spangled, moonstruck beams and furniture to fill it — there are exotic touches here. Architecture buffs will like the impressive barn with walls containing sections of the original earth construction. The Fontaines have spent two years restoring their lime-rendered C18 farmhouse, polishing wooden floors and creating a balance between the traditional and the modern. The guestrooms both have doors leading to semi-secluded corners of the garden. In cold weather, enjoy the huge open fire in the comfortable *salon*.

Rooms: 1 quadruple with bath & wc, 1 triple with shower & wc.

Price: 280 Frs (€ 42.69) for two, including breakfast.

Meals: 95 Frs, including wine.

Open: All year.

From A64 exit 16 onto D939 through Lannemezan to Galan. From village square/church, take Rue de la Baïse towards Recurt — house 500m on left.

MMap 234-40 **ASP Map No: 12**

Jean & Danièle FONTAINE
Namaste
13 rue de la Baïse
65330 Galan
Hautes-Pyrénées
Tel: (0)5 62 99 77 81
Fax: (0)5 62 99 77 81
www.sawdays.co.uk

These are indeed the chateau's converted stables and you can still come on a horse. Guestrooms are furnished so simply, with just the right lovely pieces and lots of spacey white wall, that there's almost a monastic feel to them. Carefully-chosen Indian dhurries and furniture spirited out of the château, where Madame grew up, give that dash of style. Breakfast is served in the kitchen, dinner in the dining room, children can play in the great attic room on rainy days and sleep in the 'overflow' room. Madame is a delightful, unbusinesslike, charmingly scatty hostess who unleashes an endearing giggle; her house is both elegant and simple.

Rooms: 1 triple, 1 double, 2 twin, all with bath & wc.

Price: 300 Frs (€ 45.73) for two, including breakfast.

Meals: 80 Frs, including wine & coffee.

Open: All year.

From Tarbes N21 N for 13km — small signpost on left for Tostat. Straight on for 2km. House in village centre.

MMap 234-36 **ASP Map No: 12**

Catherine RIVIÈRE D'ARC
Les Écuries du Château
65140 Tostat
Hautes-Pyrénées
Tel: (0)5 62 31 23 27
Fax: (0)5 62 31 23 27

English Nick is a wonderful host, full of life, ideas and love of good food — he wears his chef's hat magnificently and talks all the time he's cooking, which is all the time he's indoors. He and his wife, who is French, really belong in Fontrailles: they run the local music festival. Their farmhouse is a good mix of C17 architecture and new comforts (including good mattresses), the food a delicious mix of traditional French and exotic, the rooms cosy, fresh and neat. This is 'Foothills Country' surrounded by rolling farmland — a haven for birds, wildlife and walkers — the mountains are an hour's drive away.

Rooms: 2 double, 1 twin, 1 triple, each with shower & wc.

Price: 320 Frs (€ 48.78) for two, including breakfast.

Meals: 120 Frs, including wine. Children over 2 60 Frs.

Open: All year.

From Tarbes D632 NE to Trie sur Baïse (c.30km); through village to junction with D17; there take tiny D939 N for 1.5km. House signposted on left.

MMap 234-36 **ASP Map No: 12**

Nick & Dominique COLLINSON
Jouandassou
65220 Fontrailles
Hautes-Pyrénées
Tel: (0)5 62 35 64 43
Fax: (0)5 62 35 66 13
e-mail: nickc@planete.net
www.planete.net/~nickc/tourism.html

Neither airs nor graces, just good solid value. Josette is a keen decorator and her husband an artisan in wood, as you can see. The house lay abandoned for 35 years but now has a peach/ochre salon, a yellow/blue dining room, a gorgeous kitchen floor and a billiards room with huge fireplace. The hall is vast, and in stone. Bedrooms and bathrooms are large, superbly done with antiques, a mix of simple and rich fabrics, good linen and have views over the handsome park and pond. Good-value people too.

Rooms: 2 quadruple, 3 double, each with bath & wc.

Price: 320 Frs (€ 48.78) for two, including breakfast. Extra person 80 Frs.

Meals: 120 Frs, including aperitif, wine & coffee.

Open: All year except 20-31 December.

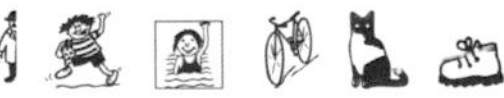

From Pau NE on D943 through Morlaas & Lembeye dir. Maubourguet. 2km before Maubourguet left on D59 to Sombrun, through village: house on outskirts on left.

MMap 234-31 **ASP Map No: 12**

Josette & Gilles BRUNET
Château de Sombrun
65700 Sombrun
Hautes-Pyrénées
Tel: (0)5 62 96 49 43
Fax: (0)5 62 96 01 89
e-mail: chateaudesombrun@sudfr.com
www.sudfr.com/chateaudesombrun

The Bolacs, warmly gracious and very French, shop at good auction houses and it shows: each bedroom has some special pieces and three have four-posters canopied with acres of flowers. After a buffet breakfast in the guest quarters, dip into the well-stocked library then, after a day exploring the Bread Basket of France (this area is, in fact, more Gers than Pyrenees), dip into the swimming pool before sharing a remarkable-value regional dinner (including home-grown salads, vegetables and herbs) in the dining room.

Rooms: 1 suite, 1 triple, 1 twin, 1 double, each with bath, shower & wc.

Price: 350 Frs (€ 53.36) for two, including breakfast.

Meals: 130 Frs, including wine & coffee.

Open: All year but booking essential in winter.

From Tarbes D935 N for 40km. In Castelnau, château is 0.5km from centre; well signposted.

MMap 234-31 **ASP Map No: 12**

Claudie & Xavier BOLAC
Château du Tail
65700 Castelnau Rivière Basse
Hautes-Pyrénées
Tel: (0)5 62 31 93 75
Fax: (0)5 62 31 93 26
e-mail: chateaudutail@sudfr.com
www.sudfr.com/chateaudutail

In a C13 hilltop stronghold, the old family house still has the dark, faded wallpapers, genuine old furniture, *objets* and photographs that are so typically *Vieille France*, unchanged in 100 years. Your host is a most appealing character too: a part-time teacher of English with a good sense of humour, he may offer French lessons, has kayaks that can be used on the nearby river Baïse and will let you use his fridge, cooker and crockery. Two of the rooms face south across a little terrace to the wooded hills, the swimming pool (most unusual in such a village) and BBQ are just across the little road and the atmosphere is so easy.

Rooms: 2 double, 1 twin, each with shower & wc.

Price: 250 Frs (€ 38.11) for two, including breakfast.

Meals: Choice 3km.

Open: All year.

Gîte space for 5 people

From Auch N124 W dir. Vic Fezensac & Mont de Marsan for 13km; left onto D374 to Biran. House is first on left after fortified gate into village.

MMap 234-28 **ASP Map No: 12**

Jean-Pierre CARLIER
32350 Biran
Gers
Tel: (0)5 62 64 62 79
Fax: (0)5 62 64 62 79

This splendid 18C Gascon farmhouse in its large lush garden has heart-stopping views south to the Pyrenees and west down the valley to the setting sun. Restored to a high degree of comfort (roll-top baths, salt-water swimming pool...) by its friendly and interesting English owners, it breathes charm and peace from cool arched terrace and antique-furnished rooms. Your hosts enjoy entertaining and Christine's delicious local dishes are made with fresh garden ingredients. This is hidden France still, with old villages, *bastides*, and fascinating architecture as well as vineyards and fabulous food. Altogether a highly civilised place to stay.

Rooms: 1 suite for 4, 1 double, 1 twin, each with bath, shower & wc.

Price: 500-600 Frs (€ 76.22-91.47) for two, including breakfast.

Meals: 200 Frs, excluding wine.

Open: All year except 2 weeks Dec-Jan.

Gîte space for 10 people

From Auch N124 W dir. Vic Fézenac for 5km; left on D943 through Barran, Montesquiou, Bassoues. After Bassoues follow D943 left dir. Marciac. Scieurac Flourès signed off this road. In village bend left by church; house 1st on right.

MMap 234-32 **ASP Map No: 12**

Michael & Christine FURNEY
Setzères
Scieurac et Flourès
32230 Marciac
Gers
Tel: (0)5 62 08 21 45
Fax: (0)5 62 08 21 45
e-mail: Setzeres32@aol.com

The Sabathiers run a real working farm rearing capons and beef cattle and the house has plenty of French *paysan* warmth. Breakfast is at a long table before a huge open hearth and there's a kitchen area where guests can cook if they like. It is all down-to-earth and clean with proper country charm. The bedrooms, which open onto the balcony overlooking the courtyard, have super old rickety wooden floors and some endearing features like Granny's wedding furniture. It all rejoices in a very French and delightfully secluded setting of gentle hills, corn fields and pastures.

Rooms: 1 double, 1 triple, 1 suite ideal for families, each with own bathroom.

Price: 230 Frs (€ 35.06) for two, including breakfast.

Meals: Self-catering facilities.

Open: All year.

From Auch, N21 towards Tarbes. 6km after Mirande, house signposted on left.

MMap 234-32 **ASP Map No: 12**

Louis & Marthe SABATHIER
Noailles
32300 Saint Maur
Gers
Tel: (0)5 62 67 57 98

On a clear day you can see the Pyrenees... and every day the rolling fields beyond the wooden terrace outside your window: God's space comes in and expands this cosy little house into a castle. Youthful and natural, Mireille is an inspired cook and a delight to be with; Olivier, though a little disenchanted with farming in the modern age, still enjoys his smallholding. They grow Christmas trees and cereals, fill their house with antique plates, prints, pictures and furniture and create a relaxed and happy family home with the essential dogs and cats and now a swimming pool — a perfect place to take the children.

Rooms: Duplex: 1 double + 1 small double (for 2 children), sharing bathroom.

Price: 240-270 Frs (€ 36.59-41.16) for two, including breakfast (reduction 3 nights).

Meals: By arrangement 90 Frs, including wine & coffee.

Open: All year.

Gîte space for 10 people

From Auch N21 dir. Tarbes for 2km; left on D929 dir. Lannemezan. In Masseube, left dir. Simorre for 4 km; left dir. Bellegarde. House first turning on left.

MMap 234-36 **ASP Map No: 12**

Mireille & Olivier COUROUBLE
La Garenne
Bellegarde
32140 Masseube
Gers
Tel: (0)5 62 66 03 61
Fax: (0)5 62 66 03 61

You are woken by an unobtrusive cockerel... an authentic rural touch. There are others: Grandma squelching around the farm in her wellies, an old pigeon tower with its original screw 'ladder', pigs, ducks, rabbits, turkeys, dinner with ingredients produced, from birth to death, on the farm — naturally delicious. The old house is part C14, the perfectly adequate guestrooms are in a modern extension — watch the moon set from your bedroom window and nip across to see the sun rise on the terrace (ignore the distant nuclear reactor glow). A genuine French smallholding, warm, friendly farming hosts, well worth the experience.

Rooms: 2 double, 1 triple, 1 quadruple, each with shower & wc.

Price: 230 Frs (€ 35.06) for two, including breakfast. Extra person 60 Frs.

Meals: 85 Frs, including wine & coffee.

Open: April to October.

From A62 exit 8 onto D953 S dir. Château de Gramont for 1.5km then fork left on D88, same direction. 3km before Gramont left following La Ferme des Garbès signs.

MMap 235-21 **ASP Map No: 12**

Simone VARGAS & Patrice GAILLARD
Ferme des Garbès
82120 Gramont
Tarn-et-Garonne
Tel: (0)5 63 94 07 81

It's hard to find fault here! The rooms could grace the pages of a magazine – lovely prints, old wardrobes, terracotta tiles. All is fresh, light and a happy marriage of old and new. Varied breakfasts and delicious dinners — regional and exotic dishes and an excellent cheeseboard. Sunflowers, farmland and a dreamy hamlet surround the C19 farmhouse which has been lovingly restored by its present owners, a Franco-Dutch family who enjoy sharing their summers here with guests. Madame is vivacious and energetic, Monsieur is calm and diplomatic, their children are delightful. Not to be missed.

Rooms: 1 suite for 2-4, 1 double, each with shower & wc.

Price: 250 Frs (€ 38.11) for two, including breakfast.

Meals: 90 Frs, including wine & coffee.

Open: July & August.

From Agen, A62 east, exit 8 dir. Gramont. After Mansonville, follow signs to Lachapelle; house on right on entering village.

MMap 235-21 **ASP Map No: 12**

M & Mme VAN DEN BRINK
u Village
120 Lachapelle
rn-et-Garonne
: (0)5 63 94 14 10 or
(0)1 39 49 07 37
l: cvandenbrink@ctr.fr

The Sellars, warm country people, left big-scale farming in Sussex for a small-holding in deepest rural France where they breed sheep, goats, poultry and rabbits using natural, traditional methods (no pesticides, no heavy machines). Their guts and enthusiasm have earned them the respect of the local community and their recipe for a simple, rewarding way of life includes receiving guests under the beams and by the open hearth. Julie will welcome you to her kitchen, too, where she creates feasts fit for farmers (organic veg and home-made goodies of course).

Rooms: 1 family room for 3/4, 1 double, each with shower & wc.

Price: 220 Frs (€ 33.54) for two, including breakfast.

Meals: 100 Frs, including aperitif, wine & coffee.

Open: All year.

From A62 exit 8 on D953 N dir. Cahors (round Valence d'Agen) for 21km; at Lamothe left on V4 signed Castelsagrat — Tondes is 1.6km along on left.

MMap 235-17 **ASP Map No: 12**

Julie & Mark SELLARS
Tondes
82400 Castelsagrat
Tarn-et-Garonne
Tel: (0)5 63 94 52 13

An exceptional working farm/B&B where quiet Gilbert will take you egg-hunting or goose-feeding of a morning. Smiling, big-hearted Michèle has won prizes for her recipes, invents sauces and makes her own aperitif. Rooms are comfortable (beware waist-low beams) but food is definitely the priority here. Fishing rods on loan to use in the pond; footpaths out from the gate; proper hiking trails a bit further away; the treasures of Moissac, lovely villages, caves, are within easy reach. *Well-behaved children and small pets welcome.*

Rooms: 2 double, 2 twin, each with bath, shower & wc.

Price: 240 Frs (€ 36.59) for two, including breakfast.

Meals: 90 Frs, including wine & coffee.

Open: All year.

Gîte space for 4 people

From Moissac, D7 dir. Bourg de Visa about 14km. Before Brassac and just before a bridge, right dir. Fauroux. Farm 2km along; signposted.

MMap 235-17 **ASP Map No: 12**

Gilbert & Michèle DIO
La Marquise
Brassac
82190 Bourg de Visa
Tarn-et-Garonne
Tel: (0)5 63 94 25 16

With the loveliest smile, Madame takes guests in as family; her dogs and cats are as friendly as she is. She greeted us from the milking shed, her hands dripping with the evidence: Le Gendre is a working farm with roaming chickens, ducks and pigs. Go lightly on lunch: dinner is uncompromisingly, deliciously 'farmhouse' with portions suitable for hard-working farmers. Your hosts are lively and empathetic, sharing their home easily, without fuss; the rustic, cluttered dayroom has a warm open fire; bedrooms are simply furnished, pleasing and spotless, breakfast coffee is in a bowl — you've found real rural France.

Rooms: 1 double, 1 suite for 4, each with shower & wc.

Price: 220 Frs (€ 33.54) for two, including breakfast.

Meals: 80 Frs, including wine.

Open: All year.

N20 south from Cahors to Caussade. Left on D926 through Septfonds. 3km beyond, left dir. Gaussou. Farm is 1km on, signposted.

MMap 235-18 **ASP Map No: 12**

Françoise & Jean-Louis ZAMBONI
Ferme du Gendre
82240 Lavaurette
Tarn-et-Garonne
Tel: (0)5 63 31 97 72

Ideas by Nathalie, action by Sean, result: the elegant simplicity of their renovated C13-C15 townhouse with its great sense of light and space in the airy hall, large spiral staircase, views through into the garden courtyard, stone walls and original old tiles. It has large, beautifully-decorated rooms, one with its own sun terrace, all with ensuite bathrooms. He, a natural host full of charm and unflappability, is enthusiastic about being here; she, originally from Belgium, quietly looks after their two children; both delight in providing extraordinary attention to their guests — some come for one night and stay for seven!

Rooms: 3 double, 2 twin, each with bath & wc.

Price: 350-450 Frs (€ 53.36-68.60) for two, including breakfast.

Meals: 110 Frs, including wine & coffee.

Open: All year.

From Montauban N20 NE to Caussade (22km); right on D926 for 7km; right on D5 to St Antonin Noble Val (12km); in town centre, follow signs 'La Résidence'.

MMap 235-18 **ASP Map No: 12**

Nathalie & Sean O'SHEA
La Résidence
37 rue Droite
82140 St Antonin Noble Val
Tarn-et-Garonne
Tel: (0)5 63 68 21 60
Fax: (0)5 63 68 21 60
e-mail: laresidence@compuserve.com

The best reason for being here is the Gorges de l'Aveyron — a paradise of clear water, cliffs, wildlife, canoeing and wild scenery. Johnny and Véronique, suitably, are sports teachers — all tan and dynamism, they encourage the active-holiday idea with great enthusiasm. They have renovated their house beyond the constraints of its origins — its rooms are simple, modern and functional, with little that is memorable or quintessentially French. But the food is good and generous and so are your friendly hosts. Very busy in summer so don't expect family intimacy then.

Rooms: 2 double & 3 twin, each with bath or shower & wc.

Price: 260-340 Frs (€ 39.64-51.83) for two, including breakfast.

Meals: 100 Frs, including wine & coffee.

Open: All year.

From Cahors, N20 to Caussade then D964 dir. Gaillac. At Montricoux, D115 towards Nègrepelisse; after 500m, signposted.

MMap 235-22 **ASP Map No: 12**

Johnny & Véronique ANTONY
Les Brunis
82800 Nègrepelisse
Tarn-et-Garonne
Tel: (0)5 63 67 24 08
Fax: (0)5 63 67 24 08

Gérard taught philosophy and Chantal taught English: theirs is a well-stocked library. They love music, too. The house was recently a working farm and the hay loft, bread oven and well are still there. You will gape in astonishment at the scale of the inglenook fireplace with all the expected oak beams plus a nail where *Grand'mère* used to hang her money hidden among the washing. A large terrace overlooks the hills (kites available); a grassy courtyard has a barbecue, table tennis and home-made exercise machines. No antiques, but we loved it for its unpretentious simplicity and the intelligent company.

Rooms: 2 triple, 1 twin, 1 double + bunk, each with bath or shower & wc.

Price: 260 Frs (€ 39.64) for two, including breakfast. Extra person 50 Frs.

Meals: By arrangement 80 Frs, including wine & coffee.

Open: All year.

From A68 exit 3 to Montastruc then onto D30 dir. Lavaur for 5km. Left on D30c to Azas; through village for about 2km; signposted towards Garrigue (D22g).

MMap 235-26 **ASP Map No: 12**

Chantal & Gérard ZABÉ
En Tristan
31380 Azas
Haute-Garonne
Tel: (0)5 61 84 94 88
Fax: (0)5 61 84 94 88

Madame Fieux gets full marks for the beauty of her reception rooms: they are big, warm and dignified in the elegant patina of age. Her house is full of old pictures, books, comfortable chairs and antiques, her visitors are immersed in the French way of life, sleep in fine rooms with views across the green oaks, enjoy her warm and genuine interest in people, manifested with "a mix of the formidable and the lovable, the dignified and the mischievous". Step out on a summer's morning and enjoy your breakfast — often with home-made cakes — in the large, lush garden. When the temperature soars head for those oaks. Lake and tennis court next door.

Rooms: 2 double, 2 twin, all with bath or shower & wc.

Price: 400 Frs (€ 60.98) for two, including breakfast.

Meals: Restaurant 4km.

Open: All year.

From Toulouse A68 dir. Albi exit 3 dir. Montastruc la Conseillère. After 1km right on D30 dir. Lavaur for 4.5km; right on D30E dir. Verfeuil & follow signs for Stoupignan: c. 1km on left.

MMap 235-30 **ASP Map No: 12**

Claudette FIEUX
Stoupignan
31380 Montpitol
Haute-Garonne
Tel: (0)5 61 84 22 02
Fax: (0)5 61 84 22 02

The Carrière family seat, designed by Guillaume Cammas who also 'did' the Toulouse Capitole, stands solid and worn on the flat farmland. Its glory is still its stupendous staircase, hung with family portraits, whence you sweep into the vast *salon* for your aperitif; way above your head, the cobwebs add to the atmosphere. The affable, disarmingly unpretentious and somewhat eccentric Baroness is happy to describe the many paintings and antiques while serving dinner. Bedrooms are small, high-ceilinged with more pictures, books, silk screens and cobwebs. Make sure you are expected as the entrance gate is locked.

Rooms: 3 double, each with bath or shower & wc. 2 extra beds available.

Price: 400 Frs (€ 60.98) for two, including breakfast.

Meals: 150 Frs, including wine & coffee.

Open: Easter to October.

From Toulouse, D1 dir. Aéroport Cornebarrieu; stay on D1 until St Paul then D87 right to Larra.

MMap 235-26 **ASP Map No: 12**

Baronne Brigitte de CARRIÈRE
Château de Larra
31330 Grenade sur Garonne
Haute-Garonne
Tel: (0)5 61 82 62 51

"The house of joy," is how Inge likes to describe her home, a fine old house beside a stream, and she is still putting the finishing touches to her most successful conversion. Forget about work, relax in the arms of Nature, fish, ride, paint — Inge will give you lessons. Passionate about horses, she trains her own and horse-keeping definitely takes priority over house-keeping. She serves good food in the pretty hall (the dining room only seats four) and offers light, eclectically-decorated, long-bedded rooms with separate bathrooms. Lovely garden, with big old shady trees, to walk or sit in.

Rooms: 4 double, each with bath or shower & wc.

Price: 200-280 Frs (€ 30.49-42.69) for two, including breakfast.

Meals: 80 Frs, excluding wine.

Open: All year.

From Boulogne sur Gesse, D635 dir. St Gaudens & Ciadoux. After about 7km, fork left dir. Ciadoux; after a few metres, left down small private road; house on right.

MMap 234-36 **ASP Map No: 12**

Ingeborg ROEHRIG
Ciadoux
31350 Boulogne sur Gesse
Haute-Garonne
Tel: (0)5 61 88 10 88
Fax: (0)5 61 88 10 88

With immense pride, knowledge and care, your host has been restoring his former abbey hospital, originally built in the 16th century, for some years and knows he has several more to do. The place oozes atmosphere and history and one feels privileged to walk in its soothing cloister and imagine one is hearing its ancient chants. The guestrooms are in fact the two gîtes in the grounds that have been restored with consummate skill, patience and taste. Christophe is a woodworker and furniture designer who also organises cabinet-making and dance workshops in the summer.

Rooms: 2 double rooms, each with bathroom.

Price: 220 Frs (€ 33.54) for two, including breakfast; extra bed 100 Frs.

Meals: 75 Frs, including wine & coffee.

Open: All year.

Gîte space for 13 people

From Toulouse, N117 to Boussens. There, D365 dir. Aurignac. In Le Frechet, follow signpost 'N.D. de Lorette'.

MMap 235-37 **ASP Map No: 12**

Christophe FERRY
Notre Dame de Lorette
31420 Alan
Haute-Garonne
Tel: (0)5 61 98 98 84/94 58 (Engl)
Fax: (0)5 61 98 98 84
e-mail: christophe.ferry@nd-lorette.com
www.nd-lorette.com

Steve is a wonderful cook, Kris a man of the theatre, together they have achieved the splendid restoration of their remote old mill where fire roars and stream flows, bedding and bathrooms are excellent, furniture country French, rugs oriental and colours simple. They are deeply involved in the local environment, preserving trees, encouraging wildlife, helping farmers and still waiting for a turbine to make heat from the river (so rooms may be chilly in winter). A very special spot, great value... and so near the Pyrenees.

Rooms: 2 triple with own bath/shower & wc; 1 double & 1 triple sharing shower & wc.

Price: 240 Frs (€ 36.59) for two, including breakfast.

Meals: 85 Frs, including wine & coffee.

Open: All year.

From Toulouse A64 to Boussens (exit 21) on D635 to the edge of Aurignac and D8 dir. Alan, turning left through Montolieu to Samouillan, then D96; signposted.

MMap 235-37 **ASP Map No: 12**

Stephen CALLEN & Kris MISSELBROOK
Le Moulin, Samouillan
31420 Aurignac, Haute-Garonne
Tel: (0)5 61 98 86 92
Fax: (0)5 61 98 86 92
e-mail: Kris.M@wanadoo.fr
www.sawdays.co.uk

A blue valentine on a quiet lane: the happy family who live here have decorated their C18 manor in quiet good taste with antiques (every piece chosen because it is the right one), lovely bed linen, gorgeous bath tiles and that blue-and-white theme — not sky or baby or royal but Brigitte's favourite French (Williamsburg to Americans) blue. It is soft, mellow, uncluttered; she is smiling, enthusiastic, young; the daughters are adorable and helpful. A dream of a place, set in dreamy countryside, where you appreciate the reality of the hard-working kitchen gardener when you sit down to dinner.

Rooms: 1 twin, 1 suite, each with shower & wc; 1 double sharing shower & wc.

Price: 250 Frs (€ 38.11) for two, including breakfast.

Meals: 80 Frs, including wine.

Open: All year except last week in Aug.

From Toulouse N117 SW past Muret for approx. 50km. Exit S on D6 to Cazères. Cross River Garonne, right on D62, follow signs for 'Camping Planturel'. House is 2nd left after camping site.

MMap 235-37 **ASP Map No: 12**

Brigitte & Bruno LEBRIS
Les Pesques
31220 Palaminy
Haute-Garonne
Tel: (0)5 61 97 59 28

So close to skiing, golfing, fishing and Toulouse's new opera house — but why go anywhere when Soulès (meaning 'sun') is here? Set among 300-year-old cedars, it has majestic gardens, a pond-blessed orchard attracting woodpeckers, owls, hoopoes and deer, a new heated swimming pool, big breakfasts till noon and *haute cuisine* dinners. The higher things in life are worshipped too: there's a baby grand, an elegant library and a fabulous antique clock collection. Denise is Swiss and a fine French cook; Arnold is English and was 'in clocks'. They are good company, their rooms are big and comfortable and they love having guests.

Rooms: 3 triple, 1 double, each with bath or shower & wc; some connecting for families.

Price: 385 Frs (€ 58.69) for two, including breakfast.

Meals: 100 Frs, including wine.

Open: All year except New Year.

From Toulouse N20 S to Pins Justaret (10km); fork right on D4 for 26km to Lézat sur Lèze. Continue 3km after Lézat — château entrance on right.

MMap 235-38 **ASP Map No: 12**

Denise & Arnold BRUN
Château de Soulès
09210 St Ybars
Ariège
Tel: (0)5 61 69 20 12
Fax: (0)5 61 69 21 68
e-mail: arnold.brun@wanadoo.fr

An isolated renovated farmhouse/hamlet that looks towards the Pyrenees. The artistic among you may care to plan your stay during one of your hostess's weekend art courses. You could stop a while, forget the maps and itinerary — you are in a world of ceramics, watercolours, weaving and sculpture... and wide-open spaces. The rooms feel right, light, not over-decorated and adorned with Dutch Jeanne's handiwork. Guests have their own living room and kitchen facilities but dinner — cooked rather well by Guy — is served *en famille* in a very laid-back and friendly atmosphere.

Rooms: 1 double, 2 triple, each with bath or shower & wc.

Price: 230-250 Frs (€ 35.06-38.11) for two, including breakfast.

Meals: 90 Frs, including wine & coffee.

Open: All year.

Gîte space for 9 people

From Belpech take road behind public gardens towards Gaudies. After 4km, at crossroads, left following Chambres d'Hôtes signposts.

MMap 235-38 **ASP Map No: 12**

Jeanne & Guy GOSSELIN
Certes
09700 Gaudies
Ariège
Tel: (0)5 61 67 01 56
Fax: (0)5 61 67 42 30

Nick lists about 200 different birds and over 50 orchids though people do come to look for just one type. He, a fauna and flora guide who really knows his stuff, and Julie, a midwife, are a thoroughly nice pair. This tiny hamlet has breathtaking views up to the mountains and across miles of fields, farms and forests; it is ineffably lovely. The simple and pretty renovated house has smallish rooms (one so tight that the loo is 3 feet from the bed!), and a cosy family living room. They'll collect you from the airport as part of a week's package.

Rooms: 2 double, 1 twin, each with shower & wc.

Price: 240 Frs (€ 36.59) for two, including breakfast.

Meals: 85 Frs, including wine & coffee.

Open: All year.

From St Girons D117 E for 7km. Just before fork for Mas d'Azil see 'Chambres d'Hôtes' sign on left. Follow signs up this tiny, metalled track for 2km.

MMap 235-42 **ASP Map No: 12**

Nick & Julie GOLDSWORTHY
La Baquette
Lescure
09420 Rimont, Ariège
Tel: (0)5 61 96 37 67
Fax: (0)5 61 96 37 67
e-mail: goldsNJ@aol.com.fr
www.ariege.com/nature/goldsworthy

Beauty without: from the lovely dining room you look straight across to a great snowy peak apparently just steps away; breakfast is wholemeal bread and home-made jam with this spectacular view. Beauty within: pretty fabrics and your hosts' own works. Goan Teresa was educated in England and paints; Alpine-born Bernard, Paris-educated, is an expert on water mammals, did his thesis on beavers, sculpts and does beautiful pencil drawings. They are a very special couple and this tiny village (pop. 60!) has an almost Alpine feel. *Children over five or babies (ladder to mezzanine).*

Rooms: 1 double, 1 single, with bath & wc .

Price: 250 Frs (€ 38.11) for two, including breakfast.

Meals: Choice 1.5km.

Open: All year.

Gîte space for 4 people

From A64 exit 20 S to St Girons. There right on D618 dir. Castillon for 12km then tiny D404 on left to Cescau. Park below church on left.

MMap 235-41 **ASP Map No: 17**

Teresa & Bernard RICHARD
09800 Cescau
Ariège
Tel: (0)5 61 96 74 24

You don't have to like horses to enjoy yourself here, but if you do you'll love it: the daughter of the family has a riding school on the spot. Guests stay in an independent ivy-clad house at this old farm in the foothills of the Pyrenees A staircase leads from a little living room (fires in winter) to clean, simple rooms — one has stone walls — with pine furniture (plus more basic rooms for groups of up to 19). Beautiful views and plenty of invigorating walks for those who prefer to use Shanks's pony. Children are made very welcome by the warm, friendly and relaxed hosts who work well together and are very interesting about local lore.

Rooms: 3 double, 1 twin, all with bath or shower & wc.

Price: 190-200 Frs (€ 28.97-30.49) for two, including breakfast.

Meals: 65 Frs, including wine & coffee

Open: All year.

Gîte space for 14 people

From Foix, D117 dir. St Girons; at top of hill, left on small D45 for 6km then left again for 1km — Cantegril drive is on the left, signposted.

MMap 235-42 **ASP Map No: 17**

Édith & Jean-Michel PAGÈS
École d'Équitation de Cantegril
09000 St Martin de Caralp
Ariège
Tel: (0)5 61 65 15 43
Fax: (0)5 61 02 96 86
www.sawdays.co.uk

Your hosts have moved on from their hippy days of communes into sharing in a rather more organised way. Over 25 years of renovation, they have made this rural idyll what it is today. Dine *en famille* in a huge living/dining room (village dances were organised here!) and share the Loizances' local knowledge — you may even be treated to their charming daughter's range of magic tricks. They are a delightful family and their home has real heart. Perfect country for summer walking and winter cross-country skiing.

Rooms: 3 double, 1 triple, all with own shower & wc.

Price: 240 Frs (€ 36.59) for two, including breakfast.

Meals: 80 Frs, including wine & coffee.

Open: All year.

From Foix D17 dir. Col des Marrous for 15km. 'Hameau de Madranque' signposted on right.

MMap 235-42 **ASP Map No: 17**

Birgit & Jean-Claude LOIZANCE
Madranque
09000 Le Bosc
Ariège
Tel: (0)5 61 02 71 29

The setting is out of this world, the house has tons of character — local stone, beams, low windows, uneven ceilings, all excellently renovated — and your hosts know what real *chambre d'hôte* means. High up at a remote edge of the world, surrounded by 70 hectares of breathtaking forested Pyrenean foothills, they raise horses and Newfoundlands, will let you join their picnics, ride their horses (if you are an experienced rider), live in their space for a while and hear their stories, in several languages, of sailing the Atlantic or the Caribbean: don't miss dining with them. Good rooms and excellent value.

Rooms: 2 double, 1 twin, 1 triple, 1 quadruple (summer only), all with shower & wc.

Price: 230-250 Frs (€ 35.06-38.11) for two, including breakfast. Book early.

Meals: 70 Frs, including wine & coffee.

Open: Mid-March to mid-November.

Gîte space for 6 people

From Foix, D17 dir. Col de Marrous. After 9km, in La Mouline left at chambre d'hôte signpost for 1.5km then right on C6, tiny unmade (but easy) track, to house.

MMap 235-42 **ASP Map No: 17**

Bob & Jenny BROGNEAUX
Le Poulsieu
Serres sur Arget
09000 Foix
Ariège
Tel: (0)5 61 02 77 72
Fax: (0)5 61 02 77 72

Don't expect silver or lace but bring your hiking boots. This old mill in its magical valley was once a *cloutier*: nails were made here. The beds are made of softer stuff and the water rushing past will lull you to sleep after that great walk. The room isn't large but there's a lovely terrace and you'll want to be out by the stream, catching trout in the right season. Your hosts will gladly harness their horse and cart to take you for a day trip in the mountains with picnic lunch on board. A simple, honest, welcoming place in a magnificent setting with a river nearby for swimming. Small pets welcome and a little cooking place you can use.

Rooms: 1 twin with shower & wc. Extra bed available. Kitchenette.

Price: 200 Frs (€ 30.49) for two, including breakfast.

Meals: Restaurant 2km; self-catering.

Open: April to October.

Gîte space for 4 people

From Foix, D21 to Ganac. After 5km take route to Micou 'Les Carcis'. Right just after small bridge.

MMap 235-42 **ASP Map No: 17**

Sylviane PIEDNOËL & Guy DROUET
Les Carcis
09000 Ganac
Ariège
Tel: (0)5 61 02 96 54

Walkers! Once you've reached the house, you'll never need to get into your car again: there are 80km of hiking trails, from easy to tough, straight from the door. It is a paradise for botanists, bird-watchers and tree insect fanatics, and your kindly hosts know those paths intimately. Layrole's most memorable features are the greenery, the riot of flowers all round the south-facing terrace and the sound of water in the background. The guestroom has an immaculate new bed, a mass of books and central heating while the Orient Express loo will appeal to train buffs. A very pretty village and good homely dinners.

Rooms: 1 double room with shower & wc.

Price: 220 Frs (€ 33.54) for two, including breakfast.

Meals: 90 Frs, including wine.

Open: Mid-April to mid-October.

From Foix N20 S to Tarascon then D618 W through Saurat. 2.5km after the café/bar at Saurat, right up steep road towards Cabus. House on right 700m, signposted.

MMap 235-46 **ASP Map No: 17**

Roger & Monique ROBERT
Layrole
09400 Saurat
Ariège
Tel: (0)5 61 05 73 24

"It is enchanting!" The great and the good want to keep it a secret but WE know that the setting is spectacular, the reception rooms are generously fireplaced, the antique chests, tables and desks are genuine and in superb condition, the bedrooms are big, airy and elegant and the bathrooms excellent. Michel, a restaurateur for 30 years, is still the finest chef within 100km and loves cooking for half a dozen. He takes his daily inspiration from the market, has twinkling eyes, says he is temperamental but may let you into his sanctum. What a welcome! And moreover, Unac church is an early Romanesque jewel.

Rooms: 1 double, 1 triple, each with bath & wc.

Price: 390 Frs (€ 59.46) for two, including breakfast.

Meals: 180 Frs, including aperitif, wine & coffee.

Open: All year.

From Foix N20 S for 33km through Tarascon to Luzenac. There, left on D2 & follow signs to Unac. Take 2nd entrance into Unac. House just down from church, 100m on right.

MMap 235-46 **ASP Map No: 17**

Michel & Simone DESCAT
L'Oustal
09250 Unac
Ariège
Tel: (0)5 61 64 48 44
Fax: (0)5 61 64 48 44

MORE FALSE FRIENDS

En-suite: can lead to terrible confusions in France. One booking for two 'en-suites', made with B&B owners became a disaster when the owners reserved their only ***suite*** for these guests: two adult couples were put into one double room leading to a 'children's' twin room leading to a shared bathroom – unhappily.
Cheminée: fireplace, flue or chimney stack (the flue is *also le conduit de cheminée). Un feu dans la cheminée* does not mean you need to call the fire brigade but *un feu de cheminée* does.
Une Commode: chest of drawers. A commode is *une chaise percée.*
Grange: simply means barn, not a big country house.
Actuel – Actuellement: A great pitfall, it means current, present – currently, presently, NOW, not As a Matter of Fact.
Éventuel – Éventuellement Possible – should the occasion arise.
Un Christmas: is a Christmas card. The French used only to send each other visiting cards with hand-written New Year greetings. The English and American custom of sending decorative cards for Christmas only caught on fairly recently and the object was naturally given the (truncated) English name.
Correspondance: connection between flights, trains, metro lines.

Rugby rouses great passions here, as do corridas and high dramas enacted beneath the Roman arches; down on the coast, traditional water-jousters get less emotional but much wetter.

Roussillon – Languedoc – Cévennes

The drive from Perpignan is historical and gorgeous and Mont Louis has changed very little since the time of Louis XIV. La Volute is on/in the entrance arch to this C17 citadel and even has a little garden. One room is a tribute to someone's talent with the fretsaw and there is a dramatic black and white bathroom. All rooms are simple, attractive, in good taste. Young and relaxed, Martine neatly combines taking good care of her guests and her two small children and has concocted a fantastically complete guide to things to do. It's a perfect base for visiting this fascinating area with its 3,000 hours of sunshine a year (do visit the solar-powered kiln).

Rooms: 2 double, 1 twin, each with shower & wc.

Price: 310 Frs (€ 47.26) for two, including breakfast.

Meals: Choice in village.

Open: All year except 2 weeks each June & Nov.

From Perpignan N116 SW for 80km. Chambres d'Hôtes signposted at entrance to Mont Louis.

MMap 235-55 **ASP Map No: 18**

Martine SCHAFF
La Volute
66210 Mont Louis
Pyrénées-Orientales
Tel: (0)4 68 04 27 21
Fax: (0)4 68 04 27 21

For 200 years, this Catalonian farmhouse has stood dramatically on its hillside of Mediterranean *maquis* and vineyards. Your hosts have built an extension and made it a perfect place for all lovers of nature, walking and good food. Lucie is a passionate cook with a repertoire (lots of organic in it) that reflects her cosmopolitan, polyglot background. Breakfast is remarkable, too. She and Jacques radiate warm, intelligent hospitality and the common rooms in the old house reflect their personalities. The superbly-equipped bedrooms are in the modern block — less romantic but utterly comfortable.

Rooms: 1 double, 1 twin, 2 triple, 1 quadruple, each with shower & wc.

Price: 330 Frs (€ 50.31) for two, including breakfast.

Meals: 130 Frs, including wine.

Open: April to September.

Gîte space for 14 people

From A9 exit 42 onto D612 W to Thuir then D615 W for 5km; left just before D58 for 1.5km. Drive on right (1km, steep, winding, paved).

MMap 235-52 **ASP Map No: 18**

Lucie & Jacques BOULITROP
Le Mas Félix
66300 Camélas
Pyrénées-Orientales
Tel: (0)4 68 53 46 71
Fax: (0)4 68 53 40 54
e-mail: lucie.boulitrop@wanadoo.fr
www.sawdays.co.uk

The plain exterior belies the almost Moroccan feel as this friendly house unfolds itself. The unobtrusive walled pool is perfect; the surrounding wild hills are the garden. Big, fresh, airy rooms have pine floors and white quilts; the cosy sitting area has a superb stereo system: your warmly generous hosts were chamber musicians. They also revel in food and wine, serve local aperitifs and wines with delicious dinners, know all the delights of cloisters, Cathar castles, mountain walks, trips to Spain. In the cottage, you may barbecue/cook your own or dine *en famille* at the main house.

Rooms: 1 dble, 1 triple, 1 family, each with shower or bath & wc; cottage for 2/3 (2 rooms, 2 bathrooms, kitchen).

Price: 300-345 Frs (€ 45.73-52.59), cottage 400 Frs, for two, incl. breakfast.

Meals: 100 Frs, including aperitif, wine & coffee. Wine-tasting menu 150 Frs.

Open: All year.

From A9 exit Perpignan Sud to Thuir. there dir. Elne for 2km; right dir. Céret for 5.5km to Fourques; right on D2 to Caixas (11km); there follow 'Mairie/ Eglise' — house by church.

MMap 235-52 **ASP Map No: 18**

Jane RICHARDS & Ian MAYES
Mas Saint Jacques
66300 Caixas
Pyrénées-Orientales
Tel: (0)4 68 38 87 83
Fax: (0)4 68 38 87 83
e-mail: MasStJacq@aol.com
www.sawdays.co.uk

This ancient *ferme-auberge* combines austerity and comfort to suit both backpacker and motorist: rooms like Fra Angelico's cells, views that go on forever with maybe an eagle circling, a swimming hole in the dammed river, owners who also raise animals and are passionate about their mountains. Sunday lunch (Catalan and French) is a riotously convivial affair; everything except the bread is home-made or home-grown and served by the two teenage children before a magnificent stone fireplace. Exceptional!

Rooms: 4 triple, 1 quadruple, 1 double each with shower & wc.

Price: 290 Frs (€ 44.21) for two, including breakfast.

Meals: 100 Frs, including wine & coffee.

Open: Mid-March to mid-November.

On French-Spanish border. From A9 exit 43 onto D115 W through Prats de Mollo and 10km beyond to Col d'Arès. Farm on left.

MMap 235-56 **ASP Map No: 18**

Michelle & Gilbert LANAU
Ferme Auberge La Costa de Dalt
Route du Col d'Arès
66230 Prats de Mollo
Pyrénées-Orientales
Tel: (0)4 68 39 74 40
Fax: (0)4 68 39 74 40

Kim is an exceptionally warm and lovely person. She and her parents, a well-travelled, cosmopolitan Scottish family, have turned their house into a perfect Pyrenean haven among some of Europe's wildest remotest landscapes. It has a magical garden full of lush vegetation and intimate sitting areas among the trees, dazzling views past snow-capped mountains down to the sea, romantic and comfortable rooms decorated with original works of art and bright scatter cushions. Two rooms offer the private bliss of walking from bed to terrace for breakfast, delivered by Kim. *Children welcome with parental supervision (pool).*

Rooms: 3 double, 3 twin, each with shower & wc.

Price: 400-650 Frs (€ 60.98-99.09) for two, including breakfast; extra bed 100 Frs.

Meals: Excellent restaurant 400m or choice in village; barbecue available.

Open: All year.

A9 to Spain, last exit before border. Drive into Céret; follow signs for 'Centre Ville' then signs for Hôtel La Terrasse au Soleil. House 300m after hotel, on left.

MMap 235-56 **ASP Map No: 18**

Kim BETHELL
a Châtaigneraie
oute de Fontfrède
400 Céret
énées-Orientales
: (0)4 68 87 21 58
(0)4 68 87 68 16
il: kimmie@club-internet.fr

A couple of young farmers who grow organic kiwi fruit, Louis and Chantal have gradually converted this old farmhouse so that it now has six large functional guestrooms. Floors are tiled throughout for coolness; furnishings are simple — almost basic — and practical; showers are small and modern. Dine on Chantal's excellent Catalan-peasant cuisine beneath the kiwi fruit trees (there may be 20-odd guests at table), share a joke with your good natured host, enjoy his spontaneous approach to running his B&B... and see the ever-beautiful Pyrenees.

Rooms: 5 double & 1 suite, all with shower & wc.

Price: 220 Frs (€ 33.54) for two, including breakfast.

Meals: 80 Frs, including aperitif & wine.

Open: All year.

From Perpignan, N114 to Elne. In village take D612 to Bages; signs after 500-600m.

MMap 235-52 **ASP Map No: 18**

Louis & Chantal TUBERT
Mas de la Couloumine
Route de Bages
66200 Elne
Pyrénées-Orientales
Tel: (0)4 68 22 36 07

Martine, who's French, and Gwyn, who's British, have made their pretty architect-designed house into a paradise for lovers of nature in general and mountains in particular — both dining room and terrace have sublime views of the Pyrenees. Gwyn is immensely knowledgeable about all things that move or grow here and can also give you an introduction to Carcassonne golf course (he plays *boules* with the local team too). Martine, warm and enthusiastic, loves cooking with local produce. Bright floral bedrooms, stylish furniture, excellent new bathrooms. "Happiness is guaranteed", say this generous couple.

Rooms: 1 double with bath & wc; 1 twin, 1 double, each with shower, sharing wc.

Price: 220-250 Frs (€ 33.54-38.11) for two, including breakfast.

Meals: 90 Frs, including aperitif, wine & coffee.

Open: All year.

From Carcassonne D118 S for 40km. At Couiza left across River Aude then left on D12 for 500m; right on D52 dir. Conilhac for 3km; right on D152 & follow yellow signs to Les Genêts.

MMap 235-43 **ASP Map No: 18**

Martine & Gwyn WILLIAMS
Les Genêts
Chemin du Pla de la Lano
11190 Conilhac de la Montagne
Aude
Tel: (0)4 68 31 45 82
Fax: (0)4 68 31 45 82

You are definitely in Cathar country now: there are donkeys and goats roaming around (children love them); the rooms are named after Cathar castles. They are ordered rather than cosy and the cool impression of alarm clocks and televisions is dispelled by the warm personal attention to your needs and the library of 1,000 books, many on the Cathars, many on cookery. Breakfast is hearty, with several types of bread, honey, cheese, home-made cakes and jams. Supper could be grilled salmon with lemon sauce and Madame's *crème caramel.* Nearby are fortified Carcassonne, medieval Foix and Mirepoix. Wonderful setting.

Rooms: 2 double, 1 twin, each with shower & wc (+ children's room).

Price: 350 Frs (€ 53.36) for two, including breakfast. Extra bed 100 Frs.

Meals: 130 Frs, including aperitif, wine & coffee.

Open: Easter to October.

From Limoux D620 dir. Chalabre for 7km then fork right on D626 (signposted Mirepoix) to Peyrefitte. Signposted from village.

MMap 235-43 **ASP Map No: 13**

Jean-Pierre & Marie-Claire ROPERS
Domaine de Couchet
11230 Peyrefitte du Razès
Aude
Tel: (0)4 68 69 55 06
Fax: (0)4 68 69 55 06
www.sawdays.co.uk

Your hosts have transformed the buildings of this charming stone-built farm into a series of wonderfully comfortable rooms. There's a real family atmosphere, lots of places to curl up with a book in house or garden and masses of interest for children when the pool palls (including lambs or foals in season). On summer evenings, parental peace is ensured by a resident babysitter so you can enjoy Michèle's delicious French cuisine and the fascinating conversation round her table. Want a cup of tea? Just "pop your head round the kitchen door and ask — any time".

Rooms: 3 double, 3 twin, each with bath or shower & wc.

Price: 450 Frs (€ 68.60) for two, including breakfast.

Meals: 129 Frs, including aperitif, wine & coffee. Children 50-65 Frs.

Open: April to mid-November.

From Carcassonne D118 S for 40km. At Couiza left on D613 12km to Arques then left on D54 dir. Valmigère for 4km. At fork, right on D70 dir. Bouisse for 2km — Les Goudis signposted on right.

MMap 235-43 **ASP Map No: 13**

Michèle & Michel DELATTRE
Domaine des Goudis
11190 Bouisse
Aude
Tel: (0)4 68 70 02 76
Fax: (0)4 68 70 00 74
e-mail: delattre-goudis@mnet.fr

The beautifully-converted farmhouse, which rejoices in huge beams, an open fireplace and impeccable taste throughout, has five pretty rooms (one for disabled), utter quiet to relax into and wonderful walks around. Diana is scatty, chatty and a superb cook, though meals, served in the enormous dining room or outside, may take second place to her genuine interest in her guests. She and Chris revel in the area, its birdlife, wild flowers, history and wine. They have lovely children and give language courses in winter. And all this just 5km from Carcassonne, 10km from an 18-hole golf course.

Rooms: 3 double, 1 twin, 1 triple, all with bath or shower & wc.

Price: 345-395 Frs (€ 52.59-60.22) for two, including breakfast (min. 2 nights June to Sept.).

Meals: By arrangement 150 Frs, including wine & coffee.

Open: All year except Feb & Nov.

From Carcassonne, D142 to Cazilhac. Left in front of 'Mairie' on D56 dir. Villefloure (bear left at cemetery). La Sauzette signposted to left after 2km.

MMap 235-39 **ASP Map No: 13**

Chris GIBSON & Diana WARREN
Ferme de la Sauzette
Route de Villefloure, Cazilhac
11570 Palaja
Aude
Tel: (0)4 68 79 81 32
Fax: (0)4 68 79 65 99
www.vtl.mnet.fr/itinerance/sauzette

You could never feel cramped in this C19 gentleman farmer's house and there's space to hide in bad weather — the bedrooms are so vast that the (fairly basic) furniture looks almost lost. Breakfast and dinner are served on the terrace in fine weather. Madame, open and welcoming, chats to guests in her attractive kitchen/dining room and enjoys their travellers' tales. Her freshly-decorated house is full of character (and new mattresses) and the huge, restful park beckons, as do nearby Carcassonne, the dreamy Canal du Midi, and the vineyards.

Rooms: 1 double, 1 triple, 1 suite for 4/5, each with shower & wc.

Price: 300-350 Frs (€ 45.73-53.36) for two, including breakfast. Extra person 90 Frs.

Meals: 95 Frs, including wine & coffee.

Open: All year.

Gîte space for 5 people

From Carcassonne dir. Salvaza airport; stay on D119 for approx. 4km more; house signposted on left.

MMap 235-39 **ASP Map No: 13**

Isabelle CLAYETTE
Domaine des Castelles
11170 Caux et Sauzens
Aude
Tel: (0)4 68 72 03 60
Fax: (0)4 68 72 03 60

The 'House on the Hill' overlooks medieval Carcassonne, just a short kilometre through the vines. A quiet haven from bustling postcard sellers, this sumptuous house, ablaze with colour inside and out, is full of pictures, lovely old furniture and treasures (hats, handmade pots, straw sandals). The wonderfully festooned bedrooms have bathrooms to match (one with a two-body shower!). Madame is open and generous, serves a fantastic array of home-made jams at breakfast on the terrace and is helped by her daughter who also made the stunning coffee table of polished cement and iron.

Rooms: 4 double, 1 apartment for 4, each with shower or bath & wc.

Price: 300-450 Frs (€ 45.73-68.60) for two, including breakfast.

Meals: 120 Frs, including aperitif, wine & coffee.

Open: All year.

Gîte space for 4 people

Go to Carcassonne Cité main gate, pass cemetery on right & follow signs Chambres d'Hôtes for 1km along narrow lane through vineyards. Well indicated on left.

MMap 235-39 **ASP Map No: 13**

Mme Nicole GALINIER
La Maison sur la Colline
Sainte Croix
11000 Carcassonne
Aude
Tel: (0)4 68 47 57 94
Fax: (0)4 68 47 57 94
www.sawdays.co.uk

Sally was born in England, lived in America and, having now adopted France completely, has thrown her energies into turning this C17 coaching inn into a well-balanced marriage of solid old French base and modern inspiration. She was an interior designer (whence daring apple green and raspberry pink in the lovely old-style dining room), is a trained cook (whence "luscious rabbit in cream and heavenly lemon mousse" at dinner), provides all possible goodies in her big, well-furnished bedrooms and loves to share her passion for, and books on, history and travel.

Rooms: 2 double, 1 suite for 4, each with bath & wc.

Price: 350 Frs (€ 53.36) for two, including breakfast.

Meals: 100 Frs, incl. wine & coffee.

Open: All year.

From A61 exit 25 onto D611 through Lézignan Corbières, zig-zag across D11 and continue on D910 to Olonzac. There, D52 to Pépieux; left just before church — house immediately on left.

MMap 235-40 **ASP Map No: 13**

Sally WORTHINGTON
Carrefour
1 rue de l'Etang
11700 Pépieux, Aude
Tel: (0)4 68 91 69 29
Fax: (0)4 68 91 69 29
e-mail: sally.worthington@wanadoo.fr
http://perso.wanadoo.fr/carrefourbedbreakfast

This is a lovely, wild, undiscovered area, well off the beaten track with masses of things for kids to do on the farm. But let's be honest about Le Fourchat, run by a mother-and-daughter team. Our inspectors have waxed lyrical about delicious meals (home-made bread, lots of home-grown fruit and vegetables) and the warmly natural welcome they've received when visiting anonymously. However, the rooms, very serviceable with all basic necessities and great for families (e.g. bunk beds), are all rather soullessly alike, arranged in a row above a living room in a converted barn. Go because it's real, not because it's smart.

Rooms: 3 double and 2 twin, all with own shower & wc.

Price: 210 Frs (€ 32.01) for two, including breakfast.

Meals: 80 Frs, including wine & coffee.

Open: All year.

Gîte space for 4 people

From Mazamet, D118 dir. Carcassonne. Right on D53 to Aiguefonde; signposted.

MMap 235-35 **ASP Map No: 13**

Véronique & Simone LELIÈVRE
Le Fourchat
Aiguefonde
81200 Mazamet
Tarn
Tel: (0)5 63 98 12 62

Madame is a delight, runs this family château with boundless energy and infectious *joie de vivre*, serves breakfast in her big kitchen in order to chat more easily to you while preparing dinner. The comfortable, lived-in bedrooms still have their original C19 charm, including a restored rare 1850s wallpaper, and turning walk-in cupboards into shower rooms or wcs was a stroke of brilliance. The interconnected, antique-filled sitting rooms are totally French and the little reading room holds hundreds of books. A country house in the style of days gone by, now comfortably worn around the edges, offering timeless friendship.

Rooms: 2 twin, 2 suites, each with shower & wc; 1 double with own shower, sharing wc.

Price: 400 Frs (€ 60.98) for two, including breakfast.

Meals: 120-130 Frs, including wine & coffee.

Open: All year.

From Revel, D622 dir. Castres. 9km along, left on D12 to Lempaut. At Lempaut, right on D46 dir. Lescout. La Bousquétarié is on your left.

MMap 235-31 **ASP Map No: 13**

Monique & Charles SALLIER
La Bousquétarié
81700 Lempaut
Tarn
Tel: (0)5 63 75 51 09
www.sawdays.co.uk

A sense of refined luxury, even opulence, pervades this beautifully-restored house where 43 large ebony beams (brought from Madagascar as repatriation luggage when the family moved back...) were used for the job. There is a happy, humorous family atmosphere with many traces of those years on exotic shores, in the cooking as well as the bathrooms. The large, pretty bedrooms are immaculate, the warm-hearted, people-loving owners are most unusual, both refined and down-to-earth, country-comfortable and artistic. *If they haven't heard from you by 8pm they may re-let the room.*

Rooms: 1 double, 1 twin, both with bath or shower & wc.

Price: 290 Frs (€ 44.21) for two, including breakfast.

Meals: 95 Frs, including wine & coffee.

Open: All year except mid-December to mid-January.

From Rabastens, D12 dir. Coufouleux. Cross river Tarn then imm'ly left on D13 dir. Loupiac. Just before village right by cemetery; skirt cemetery, fork right, follow signs for La Bonde for 1km.

MMap 235-26 **ASP Map No: 12**

Maurice & Bernadette CRÉTÉ
La Bonde Loupiac
81800 Rabastens
Tarn
Tel: (0)5 63 33 82 83
Fax: (0)5 63 57 46 54

Catherine is wonderful and does everything possible to ensure a stress-free stay here — especially for small children: early suppers, picnic lunches, a delicious breakfast menu which includes cereals — a parents' paradise. Breakfast is in a charming dining room or on the terrace. Bedrooms in this C19 manor house, built in the style typical of the region, if not big, are immaculate and pretty with good colour schemes and fabrics. It's perfectly placed for visits to the extraordinary Cathedral at Albi, wandering in the lovely local countryside or playing water games on the big lake.

Rooms: 1 double, 2 triple, each with bath or shower & wc.

Price: 300 Frs (€ 45.73) for two, including breakfast.

Meals: 100 Frs; gastronomic 150 Frs, including wine. Children 40 Frs.

Open: All year.

From Gaillac D964 N to Castelnau de Montmiral; right at bottom of village for 100m; right at sign 'La Croix du Sud', fork left dir. Mazars — house on left.

MMap 235-22 **ASP Map No: 12**

Catherine SORDOILLET
La Croix du Sud
Mazars
81140 Castelnau de Montmiral
Tarn
Tel: (0)5 63 33 18 46
Fax: (0)5 63 33 18 46
www.sawdays.co.uk

Mas de Sudre is a warm friendly house, just like its owners. George and Pippa are ideal B&B folk — relaxed, good-natured, at ease with people, adding lots of little extras to make you comfortable, enthusiastic about their corner of France. Dinners are delicious and convivial, *dégustations* can be arranged and there's a large shady garden set in rolling vineyards and farmland where you can sleep off any excesses. For the more energetic there are bikes, a pool, a tennis court, badminton and table tennis. Children are welcome and guests are encouraged to treat the house as their own.

Rooms: 2 double & 2 twin, all with own shower & wc.

Price: 300 Frs (€ 45.73) for two, including breakfast.

Meals: 120 Frs, including wine & coffee.

Open: All year.

Gîte space for 10 people

From Gaillac centre dir. Cordes. Cross railway; fork imm'ly left on D964 dir. Castelnau de Montmiral for 1km; left on D18 dir. Montauban for 400m; right on D4 for 1.5km — 1st left, 1st house on right.

MMap 235-27 **ASP Map No: 13**

Pippa & George RICHMOND-BROWN
Mas de Sudre
81600 Gaillac
Tarn
Tel: (0)5 63 41 01 32
Fax: (0)5 63 41 01 32
www.sawdays.co.uk

The sort of home we all dream of — on a hill in a beautiful corner of the Tarn, approached by an avenue of old oaks. Your heart will stir to the beauty of house and setting — and the startlingly-positioned pool. Huge dayrooms, heavy ancient doors, beams, open fires and some Louis XIII furniture. One of the rooms is richly furnished with a bathroom in the tower, the other is in brighter, simpler, Mediterranean style — both are worthy of the praise heaped upon them by visitors. And equally elegant, civilised hosts with much charming enthusiasm for the house they have lived in for 40 years and guests they have received for 30!

Rooms: 2 double, each with bath or shower & wc.

Price: 290 Frs (€ 44.21) for two, including breakfast. 2 nights min. July/Aug.

Meals: 3 restaurants in village 3km. Mini-kitchen for hire in summer.

Open: April to September.

From Gaillac D964 dir. Caussade. 4km before Larroque left on D1 for 3km. House signposted on right.

MMap 235-22 **ASP Map No: 12**

Minouche & Christian JOUARD
Meilhouret
81140 Larroque
Tarn
Tel: (0)5 63 33 11 18
Fax: (0)5 63 33 11 18

The stones of this fabulous, seriously old, house are mute witnesses to the passage from rough Middle Ages to calmer farming days and decorative flourishes from the Thornleys' travels add spice. The big, airy rooms are sensitively furnished with the perfect minimum, each has a private balcony or patio and stupendous views. Books, paintings and long, luscious walks entice you to stay (let their seven-day deal tempt you), as do the new poolside barbecue, summer kitchen and dining area. Former diplomats, the Thornleys have entertaining in their blood and Patricia's infectious laugh and sense of fun will brighten your mornings.

Rooms: 1 suite for 4, 2 double, 1 twin, all with bath or shower & wc.

Price: 300 Frs (€ 45.73) for two, including breakfast (3 nights min).

Meals: Wide choice in Cordes. Barbecue & summer kitchen.

Open: May to September.

From Albi D600 to Cordes. There take upward 'Cité' road on right of 'Maison de la Presse' for 500m; fork left dir. Le Bouysset; left at hairpin bend and right 200m on at 2nd hairpin bend into Aurifat.

MMap 235-23 **ASP Map No: 13**

Denis & Patricia THORNLEY
Aurifat
81170 Cordes sur Ciel
Tarn
Tel: (0)5 63 56 07 03

A small corner of delight on the edge of Cordes, this old house glows with the sensitive, loving care it has received. A magnificent hallway then a sweeping staircase bring you to fine, airy rooms that have original fireplaces, beams, interesting pictures, views of Cordes and are beautifully furnished (matt satin is very fitting). Your hosts are a gentle couple, maybe a little reserved at first but their dry humour warms up over dinner — most of which they'll proudly tell you they produced themselves. Children are welcome; there are games, a small park where you can picnic if you wish, and Leonard the friendly donkey.

Rooms: 1 twin, 2 double, 1 triple, 1 quadruple, all with shower & wc.

Price: 290 Frs (€ 44.21) for two, including breakfast.

Meals: 105 Frs, including wine & coffee.

Open: All year.

From Albi D600 to Cordes. There follow signs 'Parking 1 & 2'. Then signposted.

MMap 235-23 **ASP Map No: 13**

Annie & Christian RONDEL
Les Tuileries
81170 Cordes sur Ciel
Tarn
Tel: (0)5 63 56 05 93
Fax: (0)5 63 56 05 93

Looking for the complete French bourgeois experience? The huge cool entrance hall and the massive stone staircase winding up through four floors, the *trompe-l'œil* 'marble' alcoves, the high ceilings and southern colours — deep blue shutters, white walls — make it almost colonially grand. Add the owners' passion for Napoleon III furniture, oil paintings and gilt-framed mirrors and the mood is formal rather than family but above all unmistakably French. Bedrooms are antique-furnished, breakfast is on the terrace overlooking the square — good to be in a town for once with friendly, utterly French people.

Rooms: 1 suite, 4 double, 1 twin, all with bath or shower & wc.

Price: 260 Frs (€ 39.64) for two, suite 360 Frs, including breakfast.

Meals: Plenty of places in town.

Open: All year.

In centre of Gaillac, directly opposite St Michel abbey church as you come in across bridge from A68 Toulouse-Albi road.

MMap 235-27 **ASP Map No: 13**

Lucile PINON
8 place Saint Michel
81600 Gaillac
Tarn
Tel: (0)5 63 57 61 48
Fax: (0)5 63 41 06 56

You will be serenaded by birds, bees and sheep in this lovely and largely undiscovered part of France, so close to Albi and its fascinating red-brick Cathedral. Your Anglo-French hosts are welcoming and helpful — the bright, unfussy rooms may be small but the hospitality is great and their deeply converted 200-year-old farmhouse is a deliciously secluded place to stay and walk or bike out into the country. Local sheep farmers (who supply Rocquefort with milk) will show you their milking sheds if asked. The Wises grow their own vegetables and summer dinners are on the terrace overlooking the lovely Tarn valley.

Rooms: 1 twin, 1 triple, each with shower & wc, 1 twin sharing a bathroom.

Price: 230 Frs (€ 35.06) for two, including breakfast.

Meals: 95 Frs, including aperitif, wine & coffee.

Open: All year.

From Albi, D999 dir. Millau. At La Croix Blanche (25km), left down to Cambon du Temple and up to La Barthe on D163. Turn right; house is first on left.

MMap 235-27 **ASP Map No: 13**

Michèle & Michael WISE
La Barthe
81430 Villefranche d'Albigeois
Tarn
Tel: (0)5 63 55 96 21
Fax: (0)5 63 55 96 21
e-mail: michael.wise@freesbee.fr
www.angelfire.com/la/wise

All is light, sun and simplicity here in superbly wild surroundings (good walks and rock climbing). Madame is gentle, welcoming and most proud of her restored barn which houses the guest quarters. They are furnished with old country pieces, fitted with pretty curtains and new bedding, rejoice in a fireplace and a fully-equipped kitchen. She will even come to the rescue with fresh eggs for your supper. There is a lovely terrace for breakfast, which includes a different kind of bread every day, or cheese, or walnuts, or honey... Really lovely people.

Rooms: 1 double and 1 twin, each with bath & wc.

Price: 270 Frs (€ 41.16) for two, including breakfast.

Meals: Self-catering. Restaurants nearby.

Open: April to September.

From Mazamet, N112 dir. St Pons de Thomières. At Courniou, left to Prouilhe; farm on left.

MMap 240-25 **ASP Map No: 13**

Eliane & Jean-Louis LUNES
La Métairie Basse
Hameau de Prouilhe
34220 Courniou
Hérault
Tel: (0)4 67 97 21 59
Fax: (0)4 67 97 21 59

That grand façade is softened by an exotic mix of hydrangea, bamboo, palms and wisteria and it's easy to see why this sophisticated Dutch couple were seduced into leaving advertising for a simpler life. A proud old staircase sweeps up to the bedrooms which are not overdone but just right: light, roomy, marble-fireplaced, old-furnished, with super views of hills and the truly lovely garden. The young artistic owners have a flair for decoration and pride themselves on their fine French food — "those who dine here once dine every evening" — served in the soft yellow-painted, green-panelled dining room. *Pets by arrangement.*

Rooms: 3 double, 2 twin, 1 suite for 2 with kitchenette, each with bath or shower & wc.

Price: 340-420 Frs (€ 51.83-64.03) for two, including breakfast.

Meals: 130 Frs, excluding wine (50-100 Frs).

Open: All year.

Gîte space for 7 people

  35Frs   

From A9 Béziers Ouest exit on D64 then N112 dir. Castres/Mazamet/St Pons. 1km before St Pons right on D908 dir. Riols/Bédarieux. House signposted on left leaving Riols.

MMap 240-25 **ASP Map No: 13**

Monique & Reinoud WEGGELAAR
La Cerisaie
1 Avenue de Bédarieux
34220 Riols, Hérault
Tel: (0)4 67 97 03 87
Fax: (0)4 67 97 03 88
e-mail: cerisaie@wanadoo.fr
www.sawdays.co.uk

Sarah, who has just written a cookery book and Denis, an accomplished photographer, have decorative flair too, clearly visible within these golden rag-painted walls. The fine townhouse has lovely spaces, just enough antiques, careful use of light and fabrics, inviting guestrooms. You can walk, ride, climb rocks; swim, canoe in the river; follow Denis's wine trail; visit the town's unusual succulent garden — and return drunk with exertion and beauty for a superb, civilised meal on the terrace. Very special.

Rooms: 2 double, 1 twin, 1 suite, all with shower & wc.

Price: 365-445 Frs (€ 55.64-67.84) for two, including breakfast; extra bed 60-100 Frs.

Meals: Dinner 155-175 Frs, including coffee.

Open: All year.

Gîte space for 4 people

From Béziers N112 W dir. St Pons for 1-2km; then right on D14 through Maraussan, Cazouls lès Béziers, Cessenon to Roquebrun. House signposted in village.

MMap 240-26 **ASP Map No: 13**

Denis & Sarah LA TOUCHE
Les Mimosas
Avenue des Orangers
34460 Roquebrun, Hérault
Tel: (0)4 67 89 61 36
Fax: (0)4 67 89 61 36
e-mail: la-touche.les-mimosas@wanadoo.fr
http://perso.wanadoo.fr/les-mimosas/

The lovely, venerable, tree-lined Canal du Midi, loved by cyclists the world over, runs through the charming old village: your warmly friendly Australian hostess willingly houses cyclists and their mounts in this C15-to-C18 'terraced château' — it certainly does climb the hillside in terraced steps. The owners have lovingly restored the house, with its dark panelling, magnificent *trompe-l'œil* tiled hall and fine painted ceilings (with *scènes du Languedoc*). The big, comfortable rooms include 2m-long beds, power showers and much attention to authentic detail. You are only 5km from the sea.

Rooms: 2 double, 2 twin, all with bath or shower & wc.

Price: 270 Frs (€ 41.16) for two, including breakfast.

Meals: 90 Frs, including wine & coffee.

Open: All year.

Gîte space for 2 people

From Béziers, N112 dir. Agde. Pass under motorway then right on D37 into Villeneuve; house in centre opposite Hôtel de Ville.

MMap 240-30 **ASP Map No: 13**

Jennifer-Jane VINER
7 rue de la Fontaine
34420 Villeneuve lès Béziers
Hérault
Tel: (0)4 67 39 87 15
Fax: (0)4 67 39 87 15
www.sawdays.co.uk

Madame, an artist and sculptor, is an open, fun person who loves getting to know her guests and showing them her work. Her modern house has lots of artistic atmosphere and big, simply-furnished rooms, each with a few lovely things, good fabrics and a private outside space onto the green garden. The surroundings are worth the trip too: you are up on the hillside, protected by umbrella pines, above the magnificent Salagou lake — perfect for sailing, swimming on those long hot summer's days, wonderful biking, walking and riding in winter. Definitely worth staying two nights or more.

Rooms: 2 double, each with bath or shower & wc.

Price: 250-300 Frs (€ 38.11-45.73) for two, including breakfast (min. 2 nights).

Meals: Choice within 3-5km. Barbecue & picnic possible.

Open: All year.

From A9 exit 34 onto D13 N then N9 to Clermont l'Hérault (30km). In Clermont D156 dir. Lac du Salagou for 3km; fork left for Liausson — 700m along, last house on right before woods.

MMap 240-22 **ASP Map No: 13**

M & Mme NEVEU
La Genestière
Route de Liausson
34800 Clermont l'Hérault
Hérault
Tel: (0)4 67 96 30 97/
(0)4 67 96 18 46
Fax: (0)4 67 96 32 56

Not a pelican in sight, nothing out of place either on this superb estate with its mulberry-lined drive, woods, hills, vineyards and wonderful family atmosphere (the couple have a small, active child and an above-ground swimming pool). The large *auberge* dining room gives onto a covered terrace and rows of vines — just the place to try a glass of estate wine followed by delicious regional cooking. The fresh-coloured bedrooms are new and mezzanined and the delightful, hard-working owners have decorated their family house with the utmost care.

Rooms: 4 double/quadruple, each with shower & wc.

Price: 300-330 Frs (€ 45.73-50.31) for two, including breakfast.

Meals: 100-115 Frs, including wine.

Open: All year except last week in Oct.

       20Frs 

Leave Gignac centre eastwards dir. Montpellier. At the edge of town: 'L'Hérault Cuisines' on right — turn right (signed) and follow signs for 3km.

MMap 240-22 **ASP Map No: 13**

Isabelle & Baudouin THILLAYE de BOULLAY
Domaine du Pélican
34150 Gignac
Hérault
Tel: (0)4 67 57 68 92
Fax: (0)4 67 57 68 92

Monsieur keeps horses so stop on your ride to Compostela (it happens often!) or, more prosaically, on the road to Spain or Montpellier airport (the Domaine is just off the motorway so there is inevitably some road noise). It is a fine old 19th-century wine-grower's house with the remains of a 12th-century chapel. A quiet breakfast can be had in the courtyard in summer or before the kitchen fireplace in winter. Good, clean rooms and Madame is happy to take children to feed the rabbits or the old tortoise.

Rooms: 3 double, 3 twin, each with bathrooms.

Price: 200 Frs (€ 30.49) for two, including breakfast.

Meals: Wide choice nearby.

Open: All year.

Gîte space for 4 people

From Montpellier, N113 dir. Lunel. House signposted in Baillargues.

MMap 240-23 **ASP Map No: 14**

Michèle & Michel VITOU
Domaine de St Antoine
Baillargues
34670 Baillargues
Hérault
Tel: (0)4 67 70 15 58

The big gates open off the typical sun-drenched sleepy village street with its arched doorways and shuttered windows. At the back, your eye leaps straight out into the parallel vineyards and uneven hills — a festival of flaming colour in autumn. Monsieur is English; Madame is French and an artist. She is easy-going, good company and has done her house with great sympathy for its stone floors and original spaces. Her works are a bonus on the walls. It is a privilege to be her only guest, enjoy the big ground-floor bedroom that opens onto the garden and step out into the morning light for home-made fig jam.

Rooms: 1 double with bathroom.

Price: 340 Frs (€ 51.83) for two, including breakfast.

Meals: Choice 5km.

Open: All year.

From Montpellier NE on N110 dir. Sommières for 20km; D118 right to St Christol. Pass 'Cave Coopérative' on right, over small bridge, right for 800m, left Ave des Bruyères becomes Rue de l'Eglise. OR A9 exit 27 'Lunel'.

MMap 240-19 **ASP Map No: 14**

Monique SYKES-MAILLON
La Ciboulette
221 rue de l'Église
34400 St Christol
Hérault
Tel: (0)4 67 86 81 00
e-mail: cibou@aol.com
www.sawdays.co.uk

The mighty cedar protects the front, in spring a delicate yellow rose and translucent wisteria climb sweetly over the pergola at the back — echoes of a different lifestyle? Your hostess, a naturally friendly, very young grandmother, loves her Provençal village that is neither touristy nor dormitory but hums with its own genuine life. She also leaves her guests in peace when they need it — to write, to paint, to rest. Her lovely rooms are simply decorated with warm honey colours, waxed tile floors, fine pieces of furniture and good rugs. Good taste goes so far as to hide the wood-surrounded swimming pool in a walled garden.

Rooms: 5 rooms for 2 (doubles & twins), each with bath or shower & wc.

Price: 400-600 Frs (€ 60.98-91.47) for two, including breakfast.

Meals: Within walking distance; choice 2/3km.

Open: All year.

From A9 exit 26 follow signs to Aigues Vives centre; on big open square — great cedar in front of house.

MMap 240-19 **ASP Map No: 14**

Abigail BARTHÉLÉMY & Philippe GRIBINSKI
Le Cèdre
97 place Émile Jamais
30670 Aigues Vives
Gard
Tel: (0)4 66 35 93 93
Fax: (0)4 66 35 56 37

Marion has made something very special of this old C17 house: there is a slightly Moorish feel to the rooms she has lovingly put together, placing beautiful pieces of furniture and paintings to enhance their generous proportions. Her cooking also has a North African influence as well as the Provençal specialities one would expect. Candlelit dinner under the pergola in a lovely walled garden, huge breakfast the next morning including cold meats, cheese and local *fougasse* (a soft delicate bread), and the usual French delicacies — bliss!

Rooms: 1 double, 1 twin, sharing bathroom; 1 suite with bath & wc.

Price: 350-450 Frs (€ 53,36-68.60) for two, including breakfast.

Meals: 120 Frs, including aperitif, table wine & coffee.

Open: All year.

From A9 exit 26 S to Aimargues Centre. Cross roundabout with fountain down lane of plane trees for 300m. Entrance Rue de la Violette (3 cypresses behind garden wall).

MMap 240-23 **ASP Map No: 14**

Jean-Pierre & Marion ESCARFAIL
26 boulevard St Louis
30470 Aimargues
Gard
Tel: (0)4 66 88 52 99
Fax: (0)4 66 88 52 99
www.sawdays.co.uk

A *hôtel particulier* is a private mansion and Philippe receives at his with warm refinement. His rooms, all very separate and private, each named after a different local luminary (including our own Lawrence Durrell) are in traditional Provençal style: highly-polished floors, white bedcovers, a different and beautiful wall-hanging over each bed; super big bathrooms too. The magic secluded terrace garden with views over the roofs of the old town is where you have breakfast, which to Philippe is a very important moment of the day. Guests have filled the visitors' book with ecstatic comments; yours to come?

Rooms: 4 double, 1 twin, 1 triple, all with bath or shower & wc.

Price: 400-480 Frs (€ 60.98-73.18) for two, including breakfast.

Meals: 100 Frs, including wine.

Open: All year.

From Nîmes D40 W 28km to Sommières. House clearly signed in town centre — park in front.

MMap 240-19 **ASP Map No: 14**

Philippe de FRÉMONT
Hôtel de l'Orange
7 rue des Beaumes, Chemin du Château Fort
30250 Sommières, Gard
Tel: (0)4 66 77 79 94
Fax: (0)4 66 80 44 87
e-mail: philippe.de.fremont@wanadoo.com
www.sawdays.co.uk

The pool and the flower-filled garden are reason enough to stay here, so is the shady pergola for reading beneath... and the sense of having got away from it all. Edna has created something utterly English — books, pictures, trinkets, a certain kind of comfort — but it is so well done, the colours and space so carefully thought out, the day/dining room so big and pleasant, that we think you will like La Fauguière too. Breakfast is worth being on time for: it is as good as the rooms are comfortable and children are as welcome as you are.

Rooms: 2 double, each with bath, shower & wc; 1 double, 1 twin each with shower & handbasin, sharing wc.

Price: 350-450 Frs (€ 53.36-68.60) for two, including breakfast.

Meals: Wide choice 10km.

Open: All year.

From Alès, N110 S, right on D910 dir. Anduze; after 500m, left on D24 to Canaules. There, right on D149 to St Nazaire des G., right at railway bridge, up hill to 'Mairie', turn left. House at bottom of hill on left.

MMap 240-15 **ASP Map No: 14**

Edna & Ted PRICE
Mas de la Fauguière
30610 St Nazaire des Gardies
Gard
Tel: (0)4 66 77 38 67
Fax: (0)4 66 77 11 64

Where to sit in the château's large drawing room where over a dozen French chairs open their arms? The ambulant might wander onto the balcony with its panoramic views across river, dramatic viaduct and red-roofed village to the terraced hills beyond. The large elegant bedrooms have a perfect château feeling with their dark-coloured walls. Madame, one of an old French family in the silk industry who have lived here for several generations, is delightful and practical and will show you where to find really goods walks, exciting canoeing, tennis, riding, interesting wildlife spots and ancient buildings to visit nearby.

Rooms: 2 twin, 1 double, each with bath or shower & wc.

Price: 350-450 Frs (€ 53.36-68.60) for two, including breakfast.

Meals: 100 Frs, including wine & coffee.

Open: All year.

From Millau S on N9 for 19 km. At La Cavalerie left on D7 dir. Le Vigan for about 50km to Bez. Before bridge, little château signposted on left.

MMap 240-14 **ASP Map No: 13**

Françoise du LUC
Château Massal
Bez et Esparon
30120 Le Vigan
Gard
Tel: (0)4 67 81 07 60
Fax: (0)4 67 81 07 60
www.sawdays.co.uk

Warm sandstone outside, golden light inside washing over old white-painted beams, pretty acidic walls (lemon, pistachio, blue: proof of John's designer experience), easy furnishings and the amiable clutter of a family's lifetime. The heart of this rambling house is the first-floor kitchen/diner where Marie-Laure marries Mediterranean and Oriental magic to create artistic dinners for long evenings of intelligent conversation. They have gifts of hospitality, humour and interior design; a Banksia rose shades the table, the olive grove is perfect for a good read and an old Roman transhumance path runs by the house and up into the hills.

Rooms: 1 double, 1 twin with own bathrooms & kitchen; 1 double, 1 twin, sharing bath, shower, wc, *salon* & kitchen.

Price: 280-350 Frs (€ 42.69-53.36) for two, including breakfast.

Meals: 100 Frs, including wine & coffee. Use of kitchen extra.

Open: All year.

Gîte space for 10 people

From Alès D50/D129 SW to Anduze then D907 dir. Nîmes for 4km. Right on D35 dir. Quissac. 400m after Bouzène fork right; 2km to Aspères, turn right, 2nd house on left.

MMap 240-15 **ASP Map No: 14**

Marie-Laure & John MARSH
Mas des Loriots
Aspères
30140 Tornac, Gard
Tel: (0)4 66 61 88 25
Fax: (0)4 66 61 88 25
e-mail: loriots@club-internet.fr
www.sawdays.co.uk

585

This ancient abode, with flower-filled terrace, large private orchard and views of the Cévennes mountains, is home to an artist/designer couple. Supremely quiet (the only passer-by is the local winegrower) it has a choice of styles: a C11 vaulted ground-floor room with private courtyard or a first floor remodelled in the 1920s, all ice-cream colours, long, elegant windows and patterned tiled floors with private balcony. The lovely blue, big-tabled kitchen and the living room with its display of David's work add to the welcoming atmosphere. Dinner — regional or exotic — may be rounded off with organic, home-grown fruit. Art classes too.

Rooms: 2 double with bath or shower & wc.

Price: 280 Frs (€ 42.69) for two, including breakfast.

Meals: 100 Frs, including wine & coffee.

Open: All year.

From Nîmes D999 dir. Le Vigan for 27km then right to Bragassargues. House in village centre.

MMap 240-15 **ASP Map No: 14**

David & Patricia CHAPMAN
La Maison des Rêves
Le Village
30260 Bragassargues, Gard
Tel: (0)4 66 77 13 45
Fax: (0)4 66 77 13 45
e-mail: chapreves@aol.com
www.sawdays.co.uk

586

A path through the woods leads from the house to the river by the Pont du Gard, a World Heritage site — the setting is truly wonderful. Indoors, the décor is fulsome, almost whacky — a net canopy over one of the beds, hanging hats, splayed fans, silk flowers, etc. The rooms are themed. *La Provençale* has a small connecting room with bunk beds and soft toys for the younger guest. Monsieur works in Nîmes but gives all his remaining time to welcoming and caring for his guests. The new swimming pool is now an added enticement.

Rooms: 1 suite, 2 double, 1 twin with bath or shower & wc.

Price: 420 Frs (€ 64.03) for two, including breakfast. Extra bed: under 13s, 80 Frs; older 150 Frs.

Meals: Auberges by Pont du Gard 800m.

Open: March to October.

Gîte space for 4 people

From Remoulins follow signs for Pont du Gard 'rive droite'. Signposted on right 'La Terre des Lauriers'.

MMap 240-16 **ASP Map No: 14**

Gérard CRISTINI
La Terre des Lauriers
Rive Droite — Pont du Gard
30210 Remoulins
Gard
Tel: (0)4 66 37 19 45
Fax: (0)4 66 37 19 45

John, who will welcome you with exuberance to the C19 *maison de maître* he has restored with Michel, is a joiner who also has an excellent eye for interior design and decoration while Michel does the cooking and the garden. They are a delightful couple. From the classic black and white tiles of the entrance hall to the carefully-planned lighting in the bedrooms, every detail has been attended to. A very generous breakfast is served under the chestnut trees or by the pool; afterwards you can wander off to join in lazy Provençal village life, visit Avignon, Uzès or nearby Lussan, the fortified Cévenol village.

Rooms: 1 double, 2 twin, each with bath or shower & wc.

Price: 500 Frs (€ 76.22) for two, including breakfast.

Meals: 150 Frs, including aperitif, wine, coffee.

Open: All year.

From A9 exit 23 W to Uzès 19km. There D979 N for 7.5km then right on D238 to La Bruguière. House on big square next to 'Mairie' (vast Micocourier tree in front).

MMap 240-12 **ASP Map No: 14**

John KARAVIAS & Michel COMAS
Les Marronniers
Place de la Mairie
30580 La Bruguière, Gard
Tel: (0)4 66 72 84 77
Fax: (0)4 66 72 85 78
e-mail: les.marronniers@hello.to
http://hello.to/les.marronniers

Monsieur, a stonemason, restored this former medieval Templar headquarters himself; it is now a working farm. The C15 house is set among well-tended lawns. After bringing up four children, Madame attended agricultural college and raises sheep and poultry — visiting children love all the animals. The simple, comfortable rooms have fine beds, large cupboards and roomy bathrooms and there is a small *salon*. The pool has sweeping views across the surrounding countryside. A friendly, farming atmosphere, though best to avoid summer weekends when they hold wedding receptions for large numbers of happy carousers.

Rooms: 2 double, 1 twin, 1 suite for 2/4 people, all with shower & wc.

Price: 280 Frs (€ 42.69) for two, including breakfast.

Meals: Auberge 5km.

Open: All year.

   50Frs 

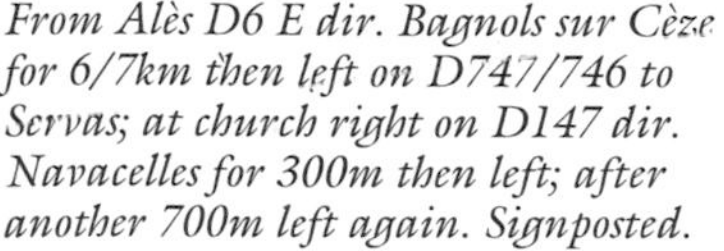

From Alès D6 E dir. Bagnols sur Cèze for 6/7km then left on D747/746 to Servas; at church right on D147 dir. Navacelles for 300m then left; after another 700m left again. Signposted.

MMap 240-11 **ASP Map No: 14**

Myriam & Daniel SORDI
Mas des Commandeurs
30340 Servas
Gard
Tel: (0)4 66 85 67 90
www.sawdays.co.uk

Madame is delightful and an excellent cook. Monsieur is a very competent potter — lovely pottery around the house and a little gallery to buy from. They run a pottery workshop as well as their *chambres d'hôtes* so the atmosphere is busy and creative with lots of interesting people about. The guestrooms, separate from the main house, are simply furnished and guests have a sitting room with a fireplace. Breakfast and dinner (on request) are served on the terrace or in the dining room. Lovely landscape of rolling hills and woods, music festivals and theatrical happenings locally: it's ideal for hikers and culture vultures as well as potters.

Rooms: 1 twin, 1 double, each with shower & wc.

Price: 270-290 Frs (€ 41.16-44.21) for two, including breakfast.

Meals: By arrangement 80 Frs, including wine.

Open: All year.

Gîte space for 16 people

From Alès, D16 through Salindres; after Salindres, left onto D241 dir. St Julien de Cassagnes; Mas Cassac signposted.

MMap 240-11 **ASP Map No: 14**

Michel & Françoise SIMONOT
Mas Cassac
30500 Allègre les Fumades
Gard
Tel: (0)4 66 24 85 65
Fax: (0)4 66 24 80 55

Climb the steps straight into the huge old kitchen to find a long wooden table on an uneven stone floor, an old sideboard along one whitewashed wall, the old stone sink along another. Touches of bright blue and splashes from pretty ochre-yellow plates punctuate the picture. This happy, intelligent couple chat easily: a warm informal welcome. They will lead you from the old kitchen to their simple stone-walled terrace and you will feel completely at ease. Bedrooms are big and uncluttered; the house is family-relaxed; dinner is good value and a chance to talk about lots of things including local culture and... wine!

Rooms: 2 double, 1 suite, each with shower & wc.

Price: 320 Frs (€ 48.78) for two, including breakfast.

Meals: 100 Frs, incl. aperitif, wine & coffee.

Open: All year.

From Alès D6 E for 27km then left on D979 beyond Lussan dir. Barjac for 1km; left on D187 to Fons sur Lussan. Entering village right at old fountain — house up street on left opposite church.

MMap 24012 **ASP Map No: 14**

Michèle DASSONNEVILLE
La Magnanerie
30580 Fons sur Lussan
Gard
Tel: (0)4 66 72 81 72

This fine rambling house, built in the 18th century as a silk-worm farm, has old stones, arches, a lovely shady courtyard. Antoine and Isabelle have created a home for themselves and their three children in their own informal and friendly image: Isabelle is an artist, her touch evident in the imaginative decoration of indoor and outdoor spaces. Breakfast is home-made jams and delicious breads on the shady terrace in summer; dinner is also served on the terrace. Isabelle is interested in cookery from all round the Mediterranean and includes North African and Greek dishes in her repertoire — all very exciting.

Rooms: 2 twin, 1 triple, 1 quadruple, each with shower & wc.

Price: 300 Frs (€ 45.73) for two, including breakfast.

Meals: 100 Frs, including aperitif, wine & coffee.

Open: All year.

From Alès D16/D579 NE to Barjac (35km), through Barjac dir. Vallon Pont d'Arc for 300m after Gendarmerie — house on right, arched doorway.

MMap 240-8 **ASP Map No: 14**

Antoine & Isabelle AGAPITOS
Le Mas Escombelle
La Villette
30430 Barjac
Gard
Tel: (0)4 66 24 54 77
Fax: (0)4 66 24 54 77
www.sawdays.co.uk

This fine old *bastide* (fortified farmhouse), built 200 years ago by Madame's great-grandfather, stands on the Ardèche River with its own private 'beach'. Rooms, some reached by the superb stone staircase, look over the romantic and much-painted ruined bridge or the squirrelly, tall-treed park where shade invites summer lingerers. Madame paints furniture, most prettily, and one room has hand-painted frieze and ceiling; Monsieur can accompany you on canoe trips (otter may be spotted) — an attractive, sociable couple who enjoy their guests. There's a small campsite on the property, but plenty of room for all.

Rooms: 1 quadruple, 1 triple, 2 double, 1 twin, each with shower & wc.

Price: 300 Frs (€ 45.73) for two, including breakfast.

Meals: In village.

Open: All year.

Gîte space for 8 people

From A7, Bollène exit onto D994 to Pont St Esprit. N86 dir. Bourg St Andéol; signposted before bridge across River Ardèche.

MMap 240-12 **ASP Map No: 14**

Mme de VERDUZAN
Pont d'Ardèche
30130 Pont St Esprit
Gard
Tel: (0)4 66 39 29 80
www.sawdays.co.uk

This magical C17 moated château (parts of it even C12) has its very own ghost, *la Dame à la Rose*. Towers overlook the monumental courtyard where Mary Stuart (later Queen of Scots) once walked. Madame runs a cultural centre and stages a summer music festival in this beautiful setting. Breakfast is in the courtyard or in the dining room. The exceptional bedrooms, with round tower bathrooms, have just been renovated with colourful details such as bright new satin canopies. The pool and sauna setup is a seductive addition.

Rooms: 3 double, 2 quadruple, 1 twin, all with bath & wc.

Price: 500 Frs (€ 76.22) for two, including breakfast.

Meals: Choice 5-10km.

Open: All year.

From Avignon, N580 dir. Bagnols sur Cèze. At junction in L'Ardoise, left along D9 dir. Laudun; signposted.

MMap 240-12 **ASP Map No: 14**

Gisèle & Jean-Louis BASTOUIL
Château de Lascours
30290 Laudun
Gard
Tel: (0)4 66 50 39 61
Fax: (0)4 66 50 30 08
e-mail: chateau.de.lascours@wanadoo.fr
www.sawdays.co.uk

A simple village home where guests have lots of space in their vaulted ground-floor suite and although it's right on the street, there's very little traffic in enchanting Pujaut. Helen and Jacques met while working in Africa, where she was a nurse and Jacques an agriculturist — they are an interesting and concerned couple (10% of their B&B income goes to development projects) and the house has many African mementoes; lots of pine, too. The pretty, peaceful, terraced garden now has a summer kitchen for guests but is not really suitable for adventurous toddlers. Super folk with whom to share good conversation over delicious suppers.

Rooms: 1 suite for 4 with shower & wc.

Price: 250 Frs (€ 38.11) for two, including breakfast. Extra bed 100 Frs.

Meals: 80 Frs, including wine & coffee. Summer kitchen.

Open: All year.

From Avignon & Villeneuve N580 dir. Bagnols sur Cèze then right on D377 & D177 to Pujaut. In village follow signs to 'Mairie' — Saba'ad is 300m into the old village from Mairie and church.

MMap 240-16 **ASP Map No: 14**

Helen THOMPSON & Jacques SERGENT
Saba'ad
Place des Consuls
30131 Pujaut, Gard
Tel: (0)4 90 26 31 68
Fax: (0)4 90 26 31 68

Mine host has created a new concept in house design: why treat horizontality as a given? Enter the main hall and then descend to the deep charms of the house. You plunge rapidly down the main shaft and follow the low ceilinged corridor reach the main reception room, a ravishingly black chamber. No views, but exquisite silence; you could hear a tap drip. The lighting is dim, by design; the décor sombre, with the odd flash of canary yellow. The furniture is Spartan, a nod to the minimalist style of the end of the millenium. Deep is your reverie, deep your adventure.

Rooms: Interconnecting suites, lined with finest bedrock.

Price: 200 Frs (€ 30.5) for two, including breakfast; group terms available.

Meals: 60 Frs, including mineral water.

Open: All year except weekends and national holidays.

From Creuse en Terre, N up valley for 1 km to La Celle d'Étin. Le Puits Dore is on the west side of the gorge. On arrival, press button on shaft and wait for lift.

Jean-Paul X. Cavateur
Le Puits Dore
30123 La Celle d'Étin
Gard
Tel: (0)4 05 06 07 08

On the wild plateau, protected by a multitude of medieval castles, the ancient hardwoods share the land with mild cows, hardy sheep and a few farmers – their ancestors ate those chestnuts, their pigs those acorns.

The Auvergne

In a beautiful, unsung part of France, cross the lovely old bridge over the Tarn into Quézac. You'd never guess Marius was a new house, it fits in so perfectly with its old stones, beams and doors and its warm, lived-in feel. Inside, if you could decorate it, it's been decorated, including a delightful mural of birds flying up the stairs. Dany and Pierre clearly adore embellishing their home, and spoiling their guests with an amazing array of delicacies from home-made *brioche* to home-grown organic veg to their speciality: *gâteau de noix* made with their own walnuts. Come hither, ye energetic sybarites.

Rooms: 3 double, each with shower & wc; 1 twin with bath, shower & wc.

Price: 250-300 Frs (€ 38.11-45.73) for two, including breakfast.

Meals: 100 Frs, including wine.

Open: All year.

Gîte space for 12 people

From A75 exit 39 on N88 E for 25km then right on N106 dir. Alès for 25km; at Ispagnac right to Quézac and follow signs in village.

MMap 240-6 **ASP Map No: 13**

Danièle MÉJEAN & Pierre PARENTINI
La Maison de Marius
8 rue du Pontet
48320 Quézac, Lozère
Tel: (0)4 66 44 25 05
Fax: (0)4 66 44 25 05

Superb for wildlife and outdoors lovers — orchids and other rare species plus canoeing, rock-climbing, hang-gliding — this is a *Gîte Panda* (providing detailed information on local fauna and flora, loaning binoculars) and Jean knows his region well. The C16 farmhouse has been restored with terracotta floors, old beams and white walls throughout. Jean made much of the pine furniture, including one splendid 'medieval' bed. The dining room has tapestries on the walls and antique farm furniture with the patina and fragrance of years of polish. Home-produced organic meat and veg are used for excellent regional meals.

Rooms: 5 double, 1 for 4/5, each with bath or shower & wc.

Price: 270 Frs (€ 41.16) for two, including breakfast; extra bed 60 Frs.

Meals: 90 or 105 Frs, excluding wine.

Open: April to mid-November.

From Millau N9 N to Aguessac. Just after leaving village right on D547 to Compeyre; left in village and follow signs for 2km.

MMap 240-10 **ASP Map No: 13**

Jean & Véronique LOMBARD-PRATMARTY
Quiers
12520 Compeyre
Aveyron
Tel: (0)5 65 59 85 10
Fax: (0)5 65 59 80 99

Here is a simple unpretentious home with a real family feel. The house is modern, the rolling Languedoc hills are wild and very ancient. You can put on your wings and join the paragliders and hang-gliders who launch themselves off a nearby cliff, or you can watch them from the safety of your breakfast table in the garden. It matters little that Henriette speaks no English: she is kind and welcoming and you can get a long way with smiles and sign language. The immaculate, simply and attractively furnished bedrooms include a suite which is perfect for a family,

Rooms: 1 double, 1 suite for 4, each with shower & wc.

Price: 240-260 Frs (€ 36.59-39.64) for two, including breakfast.

Meals: Choice in Millau 3km.

Open: All year.

From Millau D911 dir. Cahors. Just after leaving city limits right at 'Chenil' and 'Auberge' crossroads. Signposted. Follow small road for about 2km.

MMap 240-14 **ASP Map No: 13**

Mme Henriette CASSAN
Montels
12100 Millau
Aveyron
Tel: (0)5 65 60 51 70
www.sawdays.co.uk

A mini-hamlet in the calm green Aveyron where there is so much space. Two rooms, in the main house, each with a little terrace, look out over a typical old medieval château; the third, in an outbuilding, has a mezzanine; all are welcoming, two have cooking facilities. The garden is full of flowers, the view stupendous, your hosts solicitous and keen to help, providing for all your needs. The food is "outstanding and imaginative" — Pierre and Monique used to run a restaurant. *Well-behaved children and animals welcome.*

Rooms: 2 double, each with bath or shower & wc. In separate house: 2 double beds, bath & wc.

Price: 250-300 Frs (€ 38.11-45.73) for two, including breakfast.

Meals: 100 Frs, including wine & coffee.

Open: All year.

Gîte space for 8 people

From Villefranche, D922 south dir. Albi; at entrance to Sanvensa, follow signs on right to 'Monteillet Chambres d'Hôtes'.

MMap 235-15 **ASP Map No: 13**

Monique & Pierre BATESON
Monteillet Sanvensa
12200 Villefranche de Rouergue
Aveyron
Tel: (0)5 65 29 81 01
Fax: (0)5 65 29 81 01

They are the sweetest couple: warm, simple, unpretentious like their house. Their great, great-grandparents were born in Ols and their farm is a centre of activity in this small hamlet in wild Aveyron country. The biggest room is very fine with its old books and furniture and village prospect; you can sit in the pleasant garden and admire the ever-changing view. There are delightful footpaths to explore from the house or you can hire a horse or a bike locally. This is genuine farmhouse B&B at its best.

Rooms: 2 twin, 1 double, 1 triple, all with handbasins; shared bathroom.

Price: 200 Frs (€ 30.49) for two, including breakfast.

Meals: Occasionally. BBQ possible. Restaurant 4km.

Open: All year.

From Figeac, N122 dir. Villefranche de Rouergue. In Villeneuve d'Aveyron, D48 dir. Cajarc and Ols. In Ols, right following signpost for 'Chambres d'Hôtes'.

MMap 235-15 **ASP Map No: 13**

Marie-José & Gaston VIGUIÉ
Ols
12260 Villeneuve
Aveyron
Tel: (0)5 65 81 61 47

At the heart of rural France, the light plays on the fantastic shingled roofs made with stone from the ancient tumbling hillsides. Your host is a charming, well-educated farmer; his family has owned this tiny hamlet for 400 years. Views are stupendous, peace is centuries old, bathrooms are thoroughly up to date. A family-friendly scene, an open-armed welcome and in school holidays Jean's delightful children enjoy practising their English on guests. Rooms in the house are light well-furnished and share a refrigerator; the studios, with kitchens and terrace, are ideal for long stays (you may choose to do your own breakfast).

Rooms: Main house: 1 suite of 1 twin + 2 double rooms with bath/shower & wc; barn: 3 studios (1 for disabled), each with corner kitchen, bath/shower & wc

Price: Main house: 280 Frs (€ 42.69) for two; studios 300-400 Frs for two, all including breakfast; extra bed 100 Frs.

Meals: Restaurants nearby + self-catering.

Open: All year.

From Entraygues, D904 towards Mur de Barrez. 4.5km after Lacroix Barrez, right to Vilherols; signposted.

MMap 235-8 **ASP Map No: 13**

Jean LAURENS
Vilherols
12600 Lacroix Barrez
Aveyron
Tel: (0)5 65 66 08 24
Fax: (0)5 65 66 19 98

Your young hosts escaped from heaving, stressful Paris to this rural paradise. Their brilliant conversion of an old Cantal farmhouse has preserved the original scullery ledge and sink, made of vast slabs of stone, the beams, the inglenook fireplace. They now aim to convert their neighbours to better environmental (get the scrap metal off the hillside) and social (more respect for your woman?) attitudes. The rooms are well and simply done with good colours and fabrics and no unnecessary frippery; the meals are feasts, the Balleux a most interesting and happy couple.

Rooms: 1 double, 1 twin, 1 suite for 4 in main house; 2 suites in cottage; all with bath or shower & wc.

Price: 250-280 Frs (€ 38.11-42.69) for two, including breakfast; 1/2 board 195-215 Frs p.p.

Meals: 80 Frs, including wine & coffee.

Open: All year.

From Aurillac D920 to Arpajon; left on D990 for 10km (DON'T go to St Etienne de Carlat) then left dir. Caizac; signposted.

MMap 239-41 **ASP Map No: 13**

Francine & Jacky BALLEUX
Lou Ferradou
Caizac
15130 St Etienne de Carlat
Cantal
Tel: (0)4 71 62 42 37

A thoroughly restored old stone-walled, stone-shingled house, Manou's is typical of the Auvergne hills, which are ancient volcanoes where great rivers rise. She is a delight, as generous with her time as with her breakfasts: ham, cheese, three kinds of bread, *brioches*, *croissants*, home-made jam — the embroidered napkins give an idea of her attention to detail — served in the impressive dining room or the garden. Bedrooms are hung with silk, writing tables wait for you to be inspired to pen deathless prose, hairdryers hide in bathrooms; in short, every modern comfort against a timeless backdrop of drama and character.

Rooms: 2 double, 1 twin, 2 triple, all with shower & wc.

Price: 340 Frs (€ 51.83) for two, including breakfast.

Meals: Restaurant in village

Open: Mid-February to October.

From A71/75 exit 6 on D978/D996 W to Le Mont Dore (53km). Continue D996 W past 'Mairie' then 5km to Le Genestoux. House signposted in village.

MMap 239-18 **ASP Map No: 13**

Françoise Marie LARCHER
La Closerie de Manou
Le Genestoux
63240 Le Mont Dore
Puy-de-Dôme
Tel: (0)4 73 65 26 81
Fax: (0)4 73 81 11 72

Acres of parkland, a walled garden, a 12th-century vaulted chapel. The splendid rooms are utterly in keeping, from the vast, panelled, period-furnished drawing and dining rooms to big, beautiful bedrooms, with here a canopied bed, there an exquisite little dressing room, everywhere shimmering mirrors, fabulous views of ancient trees or the Puy-de-Dôme. A perfect hostess, Madame makes you feel immediately at ease and helps you plan your day over a most delicious breakfast. She can also show you how to make lace (*dentelle du Puy*).

Rooms: 3 double, 1 twin, 1 suite, all with bath and/or shower & wc.

Price: 425-555 Frs (€ 64.79-84.61) for two, including breakfast.

Meals: 150 Frs, including wine & coffee (by arrangement; not July/August.); choice nearby.

Open: April to October.

From Clermont Ferrand, A75 exit 13 to Parentignat; D999 dir. St Germain l'Hermite for 6km; signposted on right. (8km from A75 exit.)

MMap 239-20 **ASP Map No: 17**

Henriette MARCHAND
Château de Pasredon
63500 St Rémy de Chargnat
Puy-de-Dôme
Tel: (0)4 73 71 00 67
Fax: (0)4 73 71 08 72
www.sawdays.co.uk

A dream! Vaulx, a fairy-tale castle that was English during the Hundred Years' War, has been in the family for 800 years. Creak along the parquet, pray in the chapel, swan around the *salon*, sleep in one tower, bath in another. Room names are as evocative as furnishings are romantic — worthy of Sleeping Beauty, who would surely have woken up for breakfast of home-hive honey, *brioche*, yoghurt, eggs, cheese. Get to know your delightfully entertaining hosts, visit the donkey or, if you're feeling homesick, have a drink in Guy's *petit pub* with its fantastic collection of beer mats.

Rooms: 2 triple, 1 double, each with bath or shower & wc.

Price: 300 Frs (€ 45.73) for two, including breakfast.

Meals: 80-120 Frs, including aperitif & wine.

Open: All year.

Gîte space for 5 people

From A72 exit 3 on D7 through Celles sur Durolle to Col du Frissonnet. Château is the first right after the Col.

MMap 239-21 **ASP Map No: 8**

Guy & Régine DUMAS de VAULX
Château de Vaulx
63120 Sainte Agathe
Puy-de-Dôme
Tel: (0)4 73 51 50 55
Fax: (0)4 73 51 50 55

The lava of the surrounding volcanoes provided the stone flags for the dining room floor of this handsome, family house. Élisabeth is bright and enthusiastic, her interior is uncluttered, sober and furnished with antiques and soft textiles. Each room is named after an ancestor; we liked *Guillaume* best — canopied bed, Japanese grass paper, lovely Louis XV *armoire*, cabinet full of old *objets* — but they are all superb, the garden a treat for sunlit breakfasts, the cast-iron *Godin* stove warming in winter, the outbuildings full of character.

Rooms: 3 double, all with shower & wc.

Price: 300-350 Frs (€ 45.73-53.36) for two, including breakfast.

Meals: Wide choice 5-8km.

Open: All year (Nov to March by arrangement only).

From A71, Riom exit, N144 dir. Combronde & Montluçon. 2.5km after Davayat, right onto D122 to Chaptes.

MMap 239-7 **ASP Map No: 8**

Mme Élisabeth BEAUJEARD
8 route de la Limagne
Chaptes
63460 Beauregard Vendon
Puy-de-Dôme
Tel: (0)4 73 63 35 62

Peaceful at the end of a long drive, this is a special place, albeit more formal than some. The Montaignacs are elegant, immaculate and gracious, like their dining room with its panelling and breakfast silver — the epitome of Old France. Choose the ground-floor, original-parqueted, fireplaced suite or glide up the fine staircase past the ancestors to the double room. Both welcome you with antiques, old engravings, personality. Monsieur knows books-worth of fascinating history; Madame is quietly attentive.

Rooms: 1 suite for 2-4 people, 1 twin, both with bath or shower & wc.

Price: 550 Frs (€ 83.85) for two, including breakfast.

Meals: Choice within 9km.

Open: All year (by arrangement October to May).

From Montluçon, N145 dir. Chamblet; signposted on the right.

MMap 238-44 **ASP Map No: 8**

Yves & Jacqueline de MONTAIGNAC
Château du Plaix
03170 Chamblet
Allier
Tel: (0)4 70 07 80 56

The C14th origins of this gloriously isolated house, once a fortified manor, are still evident but it is a far cry from the ruin your hosts bought 30 years ago. They have restored it beautifully, making big, cosy, subtly-lit rooms that are lovingly decorated with family antiques and memorabilia and reached by a delicious spiral staircase — a treat. Their sheep graze safely in the the fields which surround the house — here, you can walk, fish and hunt mushrooms in season. The easy, good-natured Raucaz open their hearts and dining table to all; this is really somewhere you can feel at home and relax.

Rooms: 1 double, 1 twin, 2 triple, each with bath or shower & wc.

Price: 220-240 Frs (€ 33.54-36.59) for two, including breakfast.

Meals: 80 Frs, including wine.

Open: All year.

From Nevers N7 S 22km; right on D978a to Le Veudre; there D13 then D234 to Pouzy Mésangy. Signposted.

MMap 238-32 **ASP Map No: 8**

Claire RAUCAZ
Manoir Le Plaix
Pouzy Mésangy
03320 Lurcy Levis
Allier
Tel: (0)4 70 66 24 06
Fax: (0)4 70 66 25 82

Do stay a few days in this charmingly typical Napoleon III manor house, square and confident in its five acres of parkland (with tennis court) and the famous Troisgros restaurant just 8km away. There are fine walks (all levels of difficulty) to help work up an appetite for the local gastronomy. You are guest in a family home, your antique-furnished bedroom has its own character, the bath is a claw-footed marvel (plenty of towels and bathrobes to go with it) and Madame a gentle friendly widow. She loves sharing a welcome cup of something with new people and guiding them to the hidden delights of this lovely area. *Ask about pets.*

Rooms: 1 double with shower & wc; 1 suite for 3/4 with bath & wc.

Price: 350 Frs (€ 53.36) for two, 500 Frs suite for three, including breakfast.

Meals: Choice within 3km; Roanne 8km.

Open: Mid-March to mid-Nov (in winter by arrangement).

 small

From Roanne D53 for 8km. Right into village & follow signs.

MMap 239-10 **ASP Map No: 8**

Mme GAUME
Domaine de Champfleury
42155 Lentigny
Loire
Tel: (0)4 77 63 31 43
Fax: (0)4 77 63 31 43
www.sawdays.co.uk

Once upon a time, kindly Anne-Marie lived in a big town. One day she found her dream house in the Auvergne near deep mysterious woods and babbling brooks so she left the city, lovingly restored her house, installed her old family furniture and opened the door so that visitors could share her dream. So, after a delicious supper, before the roaring fire, Anne-Marie may treat you to a fairy tale of her own making. (She also offers breathing and relaxation courses.) Thus you will all live happily ever after and never forget this exceptional woman.

Rooms: 2 triple, 2 twin, 1 double, each with shower & wc.

Price: 250-350 Frs (€ 38.11-53.36) for two, including breakfast. Extra person 80 Frs.

Meals: 85 Frs, including wine & coffee.

Open: All year.

From A72 exit 4 onto D53 E to Champoly. Here D24 E to St Marcel d'Urfé then D20 S towards St Martin la Sauveté and follow signs.

MMap 239-22 **ASP Map No: 8**

Anne-Marie HAUCK
Il fut un temps, Les Gouttes
42430 St Marcel d'Urfé, Loire
Tel: (0)4 77 62 52 19/
(0)6 86 96 59 67
Fax: (0)4 77 62 52 19
e-mail: anne-marie.hauck@wanadoo.fr
www.eazyweb.co.uk/ilfut

Remote, unsung, green wooded hills, secret streams... and such a welcome! The old farmhouse exudes warmth from its rare original panelling (clock case included) to its great stone fireplace. The stables (a 15-metre tree carries the ceiling) have become a magnificent breakfast/sitting room, full of the Champels' lovely treasures. The rooms, formerly the children's, have character and individuality, from Rococo Venetian to English Country (one, amazingly, houses an engraving of Swindon!), with excellent bathrooms. And your hosts are generous, well-travelled people. A great place to stay, go for long walks, then return to a blazing log fire.

Rooms: 3 double, 2 twin, all with shower & wc (2 ensuite, 2 separate, 1 curtained off).

Price: 300 Frs (€ 45.73) for two, including breakfast.

Meals: Choice 5km. Picnics possible.

Open: All year.

From Le Puy en Velay N102 dir. Brioude for 10km then D906 dir. La Chaise Dieu for 15km then D1 through Craponne onto D498 dir. St Étienne for 3km; following signs, turn left up hill, house is 1st on left.

MMap 239-46 **ASP Map No: 13**

Éliane & François CHAMPEL
Paulagnac
43500 Craponne sur Arzon
Haute-Loire
Tel: (0)4 71 03 26 37
Fax: (0)4 71 03 26 37
e-mail: fr.champel@wanadoo.fr
www.sawdays.co.uk

Catherine, Bill and *Valentin* — a rare trio awaits you in this fairy-tale spot where the forest laps up to the edge of the hill-top village and its once-abandoned inn. The Hays left the bright lights of entertaining — he directed, she acted (opposite Peter Sellers, 007,...) — for the old *auberge* whose name was/will be Bill's in another life (they'll tell you all over dinner, in several languages). He, with great painting talent, has waved his magic wand over walls, furniture, bathtubs; she receives magnificently. Their combined sensitivities make it supremely memorable.

Rooms: 1 suite for 4, 3 double, 1 twin, each with bath or shower & wc.

Price: 290-320 Frs (€ 44.21-48.78) for two, including breakfast. Extra bed 50-70 Frs.

Meals: 110 Frs, including wine & coffee.

Open: All year.

From Clermont Ferrand A75 to Issoire exit 13 on D999 to La Chaise Dieu then S on D906 dir. Le Puy; after 100m left on D20 — follow signs for 6km.

MMap 239-34 **ASP Map No: 13**

Bill & Catherine HAYS
Chambres d'Hôtes 'Valentin'
Le Bourg
43160 Bonneval
Haute-Loire
Tel: (0)4 71 00 07 47
www.sawdays.co.uk

Once part of the ramparts of this ancient city, the old townhouse has been furnished and decorated by mother and daughter in classically French manner with proper antiques on stylish parquet floors. Dinner both looks and tastes good — true Gallic cuisine enhanced by bone china, family silver and Bohemian crystal. Hear the great organ nearby and the famous music festival (August), walk the excellent hiking paths from the back door, then return to wallow in the gentle, floral, boudoir-like comfort of La Jacquerolle.

Rooms: 2 triple, 2 double, 1 twin, each with bath or shower & wc.

Price: 300 Frs (€ 45.73) for two, including breakfast. Extra bed 80 Frs.

Meals: 120 Frs, including wine & coffee.

Open: All year.

From Brioude D19 to La Chaise Dieu. Follow signs to 'Centre Ville'; in front of Abbey turn right to Place du Monument. Park here — house is just off the square at bottom right-hand corner.

MMap 239-33 **ASP Map No: 13**

Jacqueline & Carole CHAILLY
La Jacquerolle
Rue Marchédial
43160 La Chaise Dieu
Haute-Loire
Tel: (0)4 71 00 07 52
www.sawdays.co.uk

Walkers! Join a circuit here and walk from B&B to B&B in this superbly unspoilt area; or cross-country ski it in winter. Simple, unaffected people will love Rosa, her somewhat dated décor and her fabulous home-grown, home-made food which oozes genuine natural goodness. A real old soldier, she manages the flock of milk-producing sheep, is surrounded by grandchildren and welcomes all-comers with a 'cup of friendship' before her great granite hearth. The house is warm, the rooms perfectly adequate, the hostess unforgettable.

Rooms: 1 double, 1 twin & 1 triple room, all with own shower & wc.

Price: 200 Frs (€ 30.49) for two, including breakfast. Terms for children & groups.

Meals: 70 Frs, including wine & coffee.

Open: Mid-January to mid-December.

From Le Puy en Velay, D589 to Saugues then D585 dir. Langeac, turning left onto D32 to Venteuges.

MMap 239-45 **ASP Map No: 13**

Rosa DUMAS
Le Bourg
43170 Venteuges
Haute-Loire
Tel: (0)4 71 77 80 66

In few places in France can you eat so well for so little — almost everything is produced on the farm. Bread and jam are home-made, their bees produce the honey and you can help with the milking. Bugeac is a tiny hamlet high up in the Massif Central, worth every metre you travel; the walking is wonderful and the house is a pæan to wood which Paul has fashioned into plank, wardrobe, bed and table. The rooms have wooden floors and ceilings, simple fabrics and pretty iron beds. When the snow blankets the world around it is still lovely.

Rooms: 1 double, 1 twin, 1 triple, 1 family room for 4/5, each with shower & wc.

Price: 200 Frs (€ 30.49) for two, including breakfast.

Meals: 70 Frs, including wine & coffee.

Open: All year.

From A75 exit 34 dir. St Chély d'Apcher then NE on D989 to Le Malzieu. Just after Le Malzieu right on D48/D33 for Saugues, over 'Pas de l'Ane' pass; signposted in Bugeac.

MMap 239-45 **ASP Map No: 13**

Martine & Paul CUBIZOLLE
Bugeac
43170 Grèzes
Haute-Loire
Tel: (0)4 71 74 45 30
Fax: (0)4 71 74 45 30

Country peace wafts over the pine stands and fields: the area is an 'animal refuge' where the landowner has forbidden shooting so there are lots of animals to be seen — a rarity in France. Small, simple rooms with basic pine furniture, pretty curtains, functional shower rooms and a solid stone farmhouse to enclose them. Those stones, and wood and tiles, are visible all over the house and the dining room is most welcoming — dinner is great value. The family are delightfully natural, gentle and connected to real life and the children help out with breakfast. There are no frills but you lack for nothing in a memorable setting.

Rooms: 1 quadruple, 1 triple, 2 double, all with shower & wc.

Price: 240 Frs (€ 36.59) for two, including breakfast (half-board only mid-June/mid-Sept).

Meals: 65 Frs, including aperitif, wine & coffee.

Open: All year.

Gîte space for 8 people

From Tence dir. Ste Agrève. After roundabout (between supermarket and 'Gendarmerie') D185 for 800m then left at 'La Pomme' sign & follow Chambres d'Hôtes.

MMap 239-36 **ASP Map No: 14**

Elyane & Gérard DEYGAS
Les Grillons
La Pomme
43190 Tence
Haute-Loire
Tel: (0)4 71 59 89 33

REGIONAL FOOD LABELS – À la manière de.../In the manner of...

À l'Alsacienne *With sauerkraut and sausage*
À l'Américaine *A corruption of À l'Armoricaine Armor being the Celti[c] name for Brittany with tomato sauce and shallots*
À l'Anglaise *Plain boiled*
À l'Ardennaise *With juniper berries*
À l'Auvergnate *With cabbage and bits of bacon*
À la Basquaise *With onions, sweet peppers, rice an[d] possibly Bayonne cured ham*
À la Bordelaise *Bordeaux style, with red wine shallots and bone marrow*
À la Bourguignonne *Burgundy style, with red wine onions, mushrooms and bacon*
À la Bretonne *With leeks, celery and beans (cf Américaine above for anothe[r] Bretonne)*
À la Dauphinoise *With cream, garlic and sometime[s] cheese*
À la Dijonnaise *With mustard sauce*
À la Flamande *Flemish style: cooked in beer or vinegar*
À la Lyonnaise *With onions, wine, vinegar, an[d] often sausage*
À la Niçoise *With anchovies and olives*
À la Normande *With cream*
À la Périgourdine *With goose liver and truffles*
À la Provençale *With tomatoes, garlic, olive oi[l]*
À la Savoyarde *With cream and cheese*

And four supra-regional manners:–

À la Bonne Femme *Good Woman style, wit[h] white wine, shallots and mushrooms*
À la Bourgeoise *Townswoman style, with [a] sauce of carrots, onions and bacon*
À la Ménagére *Housewife style, with onion[s] potatoes, carrots, turnips, pea[s]*
À la Paysanne *Peasant Woman/Countr[y] Woman style, with vegetables*

This valley flows past the greatest chefs of France, the woods where wild boar (and tame pigs) hunt big black truffles, and the hills where the Gauls fought so bravely their last fight against the Roman legions.

The Rhône Valley

Jean-Michel is inexhaustible: having virtually rebuilt the old mill (part of the *château*) on its spectacular ravine site where basalt prisms shimmer and the falling stream sings (and powers his generator), he is extending his walkers' dormitories, improving his superb hiking/biking itineraries, keeping donkeys to clear the land and carry small children (over five only) or hikers' packs, making lovely wooden toys, apple juice; Madame cares for five good sober rooms, serves local honey and yoghurt at one long breakfast table and the fire glows. They long for you to STAY and discover the beauty at the heart of their lovely mountain.

Rooms: 5 twin rooms, all with bath & wc.

Price: 250-270 Frs (€ 38.11-41.16) for two, including breakfast. Extra bed 100 Frs.

Meals: Occasionally 90-100 Frs, incl. wine & coffee. Restaurants 3-6km.

Open: All year.

Gîte space for 15 people

From Aubenas D104 to Vals les Bains; D578 dir. Le Cheylard. Leaving Vals, left on D243 to La Bastide sur B.; D254 dir. Aizac, past tennis courts; 300m after bridge right down sharp bend.

MMap 239-48 **ASP Map No: 14**

Bernadette & Jean-Michel FRANÇOIS
Le Château
07600 La Bastide sur Besorgues
Ardèche
Tel: (0)4 75 88 23 67
Fax: (0)4 75 88 23 67
e-mail: jean-michel.francois4@wanadoo.fr

617

How to describe paradise in one short paragraph? The setting: high, rural, hidden, silent. The views: long, of mountain peaks, inspiring. The house: lovingly restored, of stone, and wood from the surrounding chestnut forests, light, open, lovely. Bedrooms: just right. Food: organic, home-grown, imaginative... and there's lots of honey. Your hosts are warm and trusting, quickly your friends. Gil is a carpenter in winter and a bee-keeper in summer. Come up the long narrow road to walk, talk, and believe us.

Rooms: 1 suite for 5, 1 triple, 1 double, each with shower & wc.

Price: 280 Frs (€ 42.69) for two, including breakfast.

Meals: 95 Frs, including wine & coffee.

Open: All year except Christmas.

From Aubenas N102 W dir. Le Puy for 8.5km. At Lalevade left to Jaujac. By 'Café des Lorsips', cross river & follow signs 4km along narrow mountain road.

MMap 239-48 **ASP Map No: 14**

Marie & Gil FLORENCE
Les Roudils
07380 Jaujac
Ardèche
Tel: (0)4 75 93 21 11
www.sawdays.co.uk

618

Take your time: the drive up is spectacular. Then you arrive for a drink on the terrace, a gasp at the view across the valley and time to stay and unwind. Judas trees enchant, bright flowers tumble over terraces, the 400-year-old house has nooks and crannies around a small courtyard, cosy bedrooms, a magnificent vaulted sitting room, PLUS heated pool, sauna, telescope, music system, stupendous walking... Henri is smiling and positive, Jacote quieter and twinkly; they are good, interesting hosts and provide excellent food (home-made sorbets to die for) with locally-made ingredients (also for sale).

Rooms: 3 double, 1 twin, 2 quadruple, all with shower & wc.

Price: 290-390 Frs (€ 44.21-59.46) for two, including breakfast. Extra bed 135 Frs.

Meals: 110 Frs, including wine & coffee.

Open: April to December (by arrangement in winter).

From Joyeuse D203 dir. Valgorge. At Pont du Gua cross bridge and take narrow paved road up hillside to La Roche (10 hairpins in 3km!).

Map 240-3 **ASP Map No: 14**

ri & Jacote ROUVIÈRE
tite Cour Verte
La Roche Beaumont
e
4 75 39 58 88
75 39 43 00
ri.rouviere@wanadoo.fr

Add the daily gift of spectacular beauty all round, in this piece of beautiful, wooded Ardèche, to good food and good conversation with your gentle hosts in their old farmhouse (possibly built with aristocratic stones sold off by the French Revolution) and you have heaven. Myriam, Claude and their children surely inhabit a corner of paradise; come commune with them, with nature and occasionally with their parrot. Claude will ride with you (he has three docile mounts), there are magnificent walks, river pools for swimming, a special meal to come back to with home-produced cheese, honey, fruit, vegetables... many organic.

Rooms: 1 double with own shower & wc; 2 double, 1 twin, each with shower, sharing wc.

Price: 240-280 Frs (€ 36.59-42.69) for two, including breakfast.

Meals: 85 Frs, including wine.

Open: All year.

From Montélimar, N102 to Aubenas; N104 dir. Alès 16km; right on D5 to Largentière; D24 dir. Valgorge 12km then left into Rocles; 300m after church.

MMap 240-3 **ASP Map No: 14**

Myriam & Claude ROUVIÈRE
La Croze
07110 Rocles
Ardèche
Tel: (0)4 75 88 31 43
Fax: (0)4 75 88 31 43

In this glorious setting, let the wild Ardèche landscape be your playground or the backdrop for total relaxation. Take walking boots, jodhpurs, bike, canoe, hang-glider, or just yourselves, and you'll be warmly welcomed. Surrounded by almond trees, fields of lavender and mountains, this peaceful, farmhouse is truly *en pleine nature*. Monsieur has elevated 'home brew' onto a new plane, making aperitifs and digestifs to go with Madame's local dishes, eaten *en famille*. Simply-furnished rooms, each with its own entrance, vary in size and style and there's a charming stone-vaulted dayroom.

Rooms: 1 quadruple, 1 triple, 2 double, all with bath or shower & wc.

Price: 260 Frs (€ 39.64) for two, including breakfast. Extra bed 60-80 Frs.

Meals: 90 Frs, including wine & coffee (not Sundays).

Open: All year.

From Bourg St Andéol D4 to St Remèze then D362 dir. Gras. Signposted on right.

MMap 240-8 **ASP Map No: 14**

Sylvette & Gérard MIALON
La Martinade
07700 St Remèze
Ardèche
Tel: (0)4 75 98 89 42
Fax: (0)4 75 04 36 30
e-mail: sylvetlm@aol.com
www.angelfire.com/la/lamartinade/

No pretences here: if you enjoy people who have long experience of real country life, then do go and stay with the well-educated, happy and relaxed Pagis family in their creeper-clad, wisteria-hung farmhouse in this forgotten corner of the Drôme. A fountain titters in the courtyard, breakfast and dinner include home-made jams, eggs and vegetables from their superb and productive kitchen garden and, in season, truffles hunted in their own secret ways. They are generous and off-beat, the two guestrooms share a kitchen and, moreover, Jean-Jacques plays trumpet in the local salsa band.

Rooms: 1 double, 1 quadruple, sharing kitchen, bath & wc.

Price: 200 Frs (€ 30.49) for two, including breakfast.

Meals: By arrangement 75 Frs, including wine. Self-catering.

Open: March to November.

From Vaison la Romaine D938 dir. Malaucène for 4km. Left on D13 for 8km. Right on D40 to Montbrun les Bains then right dir. Sault. House 1km along on left.

MMap 245-18 **ASP Map No:**

Jean-Jacques & Agnès PAGIS
Le Chavoul
Reilhanette
26570 Montbrun les Bains
Drôme
Tel: (0)4 75 28 80 80

This welcoming young couple have been known to drive guests up the valley so they can then walk back, in the shallow river (sic), to the house, stopping for a picnic en route — the river runs at the bottom of their garden which is really fields and trees against the backdrop of those spectacular hills — superb walking country. The old house (it was Marc's grandparents') vibrates with Provençal colours — ochre outside, daringly combined reds, yellows, dusky roses, blue splashes in simply-furnished rooms inside. Valérie, who has travelled, enjoys having guests to balance her days with baby daughter Anouk.

Rooms: 2 double, 1 twin 1 triple, each with shower & wc.

Price: 230 Frs (€ 35.06) for two, including breakfast.

Meals: In Mollans 2.5km.

Open: April to mid-November.

From Vaison la Romaine D938 S for 3.5km; left on D54/D13 dir. Mollans sur Ouvèze for 8km; right on D40 for 1.2km; right on D242 dir. Veaux for 1km; right at sign.

MMap 245-17 **ASP Map No: 14**

Marc & Valérie GRENON
Les Fouzarailles
Route de Veaux
26170 Mollans sur Ouvèze
Drôme
Tel: (0)4 75 28 79 05
Fax: (0)4 75 28 79 05

Madame has been receiving guests for years now in her old farmhouse and provides honest, efficient hospitality. The bedrooms, small with rather unmatched fabrics (and one shower room curtained off), have individual entrances and refrigerators; the family suite feels better with its higher ceilings. Despite the area's vast store of cultural delights (Vaison la Romaine, Mont Ventoux, hilltop villages and wine cellars), it is for Madame's Provençal cooking that guests return. Her skills are recognised in the area and her dinner, with home-grown vegetables, round the big communal table is a most convivial affair.

Rooms: 1 double, 2 twin and 1 family suite for 6, all with shower & wc.

Price: 230-260 Frs (€ 35.06-39.64) for two, including breakfast.

Meals: 90 Frs, including wine & coffee.

Open: 15 February to 15 November.

Gîte space for 15 people

From Vaison la Romaine, D938 dir. Malaucène; after 2km, left onto D54 to Entrechaux; D13 and D5 to Mollans sur Ouvèze; D46 dir. Faucon for 2km. Turn right at sign — house 600m.

MMap 245-17 **ASP Map No: 14**

Rose-Marie BERNARD-BIR
Quartier Ayguemarse
26170 Mollans sur Ouvèze
Drôme
Tel: (0)4 75 28 73 59

The hard-working Cornillons bought this ruined 1769 farmhouse in the 1960s and have laboured diligently to create their beautiful property and the surrounding vineyards. The bedrooms have dark beams, lovely old doors over new cupboards and views out across lavender fields or the chestnut-shaded courtyard. The new double has a super-luxy bathroom, jacuzzi and an extra-big bed. The dining/sitting room, with an open fire for winter warmth after a truffle expedition, is very snug and everyone eats together at the long wooden table. There is a cleverly-hidden swimming pool, too.

Rooms: 4 double, 1 twin, 1 triple, all with bath & wc, 1 with jacuzzi.

Price: From 400 Frs (€ 60.98) for two, 600 Frs deluxe room, including breakfast.

Meals: 150 Frs, excluding wine.

Open: All year.

Gîte space for 6 people

From Montélimar, N7 for Orange. At Bollène, D994 to Suze la Rousse. There, D59 for St Paul Trois Châteaux; right on D117 to La Baume de Transit; signposted.

MMap 240-8 **ASP Map No: 14**

Ludovic & Eliane CORNILLON
Domaine de Saint-Luc
26130 La Baume de Transit
Drôme
Tel: (0)4 75 98 11 51
Fax: (0)4 75 98 19 22

The ever-delightful and energetic Prothons are still renovating their C17 coaching inn. The great high hay barn has been put to superb use: each guestroom has a mezzanine and views through one normal and one roof window to the magnificent countryside, though mezzanine stairs are VERY steep. Lots of friendly old furniture, and one room has one of the antique loos from the old house (the other is downstairs). Meals, in the family dining room or outside, are made with fresh products from the younger Prothons' farm; there are truffle weekends in winter and a welcoming fireplace. A hard-working and wonderfully friendly place.

Rooms: 3 triple/quadruple, each with shower & wc.

Price: 280-300 Frs (€ 42.69-45.73) for two, including breakfast.

Meals: 80-120 Frs, including wine.

Open: All year except 15 Dec to 15 Jan.

Gîte space for 5 people

From A7 exit 18 onto N7 S dir. Avignon for 2km then left on D133 dir. Grignan for 5km. Just before Valaurie, right dir. St Paul 3 Châteaux (D133) for 2km — house on right 200m from road.

MMap 240-8 **ASP Map No: 14**

Marie-Claire (Mick) & François PROTHON
Val Léron
26230 Valaurie
Drôme
Tel: (0)4 75 98 52 52
Fax: (0)4 75 98 52 52

The stone cross-vaulting in the dining room is wonderful and Francis has renovated the rest of the house with loving care. He has poured his energy into giving new life to old beams and tiles. He was once an engineer and knows about structures, old and new. Jackie is an artist... "And it shows", says a reader. There is a huge organic vegetable garden, producing the basics, plus fruit and eggs, for some superb meals. The rooms are perfectly simple, not a frill too many. Lively and charming people living in lovely countryside.

Rooms: 2 triple, 1 double, 1 twin, each with bath or shower & wc.

Price: 295-325 Frs (€ 44.97-49.55) for two, including breakfast.

Meals: 100 Frs, including coffee.

Open: All year.

From Montélimar D540 E to La Batie Rolland (10km). In village left onto D134 dir. St Gervais; signposted on left.

MMap 240-4 **ASP Map No: 14**

Francis & Jackie MONEL
La Joie
26160 La Batie Rolland
Drôme
Tel: (0)4 75 53 81 51
Fax: (0)4 75 53 81 51
e-mail: f.monel@infonie.fr
www.sawdays.co.uk

Walk in the enchanting park, designed by the famous C17 Le Nôtre studio, swim in the nearby river, drink in the shining views of the Vercors. Evelyne is an artist who loves people, has a permanent exhibition of well-known contemporary artists and also opens her busy, lively château to groups studying meditation, music and massage in the summer. All the food is organic and vegetarian dishes no problem. The big simply-furnished, wood-floored bedrooms have some fine antiques though the bathrooms, across the corridor, seem a little basic. The house can sleep large groups during courses but never when B&B guests are there.

Rooms: 3 twin, one with shower & wc, 1 with shower, sharing wc, 1 sharing shower & wc.

Price: 290-310 Frs (€ 44.21-47.26) for two, including breakfast (min. 2 nights).

Meals: Occasionally 90 Frs, including table wine & coffee.

Open: All year (bookings only).

From Crest, D93 to Mirabel et Blacons. Château on left as you leave village with sign 'Galerie Arbre de Vie' on wall.

MMap 245-4 **ASP Map No: 14**

Evelyne LATUNE
Château de Blacons
26400 Mirabel et Blacons, Crest
Drôme
Tel: (0)4 75 40 01 00
Fax: (0)4 75 40 04 97

Madame alone is worth the detour: her kindliness infuses her home — one that, at first glance, is coy about its age or charms; her eventful life has nourished a wicked sense of humour but no bitterness and she is a natural story-teller (she'll show you the photographs too). The slightly fading carpets and small shower rooms become incidental after a short while. Enjoy, instead, the pretty bedrooms, the peace of the lush leafy garden, which shelters the house from the road, and relish breakfast — home-made jams and cake, organic honeys, cheese- where the table is a picture in itself.

Rooms: 2 twin, 1 single/twin, each with own shower & wc.

Price: 230-275 Frs (€ 35.06-41.92) for two, including breakfast; extra bed 60 Frs.

Meals: Restaurant 2km away.

Open: All year.

From A7 Valence Sud exit onto A49 dir. Grenoble. At exit 33 right on D538a dir. Beaumont. After 2.6km, right at sign 'Chambres d'Hôtes/Chambedeau' — house 800m along on right.

MMap 244-36 **ASP Map No: 14**

Mme Lina de CHIVRÉ-DUMOND
Chambedeau
26760 Beaumont lès Valence
Drôme
Tel: (0)4 75 59 71 70
Fax: (0)4 75 59 75 24
e-mail: linadechivredumond@minitel.net
www.fleurs-soleil.tm.fr

This artistic, caring couple are deeply concerned with social and ecological issues. They have renovated their farmhouse with sensitivity and an eye for detail, using nothing but authentic materials. Art-lovers will enjoy the summer exhibitions and courses as well as Madame's beautifully-made china dolls. Guest quarters, in a separate building, have good rooms and handsome carpentry by Mado's son. Organic meals with home-grown vegetables and fruit in season are served in the vaulted guest dining room or on the terrace. A special house with a special atmosphere.

Rooms: 3 double, 1 suite for 4, all with bath or shower & wc.

Price: 250-380 Frs (€ 38.11-57.93) for two, including breakfast (2 nights min).

Meals: 85 Frs, including wine & coffee.

Open: All year.

From Chabeuil, D538 dir. Crest for 5km (ignore signs for Montvendre). Left at sign 'Les Dourcines'; house 700m on right next to 'Auberge-Restaurant' sign.

MMap 244-37 **ASP Map No: 14**

Mado GOLDSTEIN & Bernard DUPONT
Les Dourcines
26120 Montvendre
Drôme
Tel: (0)4 75 59 24 27

Madame is the grandmother we all dream of, a sprightly, delightful woman who cossets her guests, putting sweets and fruit in the bedrooms. This old stone farmhouse facing the Vercors mountains is definitely a family home (the family has been here since 1680!), so meals of regional dishes with local wine can be very jolly with family, friends and guests all sharing the long wooden table in the kitchen. The roomy, old-fashioned bedrooms have lovely walnut *armoires* and the bright, new suite has a tiny single attached for children.

Rooms: 3 triple, both with bath or shower & wc.

Price: 220 Frs (€ 33.54) for two, including breakfast; extra bed 75 Frs.

Meals: 80 Frs, including wine & coffee.

Open: All year.

Gîte space for 9 people

From A6 exit Valence Sud on D68 to Chabeuil. There, cross river and turn left on D154 dir. Combovin for 5km; signposted.

MMap 244-37 **ASP Map No: 14**

Mme Madeleine CABANES
Les Péris
CD 154 — Route de Combovin
26120 Châteaudouble
Drôme
Tel: (0)4 75 59 80 51
Fax: (0)4 75 59 48 78
www.sawdays.co.uk

Sample the simple country life at this friendly, hard-working poultry farm which has been in the family for a century. Despite 5,000 eggs to collect before breakfast, Madame always finds time to spend with guests. The bedrooms are in a separate wing of the farm with unfussy modern interiors, interesting antique beds and pretty floral linen. Meals of regional food are served family-style and include home-produced vegetables, fruit and... eggs. The setting, at the foot of Mont Vercors, is very peaceful and the whole place has been "re-harmonised using geo-biology" for everyone's better-being.

Rooms: 2 double, 1 triple, each with shower or bath & wc.

Price: 255 Frs (€ 38.87) for two, including breakfast. Extra bed 64 Frs.

Meals: 75 Frs, including wine & coffee.

Open: All year.

From Romans D538 to Alixan. Through Alixan dir. Chabeuil; on leaving village, left by 'Boulangerie', turn left & follow 'Chambres d'Hôtes Les Marais St Didier' signs for 3km — farm on left.

MMap 244-37 **ASP Map No: 14**

Christiane & Jean-Pierre IMBERT
Le Marais
26300 St Didier de Charpey
Drôme
Tel: (0)4 75 47 03 50/
(0)6 68 92 74 16
www.rent-a-holiday.com/info/imbert

They are a perfect team in their shimmeringly lovely house and garden. Renée's garden is a horticultural delight where colours run rife; Jacques wears the chef's hat: breakfast on home-made muffins, dine on refined regional dishes with fresh-picked herbs — he may join you for dessert on the covered terrace where plants flower in big pots. Bedrooms, large, luminous and immaculate, have antique headboards, open out onto the terrace or garden and have good modern bathrooms. Welcoming, life-loving people who will even put fresh fruit in your room every day.

Rooms: 3 double, each with bath or shower & wc.

Price: 350 Frs (€ 53.36) for two, incl. breakfast; babies free; 2-14 yrs 60 Frs.

Meals: 120 Frs, including aperitif, wine & coffee. Children 50 Frs.

Open: April to mid-November; winter by arrangement.

From A7 exit 15 dir. Grenoble then exit 34 dir. Chabeuil for 6km. In Alixan right at 'Epicerie' on D101 dir. Besayes for 500m, then left — 1st house on right.

MMap 244-37 **ASP Map No: 14**

Jacques & Renée CRAMMER
L'Eygalière
Quartier Coussaud
26300 Alixan
Drôme
Tel: (0)4 75 47 11 13
Fax: (0)4 75 47 13 35
e-mail: jcrammer@easynet.fr

There's a time-warp feel to this 1970s villa high above the valley outside Valence: dark floral wallpaper covers hall, stairs and bedrooms, animal skins cover floors and modern sofas, interesting modern sculptures call from *salon* and stairs. Your hostess is interesting, enthusiastic and hugely welcoming, a gift inherited from Armenian parents. Breakfast (hot croissants and home-made organic jam) on the terrace and admire the magnificent chalk escarpments of the Vercors range (beyond less attractive St Marcel). Little traffic noise can be heard. Careful: this is the B&B on the LEFT hand side of the road.

Rooms: 1 twin with shower & wc, 1 double with bath & wc.

Price: 280-320 Frs (€ 42.69-48.78) for two, including breakfast.

Meals: Vast choice in Valence 5km.

Open: All year.

From A7 exit 14; through Bourg lès Valence; left on N532 dir. Romans/ Grenoble; exit to St Marcel. At 'Place de la Mairie' left to Stop, straight across, under bridge, straight on up hill (total 1400m) — house on LEFT round hairpin.

MMap 244-36 **ASP Map No: 14**

Marie-Jeanne KATCHIKIAN
La Pineraie
383 Chemin Bel Air
26320 St Marcel lès Valence
Drôme
Tel: (0)4 75 58 72 25
e-mail:
marie.katchikian@club.francetelecom.fr

The Barrs are English and Irish but haved lived in France for 25 years so are pretty well French too. Mary, an easy, relaxed person, loves flowers and helps Greig with his wooden-toy business in winter. They have renovated their old farmhouse to give it an English feel yet preserve its utterly French character: the atmosphere is light, airy and warm as well as solid and reassuring. In the big guestroom, the beds have excellent mattresses, the views are rural, the super bathroom (across the landing but private) is blue and white with lots of pretty china bits. A very civilised place to stay.

Rooms: 1 twin with bath and wc.

Price: 300 Frs (€ 45.73) for two, including breakfast.

Meals: Good choice 12km.

Open: January to August.

From A43 exit 9 on D51 SW to Victor de Cessieu; left opposite garage on D51B to Longeville (4km). There, left up very short lane, house at end.

MMap 244-27 **ASP Map No: 14**

Mary & Greig BARR
Longeville
38300 Succieu
Isère
Tel: (0)4 74 27 94 07
Fax: (0)4 74 92 09 21

Satin cushions, swags and curly legs. your fun-loving hosts brought their standards from their previous home on the Riviera, which means you will want for nothing. Such care, attention and unbridled luxury, including superb beds and great bathrooms, may not make for a 'homely' atmosphere but the meals... Madame is not only charming, she's a stupendous cook (*bouillabaisse* a speciality). Breakfast is a banquet of home-made jams, *brioche*, cake, and more. The half-acre garden provides rest and... flowers for indoors.

Rooms: 3 double, 1 twin, 2 suites, all with own bath and wc.

Price: 450-550 Frs (€ 68.60-83.85) for two, including breakfast.

Meals: 200 Frs, including wine & coffee.

Open: All year.

From Lyon, A43 Chimilin/Les Abrets exit towards Les Abrets & follow signs.

MMap 244-28 **ASP Map No: 14**

Christian & Claude CHAVALLE REVENU
La Bruyère
38490 Les Abrets
Isère
Tel: (0)4 76 32 01 66
Fax: (0)4 76 32 06 66
e-mail: carbone38@aol.com

An Egypto-Roman obelisk amid the topiary in the garden, wine from the vines which surround the château and beautiful C17 beams to sleep under. What more could you want? Your hosts, much-travelled, polyglot and sophisticated, are genuinely keen to share their enthusiasm for the area and its wines (and will organise wine-tastings). The vast rooms, some with fine carved door frames, are eclectically and elegantly furnished (Olivier's brother is an antique dealer) and breakfast, with home-made jams, can be followed by a visit to the winery. If you want to sample *le grand style*, this is for you.

Rooms: 2 double, 1 twin, 2 suites, each with bath & wc.

Price: 600-700 Frs (€ 91.47-106.71) for two, including breakfast.

Meals: By arrangement 200 Frs, including château's own wine.

Open: All year.

From A6 exit 'Belleville' then N6 dir. Lyon for 10km then right on D43 to Arnas. Go through village — château on right after 1.5km.

MMap 244-13 **ASP Map No: 9**

Alexandra & Olivier du MESNIL
Les Jardins de Longsard
Château de Longsard
69400 Arnas, Rhône
Tel: (0)4 74 65 55 12
Fax: (0)4 74 65 03 17
e-mail: olivierdumesnil@wanadoo.fr
www.sawdays.co.uk

Come here to experience the charming, authentically aristocratic lives of your hosts: no pretence or prissiness (two screened-off bathrooms), just unselfconscious style. The richly-decorated *salon* has a piano, books and open fireplace. The richly-stocked garden has a pool, a summerhouse, a large terrace, 150 species of trees, an organic vegetable garden and a statue of Grandad. Madame is too busy cooking to eat with guests but welcomes company as she's preparing dinner. Children love it — there's a room packed with toys, and the hosts' two children to play with.

Rooms: 2 double with bath or shower & wc; 2 twin with shower & wc.

Price: 400 Frs (€ 60.98) for two, including breakfast. Extra bed 50 Frs.

Meals: 120 Frs, excluding wine (80 Frs).

Open: All year.

 50Frs   

From A6 exit Macon Sud or Belleville then N6 to Romaneche and Lancié. In village take road dir. Fleurie into Square Les Pasquiers.

MMap 244-2 **ASP Map No: 9**

Jacques & Laurence GANDILHON
Les Pasquiers
69220 Lancié/Belleville
Rhône
Tel: (0)4 74 69 86 33
Fax: (0)4 74 69 86 57
e-mail: ganpasq@aol.com

An amazing avenue of lime trees conducts you to this wholly exceptional house and hostess. Madame is a live wire, laughing, enthusing, giving — unforgettable. The house is as elegant as she is. Climb the old wooden stairs to your splendidly decorated and furnished room, revel in Persian carpets, *trompe-l'œil*, antiques, fresh flowers. Beside the complete works of Shakespeare, Madame pours tea from silver into porcelain, artfully moves the breakfast table butter as the sun rises; at night she'll light your bedside lamp, leaving a book open at a carefully chosen page for you to read after a game of (French) Scrabble. Inimitably fine.

Rooms: 1 double with bathroom & wc; 1 double, 1 twin, sharing shower & wc.

Price: 500 Frs (€ 76.22) for two, including breakfast. Child under 8 in same room free.

Meals: Good restaurant 3km.

Open: All year.

From Bourg en Bresse, N83 dir. Lyon. At Servas right on D64 dir. Condeissiat for 5km, then left at sign 'Le Marmont' into tree-lined avenue.

MMap 244-4 **ASP Map No: 9**

Geneviève & Henri GUIDO-ALHÉRITIÈRE
Manoir de Marmont
01960 St André sur Vieux Jonc
Ain
Tel: (0)4 74 52 79 74

Owners do love it when guests stay two or three days and have time to make real contact as well as discovering the area's hidden treasures.

Up there among the pointy peaks,
the Savoyards don't mix their delicious cheeses
into gooey *fondue* for the sake of the
furry marmot alone – there's enough for all.

The Alps

The clean air of the Swiss borderlands is brilliantly evident at Fleur Sauvage: a spotless, uncluttered, modern chalet that Peter, an excellent carpenter, has finished most professionally and that Evelyn has decorated in co-ordinated colours set off by big windows and white walls. They are an interesting, friendly couple, have been posted to many parts of the world, are very active in local life and are now happy to share their delight in their adopted village. In a wonderful centre for walking and watery activities, this house welcomes families and couples alike.

Rooms: 2 double, 2 twin, each with shower, sharing 3 wcs.

Price: 300 Frs (€ 45.73) for two, including breakfast.

Meals: 110 Frs, including wine & coffee.

Open: January to September.

Gîte space for 4 people

From Thonon les Bains N5 dir. Evian. Opposite Evian ferry terminal, right on D21/D52 through St Paul to Bernex (total 15km). In village, fork right on Rue de Trossy — house is 2nd after 'Boulangerie'.

MMap 244-9 **ASP Map No: 10**

Evelyn & Peter WESTON
Fleur Sauvage
Les Vernes
74500 Bernex
Haute-Savoie
Tel: (0)4 50 73 67 37
Fax: (0)4 50 73 67 37
www.sawdays.co.uk

Hospitality is a family tradition; Anne-Marie speaks fluent English, keeps horses and organises rides or walks to the Alpine pastures above the valley. The walking is indeed exceptional and you may see chamois and marmots if you go far enough. The chalet has a 'museum' depicting life on an Alpine farm in the old days. Dinner (served late to allow guests time to settle) is eaten at the long wooden table, with grandmama's recipes cooked on a wood-fired stove: "simple ingredients well prepared; delicious cheeses". Readers love it and the half-board formula includes absolutely everything.

Rooms: 1 triple with shower & wc, 5 double sharing 3 showers & 3 wcs.

Price: 200 Frs (€ 30.49) per person: half-board only.

Meals: Dinner with aperitif, wine & coffee included in price.

Open: All year.

From Thonon les Bains, D26 dir. Bellevaux; house is 2km before Bellevaux on the left — signposted.

MMap 244-9 **ASP Map No: 10**

Anne-Marie FELISAZ-DENIS
Le Chalet
La Cressonnière
74470 Bellevaux
Haute-Savoie
Tel: (0)4 50 73 70 13
Fax: (0)4 50 73 70 13
www.sawdays.co.uk

Halfway between France and Switzerland, in green, hilly country, this chalet was built by Monsieur himself. You will warm to his earthy, jovial manner and appreciate Madame's enthusiastic welcome. The guestrooms are functional, the furniture is well-worn, the first-floor room is next to the kitchen and its bathroom opposite. Dinner dishes are Savoyard with ingredients from the large kitchen garden and poultry farm (now run by younger members of the family). A chorus of readers say, "good folk, excellent value".

Rooms: 1 double with shower & own wc, 1 double with bath & wc on landing.

Price: 200 Frs (€ 30.49) for two, including breakfast.

Meals: Choice 2km.

Open: April to October.

From Annecy, N201 dir. Geneva. 1km after Cruseilles, left on D27 to Copponex. Through village, left at cemetery; sign for Chambres d'Hôtes Châtillon — 1.5km. House on right.

MMap 244-7 **ASP Map No: 9**

Maryse & Aimé GAL
Châtillon
74350 Copponex
Haute-Savoie
Tel: (0)4 50 44 22 70

Stone and wood, white paint, dried flowers and good furniture combine to give this 200-year-old Savoyard farmhouse a light, harmonious air that matches Madame's smartly energetic presence. She keeps a kitchen garden which provides fresh vegetables for her good and varied dinners and will do anything for you. Monsieur shares his extensive wine knowledge and interest in mushroom-collecting. There is an upstairs sitting room for guests with an unusual half-moon window at floor level, big light bedrooms with antique, new-mattressed, lace-covered beds and spotless glass-doored showers.

Rooms: 1 double, 2 twin, each with shower & wc (1 behind curtain).

Price: 310 Frs (€ 47.26) for two, including breakfast; extra bed 100 Frs.

Meals: 85 Frs, including wine.

Open: March to mid-November.

From Annecy, N201 dir. Geneva. 1km after Cruseilles, left on D27 to Copponex. Through village, left at cemetery; signs to Chambres d'Hôtes Châtillon. House on left.

MMap 244-7 **ASP Map No: 9**

Suzanne & André GAL
La Bécassière
Châtillon
74350 Copponex
Haute-Savoie
Tel: (0)4 50 44 08 94

Come summer carriage-driving, come winter skiing — Madame, an attractive, dynamic person, teaches both while friend Christine cooks (delectably, we're told) and runs the house. In their half of this enormous farmhouse with its distant mountain views, there are four excellent and unusually big guestrooms, each with a different colour scheme, each with pretty flower-painted mountain furniture. There are wood floors, beams, woodburning stoves and the whole house just has a fine Alpine feel to it.

Rooms: 1 triple, 1 quadruple, each with own shower & wc; 1 double, 1 triple sharing shower & wc.

Price: 220-280 Frs (€ 33.54-42.69) for two, incl. breakfast; extra bed 110 Frs.

Meals: 90 Frs, including wine.

Open: Mid-March to mid-November.

Gîte space for 12 people

From A41 exit 17 on N508 W dir. Bellegarde for c. 10km; left on D17, through Sillingy; D3 dir. Vaulx & Rumilly. House on right 2km along: pony trap outside house.

MMap 244-18 **ASP Map No: 9**

Marie-Christine SKINAZY
La Ferme sur les Bois
Le Biolley
74150 Vaulx, Haute-Savoie
Tel: (0)4 50 60 54 50
Fax: (0)4 50 60 52 34
e-mail: annecy.attelage@wanadoo.fr
http://perso.wanadoo.fr/annecy-attelage

This is a no-frills place, simple and clean, with relaxed hosts (locals who know their area well), a daughter willing to babysit and a kind micro-climate: the nearby mountains apparently attract the clouds, leaving the sun to beat a clear path to your door. Breakfast only is provided but the Martins recommend restaurants and provide a kitchen for the two rooms in the guest chalet. The rooms are fairly small and furnishings plain and simple but the garden is a pleasant surprise with swings and ropes for youngsters and there are fabulous walks to be taken. Only 10km from Annecy.

Rooms: 2 double (+ convertible sofa) in cottage, each with shower & wc; 1 double in house with shower & wc.

Price: 250 Frs (€ 38.11) for two, including breakfast.

Meals: Self-catering possible in cottage.

Open: All year.

Gîte space for 6 people

From Annecy (sud) D16 dir. Rumilly. Enter Marcellaz Albanias and go immediately left on D38 dir. Chapeiry for 1km. Right dir. Chaunu; house 100m up on right.

MMap 244-18 **ASP Map No: 9**

Claudie & Jean-Louis MARTIN
Chemin de Chaunu
74150 Marcellaz Albanais
Haute-Savoie
Tel: (0)4 50 69 73 04

This house flourishes with the loving care its owners lavish upon it. "Luxury without ostentation" is their aim and their passion for antiques, interior decorating, gourmet cuisine and entertaining ensures just that. A vast brunch for all and 4/5 course dinners on request: French-Canadian Denyse is a food journalist. The rooms are all different: the blue *Albanaise*, the raspberry *Aixoise*, the oak-beamed, four-postered *Écossaise*. You choose. Bathrooms are superb too. Beautiful Annecy with its gleaming lake, Chamonix-Mont Blanc, the towering Alps, swinging Geneva, are all nearby.

Rooms: 2 double, 1 twin, each with bath or shower & wc.

Price: 650 Frs (€ 99.09) for two, including breakfast.

Meals: By arrangement 200 Frs, including wine & coffee.

Open: All year.

Gîte space for 3 people

From A41 exit Alby/Rumilly, N201 dir. Chambéry. In St Félix, at church onto D53: pass cemetery, go 300m then left (sign for Mercy) to statue, right and imm'ly left, past farm and through gate.

MMap 244-18 **ASP Map No: 9**

Denyse & Bernard BETTS
Les Bruyères
Mercy
74540 St Félix
Haute-Savoie
Tel: (0)4 50 60 96 53
Fax: (0)4 50 60 94 65

Wood, wood and more wood, outside and in, plus lovely fabrics and furniture, make this brand new traditional-style chalet warm and reassuring. It has panoramic views south across the valley to rising green Alpine pastures and great rocky mountains. The roomy guestroom has doors to the garden and that fabulous view. Your hosts, retired contented travellers, are great fun, energetic and enthusiastic about their new house, the 135km of marked mountain trails, and their lovely Labradors who enjoy the walking too. Delightful Annecy is just two dozen kilometres and a few bends away.

Rooms: 1 twin with shower & wc.

Price: 300 Frs (€ 45.73) for two, including breakfast.

Meals: 95 Frs, including wine & coffee.

Open: All year.

From Annecy, D909 to Thones then D12 dir. Serraval & Manigod; very shortly after, take D16 to Manigod. Through village then follow signs to 'Les Murailles'. House is 4th on right.

MMap 244-19 **ASP Map No: 10**

Colin & Alyson BROWNE
Les Murailles
74230 Manigod
Haute-Savoie
Tel: (0)4 50 44 95 87
Fax: (0)4 50 44 95 87

They are a lively, friendly, happy young family — so refreshing! Myriam adores having people to stay and everyone joining in the lighthearted atmosphere. Their typical C19 farmhouse is welcoming but not smart and the family room, the hub of life at La Touvière, is cosy and pleasing. Marcel is part-time farmer (he just has a few cows now), part-time home improver. One guestroom has a properly Alpine view across the valley; the other overlooks the owners' second chalet, let as a gîte; both are small but not cramped and this is a perfect place to set out from into the walkers' paradise that surrounds it. Remarkable value.

Rooms: 2 double, each with shower & wc.

Price: 200 Frs (€ 30.49) for two, including breakfast.

Meals: 90 Frs, including wine.

Open: All year.

Gîte space for 5 people

From Albertville N212 NE dir. Megève for 21km. Shortly after Flumet, left at 'Panoramic Hotel' & follow signs to La Touvière.

MMap 244-20 **ASP Map No: 10**

Marcel & Myriam MARIN-CUDRAZ
La Touvière
73590 Flumet
Savoie
Tel: (0)4 79 31 70 11

Greet the gentle giant Danes, admire the scale of La Terrosière as you arrive — *la vie de château* is yours. In the luxuriously converted stable block there are vast antique-furnished bedrooms (you may need a mounting block for the four-poster), brilliant bathrooms, a softly embracing living room with open fire, staff to wait on you and a *châtelaine* of charm and wit to make fine food, bring superb wines from her cellar and keep you company at table. Horses exercise in the school, a tennis court, fishing lake and heated spring-water pool beckon on the 100-acre estate. Worth every centime. Oh, and it's brunch, not breakfast.

Rooms: 2 suites, 1 twin, each with bath, shower, double basin & wc.

Price: 750-800 Frs (€ 114.34-121.96) for two, including brunch.

Meals: 150 Frs, excluding wine (30-50 Frs). Self-catering.

Open: All year except August & Christmas (by arrangement).

From Chambéry N504 N via Le Bourget du Lac through small tunnel to Chevelu; left on D921 to St Paul. After r'about, 1st left. House on right approx. 1km along (large iron gates).

MMap 244-17 **ASP Map No: 9**

Mme Jeannine CONTI
La Terrosière
73170 St Paul sur Yenne
Savoie
Tel: (0)4 79 36 81 02
www.sawdays.co.uk

Blazing fires, natural wood — all pure *Savoyard*; big rooms and luxury bathrooms — such a treat. The televisions and the cardphone in the hall give a slight 'hotelly' feel, but what matter? Perched on the edge of a mountain, you have a superb view of peaks above and villages below, be you in your room, in the jacuzzi, or rolling in the snow after your sauna. After a hearty breakfast your Franco-American hostess will gladly help you map out your itinerary — mountain-lake fishing in summer, skiing in winter, superb walking all year.

Rooms: 2 suites for 4, 3 double (queen or king-size beds), all with bath or shower & wc.

Price: 550-850 Frs (€ 83.85-129.58) for two, including breakfast.

Meals: 185 Frs, including aperitif, wine & coffee.

Open: Dec to April & June to Sept.

Gîte space for 9 people

From Bourg St Maurice D902 dir. Val d'Isère through Ste Foy Tarentaise. After La Thuile left dir. Ste Foy Station and follow wooden signposts.

MMap 244-21 **ASP Map No: 15**

Nancy TABARDEL
Yellowstone Chalet
Bonconseil Station
73640 Ste Foy Tarentaise
Savoie
Tel: (0)4 79 06 96 06
Fax: (0)4 79 06 96 05
e-mail: yellowstone@wanadoo.fr

This is a year-round Alpine dream. In summer it's all flowers, bees, birds and rushing streams. In winter, you can easily reach the vast ski areas of Les Arcs and Val d'Isère, ski cross-country or snow-walk nearer to home. The cuisine is as good and honest as the young hosts, cooked in the outside wood oven in summer. Children are catered for with early suppers, son Boris is a willing playmate for them and Claude will babysit in the evening. Guests have thei own comfortable dayroom with a refrigerator. Readers love both people and food.

Rooms: 1 suite for 4/5, 1 double for 2/3, each with shower & wc.

Price: 250 Frs (€ 38.11) for two, including breakfast (reduction children & long stays).

Meals: 85 Frs, including wine & coffee

Open: All year.

From Albertville N90 to Moutiers then on towards Bourg St Maurice. Right on D87 to Peisey Nancroix; left to Peisey Centre then follow green arrows.

MMap 244-32 **ASP Map No: 15**

Claude COUTIN & Franck CHENAL
Maison Coutin
T12 Peisey
73210 Peisey Nancroix, Savoie
Tel: (0)4 79 07 93 05/
(0)6 14 11 54 65
Fax: (0)4 79 07 93 05
e-mail: clcoutin@aol.com

You can walk (and in winter you can ski) straight out onto the mountains from this dramatically-set house with its wonderful views over to Italy. Jean-Marc and Jacqueline are keen walkers, quite able to design a whole walking holiday for you — or any sort of holiday. Jean-Marc designed and built the house (he's a retired architect) with the bedrooms snugly under the eaves. There is a self-contained *appartement* with its own garden; the third person does have to sleep in the kitchen, but has sole use of the microwave and the magnificent view.

Rooms: 2 double sharing shower & wc, 1 twin with shower & wc, 1 apartment with bath & wc.

Price: 320 Frs (€ 48.78) for two, including breakfast.

Meals: Town centre 4km.

Open: 29 December to 7 April & 9 June to 9 September.

From Gap N94 NE to Briançon 85km. Entering town, left at first traffic light dir. Puy St André (4km). In village, house is 3rd on left.

MMap 244-43 **ASP Map No: 15**

Jacqueline & Jean-Marc LABORIE
Le Village, Puy St André
05100 Briançon, Hautes-Alpes
Tel: (0)4 92 21 30 22/
(0)6 84 04 11 72
Fax: (0)4 92 21 30 22
e-mail: sudalp@club-internet.fr
www.sawdays.co.uk

The ancient bits (some 800 years old) ooze history and mystery. Plays based on high spots of French history as seen from Montmaur (Mitterand was here with the French Resistance) are enacted on summer Fridays, the exhibition room has a 5-metre-high fireplace, the dining room, where you breakfast with family silver on a magnificent Provençal cloth, has superb old beams and your energetic hostess is kindness itself — she will give you a guided tour. However, the 'suites' are less grand — slightly dim and cramped with unremarkable furnishings. But romantics at heart come for the ghostly splendour of it all.

Rooms: 3 suites, each with antechamber, shower & wc.

Price: 450 Frs (€ 68.60) for two, including breakfast.

Meals: Choice 1.5-6km.

Open: April to October.

From Gap, D994 dir. Veynes. 4km before Veynes, take D320 dir. Superdévoluy; Montmaur is 2km on, visible from road. Drive along château wall then towards church.

MMap 245-6 **ASP Map No: 14**

Raymond & Élise LAURENS
Château de Montmaur
05400 Veynes
Hautes-Alpes
Tel: (0)4 92 58 11 42
Fax: (0)4 92 58 11 42

Your first taste of magnificence is the drive up. Come to La Jarbelle, in its setting of addictive beauty, to ski across country or down hills, rent your snow shoes on the spot, do some exceptional summer walks, hang-glide or just bathe in splendour. Michel, who took a half-ruined farmhouse and turned it into this atmospheric, country-warm house of welcome with small, no-frills rooms that have all you could want, is a burly, good-natured host who loves the convivial evenings around the communal table. Claude's artistry is seen in the décor (ragged paintwork...), her kindness is in the air.

Rooms: 1 double, 2 twin, 2 quadruple, 1 suite, each with shower & wc.

Price: 260-300 Frs (€ 39.64-45.73) for two, including breakfast.

Meals: 100 Frs, including aperitif, wine & coffee.

Open: All year but telephone to check.

From Gap N94 E dir. Briançon for 36km; right just before Embrun on D40 for 10km. Leaving Les Orres village on left, follow 'Station des Orres' down hill — house in hamlet, on left just before bridge.

MMap 245-9 **ASP Map No: 15**

Michel & Claude HURAULT
La Jarbelle
Les Ribes
05200 Les Orres
Hautes-Alpes
Tel: (0)4 92 44 11 33
Fax: (0)4 92 44 11 33

We the publishers, claim to offer you ar escape from the 'crushing conformity' c our age. Well, how about this? Come li in-the-round, shape your own space, become a happy, passive smoker, enjoy close contact with hosts who have learned – admirably – to survive on the edge of the throw-away society. The seating arrangements will work wonder for your posture; indeed, save the cost a visit to the osteopath in just one nigh No flimflammery here, much wigwammery, sphered space, wonderfu early morning light, a whole-hearted recreation of nomadic bliss. Come befo the planners move it on.

Price: 30 minutes tribal dance p.p., mc if owners like you.

Meals: Free for all but quantity and quality depend on aim.

Open: Always at the top.

From the valley, take upward road and climb straight as an arrow to Mont Calumet. At end of road, several white peaks are visible: Grantipi is the smallest.

Grand Chef Oeuil de Vrai
Grantipi des Arcs
Mont Calumet
05050 Plateau de Soleil Bœuf
Hautes-Alpes

The best *bouillabaisse* ingredients swim among the white Mediterranean horses; on shore, the native white ponies carry their dashing *gardians* over the Camargue, herding the great black bulls.

Provence – The Riviera

Esparron has been in the same family since the 1400s though the small garden is a shadow of its former self. Vast bedrooms, reached by a superb stone staircase, are lovingly decorated: plain walls and fresh flowers, tiles and fine designer fabrics, good antiques and lots of lamps. Slender, apple-blossom Charlotte-Anne and her two beautiful children come straight from a Gainsborough portrait (she IS English). She is attentive to everyone: husband, children, staff and guests. Bernard, with suntan, impeccable clothes and manners and pipe, adds a touch of 1930s glamour. Wonderful family, splendiferous house, vast breakfast...

Rooms: 3 double, 1 twin, 1 suite, each with bath & wc.

Price: 700-1200 Frs (€ 106.71-182.94) for two, including breakfast.

Meals: 5 minutes walk.

Open: April to October.

From Aix en Provence A51 exit 18 onto D907 then D82 to Gréoux les Bains; follow signs on D952 & D315 to Esparron. Stop and ring at château gates (once past, it's impossible to turn).

MMap 245-33 **ASP Map No: 14**

Bernard & Charlotte-Anne de CASTELLANE
Château d'Esparron
04800 Esparron de Verdon
Alpes-de-Haute-Provence
Tel: (0)4 92 77 12 05
Fax: (0)4 92 77 13 10
e-mail: bernard.de.castellane@wanadoo.fr
www.provenceweb.fr/04/ukEsparron.htm

There is a fine acacia over the terrace, the garden rambles in and out of shade; inside, there are fireplaces and decorative platters of fruit. One bedroom has lavender colour-washed walls, stripped wooden floors and good country furniture, with a rolled-edge cast-iron bath and period basin. Now to breakfast: served under mature trees with vineyards and distant mountains... try the Scottish pancakes and home-made jam. Dinner is delicious too; Michael is an imaginative chef and his sense of hospitality has been praised to the skies.

Rooms: 1 suite for 4, 3 double, each with bath or shower & wc.

Price: 350 Frs (€ 53.36) for two, including breakfast; extra bed 100 Frs.

Meals: 150 Frs, including aperitif, wine & coffee.

Open: April to October

Gîte space for 2 people

 30Frs

From Vaison la Romaine D938 N dir. Nyons for 5km then right on D46 dir. Buis les Baronnies for 4km. On entering Faucon, house on right at crossroads with D205 (blue gate & shutters).

MMap 245-17 **ASP Map No: 14**

Michael BERRY
Les Airs du Temps
Quartier les Aires
84110 Faucon
Vaucluse
Tel: (0)4 90 46 44 57
Fax: (0)4 90 46 44 57
e-mail: michaelaberry@hotmail.com

There is great character here and the chapel includes part of the Roman town wall. Monsieur has done much of the restoration himself, reproducing some of the C18 grandness. The wonderful entrance hall has its own grand piano. The very large guestrooms feature antiques, old tiles and fireplaces and two of the bathrooms, with their old-fashioned claw-footed baths, are built into the restored tower. Meals, which include home-grown fruit, are served on the terrace or in the dining room. *Big house: let the telephone ring at length.*

Rooms: 4 triple, each with bath & wc; 1 apartment/suites: 2 bedrooms, bath & wc, shower & wc, *salon*, kitchen.

Price: 550 Frs (€ 83.85) for two, including breakfast. Extra bed 80 Frs.

Meals: 160 Frs including coffee (wine 50-60 Frs). Self-catering apartment.

Open: All year.

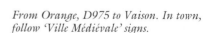

From Roman theatre in Vaison follow signs for Malaucène/Mt Ventoux. Left onto 'Chemin de Planchettes'. Signposted.

MMap 245-17 **ASP Map No: 14**

Rémy & Cécile DAILLET
Château de Taulignan
St Marcellin lès Vaison
84110 Vaison la Romaine
Vaucluse
Tel: (0)4 90 28 71 16
Fax: (0)4 90 28 75 04
e-mail: chateau@pacwan.fr

Narrow, cobbled streets lead to this fascinating, impeccably-furnished house that was once part of the C17 Bishop's Palace. The Verdiers are charming, cultivated people — he an architect/builder, she a teacher — with a keen interest in antiques and in protecting medieval Vaison from the predations of 'progress'. The guestrooms and cosy *salon* have a warm, Provençal feel. Well-presented breakfasts on the terrace come complete with French and English newspapers and, best of all, the magnificent view over to the Roman bridge.

Rooms: 2 double, 2 twin, each with bath or shower & wc.

Price: 400-440 Frs (€ 60.98-67.08) for two, including breakfast.

Meals: Choice in Vaison.

Open: All year except 2 weeks in November.

From Orange, D975 to Vaison. In town, follow 'Ville Médiévale' signs.

MMap 245-17 **ASP Map No: 14**

Aude & Jean-Loup VERDIER
L'Évêché
Rue de l'Évêché
84110 Vaison la Romaine, Vaucluse
Tel: (0)4 90 36 13 46
Fax: (0)4 90 36 32 43
e-mail: eveche@aol.com
www.sawdays.co.uk

Set among vineyards below the Montmirail hills, this simple, Provençal farmhouse has a courtyard shaded by a lovely linden tree. The views across the surrounding country and unspoilt villages are wonderful. Madame grows organic vegetables and fruit and considers dinners with her guests, in dining room or courtyard, as the most interesting part of doing B&B. Meals are also showcases for local specialities. The interior decoration is a bright version of traditional French country style with old family furniture.

Rooms: 2 suites, 1 double, 1 twin, each with shower & wc.

Price: 230 Frs (€ 35.06) for two, including breakfast.

Meals: 80 Frs, including wine.

Open: April to mid-November.

From Carpentras D7 N through Aubignan & Vacqueyras; fork right, still on D7, towards Sablet; 500m after 'Cave des Vignerons de Gigondas' turn right; signposted.

MMap 245-17 **ASP Map No: 14**

Sylvette GRAS
La Ravigote
84190 Gigondas
Vaucluse
Tel: (0)4 90 65 87 55
Fax: (0)4 90 65 36 11

The solid old aristocratic *bastide* was built on the foundations of a C12 water mill and the thick stone walls keep the house cool. There is a very big pool in the large, landscaped, tree-filled garden surrounding it (though the busy road tends to make its presence felt). Breakfast is wonderful out on the terrac or in the family dining room; dinners include Madame's Provençal specialities Her daughter and son-in-law are gradually taking over operations: what's it like now? The house is full of interesting mementoes of the owners' time in various North African countries

Rooms: 2 double, 1 twin, all with bath or shower & wc.

Price: 360 Frs (€ 54.88) for two, including breakfast.

Meals: 130 Frs, including wine.

Open: All year.

From Carpentras, D974 dir. Bédoin/Mont Ventoux; stay on this road, do NOT enter Crillon village. The mill is on the left below signpost.

MMap 245-17 **ASP Map No: 14**

Bernard & Marie-Luce RICQUART
Moulin d'Antelon
84410 Crillon le Brave
Vaucluse
Tel: (0)4 90 62 44 89
Fax: (0)4 90 62 44 90
e-mail: horisudp@imaginetfr.

Set in great walking country among spectacular fields of lavender with vast views, this fine C19 farmhouse is built around a courtyard shaded by a spreading linden tree. The family living/dining room is homely and warm with a large table and a fireplace for cooler weather. The comfortable, light-filled rooms are carefully decorated in an unpretentious mix of new and old. Monsieur is a keen cook and prepares Provençal dishes using local produce and herbs while the charming, enthusiastic Madame makes the desserts and also gives Feldenkrais (conscious movement) sessions. Stay long enough to taste ALL these pleasures.

Rooms: 1 suite for 4, 1 suite for 3, 3 triple, each with bath or shower & wc.

Price: 390-450 Frs (€ 59.46-68.60) for two, including breakfast (3 nights min).

Meals: 135 Frs, including coffee.

Open: All year except Jan & Feb.

From Carpentras, D941/D1 to Sault (41km) then D942 dir. Aurel. Just before Aurel, left at signpost.

MMap 245-18 **ASP Map No: 14**

Christian & Visnja MICHELLE
Richarnau
84390 Aurel
Vaucluse
Tel: (0)4 90 64 03 62
Fax: (0)4 90 64 03 62
e-mail: c.richarnau@accesinter.com

A genuine, long-established Provençal family: seven generations of wine-growers have breathed their first in this old C17 farmhouse. Silkworms were once bred on the estate that looks across vineyards to Mont Ventoux and Madame loves organising tastings of her own *Coteaux du Ventoux* wine. She also produces olive oil, tomatoes, beans and melons. The link between where you sleep and where you eat and swim is her very tempting kitchen. Rooms are cosy, clean and functional with tiled floors, a proper patina on walls and friezes, old doors fronting new cupboards. The old family Provençal recipes are made with wine — naturally.

Rooms: 3 double, 1 twin, each with shower & wc.

Price: 300 Frs (€ 45.73) for two, including breakfast.

Meals: 130 Frs, including wine.

Open: All year.

From Carpentras D974 NE dir. Bedoin. 175m after sign to St Pierre de Vassols, right on D224 dir. Mormoiron — signposted on left

MMap 245-17 **ASP Map No: 14**

Mme Marie-José EYDOUX
Domaine la Condamine
84410 Crillon le Brave
Vaucluse
Tel: (0)4 90 62 47 28/
(0)6 08 45 26 70
Fax: (0)4 90 62 47 28

The dining room, with its tile floors and old beams, used to be the carthorse stable and country simplicity is the theme throughout this recently-restored farmhouse. Its clean and basic rooms include good beds with Provençal covers and views over the fields. According to one of our readers, "Madame is a star with a lovely sense of humour"; fortunately she is up and shining during the daytime as well. She and her family — a gently shy husband and two teenage children — create a genuine Provençal atmosphere round the table. The fare is traditional, with home-grown vegetables.

Rooms: 5 double, all with bath or shower & wc.

Price: 280 Frs (€ 42.69) for two, including breakfast.

Meals: 80 Frs, including wine & coffee.

Open: All year.

From Apt, N100 dir. Avignon. At Lumières, D106 dir. Lacoste, then D218 to Ménerbes; second farm on the left.

MMap 245-31 **ASP Map No: 14**

Maryline & Claude CHABAUD
Mas Marican
84220 Goult
Vaucluse
Tel: (0)4 90 72 28 09

Genuine country class is here. Michel, who lives in another house 500m away, is part of a true Provençal country community: his family has lived here for generations, his father runs the farm (vineyards and cherry trees march past, honey is combed for breakfast), a friend deals with the wine, Sophie looks after guests. The irrigation pond at the front has rippled with southern light for 250 years, the old house has been lovingly restored with properly colour-washed walls, old doors and floor tiles and is refreshingly uncluttered. But modernity takes a bow with superb bathrooms and a streamlined pool.

Rooms: 2 double, 2 twin, 1 triple, each with bath & wc.

Price: 420-520 Frs (€ 64.03-79.27) for two, including breakfast.

Meals: Choice 2-5km.

Open: March to November.

From Cavaillon D973 E for 30km; left then right, through Lauris on D27 and on towards Puyvert/Lourmarin; signposted after 1km.

MMap 245-31 **ASP Map No: 14**

Michel CUXAC
La Carraire
84360 Lauris
Vaucluse
Tel: (0)4 90 08 36 89
Fax: (0)4 90 08 40 83
www.dnweb.com/carraire

Everyone's dream of what a house in Provence should be: wonderful furniture, fabrics, tiles and beams, it is all exquisite refinement. It is a former C17 staging post yet its garden is an oasis of coolness, right in the centre of pretty Lourmarin. Madame, a cultivated and interesting person and a keen cyclist, is ready to advise on routes and leads such an active life that she may just not be there to greet you or dust your room! She is now running the Villa with her daughter — and grand-daughter, who speaks perfect four-year-old English. There are bikes for guests' use and for the less athletic or the saddle-sore there's that shady garden.

Rooms: 2 double and 3 twin, all with bath or shower & wc.

Price: 350-450 Frs (€ 53.36-68.60) for two, including breakfast.

Meals: Choice locally.

Open: All year.

From Aix en Provence, N96 and D556 to Pertuis. There, D973 to Cadenet and then D943 towards Bonnieux until you reach Lourmarin.

MMap 245-31 **ASP Map No: 14**

Mme & Mlle LASSALLETTE
Villa Saint Louis
35 rue Henri de Savornin
84160 Lourmarin
Vaucluse
Tel: (0)4 90 68 39 18
Fax: (0)4 90 68 10 07

Don't pick up that broken saucer — it's part of an artist's installation. A fascinating contemporary arts centre run by a Franco-Polish couple who offer artists a spell of creative peace and sympathetic B&B guests a chance to share the privilege of an art-centred atmosphere. Pierre will even take you sketching. The old Provençal house has an authentic patina and lovely worn tiles, the sparse furniture is designer-perfect, the new apartment (bookable daily or weekly) a sheer delight, the artwork everywhere, the garden reached by a bridge across the street, the hospitality exceptionally generous and the whole feel incomparably special.

Rooms: 2 double, 1 twin, 1 apartment (with kitchen) for 2, each with bath or shower & wc.

Price: 380-450 Frs (€ 57.93-68.60) for two, including breakfast.

Meals: 140 Frs, including wine.

Open: All year except January.

Gîte space for 2 people

Saignon is 3km SE of Apt. In Saignon, park near PTT Post Office. On main street, house is on right, 30m after PTT.

MMap 245-31 **ASP Map No: 14**

Kamila REGENT & Pierre JACCAUD
Chambre de Séjour avec Vue
84400 Saignon en Luberon
Vaucluse
Tel: (0)4 90 04 85 01
Fax: (0)4 90 04 85 01
e-mail: chambre@vip.fr

Cats sit like kings on cushions in corners of this restored *mas*, but only downstairs. In an area of seething tourism and synthetic welcomes, this is proper B&B of genuine warmth and character. The owners are easy, natural, chatty and patient. The house has lots of bits and pieces — an old water pump, a royalist carving on the façade where the 1788 coin was found, an oil painting of the house by Monsieur's father, lots of local info. Simple pink or mauve rooms; copious breakfasts under plane trees or in the stupendously high old horse barn, its stone trough worn to a sculpture. Unpretentious Provence at its best.

Rooms: 1 twin with shower & wc; 1 double, 1 double/twin, each with shower & washbasin, sharing wc.

Price: 280 Frs (€ 42.69) for two, including breakfast.

Meals: Restaurant in village.

Open: April to 20 September.

From Avignon, D571 to Châteaurenard and D571 dir. Eyragues. After 1.5km take small road left opp. 'Jardin de Cécile' sign; signposted 300m to sharp narrow entrance on right.

MMap 245-29 **ASP Map No: 14**

Christiane & Robert POLI
Le Mas des Chats qui Dorment
Chemin des Prés
13630 Eyragues
Bouches-du-Rhône
Tel: (0)4 90 94 19 71

On an old cobbled street right in the heart of old Tarascon, this *maison de maître* has really ancient origins. It has been beautifully, artistically renovated without losing any of the lovely patina of stone walls and old tiles. Built round a typical ochre-hued courtyard where breakfast is served, it exudes Mediterranean age and history. The rooms have fine old furniture, beams, stone flags. Your charming hosts, new t B&B, have slipped with perfect ease int a relaxed, friendly way of receiving guests and are enjoying it immensely. Madame plans to open a little *brocante* in her generous porch entrance in 200(

Rooms: 4 double, 1 twin, each with bath or shower & wc.

Price: 420-450 Frs (€ 64.03-68.60) fo two, including breakfast.

Meals: Choice in town.

Open: March to October; by arrangement in winter.

In Tarascon centre take Rue du Château opposite the château (well signposted) — No 24 is along on right.

MMap 245-28 **ASP Map No: 14**

Yann & Martine LARAISON
24 rue du Château
13150 Tarascon
Bouches-du-Rhône
Tel: (0)4 90 91 09 99
Fax: (0)4 90 91 10 33
e-mail: ylaraison@wanadoo.fr
www.sawdays.co.uk

The interior of this manicured farmhouse is as cool as the welcome is warm from its French/Irish owners — John is big and relaxed, Christiane is trim and efficient. Natural stone, oak beams, terracotta floors and cool colours give a wonderfully light and airy feel to the house while guestrooms are carefully elegant with small, functional shower rooms. Outside, centuries-old plane trees, a vine tunnel, three hectares of cypresses and horses (why not head for the *Alpilles* mountains?) add to the magic. An oft-tinkled piano is there for you to play.

Rooms: 4 double, 2 twin, all with shower & wc.

Price: 500 Frs (€ 76.22) for two, including breakfast. Extra bed 100 Frs.

Meals: Choice in St Rémy.

Open: Easter to October.

From St Rémy D571 dir. Avignon. After 2 r'abouts, left just before 2nd bus stop (Lagoy), opp. 2nd yellow 'Portes Anciennes' sign, onto Chemin de Velleron & Prud'homme. House is 6th on right.

MMap 245-29 **ASP Map No: 14**

Christiane & John WALSH
Mas Shamrock
Chemin de Velleron & du Prud'homme
13210 St Rémy de Provence
Bouches-du-Rhône
Tel: (0)4 90 92 55 79
Fax: (0)4 90 92 55 80

Madame, who owns an antique shop, has used her knowledge and imagination to furnish this townhouse in one of Fontvieille's busy main streets with great taste. Everything here is refined and in impeccable order. Both bedrooms have beautiful antiques as well as thick woollen carpets, fine linens and large bathrooms; both overlook the small garden. There is a large, very handsome guest *salon*. Breakfast is served on old silver, a typically elegant touch. Your enthusiastic hosts enjoy sharing their love of music and Provence. *On-street parking.*

Rooms: 1 double, 1 triple, each with bath, shower & wc.

Price: 500 Frs (€ 76.22) for two, including breakfast.

Meals: Choice within walking distance.

Open: Easter to 30 October.

From Arles, D17 to Fontvieille; follow signs to 'Regalido' Hotel. House is 50m beyond on right.

MMap 245-29 **ASP Map No: 14**

Jean-Marie & Édith-Claire RICARD DAMIDOT
Le Mas Ricard
107 avenue Frédéric Mistral
13990 Fontvieille
Bouches-du-Rhône
Tel: (0)4 90 54 72 67
Fax: (0)4 90 54 64 43

A lesson in how to make a modern house feel like a charming old home, but then Jean-Pierre does run an association to promote Provençal traditions. Both he and Véronique are warmly, southernly friendly. The three ground-floor rooms with tiled floors, old beams, antiques and Provençal fabrics, look out to a garden surrounded by oak woods. One is named after *Grand'mère* Camille whose photograph hangs on the wall. The *salon* with its fireplace and antiques leads to a large roofed terrace for summer breakfasts.

Rooms: 1 double, 1 triple, 1 double/triple, each with bath or shower & wc.

Price: 310-360 Frs (€ 47.26-54.88) for two, including breakfast.

Meals: Choice 1.5-5km.

Open: All year except 5 Jan to end Feb.

From Salon de Provence D16 S to Grans (6km); left on D19 dir. Lançon de P. for 1.5km; left on Chemin des Bergers: signposted. At end of road, left on Chemin de la Transhumance; house at end.

MMap 245-30 **ASP Map No: 14**

Jean-Pierre & Véronique RICHARD
Domaine du Bois Vert
Quartier Montauban
13450 Grans
Bouches-du-Rhône
Tel: (0)4 90 55 82 98
Fax: (0)4 90 55 82 98

The Latin above the door says it all: "What you seek is here". Receiving strangers comes naturally to Michael: he began with 15 Bosnian refugees and finds endless time for his guests, providing home-made croissants, cookery classes with olive oil straight from his trees, jogging companionship, airport pick-up. His fine pink villa is filled with Provençal antiques, Berber carpets, crocheted bedcovers, sculptures by local artists and piles of books — a discovery at every turn. Plus tennis and croquet on the spot, sailing, swimming, trekking, bicycling a step away. Superior prices for superior attention.

Rooms: 2 triple, each with bath & wc.

Price: 700 Frs (€ 106.71) for two, including breakfast.

Meals: 180 Frs, including aperitif & wine. Lunch 130 Frs.

Open: All year.

From A54 exit 13 dir. Miramas on D19 to Grans 6km; right on D16 to St Chamas 9km; just before railway bridge, sharp left dir. Cornillon, up hill 2km — house on right before tennis court. Detailed plan faxed on request.

MMap 245-30 **ASP Map No: 14**

Michael FROST
Mas de la Rabassière
Route de Cornillon
13250 St Chamas, Bouches-du-Rhône
Tel: (0)4 90 50 70 40
Fax: (0)4 90 50 70 40
e-mail: rabassiere@aol.com
www.sawdays.co.uk

A fine old house, once a magistrate's summer residence, is the last trace of a huge estate that has been sold off by the city for business premises so the Bouvants' C18 manor and formal French garden and park (great old trees) are now a secret oasis. Once inside, all is fine furniture, old sepia prints and gleaming tiled floors — the elegance of bygone days. Enjoy, too, the original chapel (now a wine cellar), charming, luminous rooms and an attic sitting room full of old radios and records to be played. Also a genuinely warm welcome from your energetic Franco-Dutch hosts.

Rooms: 2 twin/double, 1 with shower & wc, 1 with bath & wc.

Price: 300-350 Frs (€ 45.73-53.36) for two, including breakfast.

Meals: 100 Frs, including wine & coffee.

Open: April to October.

From Aix A51 dir. Marseille, 3rd exit Bouc Belair; right on D59 to Pôle d'Activités Aix en Provence. After first roundabout, continue 3.4km. House on right after tennis court, opp. Maxi Livres.

MMap 245-31 **ASP Map No: 14**

Hervé & Miriam BOUVANT
Domaine du Frère
ZA Aix en Provence
13852 Aix en Provence
Bouches-du-Rhône
Tel: (0)4 42 24 24 62
Fax: (0)4 42 24 37 89
e-mail: bouvant@easynet.fr

You may have thought this intelligent elderly couple would be slowing down — they are opening more rooms! Their 1960s house (designed by Monsieur) on the beautiful, residential side of Aix, just 10 minutes walk from the centre, is modern inside, with Macintosh-style furniture and lots of cool tones of grey, blue and white in the smallish rooms. There's a pool and the big garden has tall pines and squat olive trees from which your helpful, cheerful hosts make their own oil (though the 1997 frost was painful). Children are welcome. Extra rooms may be available.

Rooms: 3 double, each with bath or shower & wc; 2 twin, sharing shower & wc.

Price: 300-450 Frs (€ 45.73-68.60) for two, including breakfast (2 nights preferred).

Meals: Wide choice in Aix.

Open: All year.

In Aix, from Pl. de la Rotonde, pass Tourist Information, turn onto Bd Victor Hugo. At top of road, left on Bd du Roi René. At 9th traffic light after Pl. de la Rotonde, turn into Rte du Tholonet dir. piscine/stade; house at second r'about, tall gateposts on right.

MMap 245-31 **ASP Map No: 14**

Mauricette & René IUNG
L'Enclos
2 av Général Préaud (Rte du Tholonet)
13100 Aix en Provence
Bouches-du-Rhône
Tel: (0)4 42 96 40 52

This modern, Provençal-style house sits high above the surrounding vineyards and orchards as if in a Cézanne: the view of the Montagne Sainte Victoire is loaded with breathtaking references. It's also a good base for a family holiday: guests have a large room with mezzanine and kitchenette in a separate little house (illustrated); there is a fine pool, table tennis, *boules* for all, the sea 45 minutes away and lovely old Aix within easy reach. The Babeys, with four sons, are relaxed and easy. One reader wrote: "A favourite — such caring and phlegmatic hosts".

Rooms: Cottage for 4 : double/twin on ground floor, double on mezzanine, bathroom and kitchenette.

Price: 360 Frs (€ 54.88) for two, including breakfast. Extra bed 120 Frs.

Meals: Self-catering. Restaurants in village 2km.

Open: All year.

From Aix, N7 dir. Nice for approx. 15 km. Left just after Château de La Bégude dir. Puyloubier; Chemin des Prés is 20m along on right. House at end.

MMap 245-32 **ASP Map No: 14**

Jean-Pierre & Sophie BABEY
Les Bréguières
Chemin des Prés
13790 Rousset
Bouches-du-Rhône
Tel: (0)4 42 29 01 16
Fax: (0)4 42 29 01 16

The C18 *bastide* seems to dominate its little hilltop on the edge of pretty Peynier. Pull the old cowbell, pass the big wooden doors and its solid red-shuttered mass surges up from its rose-filled garden. Beautifully restored *à la provençale*, it once belonged to painter Vincent Roux and memories of Cézanne live on. Roux's room (the best) has a delicious garden view, beams, terracotta tiles, a fantastic ochre/green bathroom down the corridor. The others are good too, though more functional, but the *salon* is a lovely spot. The welcoming atmosphere created by your gracious hostess is much praised. Older children welcome.

Rooms: 2 triple, 1 quadruple, each with bath or shower & wc.

Price: 360-400 Frs (€ 54.88-60.98) for two, incl. breakfast (min. 2 nights May-Sept). Extra bed 120 Frs.

Meals: In village. Summer kitchen for lunches.

Open: All year, except first 3 weeks in August.

From Aix en Provence, A8 dir. Nice. Canet exit on D6 dir. Trets. 4km before Trets, right on D57 to Peynier. There, up hill to Trets/Aubagne road (D908); left on D908; 1st right between Poste & Pharmacie. House about 50m along.

MMap 245-45 **ASP Map No: 14**

Mme Jacqueline LAMBERT
Mas Sainte Anne
3 rue Auriol
13790 Peynier
Bouches-du-Rhône
Tel: (0)4 42 53 05 32
Fax: (0)4 42 53 04 28

The Mediterranean garden is spectacularly beautiful with its tall trees, flowering shrubs and manicured lawn. Indeed, the whole place is thoroughly manicured. Monsieur, an architect, designed the large, luxurious family villa, thoughtfully integrated into its surroundings, the pool is well concealed. Rooms are decorated in Provençal style with lovely Salernes bathroom tiles and are extremely comfortable; one has its own garden with table and chairs. Monsieur is shyly welcoming, Madame smilingly efficient and the nearby medieval village of Castellet is worth a visit.

Rooms: 2 double, 1 twin, 1 suite for 4, all with bath or shower & wc.

Price: 380 Frs (€ 57.93) for two, 500 Frs suite, including breakfast.

Meals: In village.

Open: All year.

Gîte space for 4 people

From Toulon N8 dir. Aubagne. Enter Le Beausset, cross 2 r'abouts then right opp. 'Casino' supermarket & imm'ly into lane 'Chemin de la Fontaine de 5 Sous' — house signposted on left after 1.5km.

MMap 245-46 **ASP Map No: 14**

Charlotte & Marceau ZERBIB
Les Cancades
Chemin de la Fontaine
83330 Le Beausset, Var
Tel: (0)4 94 98 76 93
Fax: (0)4 94 90 24 63
e-mail: charlotte.zerbib @wanadoo.fr
www.sawdays.co.uk

The heartbeat slows as one bumps towards Garrade past fields of lavender, saffron and other relaxing aromatics, the stuff of Jean-Louis's cottage industry (enjoy his healing *tisanes*). Mother and son (whose wife works in town) run a place of peace and freedom, gently dispensing personal attention, a room to suit each personality and fine food made with their own organic vegetables (Provençal dishes a speciality). Whitewashed rooms have splashes of colour, simple furniture, good shower rooms. The vast dining room, housing a table big enough for 20, gives onto both terraces, a promise of long hot convivial evenings.

Rooms: 4 triple, 2 double, all with own shower & wc.

Price: 295-320 Frs (€ 44.97-48.78) for two, including breakfast.

Meals: 100 Frs, including aperitif, wine & coffee.

Open: April to October.

In St Maximin take D28 dir. Bras for 3km to signpost on right. From here follow narrow road 3km further.

MMap 245-33 **ASP Map No: 14**

Jean-Louis & Pierrette BAUDE
Domaine de Garrade
Route de Bras
83470 St Maximin la Ste Baume, Var
Tel: (0)4 94 59 84 32
Fax: (0)4 94 59 83 47
e-mail: garrade@aol.com
www.provenceweb.fr/83/garrade

"SUCH delightful, cultivated people". Here is a chance to stay with a warm, lively family (four teenage children) on a working farm/vineyard with a timeless feel to it. The first-class bedrooms, impeccably decorated in authentic Provençal style, and the guests' dayroom (with mini-kitchen) are in a separate wing; weather permitting, breakfast is on the terrace. Monsieur, an historian, is happy to share his encyclopædic knowledge of the monuments and sights of the area and readers simply write: "Armelle is wonderful". And this is superbly varied walking country.

Rooms: 2 twin/double & 1 suite for 4, all with bath or shower & wc.

Price: 300-350 Frs (€ 45.73-53.36) for two, including breakfast; extra bed 90 Frs.

Meals: Self-catering. Restaurant nearby.

Open: All year.

Gîte space for 4 people

From A8, Saint Maximin/La Sainte Baume exit onto D560 through Barjols. There, continue D560 for 2km dir. Draguignan; entrance opposite D60 turning for Pontevès.

MMap 245-33 **ASP Map No: 15**

Guillaume & Armelle de JERPHANION
Domaine de Saint Ferréol
83670 Pontevès
Var
Tel: (0)4 94 77 10 42
Fax: (0)4 94 77 19 04

These are happy, civilised people who enjoy having guests in their beautiful rambling stone property, leave them in peace and cook them delicious dinners. You sleep in rooms of timeless simplicity in the ancient tower (once a dovecote): exposed stones and old tiles breathe in the coolness, smart bedcovers glow, each room has its own entrance — it's almost monastic. Meals, with home-grown fruit and vegetables, are in the family dining room (separate tables) or on the terrace. There is a majestic peacock, a friendly dog, lots of pure-bred Arab ponies and... a new baby. Botanic walks, riding and visits to local wine cellars can be arranged.

Rooms: 3 suites for 3, 1 triple, 1 twin, all with bath or shower & wc.

Price: 300 Frs (€ 45.73) for two, including breakfast. Extra bed 80 Frs.

Meals: 100 Frs, including wine & coffee.

Open: All year.

From Ginasservis D23 dir. Rians for 1.5km then left on D22 dir. Esparron for 1km. Signposted 'Aubanel' on left.

MMap 245-33 **ASP Map No: 14**

Fatia & Michel LAZÈS
Aubanel
83560 Ginasservis
Var
Tel: (0)4 94 80 11 07
Fax: (0)4 94 80 11 04

Your hosts were born in this unspoilt part of the Var where beautiful views of the Alps across vineyards and hills - and genuine human warmth — await you at their modernised farmhouse (C19 foundations). The smallish bedrooms feature typical Provençal fabrics and antiques, the bathrooms are new and spotless. Breakfast is brought to you on the private terrace or in the dining room. Monsieur, a tenant farmer, loves to talk about his *métier* and village. Madame is a kindly hostess. Readers have amply confirmed this.

Rooms: 1 triple, 1 double, 1 twin, all with shower & wc.

Price: 295 Frs (€ 44.97) for two, including breakfast. Extra bed 100 Frs.

Meals: In village (1km) or 3km away. Barbecue available.

Open: All year.

From Aups, D9 and D30 to Montmeyan. There, D13 dir. Quinson. House is on left of road, 1km along; signposted.

MMap 245-34 **ASP Map No: 15**

Dany & Vincent GONFOND
Mas Saint Maurinet
Route de Quinson
83670 Montmeyan
Var
Tel: (0)4 94 80 78 03
Fax: (0)4 94 80 78 03

This delicious old manor house was built in 1760 as a silkworm farm — mulberry trees still shade the wonderful terrace that gives onto a mature garden, a meadow area with children's games, a summer pool and a stupendous view to the distant hills. Inside it is just as authentic: old tiles with good rugs, beams, white walls and simple, comfortable antique furniture. Unlike our other owners, Nicola is here four months of the year only; her Norwegian friends receive you, in perfect English, at other times. They are all delightful.

Rooms: 1 double, 1 twin, each with shower & wc; 1 double, 1 twin, sharing shower/bath & wc.

Price: 400-460 Frs (€ 60.98-70.13) for two, including breakfast.

Meals: Wide choice within walking distance.

Open: All year.

From A8 exit 13 onto N7 E to Vidauban then left on D48 to Lorgues. In main street, post office on right: right and right again (behind post office). At T-junction left into Place Arariso. Leave square on left into Rue de la Canal; house along on left.

MMap 245-35 **ASP Map No: 15**

Nicola & Mario D'ANNUNZIO
La Canal, 177 rue de La Canal
Quartier le Grand Jardin
83510 Lorgues
Var
Tel: (0)4 94 67 68 32
Fax: (0)4 94 67 68 69

Half of this gorgeous, well-restored C18 *bastide* (manor farmhouse) is yours: yours the light, airy, vineyard-view bedrooms, simply Provençal-furnished with a happy mix of antique and modern, yours the big bourgeois sitting room (little used because it's too lovely outside), yours the kitchen for picnic-making and laundry, yours a share in the great spring-watered tank for delicious natural swims. Gently confident, François runs the vineyard and the tastings. Enthusiastic and efficient, Nathalie cares for three children — and you — with sweet-natured ease. Very close to perfection, we thought.

Rooms: 3 double and 1 twin, all with bath or shower & wc.

Price: 350 Frs (€ 53.36) for two, including breakfast (min. 3 nights July & Aug).

Meals: 110 Frs, including wine (not Sat or Sun).

Open: March to October.

From A8, Brignoles exit north onto D554 through Le Val; then D22 through Montfort sur Argens, dir. Cotignac. 5km along, turn left; signposted.

MMap 245-34 **ASP Map No: 15**

Nathalie & Jean-François ROUBAUD
Domaine de Nestuby
83570 Cotignac
Var
Tel: (0)4 94 04 60 02
Fax: (0)4 94 04 79 22

In winter Madame has walking or golfing parties. At other times she gives you the chance to gasp at the beautiful views from the beautiful rooms of her beautiful house. Built with ancient stones 50 years ago, looking lots older, it stands in three hectares where she clearly enjoys both her solitude and you company. Bedrooms are Edwardian, with antique and retro furniture, or Provençal, or Modern with original paintings (some her own). Breakfast simply (home-made jam, toast and butter), alone or at a big communal table, in the delicious garden, or in the glorious 100m² salon if it's cold. *Children over 5 welcome.*

Rooms: 3 double, 1 triple, each with bath & wc.

Price: 350 Frs (€ 53.36) for two, including breakfast; extra bed 100 Frs.

Meals: Good auberge 800m.

Open: All year except January.

Gîte space for 9 people

From A8 exit "Le Luc" onto D558 dir. La Garde Freinet & St Tropez; house signposted on right after 4km.

MMap 245-48 **ASP Map No: 15**

Mme Monique FAUVET
La Gîthomière
Route de St Tropez
83340 Le Cannet des Maures
Var
Tel: (0)4 94 60 81 50
Fax: (0)4 94 60 81 50

The sea you can see has a good beach only 400m from this quiet 1960s villa. The warm-hearted, enthusiastic and tireless Didiers seem to have been born to run a happy and hospitable B&B. Two spotlessly clean bedrooms with real attention to comfort — good cupboards and bedside lights, for example — share the modern shower room. The dining room leads to a private outside terrace and thence to the garden — and guests have a key and are welcome to sit and have breakfast or a drink with the family. The hut at the bottom of the large pretty garden is Amélie's painting studio.

Rooms: Suite of 1 double, 1 twin, sharing bath, shower & wc.

Price: 360 Frs (€ 54.88) for two, 580 for four, including breakfast.

Meals: Simple places nearby, choice in Le Lavandou.

Open: All year.

From Le Lavandou D559 E to La Fossette. Arriving in village, left Ave Capitaine Thorel, left again Chemin des Marguerites. If lost, telephone for help!

MMap 245-48 **ASP Map No: 15**

Robert & Amélie DIDIER
21 chemin des Marguerites
La Fossette
83980 Le Lavandou
Var
Tel: (0)4 94 71 07 82
Fax: (0)4 94 71 07 82

Hospitable? The Dyens spontaneously de-iced our car without our asking! Their C18 château stands alone, surrounded by the vineyards where Monsieur, who is fluent in English, toils. It has a thoroughly lived-in appearance and atmosphere. Wine tastings and local produce are always available and there's usually a glass of Monsieur's own, notably the *Blanc de blancs* (white wine made from white grapes), at dinner. The rooms are big and furnished just as you'd expect. It is wonderfully civilised and relaxed and guests can swim or play tennis at the owners' little club 500m away.

Rooms: 2 double, 1 suite for 4, each with bath & wc.

Price: 300 Frs (€ 45.73) for two, including breakfast. Extra bed 60 Frs.

Meals: 150 Frs, including wine & coffee.

Open: All year.

From A8 exit Le Cannet des Maures on N558 dir. La Garde Freinet for 2km. At crossroads turn left — house 200m along.

MMap 245-48 **ASP Map No: 15**

Lucette & Paul DYENS
Château de Roux
Le Cannet des Maures
83340 Le Luc en Provence
Var
Tel: (0)4 94 60 73 10
Fax: (0)4 94 60 89 79

On sunny summer days, breakfast is eaten and life is lived on the peaceful terrace beside the pool of this modern villa. Monsieur, a very able watercolourist, personally designed the house in the Provençal style, adding extensions over the years. The spotlessly clean, if somewhat impersonal, guestrooms are named *Papillon* and *Provence*. They are light and airy and have direct access to the flower-filled garden and the swimming pool. An excellent base and there are many good local beaches.

Rooms: 1 double, 1 twin, each with shower & wc.

Price: 380 Frs (€ 57.93) for two, including breakfast.

Meals: 100 Frs, including wine & coffee.

Open: May to September.

In Fréjus N7 dir. Cannes; pass memorial to 'Morts en Indochine' on right. After 1km enter 'Les Jardins de César' development on left; 1st left is Pline l'Ancien; No 7 on left.

MMap 245-36 **ASP Map No: 15**

Yvette BERTIN
Les Jardins de César
7 allée Pline l'Ancien
83600 Fréjus
Var
Tel: (0)4 94 53 17 85
Fax: (0)4 94 53 17 85
www.sawdays.co.uk

A modern house looking out over ancient hillsides studded with gnarled olive trees, this is a place to rest between sophisticated Monte Carlo and the wild Verdon gorge. Your kindly, hospitable hosts are doing B&B for the sheer pleasure of it — feel the difference. Monsieur will tell you all about everything (in French), and will then, if you like, take you walking in the 'red' hills of Esterel. Madame is quieter with the sweetest smile. The double room is excellent, simply but thoughtfully furnished, has good storage space and lighting and shares the large spanking new shower room with the much smaller twin room. Very good value.

Rooms: 1 twin, 1 double, sharing bathroom & wc.

Price: 250-290 Frs (€ 38.11-44.21) for two, including breakfast.

Meals: Choice in Montauroux 2.5km.

Open: All year.

From A8 exit 39 onto D37 N for 8.5km; cross D562, continue for 200m then Chemin Fontaine d'Aragon on right — house signposted.

MMap 245-36 **ASP Map No: 15**

Pierre & Monique ROBARDET
Fontaine d'Aragon
Quartier Narbonne
83440 Montauroux
Var
Tel: (0)4 94 47 71 39
Fax: (0)4 94 47 71 39
e-mail: p.robardet@wanadoo.fr

These two are really worth getting to know. Eve, a slender, fascinating Medieval History specialist, has decorated her large and spotlessly clean, cool villa in her own personal 'retro' style. She and her doctor husband, Henri, provide a generous breakfast that is usually served in the lovely garden under the spreading palm tree (self-service before 8am); one of the ground-floor rooms actually opens onto the garden and the top bedrooms have a big private balcony. The house is only 15 minutes walk from old Cannes and its famous star-crossed Croisette (they close during The Festival to avoid the curling faxes strewn on the floor at 4am).

Rooms: 1 double, 2 twin, 1 triple, each with bath & wc.

Price: 480-620 Frs (€ 73.18-94.52) for two, including breakfast; extra bed 140 Frs.

Meals: Bistro 5 minutes walk; 15 minutes walk to town centre.

Open: All year except during film festival.

From A8 exit 'Cannes Centre' onto bd Carnot. At 69 bd Carnot (Le Kid café) right into Rue René Vigieno; up hill for 150m — house on right on small roundabout.

MMap 245-37 **ASP Map No: 15**

Eve & Henri DARAN
L'Églantier
14 rue Campestra
06400 Cannes
Alpes-Maritimes
Tel: (0)4 93 68 22 43
Fax: (0)4 93 38 28 53

Geographically, it's not far from the tourist shops, potteries and madding fleshpots of Vallauris but it's a world away in atmosphere. Your hosts restored this old building on a terraced vineyard when they retired from the hectic life of running a *brasserie* in Paris 15 years ago, so they understand the value of peace. The house is light, well furnished and eclectically decorated with collections of antique glass and mugs. The fabulous garden with its swimming pool is a place to pamper yourself and relax to the sound of chirruping cicadas.

Rooms: 1 double with shower & wc, 1 twin with bath & wc.

Price: 420-450 Frs (€ 64.03-68.60) for two, including breakfast.

Meals: Choice in town.

Open: All year.

From A8 Antibes exit dir. Vallauris. There follow signs 'Route de Grasse' from centre; go through 2 roundabouts then hairpin bend; at next crossroads left into forest (signed Mas du Mûrier) — 50m up track.

MMap 245-37 **ASP Map No: 15**

M & Mme G. RONCÉ
Mas du Mûrier
1407 route de Grasse
06220 Vallauris
Alpes-Maritimes
Tel: (0)4 93 64 52 32
Fax: (0)4 93 64 23 77

Panko is a riot of colour: the sheltered (no-smoking) garden has clumps of orange, yellow, mauve and scarlet flowers; real and fake flowers invade every bit of the living room and fight with the cheerful pictures filling every inch of the variegated walls; upstairs are rainbow sheets, patchwork bedcovers, painted furniture and *objets* galore, fine big towels and myriad toiletries. Big outdoor breakfasts come on colourful china. Madame's energy drives it all — she will organise your stay to a tee. It is quiet, exclusive, six minutes from the beach — superb! *Children over five; pets by arrangement; book EARLY.*

Rooms: 1 dble/twin, 1 dble/twin + 1-2 children's beds, each with bath & wc.

Price: 460-730 Frs (€ 70.13-111.29) for two, including breakfast. Reservations only.

Meals: Good choice in town.

Open: All year except Christmas & New Year.

From Antibes centre dir. Cap d'Antibes. At palm-tree roundabout, dir. Cap d'Antibes 'Direct'. At next junction, dir, Cap d'Antibes. 1st right into Chemin du Crouton; 1st left. At end of cul-de-sac left on drive. At No17, Panko is 2nd house on right.

MMap 245-37 **ASP Map No: 15**

Clarisse & Bernard BOURGADE
Villa 'Panko'
17 chemin du Parc Saramartel
06160 Cap d'Antibes
Alpes-Maritimes
Tel: (0)4 93 67 92 49
Fax: (0)4 93 61 29 32

Cascades of bougainvillea and blushes pelargonium beloved by colour-loving Riviera gardeners tumble over this modern townhouse. Antibes' sea front an easy 15-minute walk and vibrant, fashionable Juan les Pins just a few minutes more. Madame, who fills the rooms with fresh flowers, took a crash course in English before opening her rooms and takes great care of her gues she took the trouble to walk to the Pla de Gaulle to meet us to guard against any wayward wanderings. The house, garden and terrace are remarkably qui for the area.

Rooms: 1 double with salon, shower & wc.

Price: 380 Frs (€ 57.93) for two, including breakfast.

Meals: Wide choice in Antibes.

Open: All year.

In Antibes centre, from Place de Gaull take Rue Aristide Briand; left at roundabout and follow railway 600m; right into impasse with barrier, marke 'Privé'; house at end on right.

MMap 245-37 **ASP Map No: 1**

Martine & Pierre MARTIN
Villa Maghoss
8 impasse Lorini
06600 Antibes
Alpes-Maritimes
Tel: (0)4 93 67 02 97
Fax: (0)4 93 67 02 97

A new Provençal-style house on a flat, carefully planted-and-pooled piece of land. In a separate guest wing, each ground-floor room has its own patio area and shares the indoor guest sitting space (with kettle and refrigerator). Madame has furnished the rooms with taste, simple floral fabrics, plain pale walls and rugs on tiled floors. She is genuinely interested to see that you enjoy yourself, offers a welcome glass of rosé, puts chocolates on turned-down beds and serves breakfast in the pleasant conservatory overlooking the large swimming pool. She also runs a family of teenagers... *Children over seven welcome.*

Rooms: 2 double, 1 twin, each with bath or shower & wc.

Price: 320-400 Frs (€ 48.78-60.98) for two, including breakfast. Children 50 Frs.

Meals: Choice in village or St Paul de Vence (2km).

Open: All year (book ahead).

From A8 exit 48 dir. St Paul de Vence for 3km. Fork right on D536/D7 to La Colle. Right at flashing light, cont. straight down hill; 100m after telephone box on right turn right into Chemin de la Rouguière; first house on left.

MMap 245-37 **ASP Map No: 15**

Béatrice RONIN PILLET
Le Clos de Saint Paul
71 chemin de la Rouguière
06480 La Colle sur Loup
Alpes-Maritimes
Tel: (0)4 93 32 56 81
Fax: (0)4 93 32 56 81

Near the top of one of those stunning hilltop villages, the house itself is nothing spectacular but it has a sheer rock face rising above it (where mountaineers practise) and incredible views down to the sea 10km below. The terraced garden is alive with subtropical vegetation, the old Provençal house has later additions and is decorated with old furniture and good taste. Your host is a retired colonel who enjoys having guests, Madame is a management consultant of charm and intelligence and they love children.

Rooms: 2 double, 1 twin, each with bath, shower & wc.

Price: 500 Frs (€ 76.22) for two, including breakfast. Children under 10 free.

Meals: In village.

Open: All year.

From A8 St Laurent du Var exit on D118 then D18/D2210 to St Jeannet. Into village along narrow (2-way) street; fork right into Rue St Claude: No 136 is 300m along. Or park in P at entrance and walk (10 mins).

MMap 245-37 **ASP Map No: 15**

Guy & Michelle BENOIT SÈRE
L'Olivier Peintre
136 rue Saint-Claude
06640 St Jeannet
Alpes-Maritimes
Tel: (0)4 93 24 78 91

Madame radiates enthusiasm, energy and generosity — her breakfast of cheese, cereals, stewed and fresh fruit, various breads and jams is not for picking at. You can see the sea from this huge, Italianate villa smothered in bougainvillea and set in a big, peaceful garden way up above Nice. The drive up is part of the adventure and your reward is a fantastic welcome; Monsieur will skilfully park your car for you in the tiny space. Guestrooms are big, each one individually decorated with comfort unmatched by any hotel I know. The sparkling bathrooms sport lots of toiletries and a chocolate appears on your pillow at night.

Rooms: 1 double, 1 quadruple, 1 suite for 4, each with bath, shower & wc.

Price: 600 Frs (€ 91.47) for two, including breakfast. Extra bed 200 Frs.

Meals: Vast choice in town, 2km (walk down, taxi back?).

Open: All year.

Not far from Nice railway station. From Place St Philippe, under expressway & left into Ave Estienne d'Orves for 600m, over level crossing & after sharp right-hand bend, turn hard back left into private track climbing steeply to house. Telephone if lost.

MMap 245-38 **ASP Map No: 15**

Mme Jacqueline OLIVIER
Le Castel Enchanté
61 route de St Pierre de Féric
06000 Nice
Alpes-Maritimes
Tel: (0)4 93 97 02 08
Fax: (0)4 93 97 13 70

Madame, an elderly, lively and talented painter, inherited this house from an uncle, loves it to bits and wants to shar[e] it with others. It is like a dolls' house; indeed, the small single room is full of antique dolls. The main bedroom, also quite small, looks across the large, lush Mediterranean, statue-decorated, terraced garden to the Alps and has delightful French antiques, a well-equipped kitchenette and a modern shower room. Amazing peace so near the centre of Nice, and there are good walking and biking paths nearby.

Rooms: 1 double, 1 single sharing shower & wc.

Price: 390 Frs (€ 59.46) for two, including breakfast. 190 Frs single.

Meals: In village.

Open: All year.

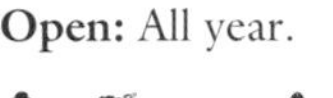

small

From A8 exit 54 Nice Nord on D14 to Gairaut. After village follow dir. Aspremont. Pass 'Auberge du Mas Fleuri' on left. Ave Panéra is 1km along on left; house a few metres down hill.

MMap 245-38 **ASP Map No: 15**

Mme Pia MALET KANITZ
Villa Pan 'É' Râ
8 avenue Panéra — Gairaut Supérieur
06100 Nice
Alpes-Maritimes
Tel: (0)4 92 09 93 20
Fax: (0)4 92 09 93 20

This is a slightly faded (imagine 80 window shutters to paint) Italianate stately home set in splendid isolation among tall trees, home to a trio of highly cultured, interesting, English-fluent people, just a dramatic, twisty drive up from the hot vulgarity of the coast. No clutter, either of mind or matter here. White-painted, colour-co-ordinated bedrooms are simply and prettily furnished with excellent wardrobes, lighting, bathrooms, and views over the vast park dotted with Madame's father's wonderful sculptures. Above his studio in the garden is the suite, perfect for a family of four. It's fine walking, riding, bird-watching country.

Rooms: 1 twin, 3 double, each with shower & wc; suite of 1 double, 1 twin, each with shower, sharing wc.

Price: 280-400 Frs (€ 42.69-60.98) for two, including breakfast.

Meals: In Sospel 3km.

Open: All year.

From Menton, D2566 to Sospel; at 'Mairie' (town hall), left dir. Col de Turini for 1.9km then left dir. 'La Vasta' & 'Campings'. Domaine is 1.3km along, hard back on right after ranch & sharp bend.

MMap 245-26 **ASP Map No: 15**

Marie MAYER & Marcel MAYER
Domaine du Paraïs
La Vasta
06380 Sospel
Alpes-Maritimes
Tel: (0)4 93 04 15 78

He is an Italian builder, so every column of his new house is turned to a T and every gnome on the entrance bridge painted to perfection. He and his English wife (she came from Yorkshire years ago and stayed...) have taken advantage of every square inch of the steep site and the views are stupendous, so what matter the insalubrious quarter of Menton you go through to get there, the rather basic bathrooms and a bit of satin overkill? It is simple, clean, welcoming and deliciously breezy by the pool in summer.

Rooms: 4 double, each with bath & wc.

Price: 320 Frs (€ 48.78) for two, including breakfast.

Meals: Wide choice in Menton.

Open: All year except Dec & Jan.

From Menton D24 dir. Castellar (NOT Ciappes de Castellar). Follow numbers (odds on left) and park above house.

MMap 245-39 **ASP Map No: 15**

M & Mme Paul GAZZANO
151 route de Castellar
06500 Menton
Alpes-Maritimes
Tel: (0)4 93 57 39 73

FRENCH WORDS & EXPRESSIONS used in this book

Mairie (town hall) and ***Hôtel de Ville*** (city hall): useful landmarks, bearing tricolour and noticeboards, easy to find in town centres.
Gîte Panda: *Chambre d'Hôte* or self-catering house in national or regional park; owners provide information about flora and fauna, walking itineries, sometimes guided walks, will lend you binoculars and even rucksacks.
Château: mansion or stately home built for aristocrats between the C16th and C19th. A 'castle', with defences and fortifications, is a ***château fort***.
Maison bourgeoise, in town, ***maison de maître,*** in the country: big, comfortable houses built for members of the liberal professions, captains of industry, trade, etc.
Bastide: a stronghold, a small fortified village or, in Provence, another word for ***mas***.
Mas: in Provence, a long, low country house, typical in its old stone walls, pan-tiled roof and painted shutters.
Malouinière: Malouin means 'of Saint Malo'; ***malouinière*** is a local style of large house built for Corsairs or wealthy fishing families.
Les Malouines is the French name for the Falkland Islands – first discovered by sailors from St Malo – whence the Argentinian name for them: ***Las Malvinas***.
Maison vigneronne, house in a wine-growing area, anything from a tiny vine-worker's cottage (often part of a row) to the estate manager or owner's residence.

Marais: marsh/marshland/wetland. The most spectacular in France is perhaps the ***Marais Poitevin*** near La Rochelle, with miles of little waterways to be explored by boat. The 4th *arrondissement* of Paris, once a miserable slum, now fast being gentrified, is known as ***Le Marais***.

Armoire: wardrobe with more or less elaborate regional-style carving (Norman, Breton, Burgundian,...) and often a mirrored front.
Lit clos: type of country bed, some used until very recently. Basically a wooden box with a canopy over the top, it held a small high double bed and doors to shut once you'd climbed in, so you could share your room with your animals and keep out the rats. Some, 'Marriage Beds', are very richly carved. Much in demand now for conversion to hi-fi cabinets, computer corners, telly tubs...
Potager: 1) kitchen garden, whence the French word for vegetable soup: ***potage***. 2) the ancestor of the hotplate: a waist-high stone structure with several dish-shaped holes in the top – the number depended on the size of the household – and a space beneath the holes to put burning embers brought over from the kitchen range.

Déguster: to taste, sample or savour; ***une dégustation:*** a tasting – of wine, oysters, any speciality. (NOT necessarily free).
A volonté: 'as much as you want'.
Viennoiserie: literally 'things from Vienna' – covers all those relatively plain flaky-pastry concoctions served for breakfast or tea : *croissants, pains au chocolat,* etc.

TIPS FOR TRAVELLERS IN FRANCE

- Buy a phonecard *(télécarte)* on arrival; they are on sale at post offices and tobacconists' *(tabac)*. Keep some small change for the (very few) non-card phone boxes; phone boxes are generously distributed throughout France.
- Public Holidays: many museums and galleries close on Tuesdays, others close on Mondays (e.g. Monet's garden in Giverny) as do many country restaurants, and opening times may be different on:

New Year's Day (1 January)	Bastille Day (14 July)
Easter Sunday & Monday	Assumption of BVM (15 August)
May Day (1 May)	All Saints (1 November)
Liberation 1945 (8 May)	Armistice 1918 (11 November)
Ascension Thursday	Christmas Day
Whit Sunday & Monday (Pentecost)	

- Beware also of mass exodus over public holiday weekends, both the first day – outward journey – and the last – return journey.

Roads and driving

- Current speed limits are: Motorways 130 kph (80 mph), RN National trunk roads 110 kph (68 mph), other open roads 90 kph (56 mph), in towns 50 kph (30 mph). The road police are very active and can demand on-the-spot payment of fines.
- One soon gets used to driving on the right but complacency leads to trouble; take special care coming out of car parks, private drives, narrow one-lane roads and coming onto roundabouts.

French Motorways *(Autoroutes)* are mostly toll-paying	*Autoroutes á Péage*
Blue road signs – motorways	*Autoroutes*
Green road signs = alternative routes or routes leading to motorways	*Itinéraires bis*

Many roads coming from the right still have priority – and drivers take it, come what may, **so expect it always!**
The mysterious command 'Use your engine braking' is a literal translation of *'Utilisez votre frein moteur'*, a sign often seen at the top of long steep motorway slopes. In English we would expect 'Keep in low gear'.

- Directions in towns
The French drive towards a destination and use road numbers far less than we do. So, to find your way in France, know the direction you want to go and the towns your route goes through; when you see *Autres Directions* or *Toutes Directions* in a town, follow towards the place name you're heading for or through.

Medical and Emergency procedures

- If you are an EC citizen, have an E111 form with you for filling in after any medical treatment. You will subsequently receive a refund for only part of your payment, so it is advisable to take out private insurance.
- French emergency services are:
– the public service called *SAMU* or the Casualty Department – *Services des Urgences* – of a hospital;
– the private service called *SOS MÉDECINS.*

AVOIDING CULTURAL CONFUSIONS & SHOCKS

À TABLE

(Don't be alarmed by all the etiquette below; making mistakes can be as much fun as getting it right!)

Breakfast

There may be only a bowl/large cup* and a teaspoon per person on the table. If so, you are expected to butter your bread *on your hand* or on the tablecloth (often the kitchen oilcloth) using the knife in the butter dish, then spread the jam with the jam spoon. This method has recently been described to us as The Only Proper Way to Eat Breakfast by an extremely aristocratic French country gentleman (tip of tongue in cheek? we're not absolutely sure).

A well-bred English lady would never dream of 'dunking' her croissant, toast or teacake in her cup - it is perfectly acceptable behaviour in French society.

* The old-fashioned bowl has now been replaced in the superior French housewife's affections by the giant-size cup with its matching saucer, the set being known as '*un breakfast*'.

Lunch/Dinner

1. EQUIPMENT

Glasses are centred at the top of the plate, not to the right, and you are expected to put your glass/glasses down in the same place each time and not allow them to wander back and forth, left to right, as the whim takes you.

Cutlery is laid concave face upwards in 'Anglo-Saxon' countries; in France it is proper to lay forks and spoons convex face upwards (crests are engraved accordingly). Do try and hold back your instinctive need to turn them over!

To the right of your plate, at the tip of the knife, you may find a **knife-rest**. This serves two purposes : to lay your knife on when you are not using it, rather than leaving it in your plate; to lay your knife AND fork on (points downwards) if you are asked to '*garder vos couverts*' (keep your knife and fork) while the plates are changed - e.g. between starter and main dish.

2. FOOD

Cheese comes BEFORE pudding in France - that's the way they do it! The proper order is -
Entrée - starter (rather than main dish à la Mrs Beeton)
Plat - main dish of meat and vegetable(s)
Salade - usually just green leaves
Fromage - can be just one perfect Camembert or a vast tray with a dozen cheeses to choose from; in very smart places, there will be a second board for goat cheese; the middle-of-the-road place has all cheeses are on one board with one knife for cow and ewe and another for goat.
Dessert - ranging from plain fresh fruit to superbly complicated creamy structures.
It is becoming more and more acceptable to serve/ask for the cheese to be served at the same time as the salad.

Cutting cheese

Cut a round cheese as you would cut a round cake - in triangular segments. When a ready-cut segment such as a piece of Brie is presented, the rule is to 'preserve the point', i.e. do not cut it straight across but take an angle which removes the existing point but makes another one.

ORDER FORM for the UK. See over for USA.

All these books are available in the major bookshops but we can send them to you quickly and without effort on your part. Post and packaging is FREE if you order 3 or more books.

	No. of copies	Price each	Total value
French Bed & Breakfast 5th Edition		**£13.95**	
Special Paris Hotels 2nd Edition		**£8.95**	
Special Places to Stay in Spain & Portugal 3rd Edition		**£11.95**	
Special Places to Stay British Bed & Breakfast 4th Edition		**£12.95**	
Special Places to Stay in Ireland 2nd Edition		**£10.95**	
Special Places to Stay British Hotels & Inns 1st Edition		**£10.95**	
Add Post & Packaging: £1 for Paris book, £2 for any other, **FREE** if ordering 3 or more books.			
TOTAL ORDER VALUE *Please make cheques payable to Alastair Sawday Publishing*			

All orders to: Alastair Sawday Publishing, 44 Ambra Vale East, Bristol BS8 4RE
For credit card orders please call 0117 929 9921.

Name ______________________________

Address ______________________________

____

______________________ Postcode ______________

Tel ______________________ Fax ______________________

If you do not wish to receive mail from other companies, please tick the box ☐ FBB5

ORDER FORM for USA.

These books are available at your local bookstore, or you may order direct. Allow two to three weeks for delivery.

	No. of copies	Price each	Total
British Bed & Breakfast		**$19.95**	
Special Paris Hotels		**$14.95**	
Special Places to Stay in Spain & Portugal		**$19.95**	
Special Places to Stay British: Hotels, Inns & Other Places		**$19.95**	
Special Places to Stay in Ireland		**$19.95**	
Shipping in the continental USA: $3.95 for one book, $4.95 for two books, $5.95 for three or more books. Outside continental USA, call (800) 243-0495 for prices.			
For delivery to AK, CA, CO, CT, FL, GA, IL, IN, KS, MI, MN, MO, NE, NM, NC, OK, SC, TN, TX, VA, and WA, please add appropriate sales tax.			
TOTAL ORDER			

Please make checks payable to: The Globe Pequot Press

To order by phone with MasterCard or Visa: (800) 243-0495, 9 a.m. to 5 p.m. EST; by fax: (800) 820-2329, 24 hours; through our Web site: www.globe-pequot.com; or by mail: The Globe Pequot Press, P.O. Box 480, Guilford, CT 06437.

Name ______________________ Date ______________

Address ______________________________________

Town ____

State ______________________ Zip code __________

Tel ________________________ Fax ______________

REPORT FORM

If you have any comments on entries in this guide, please let us have them.

If you have a favourite house, hotel or inn or a new discovery, please let us know about it.

Please send reports to: Alastair Sawday Publishing, 44 Ambra Vale East, Bristol BS8 4RE, UK or e-mail us at specialplaces@sawday.co.uk

Report on:

Entry No ______ New Recommendation ☐ Date ______________

Name of owners or hotel/B&B

Address

Tel No

My name and address :

Name

Address

Tel:

My reasons for writing are :

BULLETIN DE RÉSERVATION
Booking Form

À l'attention de :
To : ....
....
Date: ....

Madame, Monsieur,

Veuillez faire la réservation suivante au nom de : ....
Please make the following booking for (name):

Pour .... nuit(s). Arrivant le: jour .... mois .... année ....
For night(s) Arriving: day month year

Partant le: jour .... mois .... année ....
Leaving: day month year

Si possible, nous aimerions .... chambres, disposées comme suit:
We would like rooms, arranged as follows:

À grand lit ....
Double bed
À lits jumeaux ....
Twin beds
Pour trois ....
Triple
À un lit simple ....
Single
Suite ....

Nous aimerions également réserver le dîner pour .... personnes.
We would also like to book dinner for people

Veuillez nous envoyer la confirmation à l'adresse ci-dessous:
Please send confirmation to the following address:

Name: ....
Name:
Address: ....
Address.

Fax No:

FBB5

INDEX OF NAMES

INDEX OF PLACES

ENTRY NO.